# WOMEN'S WISCONSIN

# WOMEN'S WISCONSIN

## From Native Matriarchies to the New Millennium

Edited by Genevieve G. McBride

Published by the

Wisconsin Historical Society Press

www.wisconsinhistory.org/publications

Photographs identified with PH, WHi, or WHS are from the Society's collections; address inquiries about such photos to the Visual Materials Archivist at the above address.

Publications of the Wisconsin Historical Society Press are available at quantity discounts for promotions, fund raising, and educational use. Write to the above address for more information.

Printed in the United States of America

Designed by Jane Tenenbaum

09  08  07  06  05       5  4  3  2  1

Library of Congress Cataloging-in-Publication Data

Women's Wisconsin : from native matriarchies to the new millennium / edited by Genevieve G. McBride.

    v.  cm.

  Includes bibliographical references and index.
  Contents: The first Wisconsin women—Women on the Wisconsin frontier, 1836–1848—Statehood and the status of women, 1848–1868—Poverty and progress for women in Wisconsin, 1868–1888—Organized women, 1888–1910—"Forward" women in Wisconsin, 1910–1930—Women at war, 1930–1950.
  ISBN 0-87020-361-4 (pbk. : alk. paper)
1.  Women—Wisconsin—History.  I. McBride, Genevieve G.
  HQ1438.W5W64 2005
  305.4'09775—dc22

2005001067

Photographs: FRONT COVER, top to bottom, left to right: Ho-Chunk women pose for a portrait, Black River Falls, ca. 1915. WHi Image ID 10151; switchboard operator at her post, Washington Island, ca. 1915. WHi Image ID 9212; nurses pose in uniform, Milwaukee, ca. 1900. WHi Image ID 6942; CORE (Congress of Racial Equality) picket protests school segregation, Milwaukee, 1964. WHi Image ID 4993; students at Milwaukee-Downer College conduct scientific research, Milwaukee, 1900; woman working at the Badger Ordnance Works, Baraboo, ca. 1943, WHi(V51)58. SPINE: Louise Phelps Kellogg (1862–1942), longtime historian at the Wisconsin Historical Society and mentor to two generations of women historians, Madison, 1936, WHi Image ID 15343. BACK COVER: A woman photographer captures a reflection of herself, a young girl, and a woman in a vanity mirror, ca. 1900, WHi Image ID 4409.

# BRIEF CONTENTS

# CONTENTS

# FOREWORD

I am a Wisconsin woman, albeit one who was born in New York City. In the year of my birth, 1933, our nation was in the midst of the Great Depression, Franklin Delano Roosevelt had just been elected president in one of the early elections in which women had the right to vote, and Germany was on the verge of naming Adolf Hitler its chancellor. The world was lurching toward the Second World War and I, as a young girl, had the good fortune to be sheltered from the weightier problems facing our nation and the world. I spent my early years practicing English (Yiddish, the native tongue of my parents, who were immigrants from Poland, was my first language) and my teen years occupying myself with the myriad fascinations of New York City and a small neighborhood grocery store that hummed with life across the street from my family's apartment. The store — Leo's — belonged to my parents, Leo and Celia Schlanger. Its shelves were packed with a jumble of dry goods and the air was rich with the aroma of the meats and cheeses that were stocked in the deli case.

Our lives revolved around that tiny precious square of real estate on Manhattan's Upper West Side. It was where work, neighborhood, and family converged; it was our community. And, like most places that settle in our hearts, it was special not for its towering stacks of cans or its gritty tile or high glass counter, but for the people it brought together. How I delighted in the diverse group that stepped across the threshold of our little store each day: the friends and neighbors and strangers, young and old, worried and carefree. Some rushed, some browsed, some argued, some stayed sufficiently long to outline what was wrong with the world, and others stayed a bit longer and solved a few of those problems. It was untidy, unpredictable, and I loved it. And somehow I knew, from about the age of 6, that if I became a lawyer I could work with people just as interesting as my parents' customers, and I wouldn't have to stock shelves.

My work as a lawyer and a judge has indeed allowed me to find a spot at the center of a similarly lively jumble of humanity. There is nothing like the bustle and hum of business under the dome of our State Capitol and in the corridors of our many magnificent county courthouses. And as was true at Leo's, it is not the buildings but the people within them who make the court system a very special place to work. Our diverse backgrounds and perspectives increase the quality of our decisions and improve the chance of success of every initiative we undertake. So I am grateful that there has been a place for me, mindful of the sacrifices of the women and men who broke down some of the barriers along the path that I have navigated, and honored to have played a role in eliminating barriers for others.

That the child of an immigrant grocer — and a girl, no less — could become a lawyer was, I am sure, unthinkable to many of the people who crossed my parents' threshold. And indeed I might not have become a lawyer but for the fact that my father had a heart attack when he was in his early forties. He survived, but the event underscored for my parents the reality that my mother might someday have to support my sister and me on her own. They became convinced that their girls must be raised to be self-sufficient.

My parents encouraged me to get a good education, and I took their advice. I was one of a handful of women at Indiana University Law School and the only one in the graduating class of 1956. Around the nation at that time law schools were beginning to open their doors to women, and it was a very difficult change for some within the system. At Harvard Law School, which began admitting women in 1950, some professors controlled the participation of their female students by instituting "Ladies' Day" — generally, a single class each month when women students were invited to speak. And, of course, designating restrooms for women and dorms for women required substantial study and careful consideration.

I graduated high up in my class, an achievement that normally guarantees offers of employment from at least a few law firms. But the only offers that the dean of the law school thought would come my way were offers for librarian positions — which are great jobs for someone who is trained and interested in that field. When I did find a law firm willing to take on a woman — in Madison, Wisconsin — I seized the offer and stayed fourteen years. While in private practice I became a professor at the University of Wisconsin Law School, and later I left practice to become a Supreme Court justice.

If law is truly going to serve the public's interest, the profession must be opened wide to all people who wish to serve. I am happy to say that, in 2005, about half of all law school graduates are women, three of our seven Supreme Court justices are women (and we welcomed our first African American justice), and the State Bar of Wisconsin has had women presidents (one of whom also happened to be African American). But work remains to be done. There is equal access to the profession but not yet equal representation in the management of law firms and at the high end of the salary scale.

The experience of women in the law mirrors the experience of women in many professions that were once exclusively male. Women who serve in law enforcement, fight fires, drive trucks and work in trades such as plumbing, carpentry, and welding are breaking down the next set of barriers and those professions, careers, and jobs, like the law, are better for their participation. I am inspired by the young women who are rising to these challenges, and I hope that they may find inspiration, as I do, in the dozens of stories of Wisconsin women contained within Genevieve G. McBride's new anthology. I am indeed proud to be a Wisconsin woman.

— Shirley S. Abrahamson, Chief Justice
Wisconsin Supreme Court

# PREFACE

This anthology is intended to serve students, teachers, and other readers by collecting in one place a remarkable historical record by and about women's place in Wisconsin as published in the more than three hundred and fifty issues of the *Wisconsin Magazine of History* since 1917 as well as from other publications of the Wisconsin Historical Society. This overview of that extraordinary record of publication provides excerpts from dozens of far lengthier articles in their original form. Some are primary sources by historical subjects; some are secondary sources by historians who also speak from so far in the past that their voices serve almost as primary sources.

As an author and a longtime reader and admirer of many historians herein, the editor found it difficult to give up their gifted writing and attempted to respect and retain, wherever possible, their voices and the voice of their times. Editorial commentary is inserted only to provide correct factual information or inferences with inclusion of historical scholarship in the interim to better serve current readers. If the remaining content contains terms, titles, usages, or stereotypes that are uncommon in usage today, out of favor, or even offensive to readers, that content ought to be viewed in the context of the times for insight into the treatment of women at the time that the sources were created. To resolve the resulting cacophony of voices — sources and authors, historians since, and this editor — insertions are indicated typographically in different fonts, brackets, and editor's notes.

However, many women's voices still have not been heard by historians. This anthology also is intended to encourage further research for the *Wisconsin Magazine of History* on the missing majority in Wisconsin's past. In its long history, the *Wisconsin Magazine of History* has lacked scholarship on Native American and African American women, on Asian American women and Latinas, and on lesbians and women of other gender orientations. It also has lacked perspectives on women's work as homemakers, including adding to family incomes from the frontier forward by providing homes for boarders, and on women in the paid workforce in Wisconsin for a century and a half. More understandably, the *Wisconsin Magazine of History* also lags in providing a record of women's contributions in the recent past and on the place of Wisconsin women within a comparative context in the country. To attempt a more inclusive and contextual history, the editor supplemented the excerpts of articles with references to other secondary sources in extensive introductions to the first seven chapters, from the preterritorial period to the centennial of statehood. The final chapter relies not only on such secondary sources as are available on the recent past but also on primary sources in an extensive historical essay on the last half of the twentieth century and the first years of the new millennium for women in Wisconsin.

For further reference and research for readers who wish to read the articles in full, each excerpt is preceded by a citation to the original article in the *Wisconsin Magazine of History* or to each original publication by the Wisconsin Historical Society, all widely available in libraries across the state. Recent issues of the magazine also are available online on the Wisconsin Historical Society Web site, www.wisconsinhistory.org, by subscription as a member of the Society, or by purchasing current single copies at select bookstores. Several Society collections also are available online, such as Wisconsin Local History and Biography Articles from state newspapers from 1860 to 1940, Wisconsin Historical Images from the first years of photography, and Turning Points in Wisconsin History, which includes a collection specifically on women's history. Also recommended are bibliographies on Wisconsin women's history on the Web site of the University of Wisconsin Women's Studies Librarian's Office, www.library.wisc.edu/libraries/WomensStudies/.

For students and teachers, this anthology is organized chronologically in eight chapters coordinating with the common curricular calendar of a sixteen-week semester at the postsecondary level, although the organizational plan is adaptable to the many variations at secondary schools and postsecondary campuses in the state. As this anthology is intended as a reader not only for Wisconsin women's history courses but also for Wisconsin history and American women's history courses, the chapters follow conventional periodization in history, based on territorial status and statehood, political administrations — presidential or gubernatorial — and wars. However, for the purposes of this anthology, the periodization is modified for emphasis on significant points in Wisconsin women's history, such as formation of a suffrage association, or to provide chapters of similar length for curricular planning.

Also for curricular planning, contextual references are primarily from only a few, widely available, and standard sources such as the Wisconsin Historical Society's six-volume series, *The History of Wisconsin,* and also recommended for regional context is a less well-known collection, *The Women's Great Lakes Reader* by Victoria Brehm. For national context, of the many worthy and widely available readers and texts, the editor relied on *Women's America* by Linda K. Kerber and Jane Sherron De Hart and on *Born for Liberty* by Sara M. Evans, a midwesterner, because both begin with Native women rather than European settlement and, throughout, both are more inclusive of midwestern women, who are too often neglected in texts with an overemphasis on the East.

In the new millennium, perhaps a new history of Wisconsin will realize the goal of providing a truly comprehensive story of the state, with women's history comprising a representative 52 percent of its pages.

# ACKNOWLEDGMENTS

Many women of the Wisconsin Historical Society contributed their expertise to this project but none more expertly, enthusiastically, and faithfully — from its inception through three years, dozens of emails, and countless conversations on our larger vision and the most minute details — than Deborah T. Johnson, developmental editor. I also am grateful for the expertise of Diane Drexler, managing editor, and Kathy Borkowski, editorial director. However, it was a man who first conceived the idea of an anthology on women's history in Wisconsin from the pages of the Wisconsin Magazine of History. To Michael E. Stevens, state historic preservation officer, I am grateful for the opportunity to put together the initial proposal — although it evolved into far more than he envisioned. I can sincerely recommend that everyone interested in state history also canvass every table of contents of every issue since 1917 for an education in the work of the Wisconsin Historical Society.

I also am grateful to a group of historians of women at schools and libraries statewide who reviewed the proposal, reshaping this project in significant ways to provide a usable text for students and teachers — and, I hope, a usable past for every reader. The proposal reviewers' support reaffirmed the need for this project, and their suggestions resulted in the inclusion of more articles and more extensive chapter introductions. Their insistence on including recent decades, despite a lack of sufficient articles in the *Wisconsin Magazine of History* on women's history still in the making, resulted in expanding the brief epilogue that I had originally envisioned into the extensive historical essay that comprises the final chapter. Proposal reviewers included Helen M. Bannan, associate professor and director of women's studies, University of Wisconsin–Oshkosh; Catherine B. Cleary, historian, pioneer leader of women in banking, and mentor to Wisconsin women; Liz Winter Dannenbaum, adult services librarian, Middleton Public Library; Carolyn J. Mattern, archivist, Wisconsin Historical Society; Kim E. Nielsen, associate professor of social change, University of Wisconsin–Green Bay; Phyllis Holman Weisbard, librarian, Women's Studies Consortium, University of Wisconsin System; and Nancy Worcester, associate professor of women's studies and continuing studies, University of Wisconsin–Madison.

Women in every corner of the state also responded willingly to requests for information on their locales, even to the point of trekking to a cemetery on Madeline Island in northernmost Wisconsin, as did the Reverend Marina Lachecki of La Pointe. I also am grateful to the Reverend Deborah A. Block of Milwaukee, Sandy Malzhon of Lancaster, Margaret Larson of La Crosse, Elizabeth Jozwiak of the University of Wisconsin–Rock County, and others who contributed with the enthusiasm as well as the expertise that are the hallmarks of local historians across Wisconsin.

Colleagues closer to my home in the University of Wisconsin–Milwaukee Department of History contributed expertise from their fields, especially Margo J. Anderson, Merry Wiesner-Hanks, and Ellen D. Langill on women's history, Michael A. Gordon on Wisconsin history, Stephen Meyer on Wisconsin labor history, Cary Miller on Native American history, William Jones on African American history, and Joseph A. Rodriguez on local Hispanic history. The Cultures and Communities Program provided fellowship funding for developing a multicultural American history course and the collegial support of my co-instructors, program director Gregory S. Jay and Native American poet Kimberly M. Blaeser, as well as the expertise of Mary Louise Buley-Meissner, also of the English Department, on local Hmong American women. For the Morris Fromkin Fellowship in Social Justice to fund research on the Wisconsin Equal Rights Amendment of 1921, I am indebted to Peter Watson-Boone and his successor, Ewa E. Barczyk, director of libraries at the Golda Meir Library on my campus, and to then-archivist Timothy L. Ericson, now senior lecturer in information studies. For a sabbatical leave to research the Wisconsin Equal Rights Amendment campaign of the 1970s and to complete this anthology, I am grateful to the College of Letters and Science.

I also am grateful to a group of aspiring historians, the hundreds of students in my courses at the University of Wisconsin–Milwaukee, whose enthusiastic and constructive responses to reading about their foremothers also reshaped this work in progress and always revive my enthusiasm for teaching and researching women's history. My graduate students' own research educates me with every primary source discovered and every informed and insightful response offered, some of which are cited herein. I also am grateful to graduate assistants Michelle Zierhut Boyle, Stacy Smith, and Blair Thorpe for research on Vel Rodgers Phillips, funded by a grant administered by Joyce F. Kirk of the Africology Department and director of the University of Wisconsin System Institute on Race and Ethnicity at the University of Wisconsin–Milwaukee.

No students at my campus heard more about Wisconsin women's history and are more supportive than John McBride Caspari and Catherine Southmayd Caspari, my children. No graduate student gave more to this work, setting aside his own and delaying his doctoral degree, than Stephen R. Byers, my husband, colleague, and companion in the never-ending historic preservation project we call home.

Despite all of their support and suggestions, and every effort of mine, the editor alone must take responsibility for any errors that remain. But I blame the benighted plumbing, the erstwhile electricity, and the other almost-daily failings of modern technology amid the months of repairs and renovation around my home office. However, I also bless our home for serving as a reminder to be grateful that I am a Wisconsin woman today. That our foremothers made history here without computers — or even indoor plumbing and central heating — remains among many reasons for my unending awe at all that they accomplished for us.

— Genevieve G. McBride
Milwaukee, Wisconsin

# LIST OF ABBREVIATED CITATIONS

*WMH*       *Wisconsin Magazine of History*

WHS       Wisconsin Historical Society

SHSW     State Historical Society of Wisconsin (a previous name of the WHS)

WSA       Wisconsin State Archives

*HOW*      *History of Wisconsin,* the six-volume series from the WHS

# INTRODUCTION

*One of the most effective ways in which dominant groups maintain their power
is by depriving the people they dominate of the knowledge of their own history.*
— WOMEN'S AMERICA[1]

A more inclusive historical record of Wisconsin may require different definitions and
documentation than those found in traditional historiography. Historians who measure a civilization, a state, or a city by bricks and mortar rather than by bone needles and beaded belts or spinning wheels and bolts of cloth will miss women's role as builders of communities measured by other means, for women are the weavers of the fabric of society. Historians who look only to politics or laws will miss the work of women who, without legal or political power, formed their own societies and bylaws. Sources may require reading between the lines written by women socialized to silence or "womanly" modesty, even in diaries and private poems, and reading beyond the words voiced by women in newspaper interviews and oral histories. Women's words may have been misconstrued as gossip or myth, as were Native women's "origin stories" that transmitted the history of their people, writes Ojibwe historian Patty Loew. As she advises, "we must not only *read* history but also *listen* to it" for other voices and other values in the origins of the other Wisconsin — women's Wisconsin.[2]

Examples of the importance and impact of definitions in the gender politics of history in Wisconsin are the "origin stories" of the "founding fathers" of both the state and its largest city as well as many other communities. Awarded the honorific of the "father of Wisconsin" by many historians was Charles Michel de Langlade, often labeled as a French fur trader. However, his father was a French Canadian trader at Michilimackinac (now Mackinac) who married Domitilde, an Ottawa, so their son was a *métis*, with heritage both Native (not Native American, as he was born in 1729 when Wisconsin was a part of Nouvelle France, or New France) and French Canadian. The personification of both cultures, Langlade was schooled at a Jesuit mission at Mackinac, and at the age of ten, he began his military career by fighting for the French in Canada. But "he grew up in and absorbed his mother's culture," according to historian Sandra J. Zipperer. He also married an Ottawan, Agathe — as would his *métis* son and a long line of his descendants, often designated as French, who also had a proud, primarily Native American heritage.[3]

However, Wisconsin's *métis* "founding father" also was rewarded by the British for his warlike ways with land at La Baye (later Green Bay), after abandoning his first wife to marry a French Canadian and further his military career that often took him far from his home, family, and trading post. He died in 1802, but by the time of settlement from the

East, writes Zipperer, Langlade "would have deplored the advent of the Yankees, the end of a way of life, and a new world, devoid of the manners, political system, and unique culture" of the *métis*. In short, the "father of Wisconsin" would have disowned the home of his foremothers.[4]

Similarly, in the widely accepted "origin story" of Milwaukee, more is known of the alleged city founder than of his *métis* wife, who was here first: Josette Vieau Juneau, born in 1802, the year that Langlade died. For a century, historians concurred with a journalist who bestowed the honor on Laurent Solomon Juneau based solely on two criteria: property ownership in the city and citizenship in the United States. Both criteria required that the city founder be a man. However, the man who bears the appellation of "founding father" began his rise by the time-honored manner of marrying his boss's daughter and inheriting her family's Milwaukee post that might have been in her name, had she not married him before women began to win property rights. She also was ineligible for citizenship in an era when the government counted Native Americans and many *métis* as noncitizens and did not account for traders' intermarriage with the first Wisconsin women. But Josette was born in Wisconsin when her future husband was a footloose French Canadian voyageur and a "latecomer to the trade," as historian John Gurda writes. Her husband also was a comparative latecomer to Milwaukee and still was not a citizen at the founding of the city in the 1820s and for more than a decade afterward. Finally, at the age of forty, he sought citizenship only for mercenary reasons — to speculate in property in a "Wisconsin cleared of the red man's claim," as Bayrd Still states, ignoring the moral claim of Native American women as caretakers of the land, the ancestral lands of many once-matrilineal cultures in Milwaukee and across Wisconsin.[5]

That the mothers of Wisconsin, such as Domitilde de Langlade and Josette Vieau Juneau, are more logical selections as the founders of the state and its largest city may suggest how gendered history has shaped local mythology. To challenge the definitions that have enshrined their husbands may border on historical heresy, as both women are, literally, mere footnotes in many worthy state and city histories. However, one historian of Milwaukee, Kathleen Neils Conzen, argues for stability of settlement as a *sine qua non* for community formation. Had other historians also looked to less gendered criteria for founding a city (such as stability), they might have looked more closely at Vieau Juneau's husband. When the Juneaus moved to her family's store and stockade, he hardly settled down in her hometown. He was an absentee husband and father, often off on trading treks, while she stayed home to raise their fourteen surviving children — of seventeen born — and to run the family business as she was raised to do. Both spoke French, but he had to learn local dialects and the English that she already knew as a necessity for serving the next settlers and for the city's future. In another crucial role for the young city, as historian Ruth De Young Kohler writes, "her neighborly help" included serving as, literally, midwife to Milwaukee.[6]

Bringing *métis* women into history adds to more than the narrative of Wisconsin because they add complexity to basic tenets of local mythology about our modern beginnings. From the semipermanent farms, tribal villages, and trading posts of the first residents of Wisconsin, the city and the state arose from *métis* culture — the culture of Domitilde de Langlade's descendants, of Josette Vieau Juneau, of the other women whose foremothers for generations had married French Canadian fur traders and literally gave birth to a new people and a new land where *métis* women founded the founding families and worked as fur traders, too. They were here to welcome women who came from the East, the South, and Europe in the nineteenth century who next contributed their customs to their new communities in the ever-evolving culture of Wisconsin — a culture made by women as much as by the men who dominate state history, if the making of culture and history are redefined to recognize women's work as significant in community formation.

In addition to redefining history-making by different criteria, such as the founding of many institutions significant in community formation (from schools, libraries, and hospitals to parks, playgrounds, and other public spaces){m}an enterprise often considered "women's work" in Wisconsin and nationwide in the nineteenth century — a more inclusive history also may require finding different documents. The first books published in Wisconsin were the first writings in local languages and dialects of the previously oral Native culture; these led to the legacy of other accounts of the preterritorial period. Other but more mundane records may tell more between the lines, such as the account books that often were maintained by women who were wives and daughters of traders, if not traders themselves; the bylaws of women's organizations in the public sphere of the frontier of the territorial, early statehood, and Civil War eras; the diaries, letters, and other private correspondence by women; as well as many oral histories written down by descendants or documented in interviews with early settlers that were popular in the late-nineteenth-century press. During the twentieth century, increasing numbers of woman historians and writers also provided a rich historical record for the reconstruction of Wisconsin women's work in their communities.

However, although the words of those Wisconsin women were heard by historians and made this anthology possible, the voices of many other women who also made Wisconsin history have remained unheard for too long. As their story starts on the following pages, Loew's admonition to "not only *read* history but also *listen* to it" is apt advice for reading and listening well to not only her foremothers, the women who were here first and formed the first communities — the first women who made Wisconsin history — but also to all of the words of the women herein.[7] *Listen . . .*

## NOTES

1. Linda K. Kerber and Jane Sherron De Hart, *Women's America: Refocusing the Past*, 6th ed. (New York: Oxford University Press, 2004), 1.

2. Patty Loew, *Indian Nations of Wisconsin: Histories of Endurance and Renewal* (Madison: WHS, 2001), 2–5, 11; emphasis hers.

3. Sandra J. Zipperer, "Sieur Charles Michel de Langlade: Lost Cause, Lost Culture," *Voyageur, Historical Review of Brown County and Northeast Wisconsin* (Winter/Spring 1999), www.uwgb.edu/wisfrench/library/articles/langlade/.

4. Ibid.; on descendants of Langlade's second marriage, see Virginia Glenn Crane, "History and Family Values" in chapter 2.

5. Alice E. Smith, *The History of Wisconsin,* vol. 1: *From Exploration to Statehood* (Madison: SHSW, 1973), 76, 113; John Gurda, *The Making of Milwaukee* (Milwaukee: Milwaukee County Historical Society, 1999), 12–27; Bayrd Still, *Milwaukee: The History of a City* (Madison: SHSW, 1948), 5, citing "The Founder of Milwaukee," *Milwaukee Sentinel,* November 11, 1906, by editor Henry W. Bleyer; John G. Gregory, *History of Milwaukee, Wisconsin,* vol. 1 (Chicago: Clarke Publishing, 1931), 147; Edwin S. Mack, "The Founding of Milwaukee," *Proceedings* (Madison: WHS, 1906), 198; Louise Phelps Kellogg, "The Beginnings of Milwaukee," *WMH* 1, no. 4 (June 1918): 417. On matrilinealism, see also Loew, *Indian Nations,* 40–41; and Robert E. Bieder, *Native American Communities in Wisconsin, 1600–1960: A Study of Tradition and Change* (Madison: University of Wisconsin Press, 1995), 58.

6. Still, *Milwaukee,* 5; Gurda, *Making of Milwaukee,* 14–20; Kathleen Neils Conzen, *Immigrant Milwaukee, 1836–1860: Accommodation and Community in a Frontier City* (Cambridge, MA.: Harvard University Press, 1976), 42–43, 46; W. A. Titus, "Theresa, the Last Home of Solomon Juneau," *WMH* 18, no. 3 (March 1935): 308; Marion Lawson, "Solomon Juneau: Milwaukee's First Mayor," *WMH* 41, no. 2 (Winter 1957–58): 114–119; Ruth De Young Kohler, *The Story of Wisconsin Women* (Madison: Committee of Wisconsin Women, 1948), 9; see also Introduction to chapter 1.

7. Loew, *Indian Nations,* 11; italics hers.

# WOMEN'S
# WISCONSIN

*Betsy Thunder, Ho-Chunk medicine woman, February 6, 1913*

# THE FIRST WISCONSIN WOMEN

## INTRODUCTION

For thousands of years, women lived and worked in the land later known as Wisconsin — hundreds of thousands of women even in the prehistoric period, according to archaeologists, who have found many artifacts of ancient cultures. Whether men alone built mounds and mined copper near Lake Michigan or created cave drawings closer to the Mississippi River cannot be known, or whether only women made the beaded wampum belts for trade or the stone tools or the spear points for warfare that also have been found among earthen effigies and other fragmentary evidence from the past. However, archaeological and historical records suggest that women were the miners of galena, or lead, among the Ho-Chunk, Mesquakie, and Sauk living in the southeastern area along the Mississippi. Women were among the traders of the Ojibwe and other northern, more nomadic Native nations. Women were the farmers of the Ho-Chunk, Menominee, and Potawatomi societies in southeastern Wisconsin, where the climate is more conducive to agriculture. As many as ten thousand women mined, traded, tilled, and tended the land west of the Great Lakes in the 1600s, when they encountered the first French Canadian explorers who wrote the first accounts of Wisconsin almost four hundred years ago.[1]

The first accounts offer evidence that women also once led Wisconsin as chiefs of the Ho-Chunk, an ancient people whose ancestral homeland then spanned the central and southern areas from Green Bay in the east to the La Crosse and Prairie du Chien area in the west, and even south into northern Illinois. The forerunners of several other Native nations, according to anthropologist Nancy Oestreich Lurie, their women mined, farmed, and maintained large villages while men left to hunt. The Ho-Chunk also had a matrilineal society — with descent derived from the mother's line — and a system of split military and civil leadership in which women were the "peace chiefs" or civil leaders, according to historian Patty Loew.[2]

In the 1700s, the last known woman chief of the Ho-Chunk was Ho-poe-kaw, or the Glory of the Morning of Wisconsin. The sister or daughter of a chief, she succeeded him as head of their largest village, east of Lake Winnebago — and she succeeded as a chief for decades despite devastating effects of diseases from explorers and warfare with other tribes forced westward. If women rarely were warriors, nevertheless war was women's story as well. Continued epidemics and economic instability as well as conflicts caused by explorers, traders, and settlers cost women their families, crops, lodges, villages, and even their lives. Ho-poe-kaw, however, stayed all her life in her homeland and stayed in power despite devastating personal losses.[3]

Ho-poe-kaw was not unusual among Native women in marrying a French Canadian in

Wisconsin when the area was a colony of Nouvelle-France, or New France. Sabrevoir De-
scaris, an officer, arrived in 1728 but resigned his commission to work as a trader with the
Ho-Chunk. He wed Ho-poe-kaw in 1729 to "secure the trade of her tribe and their warm
and enduring goodwill," writes historian Louise Phelps Kellogg. Sadly, his desertion of his
wife and their sons seven years later also was not unusual — nor that he departed Wisconsin with their only daughter, never to return. He is now merely a footnote in family history, although the family bears a form of his name that history has made famous. Of the
Decorahs, historian Milo Milton Quaife writes that "the descendants of Glory of the Morning have been both numerous and notable, and the history of the family constitutes a remarkable record." He attributes their success to the French Canadian ancestor, reputedly
of "noble blood" in France, but did allow that Ho-poe-kaw "was nobly born" here.[4]

An explorer who met her agreed. Jonathan Carver came from Connecticut to Wisconsin in 1766, after more than three decades of Ho-poe-kaw's leadership of the Ho-Chunk,
whom he and other Englishmen called the Winnebago. He could not imagine a woman
who was a chief. Instead, in an account that was rare for the era in its inclusion of women
at all, he called her a queen.

> I arrived at the great town of the Winnebagoes. . . . Here the queen who presided
> over this tribe . . . received me with great civility and entertained me in a very dis-
> tinguished manner [for] four days. . . . I held a council with the chiefs, of whom I
> asked permission to pass through their country. . . . The queen sat in the council
> but only asked a few questions, or gave some directions in matters relative to the
> state, for women are . . . allowed to sit in their councils . . . [and] invested with the
> supreme authority. . . . She was a very ancient woman, small in stature, and not
> much distinguished by her dress from several other women who attended her.
> These, her attendants, seemed greatly pleased whenever I showed any tokens of
> respect to their queen, particularly when I saluted her, which I frequently did to
> acquire her favor.[5]

Carver apparently did acquire Ho-poe-kaw's "favor," for he wrote that "the good old lady"
showed "by her smiles" that "she was equally pleased with the attention" from the explorer.[6]

For how long Ho-poe-kaw continued as chief after 1766 is not known, nor is the date
of her death. "The rest is known only by tradition" orally transmitted by her Decorah descendants, who reported that she "ruled her village with wisdom and care," according to
Kellogg. She also writes that Ho-poe-kaw apparently never was reunited with her daughter, who "lived among the whites and was educated by her father's people" in Quebec,
married a merchant trader in Montreal, and then became as lost to history as she was to
her mother. However, a descendant would return to Wisconsin decades later. By then,
both of Ho-poe-kaw's sons had succeeded her as chiefs of a Ho-Chunk village near
Portage on the Wisconsin River, later a town called Dekorra.[7]

Fortunately, Ho-poe-kaw did not live long enough to see her descendants forced from
their homeland by the next country to claim their land: the United States. "The Decorah

family in the nineteenth century was the most powerful of the Winnebago families," writes Kellogg, as descendants signed "peace treaties" with the federal government for decades. One son of Ho-poe-kaw signed the first "peace treaty" with the federal government soon before he died in 1816. His son signed the treaties of 1828–1832, after two male cousins from Koshkonong went to Washington, D.C., to negotiate — as did his daughter, the only woman in the party and only eighteen years old. Although her name was not recorded, she was remembered in the new nation's capital. Saterlee Clark, later a U.S. senator from Wisconsin, "said she was the most beautiful Indian woman he ever saw, and that she created a decided social sensation," according to historian H. L. Skavlem. She "was spoken of in the eastern newspapers of that day as an 'Indian princess'" and called a "keen, sagacious, womanly woman." Afterward, she was known as "Washington Woman" — at least to newcomers to Wisconsin — for her social ease gained from experiences in the East, where she had visited "various exhibitions, museums, menageries, the theater," according to Juliette Magill Kinzie. The Decorah descendant "had a pleasant, old-acquaintance, sort of air . . . as much as to say, 'You and I have seen something of the world.'"[8]

It was a world that would not be theirs for long. In the 1830s, according to Kellogg, the government "could not let the Winnebago live in their ancient villages, duping them into" — or, in other accounts, altering — "a treaty by which they sold all their Wisconsin lands." The federal government forcibly removed the Ho-Chunk, first to Minnesota and later to Iowa and Nebraska, where the Decorah name decorates signs for streets and towns. However, "many refused to remain and surreptitiously made their way back to their loved Wisconsin, where some dwell even to this day," writes Kellogg, and they returned repeatedly for decades, in defiance of federal removal. However, they lacked a federal reservation and had to repurchase their homelands.[9]

Few other accounts of women's lives in Wisconsin exist from the first written accounts of the explorers in the 1630s to the establishment of separate territorial status in the 1830s. While men claimed the land for their countries, women continued to reclaim the land for their crops and to trade the furs trapped by men, until the Natives' way of life was lost owing to "involvement in the fur trade, which emphasized male activities," according to historian Patty Loew. That involvement and the influence of outsiders meant that Native women also "lost both skills and autonomy," writes historian Sara M. Evans, although as the fur trade led Native men to undertake longer trading, hunting, and trapping expeditions away from home, their villages "became a female space" in which "women stayed at home, maintaining villages and cornfields generation after generation."[10]

Another reason for loss of their matrilineal heritage was intermarriage of Native women, such as Ho-poe-kaw of the Ho-Chunk, with newcomers. Her marriage was notable only because she was among the first women to wed French Canadian soldiers, trappers, and traders. These women literally gave birth to a new land and a new people: the children of both cultures, called the *métis*. They would found Wisconsin's first settlements, which would become towns and cities, many with French names, and their descendants would bear French surnames such as that of Charles de Langlade, who is called the "father of Wisconsin" and "first white settler" in many histories, although he was a *métis*.

Others included Cadotte, Denomie, Grignon, Juneau, Rolette, Vieau — all men whose names became far better known for founding fur-trading dynasties.[11]

Little is written of the Native and then *métis* women who were here first and also founded the founding families — and often were fur traders and founders of the family businesses as well. Of some, not even their names are known, or only their Christian names after conversion. An exception was Thimatee, the daughter of an Ottawa chief, whose baptismal name became Marie or Marianne Amighissen and who married a trader named Marcotte or Marcot. Her daughters, Therese Marcot Lasaliere Schindler and Marguerite Madeline Marcot La Framboise, also were successful traders at Sault Ste. Marie on Michilimackinac, or Mackinac Island, when the Upper Peninsula and Wisconsin were in Michigan Territory. Their story is in this chapter.

The stories of many other Native women and their contributions merit mention in this collection. A woman of the Anishinabe — an alliance of the Ojibwe, Ottawa, and Potawatomi — named Athanasi, also called Catherine Cadotte, married a Frenchman in 1756 and continued their fur-trading company at Michilimackinac after his death. One of their *métis* sons, Michel, opened a trading post at La Pointe on the island of Moningwunakawning, the spiritual center of the Anishinabe along Chequamegon Bay of Lake Superior. In 1792, he married an Ojibwe chief's daughter, Equaysayway, or Traveling Woman, better known by her baptismal name for which her father renamed her island home, Madeline. Also born on Madeline Island was another Ojibwe chief's daughter, Ozhaguscodaywayquay, or Woman of the Green Glades, who wed an Irish immigrant trader named Johnston in 1793 and bore four sons and four daughters. A daughter born in 1800 and named Bamewawagezhikaquay, or Woman of Stars Rushing Through Sky, also called Jane, became better known by her pseudonym of Leelinau as the author of "origin stories" she had learned from her grandfather. A chief and storyteller of Ojibwe oral history, he was not literate; nor was Jane's mother, although she capably carried on her husband's trading company after his death. However, Jane was educated in Canada and Ireland prior to her marriage to an agent and scholar of Great Lakes cultures, Henry Rowe Schoolcraft. He and Jane Johnston Schoolcraft published a magazine on Native American cultures: *The Literary Voyager* or *Muzzeniegun,* which included the "tales" told by "Leelinau" of the life of her island people.[12]

Far to the south, the life of Milwaukee's *métis* "founding mother," Josette Vieau Juneau, spanned the half-century of her homeland's changing status from the preterritorial period to statehood. She would be her family's third generation of women who married French Canadian traders — as had her Menominee grandmother and *métis* mother, Angelique Roy Vieau — but she was the first to have been born an American, in 1802 or 1803, probably at her parents' permanent trading post near Green Bay. Sometimes still called La Baye from its founding as the first fort settlement of New France west of Lake Michigan almost a century before, the fort at Green Bay by then was under British forces' control, although they had lost to the new United States the lands then officially in the Indiana Territory. The U.S. census in 1800 found only fifty civilians at the Green Bay fort and sixty-five at a second fort settlement at Prairie du Chien. Forts also housed several hundred soldiers and their families, servants, and even slaves, although slavery was illegal in the territory; the few federal officials enforced few laws on the frontier. At least the census counted slaves — but not the "non-citizens," as many as 24,000 Native Americans, who then were living in Wisconsin.[13]

By the time that Josette Vieau Juneau was twelve years old, the British lost the War of 1812, and they finally left the forts and lands west of Lake Michigan, which were by then in Illinois Territory. By 1820, when she left her parents' post, the American government had garrisoned Green Bay, by then in Michigan Territory and home to 290 civilians. But none lived at Milwaukee, the site of one of the Vieaus' seasonal posts, as late as 1820 — the year that their daughter married their clerk, a former voyageur from Montreal named Laurent Solomon Juneau, in the mission church in Allouez. The Juneaus soon moved and made the Milwaukee post their home, although he often was off on trading trips.[14]

Josette Vieau Juneau ran their store and stockade as well as their log home. However, she hardly was alone; of their seventeen children, fourteen survived to adulthood, and their home was known for her hospitality. That Milwaukee also survived is credited to her for having negotiated a truce to avert a massacre after squatters angered the area's Potawatomis. They respected her Menominee heritage, manner, and linguistic ability, as she wore native dress and knew many native dialects, often interpreting for her husband. Also fluent in French and even in English to an extent, she welcomed "distinguished visitors" for decades after 1825, when the Erie Canal linked the Great Lakes to the East by waterway in addition to the overland route.[15]

Yet as late as 1830, when more than 3,000 non–Native Americans lived in Wisconsin, "virtually everyone" was like the Juneaus, according to historian Alice E. Smith. They were fur traders of French Canadian or Native origin — or both. But the *métis* soon became a minority amid many newcomers from the East. In 1835, the Juneaus' home was the site of the first town meeting in Milwaukee, whose population of almost 2,000 surpassed that of Green Bay. On the eve of separate territorial status in 1836, more than half of Wisconsin's population of almost 11,700 residents lived in the southeastern area. By 1846, Milwaukee alone grew to almost 10,000 residents and gained city status. Although most voters were easterners — and all were men — they elected the first settler as their first mayor. Josette Vieau Juneau, the granddaughter of one of the first Wisconsin women, was the first "first lady" of the city that was the largest in Wisconsin, then and since.[16]

Another Native American woman's place in Wisconsin history was as the first public schoolteacher. Wuhwehweeheemeew, or the Chosen One, also was called Electa Quinney. Born about 1798, she had an advanced education at a female seminary in Connecticut and taught at a mission school in New York for six years until 1827, when she followed her Stockbridge people, who had been forced west by the federal government four years earlier to Menominee land. As early as 1828, at Statesburg near Grande Kawkawlin, now Kaukauna, Quinney taught as many as forty to fifty children at a time. In 1833, she married a Mohican minister sent from Canada as a missionary to the Oneida, who also had migrated west in the 1820s. The couple next served a Seneca mission in Oklahoma, where Electa Quinney Adams worked alone after widowhood in 1844 until her remarriage to a Cherokee editor. She returned to Wisconsin, where her brother was sachem of the Stockbridge. She died in 1885 and was buried on the shore of Lake Winnebago, near the site where the Native American and newcomer to Wisconsin herself had schooled any students, regardless of whether they were Native Americans or newcomers to Wisconsin.[17]

Other schools — often private or parochial — arose at the first forts and settlements, many of them mission schools that accepted Native American students, but not their culture. By 1836, ten missionary schools with 1,300 students had opened in northern Wisconsin. A school opened for boys on Michilimackinac, but nothing comparable for girls was established until Marianne Schindler Fisher — granddaughter of Thimatee of the Ottawa — began the first boarding school in the territory. Her daughter, Elizabeth Therese Fisher Baird, later recalled that the "most estimable" Sarah B. Cadle came to Allouez near Green Bay in 1827 with her missionary brother and opened a school for the Menominee. At Little Chute, according to Alice E. Smith, the *métis* Rosalie LaBorde Dousman "devoted the greater part of her life to the education of her young Indian charges," assisted by her daughters Jane and Kate. At La Pointe, descendants of the Cadotte dynasty founded a school for their own *métis* children as well as for the Ojibwe in 1831. Among Ho-Chunk students in Prairie du Chien at a mission school opened in 1833 by a minister and his wife, girls soon outnumbered boys.[18]

However, men outnumbered women throughout Wisconsin in the preterritorial period, especially in the military culture of the forts. The wife of a government agent to the Ho-Chunk traveled with him in 1830 — and she would not travel without her piano, an artifact of her eastern women's culture, carried by men from ships to wagons on a journey of many weeks to Mackinac, Green Bay, and finally Fort Winnebago. Her piano became as famed as Juliette Magill Kinzie when she authored one of the first written accounts of Wisconsin by a woman, *Wau-Bun, the "Early Day" in the North-West*. This chapter includes the story of her courage, curiosity, and compassion in her own stories of "Washington Woman" Decorah and other Ho-Chunk women whom she met.

Women also were outnumbered by as much as three to one in the southeastern area near Milwaukee and the southwestern area near Mineral Point, where settlements arose not for the fur trade but for an even more lucrative natural resource: lead. Although early settlers found that women were "quite industrious miners" among Ho-Chunk inhabitants in the area, men were the miners of the newcomer culture — a southern culture, since most migrated up the Mississippi River, as well as a military culture. In sum, settlement signaled the onset of an unsettlingly male culture that must have only added to the discomfort of the first women on the frontier.[19]

Among them, the wife of one of the first government land sales agents, Eliza Whiting Sheldon, literally carried her youngest son into Wisconsin in 1833 while wagons carried her comforts of eastern women's culture: hundreds of books to educate her youngest children. She left her oldest daughters behind for advanced education in the female academies not yet found on the frontier, as her son tells in his account here of women's worries and sorrows of separation as well as their courage in facing sacrifices to come westward without the comfort of daughters.

Some immigrants and migrants to the southwestern mining area also contributed customs from other continents and cultures. Among the first Cornish settlers from 1827 forward was Frances T. Maynard Clyma, who had married at the age of seventeen, immigrated at twenty-one, and migrated six years later with her husband to his "diggings" near Pendarvis. As many as seven thousand more miners and family members came from Cornwall, England, including women whose colorful custom of waving dishcloths to signal dinner — pasties and perhaps saffron cake with "scalded" or clotted cream — gave the name to Shake Rag Street in Mineral Point. Even earlier, if far fewer, were African Americans from the South who came as servants with soldiers; in 1820, the census found freedmen at the Prairie du Chien fort — but apparently no freedwomen.[20]

Civilian settlers from the South also brought slaves, sometimes to freedom. The sacrifices that women made for life on the frontier — for a better life for their families and a life of freedom for others — are evident in the loneliness of letters, excerpted in this chapter, written by an abolitionist born in Connecticut who came to Wisconsin by way of Missouri in 1826. Susan Hempstead Gratiot and her husband, a prominent slave owner from the founding family of St. Louis, had to move from Missouri to manumit his slaves, including an African American freedwoman and settler known only as Jenny, whose later story is lost to history.

Other settlers who brought slaves north to escape the slave culture included a southerner named Christiana McDonald Dodge. She had lived most of her life on the ever-moving frontier of the era, from Kentucky to the Deep South states of Mississippi and Louisiana to Missouri. There, in 1801, at the age of sixteen, she married the future first governor of Wisconsin Territory. Henry Dodge moved his family in 1827 to found Dodgeville, near Mineral Point, after an upriver trek of more than a month with their eight surviving children. The Dodges also brought slaves whom they freed years later, including some of Wisconsin's first African American women settlers, although their full names are lost to history.[21]

The full name is known of one of these early freedwomen in southeastern Wisconsin, a charter member of the first known women's organization anywhere in Wisconsin. She and her husband had been bought and manumitted in the East by the influence of the Ordways, an abolitionist minister and his wife whom the newly freed couple followed to a Presbyterian pulpit in a new town in Wisconsin called Prairie Village. While some women went west with books and pianos, Lucy Ordway brought bylaws of the first nationwide women's organization, the Female Moral Reform Society, founded not long before in the East to promote the "observance of the Seventh Commandment" by eradicating prostitution and preventing sexually transmitted diseases spread by men to their wives and children. In the 1830s, she founded the Female Moral Reform Society of Prairie Village, a town of only two hundred residents. However, the organization enrolled more than a hundred women on the charter. Many signed their first names only as "Mrs.," and one signed hers only as "X." Others were mothers, grandmothers, sisters, and wives of a future governor and a future congressman. Another was former slave Peggy More, who had "good standing in society and was on terms of perfect equality," according to a historian, in the town that eventually would be called Waukesha.[22]

From La Pointe to Mineral Point to Milwaukee and points in between, the missions and mines and future metropolises then seen as progress in the new territory would mute the lessons of the land that had been learned by the first Wisconsin women and transmitted to traders, husbands, and *métis* children in the period prior to separate territorial status. True progress would be achieved only with the contributions of women as bearers and builders of culture — all cultures in Wisconsin — although neither women nor men would achieve a "perfect equality" of cultures, then or since. Nor would the contributions of many women receive mention in most Wisconsin histories.

However, at least the tribal traditions of Wisconsin's first nations were not lost. As Ojibwe scholar Patty Loew observes, their oral history of "origin stories" and "songs passed down to present generations," combined with evidence such as effigy mounds, can aid in reconstructing the past prior to written history — a past that included the first women who made Wisconsin history and their *métis* daughters as well as the newcomer mothers and daughters who came next from the East, the South, or elsewhere to Wisconsin, where women would make history again.[23]

⚜

## NOTES

1. Patty Loew, *Indian Nations of Wisconsin: Histories of Endurance and Renewal* (Madison: WHS, 2001), 40–41. Another scholar suggests that other nations, but not the Ho-Chunk, also organized in matrilineal clans; see Robert E. Bieder, *Native American Communities in Wisconsin, 1600–1960* (Madison: University of Wisconsin Press, 1995), 23. On the population estimate in 1600, see Robert C. Nesbit, *Wisconsin: A History* (Madison: University of Wisconsin Press, 1989), 12. On tribal names, See Loew, *Indian Nations;* on usage and terminology in discussion of Native cultures, see Nancy Oestrich Lurie, *Wisconsin Indians,* rev. ed. (Madison: SHSW, 2000), x–xiii.

2. Nancy Oestreich Lurie, "Wisconsin: A Natural Laboratory for Native American Indian Studies," *WMH* 53, no. 1 (Autumn 1969): 6, and "In Search of Chaetor: New Findings on Black Hawk's Surrender," *WMH* 71, no. 3 (Spring 1988): 162–183; Loew, *Indian Nations,* 40–41.

3. Louise Phelps Kellogg, "Glory of the Morning and the Decorah Family," *Madison Democrat,* February 21, 1912; Milo Milton Quaife, "Glory of the Morning," *Milwaukee Journal,* August 15, 1925; see also Lucy Eldersveld Murphy, "Autonomy and the Economic Roles of Indian Women of the Fox-Wisconsin Riverway Region, 1763–1832," in *Negotiators of Change: Historical Perspectives on Native American Women,* ed. Nancy Shoemaker (New York: Routledge, 1995), 72–89.

4. Kellogg, "Glory of the Morning;" Quaife, "Glory of the Morning;" see also Murphy, "Autonomy and the Economic Roles of Indian Women," 72–89.

5. Walter Monfried, "Fertile Wisconsin Described by Explorer Carver 200 Years Ago," *Milwaukee Journal,* October 14, 1941.

6. Ibid.

7. Kellogg, "Glory of the Morning"; "The Story of 'Glory of the Morning,'" *WMH* 1, no. 1 (September 1917): 93; M. Mornington Dexter, "The Old World of Dekorra," *WMH* 17, no. 3 (June 1934): 342. Sources also give the original spelling of the surname as Des Caris, Descarrie, Decarry, or DeKaury.

8. Kellogg, "Glory of the Morning"; H. L. Skavlem, "White Crow and His Daughter, An Indian Princess," *Baraboo News,* April 5, 1917; Mrs. John H. Kinzie, *Wau-Bun, The "Early Day" in the North-West* (New York: Derby & Jackson, 1856).

9. Alice E. Smith, *HOW,* vol. 1, *From Exploration to Statehood* (Madison: SHSW, 1973), 76; Kellogg, "Glory of

the Morning"; Loew, *Indian Nations,* 21. Centuries after Ho-poe-kaw's era, early film actress Nadonis Decorah of Mirror Lake "glorified in the distinguished blood of her husband," who was called Kanokah or White Eagle Decorah and was a Chautauqua lecturer on "legends" of the Ho-Chunk such as the life of his great-great-grandmother Ho-poe-kaw; see O. D. Brandenburg, "Indian Princess on Shore of Mirror Lake," *Baraboo Daily News,* July 16, 1921. Other Decorah descendants were veterans in every American war, including the first Ho-Chunk named to the Indian Hall of Fame: Mitchell Red Cloud Jr., a Medal of Honor recipient in the Korean War who was on a *Life* magazine cover and in *Esquire* magazine in 1951. Renamed in his honor were a La Crosse park and military sites, including one at Fort McCoy, Wisconsin. However, according to a base newsletter, Ho-poe-kaw was "the daughter of a Winnebago chief" (not herself a chief) and "Red Cloud inherited his adventurous spirit from the French side of his family." See "Red Cloud Among MOH Recipients Honered," *Triad,* Novermber 12, 1999.

10. Loew, *Indian Nations,* 8, 14, 19, 41–42; Sara M. Evans, *Born for Liberty: A History of Women in America* (New York: Free Press, 1989), 11.

11. Smith, *HOW,* 51–53, 70; Nesbit, *Wisconsin,* 54; Loew, *Indian Nations,* 15.

12. Loew, *Indian Nations,* 54; Smith, *HOW,* 62; Milo Milton Quaife, "Stories of Wisconsin: Romance of Old La Pointe," *Milwaukee Journal,* September 5, 1920; Hamilton Nelson Ross, *La Pointe: Village Outpost on Madeline Island* (Madison: SHSW, 2000), 64–65; Victoria Brehm, *Women's Great Lakes Reader,* 2nd ed. (Tustin, MI: Ladyslipper Press, 2000), 23–24.

13. Smith, *HOW,* 41–45, 164, 96–101, 165; Nesbit, *Wisconsin,* 80–81, 89–91, 138; W. A. Titus, "Theresa, the Last Home of Solomon Juneau," *WMH* 18, no. 3 (March 1935): 308; Marion Lawson, "Solomon Juneau: Milwaukee's First Mayor," *WMH* 41, no. 2 (Winter 1957–58): 114–115. Sources differ on whether he was named Laurent Solomon or Solomon Laurent and also differ on vital data on both women. Vieau, sometimes cited as Angeline and a stepmother, was born about 1766, wed in 1786, was widowed in 1852, died in 1862 or 1864, and was buried in Allouez.

14. Smith, *HOW,* 41–45, 164, 96–101, 165; Nesbit, *Wisconsin,* 80–81, 89–91, 138; Titus, "Theresa, the Last Home of Solomon Juneau," 308; Lawson, "Solomon Juneau: Milwaukee's First Mayor," 114–115.

15. Smith, *HOW,* 41–45, 164, 96–101, 165; Nesbit, *Wisconsin,* 80–81, 89–91, 138; Titus, "Theresa, the Last Home of Solomon Juneau," 308; Lawson, "Solomon Juneau: Milwaukee's First Mayor," 114–115.

16. Smith, *HOW,* 41–45, 164, 96–101, 165; Nesbit, *Wisconsin,* 80–81, 89–91, 138; Titus, "Theresa, the Last Home of Solomon Juneau," 308; Lawson, "Solomon Juneau: Milwaukee's First Mayor," 114–115. The Juneaus moved to Theresa in 1852 but returned to Milwaukee for medical care in 1855, when she died. Her husband died less than a year later, and both are buried in Milwaukee.

17. *WHC,* vol. 15, 47, 86–88; Electa F. Jones, *Stockbridge: Past and Present* (Springfield, MA: Samuel Bowles, 1854), 103–105; Nesbit, *Wisconsin,* 85.

18. Smith, *HOW,* 152–156.

19. Nesbit, *Wisconsin,* 91–92, 110, 116.

20. Smith, *HOW,* 165, 185, 494; Louis Albert Copeland, "The Cornish in Southwest Wisconsin," *WHC,* vol. 14, 305. Clyma, born in 1798, died in Monticello in 1879.

21. Nancy Greenwood Williams, *The First Ladies of Wisconsin* (Kalamazoo, MI: Ana Publishing, 1991), 5–9. Christiana McDonald Dodge moved again to Iowa, where a son became the first U.S. senator born west of the Mississippi River and a daughter wed the territorial governor before their mother died in 1865 in Burlington, Iowa, where she is buried.

22. Evans, *Born for Liberty,* 74–75; "Ladies of Days Gone By," *Waukesha Freeman,* May 18, 1899; Female Moral Reform Society File, Waukesha County Historical Society. The date of the founding of the organization in Wisconsin is cited variously as from 1834 to 1839 in undated clippings and other sources, some of which also list the freedwoman's name as Peggy Moon.

23. Loew, *Indian Nations,* 5, 8.

# Therese Schindler of Mackinac

## *Upward Mobility in the Great Lakes Fur Trade*

JOHN E. McDOWELL

WMH 61, No. 2 (December 1977): 125–143

⁂

The fur trade on the upper Great Lakes was by all accounts a risky business. . . . The trader has been portrayed, and with some degree of accuracy, as tough, volatile, and not overly ethical, with a nut-brown face and a fondness for whiskey and Indian women. . . .

Several minor but significant facets of his existence, however, are apt to be overlooked. First of all, many fur traders did not simply go off into the woods and disappear from history after the War of 1812. Some, better endowed with talent, more innovative or aggressive, become city founders, real estate promoters, bankers, politicians. Others founded local and regional dynasties which, after a second or third generation, produced lawyers, merchants, governors, and physicians. In short, there existed a high degree of upward mobility among those who trafficked in furs, and a good many sharp-witted traders sooner or later escaped the noisome Indian encampments where they had entered the trade. A second point to be made is that not all fur traders engaged in those hazardous seasonal expeditions in canoe or bateau, but rather anchored their businesses in more-or-less permanent homes and traded hardware and blanketry with the same Indian bands year after year. And finally, it is worth mentioning that some of the wealthiest and most celebrated fur traders were not men, but women.

Therese Marcot Lasaliere Schindler, the subject of this piece, embodied all three traits. She was utterly determined to rise above the circumstances of her birth and upbringing; she became one of those fur traders who operated principally from a permanent home — Mackinac Island, in her case; and despite the vicissitudes of her life and the rougher aspects of dealing with Indians and boatmen, she was a woman of strength, sensitivity, and intelligence. Her accomplishments were notable, but she was far from unique; indeed, she was but one of a trio of female traders, all personally close, who lived and dealt in furs at Mackinac. Probably the most famous of the three was her sister, Madeline La Framboise, whose name occurs in many accounts of the trade in the upper Great Lakes. The other was Elizabeth Mitchell, wife of Dr. David Mitchell. . . . All three women were aided by the fact that they were half-Indian by birth, for this enhanced their ability to deal with Indians; on the other hand, it meant, in a sense, that they had farther to climb in society to attain material success and social acceptance. Yet climb they did, the descendants of Therese Schindler becoming most prominent in Wisconsin medical and social circles and the daughter of Mme. La Framboise marrying the brother of a future President of the United States.[1]

Therese was born — so she told Henry Rowe Schoolcraft, the famous Indian agent and student of native culture — in 1775, at "Old Mackinac," meaning Michilimackinac or what is now called Mackinaw City, on the tip of lower Michigan, the strategic gateway to lakes Michigan and Superior. Her father was a North West Company "factor" or chief agent named Jean Baptiste Marcot — evidently a man of some substance since the *Mackinac Register* refers to him as *sieur,* a title of distinction. (The same source discloses that he could not sign his own name.) Her mother was an Ottawa woman, Marianne, or Marie Amighissen — sometimes called Thimatee — the daughter of Kewinaquot, a chief of the Ottawa. Therese was the second-youngest and Madeline the youngest of seven Marcot children, about four of whom nothing is known except their names and their dates of birth. One thing is certain: her father and mother were legally married. . . .

The Marcot family home was at St. Joseph, the site of present Niles, Michigan. A census taken in 1780 listed Marcot, his wife, and four children as living there. This small settlement had a population of forty-nine persons who lived in a few rude cabins in or near a fort that had fallen into disrepair. They made their living by trading. . . .[2]

However, Marcot and his neighbors did not spend all of their summers at St. Joseph. They made regular trips to Michilimackinac. . . .[3]

During her early life Therese Marcot probably accompanied her family to their winter post in the western Lake Superior country. It would have been a long, grueling trip, the journeyers being confined for days in a small boat on the dangerous waters of Lake Superior. When they arrived at their destination, they existed through the winter in another rude cabin, enduring the bitter cold of the region, fighting to keep enough food on the table while they haggled with the Indians over pelts. It was a hard life, but worse was yet to come.

In 1783 Jean Baptiste Marcot was killed by Indians at the portage between the Fox and Wisconsin rivers. The family breadwinner gone, the mother, Marianne, returned to her native Ottawa village near St. Joseph, taking her children with her. This move had a profound influence upon Therese's later life. First, she became even more inured to hardship. Although they were more prosperous than several other tribes, the Ottawa still often lived on the edge of starvation. Furthermore, the life of an Indian woman was far from easy. It was her task to prepare the meals, cure the pelts, and plant and till the fields. Therese Marcot was kept busy. . . .[4]

. . . Therese Marcot thus spent the bulk of her formative years among formidable traders, both white and red; and what she saw and learned as a young woman would stand her in good stead in later life. . . .[5]

. . . On August 1, 1786, Marianne was at Mackinac, probably on a trading venture, and took the opportunity to have Therese and her sister, Madeline, baptized. She was unable to do much more than that for her two youngest girls. While he was alive, Jean Baptiste Marcot had seen to it that his children had been sent to Montreal to be educated. But now that he was gone, Marianne did not have the resources to do the same for Therese and Madeline. They might be given the benefit of a Christian baptism, but not that of an education. Like their mother, both girls would grow up illiterate.[6]

Before she was fifteen years old, Therese was married at St. Joseph to Pierre Lasaliere, a Canadian voyageur or boatman. Documents note that the marriage was performed "before witnesses," suggesting that it was a civil ceremony or perhaps an Indian marriage by contract, as were so many French-Indian unions. In any event, in 1799, when Therese's daughter Marianne was baptized at the age of nine, only the child's mother was present. Pierre Lasaliere had left his wife and child and gone voyaging elsewhere, never to re-enter their lives.[7]

Up to this point Therese's life had been one of adversity. The "half-breed" daughter of a French trader, she had lived so long in an Indian village and as the "Indian" wife of Lasaliere that she was referred to as an "Outawas" on her daughter's baptismal certificate. There had been no upward momentum so far in her life; indeed, just the opposite. But if her troubles were not entirely over, matters were about to change for the better.

On July 12, 1804, Therese married George Schindler, a fine and well-liked Mackinac trader, and from 1805 on she made the island her permanent home. Her daughter Marianne was enrolled in a school run by Angelique Adhemar. . . . Angelique was the sister of Josette La Framboise, who was the sister-in-law of Madeline Marcot La Framboise. All of this seemingly extraneous matter is noted to illustrate how closely and complexly knit was the Mackinac community into which Therese now settled. Buffeted from place to place, she had now put down roots. Her home was just a few rods from that of her sister, Madeline. And she probably took comfort in the presence of her sister, for her mother was no longer living. She and Madeline had been close during the time they spent in the Indian village, and they would remain close the rest of their lives. Therese made relatively short trading trips from the island, but as near as can be determined she never "wintered" away from home. . . .[8]

It was both a distinctive and a pleasant place that Therese Schindler had chosen to live in. . . . In the early 1800s the village of Mackinac had a permanent population of about 250 persons, mostly of French and French-Indian derivation. French was the common language, though Indian dialects were often heard and even a little English was spoken. . . . The few Americans around, mostly in the garrison, were apt to look down upon these islanders, feeling that they were overly fond of having a good time. . . .

Except for the summers, Mackinac was a quiet place. However, when the ice went out of the strait, traders began to appear, some from as far away as the upper reaches of the Missouri River. Indians followed. It was the time when furs were sold and goods purchased for the following winter. Then, during the few warm months the island enjoys, the population burgeoned to as high as 4,000, made up mostly of shouting, singing, laughing, carousing men from the interior trading posts, all bent upon having an uproarious good time. The traders themselves gave lavish parties, each striving to outdo the other in the amount of food and liquor supplied. Mackinac was hardly ever quiet then, day or night. . . .[9]

About 1794 Therese's sister, Madeline, had married Joseph La Framboise, a member of a prominent trading family who, like George Schindler, operated in the area surrounding northern Lake Michigan. . . . [I]n 1806, while on his way to his post near present

Grand Rapids, Michigan, Joseph was killed by an Indian. Although Madeline La Framboise took over her husband's business, there remained the matter of settling Joseph's estate. . . .

. . . Therese had indeed bettered her station. George Schindler was not an inconsequential landowner at Mackinac. And there was to be another upward step in her family. Her daughter Marianne was about to make a noteworthy alliance. On July 22, 1809, she was married to Henry Monroe Fisher.

Fisher was quite a catch. He came from a wealthy Scotch family. . . . Educated at Montreal, like so many young men of that city he had gone west to enter the fur trade. He settled at Prairie du Chien and prospered, marrying a daughter of Gauthier De Niverille — a well-known name in Great Lakes history — and begetting four children: three sons and a daughter named Jane. (A beautiful, spirited girl, Jane Fisher was married successively to two famous Prairie du Chien traders, Joseph Rolette and Hercules L. Dousman.) Fisher was well liked by his fellow villagers, and he became a justice of the peace and captain of militia.

After his first wife died, Fisher met and married Marianne Schindler, taking her to his Mississippi River home. . . . Marianne presented him with a daughter on April 24, 1810. They named the infant Elizabeth Therese, and though they could hardly have expected to know it, she was to make her mark upon the history of the area. . . .[10]

. . . For the present Marianne was at Prairie du Chien, separated from her mother. But in June of 1812 she decided to visit the Schindlers on Mackinac, taking little Elizabeth with her. The visit was to last longer than she anticipated. Early on the morning of July 12, they, along with the other villagers, were routed from their beds and taken to the Dousman distillery at the western edge of the settlement. British soldiers and their Indian allies soon made their appearance upon the hill back of the fort, compelling its surrender. The War of 1812 had reached Mackinac. As Elizabeth later stated, the country was in an uproar and Indians in all directions were on the warpath. Marianne thus found that she was unable to return to Prairie du Chien and would have to stay with her mother.

This turn of events became very important in the lives of Therese and her family. Back at Prairie du Chien, Henry Fisher sensed correctly that the village would be the target of an American attack. And, although he was strongly pro-British, he did not wish to participate in hostilities against the Americans, many of whom were his friends. So he made arrangements with the wife of Michael Brisbois to take care of Jane and his youngest son; then, with his other sons, Henry and Alexander, he left for the Red River country. The Fisher family was never again reunited. . . . [A]bout 1824 . . . Fisher visited his wife and daughter at Mackinac, then went to Prairie du Chien to live with Jane, who was by that time Mrs. Rolette. He died there in 1827. In the meantime Marianne and Elizabeth had made the Schindler house their home. Historians should be grateful that they did so, for this enforced stay at Mackinac enabled Elizabeth later to record her fascinating reminiscences of life on the island. . . .[11]

. . . Therese Schindler had been plagued by hardship and trouble all her life, and more was in store. Sometime after Marianne and Elizabeth came to Mackinac — the exact time is far from certain — George Schindler lost both his health and his property. The nature of his illness is not known, but he may have suffered a stroke for he became a cripple. Schindler was finished in the trade, but he found a way to be useful nonetheless. He opened a school for boys. . . .[12]

Faced with the illness of her husband and the loss of his livelihood, Therese made the response that both her personality and her early life had prepared her to make: she carried on the fur trade. Her sister, Madeline La Framboise, had done the same thing when confronted with the death of her husband, and her success in that venture probably influenced Therese. But the larger question naturally arises, why did either of these two half-Indian women, both raised in an Indian village and both illiterate, enter the risky business of trafficking in pelts? . . . [C]ould they not have found an easier way to make a living?

In truth, there were not a great many respectable ways for a woman to make a living on the Great Lakes frontier in the early nineteenth century. Being illiterate, Therese Schindler could not even teach school. But she had been raised in the fur trade; her French as well as her Indian forebears knew the business; and her second husband had now, unfortunately, presented her with the opportunity to take over a modest but established enterprise. All this entered into Therese's decision. But perhaps the single most important factor was contained in her own tough-fibered personality. Like Madeline La Framboise and Elizabeth Mitchell, two other half-Indian women of Mackinac who made their marks in the fur trade, Therese Marcot Lasalier Schindler possessed both intelligence and an unquenchable spark of ambition to persevere, to overcome the difficult circumstances of her life. . . .

When Therese decided to carry on her husband's business, she was fortunate that there were members of her own tribe close by . . . [which] obviated the necessity of setting up a wintering post elsewhere. These Ottawa . . . were an accomplished, semiagricultural tribe. They lived in solidly constructed log cabins, and a priest who visited them in 1848 wrote that they were "generally industrious and skillful in what they undertake." . . . They were, in short, ideal customers for Therese Schindler, who could serve them by making several short trips each year to L'Arbre Croche, rather than staying in their midst all winter. Being half-Indian, she felt an affinity for these Ottawa, who in turn respected her and maintained their commercial ties with her throughout her lifetime.

So she packed her bateau (or perhaps bateaux, for a ledger indicates that there was often more than one boat) with "pieces" of goods that included firearms, knives, hatchets, tobacco, blankets, and silver ornaments. She employed five or six voyageurs to a boat, and, at first light, her trading party would paddle out of the Mackinac harbor. . . . After the thirty-mile trip was over Therese's voyageurs would quickly erect a tent for their employer and unload her trade goods. . . . Therese found time to visit with friends, exchange stories, and eat meals with a favored few. During their stay her men camped out, sleeping under the boats and existing on two daily meals of lyed corn boiled with pork. The furs she received for her goods were carefully baled and transported back to Mackinac. The disposal of the pelts there was a ritual that all appeared to enjoy. It was a battle of wits, complete with what seemed like interminable haggling over the grades of furs and the prices asked and paid. . . .[13]

Therese Schindler prospered. Her daughter Marianne kept a ledger for the years 1821 through 1824. . . . [I]t seems safe to say that Therese took in perhaps $8,000 to $10,000 a year . . . at a time when an experienced trader (one with an Indian following at that) could be hired for $1,000 per year. Like Madeline La Framboise and Elizabeth Mitchell, both of whom became wealthy in the trade, Therese Schindler supported her family very well.[14]

Shortly after the end of the War of 1812 a new organization appeared at Mackinac that had a profound effect on both Therese and her trade. This was the American Fur Company. . . . The avowed purpose of this concern was to dominate the fur trade in the Great Lakes country, and it did a thorough job. Madeline La Framboise became affiliated with the company in 1816, and ultimately Therese followed suit. In 1821 she appeared on the company rosters as trading on her own "account and risk," which explains why she was permitted to sell to other merchants. Semi-independent she may have remained, but she purchased her goods from the American Fur Company, and to it she had to sell her furs. But since the company secured practically all the traders in the district by one means or another, she hardly could have escaped its clutches even if she had so desired. . . .[15]

The presence of the American Fur Company at Mackinac had [another] effect upon the Schindler family other than influencing their trade and introducing them to rising young men who would later gain prominence in the business world. Mackinac was a fairly good place to live, considering conditions on the frontier generally, but it did lack some of the amenities of civilization.[16] It had a church, but most of the time no priest to say Mass. It had a school for boys — George Schindler's — but none for girls. Robert Stuart, resident manager for the fur company, did something about that. He believed that there should be a school for girls, and that its teacher could be found right in the Schindler house. He persuaded Marianne Fisher to open such an institution for the daughters of the company's principal employees, thereby founding (so it is claimed) the first boarding school in the Old Northwest. The pupils, ranging in age from twelve to eighteen, were taught to read and write, to keep house, and make their own clothes.[17] Marianne was thus on her way to becoming something more than just another trader's daughter. The years that followed would see her at a mission on the Grand River translating books for the Indians, at L'Arbre Croche teaching and translating, and again conducting school at Mackinac. Her work was appreciated. . . .[18]

Marianne Fisher found her life's work in teaching, Therese Schindler hers in commerce; yet neither woman ever escaped the tug of her Indian heritage. Sometimes the fact of blood was brought home in curious ways, as in 1820, when Therese Schindler looked out her window one morning and saw an Indian wigwam pitched in the dooryard. Upon investigation, she found that it was occupied by John Tanner, a "white Indian," and his Indian wife and children. Tanner was a Kentuckian who had been captured by the Shawnee when he was nine. . . .

Tanner was a sullen and bad-tempered man who never fully made the transition back to white society. He drifted from job to job, deserted his family, went to Sault Ste. Marie, and, after being accused of committing a murder, disappeared. But before all this occurred, he persuaded Therese Schindler to look after his daughters. One of them, Lucy, she adopted as an infant. The child became the darling of the Schindler household.

When she was old enough, she was educated in Marianne Fisher's school, and later she helped with the teaching. Tragically, in 1834, she perished when the lake schooner on which she was a passenger foundered with all hands on a voyage to Grand Rapids. Another Tanner girl, Martha, stayed at Mackinac until the 1840s, helping Marianne at the mission school and staying for a time with Madeline La Framboise. Finally, Tanner's Indian wife — whose name has not yet come to light — was taught by the Schindler women to work as a housekeeper, and as such she made her living at Mackinac for a dozen years before returning to the obscurity of her old life among the Red River Ottawa.[19]

The strange episode of the Tanner family, so intermixed with racial consciousness and Christian piety, was not the only evidence of the Indian influence in Therese Schindler's life. Like a great many of the Mackinac villagers with Indian blood in their veins, she carried on one of the most persistent, and pleasant, customs of aboriginal life: that of making maple sugar, which supplied the sweetening that was otherwise both scarce and expensive — and which incidentally was also a marketable commodity. Each spring about half the population of Mackinac journeyed into the woods, usually to Bois Blanc, a larger island about five miles eastward where Therese Schindler maintained a sugar camp. The settlers would begin tapping the trees about the first of March. Since she had more than a thousand trees to be cared for, Therese employed three men and two women to do the work. The sap was collected in birchbark buckets, carried by means of shoulder yokes and larger buckets to a rudely built shed, and there dumped into brass kettles suspended over open fires. Boiling to syrup took about twenty-four hours, after which the syrup was stored to be made into sugar later. After a second boiling at a different heat, the syrup was poured into molds made in the shape of diamonds, crosses, bears, rabbits, and other animals. Granulated maple sugar was kept in a mocuck, or box, of birchbark.

A great deal of work went into making sugar, but there was time for pleasure as well. After a long, confining winter it was a pleasant out-of-doors activity. And there were parties, at Therese's camp at least. This was perhaps inevitable, since her granddaughter, Elizabeth, was known as the "belle of Mackinac" and attracted much attention. At one such gathering five ladies and five gentlemen made their way to the Bois Blanc camp. . . .[20]

The name of Henry S. Baird among the guests that day is significant. He came from a family that had resided in Pennsylvania and Ohio, failing in business in the latter state. Henry had been well educated for the times and had studied law. But he suffered from ague, and when a friend suggested that Mackinac offered a more healthful climate, as well as the opportunity for self-advancement, he decided to move to the island. He arrived there on June 5, 1822. His total assets were four dollars, some books, his clothes, and the determination to make a place for himself.

That he certainly did. For a while he taught school to establish himself with the villagers. Then, in 1823, he was admitted to the Michigan bar, where he practiced among such well-known trader-lawyers as James Lockwood and Rix Robinson: men to be reckoned with. Henry Baird prospered and gained such a reputation that Lockwood accounted him the best lawyer in the vicinity. New courts were being established as settlers began moving into Michigan and Wisconsin; Baird thought he saw a greater opportunity to the west. In the spring of 1824 he visited the village of Green Bay, found that he would have no legal competition, and decided, upon the urging of several citizens, to move there.

But Baird had not been totally occupied in establishing himself as an attorney. He had . . . been seeing a good bit of Elizabeth Fisher. His attention was reciprocated, and when he returned from his visit to Green Bay, they were married in her home. The date was August 12, 1824. Elizabeth was fourteen years of age.

In September the couple left for Green Bay, which was then a rather primitive village. For a time they lived in a log house, but soon Baird bought a store that had been converted into a home. His legal practice kept him busy, and Elizabeth found that she would have to learn to speak English, as well as how to read — matters that she had neglected at Mackinac. Writing later, she did not spare herself; despite the attentions of both George Schindler and Marianne Fisher in attempting to teach her, she admitted, she had been too spoiled to study. But Elizabeth now had made a start, and she would complete the upward movement of the Schindler family in both social and literary circles. Henry Baird became a factor in the business and political life of Wisconsin, greatly aided by his wife's knowledge of the area, her ability to interpret for his French-speaking clients, and, not the least, her Indian ancestry. Finally, she made up for her earlier indifference to reading and writing by contributing several distinguished reminiscences of life among the Indians and fur traders of the Old Northwest to the *Wisconsin Historical Collections*.[21]

Elizabeth Therese Baird may have moved away from Mackinac, but that did not mean that her grandmother did not see her now and then. Henry Baird still had cases on the island, and apparently she often found a way to visit. . . .

. . . [I]n 1825, Elizabeth stayed on at Mackinac for several months to be with George Schindler, whose failing health had worsened gravely. Three weeks after she left, Elizabeth's "grandfather" died, making Therese Schindler a widow once again.[22]

Therese carried on her trade after her husband's death. But the changes wrought by the close of the War of 1812 and the entry of the American Fur Company into the Great Lakes region continued apace, affecting the texture of life in Mackinac. . . .

Other changes were also taking place. Settlers were entering both Michigan and Wisconsin, and treaties were made to remove Indian title to the land they would occupy. As a result, some of the Indians were displaced. . . . That was not all. Fur prices fell and money became scarce in the trade. . . . Of greater consequence, however, was the increased competition for furs. Many of the new settlers, while essentially farmers, found that they could earn extra money by trapping and trading for furs. The prosperity the trade had enjoyed attracted many newcomers. . . . Ruinous competition and hard times signalled an end to the palmy days of the trade. . . .[23]

And how did Therese Schindler survive these changes in the fur trade? As far as can be determined, fairly well. She had great influence with the Ottawa of L'Arbre Croche, who were but little disturbed by settlers. Marianne Fisher had both taught and translated for them, and they remained loyal to the Schindlers. In the spring Therese, who was now in her sixties, would wait for them to return from their winter hunting and then accompany them to Mackinac. She was not always well, but she carried on.[24]

Marianne Fisher continued her school teaching and mission work among the Indians of Mackinac, corresponding with her aunt, Madeline La Framboise, in Montreal and fretting from time to time about whether she should remarry. (Mme. La Framboise counseled her, rather confusingly: "I don't want to imply, however, that you will [be] unmortal in passing to the second wedding, but I am almost sure that you like better your freedom.") In 1842 she received word from Prairie du Chien that Joseph Rolette had died. Although she had not been as close to the Rolettes as had Elizabeth Baird, nevertheless she must have felt some sense of loss at the death of her stepdaughter's husband — and perhaps a sense of relief when, in 1844, Jane Fisher was remarried to Hercules L. Dousman, the Prairie du Chien fur trader and lumberman. The Dousman family was well-known to the Schindlers; Hercules had attended George Schindler's school at Mackinac before going to Wisconsin, where he became one of the wealthiest men in the territory.[25]

Madeline La Framboise, friend and confidante to the Schindler family for so many years, died on April 4, 1846. She had been a generous benefactress of Ste. Anne's in Mackinac, and both she and her daughter were buried there beneath the altar of the Catholic church.[26] Madeline's passing, like the attainment of statehood by Wisconsin in 1848, marked the twilight of the first generation of traders and settlers in the upper Great Lakes region. Therese Schindler, matriarch of a large and far-flung family, serenely held court in Mackinac, where, on one occasion at least, her home swarmed with five generations of Schindlers. In her final years she freed her slave, François Lacroix, whose mother, Angelique, had been Mme. La Framboise's slave for many years. In 1853 Marianne Fisher died, and Therese gave up her home on Mackinac so that she could live with her granddaughter, Elizabeth Baird, in Green Bay. There, on October 31, 1855, Therese Schindler died in her eightieth year. As had been her wish, she was returned to Mackinac and buried in a Catholic cemetery below the bluffs, within sight of the great inland seas on which French, British, and Americans had contested for wealth and empire.[27]

. . . Through perseverance and a modicum of good luck, Therese Schindler progressed from the fringes of a grubby trading outpost to a seat among the wealthy denizens of Mackinac; but although she and Mme. La Framboise and Elizabeth Mitchell earned respect and a measure of power on the island, their influence was both modest and localized. It was their families that achieved larger status and more lasting fame. Marianne Fisher, Therese's daughter, advanced the Schindler family through her educational and missionary work; but it was Marianne's daughter Elizabeth who completed the family's upward spiral. As the wife of Henry Samuel Baird, the first professional lawyer to practice in what became Wisconsin Territory, she achieved social prominence and a degree of historical significance that must surely have brought satisfaction to her remarkable grandmother. . . . Succeeding generations of Favills and Tenneys continue to make their marks — living testimony to the intelligence and character of their French-Indian ancestor, Therese Marcot Lasaliere Schindler.[28]

# NOTES

1. See John E. McDowell, "Madame La Framboise," in *Michigan History* 56 (Winter 1972): 271–286.

2. Obituary of Therese Schindler, in *Wisconsin Necrology* 1: 202; Edwin O. Wood, *Historic Mackinac* (New York, 1919), 2: 238; *WHC* 18: 484–485, and 19: 18; *Michigan Pioneer Collections* 10: 407; Wilbur M. Cunningham, *Land of Four Flags* (Grand Rapids, MI: 1961), 67, 72–73.

3. *Michigan Pioneer Collections* 10: 405, 599.

4. *WHC* 11: 164. . . .

5. McDowell, "Madame La Framboise," 272–273. Therese's childhood resembled her sister's.

6. *WHC* 19: 86.

7. Ibid., 19: 86n, 117, 118; 11: 164–165. Lasaliere appears in fur-trade documents as late as 1818. . . .

8. Elizabeth Therese Baird, "Reminiscences of Early Days on Mackinac Island," *WHC* 14: 20, 42.

9. *WHC* 9: 316–317; Wood, *Historic Mackinac* 2: 137, 138, 143, 168, 172.

10. Baird, "Reminiscences of Early Days on Mackinac Island," 22; *WHC* 10: 492–493; 19: 139–140.

11. Baird, "Reminiscences of Early Days on Mackinac Island," 22; Alec R. Gilpin, *The War of 1812 in the Old Northwest* (East Lansing, MI: 1958), 90.

12. Baird, "Reminiscences of Early Days on Mackinac Island," 22; Elizabeth Therese Baird, "Reminiscences of Life in Territorial Wisconsin," in *WHC* 15: 213.

13. David Lavender, *The Fist in the Wilderness* (Garden City, NY: 1964), 265; McDowell, "Madame La Framboise," 278; [Milo M.] Quaife, *Lake Michigan* [Indianapolis, 1944], 282; Bela Hubbard, *Memorials of a Half-Century* (New York, 1887), 185–186; Gurdon S. Hubbard, *The Autobiography of Gurdon Saltonstall Hubbard* (Chicago, 1921), 144–145; George Pare, *The Catholic Church in Detroit* (Detroit, 1951), 597–598.

14. "Account Book of a Mackinac Merchant," Michigan Manuscripts C, in Archives Division, WHS; *Michigan Pioneer Collections* 37: 143.

15. *WHC* 11: 373–375; 12: 154, 169; Ida A. Johnson, *The Michigan Fur Trade* (Lansing, 1919), 125.

16. Baird, "Reminiscences of Early Days on Mackinac Island," 41–42.

17. Ibid., 42.

18. Ibid., 22, 23, 54; Madeline La Framboise to Marianne Fisher, July 19, 1842, in the Henry S. Baird Papers, Archives Division, [WHS].

19. Baird, "Reminiscences of Early Days on Mackinac Island," 47–54; *WHC* 19: 134. For Tanner's life, see Edwin Jones, ed., *Thirty Years Indian Captivity of John Tanner* (Minneapolis, 1956).

20. Baird, "Reminiscences of Early Days on Mackinac Island," 28–31.

21. Ibid., 18; Baird, "Reminiscences of Life in Territorial Wisconsin," 205–213; *WHC* 7: 426–430.

22. Baird, "Reminiscences of Early Days on Mackinac Island," 55–64; Baird, "Reminiscences of Life in Territorial Wisconsin," 219–220.

23. Johnson, *The Michigan Fur Trade*, 135, 136–137, 146, 150; R. Carlyle Buly, *The Old Northwest* (Bloomington, IN: 1951) 2: 319; *Michigan Pioneer Collections* 11: 195–200; Dwight Goss, *History of Grand Rapids* (Chicago, 1906), 74–75; Joseph La Framboise to Elizabeth Baird, February 28, 1840, August 23, 1842, in the Henry S. Baird Papers; Mrs. Lyle Weldy, a great-granddaughter of Joseph La Framboise, to the author; Rhoda R. Gilman, "Last Days of the Upper Mississippi Fur Trade," in North American Fur Trade Conference, *People and Pelts: Selected Papers*, ed. by Malvina Bolus (Winnipeg, 1972), 128.

24. Martha Tanner to Elizabeth Baird, October 4, 1843, May 26 and December 2, 1844; Madeline La Framboise to Elizabeth Baird, April 26, 1845, all in the Henry S. Baird Papers.

25. Madeline La Framboise to Marianne Fisher, August 18, 1841, and July 19, 1842, ibid.

26. Baird, "Reminiscences of Early Days on Mackinac Island," 43.

27. Ibid., 42; *Wisconsin Necrology* 1: 202; Mrs. Marie Abbott to Elizabeth Baird, January 1, 1853, in the Henry S. Baird Papers.

28. Biographical sketch of Elizabeth Baird, in U.S.–WPA–Wisconsin, Wisconsin Biographies, in Archives Division, WHS; Stephen Favill, *Favill Family* (Madison?, 1899), 7, 14, 31–32; Horace Kent Tenney sketch, in *Who Was Who in America*, I; Joseph Schafer, "Henry Baird Favill: A Wisconsin Gift to Chicago," in *WMH* 24 (December 1940): 199–227.

# As She Knew Them

## Juliette Kinzie and the Ho-Chunk, 1830–1833

### MARGARET BEATTIE BOGUE

WMH 85, No. 2 (December 2001): 45–58

☙ ❧

In the published history of Wisconsin, we have in the literature of the Black Hawk War of 1832 much about military action, the pursuit of Black Hawk, the bungling and conflict between army regulars and militia, the brutality of Indian and white alike, and the terrible slaughter at the Battle of Bad Axe on the first two days of August of that year. We do not have nearly enough published about those indirectly involved and about the immediate consequences of the conflict for the people who called this area of Wisconsin home, principally the Ho-Chunk.

So it is that readers of Wisconsin history will ever be indebted to Juliette M. Kinzie for her autobiographical memoir, *Wau-Bun, the "Early Day" in the North-west,* for the insights it gives about life in frontier Wisconsin from 1830–1833, the years of Black Hawk's last resistance to white settlement. . . .

*Wau-Bun* is especially valuable because it offers perspectives on the meaning of the Black Hawk War for the Indian people living in the area to the south and east of the Fox and Wisconsin Rivers. The lives lost, the physical suffering, and the surrender of beloved tribal land combined to produce devastation for the Ho-Chunk. In *Wau-Bun,* we see these developments through the observations and thoughts of a well-educated, cultured, middle-class New England woman married to a seasoned fur trader and federal Indian agent. Both of the Kinzies had a deep affection for the Ho-Chunk, a clear understanding of their enormous problems in the face of white settlement, and a real interest in their well-being and their culture. During their thirty-three months at Fort Winnebago, Juliette and John Kinzie clearly had come to feel very critical of the way the United States government handled Indian affairs, and yet they agreed in general principle with the idea of land cessions and removal to minimize contact with white culture, which they perceived to be a degrading influence on the Ho-Chunk. The only problem with that position, given the rapid development of the continent, was that it turned out to be virtually impossible to keep the cultures from each other. But that could not be foreseen in the early 1830s.

The principal actors in the narrative are the Kinzies. Juliette Kinzie was born Juliette Magill in 1806 into a respected, middle-class Connecticut family. She attended an avant-garde women's school, Emma Willard's Troy (New York) Female Seminary, founded on the principle that women deserved an educational experience equal to that available to men. Privately she studied music, natural history, and sketching. She was very impressed by what she learned about frontier life, and when she met handsome young John H. Kinzie — fresh from Michigan Territory — at her grandparents' home in Boston, she found him most attractive. They were married in August 1830.

John Kinzie, born at Sandwich, Upper Canada, in 1803 into a family of fur traders, had served the American Fur Company at its Mackinac (Michilimackinac) Island headquarters and then at Prairie du Chien, assisted Governor Lewis Cass of Michigan with Indian treaty negotiations in 1825, and thereafter served as his secretary. His understanding of Indian languages and culture made him a natural choice in 1829 for sub-agent to the Ho-Chunk.

The tribe's ancestors had interacted with the ever-growing numbers of Euro-Americans for almost two centuries. At first French explorers and fur traders came their way. After 1800 their British fur trading allies, successors to the French in 1763, declined in influence as Americans in search of lead and farmland came closer and closer to tribal territory and even into it, precipitating abrasive and violent episodes in the struggle over who would occupy and use the land. By the time the Kinzies arrived at Fort Winnebago the tragic drama was nearing its final act.

Specifically what had brought John and Juliette Kinzie to Fort Winnebago was the Treaty of 1829 between the United States and the Ho-Chunk, a settlement following the Red Bird Uprising of 1827. This uprising occurred as the direct result of incidents between settlers — especially lead miners who came into unceded Indian territory including that of the Ho-Chunk — and the Indians who resented such intrusions. The truth about which side in the confrontations committed the most severe murderous acts will never be known. Several such retaliatory incidents led by the Ho-Chunk chief Red Bird in 1826 and 1827 led to a coordinated push by federal troops and militia from Fort Snelling in present-day Minnesota, Green Bay, and Prairie du Chien. In early September 1827 they overtook Red Bird at the Fox-Wisconsin portage, where he surrendered.

The United States built Fort Winnebago at Red Bird's surrender site to further protect the strategic, well-used Fox-Wisconsin water route between the Great Lakes and the Mississippi River. Red Bird died in prison, and the American government negotiated a series of land cession treaties with Wisconsin Indian groups in 1829, which cleared the lead fields of all Indian claims. This treaty included the Ho-Chunk, who on August 1, 1829, relinquished an enormous tract: 1.76 million acres located in present-day southern Wisconsin and additional land in northern Illinois. Part of the settlement was payment of a little over half a million dollars in thirty-year annuities. John Kinzie carried the first installment of that money to Fort Winnebago in the fall of 1830.

Juliette Kinzie opened her narrative on a dark and rainy evening in Detroit when the newlyweds boarded the steamer *Henry Clay* bound for Green Bay. They carried with them the annuity payments for the Ho-Chunk and their household possessions, among them her piano! Juliette loved music and decided the piano was a must in the home.

The first stop beyond Detroit would be Mackinac Island, near the juncture of Lakes Huron and Michigan. . . .

From Mackinac Island the *Henry Clay* moved west and southwest through Lake Michigan and into more rough, rainy fall weather before arriving at Green Bay. . . .

After a short time in Green Bay in the company of the Grignon and Baird families, with Judge James Duane Doty as their host, the Kinzies set off up the lower Fox River to make the well-known hard passage to Lake Winnebago, notorious for its many rapids. . . . The Kinzie party boarded a thirty-foot mackinaw boat manned by soldiers and three Canadian voyageurs to carry the passengers, Juliette's piano, and the silver coin for treaty payments. The furniture and housekeeping articles would follow later. In the early pages of *Wau-Bun,* Juliette Kinzie recounted their adventures of passing around the rapids of the lower Fox and making their way through the Upper Fox River swamps filled with wild rice and water birds. . . .

During this part of the trip Kinzie also noted carefully how the Ho-Chunk women gathered wild rice around the shores of Lake Butte des Morts:

> The water along its shores was green with the fields of wild rice, the gathering of which, just at this season, is an important occupation of the Indian women. They push their canoes into the thick masses of the rice, bend it forward over the side with their paddles, and then beat the ripe husks of the stalks into a cloth spread in the canoe. After this, it is rubbed to separate the grain from the husk and fanned in the open air. It is then put in their cordage bags and packed away for winter use.

On the second day of their journey beyond Lake Butte des Morts, Kinzie depicted the abundance of rushes along the shores of Lake Puckaway and described in great detail how Indian women used these to make rush matting to cover their wigwams.

> Their mode of fabricating this is very primitive and simple. Seated on the ground, with the rushes laid side by side, and fastened at each extremity, they pass their shuttle, a long flat needle made of bone, to which is attached a piece of cordage formed of the bark of a tree, through each rush, thus confining it very closely, and making a fine substantial mat. These mats are seldom more than five or six feet in length, as a greater size would be inconvenient in adjusting and preparing the lodges.

Although she could not have known so early in her journey, she did learn about the customs associated with this work and later described them in the pages of *Wau-Bun:*

> It is a species of labor usually assigned to the elder women of the family. When they become broken down and worn out with exposure and hardship, so that they cannot cut down trees, hoe corn, or carry heavy burdens, they are set to weaving mats, taking care of the children, and disciplining the dogs, with which every Indian lodge abounds.

Kinzie thus began her tale with a focus on and interest in the work of women, especially Ho-Chunk women, awarding it by her attention and description a value that is evident to readers today. . . .

. . . At last they had arrived at Fort Winnebago where they temporarily settled in an apartment in the fort, awaiting the arrival of furniture and household goods for the as-yet-to-be-built agency house.

Many of the players in the drama that unfolded over the next eighteen months were highly visible on the day of the Kinzies' arrival in October 1830. As she looked over the landscape below the fort, Juliette Kinzie saw the soldiers at the garrison, many Ho-Chunk people, and the Indian traders. . . .

. . . Kinzie discovered the status of Ho-Chunk women in their communities, one of honor and respect that is not always apparent from the contemporary descriptions of village life. Kinzie wrote of Madame Four-Legs, a member of the Fox tribe and the wife of the Ho-Chunk chief Four-Legs. She spoke the court language among all the tribes, Ojibwe. Kinzie noted, "She was often called upon to act as interpreter, and had, in fact, been in the habit of accompanying her husband, and assisting him by her counsels upon all occasions. She was a person of great shrewdness and judgment, and, as I afterwards experienced, of strong and tenacious affections."

During the eighteen months between the Kinzies' arrival at Fort Winnebago in the fall of 1830 and the beginning of the Black Hawk War in April 1832, Juliette Kinzie became acquainted with the Ho-Chunk and went on several journeys as far north as Green Bay, southwest into the lead fields, and southeast to Chicago. . . . She vividly portrayed hunger and hospitality along the way. . . .

As the Kinzies traveled north, the tensions between white miners and farmers and the Sauk and Fox Indians in the Rock River area of northern Illinois escalated. In addition to the Red Bird uprising, a result of white intrusion on unceded land, white settlement on ceded lands was also a source of trouble. The Sauk and Fox in the area had previously signed a treaty relinquishing their lands east of the Mississippi, agreeing to vacate them when settlers arrived, but they had found it very hard to leave their homes, cornfields, and burial grounds at Saukenuk, the village located near the mouth of the Rock River. While one principal leader, Keokuk, a Fox tribal chieftain, consented to the move and led all who would follow him west of the Mississippi in 1829, Black Hawk, a prominent Sauk warrior, resisted. In 1830 and again in 1831 following the winter hunt, he and his followers had returned to Saukenuk. . . .

Trouble did not follow immediately. In the face of an overwhelming force of federal troops and an undisciplined Illinois militia, Black Hawk and his followers quietly retreated west of the Mississippi under cover of darkness. The military showdown was postponed until the spring and summer of 1832.

When Juliette Kinzie's brother, Arthur Magill, arrived from Kentucky in late April 1832 by way of the Mississippi, he brought the news that Black Hawk and his followers had recrossed the Mississippi River to take possession of their old homes and cornfields. Soon, Juliette wrote, "our own Indians came flocking in, to confirm the tidings, and to assure us of their intention to remain faithful friends to the Americans." The Kinzies learned bit by bit about the Illinois Rangers' and the U.S. Army's pursuit of Black Hawk and his followers as they retreated up the Rock River, scattering throughout the countryside, eluding their enemies, their presence — or even rumor of it — causing terror. John Kinzie decided to confer with all Ho-Chunk chiefs available because he knew the Sauk would try hard to have the Ho-Chunk join them. He knew that many young warriors wanted to distinguish themselves by "taking some white scalps." Juliette Kinzie did not blame them. She explained:

> They did not love the Americans — why should they? By them they had been grad-
> ually dispossessed of the broad and beautiful domains of their forefathers, and
> hunted from place to place, and the only equivalent they had received in ex-
> change had been a few thousands annually in silver and presents, together with
> the pernicious example, the debasing influence, and the positive ill treatment of
> too many of the new settlers upon their lands.

She felt confident of the loyalty of the older members of the tribe encamped in fifty lodges around their dwelling. They had pledged to protect the family.

John Kinzie, feeling he should do everything possible to dissuade the younger Indians in his charge from joining Black Hawk, made arrangements to meet in council with the Ho-Chunk near Four Lakes, thirty-five miles to the south, the location of present-day Madison. Despite his family's pleas, he rode forth. He returned the same day. Juliette Kinzie told of the family sitting at a late hour near an open window, listening, and "with what joy did we at length distinguish the tramp of horses!" He returned with leaders' promises to try to preserve peace among the young warriors and with the knowledge that all the Rock River bands save one was determined to remain peaceful. These were said to be abandoning their villages and fields and moving north to keep out of trouble.

Rumor after rumor of "outrages" and "murders," as Juliette Kinzie put it, and reports about Sauk plans to attack Fort Winnebago floated in, increasing tension and unease dur-ing spring and early summer. The fort stood open without palisades; it lacked artillery; nothing defended the barracks or officers' quarters; and the commissary's store was down the hill, well away from the other buildings. John Kinzie and family finally convinced the military to build a stockade. The family, housed as they were outside the palisade, devel-oped a plan to use in case of attack, whereby Juliette and her sister-in-law, Margaret, and Margaret's child should go to the upstairs. Juliette, having recently accidentally shot a "blackbird on the wing," kept her "little pistols" handy at night and admittedly was ready to shoot if necessary. She rested uneasily and felt renewed terror with the arrival of every Indian party carrying news of troop and possible Sauk movements. A detachment of troops from Fort Howard arrived at the newly stockaded fort in early summer, and John Kinzie and the military agreed that every night the Kinzies should sleep inside the fort.

One incident dramatically illustrates the genuine sense of terror the women in the family felt. A group of Ho-Chunk arrived one day at the Kinzie home and asked per-mission to dance for the family. The dance began in front of the house with Juliette and her sister-in-law watching from the open parlor windows. Margaret spotted one dancer whom she believed from paint and ornament to be a Sauk, and she shared this belief with Juliette.

. . . [H]er sister-in-law had the events of the Fort Dearborn massacre fresh in mind from oft-repeated family memories. When the dancers decided to avoid raindrops and continue the dance inside the house, Juliette and Margaret fled to the upstairs room, thinking death was upon them. John Kinzie and the children refused to follow because they were having such a good time watching the dance. With the dance over, the Indians departed. As she later found out and noted, "the object of our suspicions" was "only some young Winnebago, who had, as is sometimes the custom, imitated them [the Sauk] in custom and appearance." . . .

Shortly thereafter, John Kinzie insisted that the family, all except himself, leave Fort Winnebago for the greater safety of Fort Howard at Green Bay, and so they went solemnly with a boatload of furs on July 4, 1832. They proceeded "always in profound silence, for a song or a loud laugh was now strictly prohibited," until they were far from where Black Hawk's band might conceivably be. They experienced nothing worse than a very heavy rainstorm with violent thunder and lightening and arrived at Green Bay to find people terrified that Black Hawk and his followers would come their way in search of British protection in Canada.

Juliette Kinzie vividly described the panic at Green Bay. "A portion of the citizens were nearly frightened to death, and were fully convinced that there was no safety for them but within the walls of the old dilapidated fort," even though the troops had departed for Fort Winnebago long before then. Intense heat, mosquitoes, a plague of the Green Bay fly (a kind of dragonfly), and the news that cholera not only afflicted Detroit but that it had struck General Atkinson's reinforcements in the war on Black Hawk enlivened the Kinzie party's short stay at Green Bay. After news came of the Battle of Wisconsin Heights on July 21 and the Indians' consequent retreat toward the Mississippi River, the Kinzie party returned to Fort Winnebago.

When army forces confronted Black Hawk's fleeing followers near the mouth of the Bad Axe on the Mississippi River the first two days of August, the Sauk experienced a terrible slaughter by militia, army regulars, and the soldiers aboard the steamboat *Warrior.* With so many dead, the war was over. . . . Indian rebellion and warfare in Illinois and what would become Wisconsin seemed to be a thing of the past.

The Kinzies soon witnessed the tragic consequences of Black Hawk's struggle and its impact upon the Ho-Chunk. Summoned in late August 1832 to come to Fort Armstrong at Rock Island with as many chiefs as possible, John Kinzie called them together for the journey. The purpose of the gathering was to demand further tribal land cessions from the Sauk and Fox and to make a treaty with the Ho-Chunk whereby they would cede all of their land east and south of the Wisconsin River in exchange for land west of the Mississippi. The United States accused the Ho-Chunk of encouraging and assisting Black Hawk, and the U.S. government demanded the surrender of specified tribal members accused of murdering whites; these men would be tried and punished according to white law. The federal government and the tribal leaders concluded the treaty on September 15, 1832.

To John Kinzie fell the task of persuading the chiefs to collect and surrender those prisoners, which he succeeded in doing. With due ceremony the prisoners came in a "grand and solemn" procession, winding their way up the hill to the agency house on a bright autumn day. They surrendered at the front steps of the Kinzie residence in the presence of John Kinzie and General Henry Dodge, soon to become Governor of the Wisconsin Territory. Juliette Kinzie watched the ceremonies through the window; she reported her doubts about the guilt of two prisoners but wondered about the third. The accused were imprisoned at Fort Winnebago awaiting trial but tunneled their way out of the "black hole" in late autumn.

. . . The Indians were already painfully aware of the bleak winter before them. They had abandoned their gardens and hunting grounds in the summer and moved north to avoid being accused of helping Black Hawk. By November they were very short of food, and John Kinzie tried to bring two boatloads of corn from Green Bay to the fort. He planned to stockpile these against the very lean times certain to ensue, but he failed to receive them before the freeze prevented use of the waterway. The Indians used their late-arriving annuity payments to secure extra ammunition, hoping for a good late fall and winter hunt to sustain themselves, but the hunt was poor. The Indians came straggling in all winter long to Fort Winnebago, badly emaciated and in search of food from the commander of the garrison and from the Kinzies, both experiencing extremely short rations. The Kinzies heard reports of dying Indians stretched in the road to the portage. By spring the Ho-Chunk were trying to stay alive on roots and bark. Juliette Kinzie recounted how their terrible suffering reached a nadir before the boatloads of corn reached the fort:

> We were soon obliged to keep both doors and windows fast, to shut out the sight of misery we could not relieve. If a door were opened for the admission of a member of the family, some wretched mother would rush in, grasp the hand of my infant [Wolcott], and, placing that of her famishing child within it, tell us, pleadingly, that he was imploring "his little brother" for food. The stoutest man could not have beheld with dry eyes the heart-rending spectacle which often presented itself. It was in vain that we screened the lower portion of our windows with curtains. They would climb up on the outside, and tier upon tier of gaunt, wretched faces would peer in above, to watch us, and see if indeed we were as ill provided as we represented ourselves.

Finally the boats came in sight, and with their landing and the opening of the barrels of corn, the starving time was over. The treaty-allotted time for the Indians to live near Fort Winnebago also was almost over. They had agreed to leave for their newly assigned lands west of the Mississippi by June 1, 1833, but many of them did not.

The closing pages of *Wau-Bun* leave the reader with two memorable vignettes: the appearance of one of the escaped prisoners on the Kinzies' doorstep in spring of 1833, and the departure of the couple on July 1. Juliette recognized the prisoner in company with others who had come to have the blacksmith repair their guns, traps, and tools. She told John Kinzie, who made no effort to detain him. Clearly expressing his empathy with the Ho-Chunk, he replied, "You are right, but it is no affair of ours. We are none of us to look so as to give him notice that we suspect anything. They are undoubtedly innocent, and have suffered enough already."

On July 1, amid the tears and lamentations of the Indians, the Kinzies departed for Detroit and a new life in Chicago. . . . As for the Ho-Chunk, their prospective new home was far different. They had been assigned new land west of the Mississippi in present-day Iowa, the "neutral territory" between the Sioux and the Sauk and Fox. By 1837 the Ho-Chunk would lose all their Wisconsin tribal lands by treaties with the federal government, seven and one-half million acres, roughly 20 percent of present-day Wisconsin.

*Wau-Bun,* or "The Early Day," is an intriguing title for Juliette Kinzie's book. Louise Phelps Kellogg suggests on the title page of her edited edition that in the Ojibwe language it means the dawn, or the break of day. Perhaps Kinzie named it for that wonderful morning, "bright and beautiful," at Michilimackinac following their arrival on a very stormy night aboard the steamship *Henry Clay* in September 1830.

Whatever she had in mind, that day was the dawn of a completely new experience in her life, thirty-three months among the Ho-Chunk in frontier Wisconsin. . . .

Juliette Kinzie's opinions as both sensitive observer of the Ho-Chunk and active participant in frontier life give historians a perspective to be treasured for its insights. It is interesting to touch on just a few passages from *Wau-Bun* that reveal much about Ho-Chunk culture and Juliette Kinzie, the individual. While she felt her own culture superior to that of the Ho-Chunk and initially tried to promote knowledge of the English language and Christianity among the Indians, she found it important to understand why Indians preferred their ideas and ways of life. She noted:

> As a general thing, they do not appear to perceive that there is anything to be gained by adopting the religion and the customs of the whites. "Look at them," they say, "always toiling and striving — always wearing a brow of care — shut up in houses — afraid of the wind and the rain — suffering when they are deprived of the comforts of life! We, on the contrary, live a life of freedom and happiness. We hunt and fish, and pass our time pleasantly in the open woods and prairies. If we are hungry, we take some game; or, if we do not find that, we can go without. If our enemies trouble us, we can kill them, and there is no more said about it. What should we gain by changing ourselves into white men?"

She brought the same studied approach to Ho-Chunk religion as well:

> They have a strong appreciation of the great fundamental virtues of natural religion — the worship of the Great Spirit, brotherly love, parental affection, honesty, temperance and chastity. Any infringement of the laws of the Great Spirit, by a departure from these virtues, they believe will excite his anger and draw down punishment. These are their principles. That their practice evinces more and more a departure from them, under the debasing influences of a proximity to the whites, is a melancholy truth. . . .

In just those few sentences on culture and religion she indicated an awareness of her own time with the Ho-Chunk, a time of transition and change for a culture that she valued and for which she quietly grieved, in her knowledge that it was eroding as her own Yankee culture intruded.

Yet that grief did not keep her from capturing the daily experiences she witnessed, and through her writing she helped preserve the Ho-Chunk culture. The subject of women's work remained a constant, and very conscious, theme. She recounted the scene before her when the Ho-Chunk arrived and departed at annuity payment times under the terms of the treaty of 1829:

> When the Indians arrived and when they departed, my sense of "woman's rights" was often greatly outraged. The master of the family, as a general thing, came leisurely bearing his gun and perhaps a lance in his hand; the woman, with the mats and the poles of her lodge upon her shoulders, her papoose, if she had one, her kettles, sacks of corn, and wild rice, and, not unfrequently, the household dog perched on the top of all. If there is a horse or pony in the list of family possessions, the man rides, the squaw trudges after.
>
> This unequal division of labor is the result of no want of kind, affectionate feeling on the part of the husband. It is rather the instinct of the sex to assert their superiority of position and importance, when a proper occasion offers. When out of the reach of observation, and in no danger of compromising his own dignity, the husband is willing enough to relieve his spouse from the burden that custom imposes on her, by sharing her labors and hardships.

And yet, despite the lack of power and control that Kinzie testifies to in the pages of her memoir, another example gives readers an insight into her thoughts on the resiliency and resourcefulness of Ho-Chunk women. She told with relish a tale about the mother of the elder Day-kau-ray, a very old Ho-Chunk. As Juliette described her:

> No one could tell her age, but all agreed that she must have seen upwards of a hundred winters. Her eyes dimmed, and almost white with age — her face dark and withered, like a baked apple — her voice tremulous and feeble, except when raised in fury to reprove her graceless grandsons, who were fond of playing her all sorts of mischievous tricks, indicated the very great age she must have attained. She usually went on all fours, not having strength to hold herself erect. . . . She crept into the parlor one morning, then straightening herself up, and supporting herself by the frame of the door, she cried, in a most piteous tone, — "Shaw-nee-aw-kee! Wau-tshob-ee-rah Thsoonsh — koo-nee-noh!" (Silverman, I have no looking-glass.) My husband, smiling and taking up the same little tone, cried in return, — "Do you wish to look at yourself, mother?"

Juliette told her readers that the elderly woman found the idea very funny and laughed so hard she had to sit down. Then she told him it was for one of the boys. Once she received it, noted Juliette, "She found that she had 'no comb,' then that she had 'no knife,' then that she had 'no calico shawl,' until it ended, as it generally did, by Shaw-nee-aw-kee paying pretty dearly for his joke." The old woman was indeed old, frail, and without much formal power. But, as Kinzie joyfully noted, the elderly woman had the powerful, young white man meeting all demands and enjoying himself as he did so. As a whole, Kinzie's observations show her admiration for Ho-Chunk women whom she found excellent wives and mothers who bore far more than what she believed to be a fair share of work essential to tribal life, but who managed all the same.

These few examples do little more than sample the kinds of rich social history encapsulated in Juliette Kinzie's experience living at Fort Winnebago during the years of the Black Hawk War. Readers of Wisconsin history are the richer for her efforts to portray the largest segment of Wisconsin's frontier people, men and women, as she understood them and their way of life.

*The book* Wau-Bun *fixed the Kinzie family's historical importance as founders of Chicago — and Juliette Magill Kinzie's reputation as one of its most prominent hostesses while she also reared their children, three sons and a daughter. However, she also established her reputation as an author, although her other works never had the success of* Wau-Bun, *which has remained in print in several editions since its publication in 1856. After she was widowed in 1865 and until her death in 1870, she spent much of her later years with her daughter Eleanor Lytle Kinzie Gordon of Savannah, Georgia — and enjoyed the early years of her granddaughter and namesake, Juliette Magill Kinzie Gordon Low, who later founded the Girl Scouts of America.*

# Narrative of a Pioneer of Wisconsin and Pike's Peak

THOMAS HANFORD SHELDON

WMH 12, No. 4 (June 1929): 401–422

∾৶৶

*At the age of eight, the author was an early pioneer in the Mineral Point area, site of the first sizeable settlement in southwestern Wisconsin and the first territorial capital by the time he was twenty-one. He wrote this account when he was eighty-four years old, in 1909. However, his memory was remarkable, as was his sensitivity to women settlers' sacrifices. Through him, his mother's voice is heard here.*

*Eliza Whiting Sheldon, from one of the "first families" in Detroit, Michigan, left behind two older daughters for further schooling when she came west with her younger children, one an ill infant in her arms, to help her family begin again on the frontier. Her husband, John P. Sheldon, had been a publisher of Democratic Party newspapers in New York State, and then of the first newspaper in Detroit. However, all of his business attempts failed, in part owing to his temper and editorial temperament; he even earned jail time for contempt of court. But by political patronage, he was appointed the first register of the land office in Mineral Point, the first land office to open in Wisconsin when the region was still in the Michigan Territory. He would allot land for sale to settlers in the "lead rush" for the lucrative minefields of southwestern Wisconsin.[1]*

*After a two-month-long overland journey in 1833 through four states or territories — from Michigan to Indiana to Illinois to Iowa — the family then endured two years of delay and more moves until their home was ready in Willow Springs, Wisconsin. Only a few settlers had preceded them, and by only a few years. However, these settlers, well accustomed to travel, visited each other often, which was both a burden for women and a welcome respite from loneliness on the frontier.*

*Eliza Whiting Sheldon was often on her own, owing to her husband's work. She had to tend her children through illness, but she could be grateful that her care on the overland journey helped a sickly son survive to adulthood, if barely. She was a well-read woman who helped her children gain a good education, as the ability of this author attests.*

*And while family fortunes allowed, Eliza Whiting Sheldon sent two daughters east to a female academy to gain an education that would not be available in Wisconsin to women for decades.*

∾৶৶

It was August [1833] before we began to prepare for coming West. How long father and mother had been preparing, I do not know; perhaps the winter and spring before. Jackson was president, and he appointed father assistant superintendent of the lead mines in Michigan across the Mississippi and the Galena district. Major Legate of Galena was the principal superintendent. Father sold to Sheldon McKnight, a nephew, the *Gazette* office and other property, house and lots, and prepared generally to go to the "Far West." It took all he had except his salary as superintendent to pay his debts. I knew that we were going away when I saw the Pennsylvania [two-horse] team (I thought they were elephants, being used to Canadian ponies) and wagon drawing a house. When it was loaded, I climbed up onto the boxes as far as I could get and said I was going to ride to the West that way.

Mother said, "Come down, Tom. You will ride most any way before you get there." Oh, the heavy hearts that were in our family, I do not wish to recall! Ann and Delia were to stay in Detroit, board with Mrs. Hendry, and go to school, while mother, father, and the other children were to go where they should never see them again, or perhaps see them only after they were grown women.

We smuggled our skates in with the other goods, to "skate on the Mississippi." Will, the youngest, was sick when we started, but the journey did him good and he never would have lived to the age of twenty-three if he had not taken it in the arms of mother and Jane in the months of August and September, 1833.

. . . Father drove the dearborn ("buggy" it is now called; he used to call it a one-horse wagon) with a load of hunting equipment, and occasionally mother and the baby; while we children rode in the wagon and footed it when we were tired of riding. . . .

. . . When we had passed through the door [at the village of La Porte, Indiana], the weird look of the prairie (I think it was called Rolling Prairie; at any rate Rolling Prairie came in somewhere along there) caused me to run up to the wagon where mother was, and, as in former times, seek her protection from ghosts and goblins. I kept in the wagon or near it until Rolling Prairie was passed. I had never before seen a prairie. Bushes or trees or fences had broken the view in Michigan, but I saw enough of prairie land in Indiana and Illinois before I got through. We could not wander far from the wagon on the prairie because the grass was too high and coarse, the weeds and flowers too high for little boys.

We crossed the Fox River [in Illinois] near where Ottawa now stands. I recall a boy riding a horse in front of us to guide the wagon, father following with the dearborn. The greatest depth was two feet. In places there was a rock bottom. When we came to Dixon's ferry on Rock River, where the town of Dixon now is, the wagon had to be pulled into the scow by itself. The horses and all, mother thought too heavy, and Mr. Dixon respected mother's fears against father's and Peabody's [a hired man] protestations. So the horses had to cross first with Nap, and then the dearborn, for it was a question of the fox, the goose, and the cabbage. However, Mr. Dixon was boss of the job and we all got over, kit and cargo. There were two cabins where Dixon now stands; that is, double cabins, two alongside, the space between roofed over, and floored — a common mode of building where they could afford it and the family warranted it.

The next impressive place was at the Winnebago inlet — or outlet, I fail to remember which. We drove late because it was raining, and in crossing the inlet the wagon stalled so that the horses could not pull it out. McCormick, a young man whom father had hired, came to the rescue. . . . But the cabins occurred often enough to supply us with vegetables, and McCormick proved to be a good cook. He would pick up and wash the dishes to save the poor girl or the woman from the task, and do other work. For one of them had to see that the baby did not fall over. O Pioneers, there must be a heaven for them to go to, if for nobody else! . . .

The next adventure was at Plum Creek, below Galena. We reached it after dark and found it over the banks in some places. Father took us boys over in the dearborn, but the wagon was too much property to risk, and mother did not crave drowning with the children. If it had been at the east end of the road [in Michigan] she might have ventured it. It rained all night. Mother slept in the wagon with the children; McCormick under the wagon on some hay. He said that he weighed about ten pounds less on account of the mosquitoes. Father sat up in the wagon. The wagon came over in the morning. The sun shone; all our troubles were over; and after breakfast we started for Galena, which we reached about three p.m. As we came down the hill in the sight of the town, we concluded it *was* a sight. A lot of frame buildings strung along under the bluff, covered with mud halfway up. Mother said afterward that she was half sick before, and the sight of Galena made the other half sick.

I have heard a great deal about the pioneer fathers at the old settlers' meetings, but I never heard a speech about the pioneer mothers. . . . Pioneer mothers! While they are sitting in the ox wagon tending the baby and keeping the children in order, thinking hard over past and present and prospect, pioneer fathers are riding on horses or in their buggies, with guns on shoulders, inquiring of each man they meet, "Is there any game ahead?" and talking half an hour and looking out for a place to camp. The ragged horseman passes the teamster with a "How are you?" and the wagon with a bow; and the poor woman would give a dollar to know what was ahead or to talk with somebody besides the children.

The reception in front of Bennett's tavern seemed to wipe away all tears and the memory of the fearful ride. The women hugged and kissed mother and the children (except John and me, who were men grown — one eight, the other a year and a half older). . . . There was a strong mixture of southern freedom in the crowd, and they vied with one another in attention to the poor draggled woman who showed her raising even through dirt and squalor; that she made no excuses was the proof.

Mother stayed in Galena two weeks, while father, the two boys, and Peabody went on with the wagon, three horses, and the dearborn to Dubuque. We crossed the Mississippi on Brophy's ferry at Dubuque, where we stayed one night. Next day we continued up to Peru, and the journey was over for us at least. Mother and the children came by steamer *Warrior*. . . . At Peru (a small village with eight or ten houses) it was one hundred feet wide and deep enough to carry loaded steamers, such as they were at that time. . . . The house was laid up when we got there; that is, the logs were in position and the roof on.

Father was appointed register of the land office at Mineral Point; he rode across the country to his office most of the summer and was gone most of the time. When we had the bilious fever he acted according to common sense instead of the commands of Dr. Hill. He allowed us as much cold water as he thought was good for us and washed us with cool water. We were marooned until the cool weather began and the girls, Ann and Delia, came West — which was in October, I think. We could not call it home. We were on the move to Mineral Point and said a happy goodbye to Peru. We had spent two winters and one summer in Peru, but we did not want to spend another summer there.

Dubuque was but [forty-]three miles off, and the girls and mother enjoyed the society of the village, which was free, easy, and refined. Most of the inhabitants were from the South, "down the river," sociable, generous, and hospitable. . . . Galena residents used to come to Dubuque, so when we moved to Mineral Point and Willow Springs we had many acquaintances in Galena, and mother's brief sojourn there some time before had helped to make our social circle about all we could attend to. Added to that of Mineral Point and the neighborhood, it was more than we could attend to, and mother became almost a slave to her friends because we were without hired help, except such as we could catch here and there. . . .

When we pulled out for Willow Springs, we were a merry lot with two wagons, old Nap and the dearborn, and with father for a guide. (Ann and Delia had meanwhile come "home" from Detroit and were with us.) . . .

Over the beautiful prairies and through the groves we made merry. Father drove by in the height of the gale and remarked, "After the storm comes a calm. Look out that your laugh doesn't make a cry." We boys got out when we came to a big hill after crossing the Pecatonica, and after walking nearly a mile came to a descent and a house. Here our teams were unhitched. We asked, "Why are they unhitching there?" This was about four p.m. We went down and found them all crying and father scolding them. This was our destination until Christmas. We called it Cracky House, and it went by that name as long as we were children and in the neighborhood. It had been built by a Dr. Luffborough, and was rented by father until he could get a house built on the farm a half-mile from Cracky and eight miles from his office.

Mother had always lived in a town eight miles from Mineral Point, where there was one respectable store and a tavern. How we managed with visitors I do not remember. We had a raid of visitors from Galena and Dubuque, often several at a time. Father, in common with all the old settlers, had a disposition for making friends. To invite visitors to their homes was a cardinal virtue in all of them. No matter how disagreeable the friends were in the house (all chewed tobacco and smoked), the housewife found food for all. Corn bread and bacon were standard supplies. To these were added coffee, and wild strawberries, plums, or roots which the children would gather. We endured the summer quite comfortably, and none of us was sick. Father bought three cows, and we all had to learn to milk. . . .

We stayed all summer at Cracky House, and made the best of it. A visit to Galena or Dubuque was frequent, and we often went to Mineral Point also. Father came and went every day on a white mare, except when it rained or he had neuralgia. Then he would stay in Mineral Point, because his presence as register at the land office was imperative. When it was necessary for him to stay at Mineral Point two or three days, he would take one of us boys on behind him to bring the horse back. He must have used up the dearborn at Peru, or the neighbors did. Every few days, somebody would come and say, "Major, I'd like to borry your one-horse wagon. My wife would like to visit her folks down on the Catfish;" and very likely we would not see it again for a month. . . .

We moved into the new house at Christmas time, about the time mother's suffering began. The house of logs had two pens eighteen feet in the clear, ten feet apart, finished with green oak lumber floors, doors, and casings. Underpinning for the present had to be straw, rubbish, anything to keep the snow from blowing up through the cracks of the floor.

Father bought a pair of stout shoes for mother, lined with lamb's wool. "I can never take them off until the Fourth of July." "Sleep in them," said father, and she never had cold feet from that time. We children located the house where we could see the Platte Mounds. Father put it to a vote, and the majority won; but we found before we got through the winter that father knew best. The west and northwest wind played havoc with house and folks before the winter was over. Snowdrifts were so high in front that we could not see the mounds. . . .

Ann, aged seventeen, was married about this time (November 24, 1836). Delia and Ann visited in Galena and Dubuque, and in the latter place, they were acquainted with the Gratiots. Charles G., the oldest son of Henry and Susan Gratiot, a man about twenty-five years old, was considered a great catch, and he considered it a great catch to catch Ann Sheldon. However, Miss Ann, in duty bound, came home to be married. The inhabitants of Dubuque turned out en masse for the wedding, driving forty miles in sleighs. They were great for a frolic and came regardless of expense, distance, time, roads, cold, blankets, or a place to sleep. . . . We had a field bed from one end to the other of the garret, fifty feet long and twenty feet wide, and stowed away on the floor. All who came only ten miles thought it was no job to go back; they were used to such rides after balls or weddings. It was the first and last wedding of the kind that we ever indulged in. . . . Delia married two years later, and we had a concert of tears and sniffing when the ceremony was performed, as she had had charge of the younger children after her return from school in the East, and we had a dim foreshadowing of the loss to the family in the ceremony.

The spring following Ann's marriage Delia and Jane went to Utica, New York, to finish their education at the Utica Female Academy, of which Cousin Urania Sheldon . . . was principal and Cousin Cynthia commissary general. Father had yielded to the solicitations of the two old maiden cousins, who were born teachers, knowing the girls would get good care and their physical condition would be looked after. . . . It was a good stroke of fortune for the girls. Because of their years of schooling in Detroit Jane finished in three years and Delia in two. Mary and Ellen attended the log schoolhouse and then went to Galena.[2] We boys had only the advantages the log schoolhouses afforded, but these were considerable. . . . Then, too, father was a printer and editor by trade, and his house was always full of books scientific and otherwise, papers, and magazines, and we had to be educated in forensics and politics. . . . He brought them west and they are in the old house at the homestead in Willow Springs yet. I counted seven hundred and seventy-five bound volumes, big and little. Both father and mother were well educated for that day. The library was constantly augmented by gift and purchase, and with the magazines and newspapers added it was unique for a country place. How was it possible for intelligent children to grow to a marriageable age in such an atmosphere and not become refined in *belles lettres* and in life! We children used to go to the neighbors' and see the Bible, *Pilgrim's Progress,* and a few patent office and treasury reports, and wonder where the folks got their knowledge.

. . . We were lucky to have so much time for play.

1837. The year of hard times! When the speculation in land went back on men, and the women and children had to suffer because the men, especially the well-to-do, had spent all their cash for land and were not able to pay taxes on what had made them rich. . . . There was no end of economy. Mothers made their children petticoats out of quilts. But we got used to hard times, and had enough to eat — wheat, potatoes, and all the agricultural products of a rich soil — and enough wood to keep us warm through the winter. As a general thing, however, we did not have the knack of making cloth to cover ourselves. . . . Once in a while an old woman would appear who could weave, and soon a family would be seen dressed out in homemade stuff, ringed, streaked, and speckled. . . .

*The Panic of 1837 hit hard in Wisconsin, where many newcomers had gambled all they owned in the "boom" of land speculation and soon went "bust." But only a year before, in 1836, Wisconsin had gained separate territorial status, and the southwestern area seemed promising. The territory's first capital of Belmont, near Mineral Point, had attracted politically influential settlers. The first territorial governor of Wisconsin, Henry Dodge, maintained his office in Belmont even after the new capital of Madison was named, and John P. Sheldon was one of his "henchmen." However, Dodge could not protect Sheldon from dismissal from his position in 1840, when political opponents exposed illegal sales of the most valuable land to speculators such as the governor himself. His political patrons did help Sheldon gain a governmental position again, in Washington, D.C. Eliza Whiting Sheldon apparently waited in Wisconsin for some years but eventually also went east, although letters suggest she went only as far as Detroit.[3]*

*By the 1850s, she had buried three children and contracted "consumption" (tuberculosis), according to her son's account. Eliza Whiting Sheldon died in 1856. Looking back on her tragic death her son wrote, "we were a broken family," and with her "perished all that was worth building for." Her son soon failed in business as well and went west in 1858 with the "gold rush" to Pike's Peak. But his "interests lay in Wisconsin," wrote Thomas Hanford Sheldon, who returned to pass the rest of his life in Willow Springs.*

## NOTES

1. Smith, *HOW*, 323–327, 422; see also John P. Sheldon Papers, Burton Historical Collection, Detroit Public Library. Sheldon's business failures also included promotion of an early typewriter, a predecessor of the successful model later patented in Wisconsin by another newspaper editor, Christopher Latham Sholes of Southport (Kenosha).
2. [Mineral Point would be the site of one of the first public schools in Wisconsin but not until 1840; its schoolhouse was built of brick and stone. See R. E. Van Matre, "Mineral Point Was Site of First Public School," *Wisconsin State Journal*, May 2, 1926, quoting WHS director Joseph Schafer. See also Joseph Schafer, "Origin of Wisconsin's Free Public School System," *WMH* 9 (September 1925): 27–46.]
3. Smith, *HOW*, 331–332, 422; Sheldon Papers.

# A Packet of Old Letters

FLORENCE GRATIOT BALE

*WMH* 11, No. 2 (December 1927): 153–168

*Susan Hempstead Gratiot, whose letters were saved and excerpted by a descendant, was born in 1797 in Connecticut, near the New York town of Hempstead on Long Island. Hempstead had been founded by the first of her family to emigrate five generations earlier from Hempstead, England. Her family left in 1811 for St. Louis to join a son who was Missouri's first delegate to Congress in 1812. In 1813, at sixteen years old, Susan Hempstead met and married Henry Gratiot, who was twenty-four years old, a nephew of the Chouteaus, who had founded St. Louis. He followed in their field as a fur trader until he was appointed government agent to the Ho-Chunk in southwestern Wisconsin.*

*Susan Hempstead Gratiot readied her family for the move for months while her husband and his half-brother Jean Pierre Bugnion, called John, migrated up the Mississippi River from St. Louis in the autumn of 1825 and wintered in Galena, Illinois. In the spring of 1826, John left first for New Orleans to bring his family to the north: his wife, Adèle Marie Antoinette de Perdreauville Bugnion, daughter of a former lady-in-waiting to the French queen for whom she was named, and their three children. The Bugnion family arrived before the Gratiots in Galena, where they built a log cabin large enough for the Gratiots as well. "The bond was very strong" between the sisters-in-law, wrote Florence Gratiot Bale. "Together they faced Indian warfare and danger, many times seeing their husbands depart from their home to protect the settlement." Susan's sister-in-law recalled that "Mrs. Henry Gratiot was composed, but I was terrified and never thought my children and myself safe except under the shadow of her wings."*

*Henry and Susan Gratiot and their five younger children, "twenty men to work in the mines," and their slaves, "Scipio and Jenny," arrived in Galena in 1826, after "seventy-six long, weary days for them to make the journey from St. Louis." This passage was made more exhausting for Susan Gratiot because she apparently was pregnant. In 1827, she and her husband had six younger children, one of them sickly, when they finally settled at Gratiots Grove, Wisconsin (Lafayette County).*

Old letters always have a fascination, and especially so when one can hold in his hand some that were written almost one hundred years ago. The faded paper, the ink dimmed by the passing of the years, the written sheet serving as an envelope and sealed with red wax, all form a link that binds today with yesterday, that can carry one back over the changing decades and give a fuller understanding of the pioneer days so interesting to the lead region of southwestern Wisconsin in this year 1927.

The letters before me were written in the period 1831 to 1837 by Susan Hempstead Gratiot, wife of Colonel Henry Gratiot, at Gratiots Grove, Wisconsin, to her younger brother William Hempstead, a merchant in St. Louis. It took six weeks to transport them by stage and Mississippi River boats to their destination. Sometimes they were sent by a friend who was making the journey to St. Louis.[1]

To re-animate the site of Gratiots Grove with the activity of one hundred years ago needs a keen imagination; for in its prosperity it had a settlement of over a thousand people, who were busy running its nine smelters, operating its mines, trading with the Indians, and tilling the soil, and during the Winnebago and Black Hawk wars it had a fortified stockade, which was called Fort Gratiot.

Now only a few crumbling foundations can be found beneath the growth of underbrush on the hillside where the old fort, smelters, and log cabins once stood; but on the other side of the roadway on a slight elevation, set in a magnificent growth of old trees, is the Gratiot homestead, first built in 1835 by Henry Gratiot. . . .

One of the reasons, aside from the monetary urge, for Henry Gratiot and his wife to seek a new home was that they might bring up their family away from the slavery that prevailed in Missouri. The practice was abhorrent to them and, though they owned slaves, it was against their principles, and one of the first acts of Henry Gratiot after becoming a citizen of Galena was to place on record in the courthouse of that newly organized town the release of his slaves, giving a thousand-dollar bond that "the slaves he liberated would never become a charge to the state."

In 1827 the business of the brothers was transferred from Gratiots Survey at Galena to that magnificent tract of virgin timber in the territory of Wisconsin that was later called Gratiots Grove. It was near the spot where Jesse Shull had built his mining shanty, which later became the nucleus of a town called after him Shullsburg, but which at this time was a vast prairie with heavily wooded hills encircling it. The brothers had a friendly Winnebago half-breed [*sic*] woman called Madame Catherine Myott for their interpreter and intercessor in their negotiations with the Winnebago. Madame Myott was very popular with her tribe and succeeded in making a "trade": the Gratiots to give the tribesmen in exchange for the privilege of operating mines on their ground, a large and valuable amount of goods and supplies.

It was in this settlement and environment that Susan Gratiot took up her life in pioneer Wisconsin, bringing to its uncouth and varied population her culture and refinement, her tender care of the sick, her uplifting influence upon the erring miner, her devotion to education, and above all, her unfaltering faith in the fatherhood of God and the brotherhood of man; these attributes enabled her to give courage and inspiration to those about her, and to rear her family with high ideals and education amid surroundings that were not ideal or even civilized. . . .

. . . Those were constructive, hopeful days, as one can see from the letters that follow. Their family now consisted of their older sons Charles and Edward, young boys under eighteen and twenty, who were forging ahead in the new land, going away from home to find fortune and favor in different undertakings; Susan and Mary, young daughters who must be educated, and also tenderly protected and sheltered from the rather crude social life of a mining town and camp (for Gratiots Grove was about two miles from the village of Shullsburg and twenty from Galena); Henry and Adèle, young boy and girl; and Stephen Hempstead and Eliza, tiny tots. Hempstead, being a very delicate child, was a constant care to his mother.

To understand the excerpts from these long-ago letters one must realize the hardships that were faced, the distance that lay between their home in St. Louis and the East, the

Indian troubles and ever-present peril from hostile tribesmen. As Colonel Henry Gratiot was government agent for the Winnebago and their loyal friend and helper, his family had no fear of them; but other tribes were not so friendly. The difficulty in obtaining education for a growing family and the lack of even ordinary comforts such as we have today must also be taken into account.

The first letter is dated "Gratiots Grove August 11, 1833":

My Dear Brother

Since you was here I have had one continual scene of sickness    I thought that I should have lost my babe by a long and severe inflamation of the head but he is now fast recovering and how thankfull I am to our great protecter for his kindness to us all when so many of our near and dear friend[s] have left us forever    I have not been in Galena nor seen any of our family since you left    I feel very anxious to see our Sister    she was to have come out yesterday. . . .

. . . in addition to Henry['s] goods send for me two pieces of Russia sheating one dozen of good dinner knifes and forkes and one piece of dark twilled bombazett for Winter dresses for my Girles . . .

accept the best wishes of your affectionate Sister Susan Gratiot

The second, dated September 20, 1833, begins:

I received your kind letter My Dear Brother with the most cordail pleasure and I hope I feel the sensations of gratitude to him who is the giver of every good and perfect gift that he has preserved you from sickness so far    your business exsposed you so often that we ware all anxiety but I hope that your City will now be healthy the warmest weather must now be over . . . we have been favoured so far    no heavy frost yet and the crops generally good    the Grove is lonesom and dull enough at present . . . doing good bussinness    if lead can only keep at a living price which I hope it will . . .

accept the best wishes of your affectionate Sister Susan Gratiot

The [following] letter written December 18, 1834, refers to the sacrifice made by Colonel Henry Gratiot and his wife for the education of their children. They rented their home to Mr. and Mrs. Jeremiah Woods of Galena, who conducted a boarding-school. . . . [T]his renunciation of home [illustrates] how devotedly these pioneers held to their desire for education. The log school always closely followed the building of a home, and from old letters and traditions of early schools in Shullsburg and Gratiots Grove . . . we find that there was a log schoolhouse in Shullsburg and day schools in the home of J. P. B. Gratiot prior to the school in the home of Henry. But Miss Hotchkiss, the teacher, was compelled to leave, and the school was closed; hence the following letter:

My Dear Brother

I have commenced I can not tell you how many letters since I received Yours from Galena and have tried to compose a fine speech on my surprise and disapointment and have never been able to finish one for we are all crowded in one room so by the time that I got a few lines some one would come and away with writing    but fully am I convinced of your sympathy    I could not help crying but it [is] all for the best I suppose    you would have found me in a confused place [had you come]    many blame Henry for giving up our old place before we were fixed . . . none but a parent or some such fatherly old Bachelor as you are can enter into our feeling    we had had no School since May    Susan & Mary had taken hold with a determination to learn    I could not think of sending them to Galena and if I had sent them then ther was Henry and Adelle that we must have kept at home and by giving up our place we send all to school    all Mr Wood give us is 200 per year    it is not sufficient to defray our school bills yet it is a great help and a great reliefe to my mind to know that they [are] at a place wher they can learn and I believe that they do learn    the Girles shall write you by Wm Hamilton    he says he is going to St Louis in a few weeks and you can judg for your self    Susan has studied her self sick so that she has had to leave school for two weeks but I am in hope she will be well soon    I was alarmed last week for fear of a head complaint Henry went to see Theodore in July and took the fever and has had it ever since well one day and sick one    the girles board with Mr. Wood; and now for me Old Lady Sigh has a comfortable room with a large window in it and a green chair standing to it and more work around than Ever she had but if I can only go through all and do my duty it is all I ask for . . . but can I dear William complain when I think of the hardships that my husband is so often Exposed to    if my cabin is small and poor mor than half of his time is exsposed to the cold going and coming to the mill . . .

I must now beg of you to tell my Dearest Sisters that I often think of them but have not had time to write but hope soon to write them    this move has been equal to an Indian War . . . your Sister Susan Gratiot

Near Galena, June 30th 1835

My Dear Brother

before this will reach you I hope our Sister [Sarah] and [my daughter] Susan will be safely landed [with you in St. Louis] and you will learn from Sister Beebe why Adelle was not with them so I need only say that she arrived a half an hour after the departure of the *Warrior* and Charles said that she must go with Madam La Grave . . . she goes not very well prepared    I do not know how she will leave me tomorrow to go with a stranger    her heart is very full tonight yet she will not say she dont want to go    the climate is all I dread but if you perceive that it does not agree with her I must dear William beg you to let me know    her health is very delicate and if you think that all of the Sunday School is too confining for her you must regulate that    we have had to take her from the Sunday School this spring half of the day . . . I do think that they wear the children out    they do here the children and Teachers too. . . .

I can assure you My Dear William that Henry has often wished for you    he has lately entered our farm and we are now on our own land and when we get out of our embaressment we can make a good living    Henry is about to build us a comfortable house    [It is near the section of land that he bought of Mrs. Myott.] ... Bugnion furnace draw first rate    they Exspect to put mineral in this morning    he is in high spirits and I am truely thankfull that he has succeeded ... God bless & protect you Dear Brother from all surrounding dangers is the constant prayer of your affectionate Sister Susan Gratiot

It is way past midnight.

Gratiots Grove Octr 4th 1835

My Dear Brother

Your kind letter would not have remained this long unanswered had I been at home    I received it while at Dubuques and staid [there] three weeks longer than I expected and thought every day to return    Hempstead was so lame and in such racking pain that it was difficult for me to get home with him    he has not walked a step now for a month or more and no assistance but old Jenny so that I am not mistress of my own time but I am ceartain that you will not charge my remissness to the want of affection    no Dear William your letter really exhilarated my drooping spirits and yet should I have any thing to depress my Spirits while blessed with health to perform my daily task    blessed with the best of Brothers and Sisters would to heaven I could prevent anxiety from Ever entering the hearts of friends so dear    but that is a fruitless wish but I can tell you that at present our prospects are more flattering than for years past    the Soil is ours and what we do now will be well done and a fixed home for the remainder of our days    if I could think that the short time I may remain here may continue with as few troubles as the past it would be a blessing but that can not be    old age creeps on    the children grow up and of course troubles must increase ...

Henry will be compelled to go to St. Louis to procure Genl Atkinson signture and then to Washington    the Indians have made a request of the President to let them go on this Winter to expose ther Miserable situation    that is the Indians on Rock River    they are allmost starved and naked    they did not receive a dollar at the payment by some bad mangment    there is four chiefs here now    they want Henry to go with them or for them but w[h]ether the request will be granted or not we can not tell ... it is now near one o'clock at night    I must think of going to rest. ...

❧

*In 1835, the Gratiots finally had their home for which they had hoped, and "their family all growing into useful and educated men and women, the future looked bright and full of years of content and happiness," as their descendant wrote. But while returning from Washington, D.C., in 1836, Henry Gratiot died in Baltimore. Susan Hempstead Gratiot moved to Dubuque but wrote in her last letter* to her brother in 1837 that her "new situation adds new cares and anxieties." She then returned to her "dear home" at Gratiots Grove, which, she wrote, "is endeared to me by so many happy associations and the hours spent with a melancholy pleasure and a happy anticipation of once again being all together." However, few of her eight surviving children — one had died in infancy — lived nearby. Her oldest sons found "fortune and favor" in Wisconsin; Charles wed Ann Sheldon of Willow Springs, whose family's story appears in this chapter, and Edward stayed on the family farm. Her "sickly" namesake Stephen Hempstead also stayed and married Mary Jane Chamberlin, a daughter of Beloit pioneers Eliza McBride Chamberlin and Thomas Chamberlin and sister of a sibling who later served as president of the University of Wisconsin.

However, Susan Hempstead Gratiot's daughter Eliza died at twenty years old, two weeks before her wedding day, and another daughter also died young, soon after marrying and moving to St. Louis. Her other children likewise married and moved away, ending up scattered from coast to coast. Prominent among these migrations was that of her daughter Adèle Gratiot Washburne, whose husband went to Congress from Illinois. (After his mother-in-law's death, he briefly served as U.S. secretary of state under his protégé, President Ulysses S. Grant, and then as U.S. ambassador to France, while one of his brothers was governor of Wisconsin.) Susan Hempstead Gratiot visited her daughter Adèle often, first in Galena and then in Washington in 1854, when she visited her husband's grave. Then, as had her husband almost two decades earlier, Susan Hempstead Gratiot died during her return trip to Wisconsin. She was brought home and buried in Gratiots Grove. As a nephew wrote, "truly one of the salt of the earth has gone, for she was a true woman in every sense of the word."

❧❦

## NOTES

1. In time they were given to the writer by the heirs of William Hempstead. Upon my visit to the centennial celebration and homecoming at Shullsburg, Wisconsin, in July, 1927, I devotedly carried them back to the very home spot at Gratiots Grove where they had been written so many years ago.

*Rachel Lawe Grignon (1808–1876), the daughter of English Canadian trader John Lawe and Therese Rankin, or Nekikoqua, whose father was a* métis *British army officer and whose mother was Menominee, Ottawa, and apparently also Ojibwe.*

# *2*

# WOMEN ON THE WISCONSIN FRONTIER, 1836–1848

## INTRODUCTION

Territorial status was a transitional time and an ill-defined period of political suspension without full rights of citizenship for Wisconsinites, all of which also describes women's status in the dozen years prior to statehood — and for some time afterward. Some of the first Wisconsin women, the Native Americans and part-European *métis,* actually lost status amid increasing discrimination. At the same time, some settlers won the first, tentative advances in women's rights in the territorial era and even attempted political activism on the Wisconsin frontier.

Wisconsin's separate territorial status in 1836 probably mattered little to most residents, as most were Native Americans who had lived under several flags, far from the few early settlements of newcomers along the Great Lakes and Mississippi River. Despite tribal attrition owing to the epidemics caused by contact with newcomers, the encroachment of settlers on ancestral lands, and treaties resulting in forcible removal by the federal government, Native Americans still outnumbered the fewer than 12,000 newcomers in the new Wisconsin Territory, which then included Iowa and much of Minnesota.[1]

Within a few years in Wisconsin, that ratio would reverse. The population soared to more than 30,000 by 1840, more than 150,000 by 1845, and almost 250,000 by 1848, the end of the territorial era. Native Americans apparently accounted for less than 5 percent of the population, although the census did not count many of them as they were considered "non-citizens" and did not account for traders' intermarriage with the first Wisconsin women or their children born into both cultures.[2]

For example, the likes of the *métis* Langlades, Wisconsin's Native and French Canadian "founding family," still led territorial society. However, acceptance of their Grignon descendants — especially the daughters — would decrease in later decades. Effects of discrimination are evident in the story in this chapter of a daughter of Irish immigrants, Mary Elizabeth Meade Grignon, who married well by marrying into the family in 1837. However, her daughters who resembled their father's Native foremothers faced a different fate in later decades, as they never married. Native Americans would become "outcasts" in their own lands after the territorial era, "alienated in a young state governed and inhabited predominantly by whites," according to historian Suzanne Elizabeth Moranian.[3]

The Grignon girls never knew the joys as well as sorrows of "Motherhood on the Wisconsin Frontier," a work by early women's historian Lillian Krueger also excerpted in this chapter. On the ratio of the genders, Krueger wrote, "The scarcity of weddings was caused by the scarcity of women," which meant that many men returned east to find wives willing to undertake motherhood without help for the labors of housework — or when they went into labor. As historian Alice E. Smith noted, when the only men in short supply were those with medical degrees, women's "cycle of bearing and burying children" was "harrowing" for "native-born and foreign-born alike" on the Wisconsin frontier.[4]

Few women went farther on the Wisconsin frontier than did missionary Florantha Thompson Sproat, whose letters from the first Protestant school in La Pointe, excerpted in this chapter, express longing and loss. She especially longed for her family and former life in the East after the loss of her stillborn infant. Such a loss was all too typical for missionary women, she wrote, owing to a high incidence of pregnancy but few physicians on the frontier. However, Sproat also wrote of her satisfaction in homemaking, childrearing, and teaching traders' and Ojibwe children as she learned their language and attempted to adapt to aspects of ancient Anishinabe customs. She saw that many Ojibwe comprehended "the unjustnesses of the white men" — and women — who attempted to convert them to Christianity so as to subvert their culture. Native Americans were correct in such concerns, according to historian Suzanne Elizabeth Moranian, who suggests that missionary efforts, even by well-meaning women, eventually ended in the educational "ethnocide" of Native Americans.[5]

Other children experienced happier times in the territorial era, including a young girl who would grow old with Milwaukee and make her mark on high society in the city. In a reminiscence excerpted in this chapter, Martha Eliza Curtis Fitch recalls when her mother — "a fine shot" — hunted deer for dinner in the family's farming years, when they lived in a little house on the Wisconsin prairie. The family then moved to town and moved up into the social set. "I want to tell you the fun we had," she writes of bygone days before mansions were torn down to make way for downtown office buildings, and little girls had horses for pets and learned to ride sidesaddle in the streets of old Milwaukee.

Girls in her social set first went to "finishing schools" for the equivalent of an elementary school education and to form the significant female friendships that would be important among the future matrons of Milwaukee. Then they went away for the advanced education that was still new in the East in the 1830s — an era when slightly over a third of all Americans under twenty years of age attended school at all. In Wisconsin in the territorial era, several "female academies" and "female seminaries" offering high school–level education arose across the southern area of the state, often accompanying but separate from comparable schools for boys. However, few "female academies" of the era survived. At the same time, a pioneering experiment in coeducation thrived: Platteville Academy, founded in 1839, opened new facilities for both boys and girls in 1842 and succeeded so well that the school eventually became a college and then a campus of the state university. Other boys' academies in Waukesha and Beloit became chartered by the legislature as men's colleges in 1846. Finally, in the following year, the first coeducational college in Wisconsin requested and received a charter, although Lawrence College in Appleton did not open its doors during the territorial era.[6]

The new settlers with wealth and education increasingly set the tone of "Social Life in Wisconsin," another article by Lillian Krueger excerpted in this chapter that describes the range of activities undertaken by women. If women were increasingly class-stratified, they were united in facing the Wisconsin frontier as "no place for tears," in Krueger's terms. She shows the creativity of rural women in turning the making of necessities — a winter's worth of candles or a quilt for a cold winter's night — into occasions for female companionship, while women in towns turned to "pure diversions" such as dances, especially for the first weddings of the few women on the male-dominated frontier.

The transiency of new towns, where almost everyone was a traveler or new in town, also encouraged entrepreneurial women in what would become the leading industry in the economy of the future state: tourism. Roseline Willard Peck and her husband hosted the first wedding in the new capital of Madison in their hotel, opened in 1837 to house territorial legislators — and turtles in the cellar as well, as recounted in a hilarious recollection in Krueger's account. Enterprising women elsewhere included Fredericka Levy and her husband in La Crosse, a community of only five log cabins in 1846, when they built the first frame structure to house their hotel, restaurant, and home. However, the city's first history relied on her written account but hardly noted her contribution.[7]

Krueger also shows that churchwomen on the frontier eschewed frivolous entertainments for fund-raising events, which, as in the earlier "female moral reform" movement, now can be seen as a form of training toward women's later work to gain more political reforms for the less fortunate — and then for themselves. Some women already showed a precocious political maturity on the frontier and worked for the rights of territorial inhabitants, although not yet for women's rights. In 1846, they petitioned Congress for reform of "pre-emptor" laws against speculators, often wealthy easterners who never set foot in Wisconsin but invested in its "land boom," while settlers had only a year to pay for their land. Local homesteaders sought a longer payment period, according to historian Alice E. Smith, including a "group of 123 Wisconsin women, certainly bold females for their time," petitioning for protection "from the speculator, 'who has more money in his Pocket than Humanity in his breast.'"[8]

The women were "bold" for their place and time in practicing their "one political right" of petitioning, their only means for direct participation in politics without the ballot. In early examples elsewhere, Congress received thousands of antislavery petitions from women, primarily easterners, in the 1830s. Others petitioned the legislators of eastern states for labor reform for "millgirls" and women factory workers in the 1840s. Wisconsin women's petitions to Congress, even prior to statehood, thus stand as an early example beyond the East and almost a decade before a better-known campaign for women's property rights in upstate New York by Elizabeth Cady Stanton and Susan B. Anthony. As one historian observes, such petition campaigns prepared women for their later work in the woman suffrage movement by providing practical experience in the "mechanics of the political system and methods of political discourse and persuasion."[9]

Another early example of politicized women's collective work in Wisconsin for property rights reform came in 1848 from the communal settlement near Ripon called Ceresco, of which is recalled in an article excerpted here. That women at Ceresco had the right to invest in communal land and assets suggests the logic of their request to legislators as "a more realistic appeal for land reform" than previous petitions for "pre-emptor" law reform, in Smith's opinion. However, the utopian community's unrealistic aims for women's rights failed, since holding shares in Ceresco did not spare women from house-work and other tasks — as all tasks were allotted by men.[10]

The rarity of political actions by women in the era, especially far from the East, sug-gests the reason why few documented examples merit historical attention. The rule of the land remained the "natural law" of women's submission to men. Not until the first sum-mer of Wisconsin statehood, in 1848, would Stanton and other women in upstate New York start the women's rights movement. Similar statewide work for women's rights in Wis-consin was two decades away. Most women in Wisconsin had a far higher priority in the period: the survival of their families on the frontier.

A "torrent of emigration" into Milwaukee's harbor merited mention by pioneering female journalist Margaret Fuller of New York in her travelogue, *Summer on the Lakes in 1843*. "Her reporter's eye caught the novelty and pathos of the foreigners thronging into Milwaukee," writes Smith. Fuller observed that "poor refugees arrive daily, in their na-tional dresses, all travel-soiled and worn . . . the mothers carrying their infants, the fathers leading the little children by the hand, seeking a home where their hands may maintain them." The torrent turned into a flood in 1843 when the "arrival of 1,000 to 1,400 a week was not unusual," according to Smith. Nor was their poverty, as "the privileged, moneyed few" were exceptions among the foreign-born.[11]

However, neither noble birth nor money guaranteed success or even survival in Wis-consin, as is evident for a Swedish colony whose story is excerpted in this chapter. Wealthy immigrants "reduced to absolute beggary" saw their numbers diminished by deaths of mothers and infants from "frost and cold," while a widow became "broken down before her time by severe labor and trouble." Apparently, among women colonists, only a daugh-ter sent away for adoption prospered. Others soon left, and the colony failed after its founder left Wisconsin to return to Sweden.

Most immigrants stayed, but some settlers saw Wisconsin as only another stage in their westward journey. In the southwestern area, lead production declined by the mid 1840s, as did the population in early settlements. Gratiots Grove, for one, gradually slipped from public memory and maps (see "A Packet of Old Letters" in chapter 1). Men who had "spent most of their adult years in mining" moved again, according to Smith. So did their wives, who had spent their lives in setting up housekeeping after crossing continents, oceans, and communities in America, such as the Cornish immigrants in Pendarvis and Mineral Point. Many thousands moved to copper mines in northern Wisconsin and Michi-gan, while others went west to California "to seek their fortunes in gold" on the next fron-tier of opportunity in their new country.[12]

Women's need to focus on necessities deferred discussion of women's rights to an ex-tent. However, gender issues competed on the public agenda with issues of race that would dominate political debate, even in the new territory, despite its minuscule popula-tion of African Americans. The 1840 census counted fewer than two hundred freed-women and freedmen in Wisconsin, most residing in the southwestern area settled by

Southerners. The census also found that some Southerners held eleven slaves in defiance of the law — not counting two women held by a minister's wife, who soon sold them south. In Wisconsin, some former slaves founded their own communities. In 1845, Moses and Catherine Stanton started Stantonville, now Chilton, on the Manitowoc River in Calumet County; other communities included Cheyenne Valley in Vernon County, Pleasant Ridge in Grant County, and the Outagamie County community called Freedom. The number of African Americans more than tripled to more than six hundred, none of them slaves by the end of the territorial era, although all amounted to only one-fifth of one percent of Wisconsin's population.[13]

By the mid 1840s, most African Americans in Wisconsin had migrated to southeastern cities and towns, the sites of most early antislavery activity in the state. Unwelcome in men's organizations and proscribed from a more public role, women organized abolitionist society auxiliaries, raised funds for freedmen's missions, and — although often allowed to sign only initials or pseudonyms — wrote letters to abolitionist newspapers. Some soon progressed to more political activism from the moral suasion of Wisconsin's first known women's organization, the Female Moral Reform Society of Prairie Village (see Introduction to chapter 1). In the 1850s, the women boarded — for free — an abolitionist newspaper's printers, who nobly found "living upon charity" to be "of little consequence" compared to the cause, as historian Theron W. Haight observed in 1880. He did not consider more housework to be of much consequence for women, of course.[14]

Some women in Prairie Village and elsewhere in Wisconsin did far more dangerous duty on the Underground Railroad. In 1843, the town then called Prairieville, widely known as an "abolition station," became famed for the rescue of a sixteen-year-old fugitive slave from St. Louis and for the farm women who helped her flee. Caroline Quarrelles escaped her mistress in Milwaukee. Abolitionists smuggled her to farms on the west side of that city and then miles farther west to Pewaukee on a journey that lasted for weeks, until a day when the men were away and armed slave catchers arrived. The farmwife stood down the slave catchers while her daughter hid Quarrelles in a barrel in the cellar. That night, Prairieville citizens organized the fugitive's escape, hiding her in a wagon across six hundred miles to freedom in Canada. She later learned to read and write, and Caroline Quarrelles Watkins wrote to her rescuers that she had married another fugitive slave, whose first wife had committed suicide after her children were sold away from their family.[15]

Other accounts of escapes in Wisconsin often attribute all abolitionist work to men, although women also funded, fed, clothed, and cared for fugitives. However, even evidence of men's work on the Underground Railroad is understandably unknown compared to the estimated extent of their endeavors, owing to the risk of betrayal for fugitives and accomplices alike. As a Beloit minister said to his wife in hiding a fugitive in their home, they had done "secret service before the Lord." So did a daughter of the Pewaukee farmwife, Harriet Daugherty Underwood, who married a minister in Wauwatosa, where their home was said to have had a secret room for hiding fugitive slaves. Yet even decades later, another daughter, Almira Daugherty Woodruff, would say only that she knew "several stories but knew no names" of others involved in further rescues, nor could she provide even the names of many fugitive slaves, who "dared not tell the names of masters, which were all the names they had."[16]

Although more African Americans may have found Wisconsin a way station to freedom than migrated to stay, their status figured in the first statehood debates in 1846 and raised the issue of women's status as well, if only as a figure of fun for men who met to decide the fate of women in the future state. The convention brought together "the ablest men of the territory, many of whom were advanced thinkers on social questions," according to historian Louise Phelps Kellogg. However, economic concerns motivated many male proponents of married women's property rights in the aftermath of the Panic of 1837. As Kellogg writes, "worthy families" in Wisconsin had lost their homesteads, and "many wives had lost all that they had received from their fathers," because a wife's belongings became a husband's property, subject to seizure to discharge his debts. In the ensuing debate, a less advanced thinker — a future chief justice of the Wisconsin Supreme Court — cited both "natural law" and the Bible in favor of women's legal inferiority. Nonetheless, proponents won the property rights clause in the proposed constitution (see "Married Women's Property Rights in Wisconsin, 1846–1872" in chapter 3).[17]

The "advanced thinkers" then thought they could win "universal suffrage," if only for all Wisconsin men, and went too far in proposing the extension of enfranchisement to men of color. An opponent, an Irishman with a "reputation of being a wag," offered a clause for inclusion of woman suffrage, if only for comic effect. No weighty discussion of women's rights ensued among the men, not that it mattered. Kellogg concludes that "no really serious consideration of women's right to suffrage" upon statehood occurred, only "an attempt to ridicule and embarrass" supporters to "show how preposterous it was." Clauses for women's property rights and other reforms caused controversies sufficient to doom the proposed constitution at the polls with the voters — the men — of Wisconsin, who preferred to defer statehood for two years. A second convention proposed a less "preposterous" — or less courageous — state constitution, which won voters' approval in 1848.[18]

Eventually, at the end of the territorial era, concern for people of color in the South caused more conflict among Wisconsin men — and many women — than did the rights of men of color and of women closer to home. Antislavery debates also acted to distract settlers from discussion of their denial of the rights of the first Wisconsinites in a period of increasing discrimination toward people of color within the territory and future state. Few settlers raised issues of race in more relevant debate on abolition of the settlers' own policies and practices against Native Americans, from illegal encroachment on their lands, to forcible removal from their homelands, to forcing their children from their homes to remove them from their culture. For many Native Americans and *métis* who had created a remarkable new culture in Wisconsin, the end of the territorial era marked the beginning of the end of their world.

For many immigrants, the new world undeniably was a better world. Many women who migrated to Wisconsin from within the country, especially from the South, also found a better life than they had had before. However, for many women among newcomers as well, Wisconsin by the mid-nineteenth century differed little from the worlds they had left behind, whether for better or for worse.

## NOTES

1. Alice E. Smith, *HOW,* vol. 1, *From Exploration to Statehood* (Madison: SHSW, 1973),196, 201. Within two years, with creation of the Territory of Iowa in 1838, Congress redrew Wisconsin's boundaries closer to the current status.
2. Ibid., 470, 651; Richard N. Current, *HOW,* vol. 2, *The Civil War Era, 1848–1873* (Madison: SHSW, 1976), 3.
3. Suzanne Elizabeth Moranian, "Ethnocide in the Schoolhouse: Missionary Efforts to Educate Indian Youth in Pre-Reservation Wisconsin," *WMH* 64, no. 4 (Summer 1981): 260.
4. Smith, *HOW,* 493.
5. Moranian, "Ethnocide in the Schoolhouse," 259.
6. Smith, *HOW,* 589–591.
7. Margaret Larson, *For the Common Good: A History of Women's Roles in La Crosse County, 1920–1980* (League of Women Voters of La Crosse County, 1996), 129, 185.
8. Smith, *HOW,* 432. Other women also individually petitioned the legislature in the era, as territorial legislators rather than courts granted approval for divorces. In the 1848 session alone, legislators issued twenty-four divorces; see Smith, *HOW,* 383.
9. Sara M. Evans, *Born for Liberty: A History of Women in America* (New York: Free Press, 1989), 75, 84, 103.
10. Smith, *HOW,* 432.
11. Ibid., 477, 493, 496.
12. Ibid., 429.
13. Ibid., 475; Zachary Cooper, *Black Settlers in Rural Wisconsin* (Madison: SHSW, 1994), 1.
14. Theron W. Haight, *The History of Waukesha County, Wisconsin* (Chicago: Western Historical Company, 1880), 563.
15. Dora Putnam, "The Underground Railroad in Wisconsin," *Waukesha Freeman,* September 26, 1907.
16. Ibid.; see also Leonard Sykes Jr., "Monuments Commemorate Runaway Slaves' Bravery," *Milwaukee Journal Sentinel,* October 26, 2001, on the dedication of the Tower of Freedom in Ontario, honoring fugitive slaves including Quarrelles and attended by her great-great-granddaughter Charlotte Watkins, who later returned to Milwaukee to retrace her ancestor's route. Of the variant forms of Quarrelles's surname in several sources, the one used here is the preference of her descendants.
17. Louise Phelps Kellogg to Theodora W. Youmans, "The Question Box: Negro Suffrage and Woman's Rights in the Convention of 1846," *WMH* 3, no. 3 (September 1919): 227–230.
18. Ibid.; see also Leslie H. Fishel Jr., "Wisconsin and Negro Suffrage," *WMH* 46, no. 2 (Spring 1943): 180–196.

# History and Family Values, A Good Wife's Tale

## Mary Elizabeth Meade Grignon of Kaukauna, 1837–1898

VIRGINIA GLENN CRANE

WMH 80, No. 3 (Spring 1997): 179–200

In 1856 a call went out to the pioneers of Wisconsin summoning a few of the well-known early settlers to a meeting in Madison to talk about the old days when the "Red man was seen on every hill and glade." Not surprisingly, the text of the invitation described the evolution of the frontier since Indian times in terms of the nineteenth-century idea of the March of Progress — "from savagery to civilization.". . .[1]

Among those invited to reminisce at the gathering in Madison was Charles Augustin Grignon, aged forty-eight, a widely respected ex-fur trader of French-Canadian descent, a soldier, businessman, minor government official, and head of the Kaukauna branch of the Langlade-Grignon clan, one of Wisconsin's founding families. Presumably Charles would have had much to tell about the early days in Green Bay and the Fox River Valley. His wife, Mary Elizabeth Meade Grignon, was not invited to the capital to tell her story. . . .

In the Victorian world of 1856, women were perceived as being outside of history. They were considered, at best, mere appendages to the dynamic forces of war, politics, and commerce that made up the core of nineteenth-century historical studies, ideas, and action. A woman's world was marginalized because the prevailing value system denied her access to public power. Instead, the mythology of the time — characterized by modern social historians as the "cult of domesticity" — defined woman's sphere as being in the home. There, she was to be a submissive wife who bore and reared the next generation and served her family as housekeeper, moral anchor, spiritual guide, and civilizing force.

The family, and woman's responsibilities within it, are of course central to all societies, and in all ages; but the "great man" history of America in the mid-nineteenth century treated both dismissively. By contrast, twentieth-century history has been democratized and has come to value the social dimensions of human relations as subjects worthy of scholarly study and historical analysis. In keeping with that new inclusiveness, historians have come to recognize the family as a complex and fundamental institution and woman's role in society as a critical factor in shaping a culture.[2] Within that new historical perspective, the life of Mary Elizabeth Meade Grignon can properly be viewed as a human experience that was just as important as her husband's. Her work, her role, and her status were, in truth, central, not marginal, to the history of the Wisconsin frontier and the agricultural and commercial society that emerged from it.

Mary Elizabeth Meade was born in Harrisburg, Pennsylvania, on September 8, 1818. She was the daughter of David Meade, a native of Dublin, Ireland. About 1800, David had journeyed with his sister Catherine to Philadelphia. He served in the United States navy during the War of 1812, married Lydia Walye (or Wilde), and had four children: Catherine (named for her aunt), Mary Elizabeth, John F., and Mathew.[3] The young Meade family then migrated westward in Pennsylvania, moving first to Harrisburg and then to Shippensburg and on to Pittsburgh.

In 1830, Lydia Meade died in Pittsburgh and David sent his two daughters, fourteen-year-old Catherine and twelve-year-old Mary Elizabeth, to live with their Aunt Catherine who had earlier married James Durang and moved to Zanesville, Ohio. The Meades were Irish Catholics, and Aunt Durang sent her older niece, Catherine, to school at St. Mary's Seminary, a Dominican novitiate and female academy in Somerset, Ohio. Mary Elizabeth remained with her aunt in Zanesville but kept in close touch with her sister by regular correspondence. Shortly after Catherine left for school, cholera broke out in Pittsburgh, and the two sisters worried about their distant father and brothers and "prayed for their protection." Catherine's own health was endangered in Somerset, for when she arrived at school, the place was very "sickly" with scarlet fever ("putred [sic] sore throat"), and the students who became infected were "dying fast." But the Meades all survived the epidemics and in 1833, when Mary Elizabeth was fourteen, she joined her sister as a student at St. Mary's. There, she pursued a curriculum that included music, art, literature, and religion along with what were called "useful" subjects and practical training.[4]

At the academy, the Meade sisters met and became friends with the daughters of two French-Canadian fur-trading families from the Green Bay region of distant Lake Michigan: the Grignons and the Lawes. The Wisconsin students found themselves so far from home because St. Mary's was the female educational institution preferred by the priests who served the Wisconsin area in the early 1830s. Itinerant Dominican and other missionary priests had come increasingly to frequent the waterways of Wisconsin after the 1820s, serving the Green Bay Catholic community — which included the Grignons — and proselytizing among the Indians of the Fox River region. The priests recognized the need for educated Catholic daughters of local families to serve as interpreters for their work among the native peoples and as teachers at a newly established Indian mission school at Green Bay. . . .[5]

When Catherine Meade was graduated from St. Mary's in 1834, she was persuaded by her priest in Ohio and by her Wisconsin classmates to leave her family behind and travel to Green Bay to teach at the Catholic mission school. She was accompanied on her journey to the frontier by a priest and by the daughters of the Lawe family, and when they arrived in Wisconsin, Catherine took a job at the mission school. She taught for less than a year, however, for she soon met and married George W. Lawe, the brother of her school mates. She quit her job and settled down to raise a family in her new frontier environment.

In 1836, at the end of the school term at St. Mary's Academy, Mary Elizabeth, having graduated with honors, traveled with her classmate, Sophia Grignon, to Wisconsin to visit Catherine Meade Lawe in her new home. There, Mary Elizabeth became acquainted with Catherine's husband and his family as well as with Sophia's family, the Grignons, one of whom — Sophia's brother Charles — attracted her particularly.[6]

Charles Augustin Grignon came from a world that was radically different from the culture and environment that Mary Elizabeth Meade had always known. He was a *métis* or "mixed-blood," the scion of French, Scottish, Menominee, and Ottawa ancestors. His great-grandfather was Charles Michel Langlade (1729–1801), a famous French-Ottawa soldier-warrior and imperial agent in service to the crown of France who later became known as the "Father of Wisconsin." About the time of the French and Indian War in the mid-eighteenth century, Langlade, with his Canadian wife, Charlotte Bourassa (1735–1818), his father, Augustin (1703–1771), and his mother, Clear Day Woman (d.1783) — baptized with the Catholic name Domitelle — migrated from Quebec to the mouth of the lower Fox River at Green Bay. There the Langlades acquired land and established a fur-trading post. . . .

Charles Langlade and his wife had a daughter, Domitelle [1759–1823], born at Green Bay. . . . When Domitelle was thirteen, she was married to Pierre Grignon (1740–1795), a French-Canadian voyageur employed by the Langlades. . . .

Pierre and Domitelle Langlade Grignon had nine children. . . .

Augustin Grignon (1780–1860), the third son . . . [settled] at a whitewater rapids known as Grand Cacalin. . . . About 1804, Augustin married Nancy McCrea, the *métis* daughter of a Menominee woman and a Scots fur trader, . . . at Grand Cacalin. Nancy and Augustin had five children including a son, Charles Augustin Grignon, and a daughter, Sophia. The McCrea-Grignons spoke primarily French but were multilingual, with a command of Menominee, Chippewa, and English. Augustin established a thriving fur-trade business at Grand Cacalin with a store and warehouse, docks, both a saw- and a gristmill, and an oxcart portage service for ferrying vessels and cargoes over or around the rapids that obstructed navigation at that point on the river. . . .

Nancy was a devout Catholic who provided sustenance and support for the missionaries who passed her way, but she also retained her Menominee traditions — gathering wild rice with her mother, sewing moccasins, threading snowshoes, and, in the early spring, processing maple sugar at a nearby camp in the sugarbush.[7]

Charles A. Grignon (1808–1862), the oldest son of the Grand Cacalin Grignons, was sent east to New York for an English education. . . . [In the 1830s,] the older Grignon sons took over operation of the family enterprise at the rapids.

Charles was a responsible young man. . . . He apparently managed the family business with efficiency, but not with overweening ambition for economic development or capital accumulation, and he gave himself adequate time off to pay regular visits to Green Bay for business and pleasure. It was on one of those trips — in 1836, the year that Wisconsin achieved territorial status — that Charles met Mary Elizabeth Meade, newly arrived from the East. Charles was twenty-eight years old at the time, five feet nine, with black eyes, dark hair, and dark complexion. Mary Elizabeth was just nineteen years old, petite and light-eyed, alert and vivacious. He courted her for a short time and presently they were betrothed.[8]

On New Year's Day, 1837, Mary Elizabeth Meade and Charles A. Grignon were married in Green Bay. . . . Mary Elizabeth wore an elegant wedding gown of ivory-colored silk, size five. Gifts of silver flatware and hollowware and other items traditional in the wedding etiquette of the antebellum East were lavished on the newlyweds. Charles's wedding present to his bride was a piano, an expensive and fitting gift for a young woman who was regarded by her friends and acquaintances as a "musician of ability" with a sweet singing voice. All talk on "that happy day" was about the "loveliness of the fair bride" who had left the "luxuries and comforts of civilization to brave the inconveniences" of pioneer life. . . .[9]

. . . [T]he couple decided to establish their home at the McCrea-Grignon enclave up the Fox River at the rapids and to build themselves a new house there — a house worthy of their gentry status. During the first months of their marriage, while plans for the new house were under way, Mary Elizabeth continued to live at her sister's home in Green Bay while Charles came and went as his business allowed.

Both Charles and Mary Elizabeth were active in the planning, construction, and furnishing of their new house. Mary Elizabeth recruited masons and carpenters from Pennsylvania and Ohio; Charles traveled by Great Lakes steamer to New York to buy special architectural fixtures, including a cherry stair rail, banisters, and a carved newel post. . . .

. . . The dwelling took shape as a three-story clapboard structure in Greek Revival style with a two-story portico and second-story balustraded porch. Whitewashed and handsomely furnished, it became known as the "Mansion in the Woods." Charles and Mary Elizabeth moved into their spanking new home in November 1837.[10] In sharp contrast with Green Bay, Grand Cacalin was a lonely spot for Mary Elizabeth — a tenderfoot who had spent her youth in the East and had grown accustomed to living in a busy town surrounded by friends and loved ones. When the new Mrs. Grignon moved to the frontier with her silverware, her books, and her piano, she was a new kind of inhabitant on the old Menominee land. The Indians and *métis* settlers who lived at Grand Cacalin had never before heard the sound of a piano. The voyageurs were accustomed to the fiddle and song; the Menominee, to the drum, flute, and chant. Oblivious to the rich cultural tradition that existed just outside her door, Mary Elizabeth sat alone in her richly appointed parlor and played on her piano the tunes from her music book — operatic airs, comic songs, and popular ditties of the 1820s.[11]

Her music, like everything else that Mary Elizabeth had known from her first eighteen years in Pennsylvania and Ohio, contrasted sharply with all she encountered at Grand Cacalin. She knew nothing of the Menominee people, of their lodges, their village life, or their customs. . . .

Nor did she develop a sense of oneness with her in-laws. By 1837, when Mary Elizabeth moved to Grand Cacalin, Charles's father Augustin had migrated, like other fur traders before him, deeper into the wilderness. He set up a new business establishment on Lake Butte des Morts near the relocated Menominee reservation some forty miles south of Grand Cacalin. Nancy McCrea Grignon did not move right away to be with her husband, but rather remained at home with her Menominee mother; the two women continued to live in their log houses close behind (and dwarfed by) the grand new Meade-Grignon domicile. Sophia Grignon, Charles's sister and Mary Elizabeth's classmate from St. Mary's, lived at the old McCrea-Grignon cabin with her mother, but apparently the sisters-in-law were not close friends.

The vastly different houses at the enclave were the visible signs of a cultural divide between the McCrea-Grignon family and the new Mrs. Grignon of Grand Cacalin. There were, first of all, racial, ethnic, and language differences. The Langlade-Grignon saga of migration southward from Canada differed from the more common Meade pattern of migration from east to west. Mary Elizabeth was a first-generation American; Charles was a sixth-generation American on his Grignon side, of the seventh generation on his Langlade side, and of uncounted generations on his Ottawa and Menominee sides. There was the difference of a young woman with an upbringing that fostered Irish Catholic female propriety and a mature man who was quite comfortable with his Catholic French-Indian heritage. . . .

In addition to all these dissonances of culture and relationships within the Meade-Grignon marriage, there was also the normal nineteenth-century difference in the gendered culture that separated men and women. In that era, romance and sentimentality were a kind of veil obscuring the reality of early marriage. As a rule, young brides feared sexuality. They had grave difficulty adjusting to an intimate male presence within their accustomed space. After their weddings, they tended to seek emotional support, not from their new husbands, but from their own kin and especially from female friends.

Mary Elizabeth fit the pattern. She kept in close touch with the Meades in Green Bay, to whom she sent along little gifts: a pair of stockings for brother John; and almonds, filberts, and pies for the family. The Meades in turn kept Mary Elizabeth informed about news from the "city." John believed his sister was lonely because she had become accustomed to Catherine's children and felt "lost" without them. . . .[12]

In time, Mary Elizabeth adapted to both her husband and her environment, and she and Charles began filling up the Grand Cacalin homeplace with babies. A daughter, Frances Elizabeth (Fanny) was born in 1838, and during the next twenty-four years, the Meade-Grignons had ten more children [a total of seven girls and four boys]. . . .[13]

. . . Mary Elizabeth's house was frequently full to overflowing.

The designation of her home as the "Mansion of the Woods" was a somewhat romanticized conceit, but still, the place was undeniably substantial. It was also well furnished, and the standard of living enjoyed by its owners was high for the pre–Civil War Wisconsin frontier. . . . Mary Elizabeth's piano had pride of place in the Meade-Grignon parlor. In a family where both the mother and father valued education, bookcases were more than pieces of furniture, and the Grignon library contained a large, eclectic collection. . . .[14]

. . . Nevertheless, the place was rural, the family had a farm, and Mary Elizabeth kept cows and chickens and tended a kitchen garden. As such, she was a farm woman and shared with her husband the responsibility for feeding her children and providing for them. She and her extended family in Green Bay also established and maintained an informal network for the exchange of commodities between country and city. Sharing the products of her forest, garden, and dairy was a regular part of her social relationship with

her kin, and their reciprocity was an important ingredient in her role as economic producer for her household. Brother John sent bags of chestnuts and apples from Green Bay.
. . . Grandpa Meade took a special interest in the Grand Cacalin vegetable and herb garden and every spring sent his daughter seeds, cuttings, and instructions on their culture.
Top onions and summer savory, melon seed, fruit trees, and vegetable slips were regularly
unloaded at the Grand Cacalin dock from the Green Bay cargo boat. Mary Elizabeth sent
back cabbage plants for June setting, and the Meades sent bottles from Green Bay for
some of the "good cream" from their country kinswoman's five cows.[15]

The generation succeeding the Meade-Grignon marriage (1837–1860) was a period
during which the process of Americanization of the French-Indian and farming frontier
of Wisconsin culminated, in 1848, in the admission of the territory to statehood. Grand
Cacalin became a town, renamed Kaukauna. . . . The price of all this Anglo-American
"progress" was paid largely by the Indians, the *métis*, and the natural environment. The fur
trade disappeared first, then the native peoples, and before long much of the natural
beauty of the region. The Menominee, dismissed as worthless "savages," were repeatedly
encouraged to sign treaties and move off their lands. The French-speaking *métis* were
shunted aside. . . .

. . . [But] Charles brought in a cash income which — combined with Mary Elizabeth's
substantial contributions — made possible a comfortable though by no means lavish standard of living for the Meade-Grignon family. . . .

Education, like religion, was valued as an essential by the Meade-Grignon family, and
all the junior Grignons received a basic education. Fanny, the oldest, was sent to Green
Bay for the early grades because there were no educational establishments in Kaukauna
when she arrived at primary school age. For ten years, she boarded with friends of the
family and completed her early schooling away from home. In 1853, her family sent her
to Lawrence Preparatory School in the nearby village of Appleton, where she gained
recognition for her fluent French and her musical ability. She proceeded on to Lawrence
College, was graduated in 1858, and returned three years later to teach French and music.
Nancy, the second daughter, and Gus, the third child and oldest son, were also sent to
Lawrence in the 1850s after elementary schooling in Green Bay and Kaukauna. . . .

For fun, the children made maple candy, read stories from *Gleason's Pictorial,* played
with their cats, and enjoyed sledding and sleigh rides. After a long winter on the frozen
Fox, spring was invariably a joyous time, and its beauty and warmth were a recurring
theme in Grignon letters from March until May. Spring was the time to plant flower seeds
and to appreciate the budding and "leaving" of the apple trees, the cherry, peach, and
plum. Springtime in 1853 was spoiled, however, because of what Fanny termed the "Public Works." Construction on the canal and locks just in front of the house, with all the
noise and dirt, cut off the "pretty walk down to the river" and "ruined everything." The
blasting was "terrible," and the stones that were thrown "all over the garden" by the dyna-
mite made it dangerous to be outside the door.[16]

This comfortable, family-centered world at the Meade-Grignon country home was
touched by tragedy and loss during the Civil War era, and the family that emerged in the

late nineteenth century . . . was very different from the family that Mary Elizabeth and Charles had established in the antebellum decades.

Death was the leveler. . . . The Grignons lost two babies in the mid-1850s. . . . [Soon] afterward, six-year-old Emma had an accident of some sort and suffered from the effects of that for the remainder of her life. The loss and illness of loved ones was made less harsh for Mary Elizabeth in her grief because in the mid-1850s her father David and her aunt, Catherine Durang, moved from Green Bay to Kaukauna to live with the Meade-Grignons. When they died — David in 1857, Aunt Catherine in 1858 — Mary Elizabeth was bereft. Charles suffered a loss of his own in 1860 when his father Augustin died at Butte des Morts. Mary Elizabeth's younger brother, Mathew Meade of Green Bay, enlisted in the army when the Civil War began and was sent to the western theater, and his sister and her kin were anxious about his welfare throughout the war.

Good Friday, April 18, 1862, became a memorial date in Meade-Grignon family history, for on that Catholic holy day, Mary Elizabeth lost her husband. Charles died suddenly after a short illness. He was fifty-four. His widow was forty-four. She was expecting her eleventh child at the time, and when a son was born two months later, she named the infant Charles A. Grignon Jr.[17]

During the final thirty years of her life (1862–1898), the Widow Grignon was faced with the burden of single parenthood and head of household responsibilities at her Kaukauna home. . . . She went through a period of financial crisis for a year and a half in 1863–1864 while she struggled to settle the estate and make ends meet. During that hard time, when cash was short, she borrowed money from Mary Doty Fitzgerald, a family friend. Through the remainder of the 1860s and for several years thereafter, she was slow in paying taxes and household bills and was in and out of court because of debts. She became familiar with foreclosures and sheriff's sales. She continued, for the rest of her life, to sort though the tangled threads of Charles's and his father's estates, especially Charles's share of family property.[18]

While she struggled with finances, Mary Elizabeth also had to endure a family crisis that involved her second daughter, Nancy. . . . [I]n 1866, at age twenty-six, [Nancy] married Edward Meade. . . . Then, only six months after the wedding, Nancy died following a "long and painful" illness.[19] She was the first and only of the adult Grignon offspring to precede her mother to the grave.

The pain of a daughter's unhappiness and untimely death, combined with the strain of financial pressure, made the decade after Charles's death a time of severe testing for Mary Elizabeth. As she worked through one crisis after another during that difficult period, she emerged as the matriarch of the Grignon clan, and her children rallied to her support as best they could. The family was restored to a degree of financial stability after Mary Elizabeth began to lease and dispose of family property. . . . Mary Elizabeth continued her husband's practice of contracting with the Army Corps of Engineers to sell stone from the Grignon quarry and to lease land adjacent to her house, including the pasture in the front yard. . . .[20]

After income from the army came to an end, Mary Elizabeth made money by selling

Grignon land to an entrepreneur who built a paper mill across the canal from her home. The noise and dust and ugliness of construction and of the machines and shacks and railroad tracks at the quarry in her yard were distasteful to her and her children. She questioned whether the new canal and locks had actually improved the Fox River, and whether the smoke and stench of the paper mill actually improved the land where the Menominee had once encamped, raised their children, planted their crops, and buried their dead in tribally hallowed ground.

Whatever may have been the esthetic, psychic, and health costs of canals, quarries, and paper mills for Mary Elizabeth and her family, those ugly agencies of industrial progress helped pay the taxes and the bills. From them, and from land sales and a small government pension that she received in the 1890s after years of petitioning as the widow of a Black Hawk War veteran,[21] Mrs. Grignon earned enough cash income to hold on to her house, to maintain her family in their accustomed place, and to see to it that her younger children secured an education.

. . . Throughout the 1870s, all of Mary Elizabeth's children lived at home except for brief stints away working or attending school. . . . [I]nexpensive leisure-time activities were a normal part of country life and were reminiscent of earlier times at the Grignon home; but the simple entertainment was also dictated by the chronic problem of insufficient cash income and the financial burden of a household with several unmarried daughters who earned little or no money.

Of the eight children of the family who survived into the 1870s, five of them — Fanny, Maggie, Mary, Emma, and Charles — never married or had children of their own. All save Maggie continued to live at home with their mother. In part, perhaps, because of a gender imbalance in the population produced by Civil War casualties and the westward migration of young single men, all but one of the women of the family became the traditional "old maids" of the Victorian era. It also seems possible that the younger generation may have suffered ostracism because of their mixed Indian heritage. Racism was not unknown in Wisconsin in the late nineteenth century, and all of the unmarried female Grignons except Maggie had noticeable Indian features. . . .

Mary Elizabeth seemed to have provided comfort for others; but in her widowhood, as in her early years, she herself was never quite fulfilled. In 1880, in a letter to her brother-in-law, thanking him for a gift of "blood puddings and fresh Pork," she intoned a familiar lament: "I feel lonesome." At the time, her house was full of her grown children.[22]

Three of the Grignon daughters, Fanny, Nancy, and Maggie, demonstrated an early aptitude for artistic expression — in music, poetry, and painting respectively; but, as was true for most women in the nineteenth century, none had a lucrative career. Fanny, the oldest child, quit her job at Lawrence when her father died and returned home to be with her mother and to help care for the younger children. Necessity pushed her for a time into domestic service, but she soon returned home and started making a small income as a piano teacher.[23] Nancy, who as a child wrote poems filled with images of death, died young. Maggie — who had some talent as a painter of portraits and landscapes — started school in Kaukauna when she was five. She was sixteen when her father died and her plans for advanced education were interrupted. In 1868, as soon as her mother had gained some financial equilibrium, Maggie, who was twenty-two at the time, went off to Green Bay to attend the Ursuline Academy. . . . In late 1869, Maggie finally got to Lawrence, registering first as an academic and commercial student and later entering the senior preparatory program as a student of drawing and painting. . . . She completed her higher education in 1871, and signed a contract that year to teach at the Common School in Kaukauna beginning in November, earning a salary of $35 a month. . . . She was the only daughter who gained a degree of financial independence and the only one who lived away from home during her mature years. Mary and Emma remained at home unmarried and without income. Charles, the baby of the family, was tutored by Fanny for the early grades, and then attended Kaukauna high school. He became a bank clerk in town, never married, and lived at home until his death, contributing cash income for household expenses.[24]

Of the four children of the family who married, Nancy died shortly after her marriage. Lydia, who was the fourth child in the family birth order, was married in 1883 to a clerk who worked in a dry-goods store in Appleton. She had one daughter. Gus, the oldest son of the family, attended Lawrence Academy with Fanny and Nancy in the 1850s, and after that returned home to farm. He suffered an accident in 1868, cutting his foot so badly that he bled for nine hours and nearly died from the loss of blood. He recovered, continued to farm the Grignon land, married in 1884, and established a family home next door to Mary Elizabeth's place. He remained in Kaukauna until 1894, when he moved to Nebraska to pursue a business venture. Ross, who was sixteen years younger than Gus, went to primary school in Kaukauna. . . . He was married in 1884 but had no children. He and his wife moved to Arkansas and lived there for a while, but they soon returned to Kaukauna, and he eventually put down roots as a substantial member of the community.[25]

The monetary contributions for the maintenance of Mary Elizabeth's household made by Gus, Ross, Maggie, and Fanny in their mature years eased the financial burden that had weighed on their mother during the score of years after their father's death. . . .

Mary Elizabeth, in her old age as in her youth, supported the Catholic establishment in the Green Bay region. . . . Mrs. Grignon was a pious Catholic who wore out her prayer book. . . . She strictly observed the holy days and ritual requirements of her church, and on a stormy day in April, 1898, she and Mary walked up the steep hill from their riverside home to the hilltop home of her brother Mathew to observe the forty-hour devotions of Lent. Mary Elizabeth was eighty at the time and she became ill after the strenuous walk. She was put to bed and the doctor came and diagnosed a "stroke of paralysis.". . .

. . . Mary Elizabeth Meade Grignon died on April 29, 1898. Her funeral mass was held, at her request, at Little Chute where her husband, her daughter Nancy, and the two children who had died in infancy were buried. . . .[26]

Mary Elizabeth Meade Grignon was born near the beginning of the nineteenth century and died near the end of it. She shared none of the feminist ideologies or professional aspirations of the women's rights activists of her era. . . . [S]he sought no alternative to "woman's sphere." She found her strength in a hierarchical religion rather than in a struggle for equality. Within the confines of her Catholic, domestic world, she suffered what, in the twentieth century, would come to be called the "problem that has no name." From youth to old age, she had been quietly discontented and lonely in the midst of family and loved ones. But despite the emotional price that she paid for her nurturing role, she succeeded in building that most important and fundamental of all institutions: she built a family. And what was more, she kept it intact through good times and bad.

She was one of those pioneers, mostly women, who sought to conquer the wilderness not with guns, axes, and laws but with piety and music, family and society. She did not find, nor did she seek, a central place in the histories of her time. Her work did not easily translate into formal institution-building. She founded no trading post or church; she chartered no bank or canal, wrote no laws, published no newspaper. Without congregations, corporations, or constitutions to her credit, she was forgotten as soon as the circle that had revolved around her (and depended upon her) dispersed, forgot, or died. Such silence in the historical record was true for the vast majority of women in Mary Elizabeth's time and place. For the most part, their communication was oral, not written. Their work was cyclical, not linear; informal, not structured. Memory rather than documentary history was its residue. Thus, despite their central role in the lives of those within their orbit, women only occasionally became part of the historical canon.

For those reasons, when the call went out from Madison in 1856 to Charles A. Grignon and other pioneers, inviting them to come to the capital to reminisce about the frontier days of yore, it never occurred to anyone to invite Charles's wife as well. . . .

*The last of Charles and Mary Elizabeth Grignon's children died by 1933, "and the entire Meade-Grignon branch of the family, including all spouses and offspring, were dead by 1948," Virginia Glenn Crane notes; "Ross's wife Edith was the last of the Grignons to live at Mary Elizabeth's 'Mansion in the Woods.'" However, the home built for a bride brought to Wisconsin more than a century and a half ago, on the site where her husband's family had lived since the century before, has been restored to the antebellum beauty and authenticity of its early years and is open to the public as a historic site of the Outagamie County Historical Society.[27]*

## NOTES

1. E[benezer] Childs and F. Desnoyers to "Friend C.A. Grignon," January, 1856, in the Grignon Manuscript Collection, . . . Outagamie County Historical Society (OCHS), Appleton.

2. See Barbara Welter, *Dimity Convictions: The American Woman in the Nineteenth Century* (Athens, 1976); Carl Degler, *At Odds: Women and the Family in America from the Revolution to the Present* (New York, 1980); Harvey Green, *The Light of the Home: An Intimate View of the Lives of Women in Victorian America* (New York, 1983); and John Demos, *Past, Present and Personal: The Family and the Life Course in American History* (New York, 1986).

3. There is some genealogical confusion about John F. Meade's parentage. . . . [T]he family Bible in the Grignon Collection, OCHS, has an entry listing John's mother as Catherine Meade Durang.

4. See Mary Elizabeth Grignon Obituary, *Kaukauna Sun*, May 6, 1898, and Catherine Meade to "Dear Sister" [Mary Meade], [1831?], both in Charles A. Grignon Papers, Correspondence and Records, 1816–

1952, Manuscript Division, WHS; Meade Family Bible, sampler, and William Wolf, manuscript notes and records, all in Grignon Collection, OCHS; H. B. Tanner, *History of the Streets of Kaukauna* (Kaukauna, 1929); . . . advertisement for St. Mary's, October 18, 1831, in the Grignon, Lawe, and Porlier Papers, 1712–1884, WHS.

5. . . . "Documents Relating to the Catholic Church in Green Bay and the Mission at Little Chute, 1825–1840," *WHC* 14: 162–192; Wolf's Notes, Grignon Collection, OCHS; William F. Raney, "The Grignon Family in Wisconsin to About 1860," typescript in Grignon Collection, OCHS; Samuel Mazzuchelli to Louis Grignon, May 8, 1833, and Mazzuchelli to Augustin Grignon, September 27, 1833, in Grignon, Lawe, and Porlier Papers. . . .

6. Mary Elizabeth Grignon obituary; Tanner, *Kaukauna;* Wolf's Notes and "Album presented to Mary Grignon by a Friend," July 7, 1836, both in Grignon Collection, OCHS.

7. For McCrea-Grignon history, see Augustin Grignon, "Seventy-two Years' Recollections of Wisconsin," *WHC* 3:195–282; . . . Elizabeth Therese Baird, "Reminiscences of Life in Territorial Wisconsin," *WHC* 15: 236–237; John Arndt, "A Journey from Green Bay to Menasha in June 1830," in Giles Clark, *Historic Tales of the Fox River Valley* (Menasha, 1973), 61; Grace L. Nute, *The Voyageur* (New York, 1931), 19; Marguerite Grignon to Ursula Grignon, May 25, 1829, in Charles A. Grignon Correspondence; Wolf's Notes, Grignon Collection, OCHS; Raney, "Grignon," 5 (note 20); Tanner, *Kaukauna;* Elihu Spencer, *The Pioneers of Outagamie County* (Appleton, 1895), 240; Grignon–De Langlade Genealogy, OCHS. For Langlade-Grignon history, see Grignon, "Recollections," *WHC* 3:197–261; Joseph Tasse, "Memoir of Charles de Langlade," ibid., 7:123–187; "Langlade Papers, 1731–1800," ibid., 8:209–223; Louise Phelps Kellogg, *The French Regime in Wisconsin and the Northwest* (Madison, 1925), 314–317, 377; Raney, "Grignon," 1–2. . . . For Domitelle's role as community leader, see Ursula Grignon's Recollections, in "History of Brown County," *The American Sketch Book: A Collection of Historical Incidents,* vol. 3, compiled and edited by Bella French (Green Bay, 1876) and *Commemorative Biographical Record of the Fox River Valley* (Chicago, 1895). See also Grignon–De Langlade Genealogy, OCHS; and Raney, "Grignon," 2 (note 6) and 10 (note 37).

8. . . . Raney, "Grignon," 5–6; Tanner, *Kaukauna.*

9. Mary Elizabeth Grignon obituary, and Pension Claim, July 27, 1892, in Charles A. Grignon Correspondence; *Oshkosh Daily Northwestern,* July 17–18, 1892.

10. Anna Tenney, *A Mansion Built in the Woods,* booklet in Charles A. Grignon Correspondence; *Milwaukee Journal,* May 23, 1943, clipping in Grignon Collection, OCHS; Mary Elizabeth Grignon obituary; Lee Newcomer, *A Four County Guide to the National Register of Historic Places* (Oshkosh, 1981), 46–47. . . .

11. Mary Elizabeth Grignon obituary; songbooks, piano music, and John F. Meade to "Dearest Sister" [MEG], December 4, 1837, all in Grignon Collection, OCHS. . . .

12. John F. Meade to "Dearest Sister" [MEG], December 4, 1837, Catherine Lawe to "My Dear Sister" [MEG], December 4, 1837, and the George W. Lawe Papers (1839), Grignon Collection, OCHS.

13. Grignon family Bible, Grignon Collection, OCHS; Grignon–De Langlade Genealogy, OCHS.

14. Inventory, February 29, 1864, In the Matter of the Estate of Charles A. Grignon, Outagamie County Probate Records, Outagamie County Courthouse; *Milwaukee Journal,* May 23, 1943.

15. John F. Meade to Mary Elizabeth Grignon, April 25, 1844, David Meade to Mary Elizabeth Grignon, April 23, 1855, and Fanny E. Grignon to Mary F. Meade, January 4, 1853, all in Charles A. Grignon Correspondence; David Meade to Mary Elizabeth Grignon, May 13, 1850, in Grignon Collection, OCHS.

16. The Fanny Grignon correspondence, most of it with Amanda Lawe and much of the rest with "Aunt Kate" [Catherine Meade Lawe], David Meade and Augustin Grignon, 1851–1858, provides details about Grignon family life in the 1850s, including information about religion, education of the older children, holiday celebrations, leisure-time activities, reactions to local construction, and yearnings for springtime. See especially her letters dated November 2, 1851, January 27 and March 14 and 24, 1852, January 2, February 25, March 1, May 2, and June 4, 1853, all in Charles A. Grignon Correspondence. See also recipes, inventory, and Nancy Grignon to Amanda Lawe letters, 1852–1853, ibid. Fanny's obituaries in the *Appleton Crescent,* January 15, 1916, and the *Kaukauna Times* [January 14, 1916] indicate that she attended school for ten years in Green Bay and lived with the Morgan L. Martins, who were people of substance and long-standing friends of the Grignons. For the older children's attendance at Lawrence, see *Fifth Annual Catalogue of the Corporation, Faculty & Students of the Lawrence Academy* (Milwaukee, 1854), copy in Grignon House Collection, OCHS.

17. Catherine Lawe to "Dear Father" [David Meade], November 26, 1855, Hannah K. Smith to Mrs. Grignon, April 12, 1855, and Fanny [Grignon] to Aunt Kate [Mrs. George Lawe], October 7, 1856, all in Charles A. Grignon Correspondence; Mary Elizabeth Grignon obituary; Grignon–De Langlade Genealogy, OCHS; Wolf's Notes, family Bible, Amanda Meade Grignon obituary, March 28, 1855, all in Grignon Collection, OCHS; Tanner, *Kaukauna.*

18. Tax returns and tax receipts, 1852–1897, especially redemption receipt, Outagamie County Clerk's Office to R. C. Grignon, October 26, 1887, all in Grignon Collection, OCHS. . . .

19. *Green Bay Press-Gazette,* March 25, 1867. . . .

20. . . . Quarry Contract and Agreement, June 27 and 29, 1874, . . . Quarry Lease, June 19, 1879, and Mary Elizabeth Grignon to Col. C. A. Fuller, 28 November 1880, all in Charles A. Grignon Correspondence.

21. A series of letters in the Charles A. Grignon Correspondence between Mary Elizabeth and government agents, especially A. P. Clark, recount the struggle for a pension, as do Bell to Barnes Pension Claim, March 3, 1894, Pension Certificate, March 7, 1894, and George and Catherine Lawe, Testimony Before D. J. Brothers, March 2, 1893.

22. MEG to George Lawe, 1880, Grignon Collection, OCHS. . . .

23. Jos. LaBoule to Misses Grignon, September 26, 1876, M. F. Fenton to Mary Grignon, June 21, 1909, Wolf's Notes, all in Grignon Collection, OCHS; *Appleton Crescent,* August 18, 1866, and January 15, 1916; State of Wisconsin Department of Health Bureau of Vital Statistics, Original Certificate of Death, January 10, 1916.

24. . . . Margaret E. Grignon Voter Registration Certificate [undated], and Wolf's Notes, . . . Grignon Collection, OCHS. . . .

25. For Ross, see Rossiter C. Grignon to Maggie, January 4, 1874, R. C. Grignon hunting license, both in Charles A. Grignon Correspondence; R. Grignon 1879 Kaukauna Diary, R. C. Grignon Tax Receipts for Personal Property, March 2, 1896, and scattered dates 1920–1925, in Grignon Collection, OCHS. For R. C. Grignon's election as Kaukauna Supervisor, see *Kaukauna Times,* April 10, 1896. An account of Lydia's wedding was in the *Appleton Crescent,* September 29, 1883. An account of Gus's accident was in the *Appleton Crescent,* December 19, 1868. See also Bill of Sale to Augustin D. Grignon, August 7, 1874, G. S. Albee to Kate Deuel Grignon, January 1, 1889, Kate [Grignon] to Gus [Grignon], May 30, 1890, and A. D. Grignon Kaukauna tax receipts, 1891, all in Grignon Collection, OCHS. For other details on Gus, Ross, Lydia, Mary, Emma, and Charles, see *Kaukauna Times,* March 3, 1948, and Wolf's Notes, ibid.

26. Mary Elizabeth Grignon obituary; MEG prayer book, insurance receipt ("Mama's last signature"), February 2, 1898, Western Union telegram to A. D. Grignon, April 28, 1898, all in Grignon Collection, OCHS. . . .

27. *Appleton Post-Crescent,* October 24, 1934, and Edith Grignon obituary, *Kaukauna Times,* March 3, 1948.

# Motherhood on the Wisconsin Frontier

LILLIAN KRUEGER

WMH 29, No. 2 (December 1945): 157–183 and 29, No. 3 (March 1946): 333–346

. . . This is the story of one phase of the Midwest immigration, the story of the frontier mother. Her courage, initiative, and ingenuity, though tempered by loneliness and fear, contributed in full measure to a region's birth; with no thought of self, her doing has become an epic of the American way of life. Lest we forget, and the upcoming generation learns too little about her hard-earned glory, this part of Wisconsin's frontier history, centering on the 1840s and '50s, is here retold.

The mother arrived in the Middle West from the Old World, from the seaboard, particularly from the New England and New York regions, or from the states intervening. Her infrequent letters were written to her native Scandinavia, Poland, Germany, England, or Ireland, often requiring many months to reach the old home; sometimes they took the slow route to Vermont, New York, Ohio, or Indiana. . . .

The wilderness home could be occupied within a few days, a few weeks, or after several months, depending upon its size, sturdiness, and comfort, but the description of a log cabin without the mention of snow sifting onto the attic floor and over the beds is rare indeed. Sometimes the mother remained with her children at the city of debarkation while the father and the men in his group left to look for farms in the hinterland. A very simple shelter might be built at once, and he would then return to move the members of his family in an ox- or horse-drawn vehicle to their new home.

. . . A Rock County Norwegian family lived in a hay stack for three months, and surely their completed cabin must have had a feeling of real permanence, if not elegance, about it. At times a mother's duties were carried on in and around the wagon in which they bumped to their "home," or it may have been in a crude brush shelter hastily put together. She considered herself very fortunate if she could live in the cabin or barn of a relative or friend who had preceded her to the Middle West and whose homesteading was somewhat advanced. . . .

The mother's cabin was generally of small dimensions, from 12 by 12 to 12 by 14 feet, and contained a puncheon floor — logs split lengthwise. A second room was provided by a low attic which was reached by a ladder or by wooden pegs attached to the wall. This dwelling became the mother's domain although she would fall short in the performance of her duties did not many paths radiate from her door for miles in all directions, since helping her neighbors was one of her many virtues. . . .

It mattered little whether the mother's house was situated on a well-traveled road, or on a scarcely discernible trail which wound through tall grasses, brightly flowered meadow patches, and dark forests. Almost without exception she became an innkeeper. In sparsely settled areas it had to be so, while in the older sections taverns were conducted on a business basis. . . .

Sarah Pratt, a country school teacher near Afton, Rock County, and her sister Susannah had come from the East in the 1840s to assuage the desperate homesickness of their married sister Jane Washburn. Sarah frequently noted in her diary something about the travelers who stopped at the Washburn farm. In April 1845, Sarah, Susannah, and Jane were hurrying about preparing food for fifty men, who were engaged in a barn raising. Hardly had the supper dishes been removed when a family asked if it were possible to secure lodging. The mother was in great distress from a fractured ankle which had occurred a few miles back when she had jumped from the wagon. It had been one of those extra-busy days, but Mrs. Washburn did not have the heart to turn the newcomers away, especially the suffering mother. The result was that Sarah and Susannah completed their work and spent the night at the home of a friend. The next morning it was up with the sun and back to Jane's to prepare breakfast for helpers and wayfarers.[1]

One of the hospitality centers which welcomed the Norwegians to Wisconsin was the Muskego settlement in Racine and Waukesha counties. . . .

. . .[In 1843,] the influx of Norwegians was so great that every house in the Muskego colony sheltered from fifteen to twenty persons. An epidemic raging at the time made the housing doubly difficult, but it seems Norwegian mothers found the answer. . . .[2]

Almost without exception, the religious life in the early communities had its beginnings in the little cabins, but mothering and praying had to go on simultaneously if much of the latter was to be done, and few there were who did not believe in its efficacy. . . .

Of course, there were pioneer men at the church services, but the details incident to community worship were in the mother's hands. Her cabin was swept, the altar prepared — frequently a bureau especially beautified was used — all on short notice. When a Catholic father was going her way, or a preacher on horseback swung slowly along the trail, the good news traveled with lightning speed, and shortly there were prayer and admonition and sacrament at her little dwelling. . . .

Even though the mother's house was used by the church-going community, it served still another purpose: that of the first country school. She in turn might become a teacher. These "pay" schools, as they were known, were supported by the parents whose children were enrolled in them. . . .[3]

The late Mary Davison Bradford, a Wisconsin educator of Eastern parentage, who was reared in Kenosha County, began her schooling when but a child of two. Her mother, busy with a family of six, delegated to ten-year-old Ida the care of little Mary: rather than give up going to school she took her tiny sister along. Ida began her school days . . . in the large, unplastered living room of a farmhouse more than a mile from her home. . . . The teacher was a girl of the neighborhood who did a good job in the schoolroom. . . .[4]

Maybe it was her teaching experience, begun in New York State when she was seventeen, which in 1844 encouraged young Mrs. J. T. [Marian Eliza Neill] Hamilton to take charge of the first rural school in her locality, three miles south of Whitewater. She and her husband set up housekeeping in a single room while he was building their home. Into this room some thirteen or fourteen children trooped. These she taught while keeping a watchful eye on young Frederic, less than a year old, receiving the munificent salary of $1.00 a week.[5]

Sarah Pratt could not conceive of being deprived of the little reading and writing knowledge which she possessed and "often to[o] I feel the need of more learning," she wrote in her diary.[6] It is not unusual to find similar remarks made by these young teachers, though some of them added that their work was not difficult since many boys and girls whose parents were foreign born were determined to speak, read, and write the English language, a type of instruction which was performed reasonably well, even with meager training.

Sarah's district demanded a periodic appraisal of her fitness, and her account speaks of taking an eight-mile trip "to be examined."[7] It is common knowledge that some of these examiners knew far less than their candidates, and one can almost believe some such anecdote as when an examiner, thumbing his geography, questioned, "What color is Massachusetts?" Answer, "Blue." Her inspections must have proved satisfactory since she found her pupils in good spirits and became greatly attached to them.[8]

During her short teaching career she "boarded 'round" and walked many prairie miles alone and apparently unafraid. A "neighborhood blessing," she ministered to the aged, and the ill, the overworked, and the dying in much the same way as did the frontier mother. Frail, and troubled increasingly with a cough, she gradually grew weaker and died of tuberculosis in the early autumn of 1847. . . .

Comparatively few groups of single women came to America during the first half of the nineteenth century, except for the Irish colleens who arrived with the great exodus from their homeland after the potato famine had left its blight. When these girls landed, the wealthy eastern women employed them immediately. . . .[9]

The Wisconsin mother instead of finding respite in a boarding house was forced to operate one, and sweated more, endured more backache, and added a few more hours to her day. If Providence were extra kind, she might find a hired girl! At the lead mines where help was scarce, an industrious girl could earn $100 a year in addition to her board "either as a domestic assistant, or by serving."[10] The Beloit region could not compete with the lead-region wages, where maids were paid 50 and 75 cents a week in the 1830s and '40s, a washwoman receiving a shilling a day.[11] Domestics earned from 50 cents to $1.00 a week in the vicinity of Baraboo in the 1850s, the 75-cent rate being commonly paid on a farm to "a good, strong, capable girl, sixteen to twenty years of age," and of course it was understood that here gardening and milking were part of the household tasks. Of women servants, one informant says that they never or very rarely worked in the field but that they took "care of the house, and the kitchen, and at most of the stable.". . .[12]

When Melinda Weaver was raising her two small children in the vicinity of Waukesha in the late 1830s, she greatly missed her relatives and friends, since there was no one "to be hired for love or money." Milwaukee attracted the young girls, she related, and when there was severe illness the neighbors did the best they could and took turns caring for the patients.[13]

There were frontiersmen who took notice of the endless work their wives performed. When Anson Buttles' wife was struggling with her brood of six small children on a farm near Fox Point, town of Milwaukee, . . . her husband came to the rescue[with the washing] to "save the women some hard work.". . .[14]

The wealthier housewives frequently had reason to complain about their servants. There was Caroline Green Strong, for instance. She lived in rather comfortable circumstances at Mineral Point — with the help of a maid some of the time — and was a combination housewife-secretary and a personnel manager. Her days were crowded with the many duties her husband Moses delegated to her while he was away at Madison as a member of the territorial council. Her long communications of the mid-1840s describing her loneliness — they had migrated from Vermont — were concerned especially with the shortcomings of her "men servants," of whom she had employed a long series. . . .[15]

The winter preceding, Moses had learned that it was impossible for her to get along with her "house servant." She complained:

> He has so many old batchelor notions & looks so scowling if he is asked to do little chores and errands. . . . it is quite beneath him to do errands & help little jobs for women folks . . . he is "too old to learn new tricks" — and I've worried along with him & keep the peace between us, by saying as little for him to do as possible. . . .[16]

The frontier mother could not mourn too much over her help problem; marriage was daily claiming others the same as it had claimed her. . . .

Marriage in the New World during the 1840s and '50s was given consideration even before the girls left the homeland. A concerned brother, living near Waukesha, wrote to his sister in 1851, "One can always marry (here) and at all times; but I do not consider it advisable for you to come to America merely to get married. Far better to become a maid-servant for a while in order to learn American ways and manners, the household, the language. . . ."[17]

. . . A double ceremony . . . at Muskego took place in 1844 when Mrs. Hans [Cornelia Jacobson] Heg's two sisters [Anne Jacobson Einong Molee and Aslang Jacobson Tveito] were married in the Even Heg barn. . . . [O]ne of the wedding party recalled the event many years later. "This was the way Mr. Heg had of dedicating his new barn before he put it to more common use," he said.[18]

Thus the pioneer woman's status as wife and mother was established. . . .

Much of settlement history comes from the loom of scarcity: there was a scarcity of food, of clothing, of furniture, of cabin space. But the homesteads were teeming with children. . . .

Unimpeachable proof of the fecundity of the frontier mother is contained in the federal manuscript census records. Parents were commonly credited with ten or twelve children, and if the total reached fifteen, in about as many years, it still seemed credible.

Whether Irish, Polish, English, German, Dutch, or Scandinavian, every household was generously populating the frontier. In fact many of the early accounts make mention especially of the size of the families. . . .

Anson Buttles, of English ancestry, arrived with his parents from the East and settled in Milwaukee township in 1843. After his marriage he and his wife Cornelia Mullie of Dutch (Netherlands) forebears, lived on a farm near his father and mother and enjoyed somewhat better home conditions than many of those who migrated directly from Europe. The children who played about his farmhouse were not there as an economic asset, since his journal discloses the fact that near-prosperity rode in the Buttles' saddle. He and Cornelia did well in increasing the population figures in Milwaukee County; between 1851 and 1870 there appeared eleven little Buttles.[19]

His diary told of the death by accidental shooting of his brother-in-law Paul Juneau, the son of Solomon Juneau. . . . His sister Olive and her [seven] little children were brought home to live. This must have unsettled Grandmother Buttles' housekeeping not a little since she was sixty-four and had reared her family of six. . . .[20]

. . . The death rate among the infants and younger children was high since the cabins were damp, drafty, and poorly ventilated; food was coarse and unpalatable; milk and water were often contaminated; clothing was insufficient; and income frequently too meager to allow for the visits of a doctor if one were obtainable. Among the many children's diseases entered in the census necrology section were croup, "desentery" [sic], teething, cholera, typhoid, and even "consumption," as it [tuberculosis] was then known.

Again, the mother's ingenuity had to meet pioneer medicinal deficiencies, and she did well enough with her knowledge of wild plants, berries, barks, flowers, and roots. These she collected throughout the seasons — gladly assisted by the grandmother — dried and labeled them, and kept them to be used upon short notice. In some of the settlements Dr. Gunn's medical volume was almost as sacred as the Bible and a great blessing during those hard years.

In times of emergency there was no fainting mother — perhaps she had become immunized. She knew she had to rely upon her own knowledge. At times she was a surgeon as well as a physician and fitted and bound together fingers, hanging on shreds; or removed a rusty spike from a foot, washed the wound with hot salt water and hot soda water, and saved the injured member.[21] In the winter of 1836 when a hired man froze his feet while driving hogs from Belvidere, Illinois, to the head of Lake Geneva, no surgeon was at hand. To relieve the patient's suffering the housewife took a pair of shears and amputated several of the frozen toes.[22] If a child's screams told of an unfortunate encounter with a venomous snake, the emergency remedies were applied without a moment's loss of time.

Symptoms baffled the mother at times, and perhaps it was intuitive diagnosis that brought about a cure. . . .

If the illness resulted in death, the infant was placed in a handmade wooden box. This task was assumed by a woman relative or a good neighbor, who covered the box and lined and padded it with pieces of a sheet, a white dress, or with any material which might answer the purpose. . . .

When neighborhood women took the place of doctors, who had not yet begun to practice in the backwoods, there was probably one in a region who functioned as a midwife. . . .

Dr. P. L. Scanlan, Prairie du Chien historian, wrote of a Sioux woman, by the name of Marie, who early in the nineteenth century practiced among the white residents at Prairie du Chien. Her death in the fall of 1814 was spoken of as "a great loss to this village."[23] Mrs. Charles (Mary Ann La Buche) Menard served as nurse and midwife among the French in the same settlement, and took the place of a physician before the fort was established. Even after regular surgeons were stationed at the military headquarters — when she became a competitor of Dr. William Beaumont — she continued her work in the settlement, herb treatment being among her cures. She often secured excellent results when she took to her home patients whom the physicians were unable to cure. . . .[24]

. . . Though families were large, the mortality of infants whose mothers knew nothing of professional pre-natal care was likewise great.

The then incurable "consumption" attacked families with viciousness, and one member after another lingered and passed on. Men, women, and children, of all ages, filled the cemeteries, victims of this puzzling disease. The number of children bereft of their mothers was legion. One of the most complete case histories was found in the diary entries of Sarah Pratt, who was afflicted with the disease. Hers was an almost day-by-day account, the sufferer completely debilitated toward the close of the journal.

The epidemics of smallpox, typhoid, and cholera left regions desolate; the recurring fever and ague, pneumonia (known as lung fever or inflammation of the lungs), dropsy, dysentery, rheumatism, and mental disorders were other illnesses which left homes motherless, or unavoidably neglected. . . .

. . . Fever and ague was so common that it was considered as something to be expected on the frontier, like hard work. . . .

In the fall of 1846 the disease seemed to have been especially prevalent. Mrs. J. T. Hamilton's family, in the vicinity of Whitewater, began suffering with the fever and ague shortly after she gave birth to Philena. Her sister, visiting at the home, was the first to be attacked, then her father fell ill, next her two-year-old Freddie and her mother. Two young women, both of whom were in poor health, were called in to aid with the housework. . . .[25]

. . . Shortly after the birth of a son, Mrs. Hamilton became ill with the ague, as she thought, but was unable to cure it with the usual home remedies. A physician was called but he, too, was unsuccessful, and after a few weeks she succumbed. . . .[26]

Writing of the same region, Prosper Cravath also noted the sickly season of 1846, with two to four Norwegian families living together, sometimes in a one-room house. In these crowded quarters from three to six ailing persons were barely able to move. He wrote that

in a single room, there were, at the same time, six lying around the sides of the room, unable to rise; all with a dish of water at their side and a rope extended from a joist overhead in which to rest their head when they drank, there being only two small girls, about seven and ten years old, able to render assistance. In the village, few escaped the plague. . . .[27]

It is evident that additional burdens were assumed by the frontier mother. . . . If she were spared from the attacks, she would have to carry the work of other family members. . . .

In addition to the hardships already enumerated, an especially menacing one, still unaccounted for, was loneliness. It must have taken all the self-control the mother could muster to appear stout-hearted. When her days were the busiest, nostalgia may have lost its acuteness to return with vengeance when she snatched a moment here and there to think and feel. And sometimes indulgence in the thought of her loneliness and the monotony of her Herculean struggle brought on prolonged mental illness.

. . . Would it not seem that of the newcomers the foreign-born mother, who could speak only her native tongue, suffered the greatest pain over separation, the adjustment often not completed during her lifetime?

. . . The feeling of isolation must have increased as her children hurried along the road of Americanization ahead of her. Her meager social life, at most a visit with her kinfolk and worship at the native-language church, with some opportunity for news exchange, would do little to increase her fluency of English speech. . . .

. . . John Molee . . . left this record, "My wife [Anne Jacobson Einong Molee] was often sorry she came to the wilderness of Wisconsin for her father had a fine farm and servants." The "America fever" had brought her and her family to this country.[28] The wish to return to the home that she had once known could never have been fulfilled completely since her mother and a sister had been buried at sea.

There was less gloom if the mother could tell another woman of her lonely feelings, but often there was no one to sympathize. . . .

Katharine Börner Hilgen, of Cedarburg, wrote of her loneliness to her brother and sister-in-law at Charleston, South Carolina. It was in the late summer of 1846 when she described her beautiful flowers, and the admiration given them by passers-by, which gave her much pleasure, but still she was sad. "If I only had a few good true women friends, I would be entirely satisfied. Those I miss." She sent greetings to her sister also and expressed the desire that the sister come to Wisconsin, and exclaimed, "I would like to spend a day with you all."[29] Near the holiday season of that year she again sent a communication to the same relatives, rejoicing over the prospect of her brother's removal to Wisconsin. "Then we will live our lives together in happiness." A short note to her sisters Anna and Meta contained the wish, "I hope you will come here too so that we will all be together again.". . .[30]

There was one energetic frontiersman, Bartholomew Ragatz, who developed a large Sauk Prairie farm, arriving in 1842. When evening came, he found much pleasure in looking over his many acres, and would exclaim exultantly, "It is ours, every bit ours!" This thought brought him contentment, but not so his wife. "She never complained," he said, but "somehow, her courage often failed her," and she could never bring herself to believe that the almost uninhabited prairie would one day be the place of many homes. The mill, the comfortable house as well as the beloved Alps which vanished in the misty distance as the travelers were outward bound were left forever. She never saw them again. Even with her many children, some of them adults upon reaching Wisconsin, and the good way of life which was provided for her, the change from her little European hamlet to the isolated and almost unpopulated prairie of Wisconsin left a nostalgic ache in her heart.[31]

Some immigrant families started on the trip to America in fine spirits, but unforeseen tragedies brought loneliness before they even reached their destinations. When Mrs. T. S. V. Wroolie was a small child, she crossed the Atlantic from Norway with her father, mother, and three other children. She recalled in her "Memories" that when leaving Quebec her father fell through the hatchway of the top deck to the bottom of the ship which resulted in his death. The crew took charge, and when the mother was allowed to search for the $400 which was sewed inside of the father's clothing, it was missing. The body was removed, and the family never knew the place of their father's burial.[32]

This mother, now without money and [with] the care of her four small children, depended upon the generosity of friends, whom she had learned to know en route. Delayed in crossing the Atlantic the travelers arrived late, and the relatives who had come to meet them at La Crosse had returned home. So the penniless, discouraged widow accompanied several of her traveling companions into Minnesota, where some of her children were put into private homes, and she was employed by the day, working most of the time in the fields. The bitterness of her experience in a strange land was short-lived. She died about thirteen years later. . . .[33]

Loneliness was an integral part of the mother's frontier battle. On the whole there was no turning back. As the years wore on, there was a mellowing of the feeling of loss caused by migration; as the region increased in population with the arrival of more of her relatives and acquaintances, and the narrow trails became well-traveled roads, as her children's children brought additional responsibilities, loneliness took a minor place in her life, or at least it was accepted passively. In the midst of an inquisitive and new generation she knew she must live still more courageously. There was no place for tears. . . .

∗∗∗

## NOTES

1. A typed copy of Sarah Pratt's Diary, 4, 53–54, 1845, WHS Archives.
2. Theodore C. Blegen, *Norwegian Migration to America: 1825–1860* (Northfield, MN: 1931), 128. . . .
3. William F. Raney, *Wisconsin: A Story of Progress* (New York, 1940), 424; . . . Joseph Schafer, *Four Wisconsin Counties: Prairie and Forest* (Madison, 1927), 194–221. [There were no free schools in territorial Wisconsin.]
4. Mary D. Bradford, *Pioneers! O Pioneers!* (Evansville, [1937?], 74–75, 89. [See also Bradford, "Memoirs," *WMH* 14, no. 1 (September 1930): 3–47 and subsequent issues for further installments of her autobiography.]
5. J. T. Hamilton Journal, 86, WHS Archives.
6. Sarah Pratt's Diary, 51–52.
7. Ibid., 34.
8. Ibid., 59.
9. William F. Sprague, *Women and the West: A Short Social History* (Boston, 1940), 67, 222.
10. Sprague, *Women and the West*, 75.

11. H. L. Skavlem, *Skavlem and Odegaarden Families* (Madison, 1915), 158.

12. "Christian Traugott Ficker's Advice to Emigrants (III)," *WMH* 25:472 (June 1942).

13. *Memories of Early Days* (1876), 23, published originally in the Waukesha *Plaindealer.*

14. Typed excerpts from the Buttles' Diary (1856–85, except 1863), WHS.

15. Letter to Moses Strong, Madison, Jan. 8, 1845, in the Moses M. Strong Papers, WHS Archives.

16. Ibid., Jan. 19, 1844.

17. Nicholas Wertel to his sister in Germany, Meidenbauer Papers, WHS Archives.

18. Rasmus B. Anderson, *The First Chapter of Norwegian Immigration,* 1821–1840 (Madison, 1895), 316. [See also A. O. Barton, "The Old Muskego Settlement," *Waukesha Freeman,* Sept. 7, 1916.]

19. See Summary of Family History, a typed manuscript which was compiled from the Buttles' Diary and is on file with it, WHS Archives.

20. Ibid.

21. Harriet Brown, *Grandmother Brown's Hundred Years, 1827–1927* (Boston, 1929), 157–158.

22. *History of Walworth County* (Western Historical Company, Chicago, 1882), 337.

23. P. L. Scanlan, *Prairie du Chien: French, British, American* (Menasha, 1937), 199. . . .

24. Scanlan, *Prairie du Chien,* 199. . . .

25. Hamilton Journal, 98.

26. Ibid., 98.

27. Prosper Cravath and Spencer S. Steele, *Early Annals of Whitewater, 1837–1867* (1906), 76.

28. Anderson, *Norwegian Immigration,* 317.

29. "German Pioneer Letters," *WMH* 16:436–37 (June 1933).

30. Ibid., 439.

31. Lowell J. Ragatz, ed., "Memoirs of a Sauk Swiss," *WMH* 19:189–90 (December 1935).

32. "An Immigrant's Memories," *La Crosse County Historical Sketches,* Series 7 (La Crosse 1945), 77–78. [See also Mrs. T. S. V. Wroolie, "An Immigrant's Memories," *WMH* 30, no. 4 (June 1947): 433–440.]

33. Ibid., 78–80, 82.

# La Pointe Letters

## FLORANTHA THOMPSON SPROAT

WMH 16, No. 1 (September 1932): 85–95 and 16, No. 2 (December 1932): 199–210

☙ ❧

*Protestant and Catholic missionaries opened schools in the 1830s in northernmost Wisconsin at La Pointe on Madeline Island, long a sacred site of the local Anishinabe (see Introduction to chapter 1). An in-law of the Native American and French fur-trading family of the Cadottes, Lyman Warren, invited the American Board of Commissioners for Foreign Missions (ABCFM) to sponsor a Protestant school first. In 1831, the ABCFM sent Congregationalist "missionaries and their wives, who formed a missionary family," according to historian Suzanne Elizabeth Moranian. Wives were missionaries as well, not only helping with "women's work" but also assisting with "teaching and administrative work." One such wife was Florantha Thompson Sproat, who arrived at La Pointe in 1838.[1]*

*Sproat's letters suggest that the "missionary family" could not replace her family and women friends in Middleborough, Massachusetts, where she was born in 1811 and lived a far less adventurous life than on the Wisconsin frontier. Particularly poignant are her repeated pleas for letters in reply, with news of the world she had left behind: weddings, births, women's church work. She wrote of receiving no letters for as long as a year because of infrequent mail service on the frontier. Still, Sproat was stoic even in one of her last letters here, as she cancelled plans for a visit home for her ill health, owing in part to her second pregnancy in her first years in Wisconsin.*

*Sproat apparently anticipated the hardships of life at La Pointe, where women served as each others' midwives for lack of a physician. The local American Fur Company factor had a medical degree but did not practice, so Sproat's spouse, Granville Temple Sproat, was "the doctor in common cases," as she described him. However, in an era of a high rate of pregnancy, stillbirth was all too common. Sproat apparently became pregnant soon after landing at La Pointe in the fall of 1838, but the baby was stillborn the next summer. With sad acceptance, she wrote of another missionary wife on the Wisconsin frontier who had lost six infants before two survived. Sproat suggested that the "dreaded work" of housekeeping duties also had a deleterious effect on women's health, and her letters plead for supplies — yet when a women's sewing society in Massachusetts sent dresses, the donation sold for "high prices" to instead support the mission school. Her husband helped. However, far from stores and without servants, she made most of the necessities for her family and for students.[2]*

*Missionary wives cooked, clothed, and cared for boarding students. Sproat described making a meal for two dozen children, who stood to await their supper in regimental rows, although allegedly "lighthearted" and "happy" at the school. However, she was aware of many parents' and others' unhappiness with proselytizing by missionaries to convert their children to Christianity and acculturate them into non–Native American ways. "Instead of listening to the Word," she wrote, they feared that missionaries furthered the federal government's "designs."*

*Native Americans' suspicions of the schools proved correct, of course. Missionaries relied on funding from a sometimes unholy alliance of church and state, of religious organizations and the federal government. Moranian observes that "indeed, the Protestant missionaries often assisted relations between the Indians and the government" to negotiate treaties, dispense compensation, and dispel —*

*or dismiss — concerns. In serving their faith, missionaries also served a "vital function" for the federal government as a "vanguard of approaching white civilization."³*

*The quasi-governmental role was more often the concern of missionary men, who corresponded with officials on — or occasionally against — federal policy. Yet Sproat also apparently saw no conflict in missionaries' dual service and funding sources, nor in their cooperative efforts to eradicate Native American culture — to the extent that, according to Moranian, they enlisted in ethnocide. However, the La Pointe mission apparently did not initially engage in the worst practices of the later and now-infamous "Indian boarding schools." In Sproat's time at La Pointe, some students boarded at the school, although she notes only two dozen in an enrollment of almost one hundred. Their parents apparently sent daughters and sons to board at the school voluntarily, as did non–Native American parents elsewhere, who likewise sent away their children as the preference — often the only possibility — for education on the frontier.⁴*

*Sadly, all schoolchildren then endured an era of strict discipline and corporal punishment, although teachers from the same culture as their students were well aware when they caused humiliation. At La Pointe, Sproat noted that a teacher pulled a student's hair, only to belatedly learn that the pedagogical tactic was not merely unjust but a transgression of Ojibwe tradition. The anecdote supports Moranian's criticism of Protestant missionaries as prone to "demand extreme character transformation and adoption of American customs."⁵*

*However, Moranian states that unlike most Protestant missionaries, Congregationalists attempted an unusual level of adaptation to Native culture. Among "the few attempts made by the missionaries to dovetail Indian culture with their own," they — and their métis interpreters, first Caroline Rodgers and then Elizabeth Campbell — "taught Indian children in their native tongues and made efforts to translate texts . . . into Indian languages." A well-known example at La Pointe was undertaken by Father Frederick Baraga, who began its Catholic mission school in 1835 and wrote the first Ojibwe-English dictionary and grammar in 1843. But before him, a Congregational missionary at La Pointe translated the New Testament from the original Greek into Ojibwe. Sproat also gave her first winter to learning the "beauty" of the Ojibwe language, although the school "was filled to overflowing" and needed her help.⁶*

*Florantha Thompson Sproat first had to be a student of the Ojibwe, before she could become their teacher. However, as her letters attest, she had little time for studying — or letter-writing — while tending to the "numerous cares" of her new "missionary family" on the frontier.*

~∾ ∾~

Addressed to: Cephas Thompson
Middleborough
Plymouth Co. Mass.

September 12, '38

My dear Father,

Here I am seated in our own little room at La Pointe,⁷ neat and comfortable for this part of the country. You have ere this heard of our safe arrival at this place. We are now being somewhat settled, and I begin to feel at home, altho everything about me is novel and strange. . . .

. . . [T]he school is interesting, but our brethren at [nearby missions] . . . are tried very much by the hostility of the indians, they are beginning to be stirred by the story of the oppression of their southern brethren which has reached them, they are beginning to feel that the white men will oppress them as much as they can, and are afraid that government has sent the missionaries to favour their designs. . . . [S]o instead of listening to the Word their minds are on the unjustnesses of the white men. . . . Were we to look upon these missions with the eye of sense, we should be entirely discouraged, but the eye of faith discerns in the distance . . . [that] we must have faith and patience. . . .

Sept. 20

My dear mother,

You will see by the date that it is some days since I wrote the above; the numerous cares of my family came in and hindered me from finishing. Our family is now enlarged by [missionaries] . . . who are staying with us for a week or so. . . . Should you ask me what is my field of labour on missionary ground I must say thus far it has been to entertain strangers. . . .

My assistance will, this winter, be needed in the school. I have not yet attended much to the Ojibway language, as I have no time to study, I think I shall attend to it some this winter; it is a difficult language to come at, those that have studied it say that not many can surpass it in beauty.[8] I will tell you how I spend my time. I am my own servant. I have no one to assist me, but my husband brings in wood and water. I scour my own knifes, candlesticks and tin pans, which is no small job. I make my own butter which is considerable having only one cow. We are very fond of Dutch cheese in the making of which I use all my bonny-clabber. I have made soap and have had excellent luck, could have no better. So you see I have not escaped, even this year our spring, dreaded work. It would be useless to describe my business day by day, all the etc.s. of domestic life. The articles from the Low L. [Lowell] Mass. Sewing So. were read gratefully by the mission. Mr. Hall[9] says it would be useless to try to maintain the mission were it not for donations from friends. Those little frocks were very soon sold for high prices. Calico frocks, bed quilts, comforters, skirts and woolen stockings find ready market at high prices. Everything made of white cloth the people do not like to buy. We had sent to us, this spring, a small quantity of dried apples which were very acceptable as we have nothing of the kind save what is sent by the kindness of friends. I wish you would put in my salt mortars for we have nothing of the kind here. We have to pound pepper, spice of all kinds, in a rag and salt sometimes for butter, which beside making work wastes it. . . . I think you would be pleased to visit in our new home but not more than we to have you. Write to me soon, get all to write, and write everything. Tell Olivia her portrait is looked at and talked about much.

Your daughter,

F. S.

Oct. 7. — Wednesday eve. Today we prepared a supper for the school children, 26 in number. I made a rice pudding and some pumpkin pies. It was surely an interesting sight to see so many children of the wilderness standing in perfect order by the large table with happy looks and lighthearted eating, as if they loved it.

Yesterday we had to take ten with us of the indian sisters and brothers. One of them wished me to take her daughter, a girl of 10 years. We think it not advisable to take her on account of chance (risk), tho I should like to oblige the mother. Tomorrow I go into the school to assist my husband in teaching the smaller classes. . . .

Addressed to: Mrs. Cephas Thompson
Middleborough
Mass.

June 23, 1839.

My dear Mother,

Your letter I can assure you was joyfully received, a week since. In it I found many interesting items concerning friends. When I received your letter I was just recovering from confinement, am now quite well but without my natural strength. You alone of all my friends can sympathize with me when I tell you that on the morning of May 16 I gave birth to a lovely little daughter, but God took its spirit to himself. It was perfect in form — a full grown child — but still-born. Had there been a skillful physician at hand, in an unnatural birth, they might have saved our child. After prayer had been offered a hymn sung our babe was followed by husband, Mr. Hall, Dr. Borup,[10] Mr. Baraga[11] the catholic priest and a concourse of weeping natives to a resting place on the shore of Lake Superior beneath tall trees. The event being so uncommon here it excited much feeling among the indians. I had made too much dependance, and my affections too much centered in my child. Even now, tho I know it is for the best, my heart hungers for my babe.

. . . For the human heart is the same here as in our favored and enlightened land, where many will pass their lives unconverted beneath the full blaze of Gospel light. Our school is more prosperous of late, than usual, the chief favors it, advises his band to send their children regularly. Last winter it was filled to overflowing. We have passed the winter quite alone and retired. New Years day is passed here by the indians as a holiday. they go from house to house and in return for their wishing those they call upon, "a happy new year" receive a gift — or expect one. Consequently a few days previous, I made between two & 300 cakes, planning for the indians that called that day, but we concluded it would be less trouble to notify them that, at the ringing of a bell, they might come to the school-house and there receive the cakes, tobacco, and whatever Mr. Hall had to give them. At an early hour the bell was rung, and the indians made their appearance in a regular file and marched up to the front of the house, discharged their guns, and entered, filling the school-room to over-flowing, received their presents and departed leaving their room for others who continued to come for some time. At such times I think of home and how pleased friends would be to witness such customs. . . .

[July 7, 1839]

Dear Sister, do write soon, a large sheet full about every little thing. Mother write a good letter. La Pointe is a place of about 20 acres. They are expecting about five thousand indians — a dense population. The indians feel that their great father has cheated them in the land that he has bought. They are somewhat disturbed. I wish the Americans would let the indians alone in the possession of the land. if so it would save a deal of bloodshed.

Mrs. Hall has a beautiful little babe born the last of Jan., at the birth of which she had only Mr. H. and myself as assistants, he being midwife & I nurse, so you see that I have gotten into an entirely new business. Mrs. H. is very feeble and has been so ever since her confinement. . .

"This is written for father, mother and sisters. Love and respects to all my friends."

Mar. 23. [1842]

Last night Mrs. [Harriet Wood] Wheeler gave birth to a dead child. She had been confined to her bed for two months previously, on account of convulsions and other difficulties. Again I must speak of the great necessity for women missionaries to this country, to be of good and firm health. None should come but of strong and rugged constitution if they wish to be of use.

I have today finished a little bonnet for our interpreters little girl, made from the last of the straw braid sent by your society. There have been four large and two small bonnets made from it, so it has done much good, for which you have our hearty thanks. . . .

Mar. 25

A beautiful evening although it was a stormy morning which prevented me from washing, so I have been doing a little of many things, and sitting with Mrs. Wheeler. The Indians have all gone to their sugar-making, so we have less company. I am sitting in my little bed-room, writing this on my toilette made of a packing box. Sarah Hall is rolling and tumbling over my bed and Margaret sitting in the dining room stringing rags for a rug. And now my dear friends I would like to know what you are doing   how I wish that I could see you all once more. I am more at leisure than I have been since I have been here. I teach a class of indian women for awhile in the evenings   this stopped on their going to make sugar.

April 1.

A pleasant day. I have been thinking of home some today, one whole year since I have had news from you. Are you all living and in good health? Husband is in Mr. Wheeler's[12] chamber singing with him and his wife, and it sounds as if they were enjoying it much. Deep and heavy thunder is rolling incessantly and lightening is sharp. It has been an uncommonly pleasant day. In the morning Miss Spooner[13] and myself took a walk among the hills and ravines back of the mission. I came home, stewed some cranberries, and commenced making Mrs. Hall a cap for her journey out. Then I made a large loaf of bread and baked it, and then made for our supper a small parsnip stew. Mr. Hall had, the day before, brought me 5 or 6 small parsnips, and I assure you my stew was very nice.

April 2

Our expectations have been raised this morning for a smoke signal announced that there is an arrival. When persons arrive at this place in the winter they come to the shore opposite and there make a smoke signal. Those who see it first go with canoe and bring them over. At this time we are in expectation of men that were sent for the mail, and are in hopes the smoke signals their arrival. You have no idea of our feelings at such a time. One fact I would mention — that all letters that you receive from us, fall, winter or spring are carried by men 4 or 5 hundred miles through a thick and uninhabitable wilderness with snow 4 or 5 feet deep. They go thus far before they reach any sign of habitation. they then leave the mail and return with one for this place. I hope, at this time, I shall not be disappointed by not receiving letters from you.

The mail has arrived being many [letters] for others and none for me. My disappointment is great. You dwelling in the midst of friends and comforts remember but faintly your far-off missionary daughter & sister, and she never ceases to remember you with love and tenderness. I had expected that this mail would bring a letter relative to my going home and now I must give up the fond hope of seeing you as I would not got without hearing from you first. I wrote that I thought of going with Mr. Hall but as he will not start until the middle of summer I have given up the idea as my condition would make it impossible for me to travel at that time. . . . But perhaps it is all for the best.

May 1.

A beautiful and summerlike day. It is your birthday, sister Cordelia. I have thought often of you today, and wished to know what you were about. It is the Sabbath, and, if well, I suppose you are at church. I had fondly hoped to have seen you there ere this year had passed, but that hope is gone now.

I have attended two sermons today. . . .

May 15.

I received your letter day before yesterday, my dear mother, and happy was I to have news from home. We have been agitating the question whether it were not best for me to go home . . . and return with Mr. Hall next spring. Mr. Hall thinks it necessary for me to go, for the sake of my health. He thinks my health has been failing and active measures should be taken. But Mr. Sproat thinks, as we have not written the board concerning my leaving, that the prudential committee would think it strange. Mr. Wheeler objected. He thought it would cause some talk on account of so many leaving, and also that, as the missionary work was increasing, they would need my help. So I have now given it up. It would have been a great gratification to me to have gone. . . .

Oct. 10, 1842.

My dear mother

It was with mingled pleasure and pain that we received the box from home. . . . When I came to look for letters and tokens of remembrances from home and finding only yours and Elviras containing only a few lines, and no news, I felt pained and disappointed for I had been waiting with fond hopes of great pleasure half the year, not hearing from home the time. The bedquilt gave me much pleasure. I have been looking over the squares seeing the names of different friends who are dear. give my love and thanks to them all. The articles of the box are very useful for our mission and its opperations, for which your mission has our thanks. You ask what you shall make for the coming year. I think if you will make small quilts for cradles and one or two for cribs they would be useful (I may want one myself) & quilted skirts of dark cambrick. I need one very much, they are a good thing for this country, and are never sent to us. If you could sent a pattern unmade of dark calico — I like your taste — for a dress it would be very acceptable, or pieces or remnants of any kind of calico, two or three yard pieces of fine print would be very useful. I write this to let you know what *would* be useful. I have often wished for coarse earthenware pudding dishes and plates of which we have none in this part of the country. they would be more serviceable to me than most anything else. they could come safely packed with the clothes. . . . Childrens colored stockings and childrens clothes of all kinds, are needed. . . . Best love to all friends. tell Elvira that I have written to herself, Olivia Juliet and Mrs. King without having received an answer. write oftener. a long letter.

F. Sproat

I wish you would send some fall crookneck squash seeds and some cranberry beans and some of those early tender beans the pods round, and other kinds of early summer squash seeds. You see I have written somewhat of a begging letter. I mean if you can. We never get those things.

*Later in 1842, Florantha Thompson Sproat's husband wrote to family that the mission would continue, despite federal government attempts to forcibly remove the Ojibwe by treaty. La Pointe was "thronged with company" for the coming negotiations, he wrote, with more than two thousand Ojibwe, many governmental officials, and "ten missionaries from different posts . . . part of whom stop with us so you know our hands are full," which explained why his wife was not the letter writer. Regarding their future, he wrote that the Ojibwe "agreed to sell their land but are not to be removed from it*

*at present. It can be but of little use to government excepting for purpose of minerals." Other evidence also supports the Ojibwe belief that "they were merely leasing the land, not selling it" in the treaty of 1842, according to historian Patty Loew.[14]*

*However, in 1850 the federal government ordered the Ojibwe out of their Wisconsin, which led to the tragedy of Sandy Lake. The treaty included annuity payments for the land to be made to the Ojibwe at La Pointe. Instead, officials coerced them to move by moving the site of payment to Sandy Lake, Minnesota, hundreds of miles away. "More than four hundred Ojibwe" — probably including some of the Sproats' former students — "died from starvation, disease, and exposure" en route, writes Loew, herself an enrolled member of the Lake Superior Ojibwe. They later negotiated for four reservations, and many Ojibwe stayed in northern Wisconsin, only to suffer further from "forced assimilation through [land sale] allotment and boarding schools."[15]*

*The Sproats also stayed at La Pointe, where the school seemed to be succeeding, judging by students' numbers and abilities. But the adaptive methods of their mission school soon would be abandoned by the government. "As early as 1856," Loew writes, "Ojibwe children were taken from their homes and placed in government boarding schools," primarily at Hayward, Tomah, and Lac du Flambeau, although also as far away as Pennsylvania. "Ojibwe parents had no say in which schools their children would attend," and "school officials discouraged them from speaking their language or practicing their traditional religions and customs."[16]*

*The schools mainly provided manual training and only marginal skills for work such as domestic service for Native American women. Worse, according to historian Joan M. Jensen, the schools furthered "the government's growing surveillance of the sexuality of Native women" and allowed social reformers "to intervene in domestic relations" on reservations to promote "legal marriage and divorce and persuade them to 'do away with marriage by Indian custom.'"[17]*

*Historians agree that mission schools actually failed, fortunately, in their assimilationist aims — as did government boarding schools, a failure that officials blamed on women elders. Moranian suggests that missionaries "never fully comprehended. . . that the failure of their schools was a successful attempt by the Indians to preserve their native culture." As had their foremothers for centuries, women played a significant part in cultural preservation, according to Jensen: "Government officials now became convinced that despite the work of missionaries and educators, young people were not abandoning the older customs, because when they returned to reservations, older people, especially older women, were influencing them to retain or at least adapt the older customs to what they had learned at school."[18]*

*In sum, missionaries perceived Native Americans as not only primitive but also passive and incapable of resisting assimilation and "civilization," rather than as peoples of ancient civilizations who adopted some aspects of Euro-American culture and rejected others. Yet the Ojibwe and others could not fully forestall educational ethnocide, Moranian notes, because even the most well-meaning missionary teachers "contributed to the gradual process of conversion and acculturation which few of them lived to see completed."[19]*

*Florantha Thompson Sproat lived for more than four decades after her last letter here, although she and her husband left missionary work for other adventures on the next frontier, California. He became the writer of the family as a contributor to magazines in San Francisco, where she died in 1885.*

## NOTES

1. Smith, *HOW,* 156; Hamilton Nelson Ross, *La Pointe: Village Outpost on Madeline Island,* (Madison: SHSW, 2000), 74–76, 88; and Moranian, "Ethnocide in the Schoolhouse: 244–245.

2. "Pioneer History Is Recalled by Visit Here," *Bayfield County Press,* October 6, 1916.

3. Moranian, "Ethnocide in the Schoolhouse," 247.

4. Ibid. On the onset of Indian boarding schools in the 1870s, see Nancy Oestrich Lurie, *Wisconsin Indians,* rev. ed. (Madison: SHSW, 2000), 36.

5. Moranian, "Ethnocide in the Schoolhouse," 248, 254–255.

6. Ibid., 254, 259; Keith R. Wilder, "Founding La Pointe Mission, 1825–1833," *WMH* 64, no. 3 (Spring 1981): 181–201.

7. On Madeline Island, Chequamegon Bay, Wisconsin.

8. Frederick Ayer's Ojibway Spelling Book, completed in 1833, is perhaps the first book produced wholly in Wisconsin.

9. [Rev. Sherman Hall, who, with his wife, Betsey Parker Hall, came to La Pointe Mission in 1831. *WHC,* xii, 442.]

10. [Charles W. Borup, Agent of the American Fur Company.]

11. Frederick Baraga, afterwards Bishop Baraga, founder of the Nineteenth Century Catholic Mission at La Pointe in 1835.

12. Leonard Hemenway Wheeler, who came to La Pointe in 1841, removed the Mission to Odanah in 1845, and remained till 1866, returning to Beloit where he died February 22, 1872.

13. [Abigail Spooner, who came to La Pointe Mission in 1841 and served it for many years.]

14. Loew, *Indian Nations of Wisconsin,* 60.

15. Ibid., 61.

16. Ibid., 61–66.

17. Joan M. Jensen, "Sexuality on a Northern Frontier: The Gendering and Discipline of Rural Wisconsin Women, 1850–1920," *Agricultural History* 73, no. 2 (Spring 1999): 165–166.

18. Moranian, "Ethnocide in the Schoolhouse," 259; Jensen, "Sexuality on a Northern Frontier," 165.

19. Moranian, "Ethnocide in the Schoolhouse," 259.

# A Little Girl of Old Milwaukee

## MARTHA E. FITCH

*WMH* 9, No. 1 (June 1926): 80–89

*The following recollections of a girl's first years in Wisconsin may seem reminiscent to readers of Laura Ingalls Wilder's* Little House on the Prairie *series, for a reason. Martha Eliza Curtis Fitch's first home in Wisconsin was not in Milwaukee but well to the west of town, closer to Brookfield — the birthplace of Wilder's mother in 1839. That same year, the Curtis family arrived in Wisconsin and built their own little house on the prairie, where they lived for three years.*

*Wilder's mother — "Ma" in the series, whose stories of pioneering on the prairie are said to have sometimes merged with those of her daughter — was born to Charlotte and Henry Quiner. Her father's death when Caroline Lake Quiner was seven years old begins the first book in a new series,* The Early Years, *written by Maria D. Wilkes in Wilder's style, and starting with* Little House in Brookfield, Little Town at the Crossroads, *and* Little Clearing in the Woods. *Caroline's mother moved her family in 1848 to a farm in Concord in Jefferson County, where her daughter was a schoolteacher at sixteen years old, taught for four years, and met and married Charles Ingalls. They moved near Pepin, where Laura Ingalls was born in 1867, a year before the family left Wisconsin to move farther west. Her mother, widowed in 1902, died in 1924 at the home of a daughter in South Dakota.*

*But while Caroline Lake Quiner was little more than a baby on the Brookfield prairie, a little girl living nearby moved to town — a new town then, which she recalls as old Milwaukee. Martha Eliza Curtis Fitch (1836–1937) wrote the following article for her great-grandson, Eliot Fitch Bartlett. Born a decade before Milwaukee became a city, she died a year after publication.*

In the year 1839, Father, Mother, and three little girls left Buffalo, New York, by boat for Milwaukee, Wisconsin. The father in 1836 had taken the long trip and bought a quarter-section of government land in this far-away territory. . . .

. . . When they arrived in Milwaukee, small boats came to meet them — too small for either horses or carriage, so these were sent on to Chicago and were driven up from there over the almost impassable roads. The little hotel called the Fountain House received the family and there they remained until the log cabin on the farm could be built. . . .

How plainly I can see, after all these years, the beautiful young mother and the fine-looking father coming through the big trees on their horses, just as the sun was going down, each with a gun across the front of the saddle and each with a deer strapped at the back of the saddle with its legs hanging down and its horns standing out out — for the little mother was a fine shot and could bring down her own game on earth or in the air as well as any man could. . . .

. . . Sometimes the Indians would come to the house, or rather log cabin, and sit on the ground and were given something to eat. They were of the Menominee tribe, and not warlike or dangerous, but we children never were allowed to go out to speak to them. I always wanted to . . . but the doors were bolted and the children and dogs must not go out; but we children would peep out of the windows at them. . . .

Our cabin was larger than that of any of the neighbors. There was the big room where the big fireplace was, which was kitchen and dining-room, with a small bedroom off, and here in a trundle-bed I usually slept. A trundle-bed is a box on wheels so low that in the daytime it can be trundled under a higher bed and be out of the way, and at night be pulled out again. A baby might fall out of it and not be injured. Then we had a parlor with a fine Brussels carpet, and I well remember the beautiful colors like our prized Bokhara rugs — deep red with a little white — and the mahogany sofa with little round pillows all of black horsehair, which was the fashion in those days. There was a fireplace in this room also, with andirons and bellows to blow the fire if it would not burn quickly; but we had only candles to give us light. Some were moulded in a tin mould and others were dipped in a big wash-boiler full of grease. The candles were always made at home. Mother sat beside the boiler and raised and lowered the wicks, which were tied to a stick resting across the length of the boiler. The grease was just hot enough to form a coating as down they went into it. When they were the right size they were put away to cool, and these were the "tallow dips." We had no matches. The coals were carefully covered to keep the precious fire. Tapers of paper were used to light the candles. One morning one of the neighbors came with a pan and a shovel for coals of fire, saying that their fire had burned out in the night, so he must walk a mile or more to get a starter for the fire, and his breakfast could not be cooked until his return.

We also had rooms and closets up a little pair of stairs, and how well I remember waking up in the morning and finding snow on my bedspread, and also seeing the moon shining through the spaces in the roof when I did not go to sleep at once. . . .

We always had a helper in the house, usually an eastern relative or a neighbor who came, just to oblige, and was one of the family, or a kind of guest who took care of the house. They were always kind and nice, and a sort of second mother to us. . . .

Such nice neighbors as we had! They lived a mile or more away, but that was nothing in those days. The little log schoolhouse was nearer. . . . I have no recollection of the little schoolhouse; whether or not I ever went there I am not sure, but I do remember that when I was five years old I could say the multiplication tables up to the "fives" and I had knitted a pair of stockings for myself. . . .

I want to tell you the fun we had when the springtime came and the sunshine was warmer and brighter and the snow began to melt, not enough to spoil the sledding for the men [who] brought a load of big buckets from the barn . . . and drove down through the woods toward the Menomonee River. . . . In a day or two they commenced gathering the sugar sap. . . . There was a long table with tin cups and plates, and a long dipper to stir the syrup, and the nice men would give us a cupful of the syrup, which we cooled on the snow and it was just like candy. When the syrup was boiled down sufficiently we had a "sugaring off." The neighbors were invited. It was in the evening and the moon was bright as day, and the big bonfire blazed and glowed, and made us all warm and "comfy." The neighbors came, some in sleighs and some on horseback, and boys and girls, too. They could have all the sugar they wanted to eat. . . .

When I was about six years old we moved to Milwaukee, to a house on the corner of Jefferson and Michigan streets. There we lived until our home on the east side of Jefferson just north of Wisconsin was finished. . . . Just around the corner in the same block, the northwest corner of Wisconsin and Jackson streets, lived the rector of the Episcopal Church, the Reverend David Hull. . . . His charming daughter, Eleanor Hull, had a very select school for little girls on the first floor of the very grand house, as it was then considered. I was one of the little girls fortunate enough to be accepted as a pupil. Miss Hull was very kind and gentle. I don't remember about the studying, but I well remember about the playing and the nice cookies she so often gave us. The kitchen was just back of the schoolroom, and the dumb-waiter that you pushed with your hand carried the food to the dining-room upstairs. One day it was my turn to hide in our play of hide-and-seek, and I spied the dumb-waiter, so I crept in on one of the shelves and drew the door shut. As I did so the waiter started upward and about halfway up stopped. I was delighted, for I was sure my little friends would never find me. I could hear them calling and running about, but after a little while all was quiet, so I knew they must have gone home, for this was after school, when dear Miss Hull would let us stay and play together as long as we wished. So I thought I would go home, too, but I could not move the dumb-waiter or open the door; so I began to kick and to scream and my pounding on the door soon brought the maid from the kitchen, who pulled me out safely and with a little shake told me never to do that again; this was quite unnecessary, for I had had visions of never, never getting out of this stuffy little place.

We always had fine horses that were raised on the farm. One day when I was about thirteen years old a beautiful bay pony with black mane and tail so long and heavy that it reached to the ground — I mean his tail, not his mane — was brought in from the farm. I went at once and put my arms around his neck and gave him some lumps of sugar, and claimed him for my very own. He understood and accepted me for his very own. He had never been broken, as the term is, but I was not afraid of him. He was always gentle with me and would follow me around the yard and try to find the pocket with the sugar in it. I had my saddle put on him, for I could ride, as all the girls could in those days. . . . We always rode a side saddle, and the skirt of my riding habit was long and flowing, which took time to arrange, but Billie never moved until I was ready and told him that he might, and then he would almost fly.

Billie was good for quite a long time and minded the bit quite well, but after a while he would take the bit in his teeth and run like mad — and, worse than running, he would go just where he pleased. I was not afraid of him and could stick, no matter how fast he ran, for he never kicked or tried to throw me as he did the man who fed him and kept his beautiful coat so shiny. This man succeeded in mounting him once, but he was over the horse's head so quickly that he did not know what had happened to him and he never tried it again. Dreadful stories of Billie's antics reached my family and all unknown to me it was decided to sell him. A railroad official who had admired the beauty of my precious pet came one day and bought him. I was told he tried to mount him but could not, so led him to the station, and tied him securely to a hitching-post. The trains came and the trains went, making more noise than they do nowadays, and the busy railroad official bethought him of my dear Billie. He found him lying on the ground twisted in his halter, strangled to death. His attempts to get away had been in vain and so he died. He was my faithful friend and I mourned for him as if he had been human. He was all the world to me and it was such a cruel blow to a little girl, thus to lose her pet.

About this time it was decided that it would be well for me to go East to school. A lady friend who was going East offered to take charge of me and place me in school. For two weeks again we were on the boat before we reached Buffalo. Then by rail to Utica, New York, and the nice school was, I think, four miles by stage — at York Mills. . . .

Can any one living in this age of wonders of invention realize those days without any of the necessaries of life — at least, as we now consider them? . . . And when we have only to press the button for heat and light, give a thought to the days of log fires and tallow dips, and to our earlier age when the light of the blazing fire was all the light to be had.

*Martha Eliza Curtis later attended Parker Institute in Brooklyn, New York, as a student in the collegiate department in 1855. The same year, William Grant Fitch became a teller at the new Bank of Milwaukee, at a time when the press reported that "sportsmen were shooting quail on Water Street" in the center of the city. After Martha returned home, she married the up-and-coming Fitch, who became the bank cashier, while she became the grande dame of the Fitch financial dynasty, as first their son and then their grandson became bank presidents and chairmen of the board. The Fitch family remains in Milwaukee, as does the bank that became, through a series of mergers, first the National Exchange Bank of Milwaukee, then part of the Marine National Exchange Bank, then the Marine Bank, and then Bank One. At twenty-two stories, the current bank building was the city's first skyscraper and still stands on Water Street, near the site of the house where a little girl named Martha lived happily in Milwaukee more than a century and a half ago.[1]*

## NOTES

1. "They Shot Quail on W. Water St. Back in 1854/Bank's Planned Move Unearths Files," *Milwaukee Sentinel*, April 15, 1927; Marvin J. Fruth, *The Log of the Marine: The Marine corporation, 1839–1988* (Milwaukee: Banc One Wisconsin, 1989), 29, 48.

# Social Life in Wisconsin

## Pre-Territorial through the Mid-Sixties

LILLIAN KRUEGER

*WMH* 22, No. 2 (December 1938): 156–175; 22, No. 3 (March 1939):
312–328; and 22, No. 4 (June 1939): 396–426

Before Wisconsin was carved out of the old Northwest, as well as during her territorial and early statehood days, the dominant social life found in that area may rightfully be typed "neighborly assistance;". . .[1]

. . . The supply of candles for the winter was made in fall when the aid of the neighborhood was enlisted. It is said much skill was required to make a well-shaped candle although moulds were used by some housewives. "The candles were strung on rods, six to the rod and fifteen rods to the bunch. Ninety candles were the winter's supply for a family, one for each evening."[2]

And how the mirth of the quilting party accompanied by the "good" visit, cheered many a nostalgic housewife forced to live without women companions much of the time. . . . Sometimes the men were invited for the evening and the hours passed gaily; when the young folks augmented a party, there was hunting the slipper, spinning the plate, telling fortunes, paying forfeits, and dancing.

Country life would have lost much of its freshness if the fall days had brought no neighborhood invitations to corn huskings. These were participated in by both men and women, the setting usually a large barn. Hilarity reached its height when one of the women found a red ear, for it meant a kiss from each of the men; when the latter found a red ear, he was kissed in turn by each of the women. Time passed quickly and when the last shock was husked, the workers were rewarded with a good supper. The "old folks" would then leave for home while the others would remain to dance.[3]

Neighborly assistance given at cabin and barn raisings, candle dippings, quilting parties, and corn huskings was interspersed here and there with pure diversion. . . .

In 1841 the framework for the Grafton sawmill was raised by the settlers. The occasion was a dance "given then in the largest hut standing near the falls of the Milwaukee . . . [River]." A fiddler from the community furnished the music. Nearly all the residents in the county were invited and in attendance. This dance, probably the first public one in the county, continued for two days, which meant an extra supply of food. This was prepared by the women in the Indian huts.[4]

"The tavern was the community center for dancing as well as other village gatherings," writes H. E. Cole.

On January 8, 1838, the first ball at Geneva was the dedicatory dance in the Warren Tavern. . . . One hundred men and ninety women were present and the receipts aggregated about seven hundred dollars, a great sum in those times. . . .[5]

Enterprising landlords advised the public that hay for the horses was included in the entertainment fee. . . .

Milwaukee had no end of balls, which can be accounted for in part by its large German population. Good music promotes this form of recreation, and among Milwaukee Germans excellent musical organizations were numerous. . . . In 1844 the following typical notice appears:

> The undersigned respectfully informs the ladies and gentlemen of Milwaukee, that he has made arrangements with the German Brass Band, for a musical treat every Wednesday afternoon and evening, during the summer season. . . .
>
> . . . Gentlemen who do not dance may receive one shilling in refreshments for their ticket. H. Ludwig.[6]

. . . Mary E. B. reveals: "I think I never heard of so many parties as we have had this winter" [of 1847–48]. . . .[7]

Wedding festivities, though somewhat infrequent, added their cheery note to the frontier social panorama. The scarcity of weddings was caused by the scarcity of women. . . .

*However few, women would have found many dancing partners in Wisconsin, where men far outnumbered them. The 1840 census counted almost twice the number of men compared to the number of women in Wisconsin Territory. Men still outnumbered women, six to five, at the end of the decade. Yet most Wisconsin women would have found few dancing partners — or marriage partners — of their age group. In the 1840s, two-thirds of men were more than twenty years old, while the majority of women were under twenty years of age in the territorial era.[8]*

*As pioneer David F. Sayre later wrote, "The young girls, where were they? I have been trying to count them. I can remember but nine . . . [within] fifteen miles" of his home in Porter in Rock County. Sayre wrote that he knew he had not forgotten any of the few girls in his area when he was a young man, as he was hardly grown but "not practiced in passing the girls by."[9]*

. . . Then, too, marriageable men often returned to their native states to claim their first loves; the foreign-born were accompanied by wives from the homelands in many instances. So a "bid" to a wedding feast surmounted all obstacles; the ox team and clumsy wagon, or horses if fortune smiled, were brought out for a day's absence — in some instances several days — with anticipations of much merriment. . . .

The first marriage in Dane county . . . is piquantly told: . . .

> The bride was Miss Elizabeth Allen, a tall, angular young lady, who found her way West, and filled the position of maid of all work in the Peck House,[10] where the ceremony was performed [in 1838].
>
> During the day the parties continued to work at their usual occupations, and when night came, supper being over, and the dishes cleared away, "time" was called. . . . The room was decorated with the early flowers of spring. . . .

The presents were not costly nor numerous, but they were unique and useful in a young family in a new country . . . a milk-stool . . . and a fish-hook and line. . . . The ceremony was performed in the most primitive style by Eben Peck, Esq., who had been appointed a Justice of the Peace a few weeks before, and this was his first official act.

. . . The ceremony over, the cry was "On with the dance!" . . .[11]

*The bride's workplace was the first tavern and inn in Madison, operated by Eben and Roseline Willard Peck. She was born in 1808 in Vermont, then moved in 1836 to Milwaukee and then Blue Mounds, where the Pecks had an inn until legislators told them that the capital would move to Four Lakes, renamed Madison. She made six new bed ticks to be filled with grass for guests' beds, and she moved again, although pregnant and with a two-year-old son in tow — and with four feather beds for her family. The Pecks arrived in a late-spring snowstorm in 1837 and lived under a tree until log cabins were completed. Soon, their boarders held "the first social affair in the city's history" for the new father. Future territorial governor James D. Doty dubbed the newborn "Wisconsiana Victoria," after a girl who had just begun her reign as queen of England.[12]*

*Roseline Peck apparently never missed another festive event; a "first-class violinist," she swiftly recovered to become the center of Madison social life, such as it was. "There were only six girls in Madison, and two of those were too young to 'trip the light fantastic,'" a settler said. "Owing to the scarcity of female partners" and "to fill up a set," Peck could "fiddle, dance, and call off, all at the same time" — and then serve fresh doughnuts to the dancers, too. She held a "regular dancing school twice a week . . . in the first winter in the old cabin" for "young ladies and middle-aged people." If women were few, she said, "we had . . . plenty of the other sex" after Madison became the temporary home of territorial legislators — all men — when in session.[13]*

*The Peck House also offered plenty of "other kinds of amusements," from euchre parties to canoeing parties. "I paddled my own canoe alone then, as I have since, in more ways than one," said Peck, who may have been behind some "verbal and practical jokes interspersed," she recalled, amid amusements. However, the joke was on her one winter when she went to prepare her famed turtle soup sufficient to feed her family, boarders, and dining customers at the Peck House.*

*The turtles [were] caught by cutting holes through the ice on what was called "Mud Lake." The turtles were frozen solid and rattled together like stones. They were put in the cellar to thaw before we could dress them, and, going down a few days after, I found they had thawed out and were crawling around on the bottom of the cellar.[14]*

Skating, of Dutch origin, was an inexpensive sport, and one writer claims the lack of wealth in the pioneer era brought skating into prominence. It was first adopted by men and boys, but later when women shelved some of their gentility, they too were seen on the rinks. . . .[15] A spectator describes the sport thus: "There were five hundred on the ice yesterday at one time, and we are happy to say a large number were ladies. The skating costumes adopted are beautiful, and render the icy scene very picturesque. Bright red dresses with white fur trimming — blue, brown, and green, as though it was not only necessary to skate gracefully, but to look as illuminated as possible at the same time. . . ."[16]

Those who preferred the less strenuous winter diversions found recreation in sleigh rides. . . .

*Sayre, the Rock County pioneer, recalled a sunny April day on his sleigh on the way to a sawmill, when snow still "was six inches deep . . . with mud two or three inches deep under it." In the village of Fulton, he met an adventurous group of women ready for winter's end.*

*I saw several ladies at one of the houses at an afternoon party: young married ladies as full of fun as any young girl needs to be. One of them hailed me, saying, "Won't you give us a sleigh ride?" They could not be refused. Six or eight of them . . . somehow seated themselves on the runners, among them the only woman in the region who had money. . . . [She] had gone to Milwaukee and bought a rich black velvet mantilla. I venture to say no such thing had been seen in Rock County before. Arrayed in this rich costume she seated herself on one of the crossbars of the runners. The ride was perhaps a mile through the snow and slush, the women laughing at the fun. . . . The horses stopped, and looking about, there sat the velvet mantilla with the owner in it, in six inches of snow and slush. . . . That rich velvet mantilla could never look fresh and unsoiled again. But the women had the fun.[17]*

*Women's fun was "all the more so," Sayre said, "because of their constant work of those days."*

Some aspects of social life were, and still are, peculiarly dominated by women. In the 1840s and subsequently, women were planning ways and means to aid churches and benevolent institutions. . . . A "public fair," an "at home," a "grand entertainment," "strawberry festivals," supervised by women affiliated with the Presbyterian, the Unitarian, the Welsh, the Methodist, and other denominations were listed by Milwaukee editors throughout these years. The funds were used for church buildings, for furnishing rooms of the meeting houses, supplying lighting equipment, and so on.

Of Madison in the 1840s appears this story:

There was a number of religious societies just fairly beginning . . . amongst whom the ladies were not wanting in their exertions to give pecuniary aid and prosperity to their several denominations, by the institution of sewing circles and fairs for the promotion of church objects, at whose meetings the male population was not backward in their attendance; and, for those times, were quite liberal in their weekly donations.[18]

The newspapers announced Sunday School picnics during the summer months, presumably supervised by the women of the churches. . . .

. . . Affiliation with some welfare society, however, was a happy solution for those who disliked the more frivolous pastimes; here was combined sociability and a worthy purpose. According to the report of the Ladies benevolent society in 1847 [in Milwaukee] the funds received were meager; the sum of $197.74 was used for provisions, clothing, and wood. It was announced: "Our charities have again been confined almost entirely to the suffering sick.". . .[19]

*Women had raised funds in the most meager amounts imaginable only a few years before near Green Bay, at a mission to the Stockbridge, where the Reverend Cutting Marsh reported in 1843 of "a Female Cent Society which has been in existence between two and three years, and numbers 25 members. Each member contributes one cent a week, and the avails are devoted to the cause of Foreign Missions."[20] But no matter how unprofitable or seemingly innocuous, the work of women had immeasurable impact on the social structures of Wisconsin — as significant as any architectural structures built by men, as Krueger concludes.*

## NOTES

1. Carl Russell Fish, *The Rise of the Common Man, 1830–50* (New York, 1927), 150. . . .
2. Carl Quickert, *The Story of Washington County* (Menasha, 1923), 85.
3. *Chippewa County Wisconsin, Past and Present* (S. J. Clarke Publishing Company, Chicago, 1913), 128.
4. Quickert, *Washington County,* 89.
5. H. E. Cole, *Stagecoach and Tavern Tales of the Old Northwest* (Cleveland, 1930), 108, 259–260.
6. *Milwaukee Courier,* August 7, 1844.
7. Mary E. B. to John H. Tweedy, January 31, 1848, John H. Tweedy Papers, WHS Archives.
8. Smith, *HOW,* 493–495.
9. David F. Sayre, "Early Life in Southern Wisconsin," *WMH* 18, no. 4 (June 1935): 424.
10. The Peck house was the first residence erected in the state capital. It was built near the shore of Lake Monona . . . just off the present King Street. . . . *WMH* 2: 479.
11. Consul W. Butterfield, *History of Dane County, Wisconsin* (Chicago, 1880), 681–682.
12. "People with Memories/A Cluster of Wisconsin's Early Settlers/Mrs. Rosaline Peck's 60 Years in Dane and Sauk Counties," *Milwaukee Sentinel,* March 14, 1897; "Wisconsin's Pioneers," *Wisconsin State Journal,* June 18, 1885; "An Early Madison Festivity," *Oconto Herald,* April 2, 1915; Betty Pruett, "The Genesis of Wisconsin's Capital City," *Wisconsin State Journal,* September 7, 1919.
13. "People with Memories"; see also George W. Stoner, "Early Madison," *Madison Democrat,* December 3, 1899.
14. "People with Memories." Roseline Peck eventually "tired of being a slave to everybody" as an innkeeper, and the Pecks rented the property in Madison and moved again to a farm as the first settlers of Baraboo. Her husband later left to claim land in Oregon and never returned. At ninety years of age, she died in Baraboo in 1898 at the home of her daughter with the famed name of Wisconsiana Victoria Peck Wheeler Hawley.
15. Henry Hall, ed., *The Tribune Book of Open-Air Sports* (New York, 1887), 459.
16. *Milwaukee Evening Sentinel,* February 5, 1862.
17. Sayre, "Early Life in Southern Wisconsin," 423–424.
18. Daniel S. Durrie, *A History of Madison, the Capital of Wisconsin* (Madison, 1874), 158.
19. *Milwaukee Daily Sentinel and Gazette,* November 29, 1847.
20. Rev. Cutting Marsh, "Report to the Scotland Society for June 1st, 1843," *WHC,* vol. 15, 182.

# Women at Ceresco

## JOHN SAVAGIAN

*WMH* 83, No. 4 (Summer 2000): 258–280

Mary Chase was worried. Her husband Warren was talking of moving again. . . . From his native New Hampshire, to Boston, Albany, and out the other side of the Erie Canal in Buffalo, Chase had failed stops in Cleveland, Cincinnati, and Louisville, before settling for a moment in Monroe, Michigan Territory. This was where Mary, also a New Hampshire native, met and married him a year earlier in 1837. He had almost immediately impressed upon her the need to move farther west — to Wisconsin Territory, where openness and opportunity seemed one and the same.[1]

. . . When the Chase family disembarked at Southport (later renamed Kenosha) in 1838 after a three-week, tempest-tossed journey following Lake Michigan's shoreline, they did so in the midst of a shower of eastern immigrants. . . .

. . . But their bankroll for the land, tied up in store goods and shipped ahead of them, was lost at the bottom of the lake. They arrived nearly penniless. After a frightful six months of hunger and desperation, Warren found work teaching at the village school. . . .

. . . [T]heir next move would not be the act of one family seeking to better their lot in life, but the combined efforts of over fifty families to create a unique community based in theory on cooperation and equality of labor between and among the sexes.

. . . The founders of this experiment named their community Ceresco. . . .[2] The Chases and their fellow utopian pioneers were imbued with the socialist ideas of the French philosopher, Charles Fourier, who saw communitarian living as a solution to the woes caused by economic competition. . . .

. . . [M]ost of the evidence left by the Wisconsin Phalanx — minutes, stockbooks, petitions, and letters — was written by men. Fortunately, since the early 1990s, greater scholarly attention has focused on the women who helped form these very unique frontier communities. . . .

The task of bringing the voice of the women of Ceresco, women like Mary Chase, to light remains difficult. Many of them are only recounted through the words of their husbands. . . . By examining these materials with an eye toward how women lived and worked at Ceresco it is possible to discern how the power women may have gained as housekeepers and mothers under their own roofs prior to Ceresco was denied them once they moved into the community. . . .

In the fall of 1843 the *Southport Telegraph* carried a series of articles that articulated the sanitized version of Charles Fourier's message. . . .

. . . Women who lived in separate homes, performing the "slavish drudgery" of washing, cooking, keeping up fires, and marketing, would find their work under the association system "so greatly abridged . . . that four-fifths and perhaps more of the trouble will be saved.". . .[3]

Yet the changes to be instituted by association were to ease the work load rather than fundamentally change it. . . . Clearly, the "weaker sex" under Fourier's communal system was not intended to challenge man for his job but to help to ease his burden. Women could best do this by remaining within their domestic sphere. . . .

. . . [U]nder associative living women would maintain their isolation from the evils of the world but lose their hard labor. With such intentions was the way to utopian living for the women paved.

Once Fourier's ideas were in print and in the hands of the interested citizens of South-port, the issue of association was discussed in the manner customary for the time, through the local debating society called the Franklin Lyceum. . . .[4] Chase and three other men of the Franklin Lyceum took turns arguing the pros and cons of Fourier's ideas. . . .[5]

Within a month of the debates the Southport Fourier Club was established. . . . In March of 1844, the constitution was approved, the Wisconsin Phalanx was founded, shares of common stock were issued for twenty-five dollars each, and a committee established to search for a new home. . . . The utopian journal, *The Harbinger,* published by the Brook Farm Phalanx of New York, called Ceresco's founding a "glorious beginning for the Far West," one "destined to be the scene of social beauty, harmony and joy."[6]

Not surprisingly, women, although promised a better life under Fourier's system, were not members of the board of directors. Indeed, they were not mentioned in the minutes of the newly created Wisconsin Phalanx. No known diaries or journals of the women pres-ent at the creation of Ceresco exist. . . .

. . . Warren Chase offers a glimpse of the reaction his wife had upon learning that they were selling their home and moving one hundred twenty miles north into the Wisconsin wilderness: "O dear! I am so fearful we shall not get a home of our own again, if we sell this and go up there!" When he countered that chances for his continued employment in Southport were poor, Chase remembered her reply, "Well, just as you say, but I don't feel reconciled to it; but as you have to earn all we have, it is right for you to control it.". . .[7]

Mary's apprehension about her home, however, would not be settled so quickly, for initially the women and children stayed behind as the men set up camp. . . . In June, a number of the women arrived with children in tow, including Mrs. Stuart and her five chil-dren, Mrs. Stillwell with four children, and Mrs. Martin and her four children. The resi-dency continued to grow in July, as Mary Chase and a number of other women and children set foot on what they had taken to calling "the domain." Upon her arrival, Mary's fears were confirmed. Her new home was a community house so hastily constructed to beat the approaching winter that large gaps in the boards allowed wind, light, and the eventual snow to seep inside. As even Warren Chase was forced to admit, "Well may you conjecture reader, that she was unhappy, for she had not partaken of the excitement that brought others willingly here.". . .[8]

. . . The women of Ceresco did have other opportunities to develop a voice within the new community. . . . Many women owned shares in the Wisconsin Phalanx. The average number of shares for a married woman was three. Widows usually owned the same num-ber of shares as most men, about twenty-five.[9]

Female ownership in Wisconsin Phalanx stock is significant for a number of reasons. It suggests that Ceresco's leadership was influenced by the national movement to broaden the meaning of participatory democracy to include women. . . . Ceresco's women had already taken advantage of a more liberal frontier political climate to assert their right of participation. They understood that the first step in suffrage was the ownership of property. They owned shares in the Wisconsin Phalanx for the same reason men did: to have a say in how the community was run.

Yet despite having the vote as shareholders, women were not empowered to make corporate decisions regarding the daily operation of the community. That power resided in the hands of an all-male body. Ceresco was governed by a town council officially called the Councils of Industry. The minutes refer to it simply as "the Council." All resident male members twenty-one and older were allowed to vote for the leadership of the Council, composed of a president, vice-president, treasurer, and secretary. Chartered by the territorial government, Ceresco was beholden to . . . Wisconsin's territorial laws, which restricted voting to men. This is not unusual for the times, nor for the history of the state. Despite Chase and Ceresco, Wisconsin was not known for crusading for female suffrage.[10] But while it was expected that the women of Ceresco would not be allowed to vote for leaders of the Council, neither were they present on the numerous committees that supervised the various industries and chores on the domain. One might expect men to have sat on the committees of Finances, Mechanical Business, Corporation Affairs, and Rules and Regulations, areas of work traditionally proscribed to men. Men also supervised areas in the traditional realm of women, such as Domestic Affairs. . . .[11]

The Council's influence extended beyond determining who was to run each job in the community; it also defined the type of work that was necessary for earning communal income. . . .

The Council organized its labor according to Fourier's method, which divided labor into three classes: necessity, usefulness, and attractiveness. . . . The class of attractiveness listed cooking, dining-room work, ironing, all other domestic chores, gardening, horticulture, care of fowls and bees, and the business of the Council.[12]

The work of women at Ceresco was classified by the Council in the third class of labor: attractiveness. . . . As the lowest order of labor, women who engaged in attractive work earned the least amount of money, mirroring conditions in the world outside Ceresco.

. . . Evidence also indicates that the work of women was less appreciated within the community. . . . In one instance the Council was asked to order the "man having charge of the public table" to "procure female labor necessary in and about the same week." The Council then stipulated that he pay them as little as possible.[13]

Workers were rarely paid in cash, however, for all living expenses were recorded and subtracted from each worker's pay. . . . When the charge for room and board, materials used in labor, clothing, reading materials, and other miscellaneous expenses were added up, members of the Wisconsin Phalanx usually had little money left over. Cash was so tight that it was not uncommon for a member to go before the Council asking for funds to purchase a personal item. . . . Whether it was a butcher's apron or a broom for the school-house, the Council had to provide its approval before the purchase.[14]

For women, control over their domestic finances by someone other than themselves was hardly a radical concept, but the size and impersonal nature of the male authority at Ceresco certainly was. The difficulty was further enhanced by the disparity in the gender ratio in the community. Women at Ceresco were a decided minority. In 1846 there were one hundred one males and seventy-one females. More importantly, fifty-six males and only thirty-seven females were over the age of twenty-one. While Fourier's system of indus-try promised women less toil because of cooperation, much of their work involved assist-ing an entire community. Coupled with the fact that twenty-one were mothers who oversaw the raising of seventy-nine children, it is no wonder that the women organized an auxiliary called Ladies of the Wisconsin Phalanx and petitioned the Council for "con-struction of suitable machinery for washing."[15]

Ceresco's gender disparity may also explain why single women like Charlotte Haven and her sister Harriet, who arrived in 1848, were found to be indispensable. Without chil-dren of their own, the sisters were not encumbered with family matters that took away from their work for the community as a whole. Charlotte often suggested to another sis-ter, Hannah, that for her, life at Ceresco seemed to revolve around work in the dining room. . . . [For a dance,] Charlotte made eighteen apple pies and about a hundred cook-ies. In addition to such "paid work," women were expected to minister voluntarily to the sick. . . .[16]

. . . Like her sister Charlotte, the least enjoyable place to work for Harriet was the din-ing room. "The dining room, aren't you tired of the word, is honored with my presence this week," she told her journal. One month after she and her sister arrived, the Havens weighed themselves at the mill. Harriet found she had gained three pounds, but sarcasti-cally concluded, "I think mine is all in the hands."[17]

Male supervision of the dining room proved inadequate. One year after more workers were hired, the men of the Domestic Affairs Committee stood before the Council com-plaining about problems they had with the work of the young girls in the dining room. Some of the girls were not showing up when expected and considerable food was wasted. The Council suggested that "three or four women be appointed to superintend the Din-ing Room and Kitchen to work alternatively with the girls."[18] But no one could be found willing or able to take on new duties. Finally, Isabella Town MacKay Hunter, a woman who had at the age of nineteen managed a large public house in Cornwall, Canada, with her first husband, became manager of the culinary department and the dining room.[19]

Life at the unitary table was a source of serious friction in the community. Problems with communal dining have consistently been cited by historians and interested observers as a factor in the dissolution of the Wisconsin Phalanx. . . . Warren Chase noted that of 180 members at Ceresco in 1846, only eighty boarded at the public table. The rest chose to dine in their private rooms, "though their apartments are very inconvenient for that purpose.". . .[20] [S]ome members were vegetarians and did not want "to sit at the table plentifully supplied with beef, pork and mutton." Others, he suggested, wanted to have their children sit with them "which our circumstance do not permit."[21] Isabella Hunter put much stock in the latter reason. . . . Parents, she believed, often felt uneasy about disciplining their children under the watchful gaze of others.[22] However, Chase's comment tends to suggest that discipline and training were out of the question because children ate separated from their parents. To help instill discipline, the children were taught a rhyme to recite before they began eating their meals:

With right good will,
We'll all sit still;
And eat our food
In quiet mood.

Warren and Mary Chase's son Milton sang that little ditty as he taught it to his grandchildren. But it was not with fondness he recalled his time spent dining at Ceresco. . . .[23]

On the subject of education of the young of Ceresco, there is a dearth of information. In 1847 *The Harbinger* reported that there were eighty children to ninety adults at Ceresco. . . .[24] [T]he majority of Council discussions [on children's issues] focused on education, specifically who to hire for a teacher. In 1846 Benjamin Sheldon was asked "to take care of the school boys and teach them and discipline those who are old enough. . . ."[25]

Benjamin Sheldon's teaching instructions from the Council mention only the training of young boys; girls are missing from Ceresco's limited education records. In its annual statement for 1846, the third year of its existence, the Wisconsin Phalanx reported that it was still having trouble organizing its school. With only a one-schoolroom building and no interest in teaching the children together, boys and girls were taught alternately as the summer progressed. . . .[26] It is likely that if young girls did receive any extended education, it would come, as tradition dictated, from their mothers, and at home. Of course, the definition of "home" at Ceresco was highly fluid.

Much of the Ceresco women's time was spent working in the large community house built in accordance with Fourier's principle of harmony. The Frenchman had advised the associationists to live in a large, multi-dwelling building he called the Phalanstry. The people of Ceresco called their community home the Long House. The principle of the Phalanstry dealt with economy of size as much as any harmonious benefits derived from living in close proximity. The plan was for the Phalanstry's apartments for families and singles to open into a large corridor or enclosed piazza that would connect the rooms to the workshop, library, lecture hall, kitchen, and dining room. This would not only foster greater interaction, but also save the members from having to travel from a warm room to the cold outside.[27]

While the Long House may have epitomized communal living, the supposed benefits to have accrued by such interaction never materialized. Due to the poverty of the community and the Council's refusal to go into debt for any reason, the Long House never acquired a library, lecture hall, or workshop. For the life of the community, the Long House served as the sleeping and dining quarters for approximately half the members. . . .[28]

When Charlotte Haven and her sister Harriet arrived one year after construction of the new Long House, unitary living was still a trying experience. Writing to her sister Hannah, Charlotte described the hallway of the Long House. She complained that the corridor served as both passageway and storage center for the dining room, since the builders had failed to provide a cellar:

> I shall never forget my perplexed sensations when I first passed through this mysterious passage. . . . With both hands upraised before us we groped along in darkness encountering obstacles and brushing against something, I knew not what. . . . You can walk but a few steps without stumbling against cupboards, wood boxes, floor barrels, bags of potatoes, pumpkins and thus endangering toes, noses or other prominent features, or per chance ensconced in a pan of milk or find yourself sprawling amid the contents of said barrels, bags and boxes.[29]

Unlike married women who were enjoined to the Ceresco experiment by their husbands, Charlotte Haven voluntarily had sought membership in the society. As a single woman, she was the object of a good deal of attention from bachelor members. Her unattached condition was desirable, and so was her room. When she and sister Harriet gained a private room, they received visitors nearly every day. In her letter one fall evening to another sister, Charlotte records the interruptions with periodic exclamation of "Alas!" . . . Sister Harriet noted in her journal that social opportunities were always just outside their door. "Here I am sitting alone," she wrote, "I said I was alone but one cannot be alone here when by opening either door we can see and talk at as many people as we care to."[30]

Charlotte and her sister found ample opportunity to mingle and socialize. But for others, it was not as easy. . . . Ceresco member Louisa Sheldon felt the pangs of loneliness, confessing to her sister-in-law Abigail, "I think that I have had some symptoms of it. I used to sit down and cry but I have quit that and try to work it off."[31] Louisa also touched on an unspoken problem confronting many members; the material conditions of their life were not improving as they had expected. While she rallied, claiming "if I am poor, I am contented," not everyone was as sanguine. . . .

Poor living conditions led more families to move off phalanx land. In essence they decided to farm on their own while keeping stock in the association. Their departures threatened the utopian experiment, especially since those who left could still vote on matters affecting the community. Louisa Sheldon was concerned. "We have had considerable disputing in the Association this winter," she reported to her sister-in-law.[32] To solve the problem, in 1847 the community approved, by a narrow margin, a change in its Constitution which required all members of the Wisconsin Phalanx to live on the domain. This hotly debated amendment engendered great rancor among Ceresco's members. . . .[33]

After the residency vote of 1847, the communal spirit of Ceresco was in serious trouble. . . . More families began to opt out of the Wisconsin Phalanx. The profit that stockholders expected to receive at the end of the year as dividends was siphoned off to pay the members who cashed in their stocks and moved on. Charlotte Haven left Ceresco in 1849 after marrying fellow resident Volney Mason. Instead of staying in the Long House, the newlyweds moved about fifteen miles to a small two-room house on a farm near Berlin in what is now Green Lake County. She commented to her brother . . . that the Council had decided to sell the Long House to a member. This privatization promptly raised the charge for board to 75 cents a week which, she complained, hardly anyone could afford. Even more families found it necessary to eat and "smother in their rooms," as she said.[34]

In December of 1849 the remaining stockholders of the Wisconsin Phalanx voted to sell off all the property and quit the experiment. The rapid expansion of the neighboring village of Ripon no doubt encouraged the members that dissolution would not leave them completely isolated on the Wisconsin frontier. Ripon had fast been encroaching on the utopian settlement, its citizens condemning the experiment and quick to believe any rumors about its members living out Fourier's free love principles. Ceresco residents viewed Ripon with equal suspicion. As temperance advocates, they actively petitioned against demon rum, consistently outvoted Ripon citizens on the liquor question, and in one instance forced a distillery to move out. . . .[35]

Many of Ceresco's former citizens continued to live in the area. Warren Chase and a few others attempted to reorganize the association, but within a year they gave up. Warren and Mary Chase and a few others . . . would eventually leave the area. . . . In his autobiography, Warren Chase penned a eulogy for Ceresco which concluded, "It was prematurely born, and tried to live before its proper time, and, of course, must die and be born again. So it did, and here it lies.". . .[36]

. . . The men who accepted the ideas of association were for the most part individuals who experienced difficulties adapting to the new system of industrial capitalism. They were ready and eager to try something new. . . .

. . . The women of Ceresco, by the very fact of joining in association, [also] attempted to alter the gender-defining roles of their day. But what they gained in sisterhood and more efficient labor they sacrificed in influence over the decisions affecting their own families. . . .[37]

. . . The record of women at Ceresco, while admittedly meager compared to their male counterparts, does allow for some general inferences that suggests they chafed under the changes brought on by communal life. In each instance where the women had gained power through their domestic circumstance, the structure and communal living organized at Ceresco minimized or ignored them. Women at home had some say over spending of the income for food, clothing, and household items. At Ceresco, that was the function of the Council, a board that disallowed them membership. Antebellum women were protective of their growing status as mothers of the modern family because it afforded them a sphere of influence, albeit limited and dependent, centered in *their* homes.[38] At Ceresco there was no home; it was replaced by cramped and shifting personal space, crowded dining halls, and limited recognition of women's work.

. . . The Ceresco mother was expected to play a weak second to the organization and discipline that the association promised the children. . . . The pent-up lives in Ceresco's unitary house, where families competitively vied for their individual benefits, coupled with their loss of control over the children at the public table, showed the women of the

Wisconsin Phalanx that the association's gain was their loss. At Ceresco, the individual housekeeper was only one of many housekeepers, all of whom were directed by orders from a council of men.

. . . [T]he men of Ceresco retained their traditional powers outside the home. Though they too lived "in association," they were in control of the rules and decision-making outside the home and thus were able to keep their sphere of influence intact. For the women, life at Ceresco denied them their control of the hearth. They were the ones who failed to gain from the benefits derived from the power of association. Their lack of control over family and household matters must be taken into account as a factor in the eventual demise of the utopian community at Ceresco. To have stayed under such a system would have meant losing an identity they were just beginning to understand and use to their benefit. . . .

## NOTES

1. Warren Chase, *The Life-Line of the Lone One; or, Autobiography of the World's Child,* 4th ed., (Boston: Bela Marsh, 1865), 72–76.

2. The name derives from Ceres, the Babylonian goddess of grain. Some dispute has occurred among scholars about how the members came to name their community. Joseph Schafer, "The Wisconsin Phalanx," *WMH* 19:454–474 (June, 1936), believes the name meant "in the company of Ceres" (464). David P. Mapes, *History of the City of Ripon, and of Its Founder, David P. Mapes with His Opinion of Men and Manners of the Day* (Milwaukee: Cramer, Aikens & Cramer, 1873), 87, speculates that the syllable "co" at the end was added at random for euphony. Given the stocks issued and the corporate nature of the organization, it is just as likely that the "co" was added after "Ceres" to designate the incorporation of the community.

3. *Southport Telegraph,* February 6, 1844.

4. The editors of the *Southport Telegraph* noted (December 7, 1842, 2) that public lectures and debates had increased . . . in popularity during the few years before 1842. . . .

5. S. M. Pedrick, "The Wisconsin Phalanx at Ceresco," in SHSW, *Proceedings,* 1902, 191.

6. "Well Done Wisconsin!" in *The Harbinger,* October 31, 1846, 336.

7. Chase, *Life-Line,* 118.

8. Ibid., 119.

9. Stockbook of Wisconsin Phalanx, Wisconsin Phalanx Records, WHS Archives.

10. Robert C. Nesbit, *Wisconsin: A History* (Madison: University of Wisconsin Press, 1973), 389, 395. . . .

11. Minutes for March 23, 1846, [and February 22, 1847,] in the Secretary's Record, 100, Wisconsin Phalanx Records. Kathryn Manson Tomasek, "'The Pivot of the Mechanism': Women, Gender, and Discourse in Fourierism and the Antebellum United States" (doctoral dissertation, University of Wisconsin–Madison, 1995), 259, notes that the original constitution says nothing about gender in voting rights, but the by-laws allowed only male members of the association to vote.

12. Minutes for November 15, 1844, Secretary's Record, 26–27, Wisconsin Phalanx Records.

13. Ibid., February 15, 1847, 159.

14. Ibid., March 15, 1847, 163.

15. Ibid., May 22, 1848, 29.

16. Charlotte Haven to Hannah Haven, October 26, 1848, Charlotte Haven Papers, WHS Archives.

17. Entries for October 8–19, 1848, Harriet Haven journal, ibid.

18. Minutes for December 15, 1848, Secretary's Record, book 2, 67, Wisconsin Phalanx Records.

19. Ada C. Merrill, "Reminiscences of Isabella MacKay Town Hunter," *Milwaukee Sentinel,* January 31, 1904, 4.

20. John Humphrey Noyes, *History of American Socialisms* (1870; reprint, New York: Hillary House, 1961), 423.

21. Warren Chase, "Wisconsin Phalanx," *The Harbinger,* January 8, 1848, 77. . . .

22. Article by Ada C. Merrill, *Ripon Commonwealth,* January 27, 1904.

23. Telephone interview with Frances E. Vosburgh, M.D., May 8, 1980, by Jack Holzhueter and Phil Shoemaker, incorporated in "Field Trip Report," May 14, 1980, in Holzhueter's files, WHS Archives. . . .

24. "Report on Ceresco," *The Harbinger,* August 21, 1847, 169.

25. Minutes for July 13, 1846, Secretary's Record, 40, Wisconsin Phalanx Records.

26. "Annual Statement of the Condition and Progress of the Wisconsin Phalanx, for the Fiscal Year Ending Dec. 7th, 1846," *Fond du Lac Journal,* December 31, 1846, 2.

27. "From the Phalanx," *Southport Telegraph,* March 5, 1844. . . .

28. Noyes, *History of American Socialisms,* 433–434

29. Charlotte Haven to Hannah Haven, October 26, 1848, Charlotte Haven Papers.

30. "Wednesday Morning," journal of Harriet Haven, ibid.

31. . . . Louisa Sheldon to Sister Abigail, October 1, 1847, Wisconsin Phalanx Records.

32. Louisa Sheldon to Sister Abigail, October 1, 1847, Wisconsin Phalanx Records.

33. Minutes for October 18 and 27, 1847, Secretary's Record, 196–197, ibid.

34. Charlotte Haven to William Haven, July 8, 1849, Charlotte Haven Papers.

35. Merrill, "Reminiscences," 4.

36. Chase, *Life-Line,* 128.

37. Jean Harvey Baker, "Women in Utopia," in Gairdner B. Moment and Otto F. Kraushaar, eds., *Utopias, the American Experience* (Metuchen, New Jersey: Scarecrow Press, 1980), 70, offers a comparison of women who lived in vastly different utopian communities . . . and suggests a similar dislocation of mothers occurred with respect to their central places in their families.

38. Nancy F. Cott, *The Bonds of Womanhood: "Woman's Sphere" in New England, 1780–1835* (New Haven: Yale University Press, 1977), 84; Nancy Woloch, *Women and the American Experience* (New York: Alfred A. Knopf, 1984), 116.

# The Swedish Settlement on Pine Lake

MABEL V. HANSEN

*WMH* 8, No. 1 (June 1925): 38–51

*Foreign-born newcomers to Wisconsin often had the hardest adjustment, in part owing to the poverty of most immigrants' pasts. Many faced transitions from farm life to urban life — or the reverse, in the case of the first Swedish colony — as well as learning a new language and cultural norms, even if emigrating in groups and establishing ethnic enclaves such as the settlement at Pine Lake. Most settlers succeeded, but a progressive perspective on American history neglects the stories of those who failed and went home, or stayed and suffered for the rest of their lives, especially the stories of immigrant women. "For all recent arrivals to Wisconsin, the stress of relocation was severe," writes historian Alice E. Smith. "But it was more severe for women than for men, and was perhaps worst of all for the new immigrant women from Europe," the source of the influx into Wisconsin in the 1840s.[1]*

*More than a hundred thousand immigrants constituted approximately a third of the population of Wisconsin by the end of the territorial era, and English was a foreign language for more than half of the foreign-born. More than half were Germans, who first settled in Wisconsin in 1839 and soon far surpassed the second-largest immigrant group, the Irish. Many of the Irish spoke Gaelic, although as British subjects they were considered to be English speakers. Similarly, the next-largest group from the British Isles came from England but included many Cornish immigrants with their own culture and customs, while many Welsh immigrants also retained their language. Other sizeable non-English-speaking groups included Norwegians, Swiss, and Netherlanders.[2]*

*Wherever their homelands, most immigrant women in Wisconsin had the "harsh and endless hard work" of "keeping house on a raw homestead," Smith writes. They faced the "sheer physical burdens" of frontier life, a fate shared by men — but their burdens differed. Men's tasks more often took them from home to town or were undertaken together. Women more often endured emotional isolation, far from family and friends left behind. The result often was "a sense of rootlessness that must at times have deepened into despair," as happened at the ill-fated first Swedish settlement in Wisconsin, near Nashotah in Waukesha County, where Milwaukee and Chicago millionaires' mansions now overlook the shores of Pine Lake.[3]*

*Most colonists in the settlement resembled their founder Gustaf Unonius, a recent graduate of the Swedish university of Uppsala, in having more education and enthusiasm than experience suitable for survival on the frontier. He arrived first in 1841, with or soon followed by his wife, Charlotta Ohrstromer Unonius. Her husband envisioned not simply a settlement but the first Swedish university in Wisconsin. The group got no further than assembling cedar logs on the site. Also among them was a dissenting Lutheran preacher and religious recluse who lived hermitlike in a cave. Other men had held high political patronage positions in their homeland, until the coronation of a new king, and they were not "accustomed to hard work." Many of the women had held high social positions in Sweden and were accustomed to servants. For one of the few settlers who prospered, a former baron became his servant "in order to get bread," writes Hansen. But the baron disappeared, and "no one seems to know what became of him."*

*Nor did any one of them seem to know what they would face on the Wisconsin frontier.*

*Since publication of the following early effort to trace the past of the Swedish colony at Pine Lake, its story has continued to intrigue historians. More recent research reveals that the correct spelling of the founding family's surname was Petterson (with two t's), that the first Petterson actually arrived in 1842, and that his wife and another pioneering woman in the colony arrived only a year later, in 1843. As numerous bracketed corrections of a name so often used could impede readability, they are minimized in the following; the spelling of the Petterson surname follows the original article from eighty years ago.[4]*

An interesting and romantic feature of the early settlement of this section of Waukesha County was the location of the Swedish colony that settled about Pine Lake in 1841 and subsequent years. Twelve families came over originally, including two noblemen of the realm and one baron. These people had held political positions in Sweden, but the death of the old king and the ascension of a new ruler with the consequent change in administration policies had caused them to lose their offices. All were anxious to better their conditions in some way, and so came to America, which they regarded as a land of beauty and golden prospects. The new colony was called New Up[p]sala. . . .

The early history of these people, formerly accustomed to every luxury, is one of deprivation, suffering, and lack of the actual necessities of life. Their money soon exhausted, and not knowing how to work to advantage, some of them were reduced to absolute beggary.

The first member of the colony to come over was Knut Bengt. Peterson . . . who arrived as early as 1841. . . . Peterson's family, consisting of his wife and eight children, joined him several years later. The Peterson home became a veritable social center in this colony. The latch-string hung outside, and as the settlement grew, there was always company. In that far time there were only two women in this entire section — Mrs. [Mary Nicholson] Warren and Mrs. [Charlotta Berg] Peterson. A story is told that Mrs. Warren became so lonesome and homesick that it seemed as if she could not endure it any longer, so she had Mr. [Stephen] Warren take her over to visit Mrs. Peterson. Now, Mrs. Peterson could speak not one word of English, nor could Mrs. Warren talk Swedish, but it is recorded that they had the best kind of visit, and Mrs. Warren went home feeling much happier, for the sight of another woman's face and a sympathetic hand clasp of one of her own sex. . . .

Lieutenant [Adolph von Linsfeldt] St. Sure, also a nobleman, lived over the hill, beyond the village. . . . The log house which St. Sure built for his family was one of the largest and finest of its day. . . .

The St. Sure family, who had been accustomed to much luxury in their native land, lived in most distressing circumstances for a time. St. Sure tried to break up a stony piece of land but failed completely, and in the early fifties sold the place and moved to Chicago. A story which illustrates the sad contrast in their lives in this new land is told about Mrs. St. Sure. Attired in a green velvet riding suit, sole relic of her former grandeur, she sallied forth one balmy spring day to visit her neighbor Mrs. Peterson. As she went up the pathway to the house, a great black pig followed her. Her hostess, standing in the doorway, remarked, "You have company." Turning, Mrs. St. Sure saw the ugly animal and burst into tears, saying, "And have I come to this!" Silken gowns and bare feet were not conducive to conjugal felicity either, and it is related that husband and wife were separated after leaving here, St. Sure pursuing the study of medicine, for which his fine education had well fitted him. After many years, it is said, he was called to minister to a dying woman. It was his former wife, and it is a pathetic ending to the romance of their lives that a reconciliation was effected upon her deathbed.

The most romantic interest, however, lingers about Captain [Polycarpus] von Schneidau, his wife and family. Captain von Schneidau belonged to the staff of Prince Oscar of Sweden, and was his best friend and daily companion until he became enamored of a great beauty, Froecken [Caroline Elizabeth] Jacobson, a Swedish Jewess. As it was an infringement upon the matrimonial codes of Sweden for Jew and Gentile to marry, they journeyed across the channel to Denmark, where they were united, and then came to this country, joining the colony at Pine Lake [in 1842]. Thus they began life under the most trying circumstances and innumerable drawbacks, and they endured severe hardship. They conducted a very meager business here in the way of a grog shop and grocery, and a story is related of how the beautiful Fru Schneidau would tap her whisky keg until it was about full and then fill in the Pine Lake water, keeping on until there was not much whisky left. . . . An infant son born to them at Pine Lake died from exposure to frost and cold. It was while they were suffering the greatest hardship that they were visited by Mayor Ogden of Chicago, who . . . afterwards adopted the daughter, Pauline. . . .

. . . Upon the death of Mrs. von Schneidau the father and daughter visited Europe, but returned to Chicago in the course of two years, when Mayor Ogden claimed his adopted daughter and she went to live at his home. The father lived near by in the home of a friend until his death. Pauline von Schneidau was sent east to school, and while there met a son of Leonard Jerome, whom she afterward married. . . .

A notable event in the Pine Lake colony was the visit of Fredrika Bremer, the noted Swedish novelist, in 1850. Of this visit I quote a reminiscence of Mrs. Hilda Spillman, who is a daughter of the Peterson household, and whose childhood days were spent in this historic colony. She says:

> At the time Fredrika Bremer came, it was my brother who waited upon her in Milwaukee and brought her to our home here, where my mother with her cheerful welcome and hospitable board was awaiting their arrival, and every neighbor who could come had been invited to the house. . . .

Here follows Miss Bremer's own story of the visit to the Swedish colony, taken from her book *Homes in the New World:*

> There remain still of the little Swedish colony of Pine Lake about half a dozen families, who live as farmers in the neighborhood. It is lake scenery and as lovely and

romantic as any may be imagined — regular Swedish lake scenery, and one can understand how those first Swedish immigrants were enchanted, so that, without first examining the quality of the soil, they determined to found here a new Sweden, and to build a new Up[p]sala! I spent the forenoon in visiting the various Swedish families. Nearly all live in log houses, and seem to be in somewhat low circumstances. . . .

. . . The difficulty of obtaining the help of servants, male and female, is one of the inconveniences which the colonists of the West have to encounter. They must either pay for the labor at an enormously high rate — and often it is not to be had on any terms — or they must do without it; and if their own powers of labor fail, either through sickness or any other misfortune, then is want the inevitable consequence. . . .

. . . [W]e betook ourselves to the oldest house of the colony on Pine Lake, where lived Mrs. Bergwall's mother, the Widow Peterson, and who expected us to coffee. . . .

Mrs. Peterson, a large woman, who in her youth must have been handsome, came out to receive me, bent double and supported on a crutch-stick, but her open countenance beaming with kindness. She is not yet fifty, but is aged and broken down before her time by severe labor and trouble. . . .

Her husband began here as a farmer, but neither he nor his wife were accustomed to hard work; their land was poor . . . they could not get help, and they were without the conveniences of life; they had a large family which kept increasing; they endured incredible hardships. Mrs. Peterson, while suckling her children, was compelled to do the most laborious work; bent double with rheumatism, she was often obliged to wash for the whole family on her knees.. . . [Her husband] had now been dead . . . [for five] years, and the widow was preparing to leave the little house and garden which she could no longer look after, and remove to her son-in-law, Bergwall's.

Their children, four sons and four daughters — the two youngest born here, and still children — were all of them agreeable, and some of them remarkably handsome. . . .

The old lady Peterson had got ready a capital entertainment; incomparably excellent coffee, and tea especially; good venison, fruit, tarts, and many good things, all as nicely and delicately set out as if on a prince's table. The young sons of the house waited on us. At home, in Sweden, it would have been the daughters. All were cordial and joyous. When the meal was over we had again songs, and after that dancing. Mrs. Peterson joined in every song. . . . The good old lady would have joined us too, in the dances and the polkas, if she had not been prevented by her rheumatic lameness. . . .

I was to remain at Mrs. Peterson's, but not without some uneasiness on my part as to the prospect of rest; for . . . the state of the house testified of the greatest lack of the common conveniences of life; and I had to sleep in the sister's bed with Mrs.

Peterson, and six children lay in the adjoining room, which was the kitchen. Among these was young Mrs. [Abba Peterson] Bergwall, with her little baby and her little step-son; for, when she was about to return home with Herr Lange, his horses became frightened by the pitch darkness of the night and would not go on, and she herself becoming frightened, too, would not venture with her little children. Bergwall, therefore, set off alone through the forest, and I heard his wife calling after him: "Dear Bergwall, mind and milk the white cow well again to-night." (N.B. — It is the men in this country who milk the cows as well as attend to all kinds of outdoor business.) . . .

*In her book* Homes in the New World, *feminist reformer Fredrika Bremer also wrote that Charlotta Berg Petterson said that night of her life, "Ah, Miss Bremer, how much more people can bear than can be believed possible!"[5]*

*Many of her neighbors moved on for possibilities elsewhere, and the settlement at Pine Lake failed within a decade of its founding. Even Gustaf and Charlotta Ohrstromer Unonius gave up their utopian dream, at least in America, and left Pine Lake in 1847. At first, as the first graduate of nearby Nashotah House seminary, he served as an Episcopalian minister in Manitowoc and began to prosper. They then moved to Chicago, until a visit to Sweden convinced Unonius to return to his homeland in 1858. However, the Swedish church would not accept his ordination. "There ended the poor man's dreams," writes Hansen, "for poor he was and poorer he became when he was obliged to accept a meager professorship" in Sweden, far from the site of the university he had envisioned for his New Uppsala in the new world of Wisconsin.*

*Other Swedish settlers would succeed in America. More than a million immigrants from Sweden arrived after 1850, and more than seventy percent of them settled in the Midwest.[6]*

## NOTES

1. Smith, *HOW,* 493.
2. Ibid., 488–492.
3. Ibid., 493.
4. George C. Brown, ed., "A Swedish Traveler in Early Wisconsin: The Observations of Fredrika Bremer," *WMH* 61, no. 4 (Summer 1978): 300–318, and 62, no. 1 (Autumn 1978): 41–56; Nellie Mary Warren Weed, "History of Hartland," *Hartland News,* November 16, 1934; and William F. Stark, *Pine Lake* (Sheboygan: Zimmermann Press, 1984).
5. Brown, "A Swedish Traveler in Early Wisconsin," 315.
6. William H. Rehnquist, "Remarks," Swedish Colonial Society Annual Meeting, Philadelphia, April 9, 2001. Rehnquist, Chief Justice of the Supreme Court of the United States and a native of Shorewood near Milwaukee, is a grandson of Swedish immigrants who came to Wisconsin in 1880.

*Mathilde Franziska Anneke*

*about 25 yrs old*

SHERMAN, | MILWAUKEE.

*Portrait of Mathilde Franziska Anneke, an early Wisconsin journalist*

## ⊷3⊷

# STATEHOOD AND THE STATUS OF WOMEN, 1848–1868

## INTRODUCTION

o Wisconsin women, statehood meant improvements in everyday life — roads, harbors, and other internal improvements from the sale of ceded federal lands — but no improvement in their political status. Men gained full rights with statehood, while women remained second-class citizens. Still, issues of women's status had arisen in statehood debates as at least a start toward the first improvement in their legal rights in later decades. However, other issues of significance to women, as well as the Civil War, would intervene in the 1850s and 1860s. As historian Alice E. Smith writes, "Wisconsin joined her sister states in the Union during a time of stirring events."[1]

A historic event of sisterhood that coincided with Wisconsin statehood in the summer of 1848 was the first convention for women's rights, in upstate New York at Seneca Falls. However, most Wisconsinites felt more immediate impact from other "stirring events" that Smith cites — revolutions in Europe or the gold rush in California — that simultaneously increased an influx of immigrants and an outflow of settlers moving farther west for a better life on the next frontier. In the first two decades of statehood, Wisconsin's population would almost quadruple to more than a million, despite the departure of as many as fifty thousand early settlers. The 1860 census would show that the new state's population center shifted from the southwest to the southeast, and four-fifths of Wisconsinites lived in the southern half of the state. Other trends altered little: two-thirds of all residents were native-born, one-third were immigrants, and only about 1 percent were Native or African Americans.[2]

Compared to immigration or the westward movement, the women's rights movement would not have so immediate an impact, and many decades would pass before women nationwide and in Wisconsin would begin to win the most basic rights before the law. Women had no right to retain their belongings — whether inherited before marriage or earned afterward — or the custody of their children. Even women's bodies legally belonged to men, whether their fathers at first or their husbands in the end. Many women's lives ended early, as the legal system did nothing to protect them from spousal abuse running the gamut from frequent pregnancies, which increased the risk of death in childbirth, to battering. Not until 1984, fourteen decades after the first statehood debates on women's property rights, would Wisconsin women win full equality before the law after marriage — but the first steps were taken soon after statehood, as Catherine B. Cleary observes in her article excerpted in this chapter. A schoolteacher before she became a lawyer and a historian, Cleary uses her experience and expertise to explicate complex legal concepts and historical evidence for readers unfamiliar with law and to explore the political context of the first debates on the first women's rights won in Wisconsin. Yet by the end of the era, as Wisconsin historian Richard N. Current writes, women "remained economically and legally far inferior to their menfolk, no matter what their ethnic group or social class."[3]

The need for marital property rights reform was especially evident in cases of battered women in the era, when domestic violence was a woman's personal plight, not a societal problem. "Now your sister," wrote Wilhelmina Niedenhoefer Melchior of Trempealeau County to a cousin, "my heart bleeds for her. Her husband treats her very badly." His family had no food or clothing, while he "dresses well," she wrote, "and drinks up everything." Melchior had sent money but feared that the "sot" would "get it into his hands," since any property sent to the wife was his by law. In the same year, Melchior also appealed to the parents and burgermeister in Prussia of another woman whose "life was several times threatened through the outrageous behavior of her husband so that the officers of the city and the neighbors advised her to leave him." Now "almost naked," homeless, and pregnant, the long-abused woman also was alone; her nine children, born within a seven-year span, had died.[4]

To support themselves, many women sought advanced schooling in Wisconsin in the 1850s, when few colleges or even academies admitted women students. Eastern women especially — and repeatedly — attempted to replicate the female academies and first women's colleges that they had known there. On the origins of Wisconsin's first women's college, early women's historian Louise Phelps Kellogg had access only to evidence that attributed its founding to the eastern educator Catharine E. Beecher. However, Grace Norton Kieckhefer later uncovered evidence that more correctly accords Beecher the status of a major benefactor, who motivated Milwaukeeans to transform a "select school" for girls into a women's college, but that correctly credits Lucy Seymour Parsons as founder of the Milwaukee Female College. Her story is intriguing in itself, but readers also may find it useful to compare both historians' accounts in the compilation in this chapter. While Kellogg's work remains insightful, Kieckhefer's newer information shows why revisionist history may be required.

The effect of the first women's college as a force for higher education elsewhere in Wisconsin is evident in the story of one of its first students, Lucy Huntington Fallows of Marshall, the first woman faculty member at a coeducational campus from its founding in Trempealeau County in 1859. Galesville University endured for eighty years, although always small, sectarian, and "perpetually struggling to survive," according to a historian. As "preceptress" of a "preparatory and normal department" for teacher training, she supervised a majority of students, since most were women. However, when the other faculty member — her fiancé — went to war, she went home. "Her professional career began and ended at Galesville University," according to the account, although she would remain active in campus life as a university president's wife.[5]

A significant force for women's education that historians often neglect came from those who chose careers of faith over raising families: women religious. First in Wisconsin were the Daughters of Charity, as Sisters Mary Simeon Burns, Mary Ann Paul, and Mary Ann Frances Flanley arrived in 1846 to found Milwaukee's first parish school and orphanage. Sisters Mary Sarah Ann Butler, Mary Agnes Felicitas Delone, Mary Bernard Gavin, and Mary Agnes O'Connor followed in 1848 to found the new state's first hospital, St. John's Infirmary, just before cholera epidemics swept the fast-growing harbor city in 1849 and 1850. Soon, a Milwaukee minister felt moved to import Lutheran Deaconesses as nurses for another hospital — "a hospital in this city under Protestant influence," he said.[6]

Other orders followed on the Wisconsin frontier, where some found uncommon freedom for any women. Also in 1848, Dominicans — Sisters Seraphine (Mary) McNulty, Ermeline (Mary) Routane, Mary Ignatia (Mary) Fitzpatrick, and Prioress Clara (Margaret) Conway — won a legislative charter for a girls' secondary school in southwestern Wisconsin. However, they first had housekeeping duty for priests and professors at a Catholic boys' academy. Finally, after five years, they and other sisters sent to Sinsinawa were freed to open St. Clara Female Academy in 1853. They also won considerable autonomy from male supervision with freedom from diocesan control, from wearing white habits easily soiled on the frontier, even from taking the sacraments amid a local parish controversy. They especially exercised academic freedom from standard girls' curricula then, and their rigorous schooling attracted students from as far as New York and California. The sisters became best-known for coursework in natural sciences from astronomy and botany to chemistry and physiology. Their well-equipped laboratories attracted envious faculty from the state university at Madison that still lacked legislative funding for similar facilities in the 1850s. By then, some St. Clara graduates had taken vows and already were teachers furthering girls' education elsewhere.[7]

Also in southwestern Wisconsin in the 1850s, the School Sisters of Notre Dame opened another girls' academy later called Mount Mary College upon its move near their Milwaukee motherhouse, founded in 1851 by a twenty-six-year-old immigrant from Bavaria, Mother Mary Caroline (Josephine) Friess. Not all orders succeeded so well; Irish Brigidines began a school in Kenosha but soon returned to their homeland, turning the school over to the Notre Dames, the order that became dominant in religious education by serving several thousand students statewide, no matter their ethnicity. Other orders also were brought by ethnic groups for their own schools, as in Polonia, which imported the first Polish nuns in the country, the Franciscan Sisters of St. Felix, to serve in the small town that became the largest rural Catholic parish in the state.[8]

No force for advanced education for women — or for every other reform, from abolition to woman suffrage — would be as formidable as Mathilde Franziska Anneke of Milwaukee, an immigrant "free-thinker" who fled Germany after the failed revolution of 1848. Lillian Krueger's brief biography in this chapter begins to do justice to a woman who carried her crusade for justice across an ocean. Anneke's early works in Germany influenced Susan B. Anthony, and her later journalistic efforts brought a boycott by male printers who founded the city's first union — the men who thus also made her, if inadvertently, the mother of Milwaukee's labor movement. However, the men could not silence her and apparently were only an annoyance to Anneke. She continued her campaign in print and on the podium in the East, then served as a Civil War correspondent, and later came back to Milwaukee to found a counterpart to Lucy Seymour Parsons's female seminary. Anneke's academy for German American girls eventually would merge with Wisconsin's first women's college, but few Milwaukeeans remembered her by then, according to a newspaper account. However, "gray-haired Milwaukee women" among her graduates would "look upon all questions of human rights with the independence of thought and the insistence upon exact justice" — and "exacting discipline" — of their "fiery" first teacher, "Madame Anneke."[9]

Another German exile emigrated with her "free-thinking" husband, a hero of the failed revolution, and she eventually established a new form of education for children in America that was even more significant than his far better-known accomplishments in politics. Margarethe Meyer studied early childhood education in Hamburg and also assisted a sister-in-law in founding the first kindergarten in London, where she met and married Carl Schurz. They settled in 1856 in Wisconsin, where his swift rise in reform politics led to a nomination for lieutenant governor in 1857. The next year, she founded the first kindergarten in America, mainly for their daughter, on the model she had learned in Hamburg. However, owing to nativism, her husband lost his bid for office by a narrow margin. They moved again, and she never taught again. She followed him for the rest of her brief life, as he became prominent in Republican Party politics, held newspaper positions in several cities, served as a general in the Civil War and as a senator from Missouri in Washington, D.C., where Margarethe Meyer Schurz died.[10]

A force for women's education in Wisconsin in later decades, Dr. Laura Ross, arrived in Milwaukee in the late 1850s as the state's first woman physician — and only the third in the country. The first, Elizabeth Blackwell, had graduated in New York less than a decade before, in 1849, after refusing the school's suggested subterfuge that she assume male disguise. Ross had attempted to enroll at Harvard University for an undergraduate degree but was allowed only independent studies with individual professors willing to prepare her for medical school. She then was denied admittance to medical schools until one of the first for women opened in Philadelphia. After her graduation and migration west, men again denied her membership, this time in the Milwaukee Medical Society, for more than a decade. However, Ross built a successful practice specializing in health care for women and children while also building a network of pioneering women in the professions, such as Anneke, who would work together for other women after the Civil War.[11]

The importance of education to women across Wisconsin, immigrant or American-born, is evident in two stories in this chapter from the southwestern area, where Elizabeth Moore Wallace from Eire and Southerner Letitia Abbott Wall settled. They seemingly had little in common; women of Wallace's clan were pipe-smokers, while Wall maintained the manners of one to a Southern manor born. Yet the women of Irish Hollow and Wall all were weavers who worked to support their families' farming — or, in Wall's case, her shiftless husband's fishing and drinking. Interwoven in the fabric of the women's far different daily lives were their intellectual lives, whether in Wallace's schoolhouse or in Wall's home, where she held "political conversations."

Politics intruded into the lives of other schoolgirls and women in Wisconsin in the years leading to the Civil War. At the platting of Platte River Diggings arose a community with an unusual academy, not only coeducational but also open to students of color. However, by the mid-1850s, Platteville Academy dismissed an African American girl after "threats on the part of southern students" from southwestern Wisconsin, recalled onetime student Maria Greene Douglass. A principled teacher stood up to the principal and trustees, which Douglass later recalled as "one of the most valuable object lessons" of her life. In Milwaukee, women and girls of the Free Congregational Church's Sunday school helped to hide a fugitive under the pulpit. In Bristol, the second husband of former schoolteacher Lemira Tarbell Fowler Kellogg turned her deceased first husband's academy into a tavern where she "warmed and fed" and hid fugitives in her "cellar kitchen" while schooling them for freedom.[12]

In Janesville, Augusta Tallman's girlhood diary hints that her home — where presidential candidate Abraham Lincoln stayed in 1859 — also served as another station on the Underground Railroad. Her father, a militant abolitionist, had moved his family from the East to the Wisconsin town, which had a reputation for reform. Their residence, the most costly in the state, was a stately Italian-style villa with central heating, gas lighting, and even an indoor privy. Even more unusual were a "stained-glass window which signaled to fugitive slaves" with a warning or welcome and a secret staircase that led to an attic hideaway with a trapdoor to a rooftop cupola for surveillance — or for escape to the Rock River below.[13]

However, some girls in Wisconsin grew up a world away from issues of slavery and the sectional conflict in the country. In the northwestern wilderness of Dunn County, even the Civil War "seemed far away from Wisconsin" and especially "remote to the children," writes author Carol Ryrie Brink in her classic book, *Caddie Woodlawn*. In the fictionalized account of the "tom boy" girlhood of her grandmother, Caroline Woodhouse Watkins, the slow postal service on the frontier still meant that pioneer families received infrequent "news from the outside" world.[14]

Others escaped to the otherworldly rituals of Spiritualism in Wisconsin in the 1850s. In her account excerpted in this chapter, Mary Farrell Bednarowski suggests that Spiritualists rejected organized religions of the time — a time of schism, North from South, in many faiths over the issue of slavery. They placed their faith, instead, in bizarre "rappings and taps" from beyond, communicated by famous clairvoyants including a Lake Mills girl, Cora L. V. Scott. Among the best-known believers was a Wisconsin girl who grew up near Westport to become one of America's best-loved poets, Ella Wheeler Wilcox; she penned "a particularly poignant expression" of Spiritualists' "longing for certainty" — and for loved ones lost to the "other side."

Wilcox's poetry took her far from her impoverished world in rural Wisconsin. Born in 1850 in a crossroads called Johnstown Center and raised in the town of Token Creek, she wrote in a "lean-to" on the family's log house where she recalled "looking out of my little north window with hope" when "everything went wrong with everybody at home, and all my manuscripts came back." She realized her hopes at the age of eighteen, with publication in a national magazine. However, an eastern editor ridiculed her work as popular, not literary; later critics also disparaged her poems as sentimental and stereotypical portrayals of women who aspired to no more than housewifery and motherhood.[15]

Wilcox's voice shifted as she vowed never to marry and self-published her collection called *Poems of Passion* after warnings that "a single woman" would not write "such poems" in her frank, fearless, female voice. Wilcox replied that she would not wait "to hide behind a marriage ring or a tomb" to write as she felt, a feminist sentiment that found a surprising source of support when a Milwaukee newspaperwoman, Harriet Barker "Ma" Cramer, helped Wilcox to win coverage in the *Journal*.[16] Publicity — and sales surpassing sixty thousand copies — made Wilcox a cause célèbre, and caused a publisher to take her book in 1883. Wilcox left Wisconsin for New York City, where even cosmopolitan urbanites found the woman from rural Wisconsin "eccentric" for wearing "flowing Greek robes," penning poems that the *Times* called "songs of half-tipsy wantons," and promoting Spiritualism as editor of *New Thought* magazine.[17]

However, Wilcox endeared herself to a wider public with enduring lines such as those opening "Solitude" that were inspired, she said, by the sorrowful spirit and mien of a young Madison widow: "Laugh, and the world laughs with you;/Weep, and you weep alone." Wilcox did not remain alone, and a biographer writes that "her ideas about women's lot had become less rosy" after marriage. Wilcox remained committed to her writing, with almost two dozen volumes of poetry and novels in a nearly forty-year career. To the end of her life, she also remained faithful to a Spiritualist philosophy of life and afterlife, far from the practicalities of rural life in Wisconsin. In her last letter, Wilcox wrote that she was "getting rid of old Karma" and "looked to Nirvana." After her death, letters went to her brother in Westport from her admirers who enclosed alleged "poetry that Mrs. Wilcox dictated from beyond the grave." He scoffed that the "screeds" had "helped to kindle fire in our kitchen stove."[18]

Other Spiritualists included respected Wisconsin women and men whose "longing for certainty" was understandable in uncertain times, when they sought answers in immutable laws of science instead of the laws of men that all too often led to war. Others sought political answers in the new Republican Party — attributed by some historians to origins in Ripon in 1854 — that rallied many men and boys to local militia, sometimes with tragic result that altered Wisconsin history. In the histrionics of the 1860 presidential campaign on the eve of the Civil War, Wisconsin's governor questioned the loyalty of an Irish militia in Milwaukee. The men responded with a political outing and fund-raising trip on a ship that went down on the shore of Evanston, Illinois. In the worst loss of life on the Great Lakes in the nineteenth century, the sinking of the *Lady Elgin* drowned as many as four hundred passengers and crew, primarily Irishmen. The disaster widowed hundreds of immigrant women, left more than a thousand children fatherless, and forever altered Milwaukee's ethnic future. When word reached its predominantly Irish Third Ward, wrote a reporter, "little crowds of women were congregated along the walks, some giving free expression to their grief, others offering condolence," as "sounds of mourning proceeded from every third house." A third of Irish residents lost a relative, and they never recovered their earlier, more sizeable proportion of the population in the city.[19]

More often, militiamen and boys waved the flag in torchlight processions through Wisconsin towns to display their parties' prowess while women watched. In an era when many women were proscribed from public demonstrations, the meaning of politics to women without political power is difficult to determine. In her reminiscences in this chapter, Sabra Warner Lewis Smith recalls her girlhood in Windsor, where she participated in parades and sang patriotic songs, but primarily watched from the sidelines of politics as her brother and other boys waved the flags that women had sewn.

However, the war also meant educational opportunity for Sabra Warner. When men and boys enlisted in the military, the University of Wisconsin enlisted women students to bolster enrollment. Fifteen years after its founding, the university admitted women at last, although only in teacher training at first, and then in a segregated "Female College." From her "schoolgirl's point of view," she recalls a campus where women students were not welcomed. Nor were faculty wives, as Margaret Allen writes in her reminiscence also included in this chapter. However, both turned their experiences into working for educational opportunities for other women, elsewhere in the state and at the state university.

Some Wisconsin women also found their first opportunity for direct political participation during the Civil War by petitioning Congress to abolish slavery. Women collected four hundred thousand signatures nationwide in a campaign that commenced despite the objection of a Madison woman at a national meeting of "Loyal Leagues" in New York City. She argued that organizers Susan B. Anthony and Elizabeth Cady Stanton actually had a hidden objective of women's rights, "a purely political matter" that was "obnoxious to the people" in her state. However, more than four thousand Wisconsinites, primarily women, signed on in the first "Prayer of One Hundred Thousand," followed by many more.[20]

Uncounted thousands of women on the Wisconsin home front also worked for wartime wounded, widows, and orphans through soldiers' aid societies to fill needs neglected by the government, from sewing kits to bandages. The first society in Wisconsin, in Milwaukee in 1861, soon organized statewide to improve distribution of soldiers' supplies and provide work for war widows and orphans; state women then allied nationwide with Northern women's Sanitary Commission. Women also raised funds with their customary bake sales and craft fairs but on a grander scale by contributing to a series of fund-raising fairs in Chicago. The first, in 1863, was the most massive and successful such event ever seen, attracting sixty thousand including a Fort Atkinson editor who reported to readers that Wisconsin women's work was a favorite of the Chicago Sanitary Fair. Their booth, established by immigrant Eliza Nebel Salomon of Milwaukee, the governor's wife, featured ethnic handicrafts from German women whose work alone raised $6,000 toward a total of $80,000 for the "boys in blue."[21]

The remarkable courage and capabilities of Wisconsin's best "sanitary agent" and best-known war widow, Cordelia A. Perrine Harvey, are memorialized here by Patricia A. Harrsch. The Harvey Hospital and the Soldiers' Orphans' Home in Madison owed their existence — as did many veterans and orphans — to the former first lady of the state, whose husband had died during his term as governor while investigating southern hospitals housing Wisconsin soldiers. She took up his task. Then, as she said, "with an intense feeling that something must be done," Harvey went to the White House to take President Lincoln to task, telling him that the men "must have northern air or die." Persistently, she returned for four days, finally winning approval for Harvey Hospital.[22]

The war's suffering did not end in 1865 for wounded veterans or war widows and orphans — or for the women who took charge of their care for two more years. Milwaukee women continued to care for more than thirty-one thousand men, making do in makeshift Water Street storefronts in 1865, until Lydia Ely Hewitt and her "Lady Managers" held a ten-day Milwaukee Sanitary Fair and raised almost $140,000 for a Wisconsin Soldiers' Home. The federal government finally took responsibility in 1867, taking the land that the "Lady Managers" had purchased with proceeds from their fair for one of only three national veterans' hospitals, in Milwaukee, where long rows of white gravestones still stand. By then, Madison's Harvey Hospital had closed. However, as almost half of Wisconsin's men had gone to war, and many husbands and fathers had not returned, Harvey persuaded politicians to turn the site into a state Soldiers' Orphans' Home and then served as its first superintendent, a story excerpted in this chapter.[23]

By 1868, after twenty years of statehood and years of service to men who went to war — as well to widows and orphans — Wisconsin women still had few of the rights demanded in the "Declaration of Sentiments at Seneca Falls" in 1848. Drafted by Elizabeth Cady Stanton, a judge's daughter who witnessed his inability to help women abused by both their husbands and the law, the document listed dozens of wrongs to be righted. Laws deprived women of their own property and required taxation without representation; laws degraded women in divorce; and laws denied them access to their children, to higher education, and to profitable professions.[24]

Above all, laws denied women political power to change the law. Two decades after the Seneca Falls convention, the first serious effort in Wisconsin for woman suffrage arose in Janesville, where an assemblyman called a suffrage convention after securing legislative support. He was not reelected, and legislators rejected the bill to amend the state constitution in 1868.[25]

In a far worse setback for women's rights nationwide, men from ratifying states amended the U.S. Constitution after the war, with the Fourteenth and Fifteenth Amendments, to include the word "male" for the first time. Women had hoped to work for the courts to construe the Constitution as not explicitly excluding them. Now, they would have to work for another amendment to the Constitution for woman suffrage — an amendment they optimistically called the "Sixteenth." Nationwide and in Wisconsin, women would begin anew in 1869 to work for their rights — and on their own, with the organizational expertise and experience that they had gained in reform work and in wartime relief work in the decades before.[26]

## NOTES

1. Richard N. Current, *HOW,* vol. 2, *The Civil War Era, 1848–1873* (Madison: SHSW, 1976), 40; Alice E. Smith, *HOW,* vol. 1, *From Exploration to Statehood* (Madison: SHSW, 1973), 680.

2. Current, *HOW,* 72, 76, 80–82.

3. Ibid., 123.

4. "Immigrant Letters," *WMH* 20, no. 4 (June 1937): 438–441.

5. Karel D. Bicha, "Professor, Preceptress, and Pupil: Academic Life at Galesville University, 1859–1960," *WMH* 73, no. 4 (Summer 1990): 274–286. Other sources state that she came from a family of educators, including a brother who became president of Boston University, and that she died in 1916, preceding her husband, a Methodist bishop who held several prominent positions, including the presidency of Illinois Wesleyan University. See "Bishop Fallows, Oldest Badger Graduate, Dead," *Baraboo News,* September 6, 1922; "Methodist Church, City Started in Same Year," *Capital Times,* December 30, 1928; Reuben Gold Thwaites, ed., *The University of Wisconsin; Its History and Its Alumni* (Madison: Purcell, 1900), 436.

6. Brenda W. Quinn and Ellen D. Langill, *Caring for Milwaukee: The Daughters of Charity at St. Mary's Hospital* (Milwaukee: Milwaukee Publishing, 1998), 18–24; Ellen D. Langill, *A Tradition of Caring: The History of Milwaukee's Three Primary Service Hospitals* (Milwaukee: Sinai-Samaritan Hospitals, 1999), 18, 50–51.

7. Christine Johnston-Buer, "The Sinsinawa Dominican Sisters and St. Clara Academy: Female Leaders Promoting Secondary Education for Females in Wisconsin, 1850–1900," University of Wisconsin-Milwaukee, unpublished paper in the editor's possession.

8. Sister Mary Hester Valentine, *Mother Caroline and the Higher Education of Women* (Milwaukee: Mount Mary College, 1992), 1–11; Grace McDonald, *History of the Irish in Wisconsin in the Nineteenth Century* (New York: Arno, 1976), 50–53, 220–224, 247–257; Peter Leo Johnson, "Unofficial Beginnings of the Milwaukee Catholic Diocese," *WMH* 23, no. 1 (September 1939): 1–16; see also Sister Florence Jean Deacon, "Handmaids or Autonomous Women: Charitable Activities, Institution-Building, and Communal Relationships of Catholic Sisters in Nineteenth-Century Wisconsin" (doctoral dissertation, University of Wisconsin-Madison, 1989).

9. "Mathilde Franziska Giesler Anneke (1817–1884)," in E. T. James, Janet Wilson James, and Paul S. Boyer, eds., *Notable American Women: A Biographical Dictionary, Vol. 1* (Cambridge: Belknap, 1971), 50–51; Thomas W. Gavett, "Early Unions in Milwaukee," in Darryl Holter, ed., *Workers and Unions in Wisconsin: A Labor History Anthology* (Madison: SHSW, 1999), 14; "Early German Women," June 6, 1897, and Irene Norman, "National Honor Sought for Madam Anneke," April 27, 1930, both in the *Milwaukee Sentinel.*

10. Elizabeth Jenkins, "How the Kindergarten Found Its Way to America," *WMH* 14, no. 1 (September 1930): 48–62.

11. Cathy Luchetti, *Medicine Women: The Story of Early American Women Doctors* (New York: Crown, 1998), 19–21; Dennis H. Phillips, "Women in Nineteenth-Century Wisconsin Medicine," *Wisconsin Medical Journal* 71 (November 1972): 13–18.

12. Smith, *HOW,* 589; Maria Greene Douglass, "Personal Recollections of Platteville," *WMH* 6, no. 1 (September 1922): 59–60; "Wisconsin Women Honor Their Aged Champion," *Milwaukee Journal,* October 3, 1920; Helen McVicar, "Some Pioneer Settlers of Kenosha County," *WMH* 18, no. 4 (June 1935): 398–399; "The Annual Festival of the Old Settlers," *Kenosha Courier,* August 23, 1888.

13. Rachel Salisbury, "1860 — The Last Year of Peace: Augusta Tallman's Diary," *WMH* 44, no. 2 (Winter 1960–61): 85, 90; see also Julia Hornbostel, *A Good and Caring Woman: The Life and Times of Nellie Tallman* (Lakeville, MN: Galde Press, 1996). The Lincoln-Tallman House now is a museum operated by the Rock County Historical Society.

14. Carol Ryrie Brink, *Caddie Woodlawn* (New York: Macmillan, 1935), 15, 21. Born in Boston in 1853, Woodhouse lived in Wisconsin from to 1857 to 1865. Her homestead, near Menomonie, now is in Caddie Woodlawn Historical Park, operated by the Dunn County Historical Society.

15. "Childhood Home of Ella Wheeler Wilcox," *Capital Times,* December 26, 1903.

16. Mrs. William E. Cramer, "Tells Beginnings of Noted Poet," *Milwaukee Journal,* n.d., 1919. Born to an Irish immigrant mother and a pioneering settler in Packwaukee, Cramer began her newspaper career as a proofreader in 1864, when few women were in Milwaukee composing rooms. She married the publisher,

thirty years her senior and deaf and blind, and became a leading art patron in the city, clubwoman, and suffragist. Widowed in 1901, she was president of the *Evening Wisconsin* until 1918, when it became part of the *Wisconsin News,* later bought by the *Milwaukee Journal.* In 1997, she was posthumously inducted into the Milwaukee Press Club Hall of Fame. See John Goadby Gregory, "Career of Pioneer Newspaper-woman," *Milwaukee Sentinel,* n.d., 1922; Robert W. Wells, *The Milwaukee Journal: An Informal Chronicle of Its First 100 Years* (Milwaukee: Milwaukee Journal, 1981), 71–72.

17. Jenny Ballou, *Period Piece: Ella Wheeler Wilcox and Her Times* (Boston: Houghton Mifflin Co., 1940), passim.

18. Ibid.; "Brother of Ella Wheeler Wilcox, Aged 86, Disagrees With Sister's Statements," *Wisconsin State Journal,* March 4, 1923.

19. Current, *HOW,* 277–281; Kathleen Neils Conzen, *Immigrant Milwaukee, 1836–1860: Accommodation and Community in a Frontier City* (Cambridge: Harvard University Press, 1976), 171–172; *Milwaukee Sentinel,* September 10, 1860.

20. Elizabeth Cady Stanton, Susan B. Anthony, and Matilda Joslyn Gage, eds., *History of Woman Suffrage,* vol. 2 (Rochester, NY: Susan B. Anthony, 1881), 57–66, 78–80.

21. Current, *HOW,* 392–394; Nancy Greenwood Williams, *First Ladies of Wisconsin: The Governors' Wives* (Kalamazoo, MI: Ana Publishing, 1991), 57–58.

22. Cordelia A. P. Harvey, "A Wisconsin Woman's Picture of President Lincoln," *WMH* 1, no. 3 (March 1918): 233–235.

23. Current, *HOW,* 334–335; Ethel Alice Hurn, *Wisconsin Women in the War Between the States* (Wisconsin History Commission, 1911), 173–174. The hospital, then a mile west of Milwaukee, now is the Zablocki Veterans' Affairs Medical Center, next to Wood National Cemetery, both on the city border.

24. Elizabeth Cady Stanton, Susan B. Anthony, and Matilda Joslyn Gage, eds., *History of Woman Suffrage,* vol. 1 (Rochester, NY: Susan B. Anthony, 1881), 67–74.

25. Current, *HOW,* 531–532.

26. Eleanor Flexner, *Century of Struggle: The Woman's Rights Movement in the United States,* rev. ed. (Cambridge: Harvard University Press, 1975), 146–150.

# Married Women's Property Rights in Wisconsin, 1846–1872

## CATHERINE B. CLEARY

*WMH* 78, No. 2 (Winter 1994–1995): 110–137

*By marriage, the husband and wife are one person in law; that is, the very existence of the woman is suspended during marriage, or at least is incorporated and consolidated into that of the husband. . . . —*WILLIAM BLACKSTONE, *COMMENTARIES ON THE LAWS OF ENGLAND*

*Marriage is the slavery of woman. Marriage does not differ, in any of its essential features, from chattel slavery. The slave's earnings belong to the master, the earnings of the wife belong to the husband. The right of another to claim one's earnings, constitutes one a slave.* —FRANCIS BARRY, *THE LILY* (1855)[1]

The common law, as set forth by the great English jurist William Blackstone (1723–1780), gave the husband control of his wife's personal property, tangible and intangible (including her earnings), and gave him the right to manage her real estate and receive the rents and profits for the duration of the marriage or, if a living child was born of the marriage, for his life. As a result, creditors of a husband could reach the wife's assets to satisfy their claims. English common law became law in the American colonies and, following the Revolution, in the United States and the Northwest Territory.

Beginning about 1835, various states began to pass laws recognizing a married woman's right to her own separate property which she owned at the time of marriage or which was given to her thereafter for her own use.[2] In some states, such provisions were proposed for state constitutions. Wisconsin's activities in this area were part of a national trend, but Wisconsin laws — and the debates on them — tell us about the legal and social status of women in the Territory and in the early days of statehood. They also tell us about how little Wisconsin women were involved at that time in political activity affecting them and their rights.

These early laws were not designed to enhance married women's rights but rather to provide relief from the common law which permitted a husband's creditors to reach his wife's property to satisfy his debts. The legislative and constitutional battles were fought by men with varying personal and economic interests — by lawyers seeking to protect creditors' rights and prevent fraud, by fathers seeking to protect their daughters' inheritances, by husbands perhaps ambivalent as to the impact of the legislation on their credit and their families' security but fearful of its impact on their patriarchal status. Only a few men spoke in terms of justice, and women were not yet ready to speak in their own behalf. . . .

At the risk of pointing out the obvious, it should be noted that all women did not suffer under a legal disability in the ownership of property. Unmarried women — widowed, divorced, or never married — had the same property rights as men. Early European travelers in America reached "the puzzled conclusion that American society tolerates considerable freedom for American women before marriage . . . but that this freedom vanished once women entered the married state."[3]

The question of married women's property rights first arose in Wisconsin in the constitutional convention of 1846, ten years after the issue was first raised in New York.[4] Thomas Hertell, a member of the New York legislature, had raised the issue in 1836, and the following year introduced a bill which Sarah Hale endorsed in *Godey's Lady Book*, declaring that common law "degrades the woman to the condition of the slave. . . ."[5]

Mississippi passed one of the first married woman's property acts in 1839. . . .[6] In 1845 the constitution that Texas adopted . . . contained a provision on the separate property of married women which affected what Wisconsin did the following year. . . .

In 1846, public opinion in the Territory of Wisconsin had solidified in support of statehood, and Governor Henry Dodge called a convention to form a constitution. . . . The convention consisted of 125 white male delegates. . . .

While the subject of married women's property rights was put on the agenda early in the Wisconsin convention, the committee on miscellaneous provisions did not report on it [for six weeks]. . . .[7]

[One] speaker was Edward G. Ryan, a delegate from Racine County who later attained prominence as chief justice of the Wisconsin Supreme Court. His was the most powerful statement against the first section of the bill. The Madison *Argus* reported:

> Mr. Ryan opposed the section because it was contrary to the usages and customs of society, to the express commands of the Bible that "they twain shall be one flesh": because it would encourage men to be fraudulent by secreting their property under the cover of the wife's name, and because the provision if adopted will lead the wife to become a speculator, and to engage in all the turmoil and bustle of life, liable to sue and be sued, and thereby destroy her character of a wife. . . .[8]

William Rudolph Smith, a highly respected delegate from Iowa County, expressed doubt that the section would have the demoralizing effect Ryan described, and he characterized existing law "as a remnant of the feudal system, which ought to be abolished, and the sooner the better." He introduced a simplified first section which was approved. . . .

On December 7 the article came up for a third reading. . . . Marshall Strong, a member of the Racine County delegation who had been active in the debates on the draft, took the floor to deliver a strong speech against the article as it stood and the nature of the debates on it. . . . [H]e said, "If this shall become a part of the constitution, a sense of duty will compel me to oppose the whole instrument with my utmost zeal."[9]

David Noggle, a Democratic delegate from Rock County and one of the intellectual leaders of the convention, replied to Strong's speech at some length. . . . Noggle was aggressive in his defense of the married woman's rights section, charging Strong with basing his argument on the assumption "that females, that wives are common combinations of fraud, deception and dishonesty."[10]

The convention . . . clear[ed] the way for approving the article, and that night Marshall Strong resigned as a delegate. One historian has said, "His secession marks the open split in his party in the territory, and so far as the constitution is concerned is the beginning of the end."[11]

The emotion and indeed bitterness of the public debate is evident in the comment made by the *Milwaukee Sentinel and Gazette,* a Whig paper, on a Democratic caucus held on a Sunday evening to prepare for a vote on the article: "The article itself is a disgrace to our territory, and perhaps it is proper that it should be caucused into being by a violation of the laws of God — an outrage upon the moral sense of the community.". . .[12]

. . . Near the end of the convention, a delegate from Waukesha County praised the constitution as a whole but continued, "there is one article which upsets the whole — that on the rights of married women." As one historian of the convention has written, "His constituents were not willing to leave established ways, and the old common law, and strike into an unknown area.". . .[13]

When the territorial legislature convened in January of 1847, it too debated the merits of the constitution. Public opinion indicated that the draft was in trouble, so, to keep statehood on a timetable that would allow Wisconsin citizens to vote in the 1848 presidential election, a resolution was introduced in the council (the upper chamber of the legislature) providing for a new constitutional convention if the draft was defeated by the voters in April. This gave rise to a heated debate not only on the strategy but also on the merits of the document.

On February 5, Marshall Strong, who was recognized as the leader of the opposition to the constitution, delivered a three-hour speech in the council in favor of the resolution for a new convention. . . . He described in emotional terms the impact that the freedom given a wife would have on her character and on her husband, her children and the home:

> Woman is to be transferred from her appropriate domestic sphere, taken away from her children, and cast out rudely into the strife and turmoil of the world, there to have her finer sensibilities blunted, the ruling motives of her mind changed, and every trait of loveliness blotted out. When the husband returns at night, perplexed with care, dejected with anxiety, depressed in hope, will he find, think you, the same nice and delicate appreciation of his feelings he has heretofore found? Will her welfare, and feelings, and thoughts, and interests be all wrapped up in his happiness, as they now are?

Strong pointed out that this provision came from the civil law and added, "It exists in France, and I will merely say that more than one-fourth of the children annually born in Paris are illegitimate.". . .[14]

Strong's speech received extensive press coverage, and it was printed in pamphlet form for distribution by the opponents of the constitution. . . .

A glance at the Wisconsin newspapers for the first three months of 1847 shows the tremendous interest in the constitution and the amount of activity for and against it. . . .

Milwaukee's leading Whig paper, the *Daily Sentinel and Gazette,* analyzed the positions taken on the constitution by territorial papers and letters written to them. It judged all Whig, independent, and abolitionist papers opposed and that three out of four individuals "utterly disapprove of the constitution." It also concluded that among Democrats in Milwaukee County, "the best men in the party are earnest and active in opposition."[15]

It is impossible in a few sentences to convey the vigor and emotion of the public debate on the article. . . . At a Whig meeting in Janesville, Edward V. Whiton, who later became chief justice of the Wisconsin Supreme Court, spoke against the constitution, dealing at length with the evils of creating separate interests between husband and wife: "Do you think, sir, that a woman immersed in business can bestow that care and attention upon her family which are so necessary to the comfort and even the existence of the home as we know it?" A Dane County meeting supporting the ratification of the constitution adopted a resolution which referred to the article providing the wife her separate property "in order to save her and her children, in the case of an unfortunate or dissolute husband, from want and starvation, and that this is in strict accordance with the principles of right and the honest dictates of humanity and mercy, which no honest man should either dread or fear.". . .[16]

On April 6, 1847, the voters of Wisconsin Territory rejected the constitution, 20,233 to 14,119.

A second convention to form a constitution was convened the following December. . . . The married women's property provision . . . was not included in the 1848 constitution and was considered by the convention very briefly only once . . . when a provision for married women's rights was offered as an amendment and was defeated 56 to 5. . . . [17]

One of the most notable features of the record of the forming of the constitutions of 1846 and of 1848 and the public debate on them is the complete absence of any participation by women or any indirect expression of their views. Warren Chase, a delegate from Fond du Lac County in both conventions [said] . . . :

> . . . The slavery of women was . . . even often approved and sustained by woman herself. How can she expect the "lords of creation" to give her her rights, when she does not ask for them?[18]

Even in New York, where women became active politically before they did in Wisconsin, women played a minor role in the debate on married women's property in the 1846 constitutional convention and the enactment of the first married women's property law in April, 1848.[19]

It was not until [three] months after the New York act became law, that Elizabeth Cady Stanton, Lucretia Mott and her sister Martha C. Wright, and Mary Ann McClintock . . . convened the convention in Seneca Falls, New York, which adopted the "Declaration of Sentiments" launching the women's rights movement in the United States. Among the facts listed in the Declaration to show that "the history of mankind is a history of repeated injuries and usurpations on the part of man toward woman, having in direct object the establishment of an absolute tyranny over her" were:

He has made her, if married, in the eyes of the law civilly dead.

He has taken from her all right in property, even to the wages she earns. . . . [20]

In Wisconsin, as in New York, after a married women's property provision was omitted from the state constitution, the legislature acted. Wisconsin became a state on May 29, 1848, and in the first session of the state legislature, on June 17, 1848, Senator Frederick W. Horn of Cedarburg introduced a bill "to provide for the protection of married women in the enjoyment of their own property.". . . On August 3, however, the bill was voted down, 14 to 5.[21]

The following year, Senator Horn again introduced his bill with the title "concerning the rights of married women." The bill passed the senate in spite of a little fooling around by the senators after the bill had passed. . . . Senator Alexander Botkin of Madison then moved an amendment to make the title read, "A bill to authorize married women to wear their husband's unmentionables." When this was defeated, senators Botkin and Henry Merrell of Portage voting for it, Senator Merrell then introduced an amendment to have the title read, "A bill to declare married women the head of the family." This amendment got three votes, Senator James Fisher of Crawford County joining Botkin and Merrell. In the assembly, however, the bill was defeated. Among those voting against it was Marshall Strong.[22]

In 1850 Senator Horn again introduced a bill "to provide for the protection of married women in the enjoyment of their property." . . . His bill passed. . . . Governor Nelson Dewey signed the bill on February 1, 1850. . . .

Why was Fred Horn of Cedarburg such an ardent champion of this bill? There is no clear answer to that question. . . .

But the most intriguing hint of a possible source of Horn's interest in this subject is that he was a cousin of Fritz Anneke, husband of Mathilde Franziska Anneke, the well-known radical and early feminist. When the Annekes fled Germany after the failure of the 1848 revolution, they came to Wisconsin at the insistence of Fred Horn. It is not impossible that in his correspondence with the Annekes while they were still in Germany, Horn became aware of Mathilde's growing feminism, which stemmed out of the struggle she had to gain custody of her daughter by her first marriage. In Germany she had published a book, *Woman in Conflict with Social Conditions*, which, according to one writer, "gained her a national reputation and was instrumental in changing some existing laws governing marriage and divorce."[23]

After the legislature enacted the 1850 law protecting married women's property, it came before the Wisconsin Supreme Court in a case in 1853. . . . [I]n its opinion, the court said:

The "act to provide for the protection of married women in the enjoyment of their own property," . . . certainly goes far towards clothing one class of females with strange and manly attributes; yet it is a meritorious statute, designed to remedy a supposed evil of the common law, and therefore it ought to be liberally construed.[24]

Three years later, the Wisconsin Supreme Court held that under the statute a married woman could not be sued on a promissory note she signed in payment for real estate. Holding that the statute did not give a married woman the same rights with respect to her separate property as a single woman, the court in an opinion by Chief Justice Whiton said:

> ... An unlimited power to sue and be sued, and to engage in trade and business on her own account possessed by the wife, would, if exercised, be destructive of domestic ties and entirely inconsistent with conjugal obligations.[25]

The 1850 law was an important advance for married women owning property, particularly in freeing them from the complexities of equitable arrangements. It did nothing, however, for married women whose only money was what they earned themselves. . . .

In an early case the Wisconsin Supreme Court applied the common law rule that a married woman's earnings belonged to her husband.[26] The Wisconsin legislature somewhat softened the harshness of the rule in 1855 by adding a section covering the case of "any married woman, whose husband, either from drunkenness, profligacy, or from any other cause, shall neglect or refuse to provide for her support, or for the support and education of her children, and any married woman who may be deserted by her husband." Any such woman was given the right to transact business in her own name, to collect her own earnings and the earnings of her minor children, and to use these earnings for the support of herself and for the support and education of her minor children, free from interference or control by her husband. . . . [27]

That the 1855 Wisconsin law offered only limited relief to married women was made clear. . . .

. . . [I]n 1863, the Wisconsin Supreme Court in *Elliot v. Bentley* subjected the earnings of a wife as a piano teacher to the claims of her husband's creditor, saying the wife's earnings, unlike her separate property, belonged to her husband and were liable for his debts. . . . [28] [T]he legislature did nothing for another nine years.[29]

At least part of the delay in legislation on wives' earnings was occasioned by the Civil War, when the efforts of feminists and other reformers were directed toward support of the war effort. After the war, and particularly after the exclusion of women from the Fifteenth Amendment to the Constitution, which gave black males the right to vote, women again turned their attention to their own rights. . . .

There is no record of Wisconsin women's advocacy of legislation to give married women control of their own earnings in the years preceding the 1872 law. Public opinion in Wisconsin was slow to accept the propriety of women speaking in public. . . .

No single strong female leader with an interest in the subject emerged, and the woman's rights movement was not as organized as it was in states like New York, Massachusetts, and Ohio. Nor did Wisconsin have a woman available to do the kind of organizing that Susan B. Anthony did in New York. Laura Ross (later Wolcott) was a key figure in the women's movement in Wisconsin for many years, but the demands of her medical practice undoubtedly restricted the time she had to give. While she appreciated the significance of property law, that was not her field. Dr. Wolcott wrote the chapter on the progress of women in Wisconsin for *The History of Woman Suffrage* (1882), and she gave a full account of Wisconsin legislation on married women's property rights from 1850 to 1878. But she made no mention of the involvement of any women — persuasive evidence that women were not involved.[30]

In February, 1869, the Wisconsin Woman Suffrage Association was formed in Milwaukee, and Elizabeth Cady Stanton, Susan B. Anthony, and Mary Livermore came to the city to speak at its convention. Afterward they went on to Madison, where Governor Lucius Fairchild introduced them at an evening session of the legislature. . . .[31]

The following year, in 1870, Mrs. Stanton returned to Wisconsin to speak at the meeting of the Equal Rights Association in Janesville. Lillie Peckham was also on the program, speaking on woman's work and wages.[32] It may be a coincidence, but in 1872 two legislators from Janesville introduced the bills which became the law giving women the control of their own earnings.

Senator Charles G. Williams of Janesville, son-in-law of David Noggle, who had been a vocal advocate of married women's property rights in the 1846 constitutional convention, introduced a bill in the senate "to enable married women to transact business, make contracts, sue and be sued, and to define the liabilities of husbands and wives, and enable them to testify in civil actions and proceedings." On the same day in the assembly, Alexander Graham of Janesville, whose temperance bill dominated that session of the legislature, introduced a bill "to relieve husbands from liability to pay their wife's ante nuptial debts, and to secure to wives their individual earnings.". . .[33]

The bill also incorporated a provision similar to the one in the 1846 constitution making married women responsible for their debts contracted before marriage. . . .

With passage of the 1872 law, the basic property rights of married women in Wisconsin were in place. . . .

It is hard to overstate the lack of personal dignity the common law [had] accorded married women. . . . Listen to the words of Mary Jones of Winnebago County, Wisconsin, testifying in 1865 in a suit in which she sought to get back, from her husband's creditor, property purchased in 1848 with what had been her money:

> My mother willed land in Wales to me; I sold it for about 500 sovereigns; bought the half section where we live [in Wisconsin] with the money. My husband got the deed for it. I let him have the money and he took title in his own name. I brought the money from Wales in my own trunk; he did not have it until he bought the land. I had no object in getting the land back except to have it go to my children in case of my death. . . . Good many women die in this country and if her husband should marry again, it would take the property away from her own children.

Under the common law, the court found that the money belonged to Mary's husband, and his creditor could therefore reach the land in which it was invested.[34]

In a similar case involving a widow seeking to get back from her husband's estate land purchased with money she had brought with her from Prussia, the court decided that she had no claim in equity — that getting a life estate in all of her husband's estate with the remainder going to his brothers and sisters was enough for her: "There is no pretense that such is not full and ample provision for her support and maintenance; being so, she has no ground of complaint."[35]

One final example: The Wisconsin Supreme Court, construing the 1855 law, rebuffed the efforts of a schoolteacher to collect her own wages. Evidence showed that her husband was "a careless manager, and was in debt and unable to supply the necessary wants of his wife." Nevertheless, the court held he was entitled to his wife's earnings, saying that to let her have them to support herself and her children would be a precedent under which "every poor and virtuous man who may be sick, or for any cause unable to work and provide his wife and children with necessaries, may be deprived entirely of their services, and of all control over them."[36]

Control was indeed the issue. The first laws were designed to protect a married woman's property, but the price was giving her some control over it. The constitutional debates of 1846–1847 showed that many men considered the price too high, that it threatened their status, their role in the family. . . .

Gradually, over time, the stereotypes began to break down. . . . By its actions between 1850 and 1872, the Wisconsin legislature opened the way for change for women and men, and it particularly helped married women on their road to being recognized as legitimate and respected participants in the economic life of family and community. Over time, in the eyes of the law, married women began to come alive.

A footnote to history: In 1984, a new generation of Wisconsin men and women decided to adopt a system of marital property based on a theory of marriage as "an economic partnership" and in part, ironically, on the civil law and the community property law of Texas and some other states. . . . [37]

The basis of this law is that each spouse has an equal obligation in accordance with his or her ability to contribute money or services to support the minor children or the other spouse. As the new law is careful to spell out: "Nothing in this chapter revives the common law disabilities on a woman's right to own, manage, inherit, transfer or receive gifts of property in her own name." The statutory treatment of earnings, however, is another matter altogether, for both wife and husband. Clearly, the vision of a wife as a dependent under the control of her husband, or as a "slave" whose earnings belong to another, and of married women as civilly dead in the eyes of the law, has been replaced by a new concept of the married woman as a partner of her husband — a partner endowed with new rights but also charged with new responsibilities.[38]

*Catherine B. Cleary made history herself as the first woman officer of the largest bank in the state, the First Wisconsin Trust Company, in 1949 — only two years after a senior partner of a large law practice in Milwaukee told her that the firm might find a place for her, if she would not see clients. Cleary became president of First Wisconsin Trust Company in 1969 and was the first woman to serve on boards of several major corporations in the country. She also has served as a mentor to many women, not only in her Milwaukee birthplace but nationwide.*

# NOTES

1. *Commentaries* (1765), Book I, Ch. XV; *The Lily,* July 15, 1855, . . . quoted in Ann Russo and Cheris Kramarae, eds., *The Radical Women's Press of the 1850s* (New York, 1991), 74–75.

2. For a discussion of this legislation, see Kay Ellen Thurman, "The Married Women's Property Acts" (master's thesis, University of Wisconsin, 1966).

3. Jill K. Conway, *The Female Experience in Eighteenth- and Nineteenth-Century America: A Guide to the History of American Women* (New York, 1982), 45, referring to Frances Wright, Harriet Martineau, and Alexis de Tocqueville.

4. . . . [See] *Wisconsin Revised Statutes, 1858,* Chapter 95, and *Wis. Stat. 1983–84,* Chapter 766.

5. [On Hale, see] Norma Basch, *In the Eyes of the Law: Women, Marriage and Property in Nineteenth Century New York* (Ithaca, 1982), 120.

6. Historians generally cite the Mississippi law as the first, but this may be partly a question of definition. See Richard H. Chused, "Married Women's Property Law: 1800–1850," in the *Georgetown Law Journal* 71 (1983): 1359, 1397–1400. . . .

7. Moses M. Strong, *History of the Territory of Wisconsin, from 1836 to 1848* (Madison, 1885), 524–525.

8. Milo M. Quaife, ed., *WHC* 27, Constitutional Series, *The Convention of 1846* (Madison, 1919), 631.

9. Ibid., 647. . . .

10. *Wisconsin Democrat* of January 2, 1847, quoted ibid., 662.

11. Frederic L. Paxson, "A Constitution of Democracy" in Milo M. Quaife, ed., *WHC* 26, Constitutional Series, *The Movement for Statehood, 1845–1846* (Madison, 1918), 30, 44.

12. *Milwaukee Sentinel and Gazette,* December 14, 1846.

13. Quaife, ed., *The Convention of 1846,* 702.

14. *Racine Advocate,* February 24 and March 3, 1847.

15. *Milwaukee Daily Sentinel and Gazette,* January 11, 1847.

16. Milo M. Quaife, ed., *WHC* 28, Constitutional Series, *The Struggle Over Ratification* (Madison, 1920), 590, 419, 366.

17. Milo M. Quaife, ed., *WHC* 29, Constitutional Series, *The Attainment of Statehood* (Madison, 1928), 840–841, 56, 179.

18. Warren Chase, *The Life-Line of the Lone One; or Autobiography of The World's Child* (3rd ed., Boston, 1865), 183–184. [On Chase and the Reformist community he represented, see "Women at Ceresco" in chapter 2.]

19. Several excellent books have been written on the history of the New York law on this subject. Peggy A. Rabkin, *Fathers to Daughters: The Legal Foundations of Female Emancipation* (Contributions in Legal Studies, no. 11, Westport, 1980). See also Basch, *In the Eyes of the Law,* and Stanton, Anthony, and Gage, eds., *History of Woman Suffrage,* vol. 1.

20. Stanton, Anthony, and Gage, *History of Woman Suffrage,* vol. 1, 70.

21. *Wisconsin Senate Journal* (1848), 311–313.

22. Ibid. (1849), 62, 303–305; *Wisconsin Assembly Journal* (1849), 371–374.

23. Steven M. Buechler, *The Transformation of the Woman Suffrage Movement: The Case of Illinois, 1850–1920* (New Brunswick, New Jersey, 1986), 60; "Biographical Notes in Commemoration of Fritz Anneke and Mathilde Franziska Anneke," by Henriette M. Heinzen in collaboration with Hertha Anneke Sanne (1940); . . . Mathilde Franziska Anneke to Franziska Hammacher, Milwaukee, April 3, 1850. . . . (The latter two items are in the Fritz and Mathilde Anneke Papers, WHS Archives.) . . .

24. *Norval v. Rice,* 2 Wis. 22 (1853), 31.

25. *Wooster v. Northrup et al.,* 5 Wis. 245, 255–6 (1856). Whiton had been an opponent of married women's property rights in the 1846 constitution.

26. *Connors v. Connors,* 4 Wis. 112 (1855). The wife earned money "by washing, house-cleaning and other hard labor at day's work." She invested her earnings in real estate. Her husband sold the property she bought, and the court held that she could not recover it because her earnings during marriage belonged to her husband in the absence of an agreement between them to the contrary.

27. *Laws of Wisconsin,* Chap. 49, sec. 1 (1855).

28. *Elliott v. Bentley,* 17 Wis. *591 (1863).

29. A related issue came before the Wisconsin Supreme Court several times and was decided on the same principle. These cases involved the right of the wife to recover damages for injuries she suffered through the negligence of another. The court held that she could not recover because "the time and services of the wife belong to the husband and for a loss of them he must sue alone." *Barnes v. Martin and another,* 15 Wis. *240 (1862)....

30. Elizabeth Cady Stanton, Susan B. Anthony, and Matilda Joslyn Gage, eds., *History of Woman Suffrage,* (Rochester, NY: 1882), vol. 3, 638–648. [On Dr. Laura Ross Wolcott, see Introduction to chapter 4.]

31. *Wisconsin State Journal,* February 27, 1869.

32. *Janesville Gazette,* March 17, 1870....

33. Bill 101 S; Bill 347A; Chap. 155, Laws of 1872....

34. Folio 8 of printed case and Appellants' brief in Folio 29, *Hamlin v. Jones,* 79 *Briefs and Cases* nos. 16 and 18 (Wisconsin Supreme Court Library).

35. *Fuss v. Fuss,* 24 Wis. 256 (1869).

36. *Edson v. Hayden,* 20 Wis. 682 (1866), 718.

37. Wis. Stat. Chapter 766.

38. Paper of Sen. Donald Hanaway, "An Overview of Wisconsin's Marital Property Reform," in *Marital Property Act: A Compilation of Materials* (Wisconsin Legislative Reference Bureau, Information Bulletin 84-1B-1, May, 1984).

# The Origins of Milwaukee College

LOUISE PHELPS KELLOGG

WMH 9, No. 4 (1925–1926): 385–408

# Milwaukee-Downer College Rediscovers Its Past

GRACE NORTON KIECKHEFER

WMH 34, No. 4 (Summer 1951): 210–214 and 241–242

The first college for women in Wisconsin intrigued historians including Louise Phelps Kellogg and Grace Norton Kieckhefer, both of whom contributed articles on its founding. Decades apart, their accounts differ owing to evidence discovered in the interim. Yet later evidence does not entirely eclipse earlier work. Both historians offer information and insights that are useful to current readers who may be less familiar with the era of separate schooling for women and men. Thus, this piece is a compilation of their articles on early secondary and higher education for women in Wisconsin.

"[S]chools and churches sprang up as if by magic" in Milwaukee by the time of Wisconsin's statehood, according to Louise Phelps Kellogg, although these were primarily private schools, usually separated by the sexes, until the first few public and coeducational grade schools were established in 1846. However, high school and "higher education for the West was a . . . problem," and Milwaukee parents had to "send their growing children from home, or to the private schools established under local auspices, most of which were of doubtful efficiency and uncertain tenure. One of the earliest of these private schools, and well taught while it lasted," according to Kellogg, advertised its offerings in 1841 as "ultimately designed for boys only, but females will be admitted during the first session"[1] — for economic reasons, apparently, until there were sufficient male students to support the school.

Fortunately, in 1841, the "rector of the Episcopal Society decided to supplement his small stipend by opening a school for young ladies and misses in his own home. The following year it was called the 'Milwaukee Female Academy.'"[2] And the following year, in 1843, feminist journalist Margaret Fuller visited from New York. She wrote, "this school was conducted by two girls of nineteen and seventeen years," daughters of the rector and "their pupils are nearly as old as themselves."[3] Sadly, the younger sister "suddenly died" the same year, writes Kellogg. "The school was kept up for several years by the older sister, and was one of the best of the small 'select schools' of the territorial times in Milwaukee."

Kellogg searched the Milwaukee press of the era and found a "surprising" number of "private ventures in education, as drawn from their advertisements in the local newspapers." Many were only for males, but "the 'Milwaukee Academy' . . . , for the education of young ladies and gentlemen, opened . . . in the yet unfinished Presbyterian Church" on the east side in 1843. Soon, a "Miss Calkins opened a select school for young ladies and misses on the west side, above the Union Temperance House," but only briefly, because a "notice of Miss Calkins' marriage the following June probably accounts for the cessation" of the school. Other schools for young women included a "vocal music school," which was conducted in 1846 by a busy "Mr. Dye, who had classes in Miss Jones's Ladies Seminary, Mrs. Taylor's and Mrs. Coe's select schools."[4]

Kellogg writes that "one of the best of the early private schools" was the coeducational Milwaukee Collegiate Institute, founded in 1848 but never chartered as a college despite its name. Despite its excellence, its "about one hundred and fifty students" never completed the promised four-year curriculum; its principal died, and "the school declined." By then, "the 'Spring Street Female Seminary' for the west side began in 1850 under the superintendence of the Misses Chamberlain and Ransom," and, "in 1851, Miss M. E. Kendall . . . opened a school in the basement of the Baptist Church," but both failed. "In addition to these personal ventures there were parochial schools for several churches," Kellogg writes. "Nevertheless, the school census continued to show that there were more children unschooled than were attending both the public and private schools combined."[5]

Elsewhere in the country, after "the famous Seneca Falls Convention" in 1848 — the first women's rights convention in upstate New York, which was called by Elizabeth Cady Stanton and others — women increasingly would "demand not only a share in the world's affairs, but a chance to educate themselves" by "opening the doors of the institutions of higher learning for the entrance of women." In 1833, women enrolled at Oberlin College in Ohio, as "especially in the West was the impulse strong," writes Kellogg — although in part because "where schools were few and needs great, it was economy to educate girls with boys, daughters with sons."

Elsewhere in Wisconsin, the first campuses founded in 1846 — Carroll College in Waukesha, then Beloit College — did not admit women, nor did the University of Wisconsin in Madison at its inception in 1848. But Lawrence College in Appleton "opened for both sexes" in 1849, only two years after its founding, with "the course for girls being the same as that for boys" — three girls and four boys in the first college class. As Appleton surpassed the state's largest city in progressive education, "it was time for Milwaukee to look to her laurels."

Fortuitously, Milwaukee already had become the new home of a woman educator who had earned her laurels in progressive educational institutions for women in the East. She came to Milwaukee after a group of abolitionists split from Immanuel Presbyterian and Plymouth Congregational churches in 1847, to form a Free Congregational Church, and they soon invited a minister from upstate New York as their second pastor. "With him came his wife, who a short time before had been Lucy Seymour of LeRoy Seminary" in New York, writes Kellogg.[6]

But Lucy Ann Seymour Parsons's part in founding the first college for women in Wisconsin long was neglected, with more credit accorded to its famous benefactor, Catharine E. Beecher. As later historian Grace Norton Kieckhefer writes, "the name of the redoubtable Catharine Beecher immediately comes to mind as the founding spirit of old Milwaukee College," because the campus benefited by association with one of the era's foremost educators, who also was the sister of author Harriet Beecher Stowe, and both descended from famous eastern preachers. "But had it not been for the earlier efforts of another progressive and equally valiant schoolmistress," Kieckhefer writes of Lucy Ann Seymour Parsons, "Miss Beecher might never have chosen Wisconsin as the locale for one of her experiments" in women's higher education.

Historians often portray Parsons as another of the series of women — and men — who opened schools in Milwaukee only as an interim employment, before women went on to wed and men went on to more lucrative work. However, Parsons advertised that she planned "a permanent institution of high order for the education of young ladies," writes Kellogg,[7] although Kieckhefer suggests that Parsons's "little flyer" for her first school in "a small frame building which stood at the rear of the Free Congregational Church lot," did not fully convey that "teaching was her chosen vocation" as a career educator. "She had taught with great success before her marriage," writes Kieckhefer, who found "old catalogs of Ingham University, a private seminary in LeRoy," which "revealed that Lucy Ann had taught there" prior to moving to Milwaukee — and she returned there later in life, long after her modest female seminary became Wisconsin's first women's college. Then or earlier, she even served as Ingham University's assistant principal.

Parsons "belonged in the East to a distinguished circle of progressive educators" well before she came to Wisconsin, writes Kieckhefer. She knew the "new methods" and "newest theories of the day" and knew the work of eastern educator Emma Willard — whose Troy Seminary in 1821 was the first high school-level education for American girls equivalent to that for boys. Because Parsons knew one of Beecher's brothers, she "may also have known Catharine Beecher personally before their Milwaukee meeting in the spring of 1850." As Kellogg writes, Parsons's school was influenced from the first "by the new movement in women's education that was being fostered" by Beecher.

Parsons also already knew her eventual successor in Milwaukee, Mary Mortimer, another admirer of Beecher's advancements in education for women. As Kellogg writes, Beecher "was one of the first women educators to promote physical culture for women; in a period when extreme delicacy and physical disabilities were assets rather than liabilities, she advocated reform in dress, in food, and in exercise." She promoted "a liberal education" to "precede or accompany teacher-training work" and "particularly desired to see what she called co-equal teachers; that is, a body of teachers organized on the plan of the faculty of a man's college, free from the necessity of propitiating either patrons or a supervising principal, deriving their support from some form of endowment that made possible a permanent tenure" — and women's freedom from men's supervision. She advocated "domestic economy" courses to train women as homemakers or teachers, which allowed study of science and other serious fields not offered in the typical "finishing schools" for wealthier women.

However, Mortimer had struggled financially to finish her education. An English immigrant to America as a child in 1821, Mortimer was orphaned when both of her parents died within a week, and she could not complete her studies because her oldest brother denied her inheritance for schooling. She attempted teaching at the age of sixteen. Five years later, as an adult, Mortimer started her secondary education. She eventually taught for ten years in New York, where she met Parsons.[8]

"Mary Mortimer . . . was a friend of long standing to Lucy Ann Parsons," Kieckhefer writes, as "it was in her early years at Ingham . . . that Mrs. Parsons had met" the woman who would be her better-known successor at the Milwaukee school, and "they had been fellow-teachers in [the] seminary in LeRoy, New York," before Parsons went west. In 1848, Mortimer was still at LeRoy, but she visited Milwaukee as soon as Parsons opened her seminary "and found [that] her friend" had "a very flourishing school" of "fifty scholars," writes Kellogg. In 1849, Mortimer moved west to Illinois, apparently awaiting an opening in Milwaukee, and wrote to another friend that Parsons was "progressing finely . . . [and] had more than eighty scholars at her last report to me."[9] By 1850, Mortimer "had been touring with Miss Beecher" in western states, seeking likely sites.

Mortimer "decided to remain in Milwaukee" when Beecher "accepted the invitation of Mrs. Parsons to explain her famous Plan to patrons of the Parsons seminary," Kieckhefer writes. Beecher also "offered to supply a library and scientific collection worth $1,000, and promised to return for the opening of the new school in the fall," and she "kept her promise and came again to Milwaukee early in September," writes Kellogg. But Beecher did not return, nor did easterners who pledged financial support keep their promises in later years owing to "trustees' reluctance to follow her plans to the letter" in "matters architectural" more than fiscal, which led to a "famous feud," according to Kieckhefer. But Beecher's early efforts meant that "Mrs. Parsons' seminary became in 1851 the Milwaukee Normal Institute and High School, with the high purpose of training teachers for the West." Because "the faculty disliked [Beecher's] 'high-falutin' name," Kieckhefer claims, the school soon became known as Milwaukee Female College, apparently even before the name became official in its legislative charter. Kellogg writes that the name apparently amused Mortimer, as "in a letter . . . she says, 'Have I not sent you word that we keep a Normal Institute and High School and not a Ladies' Seminary?'"[10]

Under any name, women teachers were underpaid and worked in overcrowded conditions. Mary Mortimer wrote in November 1850 that "our enterprise is young, is unappreciated. . . . It needs teachers who care for higher rewards than the salaries men can give." Kellogg reports that "the first annual catalogue of the new institution for 1850–51 shows an attendance of 188 pupils with a faculty of four regular teachers, Mrs. Parsons, Miss Mary Mortimer, Miss C. M. Moulton, and Miss E. B. Warner" and instructors in German and French, elocution, and music. However, their "higher rewards" happened "while still in the old Oneida Street house," when "the first class of two" — Mercelia V. Hatch and Maria S. Train — graduated in April 1851 "in the Free Congregational Church," since the school still lacked a facility sufficient for ceremonies.[11] As the first catalogue asked, "Why should not Female Institutions be as well officered and endowed as our colleges and in the same way?"[12]

Parsons's spouse, the Free Congregational Church pastor, had by then "returned with something over $2,000 in hand and promises of endowment for considerable sums" from "eastern friends of education." So "the trustees determined to build at once," Kellogg writes, and "adopted the plans for the building" from Beecher. The "school was housed in a building of her design," according to Kieckhefer, for "in her pamphlet of 1851, *An Appeal to Women in Their Own Behalf*, there is a picture of the building," which was "marked distinctly, 'Designed by the author.'" In 1850, Beecher "made her proposition to Milwaukee" — actually, "her speech was read for her," as she "declined to speak in public" — to fund her building plan. Men made pledges, and William Parsons "resigned his pastorate . . . to become the secretary and agent of the new school," according to Kellogg.

"Nor were the women ignored in this money-raising effort," Kellogg writes. In November 1851, "the daily press announc[ed] the formation of the Ladies' Educational Society of Milwaukee, . . . proclaiming its determination 'to make a strenuous effort to secure for our city a school of the highest order, for young ladies.'" The "record book" of "minutes of this organization" suggests "the spirit of sacrifice and the ingenuity exerted to raise funds for this first building for the college." First, "a 'Musical Festival or Soirée'" was "held in the Masonic Hall and netted $115.36 for the fund." Then "the proposal was made 'to induce members to take subscription papers for the collection of $1.00 or less from cash subscribers,'" which raised $89.32. Then "a resolution was passed asking a concert company to give a performance for their fund," which "brought in $85.80."

By 1853 the "building was erected by Milwaukee citizens at an expense of $5,740," writes Kellogg, who describes Beecher's design as a "curious pseudo-Gothic building, adorned with pinnacles and quaint battlements." But Mortimer wrote, "Our building is very beautiful and commodious."[13] Beecher had sought $10,000 from Milwaukeeans, who faced many needs in building a new city. As "one of the trustees wrote to her" from Milwaukee, "*the money is not here.*" However, Beecher also did not keep a promise from her American Women's Educational Association of $60,000 in endowment funds "to supplement the salaries of the teachers." Later, "interest on the first endowment fund was paid by a patron who failed in the panic of 1857, and was forced to rescind his promised fund," Kellogg writes.

By 1853, when the third class of graduates "was ready to leave the institution, it was no longer the Normal Institute and High School, but by act of legislature had become a full fledged college," writes Kellogg. "The institution was now legally incorporated, established in a building of its own, with a competent band of teachers" and "earnest and brilliant students."

As Kellogg writes, "A college for women was born in the West."

*Lucy Ann Seymour Parsons left Milwaukee in 1854 to found another school for Beecher in Iowa and "continued to teach almost to the end of her long life," according to Kieckhefer. The Dubuque school closed during the Civil War, when the Parsons returned east to teach at Ingham University. They and their two children are buried near LeRoy, New York.*

*Mary Mortimer led Milwaukee Female College from 1854 to 1857, when an "earnest and bril-*

*liant student" brought to the campus from Janesville was educator Emma Willard's niece, Frances. She
left Wisconsin the following year for Evanston to attend a women's college, which she later would
serve as president. But Frances Willard would become one of the most famous women in Wisconsin
and the world as the president from 1880 to 1898 of the largest women's organization in the world,
the Woman's Christian Temperance Union. At her death, flags flew at half-staff nationwide.[14]*

    *Mary and Caroline Chapin, who were sisters, led Milwaukee Female College from 1857 until "the
financial crisis brought on by the Civil War forced them at last to give up the school," writes Kieckhefer. Mortimer returned to lead the college from 1866 to her retirement in 1874. In 1876, she helped
to found the Woman's Club of Wisconsin, which still houses in its historic building in Milwaukee the
continuing efforts of the College Endowment Association, successor to the Ladies' Educational Society of the 1850s.*

    *Mortimer's successors included Louise Upton from 1893 to 1895, when Wisconsin's first college
for women merged with Downer College, founded in 1855 in Fox Lake as the Wisconsin Female College. There, principal Caroline Bodge "was to Wisconsin Female College what Mary Mortimer was
to Milwaukee," according to Kieckhefer. Bodge's successors were Mary Crowell and Ellen C. Sabin,
who became the first president of Milwaukee-Downer College (see "Ellen Clara Sabine and My Years
at Downer" in chapter 5). Sabin served the two institutions for a total of thirty years, from 1891
to 1921, a record matched by her successor, professor Lucia Russell Briggs, who served as president
until 1951.*

    *In 1951, Wisconsin's first college for women celebrated its centennial. However, it closed in 1964
and consolidated with Lawrence University, where women students still earn diplomas under the
name of Milwaukee-Downer College. Its historic buildings became part of the campus of the University of Wisconsin–Milwaukee, which started as the Milwaukee State Normal School in 1885 to provide teacher preparation, primarily for women students.*

## NOTES

1. *Milwaukee Courier,* May 1, 1841.
2. Ibid., August 18, 1841; April 27 1842.
3. Margaret Fuller Ossoli, *Summer on the Lakes, in 1843* (Boston, 1844), 167. The rector was the Reverend
Lemuel B. Hull, who had a daughter named Eleanor; see Martha E. Fitch, "A Little Girl of Old Milwaukee," in chapter 2. However, Fitch recalls the rector's name as David Hull and does not mention another
daughter or a death. The Reverend Lemuel B. Hull died in 1843; see "St. Paul's 75th Anniversary," *Milwaukee Free Press,* January 19, 1913.
4. *Milwaukee Courier,* September 21, 1842; *Milwaukee Sentinel,* December 4 and 9, 1843, March 9 and June
8, 1844, and October 3 and 10, 1846.
5. James S. Buck, *History of Milwaukee under the Charter,* (Milwaukee, 1884), iii, 118–119, 284; *Milwaukee Sentinel,* August 13, 1851. The Milwaukee schools noted above primarily served students from "Yankee" families, the settlers from eastern states. For the increasing number of German immigrant families in the city
after statehood, the German-English Academy started in 1851 — but served only boys. Similar education
for German American girls began in 1865 with the Tochter Institut; see "Madame Mathilde Fransziska Anneke," its founder, in chapter 3.
6. The Free Congregational Church's first pastoral couple, the Reverend Otis Freeman Curtis and Mar-
villa Wright Curtis, came from Waukesha. She came from a famous missionary family from the East, a tradition continued by dozens of descendants in Beloit, Janesville, Madison, Endeavor, and elsewhere across
Wisconsin, the country, and several continents; see "Church Here to Celebrate 75th Birthday," *Milwaukee*

*Telegram,* February 5, 1922, and "Curtis Family Has Long List," *Beloit News,* June 18, 1913. The Free Congregational Church later was renamed the Grand Avenue Congregational Church, which closed in 1997 when its historic building became the home of the Irish Cultural and Heritage Center in Milwaukee.

7. *Milwaukee Sentinel,* August 29, 1848.

8. Diane Long Hoeveler, ed., *Milwaukee Women Yesterday* (Milwaukee: Milwaukee Humanities Program, 1979), 23.

9. Minerva Brace Norton, *A True Teacher: Mary Mortimer* (New York, 1894), 76, 95.

10. Ibid., 130.

11. *Milwaukee Free Democrat,* April 8 and 10, 1851.

12. *First Annual Catalogue of Milwaukee Normal Institute and High School, 1850–51;* circular of August 1, 1851, Milwaukee-Downer College library [now in Lawrence College library].

13. *Milwaukee Sentinel,* June 14, 16, and 17, 1852; Norton, *Mary Mortimer,* 133, 152.

14. Ruth B. Bordin, *Frances Willard: A Biography* (Chapel Hill: University of North Carolina Press, 1986), 3–23, 50, 95.

# Madame Mathilda Franziska Anneke

## *An Early Wisconsin Journalist*

LILLIAN KRUEGER

*WMH* 21, No. 2 (December 1937): 160–167

When Wisconsin had barely attained statehood, Milwaukee already was the home of a woman journalist. A woman in the profession of journalism . . . was doubtless considered by some a curiosity, by others a courageous pioneer, and by still others a shameless interloper.

Madame Mathilda Franziska Anneke[1] was well able to bear whatever appellations the "newness" of women in that profession brought to her. She had been steeled to meet opposition a few years earlier in the Revolution of 1848 in the German Palatinate. With her husband, Captain Fritz Anneke,[2] she served in the ranks, riding her charger by day and sleeping by its side at night.

Her urge to write had found expression while still a young woman in Germany, for when her husband espoused the cause of the Revolution, [he] was imprisoned at Cologne for almost a year because of his political views and awaited trial for treason. "Madame Anneke removed the furniture and carpets from her parlors, and bringing in a printing press"[3] published the *Neue Kölnische Zeitung*, a paper supporting the Revolution, which was suppressed. This was followed by the *Frauen-Zeitung* in which she fought for the equal rights of women, whose fate was that of its predecessor.[4] "She continued to labor, until, her party losing ground, she was forced to abandon her work and fly for safety.". . .[5]

The editing of these two papers was not her initiation into the field of writing. Preceding the Revolution various yearbooks and poetical works had passed through her hands; contributions in verse from her pen had been accepted for publication; English novels had been translated by her; *Kölnische, Augsburger, Düsseldorfer,* and other newspaper editors had made use of her editorial ability. . . .[6]

. . . Her early experience [and]also her background [were] a stimulant to her literary and journalistic growth. She was born of nobility at Lerchenhausen, Westphalia, April 3, 1817, the daughter of the Karl Gieslers. . . .[7] [H]ighly educated, she showed in youth a leaning toward literature and art.[8] With leisure, education, and energy, all fortunately possessed by her, ideas were bound to come to fruition.

The principal reason for her support of the feminist movement in Germany, however, is found in her bitter experience soon after she left her happy childhood surroundings, for through it she learned of the injustices of the laws pertaining to married women.[9] At nineteen she became the wife of Herr von Tabouillot; this marriage terminated a year later. Prolonged controversy over the possession of their infant daughter embittered [her] once carefree life still more. So it was not strange that, throughout the remainder of her days, she became a staunch champion of women's rights.

With the disastrous termination of the Revolution, the German patriots took flight.
. . . [T]he security of American shores brought them hither in the autumn of 1849.[10]

What this haven represented to Madame Anneke she warmly pictured to an audience
at a meeting of the national convention of the American Equal Rights Association some
twenty years later:

> The consciousness and the holy conviction of our inalienable human rights, which
> I have won in the struggle of my own strangely varied life, . . . carried me through
> the terrors of bloody revolution, and brought me to this effulgent shore. . . .[11]

The woman's equal rights movement was gaining adherents in Wisconsin when she arrived in New York with her husband, Captain Fritz Anneke, later a colonel in the Civil war,
[and their children]. Naturally enough, when she subsequently became a resident of Milwaukee with its large German population, far removed from the revolutionary turmoil,
the ardor to write again seized her. To use her pen to advocate the equal rights of women,
especially the German-born, challenged her. She soon met that challenge by editing and
publishing the monthly *Deutsche Frauen-Zeitung* (*German Woman's Journal*) also known as
the *Frauen-Zeitung*. . . .

. . . [T]he launching of her *Zeitung* brought endless hardship. The penniless refugee
gratefully accepted the unselfish offer of the publisher of the *Volksfreund* who supplied office space, compositor, type, and paper for the first issues. Later her paper was issued at
the *Banner* press, where she employed women compositors. The employment of these
women resulted in more grief for her. . . .[12]

When the *Deutsche Frauen-Zeitung* appeared in March, 1852, a daily paper of Milwaukee
carried the following item:

> The "German Frauen-Zeitung" edited by Frau Mathilda Francisca Anneke, née
> Giesler, and issued at the office of our "Volksfreund" has just made its friendly and
> promising appearance, and we hasten to heartily welcome the esteemed editor.
> The "German Frauen-Zeitung" will appear provisionally each month at the sub-
> scription price of $1. Individual numbers cost 10 cents. The first number at hand
> is well gotten up and edited with especial care. . . .[13]

Prejudice finally confronted this pioneer journalist in physical form, namely, a German typographical union [all male] was organized on May 18, 1852, about three months
after the birth of the *Frauen-Zeitung*. A committee was named to find a means to safeguard
the printers from those who made encroachment upon the trade. This resulted in requesting the heads of printing firms not to employ women workers and to remove those
already appointed. This, of course, was a blow aimed directly at Mathilda Anneke. . . . [14]

"The dynamic woman editor now decided to meet the challenge of the union by going
on a lecture tour during the summer through nearly all of the larger cities of the United
States in order to accumulate funds to establish a small print shop of her own."[15] Of this
tour the *Wisconsin Banner* says: "Frau Mathilda F. Anneke left on a propaganda-tour in the

interest of her *Frauen-Zeitung* on last Friday. She will visit Detroit, Cleveland, Buffalo, New York, Philadephia, Pittsburgh, Wheeling, etc. . . .[16]

. . . [E]ven though her tour proved successful, her plans matured simultaneously to leave Milwaukee. In October the *Frauen-Zeitung* was issued in New York, then semimonthly in Jersey City, and later as a weekly in Newark.[17] After three years of severe editorial labor, she was compelled by ill health to abandon the enterprise.[18]

Before her return to Milwaukee permanently, she spent a happy interval abroad. Then followed her return and the successful establishment of a girls' school [in Milwaukee, her Tochter Institut]. Though she is recognized as an eminent educator, as a national figure in the feminist movement, and as an author, Mathilda Franziska Anneke's journalistic pioneering should be counted as an achievement, apart, in a career as brilliant as it was vigorous [to her death in 1884].

## NOTES

1. The references vary in the spelling of her name. Sometimes "Annecke" is used; also "Mathilde," "Francisca," "Franzeska," "Franciska," and "Franceska." The spelling adopted is from Rudolph A. Koss, *Milwaukee* (Milwaukee, 1871). [Modern historical preference for the first and middle name of "Madame Anneke" is her preference. The Germanic "Mathilde" and "Fransziska" are used in other references to her in this anthology. However, this excerpt preserves the Americanized spellings that were used in the original publication.]

2. *Milwaukee Herold,* November 27, 1884; Wilhelm Kaufmann, *Die Deutschen in amerikanischen Bürgerkriege* (Berlin, 1911), 479. . . . The Annekes were married in 1847; he was her second husband.

3. Charles Tuttle, *An Illustrated History of the State of Wisconsin* (Madison, 1875), 702.

4. *Milwaukee Freidenker,* November 30, 1884.

5. Tuttle, 702.

6. Koss, 381–382; *Milwaukee Freidenker,* November 30, 1884.

7. In some references the name is spelled "Gieseler."

8. . . . Milwaukee *Wisconsin Banner and Volksfreund,* December 4, 1884; Wilhelm Hense-Jensen and Ernest Bruncken, *Wisconsin's Deutsch-Amerikaner bis zum Schluss des neunzehnten Jahrhunderts* (Milwaukee, 1902), ii, 15.

9. Stanton, Anthony, and Gage, *History of Woman Suffrage,* [vol. 3], 646.

10. Ibid., 647.

11. Ibid., [vol. 2], 393. The association convened in New York [in] May 1869.

12. Koss, 382. . . . See Frederick Merk, "The Labor Movement in Wisconsin during the Civil War," in WHS *Proceedings* (1914), 175–176.

13. *Das Tägliche Banner,* March 30, 1852.

14. Koss, 382–383.

15. Ibid.

16. August 4, 1852.

17. Koss, 383.

18. Tuttle, *Illustrated History,* 702; *Milwaukee Freidenker,* November 30, 1884. . . . Madame Anneke recovered from this illness. . . .

# Early Farmers in Exeter

ELIZABETH MOORE WALLACE

*WMH* 8, No. 4 (June 1925): 415–422

# Letitia Wall

## *A Wisconsin Pioneer Type*

JOSEPH SCHAFER

*WMH* 8, No. 2 (December 1924): 193–198

*From Irish Hollow to Fennimore Creek, the women and men of southwestern Wisconsin saw mining decline after statehood, when "California mania" overcame thousands of Wisconsin's first settlers. In 1850 in Mineral Point alone, sixty wagons went west, and at Prairie du Chien, caravans of Norwegians crossed into Iowa. On one day in 1854, a woman watched three hundred wagons pass by and wrote, "I believe the entire population of Wisconsin is on the way to the West now." But the "driftless area" drew farmers from many places to work the land that miners had left. "Practically every adult was Swiss by birth" in New Glarus, a historian writes of the quaint and colorful Green County colony founded in the mid-1840s.[1]*

*But the Swiss bought out earlier immigrants, especially the Irish, who already had left their legacy — and far more followed. In Lafayette County, Shullsburg began as a town named Dublin, and nearby were Erin Prairie, Cork, Tyrone, and Irish Diggings. In Exeter, Green County, the second settler and first Irisher in the 1820s was trader John Doherty, who had married a Native American woman. However, he was part of an "earlier, less desperate Irish immigration," a historian writes, than in later decades when the Irish would become the second-largest immigrant group in Wisconsin — although many in the southwestern portion of Wisconsin moved west again.[2]*

*Those who fled Ireland in the famine years of the 1840s and 1850s more often emigrated en masse, even in entire villages, as Elizabeth Moore Wallace recalls in the following article. They replicated their earlier village life, including intricate intermarriages. A "cousin-bride" was a common occurrence — Wallace herself married her mother's brother-in-law — in her extensive clan of women "weavers and small farmers" who emigrated to Irish Hollow in Exeter.*

*Although Wallace came to Wisconsin as a girl, more mature and unmarried Irish women came over the ocean than in any other immigrant group, and many who wed were widowed early. The poverty of the Irish and discrimination they endured in employment led more of their men into hard labor and resulted in more early deaths. But it was murder that widowed Wallace's aunt, with seven children to educate in the rural schooling of Exeter described here. However, her aunt was "a capable woman with a strong character" and "a will of her own," who even saved a "competence for her old age" to spare her children from supporting her.[3]*

*Some women who had their husbands still had to support themselves. Another of the many Southerners who migrated up the Mississippi River to the southwesternmost county of Grant seems unlike the immigrants in many ways, as Letitia Abbott Wall was a "belle" who had married a ne'er-do-well.*

*While he lived off the land and fished on his brother's farm in Fennimore Creek, she earned a "slender living" as a weaver in Boscobel, where she often lived alone. Unlike most women in Wisconsin, Wall was childless. However, she mothered others' children, including a nephew who writes fondly of her here. He recalls her as an "intellectual" interested in politics, self-supporting, and never succumbing to self-pity even when left bereft, a widow in "broken health" but never "tragically hopeless." A woman of the South, Wall met her end "without admission of defeat or even disappointment."[4]*

*The hardships of life in Wisconsin did defeat some newcomers, even in the 1850s in the settled society of the southwestern area, and even if they were experienced farmers from eastern states. In more than a hundred letters to her prosperous parents in New Hampshire, Hannah Thompson Aldrich left a record of "seven hard years making a home and making a living" in Sylvan (Richland County) from 1856 to 1864. Finally, "sickness and bad luck" — from the financial panic of 1857, as soon as she and her husband settled in Sylvan, to the inflationary effect of the Civil War, to the harsh Wisconsin winter of 1864 — forced them to sell off all for which they had worked, to pay their fare back to the East. There, they succeeded.[5]*

*But Elizabeth Moore Wallace and Letitia Abbott Wall stayed. Their stories, if of only two women in one corner of Wisconsin, suggest the disparate backgrounds but similar strength — or better luck — that thousands of women brought to every hollow, hill, and town within Wisconsin's borders.*

⌘

# Early Farmers in Exeter

I was born in Knockahollet, County Antrim, Ireland, on May 13, 1843. We were a village of weavers and small farmers — the Lynns, Moors, Hughys, Wallaces, and Cains. All of these families except the Cains finally became related by marriage.

Ireland was just emerging from that distressing period known as the potato famine. While I do not recall any shortage of rations in our little village during my childhood, I have no doubt the restlessness and discontent of the young people, which I distinctly remember, was due to the hard times. They were keen to be off over the sea to either America or Australia, while the conservative older heads of the families were against such a change. There were many heated arguments of the question, but . . . the young people won and the exodus began. So completely was Knockahollet depopulated that not so much as one stone of the many stone houses now remains. . . .

It was in the fall of 1848 that Uncle John [Lyon] returned to Knockahollet with a deed to three hundred and twenty acres of Wisconsin land in his pocket and a glowing description of its hills and valleys on the tip of his tongue. . . .

By March, 1849, John was back in Wisconsin with his cousin-bride, Elizabeth Gambel, to help him grub a home out of the wilderness. On the same ship with them came many other young people from Knockahollet. . . . Uncle Elison Lynn . . . accompanied his brother to Wisconsin, where he found work on a farm near Mineral Point.

These Scotch-Irish were industrious and thrifty and it was not long as time was reckoned in those days — perhaps a year or two — before many of them had saved the fifty dollars necessary to pay for forty acres of Wisconsin government land.

My parents, Joseph and Mary Lynn Moor (or "Moore," as our name was written in the new world) arrived in Wisconsin early in the spring of 1851. I was then eight years old and my sister Nancy . . . was two. My mother's parents, James and Nancy Ellis Lynn, and my father's only brother, William, accompanied us to Exeter.

. . . With fifty dollars out of their scant store my parents purchased forty acres southeast of John's farm. . . . [O]ther forties [were] added from time to time. . . .

The Swiss settlement of New Glarus lay five miles beyond the wooded hills to the northwest. The old mining town of Exeter, three miles to the southeast, was the most pretentious village, but it was beginning to run down at the heels, since the mining industry had practically ceased and the clearing of the ground for farms had only just begun. . . .

Speculators were fast buying up the unoccupied land. In 1859 . . . Samuel Patterson and his wife Sally Wallace with their eight children arrived. . . . The price of land had advanced from three dollars to six dollars per acre. The Pattersons were the last of that early group of relatives to come from the old country. . . . [Six Wallace] boys and two of their sisters owned farms in "Irish Hollow," as that section of Exeter was called. Of Grandfather Lynn's family, five boys and their two sisters were established there. . . .

Alexander Wallace and his wife Nancy Lynn, my mother's only sister, with their two little girls, Mary and Anna, came from New York in 1852 and settled just east of us. His father soon followed. . . . His wife, Ann Bailey, was counted by those who knew her best a spoiled, pretty little woman. With them lived their youngest daughter, Ann Jane . . . and William, their youngest child, who later became my husband. . . .

William bought the eighty acres lying across the marsh south of us. When in 1864 he enlisted in the army, [his brother] James and his wife Eliza Annett, came out from [New] York State and took over the management of the farm and the care of the old folks. . . .

Eliza Annett Wallace [was William's sister-in-law and] was one of four orphan children who had been left to the care of their relatives in Ireland. She and her brother Willie had been brought across the ocean when very young, while the two other brothers had been left in Ireland. Willie was several years younger than his sister, and after her marriage made his home with her. They entirely lost track of the brothers; in fact, they could not remember that they had any near relatives. . . .

Uncles James Lynn and his wife, Nancy Moore (no relative of my father) bought [a] farm. . . .

Aunt Nancy was counted a capable woman with a strong character. She certainly had a will of her own and a great deal of pride, which served her well when she was left a widow in 1866 with five little boys and two girls, on a heavily mortgaged farm out there in those woods. Uncle James had driven to Monroe, fifteen miles distant, to get oak planks from which he and William were to make the beams for a long sleigh the next day. A Swiss farmer found his lifeless body. . . . His team and wagon, on which were the oak planks, were standing in the brush some distance off. There was a small hole in his forehead from which the blood oozed. He had been a quiet, sober man. His purse remained untouched in his pocket, and . . . no solution of the accident was ever arrived at. Aunt Nancy remained on the farm, educated her children, and laid by a competence for her old age. . . .

William and I built our house on his eighty acres and began housekeeping in 1865 after he had returned from the war.

Mr. and Mrs. Hare were especially good neighbors, and [had] no family of their own — their two children having died in infancy. . . .

Mrs. Hare, like many another pioneer woman, had formed the habit of smoking [a pipe] before her first child was born. Chewing or smoking tobacco was frequently recommended in those days as a cure for indigestion, irrespective of the cause. She considered it an unladylike habit and said she often prayed for strength to overcome it. Her prayer was answered by a long siege of sickness. For weeks and weeks she lay in a delirium of fever. When she recovered, the appetite for tobacco was gone and she never again took to the pipe. . . .

I had attended school in Ireland, but of course there was no school in Irish Hollow for me to attend in 1851. My father had bought new schoolbooks for me before we left Ireland, and for some time he taught me at home as best he could. The first schoolhouse in the Hollow was a little log building on the west side of the river. . . . A collection was taken up among the settlers to defray the expenses of the school. Frances Dutcher was our first teacher for a short time. Then her cousin, Frances Corey, taught the school. There were seventeen pupils representing six different families. It seems to me but yesterday they sat there on those rude benches. . . .

I spoke and read with a broad Scotch brogue, and my spelling greatly amused the other children, much to my embarrassment. My "ā's" were "å's," my "ē's" were "ā's" and my "j's" were "gaw's." You can imagine the teacher's surprise when she asked me to spell "Jane" and I promptly — for I was a good speller — replied : "Gaw-å-n-ā." But since I did not like to be laughed at, I soon learned to pronounce both words and letters in the accepted English of the time and place.

It was not long before the log building was razed and the logs were used in constructing another schoolhouse on the east bank of the river. . . .

A little ten-by-ten frame structure was at first set up at the foot of the hill. . . . In this, that first summer, school was in session long enough to entitle the district to a share in the public school fund. In the meantime the permanent building was under construction. . . . I think the men hauled the lumber from Janesville. . . .

Sarah Thayer, the first teacher in the new building, came from New York City to visit her uncle . . . in Exeter village, but remained to teach our school. She brought us many eastern ideas: she made leather flowers into bouquets covered with dome-shaped glass receptacles; she wore short sleeves and low necks in her dresses. I recall her introductory speech the first morning and how stylish we big girls thought she looked.

Abigail Corey, Malvina and Violet Avery, and I were the "big girls," and we made life miserable for the next teacher. He was a mere boy . . . and such a bashful boy! We were cruel and heartless, but we may have done him a good turn, as he gave up the unremunerative work of teaching and became a successful merchant. . . .

⟨decoration⟩

# Letitia Wall: A Wisconsin Pioneer Type

Southwestern Wisconsin, including the celebrated lead region and the territory adjacent as far as the Wisconsin and Mississippi rivers, attracted a good many settlers from the south and the southwest. . . .

The valleys of Blue River and Fennimore Creek near their junction received some pioneer settlers early in the 1850s, and among these were four or five families derived from North Carolina by way of Missouri. Two of them were families of the brothers Tillman and Alpheus Wall. . . . [T]o use his own phrase, [Alpheus] was usually "somehow or other, no 'count.". . .

There was obviously no money in the family, and under these circumstances Alpheus Wall must have been a dependent upon his brother or upon the public (unless, as some suspected, his illness was psychological and might have been cured by dire necessity), had it not been for his wife, Letitia — or 'Titia, as every one called her.

. . . Letitia [Abbott] was a belle. . . . [She] might have taken for a husband her choice of several eligible men in her own set. But she fell in love with Alpheus Wall, who was "so tall and fine looking," as she used to remark even in middle life, and him she married. In doing so she alienated her parents and cut herself off from the old home. Thus, with Alpheus and the others of his family, she found her way to the Wisconsin frontier [in about 1853 as a woman of about twenty-four years].

. . . Though brought up in luxurious surroundings, she was trained like southern women generally in the arts of spinning, weaving, quilting, and all kinds of needlework. During the Civil War, when wearing apparel became very scarce and high-priced, and the farmers of her locality found difficulty in clothing their families, these accomplishments were brought into requisition.

Aunt 'Titia observed that almost every farm had upon it a small flock of sheep, sufficient to produce the raw wool required by the family. Spinning, however, was done by only a few, and exclusively on the old-time diminutive spinning-wheel, which was too slow and uneconomical to meet the wartime emergency. She persuaded the neighbor women to buy the large spinning-wheel and taught them to use it, while for herself she procured a loom and began the business of weaving cloth. The women would spin wool for the filling, buy cotton for warp, then dye both and bring them to her to weave. Many were the suits of homespun which resulted, for she was kept busy at the loom day after day during several years.

When the war closed, farmers began once more to purchase their cloth in the stores or to buy ready-made clothing. So the demand for cloth-weaving fell away. Many pioneers, however, were then ready to leave their log houses, and when they built better homes there arose a demand for rag carpets to cover the floors. There was a period in which the sewing of "carpet-rags" was the occupation with which the industrious farm mother filled her winter evenings. Sometimes all the female members of the family worked at it, and not infrequently male members took a hand too. A small boy, if he could do nothing else, could at lest wind the ball of sewed rags. The rags were torn into narrow ribbons perhaps three-eighths of an inch in width, tacked end to end, and the resulting string was wound into a ball which grew and grew until it reached the right dimension, perhaps four or five inches in diameter, when it passed for a pound in weight. . . . [M]uch rag carpet, some of it very agreeable to the eye, was made out of the rags colored just as it happened, "hit or miss."

Aunt 'Titia now procured a carpet loom, and instead of linsey-woolsey, manufactured rag carpets for the whole countryside. An interval of several years was spent at Boscobel, where a young Scandinavian boy she had taken to rear found work in a store. Alpheus, too, performed a bit of light work now and then which brought him a few coins, and for the rest, he spent with joyous prodigality the money she earned at the loom. So, nothing could be laid by, and in a few years back they came to Tillman's farm and took possession once more of the log cabin.

. . . [I]t was a special joy to us children to go there with our mother, because it was such fun to watch Aunt 'Titia drive the shuttle with a kind of rhythmic rattle, back and forth, and to see the differently colored breadths of carpet forming under our eyes. Then, too, Aunt 'Titia loved children, and having none of her own, she adopted as hers in spirit all the youngsters of the countryside. She had not much time to talk to us, but she would snatch a few minutes now and then, and these few minutes were worth hours of waiting. For Aunt 'Titia was so kind, so jolly, and so "different" — we didn't know why. . . .

. . . It was, primarily, her extraordinary character, which harmonized with her large frame, splendid head and eyes, and aquiline countenance, as well as the dignity of her bearing and speech. In that farming neighborhood few women, even among the relatively prosperous, consistently held up their heads and looked life fearlessly in the eye. The most robust farm matrons often appeared tired, discouraged — ready to quit. Not so Aunt 'Titia. With her the hope of prosperity, if it had been experienced at all, faded early. She knew perfectly well that her slender living must come out of her earnings at the loom. Out of them, too, must come the weekly allowance of whisky and tobacco for Alpheus. . . . Want was never more than a few weeks behind her, and she had the imagination to see his grim visage. This was not a unique circumstance, for millions have been situated much as she was. What is remarkable is the way she bore up under the threat of imminent disaster. . . . The women of the neighborhood were fond of commiserating with one another over present or prospective misfortunes, sometimes sincerely, sometimes with obvious affectation. But no one would think of commiserating with Aunt 'Titia, although she worked harder than any of the rest and was obliged to do so. . . . It wouldn't do to insinuate to 'Titia that her husband was shiftless, as they would have done to others, for 'Titia was different. . . .

Aunt 'Titia was an intellectual woman. How she found time to read I know not, but she was well informed upon current topics, particularly politics. Doubtless her experience, and that of her people, in the Civil War, exerted a strong influence in keeping up her interest in politics; for though loyal in act . . . she was a rebel in spirit and she never became reconstructed. . . . She could out-talk and out-argue any man in the community on political questions, and the men were discreetly non-committal in her presence. But her information was so wide and exact that she could talk on many other subjects as well as politics, and every intelligent man delighted to converse with her.

For the women she had no end of interesting community talk. . . . She knew all the cases of young men who were "waiting on" young women and what the prospects were for marriages. . . . [S]he could give the exact day and year of birth of every boy and girl in every family within six miles of her home, for her memory in such matters was seemingly infallible; she kept track of the families who moved from the neighborhood into states farther west. . . . How she managed to gain such information, since she rarely left her cottage door, was one of the mysterious things about her which so gripped the neighborhood. Of course, she obtained it by questioning her customers. . . .

I believe Aunt 'Titia lived in the log cottage under the hill, taking care of her Alpheus, for more than twenty years. . . .

Her husband lived to a fairly ripe old age. . . . At last he passed away, leaving her free of the burden of his support, but also seemingly without the motive which theretofore had urged her to "carry on." In broken health and a spirit remote from resignation she first spent a year or two with her foster son, then entered a home for aged women. . . . There she died [in 1912, aged eighty-three years]. . . .

To almost any other woman of her time and neighborhood a life like Aunt 'Titia's would have seemed tragically hopeless, to be endured only in the spirit of self-pity. To her it was a part to be played without complaint and without admission of defeat or even disappointment. . . .

## NOTES

1. Current, *HOW,* 72–73, 79.
2. Kathleen Neils Conzen, *Immigrant Milwaukee, 1836–1860: Accommodation and Community in a Frontier City* (Cambridge: Harvard University Press, 1976), 24.
3. Current, *HOW,* 120; see also Hasia R. Diner, *Erin's Daughters in America: Irish Immigrant Women in the Nineteenth Century* (Baltimore: Johns Hopkins University Press, 1983).
4. Joseph Schafer, nephew of Letitia Abbot Wall, was born in 1876 in Muscoda, Grant County, and left school at sixteen years old to farm with his father at Fennimore Creek. He later earned undergraduate and doctoral degrees from the University of Wisconsin, was a professor of history at the University of Oregon, and was director of the State Historical Society of Wisconsin from 1920 to 1941. See "Grant County Boy at Head of State Historical Society," *Fennimore Times,* June 3, 1931, and "Dr. Schafer Dies in Madison," *Muscoda Progressive,* January 30, 1941.
5. Elizabeth Krynski and Kimberly Little, eds., "Hannah's Letters: The Story of a Wisconsin Pioneer Family, 1856–1864," *WMH* 74, no. 3 (Spring 1991): 164–195; 74, no. 4 (Summer 1991): 272–296; and 75, no. 1 (Autumn 1991): 39–62.

# Spiritualism in Wisconsin in the Nineteenth Century

MARY FARRELL BEDNAROWSKI

*WMH* 59, No. 1 (Autumn 1975): 3–19

It is customary to designate 1859, the publication year of Charles Darwin's *Origin of Species,* as the starting date of the religion-science conflict of the nineteenth century. But the battle between the churches and science over the theories and implications of evolution was merely a continuation of a struggle for authority that had been in existence, off and on, for centuries. . . . Scholarship in such areas as archeology, anthropology, philology, comparative religions, and geology led to doubts about some of the truths of Christianity that believers had always taken for granted: the creation of the world by a be- nevolent, omnipotent God; the divinity of Christ; the survival of the soul after death. . . .

The result of all this scholarship was religious skepticism in nineteenth-century culture, a gradual inability to believe in either the divine origins of the universe or in the efficacy of adhering to organized religion. The possibility that science could render religion obsolete had a liberating effect on some persons. . . .

It was during the middle of the nineteenth century, in this climate of doubt and anxiety, that American Spiritualism originated in 1848.[1] In March of that year Margaret and Kate Fox, the young daughters of farmer John Fox of Hydesville, in western New York, heard rappings and taps which came to be interpreted as evidence that the spirits of the dead were trying to contact the world of the living. . . . As news of the rappings spread . . . spirit circles[2] began to spring up in great numbers. Hundreds of people discovered that they, too, possessed the power to communicate with spirits, and the spirit manifestations began to increase in sophistication. The spirits not only rapped; they also moved furniture, played musical instruments, and poked and pinched living members of the spirit circles.

For many the spirit manifestations bespoke nothing more than a novelty, a sensational kind of parlor entertainment. But as bizarre as the spirit phenomena may seem, they nevertheless came to be interpreted by thousands as evidence that the spirits of the dead were trying to communicate with the world of the living in order to reveal indisputably that life exists beyond the grave. . . . [3] As a religion based on knowledge, then, rather than belief, Spiritualism provided an alternative to the unquestioning faith demanded by traditional religions as well as to the belief in a totally materialistic world which was seemingly demanded by science. . . .

Because Spiritualism was always a loosely organized movement, the number of followers has never been determined exactly.[4] Within several years of its beginnings, however, Spiritualism had spread across the country, and there were spirit circles in every state of the Union and in many of the territories as well.

Wisconsin proved fertile ground for [the] nurturing of Spiritualism. [By the 1860s,] spirit circles had sprung up in most cities of any size as well as in rural areas. There were regional organizations such as the Northwestern Wisconsin Spiritualist Conference which held conventions in such places as River Falls and Oshkosh and conducted summer camps at Omro. . . . Spiritualists held regularly scheduled church services in Milwaukee, Madison, Janesville, Fond du Lac, and Appleton. A newspaper, the *Spiritualist,* was published for almost a year during 1868 in Appleton and Janesville. The only Spiritualist college in the nation, the Morris Pratt Institute, was built in Whitewater in 1888, flourishing there, and later in Milwaukee, well into the twentieth century. . . . [T]he National Spiritualist Association of Churches had its headquarters in Milwaukee. And to this day Spiritualists gather in the summer for lectures, seances, and healings in the small town of Wonewoc in Juneau County.[5]

The state boasts famous and respected citizens who espoused the new belief. . . . Ella Wheeler Wilcox was a Spiritualist during part of her life, as is evidenced by much of her poetry. . . .

. . . [She] felt dismay as a child that her family expressed no great interest in the things of the spirit: "I heard the grown-ups talking in an agnostic manner about things spiritual. I recollect just how crude and limited their minds seemed to me. . . ." As she grew older, the poet concluded that her family was not "atheistical," bur rather "too advanced intellectually to accept the old eternal brimstone idea of hell and the eternal psalm-singing idea of heaven; it refused to accept the story of the recent formation of the earth, knowing science had proof of its vast antiquity; . . . so the Wheeler family was regarded as heretical by church people."[6] Ella Wheeler Wilcox considered her family typical of those whose progressive minds had outgrown the dictates of traditional religion and could not accept evidence of the existence of the spiritual world without scientific proof. . . .

Warren Chase, founder of Ceresco, the Fourier community at Ripon,[7] . . . was a particularly harsh critic of organized religion. . . .

Like many others who experimented with spirit circles in the early 1850s, Chase and his friends in Fond du Lac and Ripon did not immediately succeed in establishing contact with the spirit world. In fact, it was six months before the members of Chase's circle were able to produce raps, and then only through the mediumship of a young Presbyterian woman. . . .[8] In connection with Chase's criticism of traditional Christianity, he was convinced that the institution of marriage greatly needed reform and that women suffered most from the institution.[9] Chase recounted the story of Mrs. P. of Milwaukee, "one of nature's noble women," who divorced her husband . . . after he deserted her and their three children. Mrs. P. remarried, but her second husband died within a few weeks. "Of course," wrote Chase, "it was not the duty of any Christian to aid or comfort her, for she had broken their sacred tie of legal marriage; and they not only let her suffer, but heaped slander on her with their scorn, . . . and thus she had all against her except the few Spiritualists who alone respected, appreciated, and sympathized with her. . . ."[10]

In order to emphasize their distaste for organized religion, Spiritualists sometimes interrupted church services. On one occasion in 1851 the Sunday service at the Spring Street Congregational Church in Milwaukee was disrupted by a woman who walked to the pulpit while the minister was leading the final hymn. . . . [He] asked the woman to leave, and she walked away "with her lips mumbling some unknown tongue." The story appeared in the *Milwaukee Sentinel,* and the reporter added to it a rumor that the woman intended to pay similar visits to all the churches in Milwaukee. The woman's husband . . . denied this, however, claiming in a letter to the editor that his wife had been under spirit influence when she visited the Spring Street church and that she had no further plans for disrupting services. . . . [11]

. . . Among the more famous of the Spiritualist healers was Cora L. V. Scott (known at various times by the names of her three husbands: Hatch, Tappan, and Richmond). In 1851 Cora Scott began her healing career at the age of eleven. . . . In 1850 [her family had] moved to a farm near Lake Mills, . . . an area that was soon to become notable for a variety of Spiritualist activities. Cora Scott's first spirit experience occurred when spirits completed a school composition for her by means of automatic writing. Soon after, Cora developed the ability to diagnose illnesses while in trance under the control of the spirit of a German doctor. Apparently she was successful, for (it was claimed) she "aroused the antagonism of the regular physicians and clergymen in the neighborhood. The former were without patients and the latter lacked audiences. . . . That village in Wisconsin soon became the center of a spiritual circle that had greater power than all the professionals taken together.". . . [12] Cora Scott remained a Spiritualist throughout her life, but she pursued her career, for the most part, in New York, Chicago, and San Francisco until her death in 1923.

Because she left Wisconsin as a child, it was not Cora Scott but rather her grammar school teacher, Mary Hayes Chynoweth, who assumed the leadership of Spiritualist activities in the Lake Mills-Whitewater-Madison area. Mary Hayes Chynoweth was Cora Scott's teacher at the time of Cora's first spirit visitation. Her first reaction to the news was disapproval; she was suspicious of Spiritualism and was afraid that Cora Scott had been possessed by a devil. She received her first visitation from the Holy Spirit, or the Power, as she called it, on a night when she had refused to go with some of her family to one of Cora Scott's "test-meetings." On this evening Mrs. Hayes Chynoweth was brought to her knees in the kitchen by an unknown force, and she began speaking in tongues. She was then lifted off her feet and inspired to open the Bible and point to certain passages. She claimed that she knew very little about the Bible: "The way everybody quoted Scripture, and then put different constructions to suit themselves, prejudiced me so that I discontinued reading it; dogmas always repelled me." Nevertheless Mrs. Hayes Chynoweth was inspired to point to the account of Pentecost and the list of the gifts given by the Holy Spirit to the Apostles. Her father asked, "Do you mean it was appointed that my daughter do all this?" The answer was yes.[13]

This first visitation resulted in a career that spanned the rest of Mary Hayes Chynoweth's life, from the early 1850s until her death in California in 1905. She preached and healed and held seances, and she used her spirit powers to give personal as well as financial advice to her relatives and followers. She seems to have been a Christian Spiritualist, though, as she said, dogma repelled her. Unlike most Spiritualists, she claimed that her power was derived from the Holy Spirit rather than from the spirits of the dead. But, on the other hand, her letters and writings reveal that she believed that spirits did communicate with the living. . . . [S]he claimed that she was never alone, "and it is lively comfort to know our spirit friends are with us. . . ."[14]

Whatever the exact nature of her theological beliefs, Mary Hayes Chynoweth followed her preaching mission throughout south-central Wisconsin, to "East and West Troy, Columbus, Muckwanago, Milton Junction, Whitewater, Jefferson, and other places," all of them convenient to Lake Mills and Waterloo, where her two sons were born in 1855 and 1857. By the time the two sons, Everis Anson and Jay O. Hayes, were completing law school at the University of Wisconsin, Mary Hayes Chynoweth was firmly established as a healer and a clairvoyant, and she was well known in the Madison area. There she engaged in seances with judges, doctors, lawyers, and university professors. . . .

By the time her sons had practiced law for several years, Mary Hayes Chynoweth was using her spiritual powers for financial benefit. Acting on the advice of the Power, she urged her sons, who by this time were practicing law in Ashland, to invest $850 in a tract of land in Bayfield County and not to sell until they could get $5,000 for it. Next, the Power instructed the Hayes brothers to look for iron ore. They found it in abundance, and, along with their mother, became the owners and operators of the Hayes Mining Company, the Harmony Iron Company, and the Hayes-Chynoweth Company. . . . The *Ashland Daily Press Annual* for 1891–1892 claimed that [their success] "was very largely due to the unflinching faith and energy of Mrs. Hayes Chynoweth and her sons.". . . Whether this "unflinching faith" was based on instructions from the spirit Power, or whether the mining successes were due to the business acumen and good luck of the Hayes brothers, there is insufficient evidence to prove.[15]

By 1887, Mary Hayes Chynoweth and her sons had taken up residence in California. . . . [She] continued to be the spiritual leader of many of her Madison followers until her death in 1905. . . .

After Mary Hayes Chynoweth moved to California, [some of her clients] consulted the spirits about [their] personal [lives] through the agency of clairvoyants. One of these was Mrs. Julia Severance of Whitewater and Milwaukee, who was famous throughout the state as a Spiritualist and social reformer.[16] [Lyman] Draper sent Mrs. Severance a lock of his hair and asked her to analyze his personality through psychometric evaluation (whereby the clairvoyant assesses a person by physical contact with an object belonging to that person). Mrs. Severance advised him by letter on everything from his diet to his social life. She suggested unleavened graham bread, baked potatoes, and hot baths; she mentioned that Draper might do well to associate with younger members of the opposite sex, "in a commonplace social way, so that you can receive from them the more youthful magnetic element." Mrs. Severance informed Draper that he was attended by "a very advanced class of spirits," and that if he followed her directions he would "be able to perfect yourself in this life so that when you arrive in Spirit life you will be in condition to move right along harmoniously with your work in 'the hereafter.'". . .[17]

Underneath the more sensational aspects of Spiritualism, such as the seances, the

trance speaking, the financial predictions, and the automatic writing — those aspects of
Spiritualism which received the most publicity — lay the basic belief that . . . the individual personality would endure in the spirit world and would dwell with loved ones. . . .

It is tempting to ridicule some of the more bizarre aspects of Spiritualism, and it would
be foolish to deny that Spiritualism attracted more than its share of cranks, hoaxers, and
gulls, who sought money or entertainment or notoriety from contact with the spirits. But
it is difficult not to sympathize with the Spiritualists' longing for certainty about that most
vital of questions: does humankind survive the death of the body?. . . .[18] Only a century's
hindsight enables us to adjudge the Spiritualists as overly optimistic in their belief that science and scientific method could make known to humanity the mysteries of life and
death. . . .

## NOTES

1. Certainly there was evidence of the belief in human communication with spirits long before 1848. . . .
But the Spiritualists themselves date the beginning of modern Spiritualism from 1848. There are several
histories of Spiritualism available, although none is definitive. . . . [A] more recent volume is Slater
Brown's *The Heyday of Spiritualism* (New York, 1970). . . .
2. Spirit circles were informal groups consisting of a medium, or one who professed to have highly developed psychic powers, and several followers, usually not more than ten or twelve. . . .
3. [See] Emma Hardinge Britten, *Modern American Spiritualism: A Twenty Years' Record of the Communion Between Earth and the World of Spirits* (New York, 1870). . . .
4. E. Branch Douglas estimates the number of Spiritualists at the height of the movement as one million,
including all those who merely believed that spirit manifestations were genuine. See *The Sentimental Years*
(New York, 1934), 366–379.
5. There is no general history of Spiritualism in Wisconsin, but the WHS has an extensive collection of
material. . . . [T]he *Milwaukee Sentinel* . . . has been indexed for much of the nineteenth century (1837 to
1879) . . . for references to Spiritualist activities throughout the state.
6. Ella Wheeler Wilcox, *The Worlds and I* (New York, 1918), 66.
7. [See "Women at Ceresco" in chapter 2.]
8. Warren Chase, *The Life-Line of the Lone One or Autobiography of the World's Child* (Boston, 1857), 174. . . .
The young lady was convinced by her family and her religious superiors that the spirit phenomena were
produced by the Devil, and she abandoned her activities as a medium.
9. Almost from the beginning of their movement, Spiritualists were accused of loose living because of
their stand on marriage and divorce. . . .
10. Chase, *Life-Line of the Lone One*, 192, 194.
11. *Milwaukee Sentinel,* January 31 and February 6, 1851. [The church, later renamed Grand Avenue Congregational Church, originally was named The Free Congregational Church; see "A College for Women
Was Born in the West."]
12. Harrison D. Barrett, *Life Work of Mrs. Cora L. V. Richmond* (Chicago, 1895), 8–9. . . . [See also] R. Laurence Moore, "The Spiritualist Medium: A Study of Female Professionalism in Victorian America," in the
*American Quarterly,* 27: 200–221 (May, 1975). Moore mentions a man named Daniels as another of Cora
Scott's husbands.
13. Louisa Johnson Clay, *The Spirit Dominant: A Life of Mary Hayes Chynoweth* (San Jose, CA: n.d.), 47–48.
Louise Johnson Clay wrote the biography in thanksgiving for the cure of her mother by Mary Hayes
Chynoweth, a factor which no doubt influenced her viewpoint.
14. Mary Hayes (Chynoweth) to Mr. and Mrs. Lyman Draper, January 13, 1883, in the Draper Correspondence, Archives-Manuscript Division, WHS.
15. "Ashland and Its Iron Mines," in *The Ashland Daily Press Annual* (1891–1892), 60–61.

16. Mrs. Severance's interest in social reform earned her a reputation as a radical. The *Milwaukee Sentinel* described her as taking "the extreme radical ground" in her attempts at reform, "going if possible beyond the notions of Victoria C. Woodhull," January 13, 1874.

17. Mrs. A. B. Severance to Lyman C. Draper, September 25, 1888, in "Scrap-Book of Material on the Life, Career and Death of Lyman C. Draper," in the WHS [where Draper was director].

18. A particularly poignant expression of this longing appears in a poem, "You Promised Me," written by Ella Wheeler Wilcox to the spirit of her dead husband, [in] *The Worlds and I,* 346–347.

# My Recollections of Civil War Days

MRS. LATHROP E. SMITH

*WMH* 2, No. 1 (September 1918): 20–29

# The University of Wisconsin soon after the Civil War

MRS. W. F. ALLEN

*WMH* 7, No. 1 (September 1923): 20–29

*While their brothers went to war by the hundreds of thousands in the 1860s, and public universities in western states struggled without men students, a comparatively few women went to campus. The University of Wisconsin had opened in Madison in 1848 for men only, although the first chancellor noted a need for women students, since "the new state sorely needed trained teachers." Regents replied that they "contemplated" women students but worried "whether the liberal culture of the female mind" was worth the cost of "doubling the array and quadrupling the expense of instruction." For nine years, "nothing was done," writes historian Reuben Gold Thwaites, for "lack of funds." In 1857, regents concluded that enrolling women in teacher training — not regular college courses, as had been done at the state university in Iowa from its beginning two years before — would be "economical," and the campus ought to "prepare" for their presence.[1]*

*Wartime preparations intervened. A Normal Department opened in 1857 as a summer school for teachers and enrolled thirty women among almost sixty students by 1860, when it ended, a year before the Civil War began. But men increasingly enlisted in the military instead of enrolling in college. In 1863, regents rediscovered the "economical" aspect of women students and revived the Normal Department — this time in the regular academic year.[2]*

*One of the first women students at the University of Wisconsin in the fall of 1863 was Sabra Warner of Windsor, who writes here "from a schoolgirl's point of view" of watching from the sidelines while her brother went to the front lines, first in prewar politics and then in war. Even boys too young to vote participated in presidential campaigns in Wisconsin, where the new antislavery Republican Party emerged in the 1850s, while women sewed flags for parades. Then boys became soldiers, another test of citizenship denied to women for a century to come.*

*Yet Warner and other women would face wartime tests of their own. Within two weeks of the start of war, women formed soldiers' aid societies nationwide, as governments in neither the North nor the South were prepared to provide many supplies, from knitted socks to rolled lint for bandages. Northern aid societies soon coordinated women's work under their Sanitary Commission, which saved many soldiers' lives during and after the Civil War.[3]*

*Warner faced tests on campus, too, and not only in the classroom. As Thwaites writes, "trials still awaited the cause of coeducation at the University of Wisconsin" — and trials awaited a schoolgirl who soon followed her brothers to college and then followed her brother to war.[4]*

# My Recollections of Civil War Days

...My story is not like the one you will find in the histories of the war written by real historians but is a record of events, trivial perhaps to others, but of great interest to a schoolgirl of those days and written from a schoolgirl's point of view.

The first presidential campaign in which I had any interest, really the first one I remember, was that of 1856 when the new Republican party nominated John C. Frémont as their candidate. There was great enthusiasm all through the North and Republican clubs were organized in every city, village, and hamlet. In our neighborhood of Windsor, twelve miles north of Madison, such a club was organized. . . . [A]lthough the boys were not yet twenty-one, they attended every meeting of the club and were quite as much concerned about its success as if they had been old enough to vote. I heard many of their discussions in our home and was very anxious to have Frémont elected president. . . . We all sang songs and hurrahed. . . .

. . . [A Frémont ratification] meeting was attended by all the country round about [Madison]. A procession of wagons over three miles long was formed, decorated with national flags and banners of every description. . . . The flag which we carried was the first flag I can remember. No flags were to be bought in those days, and this one was made for the occasion by hand, with painstaking care, by Aunt Sarah Haswell, from cloth purchased at the store in Madison. . . .

Another flag I well remember was made for Rockford Seminary [in Illinois, near Beloit] soon after Fort Sumter was fired upon and used during the war and for many years afterward. . . . I [was] appointed . . . [to] a committee to purchase the cloth of red, white, and blue of which the flag was made. . . .

In Civil War days . . . the soldiers were sometimes very lonely and resorted to many methods of entertainment, one of which interested the girls at home. One day several of the boys were together and one suggested that each should put into a hat the name of a girl he knew and that then each soldier should draw a name and write a letter to the bearer of it. My name was drawn and shortly afterward I received a very fine letter from a soldier of whom I had never heard, telling of the arrangement and asking for a reply to the letter. . . .

Thus began our writing to the soldier boys, which continued for the next four years. . . . The girls in those days were patriots and anxious to do all they could for the boys in the Army who were their friends, and many of them wrote to a number and had to be very careful to put the letters in the right envelopes, for there were some instances of misplaced letters which caused sad terminations of former pleasant relationships. So the girls learned to be very careful. . . .

The women, too, were doing their part. Societies were organized for preparing articles for the Sanitary Commission and in every place the women met to scrape lint, roll bandages, make needlebooks,[5] and knit socks and all the other necessary things for the soldiers. . . . Nowhere could a girl be found who was not knitting away furiously on a blue sock for some soldier. I remember well one ride I took . . . canvassing the town of Windsor for old linen and cotton and other supplies. . . .

. . . [E]nlistment went on and in the University [of Wisconsin at Madison] the classes steadily decreased in numbers. By 1863, the regents began to fear that the University would soon be left with only the buildings and the faculty. So they decided if the young men were all going to war, they would admit the young women of the state to a Normal Department. It might help the girls and at the same time keep the faculty busy. Both objects were accomplished when the girls came in the spring of 1863. The newcomers were quite surprised, when they entered the University, to find that the men students who still remained felt humiliated over the presence of girls in the University and that some of the professors, even, did not entirely approve of the new plan. Most of the faculty, however, and especially President Sterling . . . [and] Professor Allen and Miss Moody of our Normal Department did everything in their power to make it pleasant for the girls, of whom I was one.[6] The boys roomed in North Hall, the girls in South Hall. Although our paths crossed as we went to our chapel exercises and recitations in the north end of the main building and the boys went to theirs in the south end of the same building, they did not recognize our presence and we were just as oblivious of theirs. . . .

. . . [Soon], the senior class (all but one) enlisted. . . . The boys came up from Camp Randall and spent their last evening with the girls, and we gave them the needlebooks we had made and told them how glad we were they were going, and hoped they would all return. . . .

We had exciting times in the University that spring of 1864, so many of the boys beside the senior class enlisted. . . .

There were no commencement exercises at the University that year, as the senior class was in the Army. They, however, received their diplomas just the same. . . .

*Sabra Warner left the university after a year. In May 1864, her brother was among the "many boys" who left Madison for the battlefront. Many did not return; the regiment lost more than half of its approximately one thousand men to death or disability. As officers were killed, her brother became a colonel by "battlefield promotions." But when he was wounded, losing an arm, he wrote to his sister from a military hospital in Washington, D.C. — which was typically understaffed — for "some nice little girl to wait on me, and I have concluded to send for you."*

*She left the same day from Windsor, alone, which shocked one of her former professors, whom she encountered en route in Madison; he acquired a letter from the governor to guarantee her safety. However, Warner's account suggests that she swiftly adapted to her new work as a war nurse in Washington and in Wisconsin, where she brought her brother safely back within weeks. He soon returned to his regiment and remained with it until the war's end. But she did not return to the university.*

*The Normal Department's first preceptress, Anna W. Moody, also left Madison after only a year to return to teaching in Lake Geneva, and she took Warner with her as an assistant. Moody briefly returned to Madison in 1864 to open the Normal Department's second school year, as Professor Charles H. Allen had enlisted. But when her replacement arrived, Moody returned to Lake Geneva, where Warner served as her administrator. Warner later moved to Madison, married Herbert E. Lewis of the* Wisconsin State Journal, *was widowed, and later married another newspaperman, Lathrop E. Smith, founder of the* Burlington Standard. *At the turn of the century, Sabra Warner Lewis Smith and other alumni held a reunion of the Normal Department to honor the university's first woman teacher.[7]*

*By then, Anna Moody Flack had trained hundreds of teachers across Wisconsin. Born in 1830 in Massachusetts, she grew up in the hometown of Mount Holyoke Seminary, founded in 1837 as one of the first academies for women, from which Moody graduated in 1855. She went west in 1858 with family, settling in Lake Geneva, where she started a school above a shoe store in 1859. Her hiring as preceptress of the university's new Normal Department in 1863 prompted parents in Lake Geneva to raise funds for a new school facility and higher pay to hire her back in 1864 as principal of Lake Geneva Seminary. However, she left again in the late 1860s to serve at a series of new state normal schools, including Whitewater, Oshkosh, and Platteville, prior to her marriage in 1882. Widowed in 1893, Anna Moody Flack died in Elkhorn in 1909.[8]*

*As for women students at the university after 1864, they comprised more than half of the student body in only the second year of the Normal Department but faced continuing separate-and-unequal treatment. Male students who enlisted in war had "received their diplomas just the same," in Sabra Warner Lewis Smith's words. However, the first six women graduates of the Normal Department at the end of its second year earned degrees in separate ceremonies, as did six more women in 1866. They endured despite being called "normalites" and "other unpleasant names," an alumna recalled. As another wrote, they "subordinated whatever unpleasantness might have been mingled with it . . . to get the highest education that the state offered us."[9]*

*Even that education for women came to an end. Regents considered combining the Normal Department with the high school, or Preparatory Department, claiming insufficient funding although they viewed women as "economical" enrollments. They continued the Preparatory Department but closed the Normal Department after thirteen women graduated in 1867, again in separate ceremonies.[10]*

*Regents' fiscal stringency was not the only reason for the failure of the Normal Department. Acting president Professor Sterling noted "apprehension" among alumni that the "standard of culture would be lowered" by coeducation. He reassured them of "no such mingling of classes in the higher and more recondite subjects" since men had come back from battlefields to campus. However, many of the twenty-five graduates of the Normal Department eventually went on to "higher" studies. Several would serve as "sorely needed trained teachers" in Madison, Milwaukee, and Chicago and some went on to earn bachelor's degrees. Two would earn graduate degrees and become professors at women's schools.[11]*

*Coeducation regressed further in 1866 when regents claimed that women students were a "stumbling block" in the search for a new president for the University of Wisconsin. Regents found the task "extremely difficult, if not impossible," Thwaites writes, so legislators removed the "objectionable" coeducation clause. Amended statutes stated that "the University shall be open to female as well as male students" — but under regents' "regulations and restrictions." Regents acceded to the restrictions required by an opponent of coeducation who previously had declined the presidency, Paul Ansel Chadbourne. The Normal Department was "styled the Female College," and he "prescribed an in-*

*ferior three years' course of study" for women, which "few cared to follow," with faculty in only music and art. In other subjects, women were to be seen but not heard, with "the privilege of attending lectures" but separate "recitations." As regents realized that separate classes were costly, they wanted women "instructed in any optional study for which they were prepared." Whether they were "prepared" was left to Chadbourne.[12]*

*Still, some stalwart women students at the University of Wisconsin undertook the regular curriculum in 1866, including two from Sabra Warner's hometown of Windsor: Ellen C. Sabin and Clara Bewick. Sabin would not complete her degree but, decades later, would receive honorary degrees as president of Wisconsin's first women's college. Bewick stayed, but the motherless English immigrant wrote to her grandparents, "I do not like the new arrangement" of limited library access, class chaperones, and other encumbrances upon their education, which women students endured at the state's allegedly coeducational campus.[13]*

*Women soon would find support from a formidable if unofficial campus group informally called "the faculty wives." Among them was another newcomer to Madison in 1868, Margaret Allen, whose husband had come to the campus a year before as its first professor of history. Her experience, as attested to in the next excerpt from her recollections, suggests reason for her sympathy with the welcome that women students received.*

⧼⧽

# The University of Wisconsin soon after the Civil War

To give an idea of the University as I first knew it, let me picture to you Madison as I first saw it. . . .

. . . [The campus] was the favorite camping ground for the long trains of emigrant wagons that passed through every spring, often returning in the fall with tired, discouraged emigrants. The University was no less primitive, consisting of just one building — the main building on the hill . . . while the north dormitory housed the boys in wretched homelessness, and the girls tried to add a little grace to their building, the south dormitory, by here and there in some window a white curtain or other sign of home comfort. . . . In the main building several of the professors roomed. . . .

The gymnasium was a barn-like structure. . . . The gymnasium appliances were entirely in harmony with the appearance of the building. At the time, the girls were not allowed entrance into the sacred temple, reserved for their worthy brothers, although they greatly desired to share in the physical training, and needed it, for many of them were pale and far from vigorous. . . . [They] secured Thursday afternoons for the girls to have the use of the gymnasium. . . . [T]he athletic situation, a difficult question in those days, was rendered the more difficult because of the opposition of the regents.

[Former president] Patrick Walsh in those days was the grand panjandrum of the University. . . . Patrick cared for the young professors as his children, passing judgment on their selection of wives, without fear or favor. . . . [T]heir husbands would come home from the University and tell what Patrick had said to them. I remember one crestfallen professor who had looked forward to this ordeal for his bride with pleased confidence, and who was greeted the next day after the important introduction, with these words, "Shure, professor, I can't congratulate you; you could have done a great deal better for yourself.". . .

. . . Through all this time — the period of President Chadbourne's administration — the girls were taken only on sufferance. They were here — could not be got rid of — and so President Chadbourne tolerated them, in classes by themselves. But woe to the girl who dared to walk on the boys' side of the hill, or to be seen speaking to a boy on the campus. It is curious to see how even a shrewd man may be strangely blinded on some one point. No one could have doubted President Chadbourne's shrewdness — he was as quick and alert as one of our squirrels, and always reminded me of one — but poor man, he was blind to one situation. The boys walked up the north side of the hill and recited in the south rooms of the main building, while the girls, who went up the south side, recited in the north rooms. A better place for flirtations, my husband used to say, could scarcely have been devised than the University rotunda, where these lines crossed. He could testify that the students made good use of their opportunity.

There was very little social life at the University in those early days; indeed, I think in President Chadbourne's time it was rather discountenanced, [e]xcept for an occasional reception at the home of some professor. . . . In the early days it was much more possible to have a personal acquaintance with the members of the various classes, the number was so small — in 1868 only 164, of which 34 were girls; in the preparatory [high school] department, 124 boys and 106 girls. I know that nearly every member of several of those early classes of girls had some professor's family whom she knew. . . . [M]any of the boys living their homeless lives in the north dormitory had little knowledge of the hospitality of this eminently hospitable town of Madison. . . .

. . . [T]he majority of the students who came here came with the idea that the intellectual training of the University was the object they had in view, not recreation nor social aims. Many also used every moment of their spare time in earning their living. . . . [T]he greater proportion of the students were hardworking; many were of limited means, and many even earned every dollar they used. . . .

The University appliances in the early days were of the simplest type. The [classroom] benches had been constructed not only with utter disregard of the anatomy of the human figure, but seemingly with the old monkish idea that torture and holiness went hand in hand. The students tossed all the old benches into the lake one night, and I know of several of the faculty who personally sympathized with the act, though of course they could say nothing in its praise. . . .

The sheet-iron box stoves were another primitive institution in the early times. In these was burned the greenest of green wood, bought cheap. . . . [T]he temperature of the University in those days [compared in] winter to a seat on our lake shore with one's feet in the icy water. . . .

The faculty meetings of those early days are memorable to us who climbed that long hill every Monday evening to attend them at the home of President Chadbourne. In the front parlor of that house the faculty carried on their deliberations in the early evening, while their wives, the preceptress, and the lady instructors with their work amused themselves with conversation in the back parlor. The work brought by one professor's wife was her baby. . . . [A]fter the professors came in, we were refreshed with cake and coffee. . . . The few participants who are still left have many grey hairs, but when they meet in these days, they have often a hearty laugh over the personal incidents among that cheery company who came over the University hill those winter Monday evenings of 1868–69. And though we all appreciate the wider outlook of today, and the growing power of our beloved University, we who were a part of those early days shall always give them a warm place in our hearts.

*Margaret Allen, widowed in 1889, remained for the rest of her life a "faculty wife" in Madison. In 1901, she convened other wives and women faculty at her home to found the University League. The league raised funds for a campus women's building, Lathrop Hall, completed in 1910. In 1916, the league established a loan fund for women students. In World War I, members continued to meet at Margaret Allen's home to work for the war effort. In 2001, the league celebrated its centennial and still raises funds for annual scholarships for women students.*

*As for the situation of women students after 1868, see the account by Florence Bascom in "The University in 1874–1887" in chapter 4.*

## NOTES

1. Sara M. Evans, *Born for Liberty: A History of Women in America,* 2nd ed. (New York: Free Press, 1997), 139; Thwaites, *The University of Wisconsin,* 78–80; Merle Curti and Vernon Carstensen, *The University of Wisconsin: A History, 1848–1925* (Madison: University of Wisconsin, 1949), 194.

2. Thwaites, *University of Wisconsin,* 86–88.

3. Evans, *Born for Liberty,* 114.

4. Thwaites, *University of Wisconsin,* 86–88.

5. [Sewing kits, also called "housewives" in the era.]

6. [John W. Sterling was vice-president of the university, Charles H. Allen taught in the Normal Department during the Civil War, and Anna W. Moody served as preceptress of the Normal Department in 1863–64. See Thwaites, *University of Wisconsin,* 771.]

7. "First Woman Teacher in the University Gone to Her Reward," *Wisconsin State Journal,* December 13, 1909.

8. Ibid.

9. Emma Phillips Vroman, "Pioneer Days in Coeducation," *Wisconsin Alumni Magazine* 14 (May 1913): 400–401, and Ellen Chynoweth Lyon, "Early Years of Co-Education at Wisconsin," *Wisconsin Alumni Magazine* 22 (December 1920): 5, quoted in Kristen Mapel Bloomberg, "True Woman or New Woman? Clara Bewick Colby and the Making of a Modern Suffragist," unpublished ms. in the possession of the editor.

10. Thwaites, *University of Wisconsin,* 78, 818; Curti and Carstensen, *University of Wisconsin,* 4.

11. Thwaites, *University of Wisconsin,* 80, 86.

12. Ibid., 80, 86–87, 92. A "Miss M. S. Melville" succeeded Moody as preceptress from 1864 to 1866. In 1867, the music instructor was Frances Brown and the instructor of painting and drawing was Louise Brewster, under Elizabeth Earle as preceptress and Clarissa Ware as associate preceptress. Ware succeeded Earle in 1869, and her successor was Delia E. Carson as preceptress and then principal from 1871 to 1886. Mary Ekin Whitton was principal from 1886 to 1889, as was Mary C. Bright from 1889 to 1897, when Abbey Shaw Mayhew was named Ladies' Hall mistress and Annie Crosby Emery was named dean of women.

13. Bloomberg, "True Woman or New Woman?" 10. On Sabin, see "Ellen Clara Sabin and My Years at Downer" in chapter 5. On Bewick, see "Women and the University of Wisconsin, 1869–1887" in chapter 4.

# "This Noble Monument"

## The Story of the Soldiers' Orphans' Home

PATRICIA G. HARRSCH

WMH 76, No. 2 (Winter 1992–1993): 83–120

"It is always best if you wish to secure an object . . . to go at once to the highest power and be your own petitioner."[1] With these words, Mrs. Cordelia A. P. Harvey of Madison described her efforts to secure a convalescent hospital in Wisconsin for Union soldiers. Mrs. Harvey was no stranger to coping with difficult situations. Her husband, Louis Powell Harvey, had assumed office as governor in January 1862. In April of that year, following the Battle of Shiloh, he had drowned in the Tennessee River as he left a hospital boat where he had been visiting the state's sick and wounded soldiers. After his death, his successor as governor, Edward Salomon, had appointed Mrs. Harvey a "sanitary agent" for the state. This involved her in visiting the camps and hospitals where Wisconsin soldiers were assigned, in order to inform the governor as to the physical condition and morale of the troops.

Described as "probably the most effective" of the state's agents, Cordelia Harvey "reported on the numbers of sick and wounded, arranged for transporting them home, distributed gifts and medical supplies, and made available extra surgeons and nurses."[2] When she became convinced that Union soldiers would benefit both psychologically and physically from being allowed to convalesce in hospitals closer to home, and in the healthier climate of the North, she went directly to President Abraham Lincoln. Both the president and the War Department opposed any plan that would allow convalescent soldiers to return to the North on the grounds that large-scale desertions would be the only result.[3] But Mrs. Harvey persisted. . . . Ultimately, she prevailed. In October, 1863, Harvey U.S. Army General Hospital (named after her late husband) opened in Madison, Wisconsin. Other northern hospitals were established thereafter.

When she returned from her work in the South in 1865, Mrs. Harvey brought with her several orphans.[4] She had apparently already conceived the idea of establishing a shelter for those children in Wisconsin who had been left destitute by the war. . . .

In America, by the 1860s, the problem of the care of dependent children had not yet been fully worked through. . . . Many destitute youngsters were confined to tax-supported poorhouses along with the elderly needy, the infirm, and the mentally ill; or they were bound out to "respectable families" to earn their board and keep; or, if they found themselves without homes, they might be confined to local jails on the charge of vagrancy. . . .

Orphanages had begun to appear in greater numbers. . . .[5]

In Wisconsin, several such "orphan asylums" had been established in the 1850s by private [religious] organizations. . . . [A]ll were located in the Milwaukee area and served small numbers of youngsters.[6] But in 1865 the loss of more than 11,000 Wisconsin men in a terrible war presented the statewide community with a problem of a different magnitude. Indeed, the numbers were staggering: first estimates suggested that 8,000 Wisconsin children had been orphaned. . . . [7]

The estimated number of soldiers' orphans in Wisconsin was to be reduced to 6,000 when a survey of towns, initiated by the secretary of state in late 1865, was completed.[8] Not all the orphans were destitute, but of the total number, some had lost their mothers as well as their fathers. Such children faced a grim future if family or friends were unable to assume their care. The surviving mothers of many more children found themselves poverty-stricken. The loss of their husbands had left them without any resources for caring for themselves or their offspring. . . . Such a woman might find work as a seamstress, as a laundress or a domestic servant, but how could she support a family on the wages such jobs paid — even adding to those wages the small government pension she received?

The tragedy of these widows and orphans was felt by the community at large, and particularly by the veterans who had survived the horrors of the war. . . .

. . . [T]he voices of the veterans were listened to with great sympathy. The veterans' vote was avidly courted. . . . Lucius Fairchild, former colonel of the Second Wisconsin Volunteer Infantry, who had lost an arm at Gettsyburg, was active on the political scene as secretary of state and was to run for governor . . . in the fall of 1865. . . . [9] He and many of his political friends were to assist Mrs. Harvey in her efforts to ease the plight of the destitute soldiers' orphans — efforts which resulted in the state's being presented with a *fait accompli* — an operating institution for which the state had little choice but to accept responsibility.

Harvey Hospital had closed in the summer of 1865. . . .

On September 15, 1865, the Madison common council adopted a resolution calling for a meeting of citizens to consider the purchase of Harvey Hospital for an "Asylum for orphan children of deceased soldiers. . . ."[10]

On September 27, the *Wisconsin State Journal* reported the organization of a temporary board of trustees for the Home. Members included, as president, His Excellency, James T. Lewis, Governor of the State, . . . [other influential men] and, as general superintendent, Mrs. Harvey. The institution was being organized even as fund-raising proceeded.

. . . Some $5,000 had already been raised, and it was hoped that . . . the job of raising the $30,000 deemed necessary for the project could be easily accomplished. On October 18, the paper reported that Mrs. Harvey was having "excellent success" in raising funds. . . . [[11]]

. . . A total of $12,834.69 was raised. . . .[12]

On January 10, 1866, the *State Journal* announced that the Soldiers' Orphans' Home was ready for occupancy. The board and Mrs. Harvey had apparently been overwhelmed with requests for admittance, but these were so diverse that town chairmen were being urged to help in the selection process so that the neediest children were sure to receive consideration.

. . . In mid-March . . . eighty-four children had already been admitted to the Home and were being cared for under the superintendency of Mrs. Harvey.[12]

. . . [T]he plan . . . did not receive wholehearted approval throughout the state. . . .

[The *Milwaukee*] *Sentinel* declared on page one that . . . a home solely for soldiers' orphans would be useless in just a few years and, the editorial concluded, "we cannot afford, in these days of high prices and taxes, to throw away our money under false notions of charity.". . .[13]

. . . [T]he board of trustees was to say, "We differ in opinion with those who regard its inmates as paupers and the Institution as a State Alms-House, with the sole object of supplying barely sufficient food and clothing to sustain life." Rather, the board maintained that the home should be a place of learning where "the unfortunate children of Wisconsin's patriot sons may receive such educational and moral training as will enable them to care for themselves and become good citizens.". . .[14]

On March 31, 1866, Governor Fairchild signed the bill establishing the Soldiers' Orphans' Home as a state institution. . . .[15]

[A] select committee found that the Home employed twenty-six persons as of March 1, 1867, at a cost of $557.97 per month; that the cost per child was $108.95. . . .[16]

. . . [O]nce the state assumed responsibility for the Home, the number of residents rapidly increased. In 1867, the trustees reported an average population of 280 children. By 1868, the reported average had increased to 300.[17] This was in excess of the Home's capacity. . . .

In 1872, of 262 resident children, 141 were boys and 121 were girls. The largest age group was the ten-to-fourteen-year-olds. One hundred eighty-four children had mothers who were living (fifty-eight of whom had remarried after their children entered the Home), and seventy-eight youngsters had lost both father and mother. . . .[18]

A quick survey of the residences of the children (insofar as they can be determined) shows that there were entrants from almost every county in the state. The greatest numbers came from Dane and those counties adjacent to it. . . .[19]

The *Milwaukee Sentinel* charged in the spring of 1867 that the Home's admittance practices favored Dane County. . . . A more probable explanation is transportation costs. Getting a child to Madison from any distance may have cost more than the mother could afford. . . .[20]

In later years, most of the applicants were children of school age. The mothers tended to keep their younger children at home until their need for education became apparent.[21] This was especially true of families in more remote rural areas. The schooling offered by the Home was considered to be superior to what was available in those areas, and education was probably the most important advantage offered to the residents of the Home. . . .

Under Mrs. Harvey's leadership, Miss Persis H. Torrey organized the school on April 2, 1866. By the middle of August, Miss Torrey had three assistants to help with the task of educating 244 children, the majority of whom, the superintendent noted, "were entirely unaccustomed to study or discipline in school.". . .[22]

By 1868, . . . four female teachers were employed at $25 a month. . . .[23] [E]ach teacher had responsibility for over sixty youngsters, depending upon the number and ages of the residents at any given time. . . .

No records have been found which detail the overall disciplinary practices at the Home, but they must of necessity have been very strict. . . . Indeed, some of the asylums assumed an almost military sternness. . . .[24] But there is no sense, in the reports of the superintendent or trustees, of a "military" atmosphere prevailing at the Home. Indeed, by 1873 critics were complaining of too little discipline. . . .[25]

Apparently the girls were not a problem, as they were kept busy with the housekeeping activities of the Home. They helped in the dining room and with dormitory chores, as well as in the ironing room and with the sewing and knitting. In later years, home economics courses were introduced and the girls were given the opportunity to cut and sew their own clothing. The aim was to encourage them to be both "neater in their appearance and more industrious in their habits."[26]

The boys were another matter. For them, chores around the Home were not so time-consuming. Organized into squads, they split wood, carried coal, and helped to tend the fires and keep the yard clean. . . . [27] Keeping them occupied continued to be a problem throughout the Home's existence. . . .

There were also educational opportunities outside the Home's schoolrooms. In 1867, twelve boys attended class at the Business College. . . . [28] In 1870 the Legislature approved a bill appropriating $200 per student so that six residents of the Home (one from each Congressional district) could attend Whitewater Normal School for two years.[29] The young people were selected by examination and in consultation with the state superintendent of public instruction. Ultimately twenty students were to take advantage of this program, not only at Whitewater but also at the normal schools in Platteville and Oshkosh. . . .[30] Two of the girls were sent home because they would not "submit to the discipline,"[31] but overall, the trustees considered the program to be a success. . . .

In 1872 the trustees approved setting up a telegraphy class for those boys and girls with a special talent for the program. . . . In 1873, thirty-three boys were enrolled in the class. . . .[32]

. . . [T]he superintendent was to declare in 1874 that the Home was "not a school for idlers." . . .[33]

Visitors apparently frequented the Home with some regularity. . . . Indeed, Governor Fairchild sometimes took the children on lake excursions and picnics on Sundays.[34]

On the first Monday of each month, those children who could were expected to write to their family and friends. The teachers wrote for the younger ones.[35] In 1868, the children were not allowed to go home since such visits interrupted their studies. By 1869, however, the Milwaukee and St. Paul Railroad was providing passes so that the residents could visit their mothers once a year.[36]

The 1866 bylaws had decreed that the children were not to be subjected to any religious influence of a sectarian nature. They were, however, to be allowed to attend religious services where they, their mothers, or their friends chose. . . . [37]

Throughout the Home's existence, there was considerable concern about the moral training and character development of the children. . . .

Just as the moral well-being of the children was important to the caretakers, so was their physical health, and this seems to have been an area marked by success. Among 683 children who resided in the Home during its existence, there were only twelve deaths. Of these, several were due to disease or frail health the children brought with them.[38] Emma Buelow, who died of consumption on February 12, 1870, was described as "an invalid when admitted [at age eight] in January, 1867.". . .[39]

The early years seem to have seen the greatest health problems. In 1866 Dr. L. S. Ingham reported one death and 232 cases of disease, including measles, whooping cough, and croup. In the 1867 physician's report, six deaths and 400 cases of disease were noted, with gastric fever, diarrhea, and acute opthalmia (rampant through the state) predominating. . . .[40]

. . . [A] monument was erected in the Soldiers' Rest (now Union Rest) section of Forest Hill Cemetery in Madison.[41] Dedicated to the children who had died while residents of the Home, the 8½-foot-high marble obelisk is inscribed with the names of the eight young people who are buried in the plot with Union soldiers who died at the Harvey Hospital or while in training at Camp Randall. . . .

What happened to the children who had left the home. . . .? In 1866, Mrs. Harvey had reported that twenty-five of the thirty-seven children who had left the Home that year had done so because their mothers were leaving the state; the women had remarried and wanted their children with them; or, having received pensions, they felt able to assume the care of their young ones once again. Nine boys age twelve or older, and three younger ones, had run away.[42]

. . . The board could discharge any child fifteen years or older who could support him or herself. But no child under age fifteen could be released — not even to his or her mother — without a certificate from the town chairman where the mother lived, showing she could support and educate her child.[43]

. . . [In 1867] the trustees put out a call for the citizens of Wisconsin to help in finding homes and employment for the fifteen-year-olds who had to leave the Home. Most seem to have returned to their families.[44]

. . . [By 1873] many families in the state had asked for older children who could help out on the farm or in the kitchen. But few had wanted to assume the care and expense of taking on younger boys and girls. And, in spite of the care taken in placing the children, the Home's "trust had been betrayed" in two instances, and the child had had to be returned to the Home or provided for elsewhere. In three cases, either the child or the family had been so dissatisfied with the placement that the child had been recalled until another family could be found.[45]

. . . Also, the mothers and children themselves were exhibiting a greater reluctance to participate in the placement program — a reluctance which the superintendent found not surprising. Apparently, well-qualified families had forgotten their promises to educate and care for the children as if they were their own as soon as the children were within their power. . . .

How *did* the children feel about the Home? Coming to Madison must have been traumatic for most of them. To have lost their fathers in the war, to have sensed their mothers'

grief and desperation, to have been sent away from their homes and friends and plunged
into a very large group of strangers, and then to have found themselves confined daily to
a schoolroom to which they were not accustomed — it must have been an almost overwhelming experience. The children must also have felt some confusion as to their place
in the world. As soldiers' orphans, they were "different' from other children: objects of
pity on the one hand ("Fatherless but not forsaken" was emblazoned on one schoolroom
wall), objects of an ever-mindful benevolence on the other ("We will love and honor the
state which has adopted us" was on another wall). . . . [46]

What judgment then can be made of the Soldiers' Orphans' Home? Was "this noble
monument of the patriotism and generosity of Wisconsin's people"[47] a needless institution, as the *Milwaukee Sentinel* had claimed in 1866? Or did it contribute in a positive manner to children who might have faced far more unpleasant alternatives?

Mrs. Harvey and her supporters had hoped to give some of Wisconsin's neediest children a helping hand during a difficult period in their lives and to provide them with a
background of education which would enhance their futures. . . . [I]t seems safe to assume that, aided by their years in the Home, many of the soldiers' orphans became industrious, energetic, and mindful citizens of Wisconsin and the nation. . . .

⁓⁓⁓

*Surveys of former residents of the orphans' home found that many girls had married. Others, "fol-
lowing tastes acquired in school," had furthered their educations and became teachers, and some became domestics or clerks, supporting themselves. Most younger girls were in "comfortable homes." Few
of the boys had married yet. Most became farmers; some had completed apprenticeships or were clerks,
tradesmen, or teachers; and four were homesteaders in the far West.[48]*

*By 1874, only thirty-five residents remained, the author reports, and legislators closed the or-
phans' home with provisions for placing children with mothers or other relatives, if suitable, who were
to receive $5 per month — or private orphanages that were to be paid $6 per month. Thirty children
went home to mothers, guardians, or relatives, and five were placed in other families' homes. None
went to other orphanages. Also, private bequests from donors in Chicago and London, England,
made possible pensions of $5 per month to more than a hundred mothers who had taken their chil-
dren home, as well as gifts to residents upon adulthood, which most of them eventually requested.[49]*

*As for the orphans' home, the property continued to serve as a school and as an orphanage under
other owners. Built in 1854 by a former governor, the octagonal house on Lake Monona at the foot
of Brearly Street, which had served as a Civil War soldiers' hospital and then had housed soldiers'
orphans, was damaged by fire and razed in 1895. The land later was subdivided, and one of the new
streets was named Harvey Terrace in memory of Cordelia A. Perrine Harvey.*

*Harvey, who was called "Wisconsin's Angel of Mercy" for her war service, had resigned her post
as superintendent of the orphans' home in 1867 and retired to Clinton Junction to live with her sister. In 1876, she married the Reverend Albert T. Chester and moved to Buffalo, New York, where she
taught again and was widowed again. She returned to Clinton Junction, where she died at her sister's home in 1895.[50] By then, even the youngest of the orphans for whom she had made a home were
more than thirty years old.*

❧❧

# NOTES

1. Cordelia A. P. Harvey, "A Wisconsin Woman's Picture of President Lincoln," in the *WMH* 1 (March 1918), 241. [Cordelia Adelaide Perrine of Southport, now Kenosha, was born in 1824 in New York to Mary Hebard Perrine and John Perrine, who moved to Wisconsin in the mid-1840s. Their daughter taught school prior to marrying another Southport schoolteacher in 1847. They moved to Madison in 1859, when he was elected Wisconsin's secretary of state.]

2. Current, *HOW*, 369.

3. May L. Bauchle, "The Shopiere Shrine," in the *WMH* 10 (September 1926), 29–34.

4. Bauchle, "Shopiere Shrine," 5.

5. . . . Robert H. Bremner, ed., *Children and Youth in America: A Documentary History*, vol. 1, *1600–1865* (Cambridge, 1970), 631–632.

6. *Annual Report of the Wisconsin State Board of Charities & Reform* (1880), 294–296.

7. *Wisconsin State Journal*, September 15, 1865.

8. Ibid., January 11, 1866.

9. Sam Ross, *The Empty Sleeve: A Biography of Lucius Fairchild* (Madison, 1964).

10. *Wisconsin State Journal*, September 15, 1865.

11. *Annual Report of the Trustees of the Soldiers' Orphans' Home of Wisconsin for the Fiscal Year Ending Sept. 30, 1866*, 346. [Hereinafter TR and the year.]

12. . . . *Annual Report of the Superintendent of the Soldiers' Orphans' Home for the Fiscal Year Ending Sept. 30, 1866*, 349; hereinafter SR and year.

13. *Milwaukee Sentinel*, March 20, 1866.

14. TR (1986), 2.

15. *Assembly Journal* (1866), 990.

16. . . . *Assembly Journal* (1867), 1280. . . .

17. TR (1868), 3. In 1894 the trustees report shows 287 as the largest number at any one time. TR (1894), 7.

18. SR (1870), 15.

19. ["Residents of the Soldiers' Orphans' Home," compiled by Patricia and Reid Harrsch (1991).]

20. *Senate Journal* (1867), 640.

21. SR (1870), 20.

22. SR (1866), 355.

23. SR (1868), 22.

24. David J. Rothman, *The Discovery of the Asylum: Social Order and Disorder in the New Republic* (rev. ed., Boston, 1990), 220–221.

25. *Milwaukee Sentinel*, March 19, 1873.

26. SR (1867), 16; (1868), 22; (1872), 42; TR (1872), 6.

27. SR (1867), 16 and (1868), 22.

28. Ibid., (1867), 14.

29. Chap. 49, *Laws of Wisconsin*, 1870.

30. Chap. 124, *Laws of Wisconsin*, 1871.

31. Report of James Bintliff . . . (included with the Annual Reports, 1872).

32. SR (1872), 36; TR (1872), 5; (1872), 5.

33. SR (1874), 13.

34. Ross, *Empty Sleeve*, 105.

35. SR (1868), 22.

36. Ibid., (1868), 22; (1869), 20.

37. *Rules, Regulations and By-Laws* (1866), sec. 13.

38. Causes of death included consumption, convulsions, dysentery, inflammation of the lungs, and inflammation of the brain. SR (1866–1870), passim.

39. SR (1870), 13.

40. *Physician's Report* (1866–1872). . . .

41. SR (1873), 21.

42. Ibid., (1866), 356.

43. Chap. 168, *Laws of Wisconsin*, 1867.

44. TR (1867), 3. . . .

45. SR (1873), 16–17.

46. David V. Mollenhoff, *Madison: A History of the Formative Years* (Dubuque, 1982), 151.

47. TR (1865), 5.

48. TR (1877), 8, and (1880), 6–7.

49. TR (1875), 3.

50. *Milwaukee Sentinel*, February 28, 1895; *Dictionary of Wisconsin Biography* (Madison, 1960); Bauchle, "Shopiere Shrine," 34; Williams, *First Ladies of Wisconsin*, 53–55.

*Studio portrait of one family's household staff*

## 4

# POVERTY AND PROGRESS
# FOR WOMEN IN WISCONSIN,
# 1868–1888

## INTRODUCTION

I n the post–Civil War period, the nation saw significant political and economic changes. Political change affected the South with passage of amendments to the Constitution that, for the first time, explicitly limited suffrage and other rights of citizenship to men. However, freedmen in the South would return after Reconstruction to the political status of women — that is, with no political status at all — while in the North, economic change had lasting effects as the Industrial Revolution spread west into Wisconsin. Where so recently settlers had turned frontier into farmland, now farmland turned into factories, with significant impact on the ways that women as well as men made a living.

Thousands of Wisconsin women worked in industrial sites in the late 1860s. Others had "piecework" at home, where immigrant women would not have to wear "American dress" to gain employment, as a Madison woman wrote. However, employment of women in industry increased most rapidly in the ensuing decades, as Robert C. Nesbit writes in his article, excerpted in this chapter, on making a living in Wisconsin in the era. In the 1880s, women's place also expanded into retail and business workplaces, including the oldest institution in the state and one of the largest in Milwaukee. Northwestern Mutual Life Insurance Company at last hired its first woman employee in 1880, although more than five decades would pass before the firm insured a woman's life. But the breakthrough in the workplace would change other women's lives, in part owing to the invention of the typewriter in the late 1860s by pioneering Milwaukee reform journalist Christopher Latham Sholes. Shortly before his death, his daughter-in-law remarked, "what a wonderful thing you have done for the world." Sholes replied, "I don't know about the world, but I do feel that I have done something for the women who always have had to work so hard. It will enable them more easily to earn a living."[1]

A few courageous women even earned their living in one of the most perilous and lonely fields in the period: as lighthouse keepers on the Great Lakes signaling safe harbor. Most worked without pay as assistants to husbands and fathers or, after the men's deaths — sometimes by drowning while rescuing shipwreck victims in wild Great Lakes gales — women served as "acting keepers" without full pay from the federal government until male replacements arrived. At the start of the Civil War, when men were scarce, a Port

Washington lighthouse keeper's widow so served for several months. More often, women managed routines from keeping the logs and polishing the powerful lenses to keeping beacons lit when left alone, which led some women into more dangerous duty. By the 1880s, Georgia Green Stebbins officially held the post of head keeper at the Milwaukee lighthouse, where she set a record for longevity. She moved to Milwaukee in 1874 to help her ailing father, the North Point lighthouse head keeper; her unofficial service finally was acknowledged with appointment to the post in 1881. By the end of the era, as the lakeshore eroded, she moved operations to a higher site and new home with a covered walkway to the tower, easing her work in the worst of Wisconsin weather. Stebbins served for thirty-three years, into the next century.[2]

Working-class women in Wisconsin no longer were destined only for domestic service, nor were educated women destined only for "republican motherhood," to raise sons — but not daughters — for citizenship, as historian Sara M. Evans writes. Such women could support themselves in teaching, although at less pay than men — and not in many Milwaukee schools because of resistance from immigrant German men. Women comprised two-thirds of Wisconsin teachers by 1870, according to Nesbit. By 1880, after some women won suffrage in the West, a change in Wisconsin law allowed women to run for office as school superintendents. However, that they could not vote for themselves was a paradox that would prove too typical of Wisconsin in the suffrage campaign to come. As a Racine woman wrote to the national *Woman's Journal,* suffragists "had about the same social standing" in the state "as advocates of arson."[3]

Some women seeking work in Wisconsin had little social or legal standing in the "oldest profession," prostitution. Historian Bonnie Ripp-Shucha shows that domestic abuse caused some women to become prostitutes in the dozens of brothels in the newer, northern towns. Her article on the "naughty city" of Eau Claire, excerpted in this chapter, describes a means for women to make a living in Wisconsin that hardly merits mention in most state histories. However, she also shows that prostitution is part of men's history as well, owing to their complicity as brothel-keepers and lax enforcers of the law — including lawmakers in Madison who patronized prostitutes but would not allow them, and all other Wisconsin women, to make progress toward legal protections.

If the "history of sexuality has gained respectability in recent years," as Ripp-Shucha writes, few historians have explored its part in Wisconsin's past — a violent past for women. Several historians note a notorious series of murders and lynchings in the period in Wisconsin but do not note that most arose from crimes committed against women. In 1868, a boy held for the murder of an Irish housewife was himself murdered and his corpse was lynched in Richland Center. In 1869, a mob in Monroe nearly lynched Angeline Shroyer for shooting her seducer. Another mob lynched two men for four murders near Kilbourn City, now Wisconsin Dells. That the mob also was avenging the crime of rape is recalled only rarely, and only one historian notes that the rape victim, Mary Ann Cusick Gates, was victimized again by Wisconsin's courts and sensationalist media. Although apparently neither the press nor the police interviewed her, newspapers in Milwaukee and Madison falsely accused her as the lover of the man who had raped her and murdered her husband. When the lynching case came to trial, the judge applauded the lynch mob as an "uprising of the people" but publicly "expressed his doubt that a rape had occurred."[4]

The same era also saw increasing recognition by the medical profession of the problem of sexually transmitted diseases, not only to prostitutes but also to other women and their children in the period prior to mandatory medical testing for marriage licenses. Records do not fully reflect the prevalence of many women's health conditions, owing to "the embarrassment with which people viewed such health problems as 'female complaints,'" writes historian Jan Coombs in her article excerpted in this chapter. Yet census documents and newspaper accounts dispel the myth of a pastoral life on central Wisconsin's "semifrontier," as Coombs calls it in painting a dismal portrait of even the known extent of diseases and deaths among women and children — and husbands and fathers bereft of both — in a Wisconsin where life remained hard, and often unhealthy, for the rural poor.

In another paradox of the period, the interrelated problems of health and poverty for some women and children would provide careers, if unpaid, for upper-class "society women" in some Wisconsin cities. As economic change escalated progress for some but poverty for others, women acted to augment the few governmental institutions such as poorhouses, which existed prior to federal public welfare programs. Women no longer were likely to directly bestow charity, as in the days of the Female Moral Reform Society for the rescue of "fallen women" (see Introduction to chapter 2). Instead, women now monitored and reported to governmental boards on needs to be met. A leader who typified the transition was Mary Blanchard Lynde of Milwaukee, a founder of the city's Ladies' Benevolent Society by the 1850s and the soldiers' aid society in the early 1860s. Biographer Ellen D. Langill argues that the well-educated Lynde had a precocious faith in scientific means to analyze social problems. According to historian Ann Firor Scott, that placed Lynde among "very few" women attempting "to ponder reasons for the extreme poverty they encountered and to make their own, often naive, social analysis," although no more naive than that of their male contemporaries.[5]

The spouse of a prominent lawyer and former Congressman, mayor, and state legislator, Lynde became Wisconsin's first woman political appointee in 1871 on the new State Board of Charities overseeing prisons and poorhouses. She promptly organized women to win improvements for others incarcerated in state institutions. Many of the "unfortunate women," she reported to other board members, were "victims of men who promise marriage only to betray and desert" them "when ruined," with "no refuge or shelter, and often no occupation but the life of sin." Ahead of her time, Lynde also sought retribution for "the equally guilty seducer" by "rendering" men "responsible for the maintenance of the[ir] offspring." She settled for "some provision" by the board to better prepare inmates to be self-supporting, as at the state Industrial School for Boys. Lynde led women's fund raising for a facility and lobbying for land at the soldiers' home — the same site for which they already had raised funds to care for Civil War veterans, until the federal government finally took responsibility and took the land (see Introduction to chapter 3). The Industrial School for Girls opened in 1875, run by a matron and female staff who also cared for boys too young for the other state facility.[6]

Lynde's Ladies' Benevolent Society in Milwaukee and subsequent work in the charity movement led the way in Wisconsin for the clubwomen's movement, widely publicized by a pioneering eastern woman journalist in 1868. Lynde and other city women at the nation's centennial celebration in 1876 in the East met clubwoman and poet Julia Ward Howe, the author of "Battle Hymn of the Republic" during the Civil War. They invited Howe to help found the Woman's Club of Wisconsin that took as its task, as the head of Milwaukee Female College said, the "civilizing" of their city. By the 1880s, when Milwaukee clubwomen won the appointment of a police matron for women in the city jail, Lynde became a leader in the prison reform movement nationwide.[7]

However, enrollment in vocational institutions such as the industrial school, instead of incarceration in poorhouses, did not improve the lives of some women and girls, when the courts victimized them again by committing them for acts of rape and incest against them. In her study of the "disciplining" of women's sexuality, historian Joan M. Jensen analyzed documents from the Industrial School for Girls that attest to double standards embedded in state statutes. Admission records after 1880 show that "almost ten percent of the admitted 'delinquent' girls had been sexually abused by male relatives or neighbors." She finds that women were arrested, where men were not, in the towns that "tended to tolerate an open worker culture that often included drinking, gambling, and 'whoring' by men" — as in Milwaukee, where city fathers would promote a red-light district of brothels that did business for decades.[8]

Smaller cities such as Janesville prided themselves on orderly streets "compared to the wretchedness and squalor" of Milwaukee, according to historian John A. Fleckner, but also provided women with careers as volunteers in the "burgeoning national movement to reform charity administration." In his article excerpted in this chapter, he suggests that even in Janesville's seemingly "well-ordered urban society . . . harsh poverty and suffering were inescapable features of life," viewed as inevitable and "a mark of individual deviance" rather than a failure of the economy. For example, he writes, women were sent to local poorhouses for lack of alternative support when suffering from the "debilitating condition" of pregnancy. The second charity association in the state soon arose in Janesville — where well-meaning, "well-to-do, often educated" matrons held the common "middle-class assumptions" about the poor until they learned "lessons about the complexities of poverty" amid continual economic upheavals in late nineteenth-century Wisconsin. Among the foremothers of the modern field of social work, they helped themselves as they helped others, and women's clubs arose across the state to undertake "charity work." As Fleckner writes, clubwomen "found challenging and socially useful community roles that were still largely denied them in politics, business, and the professions."

The first Wisconsin women in the professions of medicine, law, and the ministry found sufficient challenges from men in their fields. The first woman physician in Wisconsin, Dr. Laura J. Ross, had been denied admittance to most medical schools and again met discrimination from male colleagues who denied her membership in the Milwaukee Medical

Society (see Introduction to chapter 3) — until she married its president in 1869, a significant year in women's history. Earlier in 1869, in the East, Mathilde Franzsiska Anneke (see "Madame Mathilda Franziska Anneke" in chapter 3) had represented Wisconsin at the founding of the National Woman Suffrage Association by Susan B. Anthony and Elizabeth Cady Stanton after passage of the amendments to the Constitution that explicitly excluded women. Anneke returned to work with Ross, as well as with Milwaukee's first woman minister and first woman law student, in organizing the first statewide woman suffrage convention, held in Milwaukee City Hall in February of 1869. Stanton and Anthony spoke to a standing-room-only crowd of women and founded the Wisconsin Woman Suffrage Association (WWSA), which would endure for fifty years until the Nineteenth Amendment was won.[9]

Dr. Laura Ross Wolcott won election as president of the WWSA, and higher education ranked high on her agenda for women — understandably, after her experience. As she wrote of regents at the University of Wisconsin in her state president's report to Anthony and Stanton, "girls can be defrauded of their rights to a thorough education by narrow, bigoted men entrusted with a little brief authority." Her aspirations reflected the ambitions of the middle-class leaders of the women's movement. However, their aims were widely held by women and girls in the late nineteenth century.[10]

Also in 1869, in Necedah, a motherless girl who aspired to a medical career was taken out of school by a father who believed that for "girls, it doesn't make much difference." A decade of indifference from her family while Bertha V. Thomson was "boarded out" for domestic service only deferred her dream of medical training, first as a nurse and finally as a physician. She became the first "city physician," or health commissioner, in Oshkosh and the nation. Her remarkable reminiscence on achieving her dream despite discouragement and poverty is excerpted here, accompanied by Edith Dodd Culver's description of the regimen in an early nursing school from her recollections of a happier if unusual childhood in Ashland as one of the "hospital children" of a pioneering physician who introduced modern medical practices for Wisconsin women.

Discouragement and discrimination did not deter the first women from earning bachelor's degrees at the University of Wisconsin in 1869, despite delays by the university president, who refused to award their diplomas until regents forced him to relent. However, the women — including the class valedictorian — were prevented from participating in regular commencement ceremonies. The regents continued to accede to the administration by relegating most women students to the "inferior" Female College until 1874, when a new president, John Bascom, arrived on campus with his suffragist wife, Emma Curtiss Bascom, and family. Their young daughter Florence watched as her father had to rebuff regents' attempt to revive the Female College, while women soon outranked men in class standings and comprised a fourth of the student body.[11]

But women still faced discrimination at the University of Wisconsin in the 1880s, as Florence Bascom writes in her recollection, excerpted in this chapter, of her student years on her father's campus. Women students fought for access to the male bastion of athletic facilities, foreshadowing battles that would continue for more than a century, even after the federal mandate for equality in modern times known as Title IX. Bascom's account is accompanied by another by an observer of the campus in the era, one of an unsung but influential group of women who supported women students, both emotionally and financially: the faculty wives. Led by Margaret Allen, the spouse of the UW's first professor of history, William Allen, they raised funds for scholarships and other serious purposes, although her account here suggests that a faculty wife's most significant asset may have been a sense of humor, required to survive the slights of subsequent UW presidents.

The reformist Bascoms left Wisconsin after more battles with regents, especially brewers on the board, as women including Emma Curtiss Bascom led the temperance movement to new levels of success in the early 1870s, although nowhere else would women face a harder fight. Bascom served, simultaneously, as president of the state woman suffrage association and the state women's temperance organization, after the Women's Temperance Crusades of 1873–1874 brought almost one hundred and fifty thousand women nationwide into reform work, including thousands in Wisconsin. Indeed, although historians trace the crusades' origins to Ohio and the East, the first apparently occurred in Wisconsin, owing to two nationally known reform journalists, Lavinia Goodell of Janesville and Emma Brown of Fort Atkinson. Both contributed to a network of women who communicated through newspapers by and for women. Both came from New York, where Brown became one of the country's first woman publishers before she brought her family newspaper west to Wisconsin in 1856. By then, Goodell worked at her father's abolitionist newspaper and then as an editor at *Harper's* magazine, but she followed her family west in 1871. She could not gain full-time work as a journalist in Janesville, so she contributed "considerable reporting" as a freelancer to a local paper and the national *Woman's Journal*, especially on women's work for reform.[12]

Reasons for the rise in women's involvement in temperance reform included violence against women that often resulted from men's use of alcohol, also on the rise after the Civil War. But without the ballot, women had to battle by other means to reduce domestic abuse. They won saloon laws to limit the number of establishments serving alcohol and their hours, even imposing penalties for not limiting patrons' consumption, but women then had to fight for enforcement. In 1872, for example, Fort Atkinson women — with Brown's editorial backing — won a case against a saloonkeeper for flouting the law, only to lose on appeal owing to a legality. Goodell, studying law in Janesville, used her legal knowledge in July 1873, when local politicians reneged on campaign promises and granted more tavern licenses. Women wielded their only political right by petitioning — with 1,250 signatures, only 42 townswomen refused to sign — and staging public protests, with processions en masse on Janesville's streets to council meetings. They finally formed a Ladies' Temperance Union that forced local politicians to yield to pressure and liquor dealers to yield licenses.[13]

Goodell publicized women's work in Brown's *Chief* and the *Woman's Journal*, both of which reached national readerships. By the end of 1873, similar campaigns that began in the East, then spread to thirty other states and thirty cities in Wisconsin, became collectively known as the Women's Temperance Crusade. By the end of 1874, women from several states including Wisconsin founded the Woman's Christian Temperance Union (WCTU). By the end of the decade, the WCTU's presidency went to Frances Willard, formerly of Janesville, who had begun her higher education in Milwaukee (see "A College for Women Was Born in the West" in chapter 3).[14]

Goodell also won a personal crusade to open the legal profession to women in Wisconsin. The only woman in the country who had to come before a court twice to win admission to a state bar, she saw the Wisconsin Supreme Court reject her first request as a "treason" against the "law of nature" for women. Her landmark case and career are chronicled by a later pioneering woman lawyer, Catherine B. Cleary, in her article excerpted in this chapter. Cleary illuminates the brilliant but brief life of Lavinia Goodell, whose death at forty years old occurred only weeks after she won her five-year battle before the Wisconsin Supreme Court. Not for another five years would the first woman graduate from the University of Wisconsin law school, and she never practiced law (see "The Two Worlds of Belle Case La Follette" in chapter 5).

Goodell lived to see her accomplishment honored by Stanton and Anthony at the nation's centennial celebration in 1876, when her name also was entered in the annals of Congress with those of 476 other Wisconsin women, including Wolcott and Anneke. Another signatory was Lynde, whose husband served as Milwaukee's congressman and presented the Wisconsin women's petitions in support of the first federal woman suffrage bill. Then known as the "Susan B. Anthony Amendment" for its author, the amendment would not be numbered until it became law, decades later. However, Goodell died too soon to see the resurgence of the Wisconsin woman suffrage movement in the 1880s, although Fort Atkinson editor Emma Brown endured almost to the end of the decade as editor of the country's longest–lasting "temperance sheet" to endorse — almost alone in the state press — Wisconsin's first woman suffrage referendum.[15]

The surprisingly successful suffrage referendum and its later loss both were the work of the Reverend Olympia Brown, who had answered a call to a pastorate in Wisconsin two years before Anthony and Stanton — her former co-workers in suffrage campaigns — had returned to stump the state in 1880. Women met in Madison, where another suffrage referendum bill passed both houses of the legislature, to reorganize the WWSA and reelect Wolcott as president, although almost as an honorary recognition. In 1882, among the new officers was Olympia Brown, who would attempt to take over the organization. However, upon Wolcott's resignation in 1884, women called on Emma Curtiss Bascom, who served briefly before her replacement at the 1884 regular WWSA convention, widely known poet Hattie Tyng Griswold of Columbus.[16]

In 1885, with some controversy, Olympia Brown won the WWSA presidency and then led the only suffrage referendum campaign that women ever won in Wisconsin, in 1886, only to lose the law in the state Supreme Court two years later. Had the high court not again blocked women's progress, Wisconsin would have won a place in women's history as the first suffrage state east of the Mississippi River, rather than almost the last. Instead, suffragists were left only with "onerous debt" from the court defeat, as Charles E. Neu writes in a biography of Brown, which is excerpted here. The impact of the defeat on

Brown boded worse for immigrant women; she became nativist and racist for her next quarter of a century as WWSA president. Her "almost invidious" and virulent attacks on "foreign elements" among voters, Neu writes, veered toward "a real element of paranoia" that further alienated politicians and potential suffrage supporters among foreign-born or first-generation Wisconsinites who comprised two-thirds of the population, owing to ongoing immigration of Poles and Eastern Europeans in the period.[17]

By the late 1880s, some earlier immigrant women were acculturating as well as accumulating political power and wealth. In Milwaukee in 1888, heiress Lisette Best Schandein became an officer of Pabst Brewing Company, the largest brewery in the country more than a decade before, when her forefathers had helped to found the Brewers Congress to counter the Women's Temperance Crusade. She, Schlitz heiress Clara Marcel Schmitt, and a few other women of wealth became substantial stockholders and patrons of civic causes, although they made little impact on the male-dominated corporate patriarchy of Milwaukee. Nor could they — or would they, with Brown's nativism — ameliorate the work of the "liquor interests," led by the original Milwaukee brewers, who already were among the most formidable opponents of woman suffrage.[18]

Wisconsin women were not alone in nativism, or in defeatism, in the coming decades, which suffragists came to call "the doldrums" — the same decades which would become better known as the "Progressive Era," although most progress would be for men. Women would win suffrage in four states in the far West by 1896, but further referenda failed in six states — and none lost in the courts after winning at the polls, as would occur in Wisconsin. However, although political progress would be stalled, women would not be stopped. They would participate in politics, if indirectly, to influence the Progressive Era agenda for the health, education, and welfare of women and children in poverty, and thus would influence the progress of society.[19]

## NOTES

1. Richard N. Current, *HOW,* vol. 2: *The Civil War Era, 1848–1873* (Madison: SHSW, 1976), 124; "Billion Dollars in Assets Now," *Milwaukee Journal,* November 26, 1933; Frederic Heath, "The Typewriter in Wisconsin," *WMH* 27, no. 3 (March 1944): 272.

2. Victoria Brehm, *The Women's Great Lakes Reader,* 2nd ed. (Tustin, MI: Ladyslipper Press, 2000), 273–295; Terry and Sue Pepper, "Seeing the Light: Wisconsin Lighthouses," www.terrypepper.com/lights/state_Wisconsin.htm. Stebbins served into 1907. Others included Katherine Stanley at Eagle Bluff and Sherwood Point in Door County with her husband and, after his death, as assistant keeper at the latter lighthouse from 1895 to 1898; her niece Minnie Hesh Cochems as assistant keeper at Sherwood Point from 1898 to 1928 with her husband; and Ella Quick at Sand Island in Bayfield County with her husband and, after his death, as head keeper from 1903 to 1906; see Mary Louise Clifford and J. Candace Clifford, *Women Who Kept the Lights: An Illustrated History of Female Lighthouse Keepers* (Williamsburg, VA: Cypress Press, 1993), 168–169.

3. Sara M. Evans, *Born for Liberty: A History of Women in America* (New York: Free Press, 1989), 57–58; Robert C. Nesbit, *HOW,* vol. 3: *Urbanization and Industrialization* (Madison: SHSW, 1985), 470–471; Current, *HOW,* 502, 533.

4. Richard P. Durbin, "Two Wisconsin River Stories," *WMH* 77, no. 3 (Spring 1994): 192–193. Current, *HOW,* 524–525, notes the rape but not the aftermath in courts and media.

5. Ellen D. Langill, "Speaking with an Equal Voice: The Reform Efforts of Milwaukee's Mary Blanchard

Lynde," *WMH* 87, no. 1 (Autumn 2003), 18–29; "Mrs. William Pitt Lynde: Pioneer Experiences of Milwaukee Women," *Milwaukee Sentinel*, n.d.; Ann Firor Scott, *Natural Allies: Women's Associations in American History* (Urbana: University of Illinois, 1991), 25.

6. Langill, "Speaking with an Equal Voice," 23–25.

7. Genevieve G. McBride, *On Wisconsin Women: Working for Their Rights from Settlement to Suffrage,* (Madison: University of Wisconsin Press, 1993), 137–138. That no woman was protected from poverty when all lacked legal rights to property was proved by Lynde's personal experience with the vagaries of health and wealth. One of her daughters died in infancy and two sons died young, including one who was mentally ill and another with financial difficulties, which she also had in widowhood. See Langill, "Speaking with an Equal Voice," 25, 28.

8. Joan M. Jensen, "Sexuality on a Northern Frontier: The Gendering and Disciplining of Rural Wisconsin Women, 1850–1920," *Agricultural History* 73, no. 2 (Spring 1999): 143, 146–147.

9. McBride, *On Wisconsin Women,* 46–48.

10. Laura J. Ross Wolcott, "Wisconsin," in Elizabeth Cady Stanton, Susan B. Anthony, and Matilda Joslyn Gage, eds., *The History of Woman Suffrage,* vol. 2 (Rochester, NY: Susan B. Anthony, 1881), 640–641.

11. Merle Curti and Vernon Carstensen, *The University of Wisconsin: A History, 1848–1925* (Madison: University of Wisconsin, 1949), 371–379; Reuben Gold Thwaites, ed., *The University of Wisconsin; Its History and Its Alumni* (Madison: Purcell, 1900), 87–89.

12. McBride, *On Wisconsin Women,* 54–60; Ann Russo and Cheris Kramarae, eds., *The Radical Women's Press of the 1850s* (New York: Routledge, 1991); Martha M. Solomon, ed., *A Voice of Their Own: The Woman Suffrage Press, 1840–1910* (Tuscaloosa: University of Alabama Press, 1991). The Browns began publication in Cayuga County, New York, on the same day, January 1, 1849, that a group of women nearby in Seneca Falls, New York, began *The Lily,* which historians usually credit as the first U.S. newspaper published by a woman, Amelia Jenks Bloomer, although she initially served as its editor.

13. McBride, *On Wisconsin Women,* 54–60.

14. Ibid., 64, 80–82, 94.

15. *Congressional Record,* January 19, 1877, 732; McBride, *On Wisconsin Women,* 127–130.

16. McBride, *On Wisconsin Women,* 98–103, 112–115; see also Theodora W. Youmans, "How Wisconsin Women Won the Ballot," *WMH* 5, no. 1 (June 1921): 5–24.

17. Lee Weilef Metzner, "Polish Pioneers of Kewaunee County," *WMH* 18, no. 3 (March 1935): 269–280; Current, *HOW,* 423–424; Kathleen Neils Conzen, *Immigrant Milwaukee, 1836–1860: Accommodation and Community in a Frontier City* (Cambridge: Harvard University Press, 1976), 146.

18. Harry H. Anderson, "The Women Who Helped Make Milwaukee Breweries Famous," *Milwaukee History* 4, nos. 3–4 (Autumn–Winter 1981): 77; Eleanor Flexner, *Century of Struggle: The Woman's Rights Movement in the United States,* rev. ed. (Cambridge: Harvard University Press, 1975), 307–309; McBride, *On Wisconsin Women,* 78, 96, 224.

19. Flexner, *Century of Struggle,* 230–231, 256.

# Making a Living in Wisconsin, 1873–1893

## ROBERT C. NESBIT

*WMH* 69, No. 4 (Summer 1986): 251–283

*Women in Wisconsin contributed to the shift in the post–Civil War period from rural and agricultural life to urban and industrial ways of making a living — and, in part owing to the war's toll on men, many women did have to make a living in the late nineteenth century. As Robert C. Nesbit writes, population declined in ten of twenty-five southern Wisconsin counties — or would have done so but for their "urban centers that countered the actual loss of rural population" from 1870 to 1890. "Even in seemingly stable communities — stable in numbers at any rate — we now know there was a great turnover of families," he writes, as the "phenomenon" of urbanization was witnessed not only in Wisconsin but also "throughout much of the Midwest."*

*In Wisconsin, the phenomenon of women working in factories at first was mainly witnessed in Milwaukee, which already was industrializing in the 1860s. In the next decades, in smaller "urban centers," the "industries outside Milwaukee had their great period of growth," Nesbit writes. "The loss of rural population . . . was usually attributed to the lure of the cities and towns" that offered new employment opportunities in the postwar period for women.*

*Nesbit's article on working in Wisconsin was drawn from his contribution to the Wisconsin Historical Society's six-volume state history,* The History of Wisconsin, vol. 3: Urbanization and Industrialization, 1873–1893. *The following excerpts focus on women making a living in Wisconsin in the late nineteenth century.*

. . . It is hazardous to characterize the 1870s as ushering in a change of relationships between employers and employees based upon the anonymity of the swiftly growing cities and the rise of employers with workforces numbering in the hundreds. . . .

. . . Increasingly, employment opportunities were to be found in large shops owned or directed by men whose concerns were primarily with the mobilization of capital, financing the latest in technologies, and marketing their products. . . .

The employer possessed all of the advantages in dealing with labor. . . . With the premises and necessary equipment centralized under his control, the employer defined all of the terms of employment: hours, wages, standards of production, work rules, conditions of the workplace, and so forth. He was free to discriminate in any way he might choose: to exclude on the basis of ethnic origin, religion, presumed attitudes, or suspected union activity [or, of course, on the basis of gender]; or to proscribe certain behavior ranging from conversation on the job to drinking on any occasion. . . .[1]

Piecework was another common method of avoiding problems of whom to hire and what wages to pay. In Milwaukee, clothing manufacturing, including knits, gloves, and hats and caps, employed 6,700, a great many working at home rather than in factories.

This did not include an estimated 1,700 seamstresses who went to their customers. Piece-work was adaptable to many industries. Work of a disagreeable nature was often left in the hands of a minor foreman, representing one of the newer ethnic groups, who hired work-ers at his home or any place frequented by his countrymen, usually a saloon. These shops functioned in the language of the dominant group, which jealously guarded its prerog-atives by making things miserable for any outsider who might be hired on by higher authority. . . .[2]

Another deficiency of the times was that the workplace was commonly a hazard to the health and safety of the workers. This grew out of the assumption that the surroundings of the job were simply dictated by the given conditions. Factory design was an art that ar-rived late on the Wisconsin scene. . . .

Workplaces were not expected to have plumbing when most city homes and schools did not. If the job was excessively hot, cold, dirty, or dangerous, it was accepted as com-mon to the nature of the work or the circumstances of the employer. . . .

. . . A girl working as a knot sawyer in a Neenah shingle mill did find it "very hard work, and especially disagreeable in spring and fall, as the weather then is cold, and the temper-ature of the mill, quite unfavorable. During the winter months we are out of work, and therefore the employment is not such as I should wish, but I am unable to obtain more suitable work in the town. . . ."[3]

The year 1873 saw the end of a tight labor market in Wisconsin. . . . Given the low scale of wages in Wisconsin, one can appreciate that this was an environment in which a surplus of labor was the norm, except in specific local cases. . . . The seasonal nature of much of Wisconsin's industrial employment also worked to the advantage of employers.[4]

. . . In Wisconsin, where one-fourth of the industrial labor was then employed in the seasonal lumber industry and where the building trades and other industries faced harsh winter conditions, the average period of unemployment was considerably more than twenty days. . . .[5]

The insecure worker of the eighties is generally faceless at this distance, although [the Wisconsin Bureau of Labor, Census and Industrial Statistics commissioner Frank] Flower's questionnaires offer an occasional glimpse. A tailor in Milwaukee found a dull season made worse by employers who farmed out piecework to girls who did the same work [at home] for half as much — about $3 per week. . . .[6]

The greatest bargain of the time was the hired girl. E. T. Stamm remembered family life in Milwaukee in the eighties. He came from a family of eleven children. The hired girl, Albertina, was newly arrived from Germany: "We paid her two dollars a week. Well, she did the washing and she did the ironing and the cooking and everything else and then I had two older sisters and my mother, they used to help with the cooking."[7]

Frank Flower enjoyed embroidering his bureau reports from his own well-stocked kit of opinions: "A shop girl is tolerated in a certain grade of society below the 'upper ten thousand,' but the ordinary domestic or servant is not. A man of considerable standing may marry a milliner, a seamstress, a dry goods clerk or a book-keeper without totally paralyzing his 'high-toned' relatives; but if he should marry a kitchen girl, or a waiter, or a chamber-maid, no matter how fair her face, how graceful her deportment or how bright her mind, 'select circles' would be scandalized. . . ."[8]

The federal census for 1870 enumerated 25,555 Wisconsin women as gainfully employed. Domestic service accounted for five out of eight of these. By 1890 there were 81,061 women working for wages. The general population meanwhile had increased by less than two-thirds. Persons reporting gainful occupations doubled from 292,808 to 582,469, but this did not match the increase of 217.5 percent in the number of women reported as wage earners. However, by 1890 domestic service accounted for only two out of five women employed. Complaints were becoming common that domestics were hard to find, despite the influx of immigrant girls and the more numerous American-born daughters of foreign-born parents, who were presumed to be of the domestic servant class. As one editor wrote: "The phenomenal scarcity of hired girls throughout the county and elsewhere this season must lead to many serious questions. . . . That marriage is a failure may remain in the region of doubts, but no sane person will doubt that house-keeping is a failure, where dependence is placed upon the always unstable quantity of household help."[9]

The answer to the tight market for servant girls was not necessarily the social stigma supposedly attached to domestic service. There had been a great opening of other employment opportunities for women, primarily in industry. Between 1870 and 1890, the number of female industrial workers jumped from 3,784 to 12,751. Factory-made clothing and hosiery and knitting mills, centered in Milwaukee, accounted for much of the growth, but women were also finding entrée into many other fields previously considered the preserves of men. A tinware worker complained: "When I started to learn my trade there were hardly any girls employed, but now the work is done mostly by females." His was not a lonely voice.[10]

Between 1870 and 1890, the metropolis increased its share of the industrially employed women in Wisconsin from about one-third to two-thirds. By 1890 the proportion of women workers in Milwaukee industry was nearly twice that of Cleveland, half again more than in Chicago, and a third more than in Detroit. . . . There were 2,904 women reported in Milwaukee's clothing factories. Hosiery and knits employed 1,449 women in Milwaukee. . . . The manufacture of boots and shoes occupied 418. In Milwaukee, 58.2 percent of the women industrial workers were employed in clothing factories and hosiery and knits, compared to only 33 percent in Chicago. . . . [I]t is possible that there were more multiple-income families in Milwaukee. It may have had some bearing on the generally lower wage scale known to prevail there.[11]

For the wives and children of laboring men, one form or another of industrial wage earning was also available in smaller cities and even in bucolic settings. Wisconsin had quite a number of woolen mills located on minor waterpowers that traditionally exploited this labor source. There were even a few cotton mills. Cigar making was often a local industry using women and children to prepare the weed. . . . In 1887, a laboring man in Oshkosh alleged that the city's workforce was about one-fourth boys and girls under fourteen.[12]

The Janesville Cotton Manufacturing Company occupied the most imposing indus-trial building in town. . . . [In] 1880 the factory employed 250, two-thirds of them women, their median age just under nineteen. Immigrant girls and first-generation Irish- and German-Americans made up 75 percent of the women. One-third of the hands in the mill came from households headed by women, most of them widows. The remainder were mostly children of day laborers. The mill worked two shifts of eleven and a half hours, six days a week, but was never inconvenienced by a lack of available workers. Wrote a state factory inspector in 1887:

> . . . [T]here are some 300 women and children who are working 11½ to 12 hours per day and night, the night being the time most of the children are employed. The work is principally piecework; but some of them work by the day. It is a hard place to work. Young persons cannot stand the strain and long hours. . . . [T]here are many of them under 14 years of age and all have to work 11½ hours. The ther-mometer (I am told by one of the employees) averages in the heated season about 108°. . . . [I]f there is too much air stirring, the windows must be kept closed on ac-count of blowing the cotton. The dressing room thermometer (I am told) runs as high as 140° and averages 110° to 120°. (Men work here 8 to 10 hours.) I am told by employees that girls . . . are quitting on account of loss of health caused by hard work and long hours; they cannot stand the intense heat at night, and cannot get sufficient sleep in the day time. They tell me they are unanimous for a "10 hour law, pure and simple — like Massachusetts."[13]

. . . Janesville had 557 women employed in industries with a total work force of 1,639, almost double the proportion of women engaged in industry in Milwaukee. Not included was the seasonal employment in tobacco warehouses in Janesville. In 1886 the season lasted four to six months, employing mostly girls and women. "The work is done in base-ments, or on lower floors. The girls make from $6 to $12 per week. . . . [S]ome 500 fe-males and 100 males are employed. . . ."[14]

. . . [W]orking women generally, with some accuracy, were described as "working girls." . . . One federal study queried 17,427 working women of whom 15,387 were single, 1,038 widowed, 745 married, and 257 divorced or separated. Of the 17,427, only 2,509 lived away from home, in a boardinghouse or with a private family. Of the 14,918 single women living at home, 8,754 gave their earnings for the general support and 4,267 paid board at home. "In general the single woman makes and spends less than the single man." The implicit assumption was that a woman's wages generally supplemented a family income.[15]

The world of retailing, as well as the office and counting room of business and manu-facturing, was very much a male world at the end of the decade of the Civil War. The oc-cupational census of 1870 found just ninety-eight women in Wisconsin engaged as clerks and accountants in manufacturing establishments. Change did not come rapidly, but the barrier was broken initially in the retail field. By 1880, Milwaukee alone had 260 women working as clerks, sales ladies, and accountants in retailing, but only two [as] clerks in manufacturing establishments. Then the dam broke — belatedly, it would seem, since the first practical typewriter was invented in Milwaukee in the middle seventies. In 1890, 3,824 women were employed in offices and stores in Wisconsin, 781 of them as saleswomen and the remainder in offices. Stenographers and typists numbered 459, clerks and copyists in offices, 1,992. Forty-one percent of these women employed in retailing and office work were in Milwaukee.[16]

There is other evidence of the belated, and not yet wholehearted, acceptance of women in business offices and behind the store counter. A circular for Milwaukee's Spencerian Business College issued in 1890 spoke defensively:

> We favor business education for woman because we regard her as the equal of man, with the same natural right to self support. We believe in it because her entrance into business life carries with it a refining and healthful influence. . . . Much of the prejudice which has existed among business men, against the employment of women in office and counting room, has given way. . . . It is beginning to be understood that young women are in many cases preferable to young men, owing to their quickness of perception and motion, their uniform freedom from bad habits and consequent reliability. There is a demand, therefore, for those whose training fits them for book-keepers, correspondents, cashiers and stenographers.[17]

Teaching was one of the genteel occupations open to women, and they were an increasing proportion of the state's public school teaching force. In 1874 . . . women outnumbered men by two to one. By 1890 the number of female teachers had almost doubled and they outnumbered men by four to one. Numbers did not necessarily mean equity, however. Average wages for men teaching in country districts in 1874 were $47.44 per month, for women $32.13. The comparable figures for 1890 were $43.50 and $29.00.[18]

All of the county superintendents [elected] in 1873 were men. Ten years later, another barrier had been breached, as three superintendents — in Eau Claire, Iowa, and St. Croix counties — were women. By 1891, ten of the seventy county superintendents were women. But the average pay for the women superintendents, $582.50 annually, was well below the average for men in the same position, which was $823.75. . . .[19]

In 1891, there were 175 free high schools in the state, headed by 174 male principals and by Mary J. Gillan, the principal at Plainfield in Waushara County. These jobs were very evidently plums in public education. Of course, Plainfield . . . had a village population of only 459 so her salary was well below the average. Of the forty-three city superintendents, Ida M. Johnson of Menomonie and Belle Smith of Waupaca were the only women. . . . Smith received $100 annually above her regular teacher's salary. . . . Johnson supervised twenty-nine teachers . . . for an added $300 per annum. . . .[20]

The Wisconsin Bureau of Labor Statistics, established in 1883, came into existence partly out of concern that the 1879 compulsory school-attendance law was not serving its purpose. A problem was that the 1879 statute exempted from its provisions children between the ages of seven and fifteen whose "time and labor are essentially necessary for the support of an indigent parent, brother or sister.". . . [T]he superintendent of Rock

County observed in his 1886 report: "The present compulsory law is a dead letter.". . . [T]he commissioner of labor statistics . . . in his 1888–1889 report remarked testily: "The Wisconsin Bureau cannot furnish statistics of child labor, for the simple fact that there is no child labor in this state, in the strict sense of the word. Our inspectors have been very diligent in this matter, because of the annoyance created by irresponsible persons and newspapers, who keep harping upon the subject.". . .[21]

There are many inferences which one may draw about family incomes and the standard of living in Wisconsin during these years. . . .

In 1888, just over half of Wisconsin's industrial workers averaged less than $1.50 per ten-hour day. . . . One in six made less than a dollar a day, when they had work. . . . [A] Wisconsin study . . . indicated that only 3.2 percent of workmen's families had incomes over $600 annually, "while 51.6 per cent lived on less than $400.". . .[22]

There were a number of ways to augment or stretch family income. . . . [B]ackyard root cellars, smokehouses, and kitchen gardens were common in an age predating mass-produced foodstuffs. . . . Hunting and fishing also were regular sources of food. . . .[23]

Gardening, raising animals and poultry, keeping a cow, and foraging the countryside were not uncommon in the metropolis, although Milwaukee got the cows and pigs off the streets a decade or more earlier than did [other cities in Wisconsin]. The old third ward, the residential area [primarily of the remaining poor Irish immigrants in the period as well as a more recent influx of Italians who lived] immediately south of the main business district, had gardens, hen houses, and usually a shed with a cow on many of the tiny lots of the district. . . .[24]

. . . [T]he federal census . . . failed to find officially sponsored public market facilities in most Wisconsin cities. Even Milwaukee managed only a "market of small dimensions, belonging to an association of gardeners." There were, however, well-established traditional markets. . . . There was a German market on upper East Water Street where vegetables were generally cheaper and where non-Germans learned to like rye bread and new varieties of cheese and sausage. Office workers and retail clerks . . . carried baskets to work and shopped the German market. A German tannery worker remembered that he would accompany his father to a livestock market at Fourth and Vliet in the fall where they would buy a pig of 300 pounds. . . . "We tied a washline to the hind leg of [the] big pig and drove it home . . . and the whole family would get together, all the sisters and sisters-in-law. . . . One day they would make sausage here, and the next day there.". . .[25]

. . . [F]armers [brought] produce to Milwaukee to sell in the markets. . . .[T]heir wives brought dried apples on strings, berries, butter, eggs, and other items to trade at the grocers' for staples. . . .[26]

One aspect of making a living that deserves mention was the absence of leisure time for most wage earners, except that conferred by periods of unemployment. Gardening and gathering fell largely to other members of the family. . . .

Most industrial workers commonly worked a ten-hour day, six days a week. . . . In many working-class households the breadwinner was a tired boarder or even just an occasional presence. . . . This speaks volumes about the quality of life for many of Wisconsin's wage earners. . . .[27]

. . . [T]he uncertainty of unemployment did not impinge upon the farmer. . . . The wonder is that the city or the small town was assumed to act as such a lure. But farm life presented such a dull routine, and so many people in town appeared to lead interesting, well-rewarded lives. They even had time for other things than work.

For the ambitious who felt that they were equipped for better things, the years after 1873 opened many avenues, especially by way of some formal education beyond the district school. The complexities of an interdependent, industrialized society were opening new opportunities for many people [including women] — a minority, to be sure, but a growing minority.

*By 1888, of more than twenty-five thousand industrial employees in Milwaukee, more than four thousand — almost 16 percent — were women. "There were also many women in Milwaukee engaged in the needle trades who worked at home on piecework and thus were not counted," Nesbit writes. "They, of course, would have pulled down wage averages," already far lower for women than for men.*

*In Milwaukee, the wages of most industrial workers, women or men, were much lower — and the percentage of women industrial employees much higher — than in most of Wisconsin. Madison ranked first among major Wisconsin cities in wages, which Nesbit calls a measure of the capital's "minor commitment to industry" and "a measure of Madison's favorable employment pattern" for a primarily "mature male workforce." Nesbit offers a comparison with a city of similar size in the period, Racine. Industrial workers numbered more than 4,000 for 20 percent of the population of Racine, while Madison's 679 factory workers comprised little more than 5 percent of residents, which suggests Madison's aberrance in the increasingly industrial order of Wisconsin — except in employment of women. While more than 500 women made up more than 12 percent of the total industrial workforce in Racine, the 65 women in Madison industries accounted for almost 10 percent of the city's total of factory workers; in sum, women comprised almost as significant a percentage of the overall workforce in Madison as in many cities in the late nineteenth century.[28]*

## NOTES

1. Gerd Korman, *Industrialization, Immigrants and Americanizers: The View from Milwaukee, 1866–1921* (Madison, 1967), 66–67; . . . Daniel Nelson, *Managers and Workers: Origins of the New Factory System in the United States, 1880–1920* (Madison, 1975), 80–81.

2. W. J. Anderson and Julius Bleyer, eds., *Milwaukee's Great Industries: A Compilation of Facts Concerning Milwaukee's Commercial and Manufacturing Enterprises, Its Trade and Commerce, and the Advantages It Offers to Manufacturers Seeking Desirable Locations for New or Established Industries* (Milwaukee, 1892), 154–155, 205–207; Korman, *Industrialization, Immigrants and Americanizers*, 66–67; Nelson, *Managers and Workers*, 80–81.

3. Wisconsin Bureau of Labor and Industrial Statistics, *Biennial Report*, 1887–1888, 94. The girl quoted was not complaining, for her wages had increased by one-quarter in the six years she had worked at the Neenah mill, and her workday had decreased from eleven and a half to ten hours.

4. Korman, *Industrialization, Immigrants and Americanizers*, 21–37. . . .

5. . . . Wisconsin Bureau of Labor, Census and Industrial Statistics, *Biennial Report*, 1895–1896, 294–295. . . .

6. Ibid., *Biennial Report*, 1887–1888, 16, 23, 98, 109, 110. . . .

7. E. T. Stamm Transcript, Matson Holbrook Interviews [WHS Archives].

8. Wisconsin Bureau of Labor Statistics, *Biennial Report*, 1883–1884, 112–113.

9. *Fort Atkinson Jefferson County Union*, June 19, 1891. Also see Wisconsin Regional Planning Committee, *A Study of Wisconsin: Its Resources, Its Physical, Social and Economic Background* (Madison, 1934), 53; and David M. Katzman, *Seven Days a Week: Women and Domestic Service in Industrializing America* (New York, 1978), 3–14.

10. *Ninth Census of the United States, 1870: Population*, vol. 1, 764; *Eleventh Census of the United States, 1890: Manufacturing*, vol. 6, pt. 1, 628–634;Wisconsin Bureau of Labor, Census and Industrial Statistics, *Biennial Report*, 1895–1896, 324.

11. *Ninth Census of the United States, 1870: Industry*, vol. 3, 582; *Eleventh Census of the United States, 1890: Manufacturing*, vol. 6, pt. 2, 130–144, 154–165, 194–201, 334–335; . . . *Twelfth Census of the United States, 1900*: vol. 8, pt. 2, 951, 954–999.

12. Norman L. Crockett, *The Woolen Industry of the Midwest* (Lexington, Kentucky, 1970); Chicago *Knights of Labor*, March 5, 1887; Wisconsin Bureau of Labor and Industrial Statistics, *Biennial Report*, 1887–1888, 90, 238–239, 264, 314–317. The factory reports of the bureau . . . did not report city workers by age, only by sex.

13. Wisconsin Bureau of Labor, Census and Industrial Statistics, *Biennial Report*, 1887–1888, 264. . . .

14. Ibid., *Biennial Report*, 1885–1886, 499; Ibid., *Biennial Report*, 1893–1894, 44a–47a.

15. Emile Levasseur, *The American Workman*, trans. by Thomas S. Adams, ed. by Theodore Marburg (Baltimore, 1900), 336–352, 404.

16. *Ninth Census of the United States, 1870: Population, Volume I*, 764; *Tenth Census of the United States, 1880: Population, Volume I*, 886; *Eleventh Census of the United States, 1890: Population, Volume I, Part 2*, 624, 692.

17. Spencerian Business College, *Circular, 1890–91* (Milwaukee, 1890), 20–21.

18. Wisconsin Superintendent of Public Instruction, *Annual Report*, 1874, xii–xiii; *Wisconsin Blue Book, 1891*, 552.

19. *Wisconsin Blue Book, 1873*, 423; ibid., *1883*, 374–375; ibid., *1891*, 545, 548, 552. *Laws of Wisconsin*, 1875, 220–221, made women eligible for all elective school offices. This did not include their right to vote in those elections. . . .

20. *Wisconsin Blue Book, 1891*, 546–548; ibid., *1903*, 160. . . .

21. Wisconsin Bureau of Labor Statistics, *Biennial Report*, 1883–1884, 160–162; ibid., *Biennial Report*, 1888–1889, vii; Wisconsin Superintendent of Public Instruction, *Biennial Report*, 1884–1886, 195.

22. Wisconsin Bureau of Labor and Industrial Statistics, *Biennial Report*, 1898–1899, 152, 156; Levasseur, *American Workman*, 399. . . .

23. John A. Fleckner, "Poverty and Relief in Janesville," *WMH* 61 (Summer 1978): 281–283.

24. Leora M. Howard, "Changes in Home Life in Milwaukee from 1865 to 1900" (master's thesis, University of Wisconsin, 1923), 12–13. . . .

25. *Tenth Census of the United States, 1880: Social Statistics of Cities*, vol. 19, pt. 2, 672; Howard, "Home Life in Milwaukee," 27; Bill Hooker, *Glimpses of an Earlier Milwaukee* (Milwaukee, 1929), 10–11. . . .

26. Hooker, *An Earlier Milwaukee*, 9–10; Brockman Transcript, Matson Holbrook Interviews.

27. Wisconsin Bureau of Labor and Industrial Statistics, *Biennial Report*, 1887–1888, 27, 80.

28. Ibid., *Biennial Report*, 1887–1888, xix–xxv, 238–241, 245, 249, 260, 262, 278–312, 330, 333–334.

# "This Naughty, Naughty City"[1]

## Prostitution in Eau Claire from the Frontier to the Progressive Era

BONNIE RIPP-SHUCHA

WMH 81, No. 1 (Autumn 1997): 31–54

In her own day, during the last quarter of the nineteenth century, Ollie O'Dell was described in a newspaper article as "a little woman with an immense quantity of rouge, musk, and flashy jewelry on her person, also a red sailor hat tilted to the don't-care-a-damn angle on her head. . . ."[2] Ollie was not the kind of person who ordinarily makes it into the history books. She was a prostitute, and past historians would not have deemed her worthy of study.

But times and historiography have changed. The history of sexuality has gained respectability in recent years, perhaps because sexuality is now widely acknowledged as being shaped not only by nature but also by culture. Historians have come to realize that women did not enter prostitution simply because they were naturally depraved, but because society offered prostitutes few attractive alternatives.

With this new emphasis on cultural influence, the study of prostitution and sexuality falls within the legitimate purview of social history. Windows are being opened, and light shed, on a shadowy corner of American history. One such glimmer of light may be discerned by investigating the city of Eau Claire. . . .

. . . By the 1860s, lumbering was firmly established as the foundation of the community's wealth and progress, and for more than a generation Eau Claire exemplified the heyday of midwestern lumbering. . . . [B]y the 1880s, the number of loggers in the valley of the Chippewa had swelled to 7,000. . . . The city of Eau Claire grew apace. In the last quarter of the century, its population soared from 2,500 to more than 20,000. . . .[3]

. . . [P]ine logs, lumber rafts, and the men who drove them downstream were a fixture of daily life in Eau Claire. The workers were a rough lot: mostly unskilled, largely foreign-born, with Norwegians predominating and Canadians, Irish, and Germans close behind. Most were unmarried. . . . [Some] sought out the company of women — which usually meant the prostitutes who were another fixture of daily life in Eau Claire. . . .[4]

. . . Because there were relatively few females, many men could not expect to find respectable companions or wives. Prostitutes may have played a critical role in such a community because they could provide companionship as well as sex to large numbers of men. As one historian has noted, prostitution was often the first business established in lumber towns.[5] During the 1860s, Eau Claire was a pioneer settlement with little or no police supervision; prostitution operated openly, subject only to occasional outbreaks of mob violence.

The succeeding decades showed a slight equalizing of the male-female ratio: from 125.8 to 100 in 1870, and 122.1 to 100 in 1880.[6] The demand for prostitutes may have de-

creased somewhat with the presence of more women. In these decades, too, public sentiment against prostitution grew. The important change in the 1870s was that citizens began
to turn to established legal measures to stop prostitution. But many city officials could not
(or would not) even verify that such houses of prostitution existed, and in Eau Claire, as
elsewhere, most city fathers were content with sporadic enforcement of existing laws and
the occasional harassment or arrest of selected prostitutes.[7]

. . . As the public increasingly deplored the "social evil," city officials — who were still
powerless to stop it — hoped to set up an official red-light district. This would not only
give police better control over prostitution but would also keep it off the main streets —
and out of public view. . . .

Prostitution was largely clandestine. . . . However, because it was also illegal, it did
leave a public record of its existence. One index to the logging industry's influence on
prostitution in Eau Claire, for example, [is] the quarterly statistics of arrests for prostitution. . . . The number of arrests dropped significantly from April through June, when
many loggers went back home to their farms. . . .[8]

However, as with many laws dealing with vice and human frailty, enforcement was
spotty and inconsistent. Ida Barnhardt, convicted of operating a brothel at 422 Water
Street, received a sentence of two years of hard labor at the state prison. Joseph Shafer, on
the other hand, was sentenced to eight months in the Eau Claire County jail for running
a brothel, while his wife Alice was fined $100.[9]

Generally punishments in Eau Claire were not so severe. In 1880, when "two naughty
people [were] found occupying but one bed, where they should have had two," the man
was fined $7.15 and the woman $19.15.[10] Madame Duntly, who ran a house of ill repute
called the "Coffee House," was fined only $7 in November of 1875. In December of the
same year she appeared again before the criminal court; this time she received no punishment at all because she promised to leave town within the week. . . .[11]

In addition to financial penalties and imprisonment, there were other drawbacks to
prostitution. Most prostitutes naturally suffered low social status. In 1873, the *Eau Claire
Weekly Free Press* extended a degree of sympathy to Lydia Curtis, who was accused of keeping a house of ill fame: "We remember a time when Mrs. Curtis held as fair a social position as any woman of moderate circumstances in the city, and it seems as though her
terrible degradation merited a little Christian pity as well as legal punishment.[12] However,
there is no evidence that Lydia Curtis or anyone else associated with prostitution
lamented their social position or even considered themselves "degraded."

Probably of much more importance to those involved in prostitution was the degree
of danger associated with the crime. Because they operated outside the law, prostitutes received little police protection. Often Eau Claire area prostitutes and keepers of brothels
had to contend with mobs intent upon wrecking or setting fire to their places of employment. The *Weekly Free Press* seemed to advocate arson as a means of closing houses of ill
fame. . . . It was only after several people were burned to death in 1875 that the city's newspapers changed their tone and subsequently began blaming law-enforcement officials for
allowing brothels to remain open. . . .[13]

Prostitutes of course faced worse dangers than those posed by arsonists, for brothels were frequented by "some of the most desperate and dangerous characters who infest the Chippewa Valley." Fights often broke out in houses of ill fame. . . .[14]

Much more serious was the case of a prostitute whom police found "wandering in the suburbs with a gunshot wound in her face which she claimed was done at a 'place of vice in Chippewa Falls.'" On another occasion, the papers reported on the attempt by a troubled prostitute to commit suicide by ingesting a mixture of chloroform, arsenic, and laudanum.[15]

Many other hazards attended the prostitute's trade, including venereal disease, bungled abortions, alcohol and drug abuse, and the lack of sympathy accorded prostitutes by the police, the courts, and "respectable society" generally. Yet for some women the benefits outweighed the drawbacks. Undoubtedly, the biggest motivator was money. . . .

During the Victorian age, one historian has written, some people, especially early feminists, "treated prostitution as the end result of the artificial constraint placed on women's social and economic activity. . . . Inadequate wages and restrictions of their industrial employment forced women on to the streets, where they took up the 'best paid industry,' prostitution.". . .[16]

Still, a purely economic explanation does not suffice, for it fails to explain why more women of modest means did not become prostitutes. There were many differing opinions about why women entered prostitution. . . .[17]

. . . [T]he prostitute herself offered another explanation. Although money was certainly a consideration, it would also appear that several Eau Claire prostitutes were running from abusive homes. According to Dolly Patrow, who wrote a letter to John Miller asking him to arrange for her to become a prostitute at his brothel in Merrillan, a friend of hers, Christina Christofferson, . . . "said that she had no home and that her mother was mean to her.". . . Katherine Kline, who was awaiting a divorce, came to the Fox House to escape from her alcoholic husband. . . . Given the bleak alternatives presented to many women, some believed prostitution to be their best option. Dolly Patrow affirmed . . . "The girls all wanted to go.". . .[18]

. . . It seems fair to say, as one historian has written, that "no one cause, but a variety of interconnecting economic, social, and psychological factors, influenced women's choice to practice prostitution."[19]

The women who became prostitutes were as varied as the reasons they had for entering the profession, though some similarities did exist. . . . [T]he typical Wisconsin prostitute was a native-born woman of Irish or German extraction, about twenty-six years old, who had been on the streets since age twenty.[20] Many midwestern prostitutes "came from the farms . . . along with some immigrant girls who came to America looking for a better life, only to end up in the trade.". . .[21]

. . . The average age of the Eau Claire prostitute was twenty-one, slightly older than the national average, but younger than Wisconsin's average.[22] The oldest known Eau Claire prostitute was Kitty Seymore, age thirty-one, who worked in 1888 at "Hamilton's Mansion of Joy," run by Andrew Hamilton as a "dance hall" in the little Eau Claire County community of Altoona.[23] The youngest was Ann Hilpl, age fifteen, who was allegedly induced by Elizabeth Van Nostrend in 1887 "to be in and upon certain premises . . . for the purpose of . . . being unlawfully and carnally known by divers and sundry persons.". . .[24]

Two widowed and two married prostitutes reported in the Eau Claire case files that they had at least one child, and another presumably single prostitute named Minnie Summers gave birth to a breech baby while employed at Hamilton's. . . . [Two were] the mother[s] of four children. . . .[25]

Eau Claire area prostitutes often claimed alternate occupations. In May, 1888, twelve women were employed as "dancers" at Hamilton's dance hall. . . .[26]

. . . In the 1887–1888 Chippewa Falls city directory, prostitute Nellie Harrington's occupation was listed as "domestic."[27] Census takers and the compilers of city directories colluded in this deception, listing prostitutes as servants, seamstresses, or dressmakers. . . .[28] One alleged prostitute even seems to have been a teacher. A state senate report of 1899 claimed that in 1888 "Mrs. Clara Allen, a teacher in the Indian school on the Flambeau reservation, had stopped in Eau Claire about 1883 where she had a reputation as 'a sporting or fast woman.' She went by the name 'Cad Lambert.'"[29]

. . . [A] number of prostitutes were also the keepers of houses of ill fame. Both of the widowed prostitutes previously mentioned, Ida Barnhardt and Lydia Curtis, were madams. With their husbands, some prostitutes kept brothels — delicately termed "bagnios" by the editor of the *Eau Claire Weekly Free Press*.[30] Alice Shafer and her husband, Joseph, were co-keepers of a brothel in Bridge Creek. . . .[31] [T]here were at least five couples, including the Shafers, who were brought to trial for keeping houses of ill fame.

One of these couples was James McCann and Mary Haley McCann, who were married in the mid-1880s. James, who made a business of raising draft horses, owned over 200 acres of land. . . .[32] [He] also owned a house in the Town of Union, which they used as a house of prostitution. . . . Mary sued James for a divorce, claiming that he often called her obscene names, abused her, and on one occasion struck her in the face with his fist, giving her a black eye. On another occasion, James had wanted her to make a statement that a wealthy, well-respected businessman "sustained criminal relations" with her. When Mary refused to lie for James, he hit and kicked her. In the course of the divorce proceedings, it was also revealed that while she had brought a good deal of the money and property into the marriage, he had brought none.[33]

Some men kept houses of ill fame without the aid of a wife. One such brothel was "Crippen's Shebang," a house of prostitution operated by A. J. Crippen a mile or so upriver from Eau Claire.[34] Another was owned by Frank Boutin, whose occupation was listed as "laborer" in the 1885 Eau Claire city directory.[35] Charles Barker claimed that he and his wife Sadie, also spelled Satie, were not alone in running a brothel, but that they were assisted by John Gavin, a logger on the Lac Courte Oreilles reservation.[36] Alderman Frank Sebenthall even alleged that several of Eau Claire's "wealthy church men" rented houses to be used for prostitution.[37]

Little is known about the individual men who patronized houses of ill fame in Eau Claire, because the city usually did not bring charges against them. . . .

It was certainly true that some Madison men were not charged for prostitution-related acts. During the 1870 session of the Wisconsin legislature, the *Madison Democrat* reported that when a brothel was raided the "nymphs" were arrested, but the customers were allowed to depart "for fear one or both houses of the legislature would be without a quorum, if they were held!"[38] Another reason little is known about specific customers is that newspapers usually printed the names of prostitutes, but rarely if ever their patrons.

It seems reasonable to assume, however, that . . . the majority of men who patronized Eau Claire's prostitutes were workers — mostly loggers and millhands, railroad men and laborers, with a leavening of middle-class professional men. . . . One evening in 1878, two Western Wisconsin Railroad brakemen got drunk and drove a locomotive a mile east to visit what the papers coyly termed "one of those habitations of the fair but frail." Upon returning to Eau Claire, they had a fairly spectacular wreck and spent the rest of the night in jail.[39]

The case of one man caught patronizing a brothel in Chippewa Falls in 1877 caused quite a stir; the man happened to be Victor Wolf, the Eau Claire chief of police. He was found by two city policemen, but allegedly he bribed them and was let go. It is unclear whether the incident hurt the chief's career, but, according to the local papers, of the two policemen who caught him, one resigned and the other was suspended. . . .[40]

While almost everyone condemned prostitution, opinions varied about how to control it. In the ideology of the Victorian period, prostitution was tacitly tolerated as a "necessary evil." This view held that because men possessed a strong need for sex and women were to remain "pure," prostitutes performed a necessary function by satisfying men who could not act out their sexual desires within the bounds of marriage. Child-bearing, not recreational sexual relations, was the wifely ideal. In order to maintain the appearance of bourgeois respectability and marital harmony, the Victorians turned a blind eye upon adultery and commercialized vice. Indeed, some contemporaries believed that prostitution was "ultimately the most efficient guardian of virtue."[41]

. . . Even when law enforcement was deemed necessary, police were often at a loss to control prostitution. For example, in 1875, a petition signed by a number of Eau Claire women was presented to city officials, asking for the immediate closure of all brothels; but the city fathers could not even verify that such houses existed.[42] Commercialized vice, much like bootlegging and the drug traffic, tended to corrupt the police and court systems. . . . Eau Claire newspaper writers often complained about the "wide-open policy" regarding prostitution: "With officials of the city government protecting them and the police declining to interfere, these disgraceful institutions are becoming very numerous, and those who are in favor of that sort of thing will find no cause for complaint in the present state of affairs.". . .[43]

As the nineteenth century waned and many pioneer cities and former boom towns became larger and more respectable, public outrage about prostitution increased. Because the police were unable or unwilling to enforce existing laws, they increasingly attempted to keep prostitution out of the public eye. . . .[44]

It is unknown where and if Eau Claire ever formally designated a red-light district, but the city did discuss a closely related issue; namely, the regulation of prostitution by city ordinance. . . . Routine monthly "fines" (amounting, really, to monthly fees) would be imposed on keepers of houses and prostitutes, who were to be arrested only if they were found outside the specified location after a certain hour. In this manner, the city could keep track of vice and regulate its public health aspects — while gaining another source of revenue. . . .[45]

Eau Claire was not the only city in Wisconsin or the nation to implement such a policy. . . . *The Survey*, a liberal-progressive magazine of the day, expressed satisfaction that the "recent closing of the red-light district of Superior marks the end of recognized segregated vice in the state of Wisconsin." By charging prostitutes a monthly fee of $50, Superior received an annual revenue of $12,000.[46] In larger cities, this kind of levy became big business. . . .

. . . The "social purity" movement of the era attempted not only to end prostitution, but also to reform sexual attitudes. The movement attacked the Victorian ideology that sexual purity was for women only. . . . [M]ost reformers were united in their belief that there was one way to deal with what they called "the social evil," prostitution: to abolish it. . . .[47]

. . . Ironically, in their zeal to eradicate vice and crime, some of these new abolitionists reverted to extralegal measures. This was true even in Madison. . . . "Distrustful of their own police force and court system, some Madisonians turned to the Ku Klux Klan as the only force capable of driving the bootlegger, the prostitute, and the murderer from the community."[48]

. . . Despite their best efforts, reformers succeeded only in driving prostitution underground. . . . Once the brothels were shut down, the prostitute was temporarily liberated from the tyranny of madams and landlords. But the latter had provided shelter and a degree of support that the prostitute now lacked. Forced out on the streets, she was much more vulnerable to exploitation by pimps and organized criminals. While reformers struggled to lift the "working girl" out of her life of vice, their attempts often backfired, making the prostitute's situation even worse.[49]

It was one of the ironies of the Progressive Era that it was only at this point that prostitutes really became victims — not of the economy, nor of mental deficiencies, nor liquor, nor men, but of those who were trying to help them. . . . Unbound by Victorian ideology, prostitutes experienced a degree of sexual freedom unknown to most women of their day. Because they were already ostracized, they were not expected to fit neatly into societal norms of purity and submissiveness; and because they were better off financially than many of their respectable counterparts, many prostitutes attained the means to live reasonably comfortable lives.

Although it is incorrect to view prostitutes simply as victims, neither should they and their chosen life style be romanticized. . . . They were forced to satisfy the sexual appetites of strangers, which could hardly have increased their self-esteem or personal safety. They were prey to venereal disease, avaricious pimps, and corrupt policemen. Their social position — or really their ostracism — was in one sense liberating; but it also prevented most of them from ever aspiring to what might be called a "normal" home life. To be sure, some

prostitutes were married; but the profession was not conducive to marital bliss since it involved continually breaking the marriage vows, and a brothel was scarcely a healthy place
in which to raise a child. . . .[T]he prostitutes of Eau Claire were women who chose to live
outside the mainstream, reaping both the rewards and the dangers of commercialized sex.
Their lives [were] deeply shadowed and meagerly documented, but many continued in
the trade long after Eau Claire had evolved from a frontier boom town. . . .

## NOTES

1. The title's quote is from the *Eau Claire Weekly Free Press,* April 1, 1878, cited in Orry C. Walz, *Eau Claire,
Wisconsin, 1850–1880: A Case Study in Community Organization and Social Deviance, Research Notes* (Eau Claire,
WI: privately printed, 1986).
2. *Eau Claire Daily Leader,* October 19, 1877, collected in Dale Peterson, "Research Notes on Prostitution
in Eau Claire, Wisconsin, 1864–1900," in the manuscript collections of the Chippewa Valley Museum, Eau
Claire.
3. J. Rogers Hollingsworth and Ellen Jane Hollingsworth, *Dimensions in Urban History: Historical and Social
Science Perspectives on Middle-Size American Cities* (Madison, 1979), 59–78.
4. Lois Barland, *Sawdust City* (Stevens Point, WI: 1970), 45; Ruth Rosen, *The Lost Sisterhood: Prostitution in
America, 1900–1918* (Baltimore, 1982), 70; J. C. Ryan, *The Lumberjack Queens* (Duluth, 1988), 3.
5. Ryan, *The Lumberjack Queens,* 1.
6. James P. Dexter, "A Population History of Eau Claire from 1860 to 1890: A Growing County," in Eric J.
Sander, ed., *Eau Claire, New Perspectives on the History of the City: An Anthology of Undergraduate Research* (Eau
Claire, 1992), 21–22.
7. Peterson, "Research Notes on Prostitution," paraphrasing . . . *Eau Claire Weekly Free Press,* August 12,
1875; Stephen G. Sylvester, "Avenues for Ladies Only: The Soiled Doves of East Grand Forks, 1887–1915,"
*Minnesota History* 51 (1989):192.
8. Eau Claire City Council, "Proceedings," 1872–continuing, . . . Eau Claire Area Research Center, WHS;
author's conversation with Paul Bunyan Logging Camp employee, Eau Claire, October 15, 1993.
9. Eau Claire County, Records of the Circuit Court, Case Files (Eau Claire Series 50), Case #9251: *State of
Wisconsin vs. Ida Barnhardt* and Case #2781: *State of Wisconsin vs. Joseph Shafer et al.,* in the Eau Claire Area
Research Center.
10. *Eau Claire Argus,* February 5, 1880, cited in Peterson, "Research Notes on Prostitution."
11. *Eau Claire Weekly Free Press,* November 18 and December 9, 1875, and October 10, 1878, in Walz, *Research Notes.*
12. Frank Smoot, "Hunting the Soiled Dove," *Wisconsin West* (June–July, 1991), 10.
13. Ibid., 10–11.
14. *Eau Claire Weekly Free Press,* August 31, 1876, December 25, 1884, September 13, 1883, and August 9,
1877, from Walz, *Research Notes.*
15. Ibid., June 3, 1875, and July 27, 1882, from Walz, *Research Notes.*
16. Judith R. Walkowitz, "The Politics of Prostitution," *Signs* 6 (1980):125.
17. Wisconsin Vice Committee, *Report and Recommendations,* 103, 108. According to the report, [the
women's] "mental defects" were sexual perversions and abnormal sexual impulses which prevented the
prostitute from perceiving the consequences of her actions. [See also Paul H. Hass, "Sin in Wisconsin: The
Teasdale Vice Committee of 1913," *WMH* 49 (Winter, 1965–1966): 147.]
18. Eau Claire County, Records of the Circuit Court, Case Files, Case #7050: *State of Wisconsin vs. John
Miller,* and Case #8611: *City of Eau Claire vs. Mrs. F. L. Taylor.*
19. Rosen, *The Lost Sisterhood,* 143, 167.
20. Hass, "Sin in Wisconsin," 146.
21. Ryan, *The Lumberjack Queens,* 12.
22. . . . Eau Claire County, Records of the Circuit Court, Case Files, Case #4273: *State of Wisconsin vs.
Elizabeth Van Nostrend;* Case #4395: *State of Wisconsin vs. A. H. Hamilton;* Case #7050: *State of Wisconsin*

*vs. John Miller;* Case #8611: *City of Eau Claire vs. Mrs. F. L. Taylor; Eau Claire Daily Telegram,* February 12, 1896, and *Eau Claire Daily Leader,* November 27 and December 1, 1897, from Peterson, "Research Notes on Prostitution."

23. *Eau Claire Weekly Free Press,* November 1, 1883, from Walz, *Research Notes.*

24. Eau Claire County, Records of the Circuit Court, Case Files, Case #4273: *State of Wisconsin vs. Elizabeth Van Nostrend.*

25. Ibid., Case #4394: *State of Wisconsin vs. Andrew Hamilton et al.* and Case #2050½: *State of Wisconsin vs. Lydia Curtis;* and *Eau Claire Daily Leader,* May 31, June 2 [or June 26?], 1896, from Peterson, "Research Notes on Prostitution."

26. *Eau Claire Weekly Free Press,* May 8, 1888, from Peterson, "Research Notes on Prostitution."

27. *Chippewa Falls Directory,* 1887–1888.

28. Sylvester, "Avenues for Ladies Only," 292.

29. In his "Research Notes on Prostitution," Peterson quotes "Chippewa Allotments of Lands, Chippewa Timber Contracts," in *U.S. Senate Reports,* 50 Congress, 2 session (1889, no. 2710, serial 2624), 714.

30. From Walz, *Research Notes.*

31. Eau Claire County, Records of the Circuit Court, Case Files, Case #2781: *State of Wisconsin vs. Joseph Shafer et al.*

32. *Historical and Biographical Album of the Chippewa Valley, Wisconsin,* ed. by George Forrester (Chicago, 1892) 839.

33. Eau Claire County, Records of the Circuit Court, Case Files, Case #4391: *State of Wisconsin vs. James Mc-Cann et al.* and Case #6405: *Mary McCann vs. James McCann.*

34. *West Eau Claire Argus,* May 9, 1866, from Peterson, "Research Notes on Prostitution."

35. *Eau Claire City Directory* (1885).

36. Eau Claire County, Records of the Circuit Court, Case Files, Case #4798: *State of Wisconsin vs. Charles Barker.*

37. *Eau Claire Weekly Free Press,* February 23, 1899, or *Eau Claire Weekly Telegram,* February 23, 1899, from Peterson, "Research Notes on Prostitution."

38. Nesbit, *HOW,* 625.

39. Walz, *Research Notes.*

40. *Eau Claire Weekly Free Press,* January 10, 1878, from Peterson, "Research Notes on Prostitution." . . .

41. Rosen, *The Lost Sisterhood,* 5.

42. *Eau Claire Weekly Free Press,* August 12, 1875, from Peterson, "Research Notes on Prostitution."

43. . . . *Eau Claire Daily Free Press,* October 8, 1889; and *Eau Claire News,* November 20, 1889, [both] from Peterson, "Research Notes on Prostitution."

44. Rosen, *The Lost Sisterhood,* 5, 105.

45. *Eau Claire Daily Leader,* May 25, 1897, and *Eau Claire Weekly Leader,* October 29, 1893, from Peterson, "Research Notes on Prostitution."

46. "Wisconsin's Last Segregated District Closed," in *The Survey* 33 (1914): 328.

47. Rosen, *The Lost Sisterhood,* 1-16.

48. Robert A. Goldberg, "The Ku Klux Klan in Madison, 1922–27," *WMH* 58 (Autumn, 1974): 36.

49. Rosen, *The Lost Sisterhood,* 19, 3.

# The Health of Central Wisconsin Residents in 1880

## A New View of Midwestern Rural Life

JAN COOMBS

WMH 68, No. 4 (Summer 1985): 284–311

. . . For the most part, historical studies of nineteenth-century disease have focused on urban areas with their large, congested populations. Rural areas have been neglected, in part because historians assumed that widely scattered rural populations were relatively healthy. . . . In an effort to fill some small part of that historical void, this article examines health conditions in Central Wisconsin during an early period of its development.

Like many other frontier areas in the Old Northwest Territory, Central Wisconsin had just begun to experience a rapid population growth in the 1880s. As the number of residents increased, sanitation problems developed, causing the spread of disease. . . . [F]ollowing its own organization in 1875, the Wisconsin State Board of Health had encouraged local governments to establish boards of health and appoint health officers; however, few rural municipalities or towns had heeded their advice.[1] When such boards and officers did exist in Central Wisconsin, many residents . . . ignored or openly resisted measures to control their living habits. Without effective regulations to control the disposal of waste materials, protect water supplies, or enforce quarantine, infectious diseases took a heavy toll. . . .

For innumerable possible reasons, some enumerators did not report *any* illnesses or deaths in their districts. The probability that all their respondents were in excellent health or that no one had died seems unlikely, but cannot be ruled out. However, other reasons for their failure to record disease and death information deserve consideration.

The personal nature of some of the census questions must have caused considerable difficulty for some enumerators and respondents. For example, the embarrassment with which people viewed such health problems as "female complaints," alcoholism, venereal disease, mental retardation, and insanity may have kept enumerators from prying too deeply into the private lives of their neighbors, or their respondents from providing truthful answers. The 1880 census instructions to enumerators acknowledged only the possible embarrassment of respondents: . . ."It not infrequently happens that fathers and mothers, especially the latter, are disposed to conceal, or even to deny, the existence of such infirmities on the part of children.". . .[2]

Most of the enumerators would have been poorly equipped to evaluate health problems, since only one of them, a druggist, appears to have had any kind of medical background.[3] Among those who filled in the health-related questions, many resorted to folk beliefs about disease. For example, Frederick Zeller reported four stillbirths in the Town of Wausau. In three cases their mothers had fallen on the ice or were "overworked." The death of the fourth baby, whose appearance he described in detail ("head deformed, nose small, ears small, eyes near top of head"), was due to its mother having been "frightened by a rabbit while she was binding oats.". . .

Despite all these various problems, the enumerators' reports can provide many valuable insights into the health of Central Wisconsin residents. . . .

The Central Wisconsin population doubled between 1870 and 1880, suddenly growing by an average of more than 2,000 people per year. By 1880 . . . enumerators counted 54,548 persons living in their four-county area. Although the average population density was twelve persons per square mile, Portage County (because of its earlier settlement) and Marathon County (because of its size) had almost twice as many people as Clark and Wood counties.[4]

Approximately two-thirds of these residents were born in the United States, half of them in Wisconsin. Among those who were foreign born, about half came from the German Empire, which then included parts of Poland. . . . French Canadians, Scandinavians, English, Irish, Scots, Central Europeans, and native-born Americans were widely scattered throughout the area. . . .[5]

Regardless of where they lived in Central Wisconsin, the ethnic influence of the immigrants would have been far greater than census nativity statistics indicate because residents born in the United States included many young children of immigrant parents.[6] That this area had relatively more males than many other parts of the state or nation was probably due to the large number of single laborers employed in the lumber industry and on railroad construction. . . .[7]

There were only six communities of any substantial size. . . . Wausau and Stevens Point, each [had] approximately 4,000 people, and the sister villages of Grand Rapids and Centralia, [had] a combined population of slightly more than 2,000. . . . Neillsville, on the Black River, had about 1,200 people. . . . Marshfield, born of the Wisconsin Central Railroad in 1872, had only 700 residents.[8]

All six communities were remarkably similar to one another, varying some in size, number of industries and business establishments. . . . [S]aloons were in plentiful supply. . . . In every community, lawyers outnumbered doctors by at least two to one.[9]

In both town and country, Central Wisconsin residents got their water from private wells. Privy and other waste contamination of well water was a concern of state public health officials. They constantly exhorted local officials to improve sanitary conditions in their districts so as to curtail the spread of disease. . . .

Despite these warnings, animals ranged freely in most villages, munching morsels of vegetation or garbage where they found them, and leaving their own traces in payment. A few cities had passed ordinances by 1880 that prohibited the roaming of swine during all times of the year, and cows, horses, and other animals during the summer months. . . .[10]

Although farm families were usually isolated from one another, their living conditions often appear to have been equally unhealthy. In 1880 for example, an anonymous clerk . . . in Wood County reported that: "Most of the houses around here are log houses, the rooms are small, and there is generally a cooking stove in the room where all the family eat and sleep. There is usually a cellar, or a hole called by that name, where potatoes and other vegetables are stored through the winter. How such a way of living can be healthful, I can't see."[11]

Even the more substantial frame houses of well-established settlers were sometimes overcrowded. The large and multigenerational composition of Mr. and Mrs. Herman Meyer's household in the Town of Hull, Marathon County, was typical of many rural households; relatives living with this couple included two older couples, one younger couple, and thirteen children ranging upwards in age from six years, for a total of twenty-one people. When such living conditions as these were combined with the possibility of barnyard and cesspool drainage into wells, the risk of people being infected by one another, or their animals, was greatly increased.[12]

While poor sanitation was a major cause of disease and death among Central Wisconsin residents, other circumstances of life on this semifrontier can also be implicated.

Vital statistics have long been considered the bookkeeping of public health because such records as birth and death rates reflect much about a population's health. The Central Wisconsin enumerators recorded 1,936 babies, or approximately thirty-five births for every 1,000 Central Wisconsin residents. This birth rate was comparable to other areas of the state and nation.[13]

. . . Where paternity could be established, fathers of newborns were seldom teenagers, but many men were in their fifth, sixth, and sometimes seventh decades of life. For example, seventy-year-old Leander Trudell and his thirty-nine-year-old wife in the Town of Linwood, Portage County, had nine children living at home in 1880, the youngest five months old. . . . Eighty-four-year-old Jacob Mitchel, from the Town of Stevens Point, Portage County, had an eight-year-old daughter, and seventy-year-old Phillip Dumphy, in the same town, was the father of at least three children ages twelve, four, and one.

. . . However, advanced paternal age was not unusual in the nineteenth century because older men often married much younger women when their first, and sometimes second, wives died. . . . Since effective contraceptive methods were unavailable, these unions produced many babies.

Although the enumerators reported few births to teenagers or mothers in their fifties during the 1880 census year, the schedules reveal that many women had started to raise their families in their middle teens and had not stopped until they reached menopause. Repeated, sometimes almost annual pregnancies, could account for many health problems among Central Wisconsin women, including the high prevalence of "female complaints."

While the age at which men fathered children has little bearing on the health of infants, maternal age does have health implications for both the mother and child. For example, teenagers were more likely to have communicable diseases than older women; some of these diseases, especially measles during the early stages of pregnancy, can cause congenital malformations or fetal death. Conversely, women who give birth after the age of forty are more apt to suffer from such pregnancy complications as hypertension, premature or difficult delivery, and a higher maternal death rate. Their babies experience higher fetal and infant death rates because they are more likely to have congenital malformations or abnormally low birth weights.[14]

Illegitimacy had no direct influence on the health of mothers or their children, but enumerators seem to have been concerned with the social implications of this problem; unwed mothers and their offspring sometimes became paupers, requiring public funds for their maintenance and health care. Although the enumerators were not required to report illegitimate children, some felt compelled to supply such information, writing "bastard" or "bastard child" in the space reserved for occupation. George G. Oster, in the Town of Carson, Portage County, was more tactful; when a mother and baby died together of childbirth in his district, he noted that "the paternity of this child is involved in obscurity."

In addition to birth information, the population schedules show various forms of disability that afflicted Central Wisconsin residents. . . . It appears that the inability to work, rather than the condition itself, determined disability. . . .

. . . [Residents] suffering from temporary disability . . . include[d] six women who were about to give birth. Almost 600 people were recorded as being maimed, bedridden, or otherwise permanently disabled. . . .[15]

In 1880, twenty-two children from Central Wisconsin were enrolled at the Institution for the Deaf and Dumb in Delavan, and three at the Institution for the Blind in Janesville.[16] None of the children would have appeared in the Central Wisconsin census if they were living away from home. . . . [T]hese health problems were far more common than indicated by enumerators.

Congenital deafness often results when mothers have measles, encephalitis, chicken pox, or syphilis during pregnancy. . . . When deafness occurred early in life, most children never learned to talk unless given special schooling. Causes of blindness included eye diseases of the newborn (such vaginal infections as gonorrhea, when transmitted from mothers to their babies at birth, can result in infant blindness). . . .[17]

. . . [D]istinctions between mental retardation and mental illness were often confused in the 1880s. Most lay persons and some doctors haphazardly classified people with unusual or reprehensible behavior as either "idiots" or "insane." Since both these conditions were thought to be due to inheritance, or overindulgence in sex, smoking, or alcohol, this confusion is readily understandable. . . .[18] [T]he Clark County enumerator in the Town of Fremont reported that Edgar Rollins's three children, ages one to four, were all "insane." The possibility that they were all mentally retarded or misbehaving on the day of [the] visit cannot be ruled out, but it seems highly unlikely that all three of these very young children would have been mentally ill. . . .

The census counters found thirty-six people who were mentally retarded or insane, but they would not have counted many of the sixty-seven patients from Central Wisconsin who had been admitted to the Wisconsin State Hospital for the Insane at Mendota and the Northern Hospital for the Insane at Oshkosh during 1880.[19] A reluctance to divulge mental retardation or illness among family members could also account for the seemingly low incidence of these conditions in this population.

Only seventeen people were reported to be suffering from communicable diseases on the day they were visited by the enumerators. . . . (Tuberculosis was thought to be an inherited disease . . . [but] it was endemic and particularly common below the age of forty.)

In 1882, the Wisconsin State Board of Health published data it had collected from the preceding five years comparing the incidence of what it considered to be the five most prevalent contagious diseases — whooping cough, measles, diphtheria, typhoid fever, and scarlet fever — with deaths from these diseases. . . .[20] [I]t appears that more than 1,700 people (approximately 3 percent of the population) may have suffered from one of five communicable diseases during the census year.

Although they knew little about germs, public health authorities quite correctly attributed the prevalence of these diseases to crowded living quarters, poor sanitation, and disregard for quarantine measures. . . . [21]

The failure to isolate sick family members took a grim toll. John and Mary Hinky in the Town of Sigel, Wood County, lost all three of their children from diphtheria. In the city of Stevens Point, Irving and Lidia Cobb lost all three of their children to diphtheria.[22] All four children of Mr. and Mrs. J. S. Boardman in Clark County died from diphtheria within three days.[23] Less than three years later, Peter N. Christensen, a thirty-two-year-old farmer and enumerator from the Town of Lincoln in Wood County, saw his wife and four children die within two weeks after diphtheria struck his household. His only surviving child was born ten days before the death of his wife.[24]

Public health officials also blamed schools and churches for disregarding quarantine measures. . . . [T]he failure of teachers to remove sick children from the classroom incurred their special wrath.[25] They attacked churchmen and their congregations for holding elaborate funeral services for people who had died from communicable diseases because such gatherings promoted the spread of infection among mourners.[26]

Most of all, public authorities blamed the immigrants. . . . Dr. G. L. Buland from Greenwood in Clark County reported . . . that sanitary reforms had not been adopted in his community; such measures would cost money, but "the larger part of the people are Germans and very penurious."[27] Dr. W. H. Budge from Marshfield wrote to the state board: . . . "[T]he residents here are largely foreign born, and have queer ideas of personal liberty; many among them moreover are grossly ignorant."[28]

Although only one case of smallpox was reported in the state during 1880, local physicians and state public health officials held the immigrants responsible for an epidemic for this disease two years later. . . .[29] [T]he board secretary said, "We have reports that Poles and Bohemians generally object very strenuously to both vaccination and isolation, and that communities of those nationalities have been strongly scourged by Small Pox in consequence of such objections."[30]

. . . Although their comments suggest prejudice, some immigrants, especially those from the German Empire, did resist government intrusion into their lives because of experiences in their homeland. . . .[31]

. . . Whatever their reasons, these people viewed efforts to control their waste disposal and water supply, limit their activity through quarantine, or mandate smallpox vaccinations as intolerable infringements on their personal liberty. . . .

In addition to communicable diseases, Central Wisconsin residents suffered from many other illnesses. Women were prone to "female weakness," "female debility," "female complaint," "uterine colic," and "womb sickness." These diagnoses are difficult to interpret, since it was then fashionable to blame *all* illness in women on their reproductive organs.[32] Nevertheless, some of these women had suffered from birthing infections and injuries that would have left them with lifelong pain and disability. . . .[33]

Alcoholism and venereal disease must have been very prevalent, given the drinking and other entertainment habits of the railroad and lumber workers. . . . Judging by the frequent references to "gilded ladies" and "known suspicious females" in the newspapers, and repeated attempts to pass city ordinances forbidding their trade, prostitutes formed a significant part of the Central Wisconsin population.[34] Only a single case of "gunerea" was reported, but alcoholism could have been buried behind the frequent reports of "liver complaint." The lack of evidence here is best blamed on the inability of people to recognize these conditions in themselves or their reticence to confide such information to an enumerator. . . .

Town of Wausau enumerator Frederich W. Zeller found ninety-nine people (9.3 percent of his population) who were suffering from health problems. . . . [H]e found many women who suffered from female complaints and "nervous debility" (which may have been a debilitating state of anxiety). . . .

Children experienced many accidents that reflected the dangerous conditions of life on this semifrontier, including their easy access to guns and axes. Newspapers routinely issued such warnings to parents as "revolvers are ugly playthings, even for adults.". . .[35] Water wells were another hazard for youngsters. The two-year-old son of a Mrs. Fuller in Spencer was only saved from drowning by the prompt action of his mother, who "went down into the well by means of some wooden cleats on the well walls, and secured her child."[36]

An incident associated with soap-making occurred when a kettle of lye fell on Mr. and Mrs. Nathan Mane's baby boy, entering his nostrils and throat. A Clark County paper reported, "his eyes are necessarily badly damaged," but "indications are that his sight will be partially restored."[37] A rabid dog may have been responsible for the most recent tragedy to afflict the Al Plummer household. According to an 1880 newspaper, Plummer's wife had been an invalid for two years, a son had been crippled in an accident, and "now his youngest son is badly eaten by a dog.". . .[38]

. . . The mortality schedules, which listed causes of death, reveal further information about health problems.

In all, the enumerators counted 546 people who had died during the preceding twelve months. More than one-third of these deaths occurred among infants; 156 of them died before their first birthday. . . . [T]he deaths of infants . . . were probably among the most poorly reported in Central Wisconsin.

For inexplicable reasons, some parents failed to report the death of their babies; in a few cases, physicians (who had attended their births and subsequent deaths) sometimes added babies' names to the mortality forms when they signed them. Most births in Central Wisconsin, however, were attended by midwives.[39] Had these women been asked to sign the mortality schedules, they might have added other infant deaths. . . .

Despite all the diagnostic confusion that troubled both enumerators and physicians, the record clearly shows that many babies died at birth or during their first year. Bowel diseases, stillbirths, and birth defects were the major causes of death in the age group from birth to twelve months. . . .

Bowel diseases included "cholera infantum," "summer complaint," and other intestinal infections from impure water or milk supplies that caused diarrhea, dehydration, and ultimately, death. Stillbirths and birth defects could have resulted from congenital malformation, protracted delivery, maternal death, and improper use of forceps. . . .[40]

Among the mothers who gave birth during that same year, twenty-five of them died from such complications of childbirth as puerperal infection and excessive blood loss, or general debility from repeated pregnancies. Midwives assisted most women with their deliveries, but neither midwives nor physicians were then familiar with aseptic techniques to prevent infection. . . .[M]ost nineteenth-century midwives allowed birthing to proceed naturally, doing little to hasten the process; protracted delivery often resulted in maternal death from hemorrhaging or convulsions. Physicians were more apt to intervene with drugs and forceps, but their untimely use of ergot ruptured uteri, and improper use of forceps tore vaginal walls.[41]

General poor health from overwork can influence a woman's ability to survive a pregnancy and delivery. Farm women were usually overworked, but especially so in Central Wisconsin where women had to grow and preserve all their own food while tending to all the other needs of their often very large families.[42] When their husbands went off to work in lumber camps and mills for long periods of time, [women] often had to run their farms as well. Under such adverse conditions, many women failed to survive their oft-repeated pregnancies.

Among the twenty-five mothers who died that year from childbirth, six of their babies were stillborn, but nineteen babies lived on after their mothers' deaths. . . .[43]

Some of the babies were found on the census schedules living with their fathers; in other cases, they were cared for by neighbors or nearby relatives. When Catherine Keefe, from the Town of Mosinee in Marathon County, died from childbirth at thirty-one years, her infant went to stay with her husband's parents, but he kept their other six children, ages three to fifteen years, at home with him. . . . In some households where these babies were found, a woman was available to fill the role of surrogate mother — an older sister, a grandmother or aunt, or a father's new wife. In other instances, however, the father was left alone or with many other young children, none old enough to help with the baby's care.

Of the eighteen babies who were found on the census schedules, ten were still alive, but eight had died within their first seven months. Thus only slightly more than half of the babies had survived. That same year, the survival rate for Central Wisconsin babies with living mothers was 94 percent.[44]

Many of the surviving infants probably never recovered from injuries they sustained (possibly from forceps or oxygen depletion) during their difficult deliveries. Without their mothers to care for them, some babies may have been viewed as an unwelcomed burden. . . .

Families and neighbors who tried to save a motherless infant had several feeding options. Wet nurses would have been an ideal solution, but very few of the surrogate mothers had children of their own who would have been nursing. Fresh cow's milk, which was available during the summer months, could have been diluted with water and other additives then recommended by health authorities; or family recipes for paps and pandas (gruels of varying consistencies made from cooked grains, water, and sugar) could have been substituted for breast feeding.

Three commercial infant formulas, all requiring dilution with water, were on the market in the early 1800s. . . . These formulas, as well as commercial baby bottles, may have been available locally or through mail-order catalogs.[45] All of these homemade and commercial alternatives would have provided adequate nutrition and been safe if properly boiled and stored in clean containers. However, the Wisconsin State Board of Health claimed that few people were aware of such precautions.[46] It is surprising that ten infants managed to survive without the safety advantages of clean breast milk.

An incidental finding in the infant enumerations is significant for what it suggests about parental attitudes. . . . Enumerators recorded dozens of babies, some as old as seven months, who had not yet been given names. . . . Some writers contend that, with a high infant mortality, maternal bonding . . . did not take place until the child had demonstrated its ability to survive. Other writers suggest that nineteenth-century parents often left their infants nameless for many months, lest they "waste" a favorite name. . . .[47]

Babies who survived their first year then faced another major hurdle. During the next four years, they had to contend with a variety of communicable and infectious diseases to which they were particularly susceptible. Enumerators reported 102 deaths in the age group from one to five years. Here, the major causes of death were lung, bowel, and neurological infections (all similar to those which afflicted infants), as well as communicable diseases, especially diphtheria. Poor sanitation and disregard for quarantine measures were undoubtedly responsible for most of these deaths. . . .

The accidental deaths among youngsters were due to burning by fire or hot liquids and drowning in wells or rivers. [A] malignant eye tumor caused a death from cancer. [A] homicide involved two-year-old Coral Rice, Town of Pine Grove, Portage County, who was shot by his mother; she was subsequently adjudged insane. . . .[48]

Despair and resignation must have gone hand-in-hand when deaths of mothers and their babies were a dreaded but expected part of life. Since effective contraceptive methods were unavailable, many women must have viewed pregnancy as a life-threatening condition over which they had very little control. Some women faced that threat as many as a dozen times during their reproductive years.

Although maternal and newborn death rates were extremely high in the nineteenth century, doctors viewed pregnancy and birthing as normal processes involving unalterably great risks. . . . [C]oncerns would only develop after the turn of the century when pregnancy came to be viewed as a disease condition requiring medical attention.[49]

The deaths of infants and young children, sometimes all the siblings in a single family within the space of a few weeks, undoubtedly stretched parental grief to incomprehensible limits. The repeated loss of children must have seemed like incredibly cruel blows of fate when parents knew so little about the spread of disease.

Although the census records reveal few divorces, the deaths of spouses accounted for many marital dissolutions. Precise figures are not available for Central Wisconsin, but U.S. demographic records reveal that marital dissolution rates for the 1880s were almost as high as those in 1970; spousal deaths compensated for the low 1800s divorce rate. . . .[50]

. . . During the last two decades of the nineteenth century . . . rural mortality rates throughout the state remained relatively constant, while urban death rates drastically declined until the two rates approximated one another in the early 1900s.[51] Some historians contend that public health reforms accounted for the improvements in urban health, but insist that these measures had little effect on rural populations.[52] However, other historians have demonstrated that the supposedly steady rural death rate was a combination of two factors: the gradual lowering of death rates as public health reforms were slowly adopted and a gradual increase in numbers of deaths [were] reported as rural vital statistics methods improved. . . .[53]

## NOTES

1. Wisconsin State Board of Health (hereafter referred to as WSBH), *Fourth Annual Report*, 1879, xli–xlii.

2. Carroll D. Wright and William C. Hunt, *The History and Growth of the United States Census* (56 Congress, 1 session, United States Senate Documents, Vol. 14, Washington, DC, 1900), 169.

3. . . . Central Wisconsin enumerators included twenty-nine farmers, seven teachers, four lumbermen, three bookkeepers, three merchants, two carpenters, a railroad agent, druggist, publisher, store clerk, pastor, postmaster, lawyer, real estate agent, and laborer. . . . [Of the sixty-five enumerators, only one was a woman: Mrs. D. B. R. Dickson of Grant, Clark County. The author also found that "at least one-quarter of the Central Wisconsin enumerators were foreign-born. Some who were native-born probably had difficulty communicating with all non–English speaking immigrants. Foreign-born enumerators could have had problems when they encountered immigrants whose native country differed from their own."]

4. 1880 U.S. Census, *Population*, vol. 1, 84–85; 1940 U.S. Census, *Measurement of Geographic Area*, Appendix F, "Areas of the United States, the Several States and Territories and Their Counties, 1881," prepared by Henry Gannett, 106.

5. 1880 U.S. Census, *Population*, vol. 1, 534–535; 1880 U.S. Census population schedules.

6. Joseph Schafer, *A History of Agriculture in Wisconsin* (Madison, 1922), 131–137. . . .

7. 1880 U.S. Census, *Population*, vol. 1, xxxv.

8. Ibid., 367–373.

9. . . . According to the Wisconsin State Board of Charities and Reform, *Tenth Annual Report* (Madison, 1880), 238–239, Central Wisconsin had at least 150 saloons, or about one for every 350 residents.

10. [See,] . . . for example, Town of Grand Rapids Proceedings, April 7, 1868; Centralia Common Council Proceedings, May 9, 1874. . . .

11. WSBH, *Fifth Annual Report*, 1880, 137.

12. [S]ee WSBH, *Fifth Annual Report*, 1880. . . .

13. 1880 U.S. Census, *Mortality and Vital Statistics,* vol. 12, pt 2, 662, 668.

14. Although nineteenth-century doctors recognized many pregnancy complications, they did not link prepartum infections or maternal age to infant and maternal mortality. . . . Connections between prepartum infections, maternal age, and infant and maternal mortality are amply demonstrated in twentieth-century medical literature. . . . See Jack A. Prichard and Paul C. MacDonald, *Williams Obstetrics* (16th ed., New York, 1980), 763, 995–996; Edgar O. Horger, et al., Pregnancy in Women Over Forty," *Journal of Obstetrics and Gynaecology,* 49:257–261 (1977). . . .

15. The author's tabulations differ from published census reports because many errors were found in the schedules. . . .

16. *Wisconsin Blue Book,* 1881, 369–371.

17. Article by Dr. Samuel Sexton in *Harper's Magazine* (March 1880) and reprinted in the *Clark County Republican and Press,* April 2, 1880. . . .

18. WSBH, *Tenth Annual Report,* 1886, 167–181. . . .

19. *Wisconsin Blue Book,* 1881, 362, 366.

20. WSBH, *Seventh Annual Report,* 1882, 99.

21. Ibid., 90.

22. . . . 1880 U.S. Census mortality schedules.

23. *Clark County Republican and Press,* May 28, 1880.

24. George O. Jones, et al., *History of Wood County, Wisconsin* (Minneapolis, MN: 1923), 608.

25. WSBH, *Sixth Annual Report,* 1881, xii–xvi, 30–63.

26. WSBH, *Eighth Annual Report,* 1882–1884, 150–153.

27. WSBH, *Ninth Annual Report, 1885,* 109–110.

28. WSBH, *Eleventh Annual Report,* 1887, 224.

29. WSBH, *Sixth Annual Report,* 1881, xlvii–xlix.

30. WSBH, *Seventh Annual Report,* 1882, 52.

31. Kate Everest Levi, "Geographical Origin of German Immigration," *WHC,* 358–359, 362–363, 379–381. . . .

32. Patricia Branca, "Towards a Social History of Medicine," in Patricia Branca, ed., *The Medicine Show: Patients, Physicians, and the Perplexities of the Health Revolution in Modern Society* (New York, 1977), 91.

33. Judith W. Leavitt, "'Science' Enters the Birthing Room: Obstetrics in America Since the Eighteenth Century," *Journal of American History* 70 (1983):283.

34. *Grand Rapids Tribune,* February 14, 1880, June 26, 1880; *Clark County Republican and Press,* January 30, 1880; *Wisconsin Pinery* (Stevens Point), June 3, June 15, August 10, June 3, 1880; *Grand Rapids Tribune,* May 15, 1880. . . .

35. *Grand Rapids Tribune,* March 20, 1880. . . .

36. *Stevens Point Wisconsin Pinery,* May 18, 1883.

37. *Clark County Republican and Press,* May 28, 1880.

38. *Wisconsin Pinery* (Stevens Point), May 23, 1883.

39. Of 334 births recorded for the period between June 1, 1879, and May 31, 1880, and filed with the Portage County clerk, approximately fifty were attended by physicians; with the exception of a few husbands, parents, and pastors, midwives attended the rest.

40. Leavitt, "'Science' Enters the Birthing Room," 286–288; John S. Haller, Jr., *American Medicine in Transition, 1840–1910* (Urbana, 1981), 160–167.

41. Haller, *American Medicine in Transition,* 160–167; Frances E. Korbin, "The American Midwife Controversy: A Crisis of Professionalization," in Judith W. Leavitt and Ronald L. Numbers, eds., *Sickness and Health in America: Readings in the History of Medicine and Public Health* (Madison, 1978), 217–225.

42. W. W. Hall, "Health of Farmers' Families," in *Report of the Commissioner of Agriculture, 1862* (United States Executive Documents, Washington, 1862), 462–470.

43. . . . When infants survived their mothers at birth, this household information, combined with date of the mother's death, age of her baby, and nativity of the parents, made it possible to trace the fate of motherless infants.

44. . . . Thus, "only" 114 babies born to 1,911 living mothers died during their first year.

45. Rima D. Apple, "'How Shall I Feed My Baby?' Infant Feeding in the United States, 1870–1940" (doctoral dissertation, University of Wisconsin, 1981), xv–4. . . .

46. WSBH, *The Care of Infants and Young Children* (WSBH Circular No. One, Madison, 1879); Knut Hoegh, "Hints Concerning Infantile Hygiene and Dietetics," in WSBH, *Seventh Annual Report,* 1882, 151.

47. Edward Shorter, "Maternal Sentiment and Death in Childbirth: A New Agenda for Psycho-Medical History," in Branca, *The Medicine Show,* 67-88; Barbara Ehrenreich and Deirdre English, *For Her Own Good: 150 Years of the Experts' Advice to Women* (Garden City, New York, 1978), 167.

48. *Stevens Point Journal,* July 12, 1879.

49. Leavitt, "'Science' Enters the Birthing Room," 298.

50. Davis Kingsley, "The American Family in Relation to Demographic Change," in Charles F. Westoff and Robert Parke, eds., *Demographic and Social Aspects of Population Growth,* vol. I (Washington, 1972), 256. The combined U.S. marital dissolution rates for 1880–1884 were 33.0 per 1,000 existing marriages, with deaths accounting for 30.6 and divorce for 2.3. The combined marital dissolution rates for 1970 were 34.5 per 1,000 existing marriages, with deaths accounting for 19.3 and divorce for 15.2.

51. Judith W. Leavitt, "Urban Wisconsin," in Ronald L. Numbers and Judith W. Leavitt, eds., *Wisconsin Medicine: Historical Perspectives* (Madison, 1981), 168.

52. Robert Higgs, "Mortality in Rural America, 1870–1920: Estimates and Conjectures," in *Explorations in Economic History,* 10(2):177–195 (1973).

53. For example, see Henry N. Ogden, *Rural Hygiene* (New York, 1911), 6–8.

# Poverty and Relief in Nineteenth-Century Janesville

JOHN A. FLECKNER

*WMH* 61, No. 4 (Summer 1978): 279–299

∽≈⁓

. . . Janesville during the later nineteenth century seemed the very picture of well-ordered urban society. . . . As in so many other Wisconsin cities, residents of New England and New York backgrounds dominated social and economic life, though foreign-born and first-generation Americans (primarily Germans and Irish with a smattering of Scandinavians, Canadians, and British) comprised slightly more than half the population of Janesville. . . .

By 1875 Janesville was far removed from its crude beginnings. . . . [E]lm-lined residential streets [were] graced with fine homes and spired churches. Substantial brick commercial blocks lined the downtown avenues, and the city boasted five sturdy public school buildings, a handsome courthouse, and a score of lodges and voluntary associations.[1]

Despite these very genuine attractions, most residents of Janesville also knew firsthand that harsh poverty and suffering were inescapable features of life in their city. . . . [D]uring the winter of 1874, for example, a writer in the *Janesville Gazette* observed: "Our citizens are generally enterprising and industrious but it is impossible to keep hunger and want from the doors of some families. In every city in the country there are . . . a few who are doomed to suffer poverty.". . .[2]

The conditions of life in nineteenth-century America made acceptance of poverty's inevitability altogether understandable. As late as 1880 life expectancy at birth was only about forty years — approximately the figure for modern India, and less than two-thirds of what Americans now expect. Like the rest of the nation, Janesville residents suffered through plagues of smallpox, diphtheria, cholera, and scarlet fever, which left children orphaned, families broken, finances exhausted. Added to this were the hazards of industrial employment and of early railroad travel, the dangers of fire and flood, and disastrous periodic depressions in the national economy. . . .

Histories of social welfare have tended to ignore the role of self-help, forgetting the constant struggles of the poor to cope with their precarious situations. In nineteenth-century Janesville, most people believed that the poor and unfortunate could preserve a sense of personal value and public respect only by struggling to maintain an independent status. . . .

Work, when it was available, was the most obvious and acceptable form of relief from want. . . . Many of Janesville's poor and needy were women: the mothers and unmarried daughters of poor families, country girls escaping rural poverty, and widowed and abandoned wives. Rigid limits on occupations believed suitable for women further hindered them in their struggles for self-sufficiency. As a result, most poor women labored long and hard at domestic jobs — as servants, waitresses, hotel maids, seamstresses, washerwomen — for pitifully small rewards.[3]

But nineteenth-century Janesville was a growing industrial city, and increasingly the poor found work in new factory jobs. . . .

. . . [By] 1880, the [largest] factory employed some 250 people. Their median age was less than nineteen years; two-thirds were girls and young women; more than three-fourths were immigrants and first-generation Irish [or] German-Americans. One-third of all the mill hands came from homes headed by women, usually widows. The bulk of the remaining workers were the children of day laborers — the least skilled and most vulnerable of all occupational groups. . . . Work in the Janesville mills, as in cotton mills everywhere, was hard: clattering, unguarded machinery, unbearable summer heat, twelve-hour shifts, night work, six-day weeks, frequent accidents, and more. Yet, despite these hardships, the mill never suffered for want of workers. . . .[4]

As mill workers and domestic servants . . . most of Janesville's poor [women] struggled constantly to maintain themselves as self-supporting citizens. . . . [T]hese struggles also gave the poor a right to claim the "practical sympathies" of their fellow citizens when self-help no longer sufficed. . . .

Before 1886, two Janesville organizations attempted to relieve the needy of the city on a broader basis. . . . [A] series of well-attended charity balls . . . raised nearly $400 annually for the poor.

The most noted charity ball took place in 1875 at the dedication of the newly erected Janesville cotton mill. . . . To celebrate, 3,000 people jammed all three floors of the building (the machinery was not yet in place) to dine [and] dance. . . . [A]ll the proceeds were distributed among the poor of the city.[5]

A rudimentary public welfare system existed alongside Janesville's privately organized charity efforts. . . . Unlike private charity efforts, however, public welfare received little of the public attention and generated none of the community pride that surrounded private charity activities. For one thing, many people deplored the system's harsher features, including the practice of shipping out nonresidents to avoid supporting them and the appalling conditions that prevailed in the county poor house and insane asylum. . . .[6]

. . . Rock County had established its poorhouse in 1854, and by 1870 the institution was one of twenty-two in fifty-eight Wisconsin counties. The people of Janesville, like Americans elsewhere, felt somewhat ambivalent about the poorhouse as a public institution. . . . As the Wisconsin State Board of Charities put it: "While a spirit of self-reliance can be kept alive, there is with it a feeling of independence. . . . When [one is] an inmate of a poor house but a short time, all independence is lost and helplessness results." Honest observers also knew that the poorhouse served as a convenient location where society could segregate, and forget, its most helpless and desperate members.[7]

Conditions at the Rock County Poor House, located at Johnstown east of Janesville, were like those in similar institutions elsewhere in Wisconsin and the nation. In 1870 the house had six sleeping rooms without windows or ventilation, "swarming with bed bugs." Bedding was dirty; the privy emitted a "foul odor." The population at the house varied with the seasons but averaged between fifty and sixty. . . . They included the very old, the permanently handicapped (blind, crippled, retarded, and insane), and mothers unable to support their very young children. The poorhouse received some especially pitiful cases. . . . Margaret Kemp, a woman who "has staggered under the influence of liquor and has lost all womanhood and respect," entered the poorhouse at her own request. While drunk on Janesville's streets she had fled from a band of taunting boys, stumbled, and sprained her ankle.[8]

. . . [T]rue, for some unfortunates it was a final refuge in which to deteriorate and die; but many residents entered the institution only temporarily and left again for the wider world. In fact, the number "discharged" during each year roughly equaled the new admissions. Many people left the poorhouse when their debilitating condition — a broken leg, a mental disorder, an illness, or a pregnancy — had passed. . . . The length of residency in the Rock County Poor House was probably about the same as in Waukesha County, where some residents remained only a few weeks and 56 percent of the family units and 70 percent of the single individuals remained less than a year.

The staff of the poorhouse consisted of the superintendent and his family and one or two hired hands. The residents themselves did much of the maintenance and housekeeping. They also operated a 125-acre farm that in 1876 produced some 767 bushels of wheat, 1,200 bushels of oats, various quantities of other grains and vegetables, and 8,000 pounds of pork and beef. Certainly, for those who could work, there was ample opportunity to be busy. . . .[10]

This older approach to poverty and misfortune did not disappear overnight; indeed, elements of it persist today. But rapid economic and social changes in the late nineteenth century, in Janesville as in the nation as a whole, brought new ideas and practices. . . . The Janesville Associated Charities, organized in the mid-1880s, embodied many of these new ideas and practices.

The Associated Charities appeared at a critical time in Janesville's economic and social development. For one thing, a severe depression had . . . spread across the nation. The city's manufacturing firms . . . were especially hard hit. Perhaps the cruelest blow was the near failure of the cotton manufacturing company, the city's largest employer. . . . By June, 1884, even the optimistic *Gazette* admitted to a "general depression in everything."[11]

The depression of the mid-1880s had far-reaching effects on Janesville's social order. In November, 1883, cotton mill workers struck unsuccessfully for two and a half weeks against depression-induced wage cuts; two years later shoemakers in the city's second largest factory conducted a bitter five-month-long strike. These were Janesville's first prolonged labor disputes. . . .

It was within this context of economic crisis and rapid social change that a group of Janesville citizens, headed by the city's leading businessmen and their wives, organized the Janesville Associated Charities. The organization began auspiciously when about one hundred citizens — "with more ladies than gentlemen" — attended a formal organizational meeting . . . in February, 1886. They elected some of the city's most prominent residents as their first officers . . . [including] the mayor's wife . . . and a banker's wife. . . .[12]

The men and women who established the Janesville Associated Charities saw themselves as part of a burgeoning national movement to reform charity administration. . . .

The system proposed for Janesville . . . was like that operating in twenty-five to fifty other places, including Milwaukee where Wisconsin's only previous organized charitable activity had begun in 1881. . . .[13]

The Janesville Associated Charities adopted the general principles of the charity organization society movement. Using the movement's familiar rhetoric, the new organization proclaimed that its objects were "to discover and relieve the worthy poor, to discover mendicancy, expose imposture, and diminish pauperism.". . . The organization welcomed representatives of all churches, societies, and public agencies in the city which offered relief. . . . This cooperative form of organization would permit coordination of various public and private relief activities and thus "cover the city with a complete network in which all fraud shall be caught and all need discovered." Key to the new organization was a corps of "friendly visitors" which would divide the city into districts and personally visit all those seeking aid. The visitors would investigate applicants with a view to discovering their true needs, teaching them how to reach health and independence, and carrying to them "friendly social influences."[14]

. . . By careful investigation and records-keeping, the Associated Charities expected to discover the very causes of poverty while eliminating the careless, overabundant supply of relief to undeserving people that many charitable workers believed was a major cause of pauperism. "Scientific charity," its proponents believed, would reduce poverty and effect significant financial economies for the productive members of society. . . . No wonder, then, that the main support for "scientific charity" in Janesville was from the business and professional classes.[15]

The Janesville Associated Charities . . . never fulfilled its early aspirations. Some problems became immediately apparent. . . . [M]ost churches and societies never responded to the call, perhaps preferring their own informal methods to the central register of recipients and the other formalities of Janesville Associated Charities' procedures. Voluntary charity work presented other difficulties. "Our visitors are mostly women of many and varied household cares," the secretary reported in 1890, "so that they really have very little time to give to this work." As a result of such frustrations, attendance at annual meetings sometimes dwindled to less than a dozen. . . .[16]

Through it all, however, some members remained faithful. Frances Cornelia Norton Tallman — always Mrs. Edgar Dexter Tallman in public — served for years as a first ward vice-president and a friendly visitor. Born in New York state, she had come to nearby Milton, Wisconsin, as a child, and had later married into the wealthy and prominent Tallman family of Janesville [see Introduction to chapter 3]. . . .

. . . She had raised two sons to adulthood and now, largely free of parental responsibilities, she was busy in Congregational church affairs, in the social life of Janesville's best families, and in her charitable activities. Mrs. Tallman's Associated Charities work for a single year illustrated both the problems and the contributions of a dedicated charity organization society volunteer.

. . . Mrs. Tallman attended twenty-four meetings of the executive council and reported the names of seventeen needy families or individuals in her assigned area. Mrs. Tallman had visited each case personally; most she had seen several times. . . . [S]he first reported Mrs. Mary Welsh sick and her son disabled with a crushed foot. . . . [T]wo weeks later Mrs. Tallman had to ask the council for reimbursement for five dollars paid Mrs. Weaver to take meals to the Welsh family. [A month later] Mrs. Tallman informed the council of Mrs. Welsh's death.

. . . Mrs. Tallman provided necessaries for the Lightfoot family, shoes for the children in September, underclothes and bedding in December, underwear for Mrs. Lightfoot and dresses for the children the following month. In April Mrs. Lightfoot was sick and her children were again in need of clothes. The council decided to ask the county superintendent of the poor to do what he could, and Mrs. Tallman wrote Mrs. Lightfoot's sister urging her to take the children and to allow Mrs. Lightfoot to go to the county poorhouse. And so it went in case after case; shoes for the Malbon family whose father was still unable to work; food and nursing for the ill Mrs. Fitzpatrick; coal and groceries for a poor "colored family."[17]

Although Mrs. Tallman did not record her personal perceptions and reactions to all this, others who pursued organized charities work made important discoveries and contributions. In Janesville, for instance, they frequently found that "sickness or injury was the cause of misfortune," and that, located "in the midst of poverty and squalor," such suffering was almost impossible to alleviate. In response to this, and to the failure of the city government to act, Janesville Associated Charities rented a suite of rooms and engaged a nurse, creating Janesville's first successful hospital. . . . As a result, the Janesville City Hospital was incorporated in 1887. . . .[18]

Charity organization society workers learned other first-hand lessons about the complexities of poverty. The idea of helping the poor to improve themselves, an underlying principle of scientific charity, proved difficult to translate into practice. "We often find women who ask for plain sewing," reported Mrs. H. S. Woodruff . . . "and none is to be obtained. Most people hesitate to put their sewing into unexperienced hands and so the poor applicant, although willing and anxious to work, is obliged to accept alms." The Associated Charities, however, never carried out Mrs. Woodruff's recommendation for a sewing class for poor women. . . .[19]

The problem of separating "worthy" from "unworthy" poor also proved intractable. During the depression of the mid-1890's a Janesville Associated Charities report admitted that "the wisdom of the society is often severely taxed to discriminate between the unemployed and the habitually idle and thriftless who take advantage of the emergency to assert their equal rights to share the public benevolence." The case of Mrs. Street . . . was just such a problem. Mrs. Street "was discovered to be unworthy of help but it was decided for the sake of humanity to do something for her relief.". . .[20]

The experience of doing charitable work year after year gradually tempered the rhetoric of the Janesville Associated Charities, giving the organization a more humane outlook. Certainly a permanent organization, structured to direct attention to the problems of the poor everywhere in the city and to mobilize a corps of hard-working people, assisted many needy people who otherwise would have been overlooked by older informal methods of "practical charity." In Janesville, and in the nation, most of this volunteer work was done by well-to-do, often educated women for whom childrearing, sewing, and watercolors were insufficient outlets for mind and spirit. In organized charity work they found challenging and socially useful community roles that were still largely denied them in politics, business, and the professions. In the nation as a whole, the volunteer work of such charitable organizations underlay . . . the emergence of social work as a profession.[21]

. . . Yet for all the benefits that modern practices brought, much was lost in this transition. The ideas and structure of the Associated Charities reflected the middle-class assumption that to be poor was not a natural, if unfortunate, condition, but rather a mark of individual deviance. . . . Such assumptions inevitably produced a sense of self-righteousness and superiority. For example, the secretary of the Janesville Associated Charities . . . [wrote] that "one of the greatest needs of the poor is a standard of cleanly and thrifty living, a standard which they can only acquire through contact with those who, like our friendly visitors, are willing to go among them in a spirit of practical and painstaking friendliness." Similarly, . . . the secretary approvingly quoted an unnamed source: "We must be provident for the poor, who are seldom provident for themselves.". . .[22]

## NOTES

1. The standard county histories are *The History of Rock County Wisconsin* (Chicago, 1879) and William Fiske Brown, *Rock County Wisconsin, A New History* (2 volumes, Chicago, 1908). . . .

2. *Janesville Gazette*, November 30, 1874. . . .

3. The school census taker found 239 widows in the city. Ibid., September 5, 1879. The 1870 federal manuscript census in the Library Division, WHS, recorded 379 women employed in the city as domestic servants and 326 men as laborers.

4. Based on information about 228 mill workers recorded in the population schedules of the 1880 federal census, preserved on microfilm at the WHS. . . .

5. . . . *Janesville Gazette*, . . . February 10, 1875; Records of the Sack Company, Rock County Historical Society, Janesville.

6. State law required the county to aid all needy people within its boundaries. . . . [T]he statutes allowed counties to recover the costs of aiding those who did not have . . . residence by billing their home counties. The recovery process was time-consuming and frequently unsuccessful. . . . [T]he Rock County superintendents of the poor adopted a simple and common expedient: they . . . move[d] them along to another governmental jurisdiction. . . .

7. Wisconsin State Board of Charities and Reform, *Tenth Annual Report*, 1881, 235. . . .

8. Wisconsin State Board of Charities and Reform, *First Annual Report*, 1871, 23–24, 78–80; *Janesville Gazette*, June 1, 3, 23, 1875.

9. *Janesville Gazette*, January 1, 1883; figures for Waukesha County calculated from Elizabeth G. Brown, "Poor Relief in a Wisconsin County, 1846–1866: Administration and Recipients," in the *American Journal of Legal History*, 20 (April, 1976), 112. . . .

10. Wisconsin State Board of Charities and Reform, *Fifth Annual Report*, 1875, 61.

11. *Janesville Gazette*, March 18, 1886, and June 4, 1884.

12. Ibid., February 3 and 6, March 4, 1886.

13. Associated Charities Minute Books, Volume 1, minutes of meetings of January 26 and February 2, 1886, WHS Archives, University of Wisconsin–Whitewater Area Research Center. . . .

14. . . . Associated Charities Minute Books, Volume 1; . . . *Janesville Gazette*, March 4, 1886. . . .

15. Walter Trattner, *From Poor Law to Welfare State: A History of Social Welfare in America* (Glencoe, Illinois, 1974), 85–86.

16. Report of the Work of the Janesville Associated Charities in its First Two Years, November 16, 1887, and Report of the Secretary to the Annual Meeting, November 17, 1890, Associated Charities Minute Books, vol. 1.

17. Minutes of executive committee meetings, Associated Charities Minute Books, vol. 1. Throughout this period Mrs. Tallman kept a diary of her daily activities. . . . The Tallman diaries are . . . in the archives of the Rock County Historical Society [on the Lincoln-Tallman House grounds].

18. Report of the Hospital Committee, *Janesville Gazette,* November 16, 1887, . . . December 15, 1887, and January 14, 1888. . . .

19. Report of the annual meetings, November 17, 1890, and minutes of meeting, December 15, 1890, Associated Charities Minute Books, vol. 1.

20. Secretary's Report, February 25, 1895, [and] minutes of the executive committee, December 2, 1895, . . . Associated Charities Minute Books, vol. 1.

21. Roy Lubove, *The Professional Altruist: The Emergence of Social Work as a Career, 1880–1930* (Cambridge, Massachusetts, 1965), 20, and chapter two, "From Friendly Visiting to Social Diagnosis."

22. . . . Report of the secretary to the annual meeting, November 19, 1894, and November 18, 1895, Associated Charities Minute Books, vol. 1.

# Necedah in Early Days

BERTHA V. THOMSON, M.D.

*WMH* 16, No. 4 (June 1933): 412–422

# 610 Ellis and the Hospital Children

EDITH DODD CULVER

*WMH* 60, No. 2 (Winter 1976–77): 116–

*The first woman physician in Wisconsin and only the third in the country, Dr. Laura J. Ross, had arrived in Milwaukee in 1857 or 1858 and built a successful practice, but the Milwaukee Medical Society denied her membership for more than a decade (see Introduction to chapter 3). After a "bitter contest" among members — and after she married their president, a local hero for his service as the state's surgeon general in the Civil War — the medical men of Milwaukee admitted Dr. Laura Ross Wolcott in 1869, at last. She was only the first.[1]*

*Women in Wisconsin who followed her into the field of medicine, whether as physicians or nurses or midwives, also faced discrimination for decades. As Dr. Bertha V. Thomson writes in her remarkable reminiscence, she found little encouragement even to go into nursing — and finding nursing schools also was not easy in nineteenth-century Wisconsin. She had to go out of state for nursing school, and later for medical school, before she came back to Wisconsin and became the nation's first known woman "city physician," or health commissioner. Her story suggests that her success owed much to the independence she had gained from a sad childhood in Necedah after the death of her mother, who was descended from a founding family of the town. Thomson's uncle, E. S. Miner, had been Necedah's judge and postmaster and would go on to serve as president of the state senate and in Congress. However, Thomson's father was from a far different family — and a different school of thought regarding schooling for daughters.*

*Dr. Bertha V. Thomson was on her own most of her childhood and throughout her struggle to become a woman in medicine in Wisconsin, as she relates in her recollection excerpted here.*

## Necedah in Early Days

I was born at Necedah in a little house next to my aunt's large home. . . .

When I was little more than two years old, my mother died. She left five children, the youngest being only a few months old. This baby and I were boarded out wherever opportunity offered. My father . . . was a hard-working man, . . . but he was never able to accumulate a great amount of money. He was very fond of his children and though he could have had us adopted, he would not part with us. Some of the people who took care of us were very kind and some were not. I can remember each one very distinctly. Sometimes my little sister and I were at the same place and sometimes we were separated. . . . [A]fter a time my father had a home and my oldest sister kept house for us. During these times I attended school. When I was seven years old [in 1869], my father married a woman who had one child. I remember how overjoyed we were. . . .

Soon my father received an offer to [work]. . . . This . . . was . . . twenty miles north of Necedah. . . . I well remember that when this offer . . . came, my father made a remark so characteristic of a man's ideas at that time. "I don't like to take the children out of school," he said, "but as they are all girls, it doesn't make so much difference." I had one brother, a clerk in the store at Necedah. . . .

When I was fourteen years old my brother, to whom I had appealed, because, as I said, I was "growing up in ignorance," found me a place in Necedah where I could work for my board and go to school. At this age I could cook, wash, iron, make beds, mend, feed cattle, milk, make butter, and so on. . . . They moved away, and I found another place. Here I stayed for years. . . . I loved children, and as there were plenty of them in the family, I was very useful. . . . Although my aunt lived there [in the town], I was a stranger to them and I was glad to be independent. . . . Often I was very lonesome but I was determined to stay at it even if the work was hard. I used to study geography, spelling, and so on while I was washing dishes or ironing. My parents moved to Nebraska and wanted me to go with them, but I wanted to finish school. I finally graduated from high school as valedictorian. I took the teachers' examination, passed, and taught for five years [in the 1880s] in the graded schools of Necedah.

All this time I had wanted to study medicine. I saw that I could never make enough money at teaching. . . . Forty dollars a month for nine months a year was considered good pay at that time. . . . My mother was a healing medium. . . . When I went to Necedah, I heard no end of good things about my mother. . . . My desire became strong to be such a woman as my mother would have wished me to be.

. . . [When a sister in Kansas] wrote me that she was sick, I went. . . . [A] hard school year . . . nearly finished me for a time. I got a country school and taught for a few months, all the time thinking about the doctor in me, but I did not know how to manage it. Finally I wrote to the women's medical colleges in large cities like New York and Chicago telling them that I wanted to study medicine and had no money. I asked if there were any way that a girl would work her way through such a school. . . . [A] reply advis[ed] me to go to a nurses' training school. These schools were not so plentiful, and I did not know where to find one. . . . I finally discovered that there were two women physicians [in town]. . . . I called on them and explained what I wanted to do. They told me to write to the Illinois Training School for Nurses at Chicago. I did this and received a letter requesting a certificate of health and moral character. These women [physicians] examined me and would not take a cent. . . . I was accepted and started at once for Chicago.

. . . After graduating . . . I took a position in the Brainerd, Minnesota, Railroad Hospital as head nurse. This . . . afforded only a small salary, so I returned to Chicago, to private nursing, where I could make more money and get to the medical college sooner. . . .

In 1895 I graduated from the Women's Medical School of Northwestern University. . . . [I came] to Oshkosh. . . . [T]he principal surgeon in these parts . . . sent many women patients to me. [The] mayor . . . appointed me city physician. I was the first woman to hold such a position in the United States. . . . [T]he superintendent of the Northern Hospital for the Insane asked me to come there as an assistant physician. I was there for three and a half years and really opened the insane hospitals in Wisconsin to women [on staff]. They have had a woman physician there ever since.

I finally returned to Oshkosh to do private practice. . . . In the spring of 1919 the [Oshkosh] city commission elected me full-time health officer. I was the first woman, and I think the only woman, in the state to hold the position.

I have opened three positions for women. . . . [H]ence I feel that my cycle of usefulness has been quite complete.

*In 1895, when Dr. Thomson graduated from medical school, the first nursing schools finally opened in Wisconsin. The Daughters of Charity, the first women religious in Wisconsin, who had founded the first hospital almost half a century before in Milwaukee, founded St. Mary's School of Nursing in 1895. Their first graduates in 1896 marked the order's fiftieth anniversary of service in the city (see Introduction to chapter 3).[2] But a year before, near Wisconsin's northernmost border, the Ashland Training School for Nurses began in Ashland at Dodd's Hospital. One of the first in the area for women patients, its pioneering founder John M. Dodd performed the state's first hysterectomy and Caesarean section.*

*Dr. Dodd's daughter had a happy but unusual upbringing as one of the "hospital children" in an era when physicians' families resided in their medical facilities — as did their students, as she recalls. Edith Dodd Culver also happened to witness women's history in Wisconsin, as is evident in her recollection excerpted here on the strict regimen of nineteenth-century nurses' training.*

# 610 Ellis and the Hospital Children

. . . The equipment for the laboratory and dispensary was installed, and Papa began to look around for a laboratory technician, and for a group of local physicians to be associated with the hospital. Last but most important of all was the organization of a training school for nurses. . . .

Papa had begun by building a staff of six doctors, a pharmacist, and a matron, and by making his hospital available for use by other doctors. He engaged [a doctor] . . . to take charge of the laboratory and dispensary, and to teach some of the classes in the Ashland Training School for Nurses, which was incorporated in the fall of 1895, shortly after Dodd's Hospital opened. The nursing school began with six students. This number soon increased to ten, and from then on, until 1905, the classes grew in size. Students came not only from Ashland, but from all over the Middle West and from Canada.

Publicity about the school was distributed far and wide, in newspapers, circulars, lumber-industry journals, even in a 1902 calendar which bore a picture of the dispensary. As one reads a list of the requirements for entrance into the two-year nursing program it is evident that times have changed. The trainees were expected to be between twenty and thirty years of age, "strong and healthy, obedient, kind, cheerful and not given to gossip, scrupulously neat in habits, and [possessing] a common school education." Each nurse received

$120 a month for her two years' training, in addition to her board, room, washing, and uniforms. Textbooks were furnished by the school. Nurses were instructed in the best practical methods of obtaining fresh air, warming and ventilating sick rooms and keeping them in proper order, keeping utensils clean and disinfected, managing helpless patients, making beds, moving, changing, giving baths in bed, preventing and dressing bed sores, and managing positions. They observed and reported to the attending physician the state of secretions, excretions, pulse, skin, appetite, temperature, respiration, sleep, and effect of medicine and diet, and learned the management of convalescents. They administered enemas and douches, catheters and thermometers, made bandages, prepared surgical dressings, dressed wounds, applied fomentations and cups, and made and applied poultices and plasters. They arose at 6 a.m. and were required to be in their rooms by 10 p.m. unless they had special permission to be elsewhere. Loud talking and laughing in rooms and halls were not permitted; gossip was frowned upon, and, as hospital regulations stated, "nurses are expected to maintain a dignified and ladylike manner at all times whether in the hospital or elsewhere.". . .

*By the turn of the century, other women would make their mark in medicine in Wisconsin. They included Dr. Maybelle Maud Park of Waukesha, the first woman county physician in Wisconsin in 1897. In 1899, Dr. Lillie Rosa Minoka-Hill, a Mohawk and only the second Native American woman physician in the nation, graduated from Dr. Laura Ross Wolcott's alma mater, the Woman's Medical College of Philadelphia, and followed her predecessor's path to Wisconsin. Married to an Oneida, she settled on his reservation where she served for decades and was known as You-da-tent, or "she who carries aid."[3]*

*For other women in Wisconsin, full four-year medical school training finally became available seventy years after the state's first woman physician earned her degree in the East. In 1925, the University of Wisconsin School of Medicine in Madison admitted its first class; its first graduates would include six women as well as nineteen men. By then, Dr. Bertha V. Thomson had served three terms as city physician and health commissioner and also had "carried a private practice for years," as she wrote with pride. After retirement, she remained active in working for the "public welfare of the city, state, and nation" to her death in 1939.[4]*

## NOTES

1. Current, *HOW*, 528–529; Dennis H. Phillips, "Women in Nineteenth-Century Wisconsin Medicine," *Wisconsin Medical Journal*, v. 71, 1972, 13–18.

2. See Brenda Quinn and Ellen D. Langill, *Caring for Milwaukee: The Daughters of Charity at St. Mary's Hospital* (Milwaukee: Milwaukee Publishing, 1998), 11.

3. "Dr. Park Named," *Waukesha Freeman*, n.d., in women's clubs' papers, Waukesha Organizations Papers, Waukesha County Historical Society; Cathy Luchetti, *Medicine Women: The Story of Early-American Women Doctors*, (New York: Crown, 1998), 129. See also *Dr. Lillie Rosa Minoka-Hill, Mohawk Woman*, forthcoming, by her granddaughter, Dr. Roberta Hill of the University of Wisconsin–Madison.

4. "Dr. Bertha Thomson Dies," *Oshkosh Daily Northwestern*, May 15, 1939.

# The University in 1874–1887

FLORENCE BASCOM

WMH 8, No. 3 (March 1925): 300–308

In 1869, for the first time, six women earned degrees among fifteen graduates at the University of Wisconsin — almost twice as many as in any commencement class in the twenty-year history of the campus. The women had completed regular degree requirements, attending lecture classes with the men. However, the women had chaperones and separate "recitation" classes. But both were preferable to the previous curriculum of the "inferior" Female College designed by President Paul Ansel Chadbourne to replace the Normal Department that had opened the doors the university to women, although only for teacher training, during the Civil War (see Introduction to chapter 3).[1]

Regents first had promised women "appropriate degrees," then the "same degrees as graduates of other colleges" — and the same honors. Class valedictorian Clara Bewick of Windsor and another woman in her class actually had completed their degree work a year earlier. However, as Bewick wrote to her grandparents, the University deemed that "it would be neither pleasant nor profitable to have such a class graduate." She had to wait a year, teaching grade school, for the four other women to "catch up" so that they could graduate as a group. But upon completion of their coursework, according to campus historians Merle Curti and Vernon Carstensen, Chadbourne asserted that "calling young women bachelors" was an "absurdity" and denied all of the women their degrees. Regents finally forced the recalcitrant president to relent, although the delay meant that the women had to graduate in a separate commencement ceremony, setting a campus tradition that set apart their sex as second-class students.[2]

But the women graduates of 1869 proved their worth. One became a lawyer in Madison, while others left the state for careers elsewhere; one as a high school principal in Indiana, another as a college administrator in Colorado. Bewick taught Latin and history at the university in the next year but also left the state in 1872 for Nebraska — and for a national stage. Clara Bewick Colby became among the best-known activists for women's rights in the nineteenth century, as publisher of a national newspaper called the Woman's Tribune and as an officer of national and international suffrage organizations, because of the sexism that she had witnessed at the University of Wisconsin. From her "profound disappointment" at the delays and "dissatisfying arrangement" she endured to earn her degree, writes a biographer, Colby "learned that women's lives can easily be upended to suit the economic needs of men."[3]

Chadbourne left the university even sooner, in 1870. That year, when a lone woman completed the regular curriculum, she was allowed to attend the regular ceremony but not to walk across the stage to receive her diploma, as did male graduates. To criticism of the cost of women-only classes and the Female College, regents replied that they gallantly gave in to separate recitations as the "preference of the ladies," who were "conceded the privilege of a distinct ladies' education." However, as ever, regents' resistance to women was second to their reluctance to hire more faculty. Finally, "both sexes recited together" in 1871 "for the reason that there were not enough professors and instructors to conduct separate classes," writes Reuben Gold Thwaites.[4]

*But men belatedly won the battle to separate the sexes again when regents determined, as they wrote, "to provide for ladies the same facilities for college education enjoyed by gentlemen" — or at least similar facilities, with the exception of an "inside privy" in the Ladies' Hall that opened in 1871 to official fanfare. The governor announced that "now, regardless of sex, may the best scholar win," according to historians Curti and Carstensen, while regents promoted Wisconsin as "far in advance of her sister States in the noble provision which she is making for the higher education of her daughters," writes Thwaites. However, Wisconsin was neither so noble nor so advanced as to allow its daughters to graduate with its sons; nine women earned degrees in separate ceremonies in the next two years. Indeed, according to Curti and Carstensen, "the University of Wisconsin was in no sense pioneering when regents cautiously opened the back door to women," since several states elsewhere already had offered higher education with full equality for women.[5]*

*The university continued to offer the lesser curriculum of the Female College, which Lila Peckham of Milwaukee researched for a report from the state woman suffrage association to national leaders Elizabeth Cady Stanton and Susan B. Anthony. Peckham concluded that the reputations of regents and male alumni suffered as much as did women in the Female College:*

> *We find a long account of the A.B., A.M., P.B., S.B., S.M., L.B., Ph.D., to which the fortunate gentlemen are entitled after so much study. Lastly, the students of the female college may receive "such appropriate degrees as the regents may determine." I wonder how the solemn body deliberates as to whether a girl shall be A.B., P.B., or A.N., or whether they ever give them any degree at all. It makes little difference. With such a college course, a degree means nothing, and only serves to cheapen what may be well earned by the young men of the college.[6]*

*A later state suffrage leader would report to Stanton and Anthony that "owing to prejudices, it was not until 1873" — a year when no women graduated — "that complete coeducation was established" by regents. But many faculty continued to enroll men first or refused to seat women students, which effectively denied them required courses. The "gradual abolition of the dual system" took decades in some departments, delaying "complete coeducation" until the next century.[7]*

*But in 1874, Ladies' Hall became solely a residence for women students — which regents, without irony, later renamed Chadbourne Hall — and fourteen women graduated in the last separate ceremonies of the Female College era. However, all earned degrees from the university, not the Female College, and "every honor" in the commencement class "had been captured by one woman, Jennie Field," according to Curti and Carstensen. Field had taught in Boscobel before she began in the Female College but then interrupted her studies at her hometown's request to return to head its primary schools. She returned to the university "at the beginning of the coeducational regime" and graduated as valedictorian. Jane Field Bashford married a classmate, taught in Madison, and later earned a master's degree at Boston University, as did her husband, who became president of Ohio Wesleyan University — after she became the first president of the Association of Collegiate Alumnae, later called the American Association of University Women.[8]*

*New residents in the President's House on the Madison campus in 1874 proved significant for women's progress: Dr. John Bascom and Emma Curtiss Bascom, both proponents of women's rights and other reforms. She would serve as president of both the Wisconsin Woman Suffrage Association and the Wisconsin Woman's Christian Temperance Union at the same time, a decade later, near*

*the end of her husband's presidency — which ended in part owing to the Bascoms' advocacy of prohi-
bition when the original Milwaukee brewers served on the board of regents. But the Bascoms had better hopes for Wisconsin a decade before, in 1874, when their youngest daughter Florence was twelve
years old.*[9]

*A year before she became a student at her father's campus, Florence Bascom watched as her fa-
ther rebuffed a final, "reactionary movement" by a "die-hard faction" for "reviving the Female College," as Thwaites writes. A group of alumni and a regent worried less about women students'
productivity than about their reproductivity and feared the effect of higher education on "future mothers of the state who should be robust, hearty, healthy women," as the men wrote in their report that was
ridiculed in newspapers nationwide. Most regents were more fearful of the costs of separate classes;
they deferred to faculty, who stated that women students "stood the strain well."*[10]

*President Bascom stated the case more strongly, based on women's better attendance record. As his
daughter attests in her account here, "the illness excuses of the entire student body passed over the president's desk" — a student body of more than three hundred, including a third in the Preparatory Department, or high school. At all levels, women students had better health — or fewer excuses. "Young
men are not accustomed to confinement," he said, and they did not "endure the violent transition"
to academe as well as women, who "improve in strength rather than deteriorate during their college
course."*[11]

*However, women "improved" despite continued disparate access to campus athletic facilities, as
his daughter recalls in her brief account. Her recollection of "critics" of women students may refer to
a campus newspaper's resentful commentary in her freshman year, when an "Amazonian" brigade
gained access — if for only a few hours weekly — to the male bastion of the gymnasium. As for women
students' academic strength, they endured more editorial sarcasm in 1876 when women outranked
men in class standings, causing the campus press to opine that professors erred in equating women's
"gift of gab" and "quickness of perception" with "genuine intellectual power." However, in the same
year, her father announced with pride that women comprised one-fourth of the student body — at the
college level — at the University of Wisconsin.*[12]

*His daughter, in her account, also emphasizes the generally positive "attitude of the student body"
— meaning the men students — and teachers toward coeducation during her years at the University of Wisconsin.*

. . . The students in [the 1870s] were benefiting by the simple life of a small institution:
we knew and admired all of our ten professors. . . . On the faculty which we knew in 1874
were men of character and scholarship: Professor [of history and ancient languages]
William F. Allen and Professor [of geology] Roland D. Irving. . . .

. . . By training and temperament [Irving was] disinclined to coeducation, [but] in his
classroom coeducation was carried out with almost startling consistency, typified by the
seating of his students alphabetically without distinction of sex. It might be noted that in
those days the somewhat opprobrious epithet "co-eds" had not yet been fastened upon the
women. . . . It certainly is not indigenous to Wisconsin and does not fairly indicate the attitude of the student body toward the young women in my day. . . .

The discontinuance of the [high school-level] preparatory department soon depleted our numbers advantageously, and the increasing subdivision of subjects meant stronger contacts with a larger number of directing minds. . . . [T]he majority of us were in earnest about securing the training which the University offered. . . . Nor were we distracted from our main purpose by a multiplicity of social pleasures. . . .

The women lacked gymnasium drill or any form of organized athletics, except that sometime in 1878 or 1879 . . . the inadequate University gymnasium (by custom ceded to the men exclusively) was opened to the women a few hours [twice] every week. This was far from sufficient exercise, and the women suffered from lack of regular exercise unless they indulged individually in swimming, boating, or riding. There was little enough of this, but the feat of swimming from Picnic Point to our boat-house (a good seven-eighths of a mile) was accomplished by a woman in my class. It is an interesting manifestation of the attitude of certain public critics toward change, that when the collegiate training of women was first on trial there were clamorous complaints that the health of young women was being wrecked; now the same class of public critics are loudly complaining that college women are "Amazons."

Baseball was a great game among the men, and the women took a keen interest in watching the match games. . . .

Secret societies among the women were not a dominant factor in University life. Until about 1881, I believe . . . [the first sorority] Kappa Kappa Gamma had no rivals and might be accused of displaying an arrogant spirit, but it by no means exerted the influence on the campus which was wielded by the literary societies — Castalia and Laurea. These societies drew their membership at that time from two rather different groups of women, and the rivalry between the two organizations was thoroughgoing and even regulated our social intercourse. The plays, the debates, and the character parties of one's literary society were the occasion of the most intense emotions of one's University life. . . .

*Florence Bascom earned several bachelor's degrees and began graduate work at the University of Wisconsin until her father's bitter resignation in 1887. She then continued her work at Johns Hopkins University — sitting behind a screen, since faculty apparently found male classmates easily distracted — and earned a Ph.D. in 1893. She chaired the natural science department at Rockford College in Illinois and taught at the historically black Hampton Institute, at Ohio State University, and at Bryn Mawr College, while also publishing in scientific journals and serving as associate editor of the* American Geologist, *the leading scholarly journal in her field. Florence Bascom became widely known as the first woman geologist in the country.[13]*

*As for progress in physical education for women at the University of Wisconsin, see "The Wisconsin Idea of Dance: A Decade of Progress, 1917–1926" in chapter 6.*

## NOTES

1. Kristin Mapel Bloomberg, "True Woman or New Woman? Clara Bewick Colby and the Making of a Modern Suffragist," unpublished paper in the possession of the editor, 11–12.

2. Merle Curti and Vernon Carstensen, *The University of Wisconsin: A History, 1848–1925* (Madison: University of Wisconsin, 1949), 371–372.

3. Reuben Gold Thwaites, ed., *The University of Wisconsin: Its History and Its Alumni* (Madison: Purcell, 1900), 771, 778. The nine male graduates in 1869 equaled the largest group of men ever previously graduated.

4. Thwaites, *The University of Wisconsin*, 87.

5. Current, *HOW,* 506; Thwaites, *The University of Wisconsin,* 87–88; Curti and Carstensen, *The University of Wisconsin,* 194, 489.

6. Wolcott, "Wisconsin," in Stanton, Anthony, and Gage, eds., *History of Woman Suffrage,* vol. 3, 642–643.

7. Thwaites, *The University of Wisconsin,* 87–88; Curti and Carstensen, *The University of Wisconsin,* 373–379; Olympia Brown, "Wisconsin," in Susan B. Anthony and Ida Husted Harper, eds., *The History of Woman Suffrage,* vol. 4 (Rochester, NY: Susan B. Anthony, 1902), 993; John D. Buenker, *HOW,* vol. 4, *The Progressive Era, 1893–1914* (Madison: SHSW, 1998), 343.

8. Wolcott, "Wisconsin," 647; Curti and Carstensen, *The University of Wisconsin,* 271, 374; Marion Talbot, "History Aims, and Methods of the Association of Collegiate Alumnae," in *The World's Congress of Representative Women,* vol. 2 (Chicago: Rand McNally, 1894), 787.

9. McBride, *On Wisconsin Women,* 112–113.

10. Thwaites, *The University of Wisconsin,* 88–89; Curti and Carstensen, *The University of Wisconsin,* 376–381.

11. Thwaites, *The University of Wisconsin,* 88, 114.

12. Curti and Carstensen, *The University of Wisconsin,* 375–376.

13. Thwaites, *University of Wisconsin,* 360; M. L. Aldrich, "Women in Geology," in G. Kass-Simon and P. Farnes, eds., *Women of Science: Righting the Record* (Bloomington, IN: Indiana University Press, 1990), 42–71.

# Lavinia Goodell,
# First Woman Lawyer in Wisconsin

CATHERINE B. CLEARY

WMH 74, No. 4 (Summer 1991): 243–271

Lavinia Goodell of Janesville, Wisconsin, was one of the small number of women in the Middle West who opened the legal profession in the United States to women shortly after the Civil War. Most of these women — in Iowa, Missouri, Michigan, Ohio, and Indiana [and several territories] — were admitted by the courts in their states without question. Only in Wisconsin and Illinois did the state supreme court refuse to admit a woman. The opinion Chief Justice Edward G. Ryan wrote for the Wisconsin Supreme Court in 1876, denying Goodell's first petition for admission to its bar, is powerful evidence of the obstacles women faced — not the law, because that could be changed — but the widespread belief in "separate spheres" for men and women and a sense of outrage on the part of men like Ryan that any woman would dare to seek entrance into this masculine domain. Such efforts were, he said, "a departure from the order of nature" and "treason against it." But Lavinia Goodell, already admitted to the bar in Rock County, persuaded the Wisconsin legislature to remove the barrier to women the supreme court had erected; and, three and a half years after her first petition, she was admitted to the bar of the Wisconsin Supreme Court on the basis of the new law. The determination, dignity, and ability with which she pursued her goal and the support she received from unexpected sources are a bright chapter in Wisconsin history.[1]

Rhoda Lavinia Goodell was born in Utica, New York, on May 2, 1839, the third daughter of William and Clarissa Goodell. . . . [Their] daughter Maria, twelve years older than Lavinia, helped bring her up and was close to her as long as they both lived. It was Maria, after she had married and moved away, in whom Lavinia confided through long letters. . . .[2]

William Goodell was undoubtedly the greatest single influence in his youngest daughter's life. An abolitionist, editor, and reformer [as well as a minister], he shaped her interests and character, and the two of them enjoyed a close working relationship. Clarissa Cady Goodell was "much more conservative than her husband," but at the time of Lavinia's birth she was a member of the [Female] Moral Reform Society, which, in addition to its concern with moral purity, stressed work as "a safeguard to woman" so that they would not feel "their utter dependence on man."[3]

William Goodell had come to Utica from New York City in 1836 . . . to edit a weekly antislavery paper to be called *The Friend of Man*. . . .[4]

Concerns about slavery affected every aspect of the family's life. Fugitive slaves were welcome guests. The girls had pictures of kneeling slaves on work bags, pin cushions, and needlebooks with words such as, "Am I not a woman and a sister?" . . .[5]

In 1852 the family returned to New York City where William Goodell became the editor of an antislavery paper, *The Principia*. . . . Lavinia attended the Brooklyn Heights Seminary. She graduated at nineteen with a reputation as an orator and a scholar.[6]

In the spring of her senior year, she wrote her sister about what she would do after graduation. Stressing the need for women to depend on themselves, she went on:[7]

> I think the study of law would be pleasant, but the practice attended with many embarrassments. Indeed I fear it would be utterly impracticable. Our folks would not hear of my going to college; I should not dare mention it — Mamma is very much afraid I shall become identified with the "women's rights movement."

This was in 1858, eleven years before the first woman was admitted to the bar in this country and the first women were admitted to law school.[8] Her sister apparently raised objections: "false and vain ambition," "trying to be a man," "out of the common course," and so on. Lavinia denied these charges, saying that she was motivated by a sense of duty and a desire to do good and that the choice would involve sacrificing personal happiness. She concluded, "What is more womanly than the desire to defend and protect the widow and the fatherless and in a field where they have been wronged hitherto?" Mrs. Goodell never accepted the idea that Lavinia should study law, but in time Maria did because it met Lavinia's need for a "high aim."[9]

Lavinia worked in her father's office at a desk side by side with his and learned the job of editing. On at least one occasion she got out the paper when he was out of town. When publication of *The Principia* was suspended in 1864 . . . she stayed in Brooklyn. She lived with a family and taught school for several years, and then in about 1867 she went to work for *Harper's*. . . . One of her co-workers remembered her as "a shrewd, quick-witted girl, fond of humor, studious and argumentative."[10]

In January of 1870, thanks to a "competence" that Mrs. Goodell inherited from her brother, the parents were able to move to Janesville, Wisconsin, to be near their older daughter, who lived there with her husband, Lewis P. Frost. The following year Lavinia followed them, and the family's new resources made it possible for her at last to study law. Her father approved, believing she was "cut out for a lawyer.". . .[11]

Lavinia Goodell was thirty-two years old when she came to Janesville in 1871. Her years at *Harper's* had given her a sophistication intellectually and socially that would stand her in good stead. . . .

In January, 1872, Lavinia wrote her sister (who had moved away from Janesville): "I have commenced my new study & am much pleased with it." In April of the following year, she wrote, "I read no books now but law books." At that time most students, rather than attending law school, "read law," usually in a lawyer's office. . . . Some students simply prepared for the bar by reading legal treatises on their own. This was the only option for Lavinia in the beginning. "I wanted to go into a law office, like any other student, and get office practice, but human nature in these regions is not educated up to that."[12]

One firm allowed her to use its library and gave her occasional "instruction and advice in [her] study." It also employed her as a copyist. In frustration she wrote:

There were no other law students here when I commenced: just think of it! A dozen or twenty law offices suffering for the want of students to help and keep office while the lawyers were off to court, and yet they would not let me in, because I was a woman. They would sooner hire shiftless, incompetent boys . . . than take my services gratis, when they know how steady I am and anxious to learn. . . .

. . . [S]he did not blame them "as it requires so much more strength than the average man possesses to do a new thing." After a succession of young men wearied of their studies and left the firm, she commented, "I think [the partners] have had some pangs of remorse. . . ." By 1873, A. A. Jackson and Pliny Norcross were partners in the firm, and her situation improved. She wrote her sister, "Spend a good deal of time in the office now, as the men are out of town much of the time."[13]

One of the pressures on the first women in a profession dominated by men arises from their visibility because they are "different.". . . Lavinia was conscious of being in the public eye when she supplemented her reading by going to court as an observer.[14]

It is quite an innovation for me to go into court in this small, conservative, gossipy town, and requires some moral courage. . . . The community looks at me a little doubtfully as not knowing what kind of a woman I may be, but as [I] develop no other alarming eccentricity than a taste for legal studies, wear fashionable clothes, attend an orthodox church, have a class in the Sunday school, attend the benevolent society, and make cake and preserves like other women, I am tolerated. . . .

Then, as now, society expected women working outside the home to continue to carry their traditional responsibilities. . . . [But] "when a young man is studying a profession he is supposed to be doing something, if he isn't doing anything else.". . .[15]

In February, 1874, Goodell set June as the time for her admission to the bar. She gathered her courage and told Norcross what she wanted to do and asked his help. . . .

Admission to the Wisconsin bar, then as now, was based on a state statute which referred to a "person" being admitted or licensed to practice law. [But] the masculine pronoun was used throughout the statute. . . . Admission to one circuit court bar entitled the person to practice in any court in the state except the supreme court which, under the statute, made its own orders licensing attorneys to practice before it. . . .[16]

. . . Norcross made the motion in the circuit court for Lavinia Goodell's admission on June 11. Word had come that the judge was going to deny her petition on account of her sex. While waiting for the court to act on the motion, she wrote around to get precedents on the admission of women to the bar in other states. . . .[17]

. . . The judge began by noting that Goodell was a female, said he had had some doubt as to whether she could legally be admitted but, having done some studying, was convinced she might. . . . Without ruling formally on the point, the court turned the proceedings over to the examining committee of three "old and able" lawyers who questioned the candidates for over an hour. . . . The committee returned with a favorable report, and both she and [the other candidate] were sworn in and signed the roll of attorneys. . . .[18]

Like other pioneers, she felt a responsibility to women who would come after her. She wrote her sister that she hoped to do well, "for the sake of *other women* as well as for my own." . . .[19]

. . . Norcross had held out the hope of her having an office with the firm, but when the time came, his partner did not agree. Goodell, therefore, rented an office and started to practice. . . . [S]he got her first court case from some Fort Atkinson temperance women. They planned to prosecute two liquor dealers for selling liquor on Sunday, but they did not trust the district attorney whom they regarded as a "liquor man." They had failed to find a lawyer with enough courage to take their case but thought "the lady lawyer might have!" Goodell participated in the prosecution of the cases in justice court and won both. . . .[20]

While Goodell handled her cases in a highly professional manner, she was aware of the challenge having a woman as an adversary presented to her male colleagues. As she confided to Maria, "So far in my experience the masculine lawyers have acted a good deal more afraid of me than I have of them.". . .[21]

While Goodell's career as a lawyer was evolving, she was also deeply involved in temperance activities and woman suffrage. She attended the meeting in Milwaukee in October, 1874, at which the State Temperance Alliance was organized and delivered a paper. . . . The following June she attended the eighth national temperance convention in Chicago. . . .[22]

Many of Goodell's clients were women. In November, 1874, she was retained by Mrs. Lydia Burrington, a widow who was administratrix of her husband's estate. . . . [In] a claim against the estate, Mrs. Burrington consulted Goodell. . . . The claim was allowed in the probate court, and Goodell appealed to the circuit court, where she lost again. In July, 1875, she appealed the case to the Wisconsin Supreme Court. Initially the question of her being able to argue the case before the supreme court apparently did not occur to her. Under the custom of the court, a male lawyer would have been admitted automatically on the basis of his admission to the circuit court bar. . . . [23]

The hearing was held on December 14, 1875. The three-man supreme court was dominated by the chief justice, Edward G. Ryan. . . . He brought to the bench a brilliant intellect and extensive knowledge of law but also a violent temper and a record of stormy professional relationships. As a delegate to the 1846 Wisconsin Constitutional Convention, he had opposed a provision giving married women property rights as violating "both the usages and customs of society and the express commands of the Bible.". . . [see "Married Women's Property Rights in Wisconsin, 1846–1872" in chapter 3].[24]

. . . When the court convened, Goodell wrote, Ryan "bristled all up when he saw me, like a hen when she sees a hawk, and did not recover his wonted serenity during my stay. It was fun to see him! I presume I was the coolest person present." . . .[25]

Goodell's argument in favor of her admission was in three parts. First, there was nothing in the statute on admission to the bar which can be construed to exclude a woman. . . .

. . . [S]he pointed out that Wisconsin law (which provided for the admission to the

Wisconsin bar of attorneys already licensed in other states) could result in woman attorneys from other states being admitted in Wisconsin. Further, under the Wisconsin constitution . . . a woman would have the right to conduct a suit in court for herself or as agent.[26]

Goodell's second point was based on the statement of the Illinois Supreme Court . . . "that the court shall establish such terms of admission as will promote the proper administration of justice." She argued that the proper administration of justice "would be better promoted by the admission of women to the practice of law than by their exclusion," . . . [O]ne-half the human race could never obtain justice in courts where its members were not represented. . . . [27]

. . . As her third point, Goodell noted only two precedents against her. . . . On the other hand, she cited the individual women admitted to the bar in Iowa, Missouri, Michigan, Maine, the District of Columbia, and federal district courts in Illinois and Iowa. . . .[28]

After the hearing, Goodell by invitation called on Mrs. Emma Bascom, wife of the liberal president of the University of Wisconsin. It was Mrs. Bascom who suggested to her that she get the *State Journal* to publish her argument. . . .[29]

[Two days later on] December 16 the *Wisconsin State Journal* carried a story under the heading, "Lady Lawyers in Supreme Court," setting out the facts of the case and describing Goodell's demonstrated ability as a lawyer in strong terms. . . . [T]he article concluded, "the expression of attorneys so far as we have heard it is, 'Give Sister GOODELL a chance.'". . .

The justices who heard Goodell's case were members of a profession which had always been an exclusively male preserve. . . . [L]awyers continued to prize the conviviality that marked life on the circuit and to cherish the distinctively masculine culture of their profession.[30]

In February, 1876, the Wisconsin Supreme Court denied Goodell's petition for admission to its bar. The opinion was written by Chief Justice Ryan. . . .[31]

. . . [H]e went on at length about why women are not suited to the practice of law. The essence of his position is in the last two pages of the opinion:

> The law of nature destines and qualifies the female sex for the bearing and nurture of the children of our race and for the custody of the homes of the world and their maintenance in love and honor. And all life-long callings of women, inconsistent with these radical and sacred duties of their sex, as is the profession of law, are departures from the order of nature; and when voluntary, treason against it. . . .

After describing "the peculiar qualities of womanhood, its gentle graces, its quick sensibility, its tender susceptibility, its purity, its delicacy, its emotional impulses, its subordination of hard reason to sympathetic feeling," Ryan referred at length to all of the "unclean issues" and matters "unfit for female ears" which come before the courts and concluded that exposing women habitually to this kind of litigation "would tend to relax the public sense of decency and propriety. If, as counsel threatened, these things are to come, we will take no voluntary part in bringing them about."[32]

The reaction to the court's decision and especially to Ryan's opinion was immediate and widespread. The *State Journal* concluded, . . . "[i]f her purity is in danger, it would be better to reconstruct the court and bar, than to exclude the women."[33] After a somewhat jocular summary . . . the *Chicago Tribune* concluded,[34]

> And Chief Justice RYAN is glad of it, for he doesn't think the Bar of the State Courts the proper place for the exercise of a woman's peculiar qualities, or for the preservation of her purity. If the latter phrase of the decision is satisfactory to the Wisconsin lawyers, it ought surely to afford some consolation to the unsuccessful applicant from Janesville.

The *Janesville Gazette* called the decision "clearly unjust.". . .[35]

The *Central Law Journal,* while agreeing with the decision, said ". . . viewing the question [as] one of justice to women, we should say, give them a chance to earn a livelihood even at the practice of law, if any of them shall be disposed to enter upon a calling so unsuited to them.". . .[36]

On March 25, 1876, *The Woman's Journal* ran a long article on the decision by Lucy Stone, one of its editors and a pioneer in the woman's rights movement, which pointed out that women were often involved as parties or witnesses in the sordid kinds of cases to which the chief justice referred. . . . Myra Bradwell, the editor of the *Chicago Legal News* whose application for admission to the Illinois bar had been denied in 1869, printed Ryan's opinion in full with an introductory paragraph: ". . . We call the especial attention of our readers to this opinion, hoping they will read it with care, believing that it will not only aid in obtaining legislation which will allow women as well as men to practice law, but hasten the day when the right of suffrage shall be extended to women in Wisconsin."[37]

When Goodell heard about the court's decision, but before she had seen the opinion, she too focused on legislation being the next step. The case which had been argued in December was not decided until February, and she believed that the court deliberately held it up until the day after the last day for introducing bills in the legislature, thus delaying remedial legislation until the next session. But she was not beaten. "If I don't come out and give old Ryan a skinning over this, it will be because I can't, and I think I can!"[38]

In a more serious vein, Goodell wrote a long review of Ryan's opinion which appeared in Myra Bradwell's *Chicago Legal News* on March 25 and April 1. . . .

She concluded with a forceful argument addressed to Ryan's belief in separate sex roles ordained by nature: "If nature has built up barriers to keep woman out of the legal profession, be assured she will stay out; but if nature has built no such barriers, in vain shall man build them, for they will certainly be overthrown."

While Goodell was waiting for the Wisconsin Supreme Court to hear her petition for admission to its bar in November, 1875, an event occurred which had a significant and lasting effect on her life. Judge Conger appointed her to represent two indigents charged with crimes. . . . She went to jail several times to see [one] young man. Within a few weeks she wrote her sister about her thoughts on the management of criminals: "As it is, the jails are schools of vice and crime.". . . For the rest of her life Goodell took an active interest in individual prisoners and in jail reform and penal legislation. She conducted prayer meetings, Sunday school, and classes in jails, took books and newspapers to the prisoners to read, corresponded with them when they were released from jail, and tried to help them get back into society. . . .[39]

Goodell's interest in temperance related directly to her jail work. She believed that drink, along with lack of family ties, was at the heart of many prisoners' troubles. When she went to see the governor about a pardon for one prisoner, she told him she regarded the community as responsible for most crime by licensing saloons. He responded [that] it was a "difficult question," but she rejoined that "it was men's self-interest that made it seem difficult to them.". . .[40]

Maria saw her sister's emotional investment in her "boys" as an outlet for her maternal instincts, and indeed some of them did call her Mother. When Lavinia died, Maria found among her effects "hundreds of letters from prisoners, many of them touching and tender.". . .[41]

Also while she was waiting for the supreme court decision, Goodell tried a bitterly contested divorce case. . . . Goodell represented the plaintiff, who sought the divorce on grounds of cruel and inhuman treatment, and she had spent months gathering evidence. Mrs. Leavenworth, Goodell's client, testified to physical mistreatment by her husband over a period of twenty-five years and to his securing by fraud her signature on papers deeding the homestead out of his name to free it from any claim she might have to alimony. The defendant denied all of these charges, and the court refused to grant the divorce on the basis that there was "not sufficient cause for granting the decree." Goodell's diary for January 29 reads: "Finished Leavenworth case & lost it. Too mad to say any more.". . .[42]

For Goodell 1876 was a bad year, and her diary contained frequent references to "feeling blue." In January she lost the *Leavenworth* case. In February the supreme court handed down its decision denying her petition for admission to its bar. That spring she discovered she had an ovarian tumor. She did not tell anyone about it, but on a trip east that summer she consulted doctors. . . . [S]he spent a week in Philadelphia at the Centennial Exposition and also attended the Woman's International Temperance Convention. . . .[43] She went to New York, where she called on Charlotte Ray, the first black woman lawyer in the country. . . . .[44]

When Goodell returned home in August, she resumed the practice of law. The divorce case she had handled for Mrs. Leavenworth and trouble Maria was having in her marriage had made Goodell sensitive to the inadequacy of the rights of married women under the law. Her own problem in gaining admission to the Wisconsin Supreme Court bar and the legal barrier to woman suffrage as well as possible legal solutions to problems associated with liquor and jail reform all motivated her to try to get laws changed.[45]

When the legislature convened in January, 1877, she had sent eight bills. . . . One was her bill prohibiting denial of admission to the bar on account of sex. She supported this with a petition she had circulated, carrying the signatures of Judge Conger and every single lawyer in Rock County. . . . A few days later she went to Madison. . . . Again she visited with Mrs. Bascom. . . . [H]er staunch support for Lavinia Goodell could hardly have been overlooked by Madison's social and political elite. By the time Goodell went home, she was assured that her supreme court bill would be reported favorably. . . .[46]

. . . Goodell's supreme court bill passed the assembly on a voice vote, an indication of no substantial opposition. It was acquiesced in by the senate, signed by Governor Harrison Ludington, and became law on March 22, 1877.[47]

In May, after visiting doctors in Chicago and consulting a trusted doctor in New York by correspondence, Goodell decided to postpone surgery. Instead, three Janesville doctors drained the tumor. . . . Two weeks later, she was back at work. . . .[48]

Goodell's personal life changed dramatically in 1878. William Goodell died in February at age eighty-five. Lavinia closed the house in March. . . . She had noted a recurrence of her tumor as early as the previous August, and in April she went east and underwent surgery in New York. Her mother died while Lavinia was in the hospital, too weak to be told the news for some time. . . . After her operation, she weighed only eighty-eight pounds, and recovery was a long, slow process.

While she was in the East, she went to Providence in October to attend the Woman's Congress where she made two short speeches. She also participated in a woman's suffrage meeting where she delivered a long speech which was reported in the *Providence Journal*. . . .[49] Later in the fall of 1878 she returned to Janesville, rented a suite of rooms to live in, and took a desk in a law office. Soon she was as busy as her health permitted.

Over the years in Janesville, Goodell had had many contacts with Angie King. She was in the courtroom [in] 1879, when King (who had been studying law at home for many years) was admitted to the bar. Shortly thereafter the two women formed a partnership for the practice of law. Elizabeth Cady Stanton sent them large lithographs of herself and Susan B. Anthony to hang in their office. . . .[50]

In the meantime Goodell had made her second application for admission to the bar of the supreme court [of Wisconsin]. The hearing was set for April 22, 1879. By that time, Belva Lockwood . . . [had become the first woman admitted] to the bar of the Supreme Court of the United States. . . .[51]

. . . Emma Bascom and a friend were in the courtroom, a gesture of support for Goodell that reminded the court of the public interest in its decision. . . .[52]

The *Milwaukee Sentinel* commented: . . . "[I]f, on constitutional or other grounds, she is denied admission, it will be a disgrace to the State.". . .[53] On June 18 the Wisconsin Supreme Court handed down its decision. Lavinia Goodell's petition was granted. Chief Justice Ryan dissented. . . .[54]

The bar of Wisconsin was at last fully open to women. The campaign Lavinia Goodell had launched three-and-a-half years before had finally been won. . . . The great day was, however, anticlimactic for her. She wrote in her diary: "Went to Sup. Ct. Got admitted. . . . Tired from not sleeping the night before.". . .[55]

Goodell's seemingly disinterested response to her great victory may have been a product of both her deteriorating health and the loss of her parents, especially of her father, who had shared her triumphs and defeats and always been there as a source of moral support. . . .

Goodell continued to practice actively, but family ties no longer kept her in Janesville. In the fall she attended temperance conventions in Madison and Racine as well as the Woman's Congress in Madison, at which she read a paper on penal legislation. . . . She moved to Madison in the middle of November and made an office arrangement. . . . Her health was failing rapidly, but, although her friends urged her to limit herself to literary work, she said, "I shall practice law as long as I can hold together.". . .[56]

A brief entry in her diary ten days after her arrival in Madison cried out: "A day of dark, black despair. O God be merciful & let me die rather than have any more such bitter experiences!" In January she went to Milwaukee. . . .[57] On March 11 she was cheered by the news she had won [a] case, and she wrote in her diary: ". . . I have beaten the Attorney General of the State. . . . I had no assistance, so it was a *pure woman's victory!*"[58]

She was told on March 29 that there was no hope, and early on the morning of March 31, 1880, she died, a month before her forty-first birthday. . . .[59]

. . . Newspapers in Janesville, Milwaukee, Madison, and Chicago carried obituaries noting her accomplishments. The *Chicago Times*. . . emphasized her lifelong role as a reformer, speaking of her stand against slavery and her concern for the welfare of women.

Lavinia Goodell's death did not end the struggle she had begun to open the bar to women. . . . [S]ocial and cultural obstacles to men and women working together in the legal profession would not disappear in the next century. . . .[60]

. . . The legal career of Lavinia Goodell lasted less than ten years, but her life made a difference, and she still stands as a model for women lawyers today.

## NOTES

1. *In the Matter of the Motion to admit Miss Lavinia Goodell to the Bar of this Court,* 39 Wis. 232, 245 (1875); *Application of Miss Goodell,* 48 Wis. 693 (1879); James Willard Hurst, *The Growth of American Law: The Law Makers* (Boston, 1950), 255. . . .

2. . . . Maria Goodell Frost, "Life of Lavinia Goodell," . . . William Goodell Family Papers, Hutchins Library, Berea College, Berea, Kentucky. . . .

3. Ibid., 3–4. . . .

4. *In Memoriam: William Goodell* (Chicago, 1879), 26, WHS Archives. . . .

5. Frost, "Life," 7, 28.

6. Ibid., 38. . . .

7. Ibid., 40–41.

8. . . . Ellen A. Martin, "Admission of Women to the Bar," in *The Chicago Law Times,* 1:76 (1886); Lelia J. Robinson, "Women Lawyers in the United States," in *The Green Bag: A Useless but Entertaining Magazine for Lawyers,* 2:10, 13 (1890).

9. Frost, "Life," 42–43, 96.

10. *Lippincott's Magazine of Popular Literature and Science,* 23:387 (March, 1879). . . . Mary L. Booth, the editor of *Harper's Bazaar,* recruited Goodell for her staff. Rev. T. P. Sawin, "In Memoriam," *The Round Table* (1880), 25, 26

11. Frost, "Life," 96; *In Memoriam: William Goodell,* 33.

12. Letter to sister, January 22, 1872; Frost, "Life," 100–103; Hurst, *The Growth of American Law,* 256.

13. Frost, "Life," 103–104; . . . Letter to sister, February 24, 1873.

14. Frost, "Life," 102. . . .

15. Letter to Maria, November 18, 1873. Goodell at this time was also doing "considerable reporting for the *Janesville Gazette.*" Frost, "Life," 101.

16. Chapter 189, *Laws of Wisconsin* 1861.

17. She also wrote to Milwaukee to inquire about Lilly Peckham, whom she believed had studied law. *Milwaukee Sentinel,* October 11, 1871. One article said that Elizabeth (Lila) Peckham was a law student in Milwaukee but died before admission. Martin, "Admission of Women to the Bar," 76; Frost, "Life," 114.

18. Frost, "Life," 115–117; Diary for June, 1874; letter to sister, June 18, 1874. . . .

19. Undated letter, "Dear Sis," Goodell Papers, Box 15, File 8.

20. Frost, "Life," 118, 126.

21. Letter of October 8, 1874.

22. *Milwaukee Sentinel,* October 22, 1874; *Chicago Times,* June 4, 1875.

23. [Diary, November 20, 1874.]

24. Alfons J. Beitzinger, *Edward G. Ryan, Lion of the Law* (Madison, 1960); "Negro Suffrage and Woman's Rights in the Convention of 1846," *WMH* 3 (December, 1919):228–229; . . . John B. Winslow, *The Story of a Great Court* (Chicago, 1912), 328–330.

25. Letter of December 20, 1875.

26. . . . *Wisconsin Constitution,* Art. VII, sec. 20.

27. . . . [See] Eileen Boris, "Looking at Women's Historians Looking at 'Difference,'" in *Wisconsin Women's Law Journal,* 3:231 (1987). . . .

28. . . . The original handwritten brief is in the WHS Archives. Public Records Series 1633, Box No. 20. . . .

29. Letter dated December 20, 1875. . . . Emma [Curtiss] Bascom, who was active in the cause of women's rights, had no illusions about the difficulties Goodell faced. . . . [She wrote Goodell that] "this is such a conventional community that I fear you will find your path a very rough and rugged one, and I wish most sincerely I could help you." Letter dated February, 1880, Goodell Papers, Box 16, File 3.

30. William R. Johnson, "Education and Professional Life Styles: Law and Medicine in the Nineteenth Century," *History of Education Quarterly* 14 (Summer, 1974):185, 188–189 ; Hurst, *Growth of American Law,* 255, 286. . . .

31. . . . The *New York Tribune* in a long editorial which agreed with Ryan's opinion on the issues said: "We think, however, that having thus correctly laid down the law, Judge Ryan should have stopped." . . . (Reprinted in the *Milwaukee Sentinel,* March 24, 1876.)

32. . . . Ryan's opinion and the opinion of the Illinois Supreme Court and the concurring opinion of Justice Bradley of the United States Supreme Court . . . are the classic statements in American legal history on the subject of woman's sphere as it relates to women practicing law. . . .

33. February 22, 1876.

34. February 16, 1876.

35. February 18, 1876.

36. 3:186–187 (March 24, 1876).

37. March 11, 1876. . . .

38. Frost, "Life," 137–138. . . .

39. Ibid., 133–134 (140–141), 136–137 (143–144), 170 (179). . . .

40. Ibid., 171 (180).

41. Ibid., 189 (198). . . .

42. . . . The court file is in Drawer 209 at the Rock County Historical Society. . . .

43. Frost, "Life," 149 (158); Diary, June 8-16, 1876. Her certificate of admission to the Rock County bar and "Supreme Court Briefs" were on exhibit at the Exposition. . . .

44. Diary, June 26, July 22, July 24, 1876. . . .

45. . . . [Goodell's] "A Day in the Life of a Woman Lawyer," . . . gives an indication of her activities at this time. See *[Woman's Journal]* 8 (November 10, 1877):354.

46. *Diary, February 6–8, 1877 . . .* Frost, "Life," 157 (166).

47. *Wisconsin State Journal,* March 22, 1877.

48. Diary, May 18, 1877.

49. Frost, "Life," 187–188 (196–197); *Providence* [Rhode Island] *Journal,* October 19, 1878, in the Goodell Papers, Box 12, File 20.

50. *Milwaukee Sentinel,* January 31, 1879; diary, January 10, 1879; letter to sister, April 5, 1879. [On King's

earlier and equally historic career and on another pioneering woman lawyer also mentored by Goodell, Kate Kane, see full article by Cleary; see also McBride, *On Wisconsin Women*, 48, 93–94.]

51. W. Elliott and Mary M. Brownlee, *Women in the American Economy: A Documentary History, 1675 to 1929* (New Haven, 1976), 307.

52. Frost, "Life," 218; diary, April 22, 1879. . . .

53. April 25, 1879.

54. *Application of Miss Goodell*, 48 Wis. 693 (1879).

55. Frost, "Life," 136 (143).

56. Ibid., 203 (228), 205 (230).

57. Ibid., 206–207 (231–232).

58. *Ingalls v. The State*, 48 Wis. 647 (1879). . . .

59. . . . Frost, "Life," 149 (158).

60. . . . See "Ambivalence and Collegiality." In Cynthia Fuchs Epstein, *Women in Law* (New York, 1981).

# Olympia Brown and the Woman's Suffrage Movement[1]

CHARLES E. NEU

WMH 43, No. 4 (Summer 1960): 277–287

In 1878 the Reverend Olympia Brown arrived in Racine, Wisconsin, where she took charge of a small Universalist group — the Church of the Good Shepherd. Her arrival should have received more recognition than it did, for Mrs. Brown personified the kind of emancipated woman that the country was to see more of in the years ahead. At forty-three she was in the prime of a life devoted to Universalism and women's freedom. . . . Already prominent in woman suffrage circles in the East, she had now come to the Midwest, the place of her birth [in 1835], believing that in this section of the country lay the greatest opportunities for reform.[2]

. . . She had grown up on a small Michigan farm, under the influence of a mother with advanced ideas toward woman's liberties and religion. . . .

There seemed to be no question in the family over the highly unorthodox step of sending the young girl to college. In 1854 Mrs. Brown entered Mount Holyoke Female Seminary [in Massachusetts], but the religious orthodoxy and rigid discipline at Mount Holyoke did not accord with her liberal notions, especially when contrasted with the newly founded Antioch College at Yellow Springs, Ohio. Antioch . . . was coeducational, non-denominational, and open to Negroes. Mrs. Brown, who transferred to Antioch in 1856, seemed to thrive there. . . . One classmate later recalled Mrs. Brown's moral seriousness and intellectual strength during these college years. . . . She already was indignant over the inferior position of women, and left Antioch in 1860 determined to raise their status. She also left with a second and even more perilous goal — a career in the ministry — despite the determined opposition of nearly everyone.[3]

It was fortunate that Mrs. Brown chose the Universalist faith, for none of the larger Protestant denominations would ordain women to the ministry in the 1860s. The Universalists had recently opened St. Lawrence Theological School at Canton, New York, and Mrs. Brown entered and completed the course of study there, ignoring as best she could the skepticism of the school's director over her precedent-breaking action and the discomfiture caused by the prejudice of most of her fellow students. She was ordained to the Universalist ministry in June 1863, [one of the first women] in America to be ordained. . . . [W]ithin one year she was installed as pastor of the Universalist Church in Weymouth, Massachusetts.[4]

. . . Her religious belief, acquired from her mother and strengthened by her experience at Antioch, was a highly optimistic one. . . . Her faith, as revealed in her sermons, was not a particularly introspective one. . . . Primarily, she saw Universalism as a practical belief designed for a busy world in which men were in danger of forgetting about religion altogether. . . .

. . . After the Civil War she was awed by the rapid industrialization of the United States, and seemed at times to be disturbed by the hurry of American life and the superficiality of American culture. But her criticism of America was more than balanced by her enthusiasm over the new inventions and scientific discoveries coming forth in such abundance. They eased woman's burden. . . .

Mrs. Brown had no illusions about the position and attainments of American womanhood. Although women were more sensitive to the religious experience they were . . . "feeble, abject being[s]" lacking knowledge, education, and purposeful lives. Their morals were appalling, as was their physical degeneracy. . . . But "amid this wreck of intellect, this waste of God-given powers, this ruin of moral character," . . . she was determined to bend every effort to the realization of woman's potentiality. The keys to the revolution in woman's character were the ballot and formal education, both of which would teach women to think and form independent opinions.

The realism apparent in Mrs. Brown's appraisal of American womanhood was not evident in her view of American political life. Throughout her career she insisted that political questions were questions of principle, and the obvious incompatibility of this belief with political realities made her disdain politics and politicians as corrupt and immoral. "Politics," she said, "must be made a science worthy the attention of the Christian."[5]

In 1866 Mrs. Brown met Susan B. Anthony and became an ardent suffragist. She participated in the innumerable campaigns, conventions, and petitions through which women were expressing their discontent, but her real baptism into the woman's suffrage ranks came in 1876 when she toured Kansas [with Anthony] in the first state campaign for a woman's suffrage constitutional amendment. Her travels across the hot grasslands, interrupted by two or three meetings a day at widely separate settlements, were an arduous but exhilarating experience. . . .[6]

Mrs. Brown was a charter member of the American Equal Rights Association, created at the close of the Civil War presumably to advance the rights of both Negroes and women. Soon, abolitionists and suffragists were at odds over which reform should come first. Abolitionists claimed it was "the Negro's hour" and supported the Fifteenth Amendment, even though it did not include woman's suffrage. Some suffragists acquiesced in this, but Mrs. Brown, like Miss Anthony and Elizabeth Cady Stanton, bitterly denounced the abolitionists. . . . In 1868 [Brown] took the initiative in the formation of the New England Woman Suffrage Association. . . . [A year later,] Miss Anthony and Mrs. Stanton . . . formed the National Woman Suffrage Association, and their dissidents, under the leadership of Lucy Stone, formed the American Woman Suffrage Association. Both sides wooed Mrs. Brown, but she remained aloof, declaring that she wished "to work for principles, not individuals or cliques.". . .[7]

As the years passed the suffragists settled into an almost yearly routine. . . . [They] would head back to Washington, D.C., for the National Association convention. Mrs. Brown . . . became a prominent speaker at its conventions, as well as vice president at large. Some progress was being made — full suffrage in the Wyoming and Utah territories, school suffrage in a handful of states (municipal in one), the introduction of the Anthony Amendment and subsequent Senate and House hearings — but every state campaign was lost, and the cause was still not entirely respectable.[8]

In 1873 Mrs. Brown had married John Henry Willis, thus thwarting the popular stereotype of suffragists. She had, however, been deeply impressed by the arguments of Lucy Stone [to retain her own name], and continued to be known throughout her life by her maiden name. Five years later, when she received her call from the Universalist Church, the Willis family moved to Racine where . . . Mrs. Brown, in addition to her ministerial duties, plunged into local suffrage work.[9] She was elected president of the state association, and [in] 1886 seemed to have secured a significant victory — the approval of a law whereby women could vote in elections pertaining to school matters. The law appeared so promising that Mrs. Brown resigned her pastorate in 1887 and devoted all of her energies to a campaign to awaken women to their new voting rights. At the same time, dissatisfied with the narrow interpretation of the law by local officials, she instituted a suit which reached the Wisconsin Supreme Court. The court in effect invalidated the whole law [in 1888], leaving the suffrage cause in Wisconsin precisely where it was prior to 1886, except for the addition of an onerous debt and the effects of a heartbreaking defeat. . . .[10]

Mrs. Brown was forced to recast her vision of the future. She foresaw "twenty-five years of educational work ahead.". . .

It was one thing for Mrs. Brown to realize the need for a quarter of a century of effort, another placidly to accept it, for she was perplexed by the widespread indifference (especially of women). . . . The seeming irrationality of this indifference produced a sense of frustration in Mrs. Brown which began to appear as a search for the causes of failure and as an effort to produce new justifications for woman's suffrage.

. . . [B]y the late 1880s, new speech titles began to appear . . . along with new arguments almost invidious when compared with the old. The most prominent new argument — the threat of uneducated and essentially alien foreign voters to republican institutions — undoubtedly in part stemmed from numerous state campaigns (where recent immigrants were often herded to the polls by antisuffrage interests), and from her own increased contacts with immigrants after settling in Wisconsin. . . .[11]

Mrs. Brown considered it "unbearable" that women were "the political inferiors of all the riffraff of Europe that is poured upon our shores.". . . Nevertheless, her thought remained fairly coherent until the arduous woman's suffrage campaign in drought-stricken South Dakota in 1890. After her experiences in that campaign, where once again recent immigrants were marshaled to defeat woman's suffrage, a real element of paranoia began to appear in her speeches. . . . [To her mind,] the greatest threat in Wisconsin was the preponderance of foreign-born citizens at the polls. [She believed] the crux of the danger to republican institutions caused by the ignorant foreign and Negro vote was the "corruption of the ballot box," which allowed "aliens, paupers, tramps [and] drunkards" to vote while shutting out "teachers, church members, preachers [and] mothers of the republic.". . .[12]

The solution to the impending catastrophe was, as expected, woman's suffrage. . . .

This would throw the voting balance to native-born Americans since women were scarce among the foreign-born, and would also ease tension in the South by returning the whites to power. The corruption of the ballot box would be diminished, especially if states were forbidden to enfranchise noncitizens, and Protestant domination would be assured. . . .

Mrs. Brown's frustration over the perplexing failure of the woman's suffrage appeal was shared by other prominent suffragists. By 1883 Elizabeth Cady Stanton was tired of suffrage conventions. . . .[13]

. . . [She was] edging out of the mainstream of suffrage reform, which still was dominated by Miss Anthony. Miss Anthony's answer to repeated failure was more organization and agitation in an effort to keep woman's suffrage continually before the people. She had the firm support of the rising generation of suffragists, led by Carrie Chapman Catt and Anna Howard Shaw. Mrs. Brown, though sympathetic to Mrs. Stanton . . . agreed with Miss Anthony on the primacy of woman's suffrage. However, [they] differed strongly over the best means to achieve it.[14]

. . . [T]he two rival suffrage associations — the National Woman Suffrage Association and the American Woman Suffrage Association — united in 1889, ending a twenty-year split. . . . [T]he organization would undertake both state and federal work. Mrs. Brown, a firm supporter of the National [American Woman Suffrage] Association, was disturbed by the union, for she believed that [it] should continue to agitate only for an amendment to the federal constitution, allowing each state suffrage unit complete autonomy. She correctly foresaw the almost exclusive concentration of the new association upon state campaigns. . . . Mrs. Brown's protests were those of a pioneer and individualist who could not adjust to the increasing organization and subordination that younger workers thought necessary for the success of the cause.

Mrs. Brown was not a woman to make idle protests, for through her initiative the Federal Suffrage Association was founded in Chicago in 1892. . . . The most significant fact about the association was the sense of dignity its program gave Mrs. Brown and other members. They were asking for the recognition of a right already existing in the Constitution, not begging for an amendment or humbling themselves before uneducated foreigners in state campaigns. It was an assertion of dignity destined to appear in a more belligerent form later in Mrs. Brown's life.[15]

But personal tragedy cut short Mrs. Brown's protest. In 1893 her husband died and her beloved mother was stricken with a lingering illness. . . . Life became harder for her, and she was forced to give up most of her suffrage work and pleasant travels throughout Wisconsin in order to concentrate upon running her husband's printing firm. . . .[16]

At the turn of the century her mother died and Mrs. Brown, at about the same time, gave up the printing business. She once again was able to work intensively for the suffrage cause, and in 1902 with the aid of Clara Bewick Colby reshaped the defunct Federal Suffrage Association into the Federal Woman's Equality Association. . . .[17]

. . . Every year Mrs. Brown and Mrs. Colby arranged a congressional hearing at which they pleaded for a federal suffrage bill. . . . But while their organization never consisted of more than a handful of women, the National American [Woman Suffrage] Association became a powerful, well-financed pressure group with an integrated structure based on local and state units. . . .[18]

. . . Mrs. Brown's alienation from the National American Association continued to grow. In 1893 it rejected the federal suffrage idea and in 1902 showed little interest in Mrs. Brown's proposal for concentration upon Congress. She felt that National American leaders no longer needed or desired her services. There may have been some truth in this, for both National American leaders and some local suffragists were increasingly dissatisfied with the progress of the cause in Wisconsin. The Wisconsin [Woman Suffrage] Association, despite its affiliation with the National American Association, never recovered from the judicial defeat of 1888. At first Mrs. Brown ascribed the [state] association's stagnation to the distraction of women by other organizations and to the refusal of women to work for such a hopeless cause. But by 1903 she blamed the paralysis of the Wisconsin effort on outside interference, presumably that of National American leaders.[19]

The tension between Mrs. Brown [and] her co-workers . . . was brought to a head by the submission of a woman's suffrage amendment to the voters of Wisconsin, to be voted upon in 1912. Some younger Wisconsin suffragists, claiming that Mrs. Brown was too old and decrepit to lead a vigorous campaign, formed a rival suffrage association called the Political Equality League and proceeded to organize with such energy that Mrs. Brown found many of her customary financial sources diverted. Mrs. Brown objected to the[ir] "showy" methods, . . . but primarily she turned upon the younger suffragists themselves. . . .

Before their deaths, both Miss Anthony and Mrs. Stanton had experienced friction with the younger suffragists and now it seemed that Mrs. Brown, about the only old pioneer left, must also undergo the anguish of seeing younger and relatively inexperienced suffragists turn upon her. These "uneducated, half-baked women," [in her words,] coming upon the scene when the cause was respectable and popular, had not endured the hardships of the pioneers. Mrs. Brown gazed wistfully back to the time when her old co-workers lived, forgetting the differences she had had even with them. . . .[20]

The Wisconsin suffrage campaign of 1912 was lost, Mrs. Brown resigned from the presidency of the [Wisconsin] Woman Suffrage Association, and the two factions reunited soon afterwards. Her days of active suffrage work in Wisconsin ended. As Mrs. Brown herself once had said, "a nation should renew itself with every generation." However, much of her bitterness lived on. She continued to believe that the National American [Woman Suffrage] Association's methods . . . served mostly as platforms for exhibitionists. . . .

. . . She was alienated from the National American [Woman Suffrage] Association and tired of and humiliated by state campaigns. . . . [But] a sense of imminent victory was beginning to appear in Mrs. Brown as well as in others, particularly because of the repeated successes in state campaigns after 1910. Mrs. Brown's problem was how to realize this expectancy within her lifetime, so that unlike [Stanton and] Miss Anthony she would not die before her dream was fulfilled.[21]

The rise of the militant suffrage movement in 1913 under Lucy Burns and Alice Paul answered Mrs. Brown's need. . . . The militant suffragists . . . had split from the National American [Woman Suffrage] Association primarily because of strategic differences. Like

Mrs. Brown, they rejected the state-campaign approach . . . to work exclusively for a federal constitutional amendment. Their political method — more ruthless than that of prior suffragists — was the doctrine of party responsibility, which held the party in power accountable for whatever happened to woman's suffrage. Party responsibility, in its simplicity and directness, appealed to Mrs. Brown. Women had waited over fifty years, and patience, as she pointed out, had ceased to be a virtue. . . .[22]

Though Mrs. Brown was seventy-eight years old in 1913, she was, as always, ready to act upon her beliefs. She became a member of the National Advisory Council of [Alice Paul's] Woman's Party . . . and an active militant. [In] 1917, she was one of the 1,000 women who picketed the White House with large banners in a freezing rain and strong wind to make known their demands to President [Woodrow] Wilson. . . . For a woman tired of humiliation and defeat, righteous and defiant militancy was a noble, uplifting experience. Its rationality or irrationality probably had little influence on Mrs. Brown. Militancy for her was a spontaneous and unequivocal protest after years of often acute frustration.[23]

In June 1920 she marched in her last picket line at the Republican National Convention in Chicago. The ratification of the Nineteenth Amendment was completed in August, and Mrs. Brown could contemplate in peace the fruition of her life's work.

. . . Neither Mrs. Brown nor most other suffragists ever fully realized why their victory was so long overdue. In 1911 Mrs. Brown came close to at least one reason when she pointed out that "the number of people who will work for a principle which seems . . . to have no personal interest for them is very small." But she did not act upon her own insight, probably because she really never believed it. Her failure to see the inadequacy of the abstract woman's suffrage appeal is all the more striking when one views the example set by Frances Willard and the Woman's Christian Temperance Union. Miss Willard was an adroit propagandist who saw that the average woman would not want the ballot until her social consciousness was stirred by problems related to her own experience. "It is so much easier," she said, "to see a drunkard than . . . a principle." Thus she linked suffrage and temperance to a broad program including all interests pertaining to the economic, social, and political well-being of women. . . . Suffragists mostly avoided the issue by blaming the liquor interests, the foreign vote, or party hostility for the defeat and delay of woman's suffrage, hardly dreaming that the primary reason might lie in their own parochialism. . . .[24]

It is significant, from the standpoint of intellectual parochialism, that Mrs. Brown always considered Miss Anthony the "great leader of our movement.". . . But unlike Miss Anthony she lacked the personal strength to continue the same pattern of action for decades. When youthful optimism proved unfounded, anxieties and frustrations appeared which threatened to place her in the byways of the suffrage movement. . . . Mrs. Brown's failure to build a strong Wisconsin association showed her inability to gather any appreciable group of young suffragists to her banner. . . . [H]er strong desires for power contributed to a bitter conflict with younger workers in Wisconsin. . . .[25]

The fact that Miss Anthony and other early suffragists died, while Mrs. Brown lived on, makes the latter's life especially important, for it allows us to view through one woman's life the whole span of a major reform movement. . . . Mrs. Brown's life make[s] clear that the woman's suffrage movement was not a simple phenomenon, but rather a complex reform effort often readjusting its organization and attitudes — for many years in the light of constant failure, and later in that of imminent success. It was impossible for suffragists to face problems in 1910 as they had in 1865.

By 1920 advancing years clearly had mellowed Mrs. Brown. . . . Both suffrage organizations honored her and much former bitterness passed with the triumph of the cause. . . . [S]he had, after all, played a part in the evolution of American democracy. . . . She had fought hard to awaken the American people to a glaring inequality in the social and political structure of their nation, and though it is clear from our perspective that her efforts were at times misdirected, her courage, determination, and sensitivity to wrong are still impressive.[26]

*Brown died in 1926, at the age of ninety-one at her daughter's home in Baltimore, and is buried in Racine. There, a school is named in her honor, as is her church, now renamed the Olympia Brown Unitarian Universalist Church.*

*Since publication of Neu's pioneering research, recommended other sources published on Olympia Brown include her writings in Dana Greene, ed.,* Suffrage and Religious Principle: Speeches and Writings of Olympia Brown *(Metuchen, N.J.: Scarecrow Press, 1983); her daughter's recollections in Gwendolen Brown Willis, "Olympia Brown: An Autobiography," in the* Annual Journal of the Universalist Historical Society *4: 3-33 (1963); and a book-length biography by Charlotte Cote,* Olympia Brown: The Battle for Equality *(Racine: Mother Courage Press, 1988).*

## NOTES

1. Historians now — as did suffragists then — use "woman suffrage," not "woman's" (or "women's") suffrage; that is, the term is modified by an adjective, not used in the possessive case, as voting belongs to the democracy and is bestowed, not possessed, by the voters. Similarly, historians also now honor the nonrifics preferred by women; that is, in the case of the Reverend Olympia Brown, who kept her maiden name after marriage, she ought not to have been called — nor was she legally — "Mrs. Brown."
2. . . . Unless otherwise indicated, all direct quotations are taken from the [Olympia Brown Papers in the Schlesinger Library, Radcliffe Institute, Harvard University]. . . . Some use was made of the Catherine Waugh McCulloch Papers, also deposited [there].
3. Olympia Brown, *Acquaintances, Old and New, Among Reformers* (Milwaukee, 1911), 9. . . . Lucretia Effinger to Jessie Hutchinson, January 3, 1893, Brown Papers.
4. Ebenezer Fisher to Brown, June 21, 1861, Brown Papers. [Historians now recognize that the first ordination of a woman was of Antoinette Brown Blackwell in 1853 by the Congregationalists, although she was dismissed in 1854, apparently at her request; see Evans, *Born for Liberty*, 103. Historians also now suggest that Lydia Ann Moulton Jenkins may have been the first Unitarian woman minister, if ordained in 1860; see David Robinson, *The Unitarians and the Universalists* (Westport, CT: 1985).]
5. *Services at the Ordination and Installation of Reverend Phebe A. Hanaford*, ed. by Olympia Brown and John G. Adams (Boston, 1870), 46.
6. . . . Stanton, Anthony, and Gage, *History of Woman Suffrage*, vol. 2, 259.

7. William Lloyd Garrison to Brown, January 3, 1868, Brown Papers; . . . *Acquaintances,* 75–79; Brown to Lucy Stone, November 8, 1869, Brown Papers; Brown to A. E. Weston, April 21, 1871, Brown Papers.

8. Susan B. Anthony and Ida Husted Harper, eds., *History of Woman Suffrage,* (Rochester, N.Y.: 1902), vol. 4, passim; Carrie Chapman Catt and Nettie Rogers Shuler, *Woman Suffrage and Politics* (New York, 1923), 107–131.

9. [The Willeses came from Bridgeport, Connecticut, where Brown was called to a pastorate in 1870. In Wisconsin, John H. Willis was publisher and editor of the *Racine Times-Call.* They had two children; Gwendolen Brown Willis taught at Milwaukee-Downer College and Bryn Mawr School in Baltimore, and Henry Parker Willis became a professor at Columbia University.]

10. Anthony and Harper, *History of Woman Suffrage,* vol. 4, 985–993; *Wisconsin Citizen,* September, 1889.

11. Brown, *Acquaintances,* 67–68; Anthony and Harper, *History of Woman Suffrage,* vol. 4, 61; *Woman's Tribune,* March 8, 1890.

12. Anthony and Harper, *History of Woman Suffrage,* vol. 4, 148–149; Catt and Shuler, *Woman Suffrage and Politics,* 114–117.

13. Alma Lutz, *Created Equal: A Biography of Elizabeth Cady Stanton* (New York, 1940), 260 *ff.*; . . . *Wisconsin Citizen,* March, 1890.

14. Lutz, *Created Equal,* 261.

15. *Democratic Ideals, A Memorial Sketch of Clara B. Colby,* ed. by Olympia Brown (Federal Suffrage Association, 1917), 58–71.

16. *Wisconsin Citizen,* April, 1893.

17. Ibid., June and July, 1900; *Woman's Tribune,* January 17, 1903.

18. *Democratic Ideals,* 72–78; *Woman's Tribune,* April 11, May 23, May 30, and June 20, 1903; Mary Gray Peck, *Carrie Chapman Catt, A Biography* (New York, 1944), 105*ff.*

19. Ida Husted Harper, *History of Woman Suffrage,* vol. 6, (New York, 1922), 699–708; Anthony to Brown, December 22, 1899, Brown Papers; *Wisconsin Citizen,* June, 1903.

20. Alma Lutz, *Susan B. Anthony, Rebel, Crusader, Humanitarian* (Boston, 1959), 274–280; Brown to Ida Husted Harper, quoted by Harper to Brown, 1917 (no month), Brown Papers. . . .

21. *Wisconsin Citizen,* July and August, 1909.

22. *Equal Rights,* October 30, 1926; Inez Haynes Irwin, *The Story of the Woman's Party* (New York, 1921), 1–37; *The Suffragist,* March 31, August 25, 1917, and September, 1920.

23. Irwin, *The Story of the Woman's Party,* 204, 313, 388.

24. Brown, *Acquaintances,* 105–106; Mary Earhart, *Frances Willard, From Prayers to Politics* (Chicago, 1944), passim.; *Wisconsin Citizen,* May, 1892. . . .

25. . . . *Wisconsin Citizen,* May, 1892, January, 1902, April, 1906.

26. Ida Husted Harper, ed., *History of Woman Suffrage,* vol. 5, (New York, 1922), 610, 615; *Equal Rights,* October 30, 1926.

*Ellen Clara Sabin, pictured in 1931, ten years after her retirement as president of Milwaukee-Downer College*

# 5

# ORGANIZED WOMEN, 1888–1910

## INTRODUCTION

The Progressive movement, born in Wisconsin, gave a name to the turn of the centuries from the nineteenth to the twentieth. Those years were the "most momentous in Wisconsin history, so alive with the promise of constructive change that they are known to history as 'the Progressive Era,'" writes historian John D. Buenker. Wisconsin served as a "laboratory of democracy" for "a system that would ensure every citizen's economic security and enhance every citizen's quality of life" — and accomplish this end "without destroying the fundamentals of democracy and capitalism." The state so altered in "fundamental and permanent ways," writes Buenker, that "'progressivism' became a watchword, a touchstone, a totem of almost mythic power" in Wisconsin to this day.[1]

It is paradoxical, perhaps heretical, to suggest that there was not a Progressive Era for Wisconsin women, for whom "progressivism" was a myth even in the era of its making. They fell further behind their sisters in many states in economic security and permanent power in fundamental ways of life in Wisconsin, especially in lack of legal protection for girls. The state raised the statutory "age of protection" from ten years of age to fourteen in 1887. But by 1889, Wisconsin went backward by lowering the age to twelve and reducing the sentence to a year for rape if a girl "proved" a "common prostitute." Records of the Industrial School for Girls, the state institution started by women (see Introduction to chapter 4), reveal growing numbers of inmates, including incest victims; counties' committals increased — as did "vigilante justice," writes Joan M. Jensen. A father who battered his family was lynched in Trempealeau County, a father escaped tarring and feathering in Taylor County but was caught and convicted for rape, a Wood County father went free despite "ruining" a daughter who became a "common plaything," but "community indignation" came too late for a Waushara County girl who died from an abortion. Communities "patrolled and controlled sexual activities" with "chivarees," "whitecapping," and other public humiliations, and local courts locked away girls "in need of care and control," although not for prostitution, but because their mothers worked in brothels that a Lincoln County minister called "slaughter pens in the Wisconsin woods." As a petition to the legislature put it, the public feared "inherited vicious tendencies" in girls in an allegedly Progressive Era.[2]

Public outcry also caused a campaign to raise the "age of consent" across the country and succeeded in many states, but legislators hardly heeded women without the ballot in Wisconsin. Vie H. Campbell of Evansville, the president of the Wisconsin Woman's Christian Temperance Union, wrote an article in the nationally circulated *Arena* in which she called the laws "a blot upon our statute books" and "a disgrace to our boasted civilization"

for abandoning "girls who fall into that life that is worse than death." The Reverend
Olympia Brown of Racine, the president of the state woman suffrage association, wrote
that Wisconsin was "believed to be the only case on record where the age of protection has
been lowered" rather than raised.[3]

Wisconsin women also fell behind in legal rights when Brown lost her battle for the
ballot. In 1890 the Wisconsin Supreme Court ruled against the suffrage law that women
had won in 1886. The men on the bench sent the bill back to legislators for rewording, a
task that would take male lawmakers more than a decade and, even then, result in only
partial, "school suffrage." While Wisconsin women waited, Wyoming entered the union as
the first state with full woman suffrage in 1890, and a few other western states followed —
only a few, owing to intervening economic events.[4]

In the ensuing decade, the nationwide depression of 1893–1897 wreaked fiscal havoc
on women and families across a Wisconsin with a rapidly industrializing economy. The
number of factory workers would triple statewide from 1890 until approximately 1910,
when Wisconsin ranked ninth among states in manufacturing, which grew three times
faster than farming during those decades — as did wages, although not for women.
"Progress" in the Progressive Era, writes Buenker, "exacted a heavy toll on those with
little or no capital, skills, education, or organization."[5]

If the Progressive Era did not mean political progress for most women, that the
decades from 1890 to 1910 hardly deserve their characterization by woman suffragists as
"the doldrums" was demonstrated by the least educated and economically secure women
in Wisconsin. The state's women workers were "largely young and single, of recent immigrant stock, and remained in the workforce for a relatively brief period — five years or
less," writes Buenker. Even a lifelong working woman was "regarded as a mere sojourner"
and treated as "temporarily outside her natural sphere, of limited usefulness, whose earnings were purely supplementary, and whose existence posed a threat to male workers'
livelihoods" — although women in the state still earned half the average wage paid men
in Wisconsin. Few women worked in skilled or supervisory positions; by the end of the era,
95 percent of women worked in fewer than fifty of more than three hundred occupations
in the census. However, as early as the 1830s, women elsewhere organized strikes, and one
led to the largest labor uprising in the antebellum era.[6]

Women on picket lines were new to Wisconsin in the Progressive Era, when they were
unwelcome in labor unions, although some immigrant wives, mothers, and sisters of workers exhibited remarkable assertiveness and organizational skills in support of a strike in
Oshkosh. Nativism and sexism spurred the press to denounce the women as "the very pictures of anarchy," the title of historian Virginia Glenn Crane's account excerpted here.
The Oshkosh strike of 1898 also became legendary, but in labor history, for famed lawyer
Clarence Darrow's defense of a male union leader. In histories of women and of Wisconsin, the stories of wives, mothers, and sisters of strikers long were lost — or deliberately
buried, as Crane discovered.

Middle-class women made more enduring progress in employment. The turn-of-
the-century census found more than 150 women physicians, almost two dozen women

lawyers, and nearly 650 women-owned businesses. The male bastion of banking also fell in the 1890s. Women finally wielded power in the world of finance — at least in the small town of Burlington, where the founder of Meinhardt Bank died soon after its opening in 1891. His daughter Eda carried forward her father's legacy for the next forty-three years, and her mother Eliza became bank president in 1897. By then, their friend Florence Cooper Hall had become president of the neighboring Bank of Burlington upon her widowhood in 1895. It remained open despite a difficult recovery from the depression of 1893–1897 — and a difficult bank examiner who wrote that "a woman ought to know better than to try to manage a bank." Progress was slower in larger cities; Blanche Hambright became the first woman hired at a Milwaukee bank, Marshall & Ilsley, in 1900. But bankers statewide hailed Lotta Smith, hired in Mazomanie in 1902, for foiling a bank robber by dropping to the floor, an act which earned the bankers' award for bravery.[7]

More commonplace was the unpaid work of myriad middle-class women in many communities across Wisconsin — and in the most massive movement of the Progressive Era nationwide, the women's club movement. Most were not woman suffragists — or at least, not yet — but were exemplars of the era's much-heralded "New Woman," who had an advanced education and a career, occasionally in a profession, but more often as an unpaid volunteer in "club work." Some, such as Clio in Sparta, the earliest women's literary society in the state in 1871, started as "culture clubs," others as "study clubs," but all were ostensibly apolitical. However, women's clubs acted as an "ideological cover" for community activism and eventually even suffragism, according to historian Karen J. Blair, as many clubwomen moved from the "private sphere" of the home into the "public sphere" of political activism.[8]

The significance to women of educating themselves in their clubs, for lack of formal opportunities with few women's colleges in Wisconsin, cannot be overstated. Nor can their support of women artists and authors from Wisconsin. Some, such as Georgia O'Keeffe, born in 1887 to Irish immigrant Sun Prairie dairy farmers, left Wisconsin too soon. However, her later focus on nature in her pathbreaking paintings is said to reflect the influence of her early years, growing up amid the cycles of the seasons so marked in her birthplace and the encouragement of her first art instructor, a Sun Prairie schoolteacher boarding in her family's home before O'Keeffe went to boarding school.[9]

An Oshkosh matriarchy became famed for literary and artistic accomplishments, beginning with Elizabeth Farnsworth Mears from Fond du Lac, a poet and author under the pen names of "Ianthe" and "Nellie Wildwood," who encouraged creative ambitions in her daughters — as did clubwomen. Mary Elizabeth Mears also became an author, and Louise Mears Farge illustrated books. But Helen Farnsworth Mears became the most famous member of her family for winning a national competition in 1900 to sculpt the first statue in the nation's capitol of a woman, Frances E. Willard (see Introduction to chapter 4). Helen Farnsworth Mears already had won acclaim for her "Genius of Wisconsin," a statue that still stands in the state capitol but debuted at the state building at the Columbian Exposition in 1893. So had the statue named for the state motto, "Forward," by Menasha-born Jean Pond Miner of Madison, which now stands in the Wisconsin Historical Society's lobby. Miner's commission came from Janesville's Ladies Afternoon Club, while Mears was commissioned by the Woman's Club of Wisconsin, successor to a self-improvement society founded in 1876 as the Ladies Art and Science Class of Milwaukee Female College, later the College Endowment Association to fund scholarships for women.[10]

Other groups also formed to raise funds for scholarships for women. By 1894, graduates of the Female College and of the University of Wisconsin gained numbers sufficient in Milwaukee to found the state chapter of the Association for Collegiate Alumnae, now the American Association of University Women. Of eight founders, three also held master's degrees. A year earlier, in 1893, Kate Asaphine Everest had earned the first Ph.D. awarded to a woman at the state university. The Fond du Lac native became an instructor — the lowest faculty level — in history at Lawrence College in Appleton, after at first finding employment only as a high school teacher in Milwaukee.[11]

Fortuitously, Wisconsin's first women's college and state clubwomen both effected mergers in the mid-1890s that allowed them to combine forces. Clubs acted autonomously until formation in 1890 of the General Federation of Women's Clubs, which claimed more than one hundred thousand members nationwide in five years. They fostered the founding of even more clubs, including more than half of the almost seventy that sent representatives to the first convention in 1896 of the Wisconsin Federation of Women's Clubs, founded by Lucy Smith Morris of Berlin.[12] Another early force in the federation who sought her cohorts' support was educator Ellen Clara Sabin of Sun Prairie, who was among the first women students at the University of Wisconsin and had returned recently to the state to head a college (see "The University in 1874–1887" in chapter 4 ). A former student of Sabin, Neita Oviatt Friend, produced a humorous memoir of her "days at Downer," which is excerpted here. Interspersed with her recollections of students' girlish pranks on their president is the story of Sabin's struggle to strengthen women's higher education in the state.

Sabin merged two institutions to form Milwaukee-Downer College in 1895 and moved to a new campus funded in part by Wisconsin clubwomen. Milwaukee clubwomen proved their fund-raising ability that year with a "charity edition" of the *Milwaukee Journal*, printed on silk. Although it emulated similar enterprises elsewhere in the era, Milwaukee's especially ambitious edition enlisted hundreds of clubwomen who sold a record amount of advertising and trained for weeks to cover newsroom tasks for a day. Their record-setting edition totaled fifty-six pages, seven times the usual size and the largest ever printed in the state. Regular copies sold for five cents, more than twice the usual price, while silk copies went for $100 to raise a total of $3,775 for the city's welfare fund. A Minnesota paper praised the clubwomen's work as professional, although "prov[ing] little as to the actual ability of women to conduct a newspaper that shall give news."[13]

However, the "managing editress" was Ida Mae Jackson, who already had begun to breach the barriers of big-city journalism in Milwaukee despite a male colleague's claim on "clubwomen's day" that a "newspaperman's nature could never stand the strain of so much decorum." From 1890 to 1894, Jackson was the part-time "club editor" at the *Journal* and then its first women's editor as well as the first woman reporter on "hard news." The first woman writer for the *Journal*, Nellie Bartlett, had worked for free, and the paper also had hired editorial writer Mary Stewart in 1890 on a freelance basis. But the era of the newsroom as a male bastion ended forever by the end of the century. In 1899, Zona Gale joined the *Journal* full-time; born in Portage in 1874, she was a graduate of the University of Wisconsin in Madison with both bachelor's and master's degrees. Edna Ferber from Appleton followed, although both stayed only briefly at the paper before they headed east and began careers in fiction for which they won Pulitzer Prizes. Another journalist from Monroe, Janet Jennings, won headlines nationwide for her first-person accounts from the front when pressed into service in the Spanish-American War as a nurse on a ship where she witnessed military corruption. Her exposés led to congressional hearings. Such stories — and success stories — encouraged many women to enroll in one of the first journalism schools, opened at the University of Wisconsin early in the century.[14]

Women students at the state university never neared their numbers at state normal schools. New campuses opened at Stevens Point and Superior in the 1890s, when a new gymnasium at the state university in Madison also opened — for men only. The contrasting treatment was "a notable case of quite forgetting the girls," as a state schoolteachers' journal editorialized. The University of Wisconsin facility was "one of the finest in the United States," with "everything that modern ingenuity has devised for the physical culture of men" — but "not the slightest provision was made for women." Historian Christine A. Ogren observes that, although "athletics was the area of activity perhaps most touted for fostering leadership and teamwork skills," UW women had "fewer opportunities than men to lead and work in teams." At state normal schools, "on the other hand, gender equality characterized not only intellectual and social relations but also the development of teamwork and leadership skills" in athletics and other activities. When another normal school arose at La Crosse in the new century, a "bloomer brigade" already played intramural football at Oshkosh, and several campuses competed in basketball. Women also won top positions in student government at state normal schools. However, according to Ogren, "gender separation and lower status for women" would continue to characterize the state university for decades to come.[15]

From scholarships at colleges and normal schools to parks, playgrounds, and hospitals, many monuments to the civic work of hundreds of women — or "municipal housekeeping," as they called it — still stand across the state. But closest to clubwomen's hearts across the country were their beloved free public libraries. In an article excerpted in this chapter, biographer Earl Tannenbaum attributes the founding of libraries statewide to Lutie Stearns, one of the first graduates of Milwaukee Normal School. However, Stearns credited clubwomen for their help in her campaign on behalf of a public unable to pay dues for the previous, privately held "subscription" libraries. The new patrons of free public libraries included working-class adults, especially immigrants, and children from families in poverty, such as Stearns's students in her first career as a schoolteacher. Her literacy crusade led to the formation of the Wisconsin Free Library Commission, whose staff Stearns joined to stump the state. With her unpaid cadre of clubwomen, she founded 150 public libraries — three-fourths of libraries in the state — and 1,400 traveling libraries.

Far more dire needs of women and children in destitution, especially after the depression of 1893, motivated many middle-class clubwomen to venture into the "public sphere" for the first time. As historian Sara M. Evans writes, an increasingly class-stratified society in the nineteenth century meant that the "worlds of the working class and genteel women rarely overlapped" until the effects of the economic upheaval caused "respectable people of middling means and substantial education in the North and Midwest cities and towns" to "create voluntary associations on a new scale," a new "public space located between the private sphere of the home and public life of formal institutions of government" in an era prior to welfare programs. In the greatest peril were women and children, "with little re-course in the event things went wrong" — except poorhouses, as portrayed in Michael Lesy's *Wisconsin Death Trip,* on the desperation in rural areas after the depression of 1893.[16]

The shortcomings of such semipenal institutions as poorhouses spurred the spread of the "charity movement" from Milwaukee to smaller communities where women widened their earlier public health campaigns. Bank failures in 1893 both exacerbated needs and delayed funding in Milwaukee for the Children's Hospital, one of the first in the country, that finally opened in 1894 owing to the leadership of six society clubwomen in the city and physician Dr. Frances Sercombe.[17] Legions of clubwomen enlisted statewide in the drive to eradicate a leading cause of death at the time, as historian Mary Ellen Stolder dis-cusses in her article on the antituberculosis campaign, which is excerpted in this chapter. She shows the significance of local leadership, proving that one woman could make a dif-ference in whether a community led or followed progress. However, Stolder's study also shows an advantage of localizing history in her discovery that Jennie Damon Whittier Shoemaker of Eau Claire differed from stereotypical portrayals of clubwomen as middle-class and middle-aged, overeducated and underemployed, seeking escape from house-wifery into the public sphere. Instead, Shoemaker was a divorcée and working mother, which may have accounted for her awareness of economic inconstancy in women's lives. Stolder's article also illuminates the increasing interactions of women across social classes, as benevolent work for the betterment of others brought voluntaristic women in contact with working women in public health careers as well as with the needy women and chil-dren in their care.

However, helping other women did not mean welcoming them as equals, as the Gen-eral Federation of Women's Clubs (GFWC) made clear in its infamous "Milwaukee Bien-nial" convention in 1900. More than a thousand women came from across the country, including a clubwoman of color whose plans to cross the "color line" were anticipated; thousands of members of the press also came to cover the "Ruffin incident." Josephine St. Pierre Ruffin, editor and publisher of the magazine of the National Association of Col-ored Women's Clubs, which she had founded, also belonged to prestigious "mixed-race" clubs in Boston and the board of her state federation. She came to the convention as a duly credentialed and dues-paying delegate, only to be turned away by the GFWC at the doors of Milwaukee's elegant Pfister Hotel. Polite debate escalated into open conflict, hardly customary among clubwomen and dismaying delegates.[18]

Most reporters reveled in covering the national federation's infighting, but not one who was both a Wisconsin clubwoman and a "women's page" columnist. The head of the federation's press committee for the convention, Theodora Winton Youmans of Wauke-sha, denounced the southern delegates who had won the day with the decision to turn Ruffin away (see "Theodora Winton Youmans and the Wisconsin Woman Movement" in chapter 6). However, her own state federation also earned Youmans's scorn for rejecting an application from a local African American club in southeastern Wisconsin. The African American club was formed in the region where nearly three-fourths of new residents of color were part of the Great Migration from the South settled by the turn of the century, although still a miniscule community even in Milwaukee. The accommodationist editor of the local black press, the *Wisconsin Weekly Advocate,* enraged his "colored elite" con-stituency by editorializing that clubwomen of color ought to "toil for the uplifting of the race," meaning the uplifting of African American men. Although the reaction of his wife, clubwoman Clara C. Montgomery, is not known, the women on his staff — Lillian Maxey, apparently Wisconsin's first woman journalist of color, and her assistant, Sadie Johnson — left soon afterward. Reasons for their resignations were not given in the *Advocate.*[19]

The turn-of-the-century clubwomen's convention in Milwaukee is seen as a turning point in women's history, but not a turn for the better. That white clubwomen "shared the nativist and racist ideas of men of their class," as Gerda Lerner writes, is measurable in the actions of members of the all-male Wisconsin legislature who debated bills outlawing miscegenation, or intermarriage, three times in the next decade — and in the actions of the all-male courts in Wisconsin where, as Buenker writes, "one white woman was sent to an asylum when she attempted to marry a black man." Lerner, the preeminent historian of women and professor emerita of the University of Wisconsin–Madison, writes that the General Federation of Women's Clubs "followed the spirit of the times in turning away from the race issue" and was not alone among women's organizations in doing so. How-ever, the action by one of the largest women's organizations in the country was a failure in leadership with divisive impact on the larger women's movement for decades, writes Lerner, as the "constant compromise of suffrage leaders with the southern viewpoint on the race issue inevitably led to discriminatory practices and racist incidents" similar to the "Ruffin incident."[20]

Nor were women of color alone in enduring discrimination in Wisconsin, as club-women also enforced de facto policies based on ethnicity and even anti-Semitism. Women of Hebrew heritage also were not welcome in the Wisconsin Federation of Women's Clubs. In Milwaukee, early German American Jewish women's societies provided charita-ble services, even a bathhouse next to the Schlitz Brewery by channeling excess hot water from the bottling plant. In 1900, led by Lizzie Black Kander, the women founded a mis-sion for the influx of almost eight thousand Eastern European Jews living in overcrowded conditions. Kander had been born in 1858 to immigrants in Milwaukee and recalled, "I was trying to teach a group of young foreign girls in a crowded neighborhood how to cook simple and nutritious food, yet have it attractive and inexpensive, as we prepare it in America." However, high school girls in her after-school classes spent so much time copy-ing recipes instead of cooking that she sought the sum of $18 to print cookbooks. When men on the mission board refused her request, Kander organized a favorite fund-raising project of clubwomen everywhere in the era: the sale of cookbooks.[21]

In 1901, the first edition of *The Settlement Cookbook* soon sold out its first run of one thousand copies — as have thirty-four editions in the century since. Total sales of the country's most beloved cookbook, which is still based on basic instructions for newcomers to America and adaptations of ethnic recipes, exceed two million copies. After the success of their first edition, sold at fifty cents apiece, Kander and her "cookbook committee" soon incorporated as a company, moved from her home to office space, and hired office help, as cookbook profits continued to support the Jewish Community Center, the current successor to the Abraham Lincoln Settlement House built on another site bought by the women in 1910.[22]

Some new immigrants resented earlier German American settlers for their attitude toward "old country" culture, but not a girl named Goldie at the settlement house, who would grow up to found a new country, far from the discrimination she had witnessed in her homeland — and again in Wisconsin. Born in 1898, Goldie Mabowehz had fled with her family from a rise in pogroms in Russia for freedom from religious persecution in America, where they moved in 1906 to Milwaukee's Walnut Street, known as "little Hester Street." She never forgot a neighbor's threat to "knock some Jewish heads," nor that her grade school required her to learn German and sing "Deutschland Uber Alles" almost daily. However, Goldie enjoyed the settlement house entertainments for children, and upon her return to the city to see her former Fourth Street school, renamed in her honor, she expressed fond memories of Milwaukee. "Here I found freedom, kindness and cleanliness," she said. "Here I first experienced a lack of prejudice." A stellar student, she taught Yiddish at a *Folk-Schulen,* or folk school, and started teacher training at the Milwaukee Normal School, now the University of Wisconsin–Milwaukee, where her Zionist activism gave her a new goal. She soon married and left the city that had taught her the value of freedom, to found kibbutzes and then a country, Israel, where Golda Meir became prime minister in 1969.[23]

Other women entered the political sphere in Wisconsin during the Progressive Era, if only as their husbands' "helpmeets," a popular term of the time. In her essay excerpted here, historian Nancy Unger explores the life of Belle Case La Follette and the love of her life: the founder of the Progressive Party, "Fighting Bob" La Follette. As a congressman's wife and the First Lady of fin de siècle Wisconsin, as a contributor to their magazine, and as his de facto campaign manager, she often sublimated her own wishes and will. The first woman graduate of the University of Wisconsin Law School in 1885, she never practiced law; instead, she turned her considerable intellect to her husband's career. She also turned her "finely honed social conscience," Unger writes, to "work for the betterment of society comfortably behind the scenes." Unger sees even her sincere and significant support of suffragism as "a way of protesting being so dominated by her husband's needs" — and a way to win political support from the Progressive-minded women who eventually won the ballot.

Almost two decades sooner, clubwomen led the campaign to regain at least "school suffrage" in Wisconsin, which in 1902 allowed women to vote in school-related elections —but in separate ballot boxes. "Subsequent legislatures expended a great deal of heat and shed little light on the issue," according to Buenker. The men refused woman suffrage bills in every biennium, by various means; they defeated three bills for full suffrage in 1903 alone and another for municipal suffrage in 1905. Although suffrage was "the only electoral reform issue of any substance" before legislators for the rest of the decade, writes Buenker, women still "ran into a stone wall." Another bill died in 1907, while in 1909, the assembly first "killed a similar bill through the device of indefinite postponement," then refused to consider it when the senate passed the measure and sent it to the assembly again.[24]

In Milwaukee, women had won appointment of clubwoman Mary Freeman Merrill to the city's school board in 1895, and then they campaigned for the board to become elective. In 1907 one of the first women to win election to the Milwaukee School Board was Lizzie Black Kander. Her settlement house programs for children soon expanded into public schools, the forerunners of Socialists' recreation centers that presaged their pioneering evening adult education for immigrants.[25] The first Socialist woman on the Milwaukee School Board, Meta Schlichting Berger in 1909, soon became its president — apparently the first woman to head a major city school board in the country. Also among the first graduates of the Milwaukee Normal School and briefly a teacher, she had become but a *hausfrau* and helpmeet to her immigrant husband, Victor Berger, the city's most prominent Socialist politician. However, unlike Belle Case La Follette, Berger was not one to sublimate her will for long; her determination to be part of her husband's political life led to her own thirty-year political career, as she described in her autobiography, whose introduction by editor Kimberly Swanson is excerpted here. Swanson provides a context within which to understand both the private and public spheres of an early and controversial political couple's evolving partnership.

As Wisconsin's Progressive Era waned, and Milwaukee's Socialist era began, Meta Schlichting Berger's political career contrasted with the life that Belle Case La Follette lived for others, despite their similarities. Such varied approaches to progress for women foreshadowed the final, colorful but divisive decade to come in the Wisconsin woman suffrage campaign. Women took divergent paths into the public sphere and worked together in the clubwomen's movement and municipal campaigns, in the working-class labor movement and consumers' campaigns, and in the suffrage movement and political campaigns. They already had won progress beyond politics, well before they brought their political expertise and experience into a seemingly single-minded mass movement for woman suffrage after 1910.

And Wisconsin woman suffragists would succeed, not only winning the ballot but also making history nationwide in the next decade. However, as Buenker writes, their state was "from the beginning a volatile mixture of natives and newcomers, but rarely more so" than in the first decade the new century. Wisconsin suffragists would diverge again, even sooner than woman suffragists elsewhere, and the seeds of their schism already were evident in the Progressive Era.[26]

NOTES

1. John D. Buenker, *HOW*, vol. 4, *The Progressive Era, 1893–1914* (Madison: SHSW, 1998), v, ix.

2. Joan M. Jensen, "Sexuality on a Northern Frontier: The Gendering and Disciplining of Rural Wisconsin Women, 1850–1920," *Agricultural History* 73, no. 2 (Spring 1999): 144–146, 151, 156–158.

3. Vie H. Campbell, "Why an Age of Consent?" *Arena* 69 (April 1895): 295–288; Genevieve G. McBride, *On Wisconsin Women: Working for Their Rights from Settlement to Suffrage* (Madison: University of Wisconsin Press, 1993), 131–132.

4. Buenker, *HOW*, 10, 80; McBride, *On Wisconsin Women*, 131, 184; Eleanor Flexner, *Century of Struggle: The Woman's Rights Movement in the United States*, rev. ed. (Cambridge: Harvard University Press, 1975), 163, 228.

5. Buenker, *HOW*, 10, 80.

6. Ibid., 146; Sara M. Evans, *Born for Liberty: A History of Women in America* (New York: Free Press, 1989), 83, 99.

7. Catherine B. Cleary, "Wisconsin Women Become Bankers in the Twentieth Century," *Wisconsin Banker* (December 1999): 4; Ruth De Young Kohler, *The Story of Wisconsin Women* (Madison: Wisconsin Women's Centennial Commission, 1948), 50–52, 104.

8. McBride, *On Wisconsin Women*, 137; Buenker, *HOW*, 335; Karen J. Blair, *The Clubwoman as Feminist: True Womanhood Redefined, 1868–1914* (New York: Holmes & Meier, 1980), 1–5; see also Theodora Penny Martin, *The Sound of Our Own Voices: Women's Study Clubs, 1860–1910* (Boston: Beacon Press, 1987).

9. Kohler, *Story of Wisconsin Women*, 72–73; Roxana Robinson, *Georgia O'Keeffe: A Life* (New York: Harper and Row, 1989), 1–11.

10. "Winnebago County: It Surpasses All Others in Wisconsin in Literature, Art, Music, and the Stage," *Oshkosh Northwestern*, June 13, 1908. "Forward" stood outside the state capitol for a century but was threatened until its rescue in 1995 by Wisconsin women who raised funds for a replica at the capitol and for relocation of the original.

11. Kohler, *Story of Wisconsin Women*, 104; Reuben Gold Thwaites, *The University of Wisconsin: Its History and Its Alumni, 1836–1900* (Madison, J.N. Purcell, 1900), 729.

12. McBride, *On Wisconsin Women*, 153, 157, 165–166, 185.

13. Faymarie Pluskota, "Women's Day: The Charity Edition of the *Milwaukee Journal*, February 22, 1895," unpublished paper in possession of the editor. Prized by collectors, a Milwaukee clubwomen's "silk edition" sold for $400 in an auction in 2004.

14. Ibid.; Frances Stover, "Ida Mae Jackson Chalked Up Numerous Newspaper Firsts," *Milwaukee Journal*, December 26, 1945; McBride, *On Wisconsin Women*, 156–157; Robert W. Wells, *The Milwaukee Journal: An Informal Chronicle of Its First 100 Years* (Milwaukee: Milwaukee Journal, 1981), 21, 32, 60; John Evangelist Walsh, "Forgotten Angel: The Story of Janet Jennings and the *Seneca*," *WMH* 81, no. 4 (Summer 1998): 267–293.

15. Christine A. Ogren, "Where Coeds Were Coeducated: Normal Schools in Wisconsin, 1870–1920," *History of Education Quarterly* 35, no. 1 (Spring 1995): 3, 17, 21, 25.

16. Evans, *Born for Liberty*, 67–69; see also Michael Lesy, *Wisconsin Death Trip* (New York: Pantheon, 1973). On state clubwomen's later campaigns, see Janice C. Steinschneider, *An Improved Woman: The Wisconsin Federation of Women's Clubs, 1895–1920* (Brooklyn, NY: Carlson, 1994).

17. Kohler, *Story of Wisconsin Women*, 84–85.

18. Genevieve G. McBride, "The Progress of 'Race Men' and 'Colored Women' in the Black Press in Wisconsin, 1892–1985," in *The Black Press in the Middle West*, ed. H. Lewis Suggs (Westport, CT: Greenwood Press, 1996), 331–334.

19. Ibid.; Buenker, *HOW*, 186; Joe William Trotter Jr., *Black Milwaukee: The Making of an Industrial Proletariat, 1915–1945* (Urbana: University of Illinois Press, 1985), 21, 29–33; see also Kohler, *Story of Wisconsin Women*, 101.

20. Gerda Lerner, *The Majority Finds Its Past: Placing Women in History* (New York: Oxford University Press, 1979), 104; Buenker, *HOW*, 198–199.

21. Jan Uebelherr, "100 Years of The Settlement: Classic Cookbook Began with Humble Mission of Assimilating Immigrants," *Milwaukee Journal Sentinel*, April 17, 2001; quote in Angela I. Fritz, "Lizzie Black Kan-

der and Culinary Reform in Milwaukee, 1880–1920," *WMH* 87, no. 3 (Spring, 2004): 36–49.

22. Fritz, "Lizzie Black Kander," 44–49.

23. "Milwaukee Landmark, Jewish Ghetto, May Soon Pass Away," *Milwaukee Leader,* May 22, 1918; Ralph G. Martin, *Golda: Golda Meir, the Romantic Years* (New York: Charles Scribner's Sons, 1988), 4, 21–29, 55–73; quote in Marian B. McBride, "Sentimental Journey," *Milwaukee Sentinel,* October 1, 1969.

24. Buenker, *HOW,* 511–512.

25. McBride, *On Wisconsin Women,* 156; Elizabeth Jozwiak, "Socialism, Free Speech, and Social Centers in Milwaukee," *WMH* 86, no. 3 (Spring 2003): 10–21; see also Mrs. Simon Kander Papers, WHS Area Research Center, Golda Meir Library, University of Wisconsin–Milwaukee.

26. Buenker, *HOW,* 179.

# "The Very Pictures of Anarchy"
## Women in the Oshkosh Woodworkers' Strike of 1898

VIRGINIA GLENN CRANE

WMH 84, No. 3 (Spring 2001): 45–59

In 1898, a strike by woodworkers in Oshkosh generated some of the most dramatic moments in the history of women in Wisconsin. Immigrant working-class women participated in the strike as wage workers and helpmeets, as street fighters and political operatives. The outcome failed to improve wages and working conditions materially, or to change the character of Oshkosh in any significant way, but the events of the summer of 1898 comprise a compelling story of traditionally marginalized women who, for a fleeting moment, spoke truth to power and challenged the hierarchies and conventions of their culture.[1]

At the end of the nineteenth century, Oshkosh was a lumbering center with a population of about 28,000. It had long been known as the "Sawdust City" and was dominated economically by seven large companies that manufactured doors, blinds, window sashes, and custom millwork. The Paine Lumber Company, the largest of these, and the other six . . . employed about 2,000 woodworkers in their factories and yards.

The woodworkers, like other industrial laborers in the city, were mostly German, Irish, Polish, or Danish immigrants. They were separated from their employers and from each other by ethnicity, class, and culture. . . . In that working-class community of modest frame houses on unpaved streets, the residents spoke a common language but were divided into Prussian Lutheran and Bohemian Catholic neighborhoods and parishes. The millowners — English-speaking Presbyterians and Methodists — lived a world away . . . in finely crafted Victorian houses set along paved, elm-shaded boulevards.[2]

In 1898, George Milton Paine of the Paine Lumber Company was the corporate monarch of Oshkosh. He dominated the city's millwork industry and employed over 750 woodworkers — about a third of the total. . . .[3] Throughout the 1890s, he and other local lumber company executives imported cheap foreign labor, repeatedly cut wages, and hired women and children for half the pay that men received. Wages in the local millwork industry were so low — about ninety cents for a ten-hour day — that the international labor press referred to Oshkosh as the "slave wage capital of the world." Advanced technology made possible machine operations that reduced the need for skilled laborers, and by 1898 about a fourth of the experienced woodworkers in town had been displaced by women and children. At the Paine mill, one or two fathers had been discharged from their jobs and replaced by their daughters.

Local woodworkers, hampered by the disproportionate power of labor and capital as well as their own cultural divisions and the conservatism of their churches, were slow to organize unions. Eventually, however, they established four locals, united under a Woodworkers' Council, and affiliated with the American Federation of Labor. . . . [They] turned for help to Thomas Kidd, general secretary of the AFL's International Machine Woodworkers' Union.[4]

. . . In the mid-1890s he repeatedly responded to invitations to Oshkosh to confer with leaders of the emerging union movement. When he investigated wage levels at the mills and observed sixteen-year-old girls at Paine operating lath ripsaws and lifting heavy pine and hardwood doors for veneering, glazing, and molding, he publicly declared that no other city in the nation was as "disgraced" as Oshkosh by "pauper wages" and by the number of women and children working like "serfs" in the factories. He succeeded in unionizing a majority of the [male] woodworkers, but he failed in his effort to negotiate with George Paine and the other millwork manufacturers. Reluctantly, in the spring of 1898, he agreed with the workers that a strike was necessary.[5]

Prior to calling for a walkout, the Woodworkers' Council sent a letter to the millowners demanding a pay raise, recognition of the union, and the abolition of female factory labor. The demand that women be removed from the mills was, no doubt, a local reflection of the AFL's national position that female workers were competitors for jobs — and therefore a threat to male wage levels — and that men were entitled to a family wage adequate for the support of wives and children. Nineteenth-century society was patriarchal, and the notion that a woman's place was in the home cut across class, ethnic, and religious lines. The woodworkers of Oshkosh were too far removed from the ideological radicalism that existed elsewhere in the country to articulate a class-based attack on capitalist greed and a forthright assertion of the economic self-interest of all working people. They were also too remote from emerging feminist ideas to demand equal pay for equal work. Their conviction that male responsibility and prerogatives were being eroded led them to focus exclusively against women and, in their demands, to raise no objections to child labor or to new immigrant workers whose meager wages also posed a threat to their livelihoods.[6]

Upon receiving the letter from the Woodworkers' Council, George Paine "assigned it to the wastebasket." He persuaded his fellow industrialists to do the same and to deal as one with the unexpected audacity of their laborers. When the union received no response from the manufacturers, the members voted to strike. On Monday morning, May 16, 1898, woodworkers at the seven millwork factories walked off the job.

The strike lasted fourteen weeks. . . . [7]

During the long conflict, female woodworkers were almost invisible. On those rare occasions when they appeared in the record at all, they were found on both sides of the line, either as strikers or strikebreakers. Resentment against the union, coupled with sheer economic necessity, no doubt impelled many women to continue working. Whatever the individual motivation, women were prominently listed in the press as strikebreakers in the first days of the walkout. At McMillen [Company], females made up half the diminished work crew of thirty; at Paine, forty-three nonunion employees, "including girls," showed up for work. In contrast with these workers who sided with the company, other female factory operatives walked out with the men. When the union made a final count of strikers after the first week, among the 1,600 listed were fifty "girls."[8]

But female woodworkers were by no means the only women involved in the struggle. Indeed the success of the labor action depended, in large part, on the support of union members' wives and mothers. Local newspapers tended to depict the striker's wife as a desperate, hungry, stoic drudge, but Thomas Kidd preferred to idealize her as a loyal helpmeet and to enlist her in the cause of labor. He invited the female members of strikers' families to a mass union meeting on the first Sunday of the strike and pleaded with the women to stand by their men. "Ladies" became a regular fixture at all the union's subsequent public gatherings, and supportive women became the keys to family survival during the long summer months without income.[9]

While most working-class women remained in the domestic sphere, an assertive minority chose instead to play an active public role, and it was those few who gave the Oshkosh woodworkers' strike its most dramatic and historic moments. . . . [W]omen who had been attending union meetings had come to believe that scabs undercut labor solidarity and betrayed working-class interests. A small cadre of activists among them decided that, while union men were under fire, women could fill the breach and remove the strikebreakers from the workplace.

Their strategy was simple and direct. A single woman possessed little power, but a mob of women, accompanied by union men and boys, could congregate en masse at the gates of each of the open mills in turn and harass the scabs as they entered the yards in the morning and left in the afternoon. Unrestrained by middle-class prescriptions about female propriety, bold working-class women could freely take to the streets and use a woman's traditional weapon: verbal aggression. Scabs might hesitate to use violence against women, and the police would surely not arrest and jail the mothers of children. Once the scabs were gone, the scant remaining work crews might be pressured into staying home. The mills would then close, and the strike would be settled. When working-class women began thus to think strategically, their decisions suddenly and unexpectedly took on the dimensions of public policy — a far remove from the idea of woman as merely a helpmeet.

One leader of the group that devised this plan was Louise (Lizzie) Wilhemina Neumann Hando, a sixty-four-year-old widow who had migrated to Oshkosh in 1872 from Posen, in Prussia. She came with her husband, Gottlieb, who went to work at the McMillen factory. Lizzie learned to read English, though she never learned to write or speak the language. . . . Lizzie gave birth to nine children, five of whom survived to maturity. When the strike began in 1898, she was living with two of her unmarried offspring: her only daughter Etta (Edna or Ethel), an educated, well-spoken eighteen-year-old, and her son Fred, a striking woodworker. . . . Etta Hando was a close associate of her mother's in planning policy and strategy for the group.[10]

Caroline Lange Pomerening, a prominent participant with the Handos in the women's organization, was a fifty-one-year old, Prussian-born, bilingual immigrant who had moved to Wisconsin in the 1870s. She married Herman Pomerening, a woodworker, and they had one child, daughter Minnie. The family originally lived in a Prussian neighborhood . . . and belonged to the same Lutheran church the Handos attended. . . . In

1898 Caroline was a housewife; her husband was a striking woodworker; her daughter, a domestic servant.[11]

Emma Kunzendorff, another leader of the women's group, was the daughter of a French father and Swiss mother who had emigrated from France in 1870. Emma learned to read, write, and speak English fluently and in 1881 married Henry Kunzendorff, a Russian-German carpenter. After fourteen years of marriage, she gave birth to her only child, a son. When the strike began, Emma was thirty-eight, her son was a toddler, and Henry, who worked at the Gould factory, was president of the German Machine Woodworkers' Union #57. . . .[12]

Women such as these, and the recruits who followed them into the streets, seemed the least likely group in Oshkosh to emerge as a force in shaping the history of a city. . . . Several, like Lizzie Hando, had little education and could speak no English. They were not, in the terminology of the time, "gainfully employed," though of course, like most women, they performed unpaid domestic labor at home. They were not radical ideologues but conservative mothers, wives, daughters, and sisters who acted in support of their striking menfolk. Informal socializing in neighborhoods, churches, and at union meetings no doubt helped forge their solidarity and formed the basis for their collective identity and labor militancy. . . .

The first target, the Radford Company, was located at the north approach to the Wisconsin-Ohio Street bridge. . . . When the mill whistle blew at six o'clock on the afternoon of June 22, signaling the end of the workday, a throng of south-side men, women, and children — with women making up about half the gathering — poured out of their houses. Within five minutes, they assembled at the south approach to the bridge. When the scabs started across the bridge, angry women in the crowd greeted them with a din of hisses and hoots and a volley of rotten eggs. Police soon arrived to escort the strikebreakers to safety but were confounded by the spectacle of "ladies" behaving in unusual ways. The officers used no force and were quickly swept aside by the multitude. Only when all the frightened workers had made their way home through the hail of eggs and epithets did the crowd disperse.[13]

The following morning, the demonstrators reappeared — this time at the Morgan mill. . . . "[F]ollowing a preconcerted plan of action," [they] assembled near the mill. When strikebreaking workers came into sight, the street in front of the entrance and at the south ramp to the bridge quickly filled curb to curb, and women demonstrators "took complete control of the thoroughfare." Several of them carried handkerchiefs filled with eggs described by one observer as "back numbers . . . in various stages of incubation." Others had pouches of sand tied in front of their aprons or paper sacks filled with salt or pepper to throw into the eyes of the opposition. A few, armed with clubs and urged on by the crowd, "swung up and down the street," halting pedestrians and chasing away any man dressed in laborers' clothes who was not recognized as a union member. During lulls in the action, knots of women stood or sat at the curb talking animatedly in German and "broken English" about the strike and what they would do to the next scab who appeared on the scene. At the first sight of this mass of protesters, most strikebreakers . . . stopped short of the mill. . . . The police tried and failed to disperse the crowd, and only when it was announced that both Morgan and Radford would close as a result of what the papers labeled "the riots" did the demonstrators melt away. McMillen and Paine were still operating, however, and word passed along the street that McMillen would be the next target at closing time.[14]

City officials heard about the demonstration planned for the afternoon and, at midday on June 23, an agitated Mayor [Allison Baptist] Ideson proclaimed: "Oshkosh is in the hands of a mob." Sheriff Florian Lampert deputized strikebreakers and volunteers, armed them with tin stars and billy clubs, and dispatched them to the targeted mill. All through the afternoon, crowds of reporters and curious spectators also gathered at the McMillen gates in anticipation of the excitement to come.

Shortly before five o'clock, about a thousand demonstrators arrived at McMillen's and formed a solid mass outside the fence that surrounded the plant. A few men and teenaged boys were in the assemblage, but women were in the majority. The whole group seemed to be led by a half-dozen women, especially one who had been conspicuous at the Morgan mill that morning. Without doubt, this was Lizzie Hando. Accompanied by her son Fred and daughter Etta, and her friends Caroline Pomerening and Emma Kunzendorff, Hando had her troops under "tight control." Witnesses later described them as "deliberate & cool as if they were going to a picnic."

When the mill whistle blew, marking the end of the workday, McMillen strikebreakers began emerging from the factory. At the sight of these hated scabs, the crowd began to chant. Unnerved, the workers promptly retreated into the mill. They soon regrouped, however, and a few bold ones reemerged, armed with planks and stones. They were led by mill engineer Edward Casey, a husky sixty-seven-year-old Canadian of Irish heritage. Casey reeled out the company fire hose, opened hydrants, and directed a powerful torrent of cold water through the fence. The soaked demonstrators, in a fury, wrenched the factory gate from its fastenings and smashed it to the ground, then swarmed though the breach into the millyard. There was a short, confused clash. The scabs were quickly overwhelmed, and most of them fled back into the mill. Casey dropped his hose but picked up a heavy plank and stood his ground. Jimmie Morris, a sixteen-year-old striker and Paine Company painter who was in the van of the surging crowd, turned his head and shouted: "Look at them. The women are fighting harder than the men." At that moment, Casey struck Morris on the head with his club. The boy fell to the ground. The tumult stopped and Casey bolted into the mill. As friends bore the unconscious youth away, the demonstrators instantly became "a different people." A "deep terrible growl reverberated in the air" and a chilling chant went up: "Engineer! Engineer!" "Bring out Casey." "Arrest Casey." "He has killed the boy."

Police and deputies, who had previously tried and failed to disperse the crowd, were now reinforced by a new contingent of sheriff's deputies. Trouble broke out afresh, however, when one of the deputies was recognized as a strikebreaker at Paine. Lizzie Hando and others promptly accosted him. The deputy hit Mrs. Hando on the head with his billy club. She was removed to the sidelines but was replaced by other women warriors who soon put to flight the offending scab and the sheriff's entire force.

Regular police officers on the scene were aware that the women who now controlled the yard would not disperse until Edward Casey was removed from the mill. Accordingly, they negotiated an agreement whereby the crowd would keep still while a police squad entered the factory, arrested the engineer for assault, and escorted him safely to jail. All went well until Casey, pale with fright, emerged through the doors surrounded by a flying wedge of officers. As the cordon moved forward, a roar went up from the crowd and a shower of missiles rained down on the police and their prisoner, who were dripping with eggs when they reached the patrol wagon and galloped away. After Casey's removal, the angry women began clamoring for the strikebreakers still trapped in the mill. A committee of striking union men rescued them by following the police tactic of negotiating an agreement with the demonstrators. By its terms, the scabs would be allowed to leave the grounds without harm if they promised not to return to work the following day. The hapless strikebreakers promised to stay at home and, guarded by the strikers, eventually departed, with only harsh words from the women to mar their exit.

Shortly afterward, McMillen's superintendent announced that the company would close its factory. The crowd began to disperse amid whispered reminders that the Paine Lumber Company would be the target for the last of the demonstrations the following morning. . . .

Shortly after ten o'clock, Jimmie Morris died of a fractured skull. News of his death spread swiftly. Angry men and women poured out of their houses on the south side and milled about the streets all over town. When police authorities heard that there was talk in the crowds about lynching Edward Casey, they "spirited" him "out of the city in a hack."[15]

In assessing blame for the riot, local pundits cited insurgent strikers or Thomas Kidd. One ethnocentric observer explained that the mob was made up of "a type we do not often meet with in this country . . . mostly Polish & Bohemians, dark skinned & dark eyed, fierce, cruel & pitiless." The *Milwaukee Sentinel* echoed this xenophobic theme, blaming "vicious" foreigners and the "perfect viragoes" who led the mob.[16] There was at least one element of truth in this diatribe. Immigrant women had indeed instigated, planned, and led the demonstrations without the benefit of masculine brawn or brain. The local patriarchy was unprepared for the sight of women leading men, much less attacking them and taking charge of public space, but that was what the female protesters had done. Disregarding the nearly universal weight of gender and class bias in their society, and without the confidence-building weapons of socialist or feminist ideology, these wives and mothers and sisters of the strikers demonstrated that organization and militancy were not exclusively a male preserve. Their aims were traditional, but their actions were radical. They asserted themselves as active agents in supporting the family economy, not as breadwinners but as street fighters. They chose anger and action over despair and helplessness.[17]

. . . [T]he initiative in the woodworkers' strike had passed from the control of the manufacturers and the woodworkers' union to the women's action group. It was a moment fraught with irony. George Paine closed his factory to prevent the demonstration planned for Friday morning. Asked by a reporter why he could not "control" the dissident women, Thomas Kidd responded that he could nothing with women who were "making the trouble" since they were not union members subject to union discipline. City officials proclaimed that "nothing short of military rule would have any effect on the excited mobs," and they asked Governor Edward Scofield — himself a former lumberman — to send in the national guard.[18] The last time Wisconsin state troops had been dispatched to protect manufacturers in a labor dispute was in 1886 at Bay View near Milwaukee. On that occasion, guardsmen had fired into a crowd of striking ironworkers and killed five. Despite that bloody episode, the governor agreed to the request, and the morning after the McMillen riot — Friday, June 24 — Oshkosh was under military occupation. Infantry, cavalry, and artillery units armed with rifles and Gatling guns took up positions at the Paine Company gates and at the other mills and prepared for the next confrontation.

Emma Kunzendorff was up early that morning, mobilizing the south side women's corps. . . .

*At the request of the union organizer, Kunzendorff and other women called off the planned "scab at-*
*tack." But in response to hostile press coverage, Kunzendorff took up her pen and wrote to a local*
*paper in defense of the strikers. While troops and guardsmen protected the city and factories, the city*
*remained quiet for a week as, according to a local paper, "reporters who came from afar . . . were dis-*
*appointed that not even a 'quarrel with an ill-tempered woman' could be found." The week was also*
*marked by a massive public funeral to Jimmie Morris that received little coverage.[19]*

. . . The other Oshkosh event of consequence during the military occupation was a criminal prosecution. Oddly enough, it had nothing to do with Edward Casey, whose lawyers had succeeded in getting his case postponed and shifted out of town. Rather, on Monday morning, June 27, [the] district attorney . . . inaugurated criminal proceedings against alleged riot leaders. About thirty "foreigners," most of them women, were named as targets for investigation, and warrants were issued for the immediate arrest of Lizzie Hando and Caroline Pomerening. Charged with unlawful assembly and riot — a felony punishable by a sentence of three to seven years in prison — the two women were jailed and promptly bailed out by union supporters. . . . In reporting these proceedings, the *Oshkosh Enterprise* approvingly echoed an Appleton editor's opinion that it was disgraceful for a woman to become a "mobite." If she "unsexed" herself in that manner she should expect to face the "policeman's club, the discharge of musketry or the Gatling gun."[20] Transgressive women obviously had the power to disturb as well as disrupt. . . .

The Hando-Pomerening hearing on July 13 attracted the attention of masses of southside women who packed the municipal courtroom at city hall and jammed the streets outside. Witnesses for the prosecution were police officers and deputies, one of whom identified the defendants as ringleaders at the McMillen riot. During the testimony, there was a "continual shaking of heads and whispered contradictions" from the audience. When Judge Arthur Goss found the evidence sufficient for a trial and formally closed the proceedings, pandemonium broke loose. Mrs. Pomerening shouted, "They lied! They lied! . . . There is a God in heaven and I'll have my witnesses here if I have to take it to the higher court." She then broke into German and delivered what one reporter on the scene described as a tirade. Lizzie Hando hotly denied the witnesses' testimony about her role at McMillen's, and her daughter Etta corroborated her account. One "comely," "neatly dressed," "sincere" young woman — perhaps Etta Hando — attracted the reporter's attention because she was "rather refined and intelligent appearing" and spoke good English. When a cluster of German-speaking women from the audience crowded around — all talking at once, accusing the state's witnesses of perjury and vowing to take the stand for the defense — the linguistically challenged reporter dismissed their contributions as the "most indescribable babble." The noisy crowd moved toward the exit, where they encountered one of the deputized scab witnesses. "Shrieking" and "calling names," they shook their fists in his face and let him know, in several languages, how he stood with them. The reporter surmised that the municipal court had never before been the scene of such great excitement — a replay, as it were, "of the McMillen riot without the eggs."[21]

The Hando-Pomerening trial was set for August 3. Coincidentally or by design, the manufacturers chose that day to reopen their mills. When the whistles blew and small crews of strikebreakers returned to work, all was quiet on the streets. The women who might have been at the factory gates harassing strikebreakers chose instead to attend the trial at city hall and show support for their leaders. Testimony went on for two days, and the court recessed. No session was scheduled for Friday, August 5, and early that rainy morning a crowd of men and women — said to have been composed largely of the "troublesome foreign element from the terrible Sixth ward" — gathered outside the gates at the Morgan mill and prepared once more to put the scabs to flight. When police clubbed their way through the crowd and began hauling men off to the patrol wagon, a dozen or so of the "toughest looking women eyes ever looked upon" emerged from hiding places and surged forward, determined to protect their men. A reporter at the scene described the combatants as "wild-eyed" Bohemian and "Dutch" [for *Deutsch*, or German] women, the "very pictures of anarchy." They wore varicolored kerchiefs around their hair, and some had "no stockings but wore flapping slippers." A few carried umbrellas. Others had stones or clubs. One was reportedly armed with a "big bottle of gin." In the clash that followed — said to have been the most serious between the police and civilians in the history of the city — the women fought hand-to-hand with the arresting officers until they were bested and dragged off to the city lockup. Nine women — most of them Bohemian Catholics, recent immigrants, residents of the Sixth Ward, and wives of Paine strikers — were jailed and charged with unlawful assembly and riot. . . . [22]

⚬

*Afterward, Kidd was arrested for criminal conspiracy, and the women activists now became the negotiators and mediators. The next day, Caroline Pomerening led a large delegation of women to demand meetings with Mayor Ideson.*[23]

⚬

. . . The delegation described for the mayor the impact of what they called "pauper wages," thus forcing [him] . . . to hear firsthand about the suffering of his constituents' families. . . . [He] expressed his opinion that the minimum wage in Oshkosh would be raised by at least ten cents a day.[24]

What came next was even more extraordinary. A body of fifteen or twenty members of the delegation proceeded directly from city hall to the Paine Lumber Company to confront George M. Paine. . . . When curious pedestrians saw a band of working-class females striding briskly toward the Paine mill, they anticipated another street fight and tagged along to "see the fun." At the company office, the women stood outside the window and shouted for Paine to meet with them. A corps of uninhibited females making an appointment in such an unorthodox manner may have startled the millowner, but he eventually agreed to meet them, though only in groups of four. The selected delegates reportedly elicited from the city's industrial giant a promise that, when the strikers returned to work, he would take no retaliatory action against them.[25]

One city editor concluded of these meetings that "nothing came of them." He clearly knew nothing of gender politics. Something was indeed accomplished that day, when poor and hitherto voiceless immigrant women discovered that they could challenge corporate capitalism and myopic government with dialogue as well as rotten eggs. Oshkosh women, for the first time in the city's history, confronted official power without apology or self-abnegation. . . . They spoke plainly and articulated their demands. They contested prevailing notions about class and gender. They behaved, in short, like citizens who expected the government of a republic to be responsible to the needs of its people.[26]

Emboldened by this first taste of political action, the south-side women "adopted a novel plan of settling the strike" by talking to each of the millowners in turn. Whether this new mediation effort was a decisive factor in ending the strike cannot be determined, but within a week after the first city hall meeting, proprietors at each of the companies began holding de facto collective bargaining sessions with committees of their striking employees. . . . [O]nly about half of the 1,600 or so woodworkers who had walked out in mid-May were still on strike. . . . At least 700 others had left town in search of work. In August, when individual settlements were negotiated with each of the companies in turn and approved by the union, all the remaining strikers returned to work. Modest pay increases were granted at three of the mills, but none of the settlements included recognition of the union. On August 19, after three months of hardship and strife, the Oshkosh woodworkers' strike came to a close.

Much of the city rejoiced that the crisis had passed. . . .

*Although the strike was over, criminal proceedings for Thomas Kidd, Caroline Pomerening, Lizzie Hando, and approximately thirty others still went forward. Pomerening was acquitted at her trial. Hando had two trials, which both resulted in deadlocked juries before charges were dropped. Eventually, charges against all but Kidd were dismissed.[27]*

. . . In practical terms, the woodworkers' strike was a failure. Wages were raised at selected companies by a few pennies a day but, overall, the millowners prevailed. Union leaders were blacklisted and union strength eroded. The exploitation of women workers continued as before. . . . [28] Jimmie Morris lay in an unmarked grave, and Edward Casey was tried and acquitted for the boy's murder.[29] Lizzie Hando and her cohorts gained nothing from their moment of heroic struggle, and all died in obscurity.[30] Working-class wives and mothers throughout the city sank back into domesticity and silence. The millowners enticed a new cohort of workers from eastern Europe as cheap, nonunion labor, and when the newcomers settled into neighborhoods adjoining the old Bohemian community, all the old provincial and religious enmities that had divided laborers in the past were revived. After 1898, as before, Oshkosh remained a patriarchal, cheap-labor, antiunion town.

Yet despite this grim reality of loss and retreat, the naïve and courageous pursuit of an unattainable goal of equality by a powerless working-class community makes the story of the Oshkosh strike all the more compelling. In human terms, it succeeded as one of those rare instances when oppressed men and women broke through the barriers of class and culture and seized their rights as autonomous citizens. Female wageworkers sought labor solidarity across gender lines. Strikers' wives and mothers, sisters and daughters stood firm for the union. An intrepid band of working-class women liberated themselves from their "place" in the kitchen and beside the cradle. They took a new position — on the street and in the council hall — where they dictated policy and held government officials and lumber barons accountable for their actions. Most important, they shredded the fabric of that most universal of nineteenth century myths: the inferiority and weakness of women. . . .

⁂

*Lizzie Hando died in 1917 at the age of eighty; Caroline Pomerening died in about 1920 at the age of seventy-four; Emma Kunzendorff's date of death is not recorded. All remained in Oshkosh, as did George Paine. He died in 1917, when his son inherited the company — and his father's poor relations with workers. Nathan Paine "beat back a strike in 1920," cost workers their savings with the collapse of a company bank in the stock market crash of 1929, and during the Great Depression of the 1930s, he continued to build a mansion that became known as one of "America's castles." But after bomb threats, Nathan and Jessie Kimberly Paine soon donated to the city the building and grounds, now known as the Paine Art Center and Gardens.*

*The case of criminal conspiracy against union organizer Thomas Kidd became "one of the most celebrated trials in Wisconsin history," writes Crane. Kidd was defended by Clarence Darrow, "a formidable opponent who attracted national press attention wherever he went," and he went into the courthouse with a summation that "was published worldwide and became a pivotal declaration of human rights" for workers, according to Crane.*

*She writes a searing summation of Darrow's defense:*

*Darrow had stood Oshkosh on its head, reducing the millowners to a clique of bonded males swollen with mediocrity and guilty of perjury, bribery, and criminal conspiracy. . . . In the course of diminishing the mighty, Darrow had also elevated the humble, transforming a seemingly unsuccessful labor action in a relatively obscure place into a drama of struggle, endurance, and principle. Through the power and poetry of Darrow's language, the Oshkosh woodworkers' strike became an epic that, for a moment at least, pushed back the darkness and ennobled the human spirit.*

*After Darrow's two-day summation, the jury acquitted Kidd. Then, "for a hundred years," writes Crane, "the strike was virtually obliterated from the community memory in Oshkosh, and most people grew up knowing little or nothing about this epochal event in their city's history," even when workers finally had won a union at the Paine mill in the mid-1950s.*

*However, the power and poetic justice of the past still have a hold on Oshkosh. In 1998, when her book was forthcoming and a play based upon her book was to be performed, Crane writes, "a representative of the Oshkosh chamber of commerce warned me that the city would not countenance" the projects. The book was published and the play was performed about the immigrant women whose faith in democracy ought to have instilled pride in the city fathers of Oshkosh.*

## NOTES

1. This article is adapted from the author's book, *The Oshkosh Woodworkers' Strike of 1898: A Wisconsin Community in Crisis* (Oshkosh: Wisconsin Sesquicentennial Commission, 1998), which contains more detailed documentation. . . .

2. Wisconsin State Bureau of Labor and Industrial Statistics, *Eighth Biennial Report, 1897–1898* (Madison: Democrat Printing Company, 1899), 964–967, 346–347; . . . U.S. Bureau of the Census, *Abstract of the Twelfth Census of the United States* (Washington, 1900), 104, 110, 113, 126–127, 357; . . . Winnebago County Naturalization Papers, Area Research Center, Polk Library, University of Wisconsin–Oshkosh; *Oshkosh Directory, 1898–99* (Oshkosh: Globe Printing Company, 1898); Clarence Jungwirth, *The "Bloody Sixth Ward": A History of the Sixth Ward in the City of Oshkosh from 1880–1940* (Oshkosh: Clarence Jungwirth, 1991).

3. George M. Paine, "Recollections" . . . in the Paine Lumber Company Papers, Paine Art Center, Oshkosh. . . .

4. . . . Data for this study on wages, working conditions, and unionization came principally from union sources. See, for example, . . . the Thomas Kidd Scrapbook, WHS Archives. . . . Lumber company records seem to exist only for the Paine Company. Paul Cigler of the Wisconsin Labor History Society . . . states that the volumes for 1898 that might have supplied critical employment information for the history of the strike are missing from the collection.

5. "Autobiography," in Kidd Scrapbook; *Oshkosh Times,* 25 October 1898; Kidd to August McCraith, 5 May 1896, and Kidd to Frank Morrison, 16 and 27 September 1897, both in the American Federation of Labor Papers, WHS Archives (hereinafter AFL Papers); Deirdre Moloney, "Thomas I. Kidd and the Oshkosh Strike, 1898" (unpublished Labor History 902 research paper, University of Wisconsin–Madison, 1988); *International Wood Worker* (November–December 1898).

6. *Oshkosh Enterprise,* 14 May 1898. The position of early unions on women wage workers is treated in Alice Kessler-Harris, *Out to Work: A History of Wage-Earning Women in the United States* (New York: Oxford University Press, 1982). . . .

7. . . . Information for this study on day-to-day strike activity and millowners' responses derives in large part from Oshkosh's three newspapers [hereafter, the *Enterprise,* the *Northwestern,* and the *Times.*] . . .

8. *Enterprise,* 17 and 18 May 1898; *Northwestern,* 16, 17, 18, and 20 May 1898. . . .

9. *Northwestern,* 21 and 23 May 1898; *Enterprise,* 23 May 1898. . . .

10. Confirmations, 31 May 1877 (263 #18), 8 January 1880 (267 #44), 23 Sep. 1895 (291 #47); Marriages, 23 July 1892 (392 #14) and 8 June 1898 (409); Funerals, 6 June 1897, all in Peace Evangelical Lutheran Church Records, Oshkosh Public Library; Marriage Records, 16 August 1887 (7:15 #250), July 1894 (8:85 #716), 8 June 1898 (8:362 #2375); Death Records, 6 June 1897 (5:73 #437), all in Vital Records Office, Winnebago County Courthouse, Oshkosh; Wisconsin Census (1895); U.S. Census, 1880 (#102), 1900

(81/139/5/92); Oshkosh city directories, 1876–1898; Winnebago County Naturalization Papers, 22 October 1884 (#7910).

11. Marriages, 10 January 1874 (385 #1), Peace Evangelical Lutheran Church Records; Marriage Record, 10 Jan. 1874 (1:608 #4160), Vital Records Office, Winnebago County Courthouse; Oshkosh city directories, 1879–1898); Wisconsin Census (1885 and 1895); U.S. Census, 1900 (80/5/132/76); Winnebago County Naturalization Records, 29 October 1888 (#8874).

12. U.S. Census, 1900 (81/3/140/42); Oshkosh city directories, 1883–1898.

13. *Times,* 23 June 1898; *Enterprise,* 23 June 1898.

14. *Enterprise,* 24 June 1898; *Northwestern,* 23 June 1898; *Weekly Times,* 25 June 1898; *Chicago Record,* 24 June 1898.

15. *Times,* 24 and 28 June, 22 and 27 October, 8 and 9 December 1898; *Weekly Times,* 9 July 1898; *Enterprise,* 23, 24, 27 and 28 June, 13 and 21 July, 22 and 27 October 1898; *Northwestern,* 24 and 28 June, 8 and 13 July, 22, 25, and 26 October, 6 and 8 December 1898; *Chicago Record,* 24 June 1898; Lee Baxandall, "Fur, Logs, and Human Lives: The Great Oshkosh Woodworker Strike of 1898," *Green Mountain Quarterly* 3 (1976): 24; St. Peter's Catholic Church Death Index (May 1882–February 1925), Archives, Office of the Green Bay Archdiocese, Green Bay, Wisconsin.

16. *Milwaukee Sentinel,* quoted in Baxandall, "Fur, Logs, and Human Lives," 23; Ben J. Daly to his brother, 30 June 1898 (File 131.1-Unions, Strikes), Archives, Oshkosh Public Museum.

17. . . . My approach to the militant Oshkosh women of 1898 borrows from Eric Hobsbawm's . . . argument that women's family life rather than their work experience had the major impact on their behavior and consciousness, and that their family role served as a conservative force in molding their behavior. . . . See [Eric] Hobsbawm, "Man and Woman in Socialist Iconography," *History Workshop* 8 (1978): 121–138. . . .

18. *Northwestern,* 24 June and 5 August 1898; *Times,* 24 June 1898; *Enterprise,* 24 June and 8 August 1898.

19. Mrs. H. Kunzendorff to the Editor, *Enterprise,* 27 June 1898; *Enterprise,* 14, 17, and 27 June 1898; *Northwestern,* 27 June 1898; St. Peter's Catholic Church Death Index (1882–1925); Riverside Cemetery Records, Oshkosh; Oshkosh city directories, 1879–1898.

20. *Enterprise,* 27, 28, 29, and 30 June 1898; *Times,* 25 and 28 June 1898; *Northwestern,* 27, 28, and 29 June 1898.

21. *Enterprise,* 13 July 1898; *Times,* 14 July 1898; *Northwestern,* 13 July 1898.

22. *Northwestern,* 5 August 1898; *Enterprise,* 5 and 10 August 1898.

23. *Times,* 7 August 1898; . . . .

24. *Enterprise,* 6 August 1898.

25. *Enterprise,* 9 August 1898; *Northwestern,* 9 August 1898; *Times,* 9 August 1898.

26. See . . . Mary P. Ryan, *Civic Wars: Democracy and Public Life in the American City During the Nineteenth Century* (Berkeley: University of California Press, 1997); and Carroll Smith-Rosenberg, "Hearing Women's Words: A Feminist Reconstruction of History," in her *Disorderly Conduct: Visions of Gender in Victorian America* (New York: Knopf, 1985).

27. *Enterprise,* 21–24, 26–27, and 29 September, 3 and 18 October 1898; Criminal Docket, Municipal Court, City of Oshkosh and Winnebago (25 May 1895–24 June 1909), 1: 106, 127–128; . . . File #107, 1: 108–109, 130–132; Chicago Record, 14, 16–19, 21, 24–28, and 30–31 October, 1 November 1898, [Oshkosh Public Library]; *Northwestern,* 29 September, 1, 10, 14–15, 17–22, and 24–29 October, 2–3 November 1898; *Enterprise,* 14–15, 17– 22, 24–29, and 31 October, 1–3 November 1898; *Times,* 15, 16, 18–22, and 25–28 October, 3 November 1898. . . .

28. AFL Internationals, Wood Workers-America folder (Box 220), United Brotherhood of Carpenters and Joiners of America Papers, Archives and Manuscripts Division, University of Maryland at College Park.

29. . . . See "Paine Story . . . Is One of Industrial Genius," *Wisconsin Magazine,* (Oshkosh edition, December 1950), 24–26; and Robert W. Ozanne, *The Labor Movement in Wisconsin: A History* (Madison: SHSW, 1985), 19–25.

30. In the end, no party on either side of the struggle was ever legally sanctioned for any of their strike activities. See the *Northwestern,* 5–8, 10, and 12 December 1898; and the *Times,* 8, 9, and 11 December 1898.

31. . . . See U.S. Census, 1900 (80/5/132/76, 81/3/140/42, 81/139/5/92); Oshkosh city directories, 1900–1920; Funerals, 3 October 1917, Peace Evangelical Lutheran Church Records.

# Ellen Clara Sabin and
# My Years at Downer

NEITA OVIATT FRIEND

WMH 59, No. 3 (Spring 1976): 179–191

☙ ❧

*"Between the years 1891 and 1921, hundreds of young women in Wisconsin came under the influence of a remarkable educator," writes editor and historian John O. Holzhueter in his introduction to this reminiscence by a former student of Ellen Clara Sabin.*

*Before she became a teacher, Sabin already had made state history as among the first women students at the University of Wisconsin. Born in Sun Prairie in 1850, raised in Windsor, she taught ten younger siblings until she enrolled, at only sixteen years old, in the university's Normal Department for teacher training in 1866 (see "My Recollections of Civil War Days" in chapter 3). Sabin began teaching in Sun Prairie and became an elementary school principal in Madison, at only nineteen years old, in 1869 — the same year that six of her former classmates at the nearby campus earned the first bachelor's degrees awarded to women (see "The University in 1874–1887" in chapter 4).*

*Sabin never earned a regular degree but eventually was awarded an honorary degree for a career that culminated in college leadership. She left Wisconsin in 1872 with her family for Oregon. Within a year, she was principal at a "tough waterfront school," writes Holzhueter, and police "issued her a police badge as a guarantee of safe passage" when she visited students' homes. Within five years, she became Oregon's state superintendent of public instruction. By 1891, Sabin's reputation led to her return to Wisconsin as president of the struggling Downer College for Women in Fox Lake. By 1895, according to Holzhueter, the campus "was flourishing in all ways except the financial."*

*In 1895 in Milwaukee, the first college for women in Wisconsin was succeeding but seeking a new president and a new campus. Women trustees at Milwaukee Female College wanted Sabin. She immediately mediated the merger while moving the Milwaukee-Downer College campus from a sole building downtown to a parklike setting on the city's northern border, "near the end of the streetcar line" that became an avenue named Downer. Sabin supervised construction of a forty-acre complex of buildings bordered by the Downer Woods, reorganized the curricula of both the college and its high school–level seminary, and launched a campaign for better facilities for the study of science, an ambition which she would attain under the guise of "domestic science."*

*The domestic science movement began decades before across the country at the impetus of Catharine Beecher, a major benefactor of Milwaukee Female College. She had asserted that "a woman needed not only a rounded education, but a training as technical as that of a lawyer or a doctor" to be a "domestic scientist." Beecher's first books established a field of study that first was taught on a few campuses elsewhere in the country by the turn of the century, but not yet in Wisconsin.[1]*

*Sabin would establish not only studies in domestic science but also the first degree program in the field soon after 1905, when a new student named Neita Oviatt of Oshkosh came to the new campus. She would be in the last class to graduate from the seminary as Milwaukee-Downer became separate to become a "bona fide collegiate institution." Seventy years later, she still recalled details of her years at Downer and the much-admired "Miss Sabin."*

. . . I met [Miss Sabin] every morning, rounding the corner from her rooms [in Holton Hall] to join faculty and students hurrying through the long corridor and down the stairs to 7:30 breakfast.

She looked taller than her actual height because of her erect carriage and broad, square shoulders. . . . She had a firm but light step. You could not watch her walking briskly through the halls, her floor-length skirts swishing around her ankles, without catching the rhythm of that walk. . . .

Holton Hall, the largest of the dormitories, was the center of social activities. The large drawing room was beautifully furnished by the women trustees. Even the two small reception rooms were attractive, though less elegant. Here a young girl could properly receive a young man, with the approval of her parents, from seven in the evening until the lights "winked" at ten o'clock. . . .

That year, 1905, marked the fifth anniversary on the new campus. The beautiful Elizabeth Greene Memorial Library was now open to college students and fourth-year girls who were to graduate. The college girls had their own McClaren Hall, complete with dining room. The power plant for central heating and laundry had been completed and the new Plankinton Infirmary was under construction. This building would serve both college and seminary.

As a matter of convenience and economy, the only scheduled time for all seminary and college students and faculty to assemble together was for chapel service every morning at eight o'clock. None except those who were lucky enough to have the experience could realize the tremendous advantage to the seminary girls in being part of a college regime. In some instances seminary fourth years [or seniors] were permitted to take advanced courses in German and French with college students. . . .

. . . The close association with the faculty in the dining room too was a most valuable "fringe benefit," especially for the girls who were required to speak only French or German when seated at the table with their foreign-language instructor.

. . . [Miss Wollpert, the German teacher, had] received high degrees in German universities. There was no doubt in her mind that Germany had much better schools than we had in the United States, but she was at Milwaukee-Downer College to teach American girls to speak German, and that she did to her great credit. Obviously and understandably she was partial to the girls of German families who still spoke German in their own homes. We of white, Anglo-Saxon, Protestant ancestry were tolerated and taught. . . .

. . . [Mlle. Haberstitch, despite her German surname] insisted that she was French — all French — which no one doubted. She was a handsome woman, tall, stately, with white hair beautifully styled, and her clothes were the envy of every girl. Her English was so garbled with French, that even the poorest French student found it easier to learn French in a hurry than to attempt conversation in English. All of her students spoke excellent French. . . .

Silent hour was torture at first, but we soon learned to look forward to the quiet time to be alone with our thoughts. This was only one of the many intangible habits we acquired under Miss Sabin's wise guidance, which some of us carried into adult life. Imagine having to stay in our rooms from two to six [o'clock in the evening] every Sunday!

We had to observe silent hour if we were in Holton Hall, but we could accept invitations to homes of the day students or other friends in Milwaukee, with written permission from our parents. . . .

Almost overnight, pompadours came in. Every female in the civilized world had to have her hair "dressed" like that of Madame Pompadour of the French court. American hairdressers (stylists would be the word today) were quick to invent a practical means for those women beyond the reach of a hairdresser financially or geographically. Their new contraption was called a *rat,* which was made of woven wire mesh like window screening and was about the size and shape of a link of bologna sausage They were of various sizes and came in black, brown, pale gold and silver. The ends had loops of tape which could be tied together with a short shoelace at the back. To fasten one in place, the hair was brushed down over the face and back, the rat tied on, and the long hair pulled up and tucked in neatly all around the rat. After a week's practice, it was easy. This accomplished, the next addition was *puffs*. They were about the size of a doll's wig of real hair, could be rolled up to the desired size and pinned on, as many or as few as personal choice demanded.

One day at chapel, Miss Sabin announced that there was a real problem throughout the school — increasing tardiness at breakfast. She had looked into the matter carefully and had decided the cause might be the additional time it took to produce the extravagant hair styles that were appearing every day. The only solution she could see was to have rising bell rung at 5:30 instead of 6:30. She would give the student body one week to remedy the situation.

The next morning every seminary girl in Holton Hall came to breakfast with her hair slicked back from her forehead and pinned up in a knot at the back, exactly as Miss Sabin wore hers.

. . . [There were] roars of laughter. . . .

The following days all girls were on time for breakfast and all rats were in place. . . .

It had been Miss Sabin's ambition, from the time she took the presidency of Downer College . . . , to revive the excellent course in Home Economy that had flourished there under Mary Jarvis, her immediate predecessor. In 1901 the trustees had granted . . . the use of two rooms in the Merrill Hall basement and permission to use the chemistry laboratory on the third floor. This was a start, though meager. At about the same time the idea of a Domestic Science or Home Economy course took root throughout the state in normal and high schools, but trained teachers were in short supply.

Miss Sabin provided the answer to that by introducing a teacher training course for college girls. This was a two-year course leading to a teaching certificate. But if a student took it in conjunction with her regular four-year college course, she would graduate with her B.A. degree plus the teaching certificate. Enrollment increased steadily, and so did the crowding in the basement, but still there was no physical evidence of the Home Economics department other than the aroma of fresh bread coming up the stairs.

Whenever Miss Sabin had been called upon to make a public speech on education, or women's rights, or whatever, she always managed to mention her hope for a professional college course in Home Economics. She had a subtle and charming way of dropping a hint at just the right time and place, such as when she addressed the state Federation of Women's Clubs in 1902. It was at this meeting that Mrs. J. Alfred [Helen Cheney] Kimberly of Neenah picked up the "hint" that started a $10,000 endowment fund for Home Economics [to be matched by clubwomen]. . . . [2]

. . . The new building — Kimberly Hall — was dedicated during commencement week in 1908. Now with ample space, the most up-to-date equipment and laboratory, Miss Sabin announced in the 1908–1909 catalog under Home Economics: "In addition to the two year diploma course, the college will introduce a four year course leading to the degree of *Bachelor of Science.*" This was a distinct honor, for Milwaukee-Downer College was the first women's college to offer a four-year degree in Home Economics.

It had been general knowledge for some time that Milwaukee-Downer College could not rank as a bona fide collegiate institution as long as it maintained a preparatory [high school-level] department, and the time would come for complete physical separation. That time came in 1908, when construction started for new seminary buildings across Hartford Avenue and directly opposite our horseshoe drive. When school opened in September, and I realized the full meaning of these buildings, the thought struck me: my class, the fourth years, would be the last seminary class to graduate from this beloved campus. But this was progress, Miss Sabin reminded us. Progress was always a movement ahead . . . progress meant change.

We welcomed the change in our status as fourth years. We were now permitted to study in the beautiful Elizabeth Greene Library, but we could not draw books. We could go downtown into the big Milwaukee stores without a chaperone, if there were at least three of us. But the happiest times were when Miss Sabin invited us to have tea in her suite on wintry days when the weather was too cold for walking. There were never more than four girls. Miss Sabin was always informal, and cordial and willing to talk a little about herself. Since commencement was very much on our minds, we asked her one day to tell us about hers.

"I never had any." She spoke softly, then continued. "You see, I never graduated from anything. I spent a lot of time in classes and libraries, just getting educated. But," she raised her voice, "I don't recommend such a course to you!" . . .

. . . When most women of fifty years were beginning to think of retiring, she moved into the new Milwaukee-Downer campus and began the most strenuous years of her life. It took another twenty years of her efforts to help integrate academic work with nurses' training, leading to a Bachelor of Science Nursing degree. It had been a long life's work. Beginning with *McGuffey's Readers* in a rural schoolhouse, Miss Sabin had fought and won struggles to raise homemaking, teaching, and nursing to the status of professions worthy of four-year college degrees. No longer were they just jobs. At seventy years of age, Miss Sabin reached her goals and resigned as president of Milwaukee-Downer College. . . .

In retirement, Sabin remained active in the American Association of University Women and in the state chapter of the League of Women Voters, as she had in its predecessor organization, the Wisconsin Woman Suffrage Association. She also served on the state board of education but continued to teach Bible classes, as she had at Milwaukee-Downer College, where a chair in religious education was endowed in her name. A science building also was named for her in 1928. More than two decades later, in 1949, Sabin died at the age of ninety-eight.

Sabin's thirty-year record of service as president of Milwaukee-Downer College was matched by her successor, Lucia Russell Briggs, Ph.D., who served as president until Wisconsin's first college for women celebrated its centennial in 1951. However, little more than a dozen years later, in 1964, the college closed and consolidated with Lawrence University, where women graduates to this day receive diplomas from both Lawrence and Milwaukee-Downer College.[3]

The legacy of Ellen Clara Sabin and other pioneers in women's education lives on in Milwaukee. The Downer seminary merged with other secondary schools tracing back to the Tochter Institut (see "Madame Mathilda Franziska Anneke" in chapter 3), to become the University School of Milwaukee. The state bought the Downer buildings, now part of the campus of the University of Wisconsin–Milwaukee, which had started as Milwaukee State Normal School in 1885 with the same mission as that of the first women's college in Wisconsin: to provide teacher preparation, primarily for women students.

In 1909, when Friend was a "fourth year," the normal school also moved from downtown Milwaukee to a site next to the Downer campus, on the same trolley line, to serve the city's daughters who could not afford a private college education. One Russian Jewish immigrant to Milwaukee, Goldie Mabowehz, never graduated from the normal school but became the prime minister of Israel — and the most famous alumna of any Wisconsin campus. The Golda Meir Library at her alma mater, now the University of Wisconsin–Milwaukee, stands across the street from the site of Helen Cheney Kimberly Hall, since demolished. However, many historic Downer buildings still serve University of Wisconsin–Milwaukee students, and the Downer Woods nature conservancy now is protected by state statute. Holton Hall now houses offices, classrooms, and the "drawing room," which was recently reopened for student use after refurbishing to resemble the original decor donated decades ago by Downer trustees, including an oil portrait of Sabin. Another building, once destined for demolition but also recently remodeled, again houses science departments and still bears the name of a remarkable educator: Ellen C. Sabin Hall.

Her legacy also lives on in other remarkable women still well-known in Milwaukee as — despite their years — the "Downer girls," a group given "intangible courage and self-confidence" by Sabin, as her biographer wrote here. Their indomitable spirit also inspired another writer, Maud Hart Lovelace, to use the campus as a locale in the "Betsy-Tacy" series of girls' books, recently reissued to mark the sixtieth anniversary of publication. In Betsy in Spite of Herself, the heroine visits Milwaukee-Downer Seminary "day student" Tib "Browner" Muller, said to be based on Lovelace's girlhood friend Marjorie "Midge" Gerlach; she could have been a classmate of Friend's, as the book is set in 1907, her era here. The period piece still brings touring "Tacyites" to the campus and other sites in the series such as the Pabst Theater. Other readers who revel in the books include writers Judy Blume *and Anna Quindlen, who calls the character an early "feminist icon" and became an admirer of the series because "Betsy" is treated seriously as a girl who wants to grow up to be a writer, and never, in any of the many tales, is told that she cannot realize her goal.*[4]

*Neita Oviatt Friend also had ambitions to be a writer and heeded Sabin's admonition to "do your best, give your best, use the good sense God gave you." An officer and editor of the Wisconsin Regional Writers Association, she authored articles on local history, short stories, and children's stories. She also gave anonymously to many good causes, including the Wisconsin Historical Society. A member of the board of curators for more than twenty years, Friend worked for the founding in 1959 of its Circus World Museum in Baraboo. In 1976, at the age of eighty-six, she still was writing at her Pine Lake home. This "historical sketch," which reached sixty pages before revision for publication, was her last work. Neita Oviatt Friend died in 1984.*

## NOTES

1. Evans, *Born for Liberty,* 71; Flexner, *Century of Struggle,* 31.
2. [Helen Cheney Kimberly continued the project and also endowed a scholarship fund in her name. On the future of the field of home economics on another campus in the state, see "Nellie Kedzie Jones's Advice to Farm Women" in chapter 6.]
3. For Sabin's correspondence with her successor at Milwaukee-Downer College, see Virginia A. Palmer, "Faithfully Yours, Ellen C. Sabin: Correspondence Between Ellen C. Sabin and Lucia R. Briggs from January 1921, to August 1921," *WMH* 67, no. 1 (Autumn 1983), 17–41.
4. Maud Hart Lovelace, *Betsy in Spite of Herself* (New York: HarperCollins, 2000). Blume and Quindlen authored forwards for new editions, Blume for *Betsy and Tacy Go Over the Big Hill* and Quindlen for *Betsy and the Great World.*

# The Library Career of Lutie Eugenia Stearns

EARL TANNENBAUM

WMH 39, No. 3 (Spring 1956): 159–165

*Lutie E. Stearns moved to Milwaukee from Massachusetts with her family at the age of five. The youngest of eleven children, including ten girls, Stearns was born in 1866, so she had missed "the suffering of my mother's brood . . . during Civil War days" when her father served at the front. He had "received his small pay irregularly" and sent little home. So her mother had supported her family by braiding straw for hats for "a few pennies a yard" while her children slept. "After the war was over, her locks were gray," Stearns later wrote.[1]*

*Stearns's mother educated her daughters on women's rights, inspiring her youngest daughter to start her career as a public speaker early, and from an unusual podium. "I made my first plea for Woman Suffrage at ten years of age from the top of the wood shed in the backyard of our Milwaukee home," Stearns recalled. "Mother had heard Susan B. Anthony the day before and had given me her arguments, which were so convincing to my juvenile mind that I decided to let the children of the neighborhood have the benefit of them. When suffrage was finally won, forty-four years later, a friend . . . telephoned me, telling me that she had heard my original plea and congratulated me on my final victory!" But it would be years before she would speak in public again, because Stearns suffered from a lifelong severe stutter that she blamed on an overly critical teacher in a "one-room country school" near the Soldiers' Home, where her father served as physician and surgeon (see "'This Noble Monument'" in chapter 3).[2]*

*However, her unhappy home life also may have had a role in her diffidence. Her family moved into the city in the 1880s, when her father became Milwaukee's municipal health officer. But he "suddenly deserted the family," divorced her mother, moved back to Massachusetts, and remarried when Stearns was a high school student. Her mother never "made mention of the desertion" but did ensure that Stearns finished high school and enrolled in the first classes at Milwaukee State Normal School, now the University of Wisconsin–Milwaukee.[3]*

*Stearns's teachers eased her "extreme sensitiveness" about public speaking and gave her courage to undertake teaching after she graduated in 1886. She taught in the Milwaukee Public Schools for two years, for a salary of $15 per month. With few materials she faced her first class, a fourth grade of seventy-two children — and only sixty-four seats — for which "there was but one reader for the room, no supplementary reading matter, nor any sort of a school library," she recalled. So began her speaking career as a fund-raiser, despite her "speech defect." As Stearns wrote, "no one knows the agony I endured in my first public talks through my stammering and stuttering." Yet no one could stop her from speaking thousands of times for her causes in coming years, starting with a series of lectures at her school to raise $75 for reading materials. "I also begged and borrowed books from my friends. For bookcases, I used soap boxes," she wrote.[4]*

*Stearns also turned to one of the first "free libraries" in the state, in Milwaukee. Most libraries then required subscription fees of twenty-five to fifty cents every three months, more than most working women, men, or families could afford. For the next two years, after school every week, she "would take three boys and six market baskets and travel by horse car to the Public Library," which was then on a second floor over a Milwaukee storefront. Stearns's enterprise impressed the head of the circulating department, Minnie M. Oakley, who soon left her position for one at the Wisconsin Historical Society and suggested the schoolteacher as her successor.[5]*

*Stearns modestly credited another member of the Milwaukee Public Library staff, Theresa West, with founding the Wisconsin Free Library Association in 1891, when only thirty-five free libraries had started in the state and 80 percent of residents lived in rural areas with no access to library books. However, Stearns downplayed her own role as an officer of the association in lobbying for a state law to fund the founding of free public libraries, according to author Earl Tannenbaum. He attributes passage of the law in 1895 to Stearns as secretary-treasurer of the association. With the enabling legislation, she became the first secretary of the subsequent Wisconsin Free Library Commission and then, in 1897, its first salaried staff member. Similarly, as he wrote regarding the traveling libraries that she started statewide for rural readers, "she was not the originator but rather the missionary who believes in an idea, develops it, and works unselfishly to make it a reality." In sum, writes Tannenbaum, Stearns was "an apostle of progress in a world of change" in Wisconsin.[6]*

*His brief biography follows, the story of a little girl who never lost her stutter but still grew up to become a legend to librarians nationwide and left her legacy in towns across the state, where hundreds of libraries began because Lutie E. Stearns had spoken there.*

In library history the legend of Lutie E. Stearns is confirmed by the story of her activities during the period 1895–1914 when she worked for the Wisconsin Free Library Commission. An apostle of traveling libraries and free libraries, she, like other library pioneers of her time, channeled all of her amazing energy into the promotion of library service. . . .

To get a better understanding of Lutie Stearns's work, it is necessary to consider briefly the time in which she lived. It must be remembered that during the latter part of the nineteenth century the United States was seething with social improvement movements of all kinds. . . . From the lyceum, the chautauqua, women's clubs and university extension enterprises came educational leaders who wanted to bring literacy and culture to the foreigner, the working man, and the farmer. Social reformers zealously advocating better working conditions, penal reforms, and woman suffrage also saw the need for brightening the lives of the poor and for combating the big city vices of drink and delinquency.

The library movement fed upon and was a part of all of these. The library could educate. It could help combat delinquency and vice by furnishing a pleasant place for young working people to spend their leisure hours. And as the library was part and parcel of this broad social movement, so was Lutie Stearns a vital part of the library movement — both as a manifestation and as a motivator. Many other leaders rose to meet the challenge of a world changing for the better. Though much of her work was done in Wisconsin, it had significance in the national library movement, whose growth was being promoted by philanthropists. With the experience she gained in the field, she could pass on to other librarians valuable firsthand accounts of how to expand library service by means of traveling libraries. Thus she was able to inspire librarians all over the country with her ideas that she did not hesitate to promulgate at state, regional, and national association meetings. . . .

From the beginning she was firmly convinced that she should spend most of her time in the undeveloped areas of the state — the north and the northwest — for here the farmers and lumberjacks lived in comparative isolation and they were the ones who needed the services of the state. As she saw it, the first duty of the Library Commission was to nurture and foster the small library. Only by liberally sprinkling collections of books everywhere could they hope to reach the people. So wherever she went there sprang up in her wake traveling libraries, library stations, and public libraries. Library stations were placed in rural post offices, homes, schools, lumber camps, and factories.

. . . Her official reports on her community visits are revealing. One series of reports covers the seven-year period 1896–1903. During this time she visited 130 towns and cities at least once, usually several times. These visits included a lecture to arouse interest and follow-up visits to capitalize on the aroused interest. A typical laconic report reads: "F. A. Hutchins [chairman of the Wisconsin State Library Association] first interested citizens in establishment of library. L. E. Stearns lectured Sept. 19, 1896. Visited Jan. 4 '99, June 1903, and November 1903. Miss Gattiker organized the library."

[Stearns's] many services ranged from helping to found libraries to advice on library problems in general. She conducted surveys, recommended procedures for better library service, advised and did the detailed work for obtaining Carnegie grants, assisted local librarians in book selection and in getting trained librarians (the commission operated a library school and training institutes), and met with local town councils.[7] Wherever possible she tried to convert subscription libraries to free libraries. She spoke at library dedications, attended cornerstone ceremonies, and recruited librarians. In one period, from January to June, she gave fifty-six lectures. No work, as long as it was concerned with libraries, was too much for her. Her activity and vitality seemed boundless. Consider the conditions of travel during these times. Then consider that she covered distances and maintained rigorous schedules that would be difficult to keep today in spite of our modern means of transportation. A sample week's itinerary showed that she covered approximately 550 miles in northern and central Wisconsin.

Besides her work within Wisconsin, she visited library associations over the country promoting and arousing interest in the kind of work she was doing. She appeared before associations in Iowa, Illinois, Canada, Massachusetts, Pennsylvania, and the District of Columbia, explaining how traveling libraries could be started and maintained. She also wrote innumerable articles on the subject in the *Wisconsin Library Bulletin* and the *Library Journal.* For her, this work with people was a great adventure. She managed to convey her own enthusiasm to young aspiring librarians whom she recruited in the schools and colleges of the state. Some of the older librarians in Wisconsin explain that they became librarians because of Lutie Stearns. One of these recalls some of the "awe and wonder" with which she, a girl of thirteen, listened to her "proclaim the gospel of the Village Library."

The history of the growth of the traveling library system in Wisconsin is a history of Lutie Stearns's work. . . . Private donors, including individuals and associations, especially women's clubs, provided the money for traveling libraries in these early days. In 1903 the Department of Traveling Libraries within the commission, with Lutie Stearns as its chief, was created. With such funds as were authorized, the department was able to build up its own book collection. . . .

The Department of Traveling Libraries had three different sizes of libraries that circulated — one of 30 volumes for the "isolated hamlet;" one of 35 for the regular stations; and one of 100 which was rented to smaller public libraries at the rate of $12 for six months. Selecting books carefully, she established well-rounded collections of current popular fiction, nonfiction, and children's books. Individual requests for titles were also honored.

Another important activity of the department was the circulation of study libraries to clubs and interested groups. These study libraries consisted of selected books and detailed study outlines on some phase of art, history, literature, or some other subject. Actually they were a forerunner of and afterwards a part of the vast [University of Wisconsin Extension] program which came into being in the early 1900s. Other special collections included foreign-language libraries made up of thirty-five volumes each written in German, Yiddish, Danish, and Norwegian, which were rented to foreign-language groups at the rate of $7 for six months.

All of these services were developed and administered by Lutie Stearns. Before her department was organized in 1903, she had been busy for seven years promoting library work of all kinds. Now as administrator and actually the only field worker of her department (an assistant took over the work with women's clubs in 1914), her scope became somewhat narrower. As a result she chafed a bit at the reins.

When she resigned her position with the Wisconsin Free Library Commission on September 4, 1914, and thus ended twenty-five years of library work, she did not do so on a sudden impulse. . . . Years of working for social and educational improvement in Wisconsin had made her eager to strike out on a wider scale. She was passionately devoted to the cause of women's rights. . . . Then, too, at forty-eight she was beginning to get physically tired of keeping crowded schedules and driving over rough roads. She had had a serious illness in 1913, and early in 1914 her mother and a sister died — a double blow which caused her to have a nervous breakdown. There was also a hint of friction between herself and the then secretary of the commission. At any rate, all these reasons combined to make her a "free lance," as she called it. Though she severed her official connections, she offered her services as a lecturer for the Library Commission.

As she turned toward her new career, she could look back with no regrets upon her accomplishments. It is estimated that she had effectively aided in establishing 150 free public libraries and 1,400 traveling libraries, including 14 county systems. Her main contributions as a library pioneer were undoubtedly in the field of public libraries, traveling libraries, and library extension work. But she had many other ideas about library work, which she tried to promote. When she was a young librarian in the Milwaukee Public Library she became interested in work with children. She advocated children's read-ing rooms, good selection of children's books, and teacher responsibility for guiding their reading. Always she insisted that the library should keep up with modern times, that it should be a community center, that it must actively compete with the movies, dance halls, cars, and card playing for the leisure time of the people. . . . Libraries should use modern methods of advertising. They should have open shelves, cheerful rooms, and attractive books. . . . She realized the importance of educational films and their use in libraries as early as 1913. . . . [S]he pointed out in an address to a local library association that educational films existed, that they were available, and that they should be used by librarians. . . .

Having resigned from the commission and nearing middle age, Lutie Stearns could have stopped for a while and rested on her laurels. However, she launched out upon a new career for herself. She became a leader in the women's clubs of her state and nation. And she devoted herself to lecturing and public service. It is interesting to note her newfound sense of freedom after she had left the Library Commission and had lectured for a month. She made delighted reference to her first month's venture, that netted her $325. . . .

. . . [I]n her personal life, she was shy and retiring. She never wanted publicity for herself. For her pet projects she could not get enough. Once, when asked for a publicity photograph she answered: "First as to the photograph — I never yet have had my picture in the Milwaukee papers, as I object to that sort of publicity. I am perfectly willing to have *library* work exploited, but the personal side I have always tried to keep in the background." . . .

. . . She said what she had to say firmly and directly. For example, in 1917 she became involved in a public dispute concerning working conditions in the Milwaukee Public Library. At her own expense she had printed "An open letter on the public library situation" which was addressed to the chairman of the library board and which explained her views in no uncertain terms. Characteristically, this notice appeared at the end of the letter in bold-face type: "Notice to woman wage-earners: I shall be pleased to be informed of any abuses of woman in industry, store, or elsewhere, as to under-pay, working conditions, or otherwise. . . . "[8]

*Stearns remained unstoppable. "In all my later work and campaigns for various causes, I felt that I had something to say that might be of help, and I determined that my difficulty in speaking should not be an impediment," she wrote. She learned to write speeches in a selected vocabulary that for page after page avoided what she called "the vexing consonants."[9]*

*Stearns also battled skin cancer but toured thirty-eight states in two decades, lecturing on women's rights and working in woman suffrage campaigns in Iowa, Missouri, and Texas as well as serving as an officer of the Wisconsin Woman Suffrage Association in its last decade. She turned to women's work for world peace, touring Europe and studying at the Institute of the League of Nations in Geneva, Switzerland, and at the headquarters of the Quakers, her faith.[10]*

*Stearns returned to the United States at the start of the Great Depression, which caused a decline in her lecturing but led to another career as a freelance writer. A letter she wrote to the* Milwaukee Journal *on the plight of farmers brought a response from a farmwife that Stearns ought to write "again and again" to the paper. Editors agreed, especially legendary women's clubs editor Louise Cattoi, who hired Stearns as a contributing columnist. "As a Woman Sees It" ran from 1932 to 1935, even during Stearns's hospital stays owing to recurring skin cancer.[11]*

*Among her many honors, Lutie E. Stearns received a special accolade in 1942, the year before her death, from the American Library Association for service to the public and the profession in promoting and founding free public libraries in Wisconsin and nationwide. Almost six decades after her death, in 2000, the organization honored her again by naming her to its first-ever National Advocacy Honor Roll. As for her legacy, a national library ranking system also assessed Wisconsin in the top ten states in the nation for the quality of its libraries in 2000.[12]*

≈⊙≈

## NOTES

1. Lutie E. Stearns, "My Seventy-Five Years, Part I," *WMH* 42, no. 3 (Spring 1959): 212, and "My Seventy-Five Years, Part II," *WMH* 42, no. 4 (Summer 1959): 284.

2. Stearns, "My Seventy-Five Years, Part II," 282.

3. Stearns, "My Seventy-Five Years, Part III," *WMH* 43, no. 2 (Winter 1959–1960): 97.

4. Stearns, "My Seventy-Five Years, Part I," 215.

5. Ibid., 215–216. Oakley was born in Madison and began her library career in 1879 at the Madison Free Library, later served as assistant librarian of the Wisconsin Historical Society from 1889 to 1908, and then served at libraries in Seattle and Los Angeles, where she died in 1915.

6. Ibid.

7. [Andrew Carnegie, an immigrant from an impoverished family in Scotland who blamed their poverty in part on his father's illiteracy, then became a billionaire in America and donated $65 million during his lifetime alone for the founding of almost two thousand free libraries in the United States and many hundreds more around the world; see Theodore Jones, *Carnegie Libraries Across America: A Public Legacy* (Washington, D.C.: Preservation Press, 1997).]

8. . . . [Stearns's] "words — in speeches, articles, pamphlets, and letters — supplied firsthand accounts of her ideas and activities." [Records of the Wisconsin Free Library Commission, Wisconsin Free Library Association, as well as the *Wisconsin Library Bulletin,* and the *Library Journal* are in the WHS Archives.]

9. Stearns, "My Seventy-Five Years, Part III," 97.

10. Stearns, "My Seventy-Five Years, Part III," 99–105, 285–286.

11. Cattoi, of Hurley, covered women's news for the *Milwaukee Journal* for more than fifty years, starting in 1918; see Wells, *The Milwaukee Journal,* 450.

12. Dan Benson, "State Libraries Rank 9th in U.S. Rating," *Milwaukee Journal Sentinel,* October 6, 2002.

# Consumptive Citadel

## *The Crusade Against Tuberculosis in Eau Claire County, 1903–1917*

MARY ELLEN STOLDER

*WMH* 77, No. 4 (Summer 1994): 264–294

. . . Today most Americans believe it is the government's responsibility to protect the public's health as well as its property. But such was not always the case. In the late nineteenth century, a handful of states — with Wisconsin in the vanguard — entered the arena of public health and inaugurated a number of remarkably effective measures against a disease that was, in its time, a leading cause of death: tuberculosis. . . .

Tuberculosis (also known as *consumption* and, more technically, as *phthisis*) is an infectious bacterial disease, not highly contagious, but nevertheless communicable. The bacillus enters body tissues, forming tubercles (nodules), most commonly in the lungs. At the turn of the century, tuberculosis was regarded as "mysterious . . . intractable and capricious . . . an insidious, implacable theft of life."[1] "The wasting disease" was associated with overcrowded cities and slum conditions.

The virulence of the disease in densely populated industrial areas was never refuted. However, in 1911 medical experts were startled and perplexed by the findings of a survey of rural Dunn County, Wisconsin, which indicated that the incidence of tuberculosis in a sparsely populated rural county was in many instances higher than in Milwaukee. The evils of overcrowded dwellings and poor ventilation were just as deadly in the rich farmlands of western Wisconsin as they were amidst urban congestion.[2]

. . . Humans were most commonly infected by the repeated inhalation of contagion-laden air in the vicinity of the sick, who coughed up infectious sputum. But the dairy cow also played a role. In Wisconsin in the 1890s the public health campaign almost exclusively addressed the bovine transmission of tuberculosis through infected milk. Another target for public health intervention was damp, poorly drained soil — "the miasmic theory of disease regarded dampness and stagnant water as generators of epidemic diseases.". . .[3]

Still, in 1903, no cure was in sight. Rest and nourishment, as part of a monitored regimen, seemed to stem deterioration, though most physicians regarded death from tuberculosis as all but inevitable. Gradually the care and treatment of tubercular patients shifted from the home to institutions, [with] trained medical personnel. . . .

This transition from home treatment to institutionalization hinged upon the growing realization that victims of the disease might infect other members of a household. This became the primary argument for creating sanatoriums where infected individuals could be isolated from the healthy.

Before the establishment of a sanatorium in the western city of Eau Claire in 1913, a visiting nurse could only assist impoverished families to care for the far-advanced patient at home. Nurses relieved the burden of caretaking and provided nourishing food, relying on local charitable organizations for donations. They taught family members to destroy sputum expectorant by burning paper receptacles or disinfecting metal basins. They provided comfort and counsel as best they could. And while awaiting a fatal hemorrhage of a patient's ravaged lungs, they could only hope that the terrified children in the household would not witness the final, suffocating death throes of a family member.

As one Eau Claire mother said to visiting nurse Sarah West Ryder: "You don't know what it is to see someone you love just dying by inches, week by week, month by month, to see them growing paler and thinner, and to see them suffering with that racking cough . . . to see the color creep into the wasted cheek as the fever rises and the eyes grow bright. Oh, it is awful." . . .[4]

*After attempts to require reporting of cases failed, owing to economic repercussions for patients and for physicians, a sanatorium movement slowly advanced during the first decade of the twentieth century. Five years after Governor Robert M. La Follette appointed a gubernatorial commission, followed by legislative debate, the state finally built its first public sanatorium — known as "Statesan" — near Wales in rural Waukesha County in 1908. In the same year, twenty-two citizens founded the Wisconsin Anti-Tuberculosis Association (WATA) and immediately raised funds through a Christmas Seal campaign, only the second in the country — and soon the most successful such campaign in any state. Then WATA successfully lobbied for two laws enacted in 1911 that permitted counties to create their own sanatoriums and to provide funds for the care of indigent consumptives; the latter law was the first of its like in the nation. Wisconsin's fight against tuberculosis attracted considerable talent, especially two women: WATA's Edythe Tate, who provided the impetus for local campaigns, and Eau Claire's Jennie Shoemaker.[5]*

Jennie Damon Whittier Shoemaker was both an extraordinary woman and a social anomaly in her time: a divorced, working mother. When "The Christmas Seal Lady" died in 1951, a heartfelt tribute celebrated the life of a pathfinder, a woman deeply admired by both sexes, a true community matriarch richly endowed with an abundance of optimism and vigor. And of all the achievements cited in her obituary, the foremost was her much-esteemed leadership of the sanatorium campaign against tuberculosis. By all rights, when the Mt. Washington Sanatorium opened its doors in 1913, it should have been named after Jennie D. Shoemaker.

She was born on February 15, 1863, in Clemansville, Winnebago County, the daughter of Duwitt Damon and the former Julia Ann Wright. In 1894, at age thirty-one, Jennie moved to Eau Claire with her husband, Horace D. Whittier. The couple had two sons, Hugh, born in 1884, and Josiah, born in 1887. Jennie found employment as a school-teacher and was soon promoted to principal at one of the ward schools. . . . By 1898, the marriage had soured, and it ended in divorce in 1900.[6] Three months later, in September of 1900, Jennie remarried attorney Arthur H. Shoemaker, who was later Eau Claire city attorney. The partnership lasted until Arthur's death in 1950. The couple had one child, a daughter named Geanne Damon Shoemaker, born in 1903. The family later moved to a distinctive cobblestone house on Eau Claire's State Street, which remains today as a historic landmark.

After the birth of her daughter, Mrs. Shoemaker became a social and political activist nonpareil. She was a founder of the Eau Claire Anti-Tuberculosis Association and president of the Eau Claire Woman's Club during 1910–1911, 1914–1915, and 1924–1925. Her statewide prominence mounted with her election to several state offices, culminating in the presidency of the Wisconsin Federation of Women's Clubs in 1924. She is credited also with the founding of the *Wisconsin Clubwoman,* the journal of the state women's clubs, and she managed the magazine as editor until 1939. Her public involvement took her to New York City several times, representing such organizations as the Child Welfare League of Wisconsin and the district delegation to the 1939 New York World's Fair.[7]

Shoemaker's consummate skill as a grassroots community organizer became well-known. When she voiced her conviction, at a meeting discussing the need for a school nurse, "What we need in Eau Claire, we can get," the community took pause and listened.[8] The WATA appointed her to two terms on its board of directors. In 1914, she was the only woman to be elected to the board and the only member north of La Crosse or Madison. . . .

Though her personal motivations remain unclear — did she perhaps have a consumptive history in her family? — Jennie Shoemaker was crucial to the city's tuberculosis crusade. . . .

Eau Claire initiated action against consumption remarkably early. Mary McGrath, a wealthy widow and the daughter of lumber baron William Carson, organized the fist Visiting Nurse Association in Wisconsin in 1903. The visiting nurse, the precursor of today's public health nurse, provided bedside care to indigent families. The nurses' caseload not only included consumptive individuals, but also those stricken with common "visitors" such as diphtheria, scarlet fever, smallpox, and the dreaded typhoid fever.

McGrath had contacted the Henry Street Settlement of New York City to serve as a guide. At her own expense, she placed a nurse in training with the Chicago Visiting Nurse Association for three months. When Bertha Sofisberg completed the course, she was provided a salary of $50 a month and supplies for her daily rounds. Most commonly these included eggs, milk, and McGrath's homemade jelly. The VNA held monthly meetings and published an annual report in the local newspaper. Another notable accomplishment of this popular philanthropic organization was the sponsorship of a summer tent colony for consumptives, a decade before the availability of local sanatorium care.[9]

In 1905 a group of reform-minded citizens [in Eau Claire] formed the local voluntary society devoted exclusively to the battle against tuberculosis. . . . Several women were involved, including Jennie Shoemaker. . . .

The local association [in 1908] . . . engaged the Woman's Club to conduct the Christmas Seal campaign. In 1910, Eau Claire had sold more seals per capita than any other association in the state and earned two prizes from WATA: a public fountain and one month of service from the WATA's pioneering nurse, Sarah West Ryder. Both had far-reaching effects on the anti-tuberculosis movement in the city. When Eau Claire schools opened in the fall of 1910, each was equipped with a new "bubbler" — meaning a drinking fountain — which was installed near the library; and common drinking cups in public places were prohibited by law.[10] The new health nurse spent all of April 1911, in Eau Claire, coping with fifty consumptives and discovering eleven new cases of TB. In her report, Sarah Ryder noted the conditions in a local hospital ("scandalous") and expressed grave concern about local housing conditions, particularly at a group of poorly ventilated dwellings. . . . She devoted her efforts to house calls, case findings, and the supervision of disinfection. This last effort involved the use of a fumigation wagon: an airtight box on wheels housing a formaldehyde gas generator that propelled germ-killing gases onto furniture and bedding.[11]

After Nurse Ryder's departure, a Miss Morud, the first municipal tuberculosis nurse in Wisconsin, set to work in May 1911. Shortly after taking office, she nursed sixty-two patients, noting in her report that incomplete registration was a problem.[12] She distributed bedding, cots, tents, and sputum cups and provided bedside care and home education. She also alerted the local association that ailing consumptives were applying for admission at Statesan. Soon after well-publicized appearances by Edythe Tate of WATA, Dr. [Everett] Mason, and Mayor [J. B.] Fleming urging action, the county board in March 1912, passed a resolution to erect a sanatorium. . . .

. . . In characteristic fashion, Jennie Shoemaker adroitly stepped in and brokered an agreement with the county board: private donors would furnish all the equipment with another fund-raising campaign. Relieved of part of the capital expenditure, a grateful board accepted the offer. . . .

Many community groups became involved in the sanatorium plans. The summer and fall of 1913 was a busy fund-raising frenzy, with ice-cream socials and band concerts held to raise money. A list of needed furnishings was published by the local association. . . . The Woman's Club sewed fifty rugs to cover the wooden floors. . . .

Finally, the dream became a reality. Eau Claire now had one of seven public sanatoriums in the state. . . .

Mt. Washington Sanatorium proudly opened its doors on Monday morning, December 15, 1913. Several Eau Claire County residents were awaiting acceptance. One of the original admissions was a young Eau Claire woman, Signa Lyngaas. . . . Her admission had been approved by probate judge George Blum.[13] Miss Lyngaas would be the first among hundreds who could not afford sanatorium care. By mid-January of 1914, the census had increased to twenty . . .[including four] county residents transferred from Statesan. . . .

Lucy Ramstead, a registered nurse from Minneapolis, became the first superintendent of the sanatorium. A graduate of Eau Claire High School and the Minneapolis City Hospital, she had several years of relevant clinical experience.[14] She lived in the quarters provided on-site, along with three other staff members. For whatever reason, she apparently did not find the situation satisfying and resigned in April 1914, remaining until Mildred H. Lucia, R.N., could replace her in August. Mrs. Lucia settled into the sanatorium routine, remaining at her post for over a decade. Roy Mitchell, the sanatorium's first staff physician, tendered his resignation in less than six months. John F. Farr replaced him in February 1915.[15]

Under the vigilant care of these administrators, the patient routine followed the common precepts of the day: plenty of rest, fresh air, and a nourishing diet. Most patients were young adults, but Mt. Washington could also claim the largest number of children in any state sanatorium. By July 1914, thirteen children lived there, the youngest a child of two named Bruno, regarded by staff and patients alike as their special "pet."[16]

Children had a slightly different treatment protocol to follow: a total of three hours of play precisely interspersed with meals and lengthy rest periods. Brief outdoors walks on the slope of Mt. Washington constituted the prescribed exercise for adults. . . . [17]

Despite these little pleasures, sanatorium life was not entirely a carefree retreat from the world. Tubercular patients coped with homesickness, protracted boredom, lack of privacy, and well-founded fears of further deteriorating health. Sometimes the disease splintered and scarred families; older children were forced to work while a stricken breadwinner worried about the prolonged period of recovery ahead. Indeed, many patients, for reasons that are not entirely clear, left the Mt. Washington Sanatorium while still infectious. . . .

*The sanatorium served increasingly large numbers of patients, and trustees approved additions to the building. Despite these efforts, as many as one in four patients died in early years. The women of Eau Claire were enlisted, especially the "enlightened" Eau Claire Woman's Club, in the fight against tuberculosis as "missionaries of brightness and sanitation," according to the* Eau Claire Leader. *The clubwomen already regularly donated reading material and gifts at Christmastime for patients; they now undertook prevention campaigns in the community such as "Clean City Day" and — as ever — sponsored the annual Christmas Seal campaigns.[18]*

The proceeds from the sale of Christmas Seals in Eau Claire would provide milk, eggs, and warm clothing for the municipal tuberculosis nurse to distribute. With that in mind, legions of stalwart children diligently canvassed neighborhoods hoping to surpass the previous years' receipts. . . .

Despite the success of the annual Christmas Seal campaigns, other services offered by the WATA failed to attract a following in Eau Claire. The state organization painted a rosy picture of "open air" schools, but nothing could convince Eau Claire skeptics of its therapeutic merits.[19] By contrast, in southeastern Wisconsin, particularly in several Kenosha schools, classes were conducted outdoors, even in the most frigid weather. Selected students were also fed a nutritious diet as part of the program. Not surprisingly, tubercular children (or those exposed to the disease) who followed the supervised regimen gained weight.[20] Perhaps it was the Arctic-like northern Wisconsin climate that deterred the Eau Claire association from pressing the campaign. Even the sanatorium had second thoughts about the curative properties of cold air. As the sanatorium's annual report admitted in 1917, "In the fall of 1916, we had the east porches glassed in and heated. We received so many patients in advanced stages who cannot endure the extreme cold, we found it necessary to do this."[21]

In Eau Claire, as elsewhere, the crusade against TB was clearly strengthened by women's clubs. Across the United States, these groups were influenced by the currents of progressivism and shifted their focus from cultural pursuits to unorganized areas such as the tuberculosis crusade.[22] The local tuberculosis association was to some extent a paper organization under the auspices of Associated Charities, which itself was an auxiliary organization of the Woman's Club. In Eau Claire, the club became quickly identified with the tuberculosis movement and raised a total of $3,081.10 for the founding of the county sanatorium.[23]

Jennie Shoemaker, as club president in 1915, resumed the seal campaign after a two-year hiatus. . . .

. . . And the 1917 seal campaign proved to be one of the best yet. But the anti-TB crusade had to share the spotlight with other events. The "boys" of Company E of the Wisconsin National Guard, just back from the punitive expedition on the Mexican border to be remobilized for European trench warfare, rightfully claimed most of the community's attention. And, as might be expected, Liberty Bonds competed with Christmas Seals for public support. In view of these momentous worldwide events, how was the WATA to sustain interest in another war — the war on consumption? . . .

. . . Robust sales of Christmas Seals reaffirmed the efforts of the WATA and the tremendous spirit of sacrifice among the public. In due course the khaki-clad boys of Company E embarked across the ocean, Liberty Bonds sold well, and local housewives declared a "kitchen war on Kaiserism."

In the wake of the Great War, the Eau Claire association continued its commitment to education and the provision of services, guided by the capable hand of the WATA. Traveling clinics were initiated in Wisconsin in 1919, using a cadre of recruited physicians who traveled around the state to examine contacts of tubercular victims. In Eau Claire, physicians examined 206 persons in 1921, of whom twenty-eight were found to be active cases. In 1922, 449 Eau Claire residents turned out for the clinic; eighty-five were found to be infected. . . . [24] Though the prospect for a cure seemingly remained remote, the death rate from tuberculosis steadily declined. It took a generation, but in 1962, the denouement of the WATA crusade was announced. . . . [25]

. . . Finally, on September 1, 1974, Mt. Washington Santorium formally ceased operations. . . . [26]

What conclusions may be drawn from the crusade against tuberculosis in Eau Claire? First, a local elite, sincere protagonists of progressive ideals, provided generous working and financial support. No one doubted that the battle was worth fighting; few balked at the cost. Second, the sanatorium, in its formative years, provided humane, compassionate care. In the sanatorium itself, there was a high rate of mortality and morbidity, for a cure was far from certain. Third, Jennie Shoemaker was right: in 1915, what Eau Claire needed, it could get. Even as wartime obligations loomed, the citizens of Eau Claire summoned the wherewithal for the tuberculosis crusade. Tuberculosis was sometimes a subordinate concern, but it was never neglected.

. . . [I]n recent years a number of core assumptions about La Follette and other progressive reformers have been questioned by revisionist historians. Were these exalted reformers on the side of the angels or were they, after all, self-promoting elitists guided by less charitable motives?

As in most human affairs, the actions of the progressive reformers did not always correspond to their rhetoric. Indeed, as Michael Kammen has written, "in their heart of hearts they were deeply conservative and only advocated moderate reform as a means of forestalling much more radical change . . . [and were] basically committed to the status quo. . . . " Still, however tangled and conflicted their motives, these crusaders and reformers represented a "unique and transitional generation." Somehow they "differed in temper from those who preceded and those who followed them."[27]

Tuberculosis threatened many lives. To their everlasting credit, the progressives recognized the threat and did not shrink from what they viewed as their duty in meeting it. . . .

*Jennie Damon Whittier Shoemaker devoted decades to civic betterment and beautification in Eau Claire. "The Christmas Seal Lady" also initiated a community tradition with the city's first municipal Christmas tree in 1915, then chaired the local council of defense during World War I and made Eau Claire a model of wartime mobilization, according to author Mary Ann Stolder. "The trees along the highway from Eau Claire to Chippewa Falls were another of her inspirations," planted by the woman's club "in tribute to the doughboys serving in France." Shoemaker also was a suffragist, and after the war, she served as an alternate delegate to the Republican national convention in 1920 — the first year that Wisconsin women had the right to vote in a presidential election.*

*A decade later, during the Great Depression when her neighbors needed employment, Shoemaker helped to organize a $100,000 job fund for the city of Eau Claire. She gave decades more to her community until her death in 1951, at the age of eighty-eight. The* Eau Claire Leader *eulogized that "there was not a worthwhile project in the city of Eau Claire that Mrs. Shoemaker was not leading," and concluded that "it is hard to realize that no longer will civic leaders be able to say: 'Let's ask Mrs. Shoemaker.'"[28]*

## Notes

1. Susan Sontag, *Illness as Metaphor* (New York, 1977), 5.

2. Harold Holand, *House of Open Doors* (Milwaukee, 1958), 63–64. For the original study, see Katherine Gedney Pinkerton, "The Tuberculosis Situation in Dunn County, 1911," in the Wisconsin Lung Association Papers, box 9, file 8, WHS Archives.

3. Michael E. Teller, *The Tuberculosis Movement: A Public Health Campaign in the Progressive Era* (New York, 1988), 14.

4. *Crusader,* December 1911.

5. Teller, *Tuberculosis Movement,* 50, 71–73; Holand, *House of Open Doors,* 33, 69–76; Louise Fenton Brand,

"Epic Fight: Wisconsin's Winning War on TB," in the Wisconsin Lung Association Papers, 66–67, 136–137, manuscript no. 772, box 4, folder 20, WHS Archives; Harold Holand, "Twenty-Two Against the Plague: The Founding of the Wisconsin Anti-Tuberculosis Association," *WMH* 42 (Autumn 1958):29–54; *Eau Claire Leader,* December 11, 1915.

6. Eau Claire County, Circuit Court, Record No. 7029, in the Area Research Center, University of Wisconsin–Eau Claire.

7. *Eau Claire Leader,* July 24, 1951; *Milwaukee Journal,* July 24, 1951.

8. *Eau Claire Leader,* March 30, 1915. . . .

9. Holand, *House of Open Doors,* 91.

10. Lois Barland, *The Rivers Flow On: A Record of Eau Claire, Wisconsin, from 1910–1960* (Stevens Point, 1965), 258.

11. Executive Secretary's Report, 1911, box 1, folder 5, Wisconsin Lung Association Papers.

12. *Crusader,* April 1912.

13. Eau Claire County, Probate Court, Record No. 3750, in the Area Research Center, University of Wisconsin–Eau Claire; . . . *Eau Claire Leader,* July 15, 1914.

14. *Eau Claire Leader,* November 12, 1913.

15. . . . Mt. Washington Sanatorium, Board of Trustees Minutes, October, 1914, Eau Claire Center of Care, Eau Claire.

16. *Eau Claire Leader,* July 15, 1914.

17. *Crusader,* January 1914.

18. *Eau Claire Leader,* April 22, 25, and 26, and May 2, 1914, and December 18, 1915.

19. Ibid., August 15, 1916.

20. Teller, *Tuberculosis Movement,* 113–116.

21. Eau Claire County, Annual Reports of the Eau Claire County Asylum, the County Poor Farm, and Mt. Washington Sanatorium, 1916–1917. Area Research Center, University of Wisconsin–Eau Claire.

22. Teller, *Tuberculosis Movement,* 48.

23. Eau Claire Woman's Club, Annual Announcements, 1916–1917.

24. Wisconsin Lung Association Papers, 1924, box 1, folder 2.

25. Tuberculosis Scrapbook (1945–1949), vol. 1, series 904, Wisconsin Lung Association Papers. . . .

26. Mark Wilkum, unpublished manuscript, July 8, 1985, Eau Claire Center of Care. . . .

27. Michael Kammen, *Mystic Chords of Memory: The Transformation of Tradition in American Culture* (New York, 1991), 66, 271.

28. Barland, *Rivers Flow On,* 210; *Eau Claire Leader,* July 25, 1951.

# The Two Worlds of Belle Case La Follette[1]

## NANCY UNGER

*WMH* 83, No. 2 (Winter 1999–2000): 83–110

Belle Case La Follette, it has been frequently noted, was deemed "my wisest and best counselor" by her husband, Wisconsin progressive great Robert M. La Follette. She chose to fulfill that counselor's role in remarkable ways throughout their forty-three years of married life, perhaps most significantly by earning a law degree, yet never practicing law herself. This decision was one of many that allowed her to function as her husband's equal in the professional matters that affected him publicly, while reserving for herself a more private and personal role. . . .

In an obituary entitled "Wisconsin's Matriarch," Belle Case La Follette was hailed by the *New York Times* as "perhaps the least known, yet the most influential of all American women who have had to do with public affairs in this country." In a separate story, the *Times* credited her low public profile to the fact that "her personality along with her work was merged in the fame of her menfolk."[2] In truth, Belle Case La Follette was . . . an important reformer in her own right.[3] Throughout her life, she spoke in support of world disarmament and civil rights, but always and most avidly for women's rights. All three, she believed, were inextricably bound together: "This business of being a woman is, in many ways, like being a member of a despised race.". . .[4]

Even those who have not overlooked Belle La Follette's reform contributions have tended to romanticize her character while ignoring important social contexts. . . . Which of her choices are revealing of her particular personality and which the result of the unique intersection of her time and place in history, especially as determined by her class, gender, and race? For the life of Belle La Follette reveals the great changes that affected American women as the gender prescriptions of the early to mid-nineteenth century gave way — or rather, led the way — to the challenges and reforms of the twentieth. . . . She struggled mightily with the strengths and limitations that each century's prescribed gender roles had to offer a woman of her position and class. . . .

. . . Ideally, [women's] pure, domestic, feminine world was wholly divorced from the tainted masculine world of politics, business, and money. In reality, however, the two worlds intertwined. Women discovered that to protect their sole basis of power, they often had no recourse but to immerse themselves in the world of men. . . . The course from domestic to public life was a long and often convoluted one, but it was a journey a vast number of women felt they had no choice but to undertake. . . .

Belle Case, like so many other women born in the mid-nineteenth century, would inherit these conflicting messages and struggle with them. She viewed women as significant contributors to society, never as weak or ornamental, and her strong beliefs can be traced to her family's influence and support. As a child, she idolized her grandmother, Lucetta Moore Case, for her calm, capable response to life's demands. Even before Belle's birth [in 1859], women like her grandmother were beginning to become politically active, establishing the tradition of reform in Wisconsin, laying the foundation upon which Belle would later build. . . .

During the formative years of Belle's early childhood . . . Wisconsin women seasoned by the abolitionist movement pounced upon the growing evils of alcohol consumption. In their temperance crusades, they honed their organizational skills and concentrated their forces. . . . Demands for votes for women in Wisconsin would follow on the heels of one of the most active temperance crusades in the country [see Introduction to chapter 4]. . . .[5]

Belle would come to admire Wisconsin's various activists and add her own steady, calm voice to the call for myriad reforms to benefit women, but as she left for the University of Wisconsin in 1875, the bulk of her heroes could be found closer to home [in Baraboo]. In addition to her strong and self-sufficient grandmother, Belle Case greatly revered her own parents, Anson and Mary Nesbit Case. They were farmers who placed a high value on a university education and gladly sacrificed to ensure that their only daughter benefit from such an experience. . . . She excelled in her studies: although she was more than four years younger than her future husband, the two were in the same class and she, in sharp contrast to Bob, finished near the top. Exceedingly conscientious, Belle never missed a class or was late. . . .

. . . In her senior oration, "Learning to See," Belle criticized adults for subverting children's natural curiosity by insisting that they conform to preconceived standards. Her speech won the prestigious Lewis Prize for the best essay or oration produced by a member of the graduating class and was delivered at commencement in the assembly chamber of the state capitol [in] 1879.[6]

Belle and Bob were initially attracted to each other by their mutual interests in speech and reform, in addition to their similar rural backgrounds. They began to see each other regularly, meeting frequently to work on various speeches. . . . Reluctant to commit herself romantically, Belle preferred to keep their relationship purely on the level of friendship, "free from sentiment, so lighthearted and joyous," at least until they had finished college. "Mamma laughed when I proposed to her," Bob would later tell their children. His persistence paid off at the end of their junior year, although the engagement was kept a secret for almost twelve months.[7]

[Bob] La Follette's diary for 1879 includes entries for only a few days, but it reveals the sharp contrast between his feelings for women in general and his feelings toward Belle Case in particular. Within its pages he staunchly maintains the prescribed gender standards of the day in romantic, flowing language: all women are inherently weak, helpless, tender, virtuous, and consumed with yearning to be fulfilled by a home and family. By contrast, men are physically and intellectually stronger. Although frequently ruled by crude passion, they remain the "natural guardian and chivalrous protector" of women. Such notions, however romantic and chauvinistic, were contradicted by Belle's obvious reluctance, despite their engagement, to fully and openly commit herself to him. Bob's idealistic certainty and eloquence on the true nature of woman disappeared completely when he wrote about Belle, rendering him an insecure, anxious man in the throes of a love he feared was unrequited. . . . [8]

Upon graduation, Belle both taught and served as assistant principal at Spring Green High School, thirty miles west of Madison. She enjoyed immensely the sense of independence, pride, and accomplishment it brought her and was reluctant to spend time with her fiancé. Bob's diary entry describing their first weekend visit reveals a most unhappy and insecure suitor. . . .

. . . In a striking reversal of the prescribed gender roles, her pleasure mattered more to him than his own, and he seemed to be almost completely at her mercy. . . .

More than two years after these diary entries were recorded, Belle Case overcame her reluctance and married Bob. Perhaps his resentment of Belle's coolness during their long engagement contributed to Bob's having to make a note to "remind" himself to attend the ceremony, ostensibly because he was so immersed in his duties as the new Dane County district attorney. The ceremony was held New Year's Eve, 1881, in the Case home in Baraboo. It was attended only by the two families and a Unitarian minister, who honored Belle's request that the word "obey" be omitted from the marriage vows. Immediately following, Bob returned to his office to complete his day's work. The newlyweds spent their honeymoon in their new home on West Wilson Street [in Madison], also occupied by Bob's mother . . . [and] Bob's sister and brother-in-law. Any tensions, conflicts, or jealousies created by living with these family members were zealously repressed. Belle's mention of her mother-in-law's sarcasm and tendency to "fret and scold" is the harshest criticism preserved. . . . Belle and Bob preferred to perceive the arrangement as only temporary although it remained their primary residence for the next nineteen years. . . . [9]

. . . In September of 1882 . . . she gave birth to a daughter, Flora Dodge, called Fola, who remained an only child for the next thirteen years. When Bob spent evenings at home reading law books, Belle joined him. . . . Bob's desire to have her as a helpmeet, combined with her confidence in the myriad abilities of women, led her to enroll in law school the same year that Fola was born. This move satisfied many of her needs: she excelled in an almost wholly male discipline far removed from her prescribed gender sphere, demonstrating the intellectual equality of women; she was better able to understand, counsel, and influence her husband; and she was no longer left alone all day in the house with her female in-laws and a new baby. Belle was determined, not only from the beginning of her marriage but from the very beginning of motherhood, to have a hold in both the professional and personal worlds. "The supreme experience in life is motherhood," she declared unequivocally; yet she noted, "It did not require much urging to convince me I could do so [study law] without rejecting my child and other home duties."[10]

In 1885 Belle Case La Follette became the first woman to graduate from the University of Wisconsin Law School. Although she never practiced law, she was an excellent student, and a brief she wrote for her husband in the 1890s broke new legal ground and won his case before the state's supreme court. . . . [11]

Belle's enthusiasm for sweeping liberal, even radical, change never faltered. . . .

Belle took on new challenges throughout her lifetime and championed causes ranging from the Montessori system of education to pure food and drug legislation and wage and prison reform. For ten years, until overwhelmed by her duties as governor's wife, Belle was president of the Emily Bishop League, a group devoted to exercise, pure foods, and the more "natural" way of life she had so strongly advocated during her college years. She jogged regularly and further defied convention by abandoning stays and corsets for more comfortable, looser-fitting garments.[12]

Belle's professors encouraged her to pursue a career in writing, advice she later regretted not heeding. She wrote hundreds of articles over a period of more than fifty years, primarily for *La Follette's Magazine*. . . . By accepting the utility of a "woman's page," distinct from the political focus of the rest of the magazine, Belle implicitly acknowledged acceptance of woman's separate sphere, yet many of the subjects she chose to address reveal a rejection of its confines. Within the pages of *La Follette's*, she skillfully bridged the traditional domestic concerns of women with their new, enlarged public role.

Perhaps her most courageous columns were written in response to the plight of African Americans. . . . [13]

Belle received magazine subscription cancellations as well as hate mail, some of which she published in the pages of *La Follette's*. Undaunted, she spoke to black as well as white audiences against lynching, racial segregation, and the disenfranchisement of women and African Americans. . . . [14]

When it came to civil rights and other subjects about which she felt passionately, Belle, like her husband, was an energetic speaker. Although her style was somewhat quieter, people often remarked that the two resembled each other both on and off the speaker's platform. Belle contrasted dramatically, however, with her husband in other areas. Their son Phil noted, "People who knew [Belle] in her younger days reported her as being gay, high spirited, and having the most contagious laugh they ever heard."[15] Belle's writings, both personal and public, reveal someone very different. Conscientious, highly principled, and self-disciplined, Belle appears earnest, sincere, and extremely serious. . . . In contrast to her husband, Belle rarely displayed much facility for fantasy or levity even in private. In her speeches and in her letters to the family, jokes, teasing, or any general attempt at humor are conspicuous by their absence.

Following his oft-quoted assertion in his autobiography that Belle was his "wisest and best counsellor," Bob added, "That this is not partial judgment, the Progressive leaders of Wisconsin who welcomed her to our conferences would bear witness. . . . " In his later years, [Bob] spoke of "when we were governor.". . .[16]

. . . Belle's early objections to her husband's political career were not based merely on her own discomfort with public speaking. When Bob proposed to run for Congress [in 1884], Belle's "instinctive love of home and the dread of change led me, in a mild way, to take the negative side of the argument.". . .[17]

This minimization of conflict is typical of Belle, but also typical was her very real desire to keep out of politics and remain in the safe, secure, familiar lifestyle already established and so heavily touted by the women's prescriptive literature of the day. . . . When Bob considered running for the governorship again in 1898 after his first unsuccessful attempt in 1896, he believed he must fight for "the interests of better methods and better government for Wisconsin" or "quietly retire from the field and attend to 'private business.'" Claimed Bob, "The latter will be an alternative easy for me, as in so doing I will simply yield to the entreaties of Mrs. La Follette."[18] Yet ultimately Belle chose not to insist that her husband forsake his political ambitions, a decision that reveals her sense of responsibility to support his efforts to improve society.

Belle claimed in 1916 that the six years in the governor's residence [from 1900 to 1906] had been "the most taxing from a woman's standpoint," citing personal threats against the family and "the continuous and merciless fire of newspaper criticism." During Bob's many years in federal service [1885 to 1891 and 1906 to 1925] she so disliked the constant shuttling between Washington and Wisconsin that she and the children occasionally remained in Madison when Congress was in session. During one such separation Bob urged her to rest up in order to meet the demands of life in Washington in the coming year. She replied that it was not the social obligations she dreaded, but "the intense interest in you [which] seems too much for me at times.". . .[19]

At times during the first half of their marriage, Belle seems to have wholly internalized the prescribed sphere of "true womanhood": "Whenever I get discouraged I always think there is nothing I would rather be than your wife and the mother of your children and I have no ambition except to contribute to your happiness and theirs and to your success and theirs." Such internalization brought anxiety and feelings of inadequacy: "[S]ometimes I feel I am not well adapted to home making and the constant efforts to hold myself and keep my balance in the midst of so many distractions wears me out.". . .[20]

Belle's high standards made her approval all the more desirable during Bob's periods of relatively good health, but during his many illnesses, she responded maternally and generously. . . . Belle viewed herself as a guardian of her husband. Rather than insist he be responsible for his own habits and their negative effects, she claimed, "I had to be the ogre and insist on his getting sleep." . . . Throughout their marriage Bob often took on the persona of an irresponsible, sometimes naughty child, with Belle playing the frustrated but loving mother. In keeping with this relationship, Bob often addressed Belle as "Mama," in his letters, and on at least one occasion closed with "I am always your boy."[21]

A tacit acceptance of constant debt, internalized feelings of anxiety and guilt over household finances, an acceptance of the role of monitor, and ultimately the role of "Mama" for her husband: all are reflections of attitudes and beliefs that existed as the norm for many nineteenth-century women. But a major shift in the way she perceived both herself and her husband occurred within Belle La Follette. . . . As Belle entered her middle years and the strict gendered spheres that created her nineteenth-century perceptions of the ideal woman began to expand and transform, she relieved herself of certain responsibilities. She no longer saw her husband's various frustrating behaviors as indicators of her own failures, but as qualities of his personality that she was entirely unable to change, no matter how sincere and well-intentioned her efforts. . . . As Belle's love for Bob matured, being his wife involved increasing acceptance of his faults as well as his admirable qualities, and an intensification of her own efforts to carry out desired social reforms in addition to supporting his.

The reasons for Belle's advocacy of woman suffrage are certainly in keeping with the strains she endured as Bob's wife. . . . A bright woman forced to lead a lifestyle different from that which she truly desired, her work on behalf of women may be seen as a way of protesting being so dominated by her husband's needs; of expressing her rebellion against the unfairness of being thrust against her will into public life; of being continually in debt, and having to suffer with her husband the controversy and criticism which often only he had evoked.

The expression of suffragist views allowed Belle a forum to protest her subserviency to her demanding husband without incurring his wrath but instead generating praise and approval. And yet, when she addressed the Senate Committee on Woman Suffrage on April 26, 1913, Belle's message was temperate. Her emphasis was that equal suffrage "will make better homes," for "home, society [and] government are best when men and women keep together intellectually and spiritually.". . .[22]

To Bob's great chagrin, Belle steadily refused to campaign for him directly. . . . Belle's refusal remained firm . . . until 1924, when she campaigned actively in her husband's presidential race.[23]

For all Belle's dislike of public life with its chaos and uncertainty; her frequent urgings that her husband not work so hard; and her criticisms of his strategies and policies, she labored tirelessly on his behalf. According to their daughter, Fola, "[Belle] prepared briefs for his law firm and followed his legal and legislative work with professional understanding.". . . Belle spent a great deal of time performing such routine, time-consuming chores as addressing and stuffing envelopes; personally responding to constituents' mail; and tracking down late shipments of campaign posters, pamphlets, and the like. Her work with the mailing lists made her familiar with names and addresses of constituents, enabling her, she said, "when I accompanied Mr. La Follette on his campaigns through his congressional district to sometimes jog even his excellent memory with a hint as to 'who was who.'" During the congressional years, and during his three terms as governor, there were few important conferences in which she did not participate — probably none that he did not share with her. . . .[24]

. . . Following Bob La Follette's death in 1925, his widow was urged to pursue his Senate seat. Belle favored women sharing the responsibilities of high office and was deeply mindful that her virtually assured election might pave the way to the Senate for other women. Nevertheless, she stated in no uncertain terms, "At no time in my life would I ever have chosen a public career for myself. It would be against [my] nature for me to undertake the responsibilities of political leadership." At the age of sixty-six, Belle Case La Follette knew herself well. The finely honed social conscience and sense of "womanly" duty was no match for her discomfort in the public eye and "womanly" longing to work for the betterment of society comfortably behind the scenes, within the safety and security of home.

. . . An assessment of her character . . . was offered at her funeral [in 1931] by another journalist and family friend, Lincoln Steffens, who better understood the social, political and personal crosscurrents perpetually buffeting this complex woman. Calling her "historically and romantically the woman triumphant," he paid tribute to this "great woman, this Belle La Follette, great as great men are great. She too was a statesman, [a] politician: she could act but she was content to beget action and actors. She played, herself, the woman's part; she sat in the gallery in the Congress or at home with the children and the advisors. She could but she did not often make the speeches or do the deeds." Steffens assessed Belle's life from the time when "a pretty young girl with a gypsy spirit . . . found her man": "She wanted to fly. She inspired flight and she bore fliers, but she herself — Belle La Follette — walked all her life on the ground to keep the course for her fliers. That was her woman's victory; that was a woman's tragedy, too."[25]

*On Belle Case La Follette's legacy in the triumphs and tragedies of the next generation of Wisconsin's most remarkable political family, see "Changes and Choices" in chapter 7.*

## NOTES

1. [The original article was] adapted from the chapter "Belle Case La Follette: Women's Victory, Women's Tragedy" from *Fighting Bob La Follette: The Righteous Reformer* by Nancy C. Unger, ©2000 the University of North Carolina Press.

2. *New York Times*, August 20, 1931, 18–19.

3. See Lucy Freeman, Sherry La Follette, and George A. Zabriskie, *Belle: A Biography of Belle Case La Follette* (New York, 1986) and Bernard A. Weisberger, *The La Follettes of Wisconsin: Love and Politics in Progressive America* (Madison, 1994). . . .

4. Belle Case La Follette (BCL), Speech, "On Segregation," January 5, 1914, Belle La Follette Papers, Box D, File 40, La Follette Family Collection, Library of Congress. . . .

5. McBride, *On Wisconsin Women*, 60.

6. David Thelen, *Early Life of Robert M. La Follette* (Chicago, 1966), 41. Belle revisited this theme in *La Follette's Magazine* 5 (April 1913), 6.

7. Belle Case La Follette and Fola La Follette, *Robert M. La Follette: June 14, 1855–June 18, 1925*, (2 vols., New York, 1953), 1:33.

8. Robert Marion La Follette, diary, undated entry for 1879, . . . Robert La Follette Papers, Box B, File 1, La Follette Family Collection, Library of Congress.

9. La Follette and La Follette, *La Follette*, 1:110.

10. Freeman, La Follette, and Zabriskie, *Belle*, 23.

11. McBride, *On Wisconsin Women*, 229. . . . See Edward Reisner, "First Woman Graduate: Belle Case La Follette or Elsie Buck," *Gargoyle* 22 (Winter 1991–92) (University of Wisconsin Law School Forum), 10–11. . . .

12. BCL speech, . . . Belle La Follette Papers, Box D, File 40, La Follette Family Collection, Library of Congress. . . .

13. . . . See also BCL, "Colored Folk of Washington," *La Follette's Magazine* 3 (August 5, 1911), 10; "The Color Line," *La Follette's Magazine* 5 (August 23, 1913), 6–7; "Segregation in the Civil Service," *La Follette's Magazine* 5 (December 13, 1913), 6; "Color Line to Date," *La Follette's Magazine* 6 (January 24, 1914), 6–7.

14. BCL, "Color Line to Date" *La Follette's Magazine* 6 (January 24, 1914), 6–7; "Fair Chance for the Negro," *La Follette's Magazine* 6 (April 11, 1914), 6; "Segregation in the Civil Service," *La Follette's Magazine* 6 (December, 1914), 10. . . . [*La Follette's Magazine* was later renamed *The Progressive* and remains in publication.]

15. Philip Fox La Follette, *Adventures in Politics: The Memoir of Philip La Follette,* ed. Donald Young (New York, 1970), 2. . . .

16. Robert Marion La Follette, *La Follette's Autobiography* (Madison, 1913; reprint Madison, 1960), 135; Freeman, La Follette, and Zabriskie, *Belle,* 61. . . .

17. BCL to Robert M. La Follette, March 26, 1917, Box A, File 20; BCL to Robert M. La Follette, July 20, 1914, Family Papers; Box A, File 13, La Follette Family Collection, Library of Congress; La Follette and La Follette, *La Follette,* 1:58.

18. . . . Robert La Follette to A. R. Hall, November 6, 1897, 9:324, Robert La Follette Papers, WHS.

19. BCL, Speech, "Our Story," February 5, 1916, Belle La Follette Papers, Box D, File 41; BCL to Robert M. La Follette, January 2, 1907, Family Papers, Box A, File 5, La Follette Family Collection, Library of Congress. . . .

20. BCL to Robert M. La Follette, August 16, 1905, Box A, File 3. . . .

21. . . . La Follette and La Follette, *La Follette,* 1:72; . . . Robert M. La Follette to BCL, August 7, 1903, Box A, File 2; and September 30, 1897, Family Papers, Box A, File 1, La Follette Family Collection, Library of Congress. . . .

22. BCL, "A Question of Democracy," *La Follette's Magazine,* 5, (May 10, 1913), 6. . . .

23. *Los Angeles Evening Herald,* April 26, 1912. . . .

24. La Follette and La Follette, *La Follette,* 1:x; BCL, "What It Means to Be an Insurgent Senator's Wife," *The Housekeeper,* November 11, 1911. . . . [Robert M. La Follette also had run as an insurgent Republican for the presidency in 1912.]

25. . . . BCL to Edna Chynoweth, July 28, 1925, Family Papers, Box A, File 31, La Follette Family Collection, Library of Congress; Lincoln Steffens, "The Victorious Mother," *The Progressive* 49, Belle La Follette Memorial Edition (November 1931), 2. . . .

# A Milwaukee Woman's Life on the Left

## *The Autobiography of Meta Berger*

KIMBERLY SWANSON

*The following excerpt is from Kimberly Swanson's introduction to the book,* A Milwaukee Woman's Life on the Left: The Autobiography of Meta Berger *(Madison: SHSW, 2001).*

In 1909 the Socialist Party of Milwaukee nominated Meta Berger as a candidate in the . . . election of school board directors. "Surprised, shocked and frightened" by the nomination, she wired her husband, Socialist Party leader Victor Berger, asking him what to do. He advised, "Do nothing, except to accept the honor. You won't be elected anyway." She accepted the nomination and, despite Victor's prediction, won the election.[1]

Meta Berger's election to the school board launched her career in educational administration and social reform. A shy housewife and mother who joined the Socialist Party, held political office, and became influential in suffrage and peace groups, Meta participated in many of the most significant political and social movements of her time. In partnership with her well-known husband, she chose an exciting and demanding life of public service over conventionality and respectability. Through her political involvement she witnessed the rise and fall of the Socialist Party, the early twentieth-century women's rights movement, and the patriotic hysteria and repression of World War I. . . .

Meta Berger was a determined and spirited woman. Although she portrayed herself as insecure and "stupid" in her youth, she had the strength to educate herself, to speak openly of her convictions, and to stand up to a domineering husband. Her autobiography chronicles her transformation from dutiful wife to confident activist, revealing both her fears and her enduring hope for the future.

Meta Schlichting was born February 23, 1873, in Milwaukee, the second of five children. Her German-born parents, Bernhard and Matilda Schlichting, had immigrated to the United States as young children. Meta's father was a Civil War veteran, a bookkeeper, and a local politician. An agnostic, he helped his daughter to "unlearn" religious lessons. He served as a Republican member of the Wisconsin Assembly in 1875–1876 and held an appointed position on the Milwaukee board of education from 1878 until his death in early 1884. Meta was ten years old when her father's death plunged her middle-class family into poverty, forcing her mother to take in boarders and her older sister to go to work as a clerk.[2]

A year before his death, Bernhard Schlichting had interviewed a recent immigrant from Austria-Hungary, Victor Berger, for a teaching position in the public schools. Victor accepted the position as German instructor and developed a friendship with the Schlichting family that continued after Bernhard's death. Meta, who was thirteen years younger than Victor, attended the school in which he taught; she studied German language and

literature in his classroom. The German language was hardly foreign in turn-of-the century Milwaukee: the city had a thriving and well-established German-speaking community,
and residents considered their city the "most German in the United States." . . . When Victor began courting Meta, he took her to German-language plays, and when he founded
his first newspaper, the *Wisconsin Vorwärts,* he published it in German.[3]

Meta trained as a teacher at the Wisconsin State Normal School in Milwaukee, thus
qualifying for one of the few professions open to educated women. She graduated in 1894
and taught primary school for three years. In December 1897, at age twenty-four, she resigned her appointment to marry Victor Berger, who was thirty-seven. Her first daughter,
Doris, was born one year after the wedding, and her second daughter, Elsa, was born in
1900. Meta's three-year-old nephew, Jack Anderson, also joined the family after the death
of Meta's older sister, Paula, in 1902.

In the early years of their marriage, the Bergers experienced a period of "adjustment
and readjustment," as Meta phrased it, when their initial expectations of marriage conflicted. She valued financial security and hoped for a cooperative relationship, but Victor's
income was irregular, and his political work often kept him away from home. . . . Victor,
more traditional in outlook, expected Meta to accept his decisions and share his goals and
interests. He had little patience for her political naïveté and no intention of relinquishing
his leadership role in the burgeoning socialist movement. Raised in a poor but culturally
middle-class family, Meta felt uncomfortable at socialist rallies and ignorant among Victor's well-read, intellectual friends.

Even more distressing to her was the flattering attention paid him by other women as
a result of his stature in the socialist movement — attention that he probably failed to
discourage. Meta referred only indirectly in her autobiography to Victor's flirtations or
affairs with other women, but her daughter, Doris, wrote quite bluntly in her unfinished
biography of her father that he had been unfaithful. One of his affairs, according to Doris,
was with a maid, Anna, who confessed her involvement with Victor at the lunch table in
Doris's presence.[4]

Meta was determined to improve her marriage and to become "something more than
Mr. Berger's house-keeper." In an early attempt to participate more fully in his life and all-
consuming work, she followed Victor to a Socialist Party convention in 1904. "Perhaps you
think this didn't take a certain amount of perseverance!" she wrote in her autobiography.
"To a person of my temperament it took all I had." Somewhat to her surprise, the convention inspired her, unlike the books she had tried to read and the discussions she had over-
heard. . . . At her insistence, she accompanied Victor to additional conventions. . . . Slowly,
Meta came to appreciate Victor's work for social and economic change. Although in 1907
she still doubted whether his sacrifices for the "rabble" were worthwhile, by 1910 she was
writing to him that "the time . . . when I thought that if you gave up your work and devoted yourself to money making I would be happy . . . is past."[5]

Meta's marriage evolved along with her commitment to socialism. In the early years of
their relationship she deferred to Victor in many ways because of his greater age and experience. When Meta questioned Victor about political issues, "sometimes he just laughed

at me and said, '*Du bist eine dumme Gans*'" [You are a silly goose]. . . . She always accepted Victor's theories, but she began to offer her own ideas on many practical matters as she gained administrative and political experience. . . . She also challenged Victor at home, where they argued about childrearing methods and his flirtations or infidelities. . . .[6]

As she approached middle age, Meta forged a real partnership with Victor. Working together in the socialist cause, they became "more than husband and wife," she wrote. "We became comrades in the real sense of the word, and as a result we certainly were happy.". . .[7]

Meta's 1909 election to the school board, which first thrust her into a public role, was a sign of the Socialist Party's growing political momentum in Milwaukee. . . . Shortly after the Socialists swept the city government [in 1910], Victor was elected to Congress, the first Socialist in the nation to serve in that role. . . .[8]

Meta eventually took advantage of the opportunities for public service that her marriage provided. At her first school-board meeting she felt so ill prepared that she asked a fellow Socialist to signal to her — discreetly — how to vote, but she learned quickly and soon enjoyed the work. In her autobiography she portrayed Victor as supportive of her school board service, but in a 1913 letter he expressed some doubts: "When I am alone and thinking the matter over — then it always comes to me again that I *don't want* either you or the children to take a prominent part in public life. . . . *You* are not adapted to it at all, — although (I am sorry to say) that you have acquired a little taste for it through your work on the school board. When your term is over I don't want you to run again." Meta ran for office again anyway in 1915 and was reelected. She ran and won three more times in succeeding years and served a total of thirty years on the school board before her retirement in 1939. In 1915–1916 she served as president of the board. By this time Victor had accustomed himself to her public role, and he noted with pride her accomplishment in a letter to his daughter, Doris: "Sometimes I wonder whether you girls sufficiently prize the fact that your mother is the first woman in *America* who has ever achieved the honor of being elected president of a school board. And the first Socialist president at that, — man or woman."[9]

As a school director, Meta supported progressive measures such as playground construction, "penny lunches," free textbooks, and medical inspection of schoolchildren. She was also a teachers' advocate and worked for their tenure, a firm salary schedule, and a pension system. Though she was not always successful in her efforts — she failed, for example, in her attempt to provide free textbooks — her fellow school directors nonetheless respected her "clear thinking, fresh interest and enthusiasm, [and] consideration for Board employes." Her work for the school board eventually led to appointments to the Wisconsin State Board of Education (1917–1919), the Wisconsin Board of Regents of Normal Schools (1927–1928), and the University of Wisconsin Board of Regents (1928–1934).[10]

Meta participated in Victor's work as well. She advised him informally and assisted in the office of the *Milwaukee Leader,* the socialist daily newspaper he founded in 1911. During election campaigns, she supervised literature distribution and helped to formulate strategies, eventually gaining enough confidence to "scold" party members for running a poor campaign or to lament decisions made while she was ill in bed. After Victor's death, she was elected to his seat on the Socialist Party's National Executive Committee, an honor accorded very few women.[11]

Meta's efforts and skill also brought her influence outside educational and party circles. She joined numerous reform organizations and frequently accepted leadership positions in them. Prior to passage of the Nineteenth Amendment in 1920, she participated most notably in suffrage organizations. She joined the Wisconsin Woman Suffrage Association (WWSA) in 1914, serving as second vice-president for one year and as first vice-president for two years. The middle-class suffrage leaders found Meta's political and administrative experience valuable, but as a Socialist she felt an "undercurrent of suspicion and distrust." She resigned from the organization in 1917, noting candidly that the WWSA was "not sufficiently radical to suit me." She disagreed with the group's tactics and, more importantly, with its strong support for World War I. A week after her resignation she established a chapter of the National Woman's Party, a competing suffrage organization, and soon afterward shared a podium with the first woman elected to the U.S. House of Representatives, Jeannette Rankin of Montana. In the following decades, Meta turned to peace work, serving on the national committee of the Women's International League for Peace and Freedom (WILPF), an organization established and led by social reformer Jane Addams. Meta valued efforts to secure peace but found the WILPF unimpressive. "Generally speaking," she remarked, "it is a conservative group, well meaning but not courageous."[12]

In her suffrage and peace work, Meta joined millions of educated middle-class female reformers who built a large network of organizations in the late nineteenth and early twentieth centuries — organizations ranging from temperance campaigns to settlement houses to suffrage associations. These women created a place for themselves in public life and shaped their society, but they kept their organizations distinct from those of men. In fact, many justified their involvement in social and political affairs by pointing to their feminine values and by using metaphors about motherhood. These reformers [called "social feminists"] sought to improve the condition of women and of the working class, but they did so without directly challenging the gender or economic systems.[13]

However, Socialist women — even those of middle-class origin, like Meta — identified with the working class and questioned economic arrangements. Socialist women were also more likely to question social traditions. Socialist women did build organizations separate from men, but a few women of Meta's generation succeeded in achieving influence within the regular party organization and urged other women to follow suit. Meta may have found rhetoric about so-called feminine values resonant or useful at times, but she nevertheless took at face value the party's pledge of sexual equality. She demonstrated her commitment to expanding women's roles through her educational and suffrage work, for example, by defending the right of married women to teach. She once criticized a fellow Socialist for making a "purely moral" argument in favor of woman suffrage, meaning that she disapproved of arguments for change based solely on supposed moral differences between men and women. A firm proponent of equal rights, Meta may have sensed that emphasizing differences hindered rather than furthered women's integration into public life. . . .[14]

Meta was decisive and politically adept in her middle and old age. A woman of action, she knew how to get things done. She managed a household, often in her husband's absence, raised three children, and served as an adviser to her temperamental husband — all while pursuing her own career on the school board and in reform. Although she had never expected anything more than a conventional life, after her initial election to the school board she pursued her career in public service with great zest. "In spite of her gentle and helpful personality," Doris wrote, "Mama was really not essentially domestic. She fooled people. In a way she fooled Papa. She was wholly without domestic interests. And not as meek as she seemed." This comment suggests that Meta, like many of her fellow reformers, used an image of domesticity to help achieve her ends. But as Doris noted, though Meta was generally pleasant and respectful of others in her work, she was also quite capable of defending unpopular positions. Exemplifying her forthrightness is the speech she made on her first day as a regent for the Wisconsin normal schools: "I finally told the board that I personally [believed] that by figuring [budgets] so closely that we positively allowed the schools to deteriorate. . . . If we maintain a fire-trap then the refusal for the money to repair such conditions must be theirs. . . . Well, — I guess I threw a bomb alright enough. The whole board was up in arms at once and didn't know just what to do with such an unruly member.". . .[15]

The United States' entrance into World War I dramatically changed the Bergers' lives. Meta and Victor opposed American involvement in the war and were shocked by the repressive measures used to squelch dissent. The day after Congress declared war on Germany in 1917, the national Socialist Party made a formal statement of opposition to the war. This action provoked a wave of anti-Socialist sentiment throughout the country, but in Milwaukee — long identified with both German culture and with socialism — feelings ran particularly high. . . .[16]

These war years were traumatic for Meta Berger. Her antiwar activism and German heritage provoked hostility in suffrage meetings and in the school superintendent's office. Angry war supporters anonymously threatened her and vandalized her home. Despite such treatment, the withdrawal of mailing rights from Victor's *Milwaukee Leader* caught her by surprise, and his arrest and indictment turned her shock to fear. Indicted by the federal government for publishing antiwar editorials, Victor and four other Socialists were tried in Chicago during . . . 1918–1919. All five defendants were convicted. . . . At the close of the trial, Meta played a central role in collecting bond money to secure the defendants' release during the appeal process. She returned home exhausted and disillusioned, and in later years she frequently remarked that her hair had turned white during the course of the trial. Her only pleasant memory of the Chicago trial was a quiet Christmas Eve at Hull House with pacifist and social reformer Jane Addams, who had closely followed the trial.[17]

Victor's troubles continued. [He was] elected to Congress by the Fifth District of Wisconsin in the fall of 1918, [but] Congress refused to seat him. . . . Milwaukee's Socialist Party nominated Victor to run again in the ensuing special election, and the voters stubbornly elected him once more. Congress barred him a second time, leaving the Fifth District without representation for the remainder of the term. [During the next term, Victor's conviction was overturned by the Supreme Court in a landmark case in 1921.]

Elected to Congress again in 1922, after wartime emotions had cooled, Victor took his seat without debate and served three full terms before losing office in 1928. Meta resided in Washington during part of his congressional service but continued to serve on educational boards in Wisconsin. In Washington she was restless. . . . She joined new organizations to keep busy and to serve. . . .

*During the 1920s, still embittered about her family's wartime travails, Meta Schlichting Berger traveled widely to Asia and to Germany with her husband. She was home in 1924 to accept a position on the WILPF's national board and to help organize the Progressive Party campaign that nominated Wisconsin Senator Robert M. La Follette for the presidency and took great interest in the careers of her daughters; Elsa became a physician and Doris a lawyer.*

*However, after Victor's sudden death in 1929, Meta traveled again as a delegate to a women's peace conference in Switzerland and to the Soviet Union. Her relationship with the Socialist Party became strained as a result of her subsequent public sympathies with Communist organizations although, as Swanson writes, Berger was "never a theorist — indeed, she never read the works of Karl Marx" and had "left the interpretation of events to Victor." But in 1940, she resigned from the Socialist Party that the Bergers had built. By then in poor health, she had retired from public life and resigned from the Milwaukee School Board in 1939 to move to her Thiensville farm with her daughter Doris and her family. In 1944, Meta Schlichting Berger died at home.*

Throughout her life, Meta Berger juggled many responsibilities — marriage, child raising, school-board service, political and reform work — more or less simultaneously. Naive and uncertain in her youth, she grew to become a confident and capable woman who thrived on activity and made a strong effort to improve the lives of Milwaukee's schoolchildren and working people. . . . [In the last year of her life, at] age seventy, she looked back with pride on her development from politically uninvolved housewife to public figure. . . . [H]er choices and accomplishments stand as an example of what a determined and spirited woman of her era could do.

## NOTES

1. [Another woman, Annie Gordon Whitnall, also was elected in 1909 and later declared as a Socialist. The first woman on the board, when seats were appointive, was Mary Freeman Merrill in 1895; see McBride, *On Wisconsin Women*, 156.]
2. Miriam Frink Notes, 1943, Victor L. Berger Papers (VLB Papers), WHS.
3. Bayrd Still, *Milwaukee: The History of a City* (Madison: SHSW, 1948), 257–278.

4. Doris Berger Hursley, biography of Victor Berger, ca. 1926–1980, rolls 12–13, Victor L. Berger Papers (microfilm edition, 1994), WHS, hereinafter cited as VLB Papers (microfilm).

5. Doris Hursley, interview with Meta Berger, 1936, roll 33, VLB Papers (microfilm); Michael E. Stevens, ed., *The Family Letters of Victor and Meta Berger, 1984–1929* (Madison: SHSW, 1995), 86, 105.

6. Stevens, ed., *Family Letters*, 116, 138, 172, 174; Hursley, biography. . . .

7. Elsa Berger Edelman, "The Second One," ca. 1973, roll 13, VLB Papers (microfilm), 4. . . .

8. Marvin Wachman, *History of the Social Democratic Party of Milwaukee, 1897–1910* (Urbana: University of Illinois Press, 1945).

9. [Hursley, biography]; Stevens, ed., *Family Letters*, 157, 192.

10. "Twenty-two Years Ago . . . ," ca. 1931; "Mrs. Meta Schlichting Berger Served the Children of Milwaukee . . . ," July 5, 1944; both roll 33, VLB Papers (microfilm).

11. Stevens, ed., *Family Letters*, 361.

12. "Mrs. Berger Dies, Aged 71," *Milwaukee Journal*, June 17, 1944; Stevens, ed., *Family Letters*, 339.

13. Mary P. Ryan, *Womanhood in America: From Colonial Times to the Present* (New York: Franklin Watts, 1983).

14. Mari Jo Buhle, *Women and American Socialism, 1870–1920* (Urbana: University of Illinois Press, 1981); Stevens, ed., *Family Letters*, 151.

15. Hursley, biography; "Mrs. Berger Dies, Aged 71," *Milwaukee Journal*; Stevens, ed., *Family Letters*, 376–377.

16. Still, *Milwaukee*, 455–464. [See also Sally M. Miller, *Victor Berger and the Promise of Constructive Socialism, 1910–1930* (Westport, CT.: Greenwood, 1973).]

17. "Mrs. Berger Dies, Aged 71," *Milwaukee Journal*.

*Sculptor Jean Pond Miner working on her statue, "Forward,"
in the Wisconsin Building at the World's Columbian Exposition
in Chicago, 1893. The original statue, which symbolizes
Wisconsin's state motto, stands in the lobby of the Wisconsin
Historical Society headquarters in Madison.*

## ᘒ6ᘓ

# "FORWARD" WOMEN IN WISCONSIN, 1910–1930

## INTRODUCTION

The second decade of the century began as the Progressive movement peaked and began to wane, but the decade ended with the beginning of the woman suffrage movement in its "truest meaning," wrote Wisconsin leader Theodora Winton Youmans, because women had the ballot at last. How Wisconsin women won the historic first ratification of the Nineteenth Amendment provides perhaps the most paradoxical example of politics in one of the last holdout states, the "Progressive state." Suffragists won support for a federal amendment only because they still had not won a state amendment, when women elsewhere had to restart state organizations for ratification in 1920. How Wisconsin women then used their new electoral power to win the nation's first Equal Rights Amendment provides another example of their political prowess learned over long decades of suffrage campaigns. However, how Wisconsin women fared in the next decade after the Nineteenth Amendment, when they ran for political office, proved the truest test — not only of women but also of Wisconsin's "progressive" men and their movement.

That Wisconsin was "the most Progressive state in the Union" by 1910, writes historian John D. Buenker, owed much to the work of women — "tens of thousands of Wisconsin women." They "played a vital role in passage of most of the major legislation that distinguished Wisconsin progressivism," he writes. "But they lacked the right to vote" until after millions of women elsewhere had preceded them to the polls. Like suffragists everywhere, Buenker finds it "hard to believe that Wisconsin progressives could not have enacted woman suffrage if they had regarded it as a high-priority issue, since they enacted so many other reforms" with women's help.[1]

Other progressive legislation, which peaked in 1911, had helped Wisconsin women and families — if not at the polls, then in the workplace. Because of progressive laws put in place in 1911, the use of child labor peaked in 1910 with almost twenty-five thousand workers in the state under the age of fifteen, and a state study found that more than a fourth of children under fourteen were not in school. "Of all the work-related social and political issues in the period," Buenker writes, "none was more momentous than employment of children and women." Women's clubs and religious groups so "relentlessly aired the issue" that legislators passed the landmark child labor laws in 1911, and the number of underage workers decreased by a third within a decade. But their mothers would not fare as well when political debate on "the changing role of women in the workplace proved to be more portentous," writes Buenker.[2]

By 1911, women comprised a fifth of the workforce in Wisconsin, where almost a fourth worked for pay, although that did not count farm women or account for house-work awaiting all women at home. Nationwide, employed women earned half the income of men, although many women worked as many hours; farm women worked without pay for an average of sixty-three hours a week. In Wisconsin in 1911, women won a minimum wage and a ten-hour workday and fifty-hour workweek; whether rural or urban, they also averaged fifty hours weekly on housework, according to first studies by "efficiency experts" on "scientific motherhood." They measured little change for decades despite the well-advertised advent of allegedly "labor-saving appliances."[3] Wisconsin legislators would prove to be about as reliable when they used the "protective legislation" against working women a decade later.

Farm women, the often-forgotten female workers, remained a majority of Wisconsin women well after the 1920 census found, for the first time, most Americans residing in urban areas owing to immigration and rural migration. Urban populations grew at an even greater rate than the growth rate of the state, where Wisconsin's "New North" of late settlement became known as "the land of ten thousand failures," and southeastern coun-ties of Milwaukee and Waukesha each lost more than a hundred farms in the next decade to urban expansion and the new suburbs. However, rural areas remained in stasis despite a wider availability for women of the new "ready-made" apparel through traveling "trunk-shows" that featured the fashionable new higher hemlines and high heels. Vendors ped-dled fewer patterns, yard goods, and notions for home sewing, according to a study of "fashion change in a northwoods lumbering town," Ashland, that analyzed local advertis-ing. Ads already anticipated the "flapper" look — as did the Wisconsin Woman's Christian Temperance Union, which resolved at its 1912 convention that the footwear was a menace to the health of women. Other "well-publicized attractions of the metropolis were often compelling," as historian Paul W. Glad writes, "to young men and women of isolated farms and rural villages." In the metropolis of Milwaukee, the city alone had population in-creases of more than 22 percent from 1910 to 1920 and more than 26 percent again by 1930, reaching more than half a million residents.[4]

Immigration into the state remained strong until war and restrictive quotas slowed the rate, but the tragedy of the *Titanic* in 1912 meant a Swiss woman sailing in steerage never reached New Glarus. At the age of eighteen, Josefine Arnold-Franchi died only days from her destination, as did her husband and another third-class passenger from Switzerland headed for Milwaukee, Maria Kink. One of her brothers also died; another survived in one of the last lifeboats with his wife and their four-year-old daughter, and Louise Kink Pope of Lannon lived another eight decades. Jennie Howard Hansen of Racine also was in steerage and survived, but the bodies of her husband and the other immigrants to Wis-consin never were found.[5]

However, sailing first-class in the finest staterooms did not guarantee a safe harbor for a daughter of an Irish immigrant factory worker who had left her native Milwaukee for Montreal only four years before at the age of twenty-one, when she married well into wealth. In one of the first lifeboats with her two-year-old daughter but separated from her infant son, she gave up their seats to find him, unaware that he was in his nursemaid's arms in another boat. He was orphaned when Bess Daniels Allison, her husband, and their daughter died. Other passengers in first class and in the first lifeboats who survived included Vera Gillespie Dick of Milwaukee and her husband, and Daisy Minahan of Green Bay and her sister-in-law, but not Daisy's brother. Lillian Thorpe Minahan of Fond du Lac buried him before she reached the age of forty. Obituaries and first-person accounts filled newspaper columns for weeks as readers in Wisconsin and nationwide relived the disaster.[6]

Searchers recovered the body of the founder of the Great Lakes Shipping Company, Edward G. Crosby, only after his widow, Catherine Halstead Crosby, filed an affidavit from Milwaukee that was entered as testimony in congressional hearings on the *Titanic*'s fate. "My husband was a sailor all his life" and had seen signs of "ice fields" earlier in the day, she said, so he sent her and their daughter Harriette to the deck without hesitation. They never saw him again. In the lifeboats, "there were no lanterns, no provisions, no lights, nothing at all in these boats except oars," but in the darkness of night, Crosby heard explosions and "the terrible cries of the people" — her husband and more than fifteen hundred people left behind, mainly immigrants.[7]

Newcomers also came to Wisconsin from the South, although the "Great Migration" of African Americans came late to the state. Still, they numbered more than five thousand by 1920 in Wisconsin, most settling in its cities — from a few hundred in Madison, Kenosha, and Racine to several hundred in Beloit to more than two thousand in Milwaukee, although still less than .5 percent of the city's population. They remained little more than 1 percent of residents despite a 236 percent increase in their population, numbering seventy-five hundred in the city of Milwaukee by 1930, but African Americans already experienced ever more entrenched segregation in every city — and the emergence of the Ku Klux Klan in the state in the 1920s. Mass rallies in Milwaukee drew as many as fifteen thousand attendees, but elsewhere in the state, with few people of color to hate, Klansmen burned crosses in nativist and anti-Catholic attacks against Poles in Rusk County and Italians in "the Bush" area of Madison.[8]

The *primeros,* or "first arrivers," from Mexico also met a mixed welcome, as many men migrated alone for work, some for jobs in agriculture but more for work at Milwaukee's railroads, foundries, and tanneries. In the 1920s, they numbered as many as two thousand in the city, including four hundred women and children. As more families followed, they created a *barrio* of businesses, organizations, and their beloved parish of Our Lady of Guadalupe that served as many as four thousand Mexican Americans by 1930. Some had fled as refugees from the Mexican revolution — but all rural migrants fled farm life, whether in Wisconsin or elsewhere, for "the enticements of ready employment and high wages," as Glad writes — or any wages for farm women. More enticing may have been the idea that "living in the metropolis continued to be easier as well as more exciting than living in the country."[9]

Village life offered few more attractions. A rural state schoolteacher's letters attest to frustration from "the numbing dullness of the small town," Glad writes. The teacher wrote of reading as her only recreation and of refusing to serve as "a drawing card" at the new public dance halls or to descend to the depths of immorality at the new "moving pictures," which were "disgusting." If lonely, she was not alone in her views. A Lutheran pastor proclaimed the new medium of "the movies" as "poisonous" for popularizing lust and murder, a male writer denounced "photo-plays" as "dedicated to licentiousness," and the lieutenant governor called on clubwomen to coordinate a campaign against films for "the preservation of good morals and a healthful society." However, women were warned not to forsake rural life for wicked cities; concern for their fate led legislators in 1914 to investigate "white slavery" in Wisconsin but found insufficient evidence of prostitution for prosecution (see "This Naughty, Naughty City" in chapter 4).[10]

At least one Wisconsin girl literally ran away from rural Portage County to join the circus, as a "tattooed lady," for a lifetime of travel. Anna Mae Burleson Gibbons, born on her family farm in 1893, recalled that her "parents were very poor," and the nearest village of Linnwood didn't even have a "moo'm picture show." But soon after 1910, the carnival came to Stevens Point. She "done her chores" and went to the "freak show," where a tattoo artist easily talked her into life far from the farm. "What he wanted more than anything else in the world was to have somebody who could inspire him," she said. "I wanted to leave home and see the world." She married Charles "Red" Gibbons, who started her career with a small tattoo on her wrist and a stage name. As "Artoria," she never missed a show for more than fifty years and was "a very dear, sweet old lady," according to a circus manager. However, she missed "the life" after she retired in her seventies to care for her husband. It was "a nice way to make a living" and meet unusual people, she said.[11]

Another Wisconsin girl who grew up in Portage made her small town in Columbia County famous in her barely disguised fiction about "Friendship Village." Zona Gale, the onetime reporter for the *Milwaukee Journal,* moved to New York and became famed for her "saccharine studies" which, according to historian Henry Forman, were "far more sentimental than great fiction ought to be." However, he deems her "an entirely different writer" after she returned to her hometown. According to Glad, her "more realistic and sometimes mordant criticism of society in rural communities" culminated in 1920 with the novel *Miss Lulu Bett.* The best seller became a Pulitzer Prize–winning play on a rural woman who became her "family beast of burden," in Gale's words. As Glad observes, Gale wrote of "frustrated village people struggling to surmount the incessant gossip and uninspiring monotony of country towns." Yet in the waning towns, where residents "mounted the ramparts in defense of village and rural ways of life," readers "never fully comprehended what such writers were up to in their revolt," writes Glad, and Zona Gale remained "always associated with the sweetness, serenity, and neighborliness of idealized rural communities."[12]

A career in writing continued to attract increasing numbers of women into college in Wisconsin, especially with two of the earliest journalism schools in the country. They comprised the majority of students in journalism at the University of Wisconsin and at Marquette University in 1920, when Aileen Ryan started her studies in Milwaukee. The *Journal* offered her a summer job a year later, and she never left the newsroom — a newsroom segregated by gender then — except when she went to New York and Paris. She became fashion editor at the age of twenty-four, when Milwaukee was a major textile-manufacturing center. More than forty years and many national honors later, she retired but still could not join the men-only Milwaukee Press Club. Inducted in its Hall of Fame a decade after women were admitted, Ryan refused because she had not been welcome when she was a working journalist.[13]

Journalism was a second career for pioneering home economics professor Nellie Kedzie Jones, yet few advice columnists wrote with her familiarity of farm life or her wit, which won the farmwife from Wisconsin a national readership well before 1920. Her columns, excerpted here, provide historians with a wealth of detail on the daily life of the rural housewife. In the form of letters to a fictitious niece and in a "deceptively down-to-earth and good-humored" style, according to biographer Jeanne Hunnicutt Delgado, Jones gave advice with a serious purpose so a woman would not find herself "an overworked piece of farm equipment." The column ended when her own overworked family left the farm for the city of Madison, where she returned to teaching and reached rural women in a new post with the University of Wisconsin Extension. The program expanded "short courses" for farmers by 1911, when the first woman was certified, although without one required course: an "embarrassed" or perhaps too-literal faculty excused the woman from lectures in "animal husbandry."[14]

As a mother, Jones penned a poignant missive that pleaded with readers to release farmers' daughters from "prudish notions" of the past and rear them as "tomboys" to grow into "strong women" in an era when women's average life expectancy was less than fifty years. Others in the press also worried, in the words of the *Wisconsin Agriculturist,* that "girls in farm communities were so ground down by hard work that they do not know how to play." The *Wisconsin Farmer* encouraged rural electrification for the new home appliances — rather fancifully, at a time when electric companies connected to fewer than a fifth of state farms — in hope that "the daughter in the improved, country home does not seek to escape it," if only she could electrify her new hair curler.[15] A University of Wisconsin study in 1922, *Rural Life,* stated that "the farm-bred girl" was reluctant to "repeat the experiences of isolation and drudgery endured by her mother" as well as the dearth of medical care, continuing to cause high rural rates of death in childbirth.[16]

Jones joined other faculty women who shared her concern for women's health in the era. Women had won from legislators in 1909 a revision of state law to admit women to the University of Wisconsin without "regulations and restrictions as the board of regents may deem proper." The university — a sports-conscious campus even then — accepted women's access to athletic facilities and offered a "female curriculum" in physical education, although limited to calisthenics and a few sports — a far cry from the "Happy Hunting Ground of retired athletic trophies" at Oshkosh Normal School, according to its yearbook in 1915. As Christine A. Ogren writes, women "worked together to score touchdowns, goals, and runs as well as baskets" and began to organize leagues of their own at state normal schools by 1915, while their sisters at the state university watched from the sidelines. Yet even normal school women saw signs that "gender equality was disappearing" due to increasing societal emphasis on men's sports in the era.[17]

However, other disparities in higher education for women were disappearing as legislators recognized the academic level of state normal schools and their teachers, especially educator Mary Davison Bradford. Born in 1856, she began her teaching career at the age of sixteen in rural Kenosha County and became its superintendent of schools in 1910. She already had taken her agenda for childhood education to clubwomen statewide and soon attracted nationwide notice for programs from school breakfasts and kindergartens to vocational training and health courses. In 1911, the legislature authorized college work at state normal schools comparable to two years at the university; although normal schools' regents retreated at times, legislators raised the schools' status to state teachers colleges offering four-year bachelor's degrees in education in 1926. By then, racial inequities in education also were lessening as African American women began enrolling at the Milwaukee campus.[18]

However, as Mary Lou Remley writes in a paean to another innovative educator, which is excerpted here, Margaret N. H'Doubler managed to improve physical education for women at the state university, if under the guise of a degree in dance. Her courses enrolled many more students, including men, while also fulfilling the purposes of public higher education as perceived by both academics and legislators. H'Doubler developed an academic philosophy grounded in theories of physical movement balanced with practicality by providing teacher preparation. Within a decade, H'Doubler published works on her theories and won a major in dance as well as honors nationwide, where former students continued her work in developing the "Wisconsin Idea" of dance.

Another faculty woman earned international acclaim for expanding the experimentation inherent in the "Wisconsin Idea" well beyond state borders to bring peace to the world. Julia Grace Wales came to the campus a decade before war began in Europe in 1914. A "young, idealistic Shakespearean scholar," she conceived a plan for countries to "consider the possibility of peace" through "continuous mediation." Her plan presaged President Woodrow Wilson's later proposal for a League of Nations, as historian Walter I. Trattner observes in his article excerpted in this chapter. As American involvement in the war grew, Wales hoped to "be taken seriously as well as kindly," and she was. Famous pacifists from Jane Addams to Henry Ford funded her expenses for international peace conferences. However, even Wales eventually abandoned her pacifism and supported the war effort.

That Wales had proposed a plan for American involvement in peace, prior to American involvement in war, is evidence that the conflict came earlier than elsewhere to Wisconsin, which still had the seventh-largest population of foreign-born residents of any state. More than half had German heritage, and many "viewed with horror war with the Fatherland," writes Glad. However, others viewed them as suspect amid wartime hysteria, especially in Milwaukee. Many *hausfraus* may have suffered in silence, while prominent Progressive and Socialist women suffered public attacks for their neutrality. The Milwaukee School Board's Meta Schlichting Berger (see "A Milwaukee Woman's Life on the Left" in chapter 5), the spouse of the only Socialist in Congress, suffered threats to her home and family. Other suffragists endured editorial denunciations for demurring from a "preparedness parade" in the city in 1916.[19]

However, first to enlist on the homefront upon American entry into the war in April 1917 was the Wisconsin Woman Suffrage Association, foreswearing the movement's historic pacifism as a calculated ploy to win political support for suffrage. For other women, patriotism was sufficient reason for planting "Victory Gardens," knitting soldiers' socks, saving to buy Liberty Bonds, or enrolling as student nurses. Although women were not allowed in the military, more than four hundred Wisconsin women served overseas as Red Cross nurses, and six women from the state died overseas, although not near combat. No women signed on to support the war more sincerely than the mothers, sisters, and spouses of more than one hundred twenty-five thousand Wisconsin men in the military. At the war's end, women also celebrated the armistice. A *Milwaukee Journal* reporter wrote that "women were placing their feet on the 'rail' beside the men and taking 'theirs' in the true spirit of democracy" — or taking their last drop before Prohibition. But passage of the Eighteenth Amendment already had given a reason for rejoicing, if in a more sober manner, to the more than ten thousand Wisconsin members of the Woman's Christian Temperance Union at the time.[20]

Women's wartime training served Wisconsin well when a worldwide pandemic hit the home front in 1918. Disease took more lives — more than twenty million — than all military deaths in the war. Wisconsin had almost 8,500 fatalities, more than three times the total of almost 2,650 military deaths from the state, which ranked fourth highest among all states in war losses.[21] However, Wisconsin had one of the lowest state death rates from the disease, as "fighting influenza became as important a patriotic duty as cursing the Kaiser," writes historian Steven Burg in his article excerpted here. Standard state histories hardly mention the flu's "terrible swath" through Wisconsin as the war neared an end in November 1918 — except for the flu's use as an excuse by the Anti-Saloon League to foment further attacks on Germans and their "Kaiser brew." News of peace "probably contributed to [the] faint presence in . . . popular memory" of the flu epidemic, he writes. But for Burg's research, even less would be remembered of the role of women. County health nurses visited the sick, as did city teachers, since all schools closed. "Young women from wealthy families" with automobiles served as ambulance drivers in Milwaukee, while members of a Woman's Motor Squad in hard-hit Wausau helped "exhausted mothers" of "multiple sick children." Emotional effects of the epidemic remain immeasurable, according to Burg, but women's efforts contributed to preventing "the worst public health calamity in modern Wisconsin history from being much, much worse."

A volunteer nurse at Madison General Hospital, which she had helped to found as well as the city's first synagogue and Woman's Club, witnessed the worst of the epidemic when an infant born to an influenza patient became an orphan. Rachel Szold Jastrow and her husband, a University of Wisconsin psychology professor, adopted the boy. They had opened their childless home to students for decades, despite warnings from other faculty wives, but the "students were not as bad as many supposed them to be," she wrote. "One young man confessed that he had been here over two years and had never in that time known a woman well enough to exchange a word. Another had been here over four years with a similar experience, and this in a coeducational institution!" Raised in a rabbi's female-dominated family of five daughters, Jastrow was second oldest. Her elder sister, Henrietta, had founded Hadassah, an American women's organization for "pragmatic Zionism," in her words, such as funding hospitals — for both Jews and Arabs — as well as schools and farms in Palestine for decades, prior to its independence as Israel. In 1919 in Madison, Rachel Szold Jastrow founded one of the first Hadassah chapters outside of the East.[22]

Jastrow also typified women who joined the woman suffrage campaign in its last decade, which culminated in Wisconsin with the historic first ratification of the Nineteenth Amendment. All came into the campaign from women's clubs and other civic work, which both taught women the need for the ballot and trained them in the political strategies and the publicity-conscious tactics — from massive parades to mass protests — that characterized the campaign after 1910. All such "second-generation suffragists" almost abandoned other clubs and causes in a single-minded drive to win at all cost, with their strategic support of the war. Also all too typical was the schism among suffragists over leadership, a struggle over larger strategies that had existed from the first decades of "the struggle." In 1910, Ada James of Richland Center failed to wrest control of the almost-moribund Wisconsin Woman Suffrage Association (WWSA) from its first-generation leader, the Reverend Olympia Brown (see "Olympia Brown and the Woman's Suffrage Movement" in chapter 4). James founded the Political Equality League to lobby the legislature for only the second statewide referendum on woman suffrage — a family tradition, as her uncle had sponsored the first referendum bill when he served in the legislature, and her father had inherited the Richland Center seat and sponsored the second bill.

James's success in winning the first referendum in a quarter of a century soon enlisted other younger suffragists, clubwomen all, although some were atypical of their time as career women whose professional expertise and political experience proved useful in finally winning woman suffrage: Belle La Follette, Meta Schlichting Berger, Zona Gale, Jessie Jack Hooper, and pioneering woman journalist Theodora Winton Youmans of Waukesha, soon to be Brown's successor as the last president of the WWSA. The story of her life and leadership in the campaign's last, significant seven years is excerpted in this chapter. The article focuses, as did Youmans despite further schisms among suffragists in war-torn Wisconsin, on a turnaround in public opinion formation from the failure of the referendum in 1912 to the success of their race to ratification in 1919. At that time, as Youmans wrote, women finally won suffrage only because "it was taken out of the hands of the male voters of Wisconsin by the federal government."[23]

Suffragists still had to win full citizenship and stayed organized — or reorganized — as the League of Women Voters, which in Wisconsin adopted the state motto of "Forward" as its own. The new name came from the first national suffrage organization's last president, Ripon native Carrie Chapman Catt. In Wisconsin, Jessie Jack Hooper served as the first president of the state League of Women Voters. However, in the final schism among suffragists, Ada James had formed a state chapter of the National Woman's Party. But both worked to win women to the polls and into political office, as Lawrence L. Graves writes in an article excerpted here on Hooper, James, and their organizations' ongoing struggle in the post-1920 period, when "some women fairly seethed with desire to participate in politics."

Hooper ran for Congress in 1922 but lost without the promised support from men in her party. She would have been one of the first women elected to the U.S. Senate, although women had served in the U.S. House of Representatives since 1917. In Wisconsin, whether any Democrat could have defeated Robert M. La Follette in any race is doubtful. When he died in 1925, his widow also had served forty years in public life; asked to serve out his term, she refused (see "The Two Worlds of Belle Case La Follette" in chapter 5). Their oldest son inherited the seat in a special election. However, had Belle Case La Follette known that Wisconsin would be the last state with a woman in Congress, and not until the end of her century — and that Wisconsin has yet to send a woman to the U.S. Senate — women's history might have been otherwise.

Even in Wisconsin, no woman would win a seat in the upper house of the legislature for half a century, although several soon won seats in the assembly. Youmans was among the first to run for the legislature. Like Hooper, she saw similar lack of support from her party when she ran on the Republican ballot for the state senate in 1924. However, three women won seats in the lower house of the legislature that year: Mildred Barber of Marathon, Hellen M. Brooks of Coloma, and Helen F. Thompson of Park Falls. Four decades later, Mildred Barber Abel recalled that she ran on a "daring ticket" for the time, if not for Wisconsin: she was an anti-Prohibitionist, so she was made welcome by the men who "resented" another woman legislator "who wore the white ribbon of the Woman's Christian Temperance Union" in the assembly. Among Abel's supporters in the legislature was her father. Even as a "little girl," she was "literally raised in politics" and had "politicked with him all over the state." By 1924, her mother had her own political post as Marathon's postmistress, so Abel "kept house" in Madison for her father and his cronies, who encouraged her to run. However, she declined to run for a second term as "assemblyman" — a term that remained unaltered — as did Brooks. But Thompson won re-election in 1926. The most winning political woman in Wisconsin in the period was Mary Kryszak of Milwaukee, elected to the assembly in 1928 and to six more terms by 1944.[24]

Mabel Raef Putnam of Milwaukee may have been the most astute political strategist among Wisconsin women for winning the country's first Equal Rights Amendment (ERA) in 1921, when the state legislature still was all-male. As James's successor as head of the National Woman's Party in the state, Putnam put together a relentless publicity blitz for its proposed ERA and her subsequent bill. She formed a coalition with the League of Women Voters and other organizations across the state, from a Polish Housewives Association to the formidable if unofficial group of "faculty wives" of the state university. In Madison, women also won the backing of Anna Carrier McSpaden Blaine of Boscobel, the wife of the new governor. He heeded her advice on winning the new women voters, well aware that they "would be instantly aroused by any attempt to legislate them back into the condition of legal inferiority from which they have emerged," as Putnam put it.[25]

Her coalition came to the state capitol to conduct a whirlwind campaign in only weeks — and won. As Putnam wrote in a press release, state women now had "the same rights as men" — not only suffrage but also "such matters" as jury service, choice of place of residence, child custody, "and in all other respects." Headlines hailed her law nationwide, while local newspapers featured the first women on Wisconsin juries in 1921 including the first "Madam Foreman," who served in Waukesha County. In several court cases, the Wisconsin ERA did offer women a legal defense against gender discrimination; for example, women teachers no longer had to leave work when they wed, and a divorced mother whose husband had left the state won the right to use her residence for in-state tuition rates for her son at the state university.[26]

However, the same men in the legislature who had passed the law in 1921 turned it against women working for them in 1923. Putnam based her bill, perhaps prematurely, on early versions proposed by the National Woman's Party that did not preclude "protective clauses" in Wisconsin laws to limit women's workdays. Reassuring as it was for voters to know that their legislators worked long hours, lawmakers used the law won by women to let the women working for them go rather than enact an exemption. The experience with the Wisconsin ERA proved useful as the National Woman's Party unveiled a new version in 1923 — an ERA without any exceptions that was passed by Congress half a century later but was never made federal law.[27]

Passage of the historic Wisconsin ERA had made headlines nationwide for the National Woman's Party, but the passage of time would prove that the more moderate League of Women Voters had the staying power in the state. "Patience and moderation seldom inspire headlines," as Glad writes, so the league often went unsung for working to politicize women's place in Wisconsin. Historians also "have understated achievements of women as a political force in the postwar decade," focusing on their schisms instead of their gender solidarity in combining forces by building bipartisan consensus and coalitions. But women would continue to expand their efforts beyond the suffrage movement to move forward in Wisconsin, despite decades of further defeats amid the protracted demise of the Progressive movement — for all the good it had done them.[28]

## NOTES

1. John D. Buenker, *HOW*, vol. 4, *The Progressive Era, 1893–1914* (Madison:SHSW, 1998), 514, 606–607.
2. Ibid.
3. Ibid., 37, 66, 268–270, 549–550; Susan Strasser, *Never Done: A History of American Housework* (New York: Henry Holt and Company, 1982), 263–281.
4. Joan M. Jensen, "Sexuality on a Northern Frontier:" The Gendering and Disciplining of Rural Wisconsin Women, 1850–1920, *Agricultural History* 73, no. 2 (Spring 1999); 161, citing Dorothy Behling, "Fashion Change in a Northwoods Lumbering Town, 1915–1925," *Dress* 9 (1983), 32–40; Sara M. Evans, *Born for Liberty: A History of Women in America* (New York: Free Press, 1989), 161; Buenker, *HOW*, 27, 75; Paul W. Glad, *HOW*, vol. 5, *War, A New Era, and Depression, 1914–1940*, (Madison: SHSW, 1990), 220–221.

5. Jo Sandin, "'No Matter What Happens, Be Brave,' Fond du Lac Man Told His Wife," April 19, 1998, and Arthur Abernathy, "Survivors Tell Story of Horror," April 21, 1998, both in the *Milwaukee Journal Sentinel*.

6. Sandin, "No Matter What Happens;" Abernathy, "Survivors Tell Story of Horror."

7. Sandin, "No Matter What Happens;" Abernathy, "Survivors Tell Story of Horror;" see also Jack Winocour, *The Story of the Titanic as Told by Its Survivors* (London: Dover, 1960); Donald Hyslop, et al., *Titanic Voices: Memories from the Fateful Voyage,* reprint ed. (New York: St. Martin's Press, 1997); and *The Titanic Disaster Hearings: The Official Transcripts of the 1912 Senate Investigation* (New York: Pocket Books, 1998).

8. Glad, *HOW,* 88, 125–126, 221, 224, 306; Buenker, *HOW,* 186, 195–197; Joe William Trotter Jr., *Black Milwaukee: The Making of an Urban Proletariat, 1915–1945* (Urbana: University of Illinois Press), 40, 138.

9. Joseph Rodriguez, *Nuestro Milwaukee: The Making of the United Community Center* (Milwaukee: United Community Center, 2000), 5–10.

10. Glad, *HOW,* 255–256; Jensen, "Sexuality on a Northern Frontier," 154.

11. Amelia Klem, "'Say, Have You Met Lydia?' A History of American Tattooed Ladies of the Circus, Sideshow, and Dime Museum, 1882–1995" (master's thesis, University of Wisconsin–Milwaukee, 2004), 106–111.

12. Henry James Forman, "Zona Gale: A Touch of Greatness," *WMH* 46, no. 1 (Autumn 1962): 32–37; Glad, *HOW,* 230.

13. Genevieve G. McBride, *On Wisconsin Women: Working for Their Rights from Settlement to Suffrage* (Madison:University of Wisconsin Press, 1993), 303; Eldon Knoche, "Ryan Was Fashion Reporting Pioneer While at Journal," *Milwaukee Journal,* September 24, 1995. Ryan accepted induction into the Milwaukee Press Club's Hall of Fame six years later in 1987.

14. Buenker, *HOW,* 61.

15. Glad, *HOW,* 225.

16. Buenker, *HOW,* 37. Often, the only data reported are for white women, whose life expectancy if born in 1910 was age 52, an increase from age 49 in 1900; for black women, life expectancy increased to only age 38 from age 34; see U.S. Census Bureau, *Current Population Reports: Special Studies: 65+ in the U.S.* (Washington, D.C., 2001).

17. Christine A. Ogren, "Where Coeds Were Coeducated: Normal Schools in Wisconsin, 1870–1920," *History of Education Quarterly* 35, no. 1 (Spring 1995), 10, 21. Legislators also added another state normal school in Eau Claire in 1916.

18. Ibid., 10; Mary Davison Bradford, "Memoirs," *WMH* 14, no. 1 (September 1930) through *WMH* 16, no. 1 (September 1932); also published as *Pioneers! O Pioneers! Her Autobiography* (Evansville: Antes Press, 1932); Jack Dougherty, *More Than One Struggle: The Evolution of Black School Reform in Milwaukee* (Chapel Hill: University of North Carolina Press, 2004), 20.

19. Buenker, *HOW,* 186; Glad, *HOW,* 1–2; McBride, *On Wisconsin Women,* 267.

20. McBride, *On Wisconsin Women,* 279, 286; *Milwaukee Journal,* November 11, 1918.

21. Glad, *HOW,* 57–58.

22. Alexandra Lee Levin, "The Jastrows in Madison: A Chronicle of University Life, 1888–1900," *WMH* 46, no. 4 (Summer 1963): 243–256; Sarah Blacher Cohen, "Henrietta Szold as Muse," *Hadassah* 83, no. 6 (February 2002): n.p. Another early Hadassah chapter was in Appleton. Cohen, a native of Appleton, also coauthored a play on Henrietta Szold.

23. McBride, *On Wisconsin Women,* 293.

24. Glad, *HOW,* 118; Marian McBride, "Political Pioneer," *Milwaukee Sentinel,* February 24, 1965.

25. Mabel Raef Putnam, *The Winning of the First Bill of Rights for American Women* (Milwaukee, 1924). A copy of the privately published book is in the editor's possession. See also Genevieve G. McBride, "'Forward' Women: Winning the Wisconsin Campaign for the Country's First Equal Rights Amendment, 1921," in Steven Burnham, ed., *The Quest for Social Justice III: The Morris Fromkin Memorial Lectures, 1991–2003* (Milwaukee: University of Wisconsin–Milwaukee Press, 2005).

26. Putnam, *The Winning of the First Bill of Rights.*

27. Nancy F. Cott, *The Grounding of Modern Feminism* (New Haven, CT: Yale University Press, 1987), 120–125.

28. Glad, *HOW,* 111–112.

# Nellie Kedzie Jones's Advice to Farm Women
## Letters from Wisconsin, 1912–1916

JEANNE HUNNICUTT DELGADO

*WMH* 57, No. 1 (Autumn 1973): 3–27

*Nellie Kedzie Jones may have made her first visit to Wisconsin at the turn of the century, when the board of the Wisconsin Federation of Women's Clubs invited the pioneering professor in the new field of home economics to speak to its 1901 annual convention. By the end of the convention, clubwomen not only backed the board by a wide margin in a fund drive for a department of domestic science at Milwaukee-Downer College (see "Ellen Clara Sabin and My Years at Downer" in chapter 5) but also voted to undertake a petition campaign for a chair in home economics at the University of Wisconsin in Madison.[1]*

*Legislators funded a Department of Home Economics in 1903, when the university hired Caroline Hunt as the department's first professor (and the lowest-paid professor on campus). Her curriculum — popularly called "The Bride's Course" — included coursework in the sciences, economics, and humanities. She also began short courses called "Housekeepers' Conferences" for the public. However, Hunt departed in 1908, and the department moved from the liberal arts to the College of Agriculture, where Professor Abby L. Marlatt arrived in 1909 and endured for thirty years. The first graduate in home economics was Sarah Augusta Sutherland in 1910, when candidates had to complete theses; hers was "A Study of the Methods of Cooking the Rump of Beef Showing Cost, in Market Cost, in Preparation and Loss in Cooking." In 1911, Katherine Agnes Donovan earned the first master's degree for her thesis, "A Study of the Infant Mortality of Madison."[2]*

*Also in 1911, another nationally recognized home economist, Nellie Kedzie Jones, moved to Wisconsin, on Smoky Hill Farm near Auburndale, back to her rural beginnings. Nellie Sawyer had been born on a farm in Maine in 1858 and moved with her family to Kansas, where she earned a bachelor's degree at the new Kansas State Agricultural College. She taught school for five years until 1881, when she married and moved to Mississippi. Within seven weeks, she was widowed. In 1882, her alma mater invited her to return as an instructor in "household economy"; in 1883, she earned a master's degree from Kansas State, where her thesis was "Science in a Woman's Life."[3]*

*Kedzie was named Kansas State's first woman professor. As Jeanne Hunnicutt Delgado discovered, Nellie Kedzie "was to found, administer, and teach all courses in a new department of domestic economy which was to supersede the college's simple offering of a sewing and cooking course. The difficulty in organizing a new domestic economy department was, as she later said, that 'there was no such thing.'" However, with her "remarkably practical imagination," Kedzie "imagined the best and easiest way for a woman to keep an efficient and pleasant home, considered in detail what knowledge was needed," and then planned her courses. Kedzie soon "became a favorite lecturer on homemaking, particularly at farmers institutes, where the farm women . . . recognized the worth of practical suggestions for lightening their work loads," writes Delgado. In her fifteen years at Kansas State, Kedzie also was "often invited to speak at academic institutions on the idea of adding home economics to the curriculum" and built a popular and prosperous department, to the point that the legislature awarded funds for a Domestic Science Hall in 1897. However, owing to political shifts on the board of regents, they fired the entire faculty at Kansas State that year. After she departed, the new building was named Nellie Kedzie Hall.*

*She joined the founding faculty of Bradley Polytechnic Institute in Peoria, Illinois, and taught there from 1897 to 1901, when she married the Reverend Howard Murray Jones, a history professor and vice-president at Kentucky's Berea College, where she taught for two years. When he resigned in 1903 to return to the ministry, they moved to Michigan and then to Minnesota, while she continued her lecturing career around the country and was director of the annual State Fair School of Home Economics in Illinois. When an infant was left with the minister for adoption, Nellie Jones became a mother for the first time, at the age of forty-eight; three years later, their daughter nearly died due to polio. Her husband resigned his ministry, and the family moved to the Wisconsin farm.*

*"Even from the farm," writes Delgado, Jones "was called away by her reputation as a teacher and lecturer," and "every winter she 'rode circuit' to produce Farm and Home Week at five different Midwestern colleges." By 1912, Jones also had begun her journalistic career as a columnist, as her biographer writes here from her research in the Nellie Kedzie Jones Papers and Howard Murray Jones Papers in the WHS Archives, including the excerpted "Country Gentlewoman" columns, as part of a long-term project to provide authors of the six-volume* History of Wisconsin *series with insight into rural life.*

During the years 1912 to 1916, rural women all over America anticipated the arrival of the next issue of *The Country Gentleman* — and its page of advice emanating from a farm in Marathon County, Wisconsin. Deceptively down-to-earth and good-humored in style, the columns, presented under the title "The Country Gentlewoman," were entirely serious in intent. Through them Nellie Kedzie Jones was attempting to share some of the basic precepts and principles she had acquired in her distinguished career as a pioneer in the developing field of home economics. . . .

[Her advice] was particularly vivid in a series of these articles written as letters to an imaginary young niece named Janet from her loving "Aunt Nellie." Janet, with husband Ben, was supposed just to have moved to an old farm with an unimproved house. . . . Since Janet was raised in a city, "Aunt Nellie" could write detailed basic advice which might have been insulting to a farm-bred girl — or "County Gentlewoman" reader — who believed she had no reason to reconsider her basic household arrangements. . . . [H]er letters described in humorous detail very real Midwestern farm household routines, equipment, and follies. . . . "Aunt Nellie's" basic message was that a farm wife must spare herself in any small ways she can contrive — she will never be liberated from an overwhelming work burden, but she can organize it so that she does not metamorphose into an overworked piece of farm equipment.

. . . [I]n imparting that advice, Nellie Kedzie Jones unintentionally provided a nostalgic glimpse into the farm life of [the early twentieth century], before the rapid expansion of technology had changed the face of rural America.

Dear Janet:

Start with the kitchen. For the next twenty years more of your waking hours will be spent in it than out of it. Your kitchen, in the first place, is altogether too big. It is typical of the way our fathers and grandfathers built kitchens, when the husband and the carpenter did all the planning for the woman who was to do her life-work there.

Cut up that kitchen of skating-rink dimensions into at least three rooms — a modern kitchen, a laundry, and a storeroom. . . .

One-half of the old kitchen will make the new kitchen. Take about two-thirds of the other half for the laundry and the remaining third for the storeroom. A storeroom on the kitchen level saves many journeys to the cellar and cuts out much lugging up and down, which has been the death warrant for generations of farm women. . . .

. . . Th[e] laundry-washroom I have found to be one of the most convenient and necessary things in a farm home, yet it is not common. When a farmer's wife is rushing to take up a meal and get it onto the table on time, to have hired men crowd into the kitchen to wash up is an abominable nuisance, especially when hats, coats and boots have been in the stable or other unappetizing places. . . .

We agree perfectly on the matter of the kitchen range. The best is none too good. You had better economize anywhere else than on that. Good cookery is impossible on a poor stove. . . .

I prefer a range on legs to one on a solid base, for it heats the kitchen floor better and I do not bump my toes against the base. Be sure to get a range with a large reservoir. In cold weather, with chicken mashes to make, calf feed to prepare, and dairy utensils to wash and scald, you can't have too much hot water. Get a range as plain as possible. Much nickeling, curlicues, scrolls and gingerbread work generally are a pest to keep clean and are often, from an artistic standpoint, atrocious. A plain surface is easier to black and to clean. . . .

. . . The placing of the sink at exactly the right height is a matter of vital importance. . . . Even the tables that have been worked out as standard for women of various heights need personal testing, for two women of the same height have different length arms. Barbers and dentists have chairs that shift up or down easily to get the comfortable place for work, why should not women care as much for their own comfort? . . .

Provide two wooden stools, a high one and a low one, and a low, light rocking-chair. You see, I want you to take it easy while you work. This advice, the best I shall ever give you, my dear niece, "Take it easy while you work," is a slogan that ought to be hung in the kitchen of every farm woman.

The little rocking-chair back in the corner, out of the way most of the time, is a wonderful comfort as you do a little mending or are waiting for your baking to finish. These little snatches of rest, when you get your weight off your feet, are life-savers, and should be sown in during the day's work, always long on a farm, like commas sprinkled over the printed page. . . .

In a box on an upper shelf keep a good nail hammer with claws, a few nails of different sizes, tack hammer, pinchers, screw driver, box of tacks, ball of fine twine, ball of coarse twine, and a spool of fine wire. As you begin to get accustomed to the use of tools and feel the joy of being independent of men's help I know you will add other light tools. Have a carborundum or emery wheel for fast sharpening and a fine gritted whetstone to finish the edge. It is real fun to work with razorlike knives. . . .

. . . My choice of a washing machine would be one on the pneumatic principle. Get the hotel size. The cost is but little more, and with a man to run it you can double the output in the same time. You must have two wringers, ball bearing.

The telephone is a most essential part of the kitchen equipment, but on a farm I have found it best to have it near the kitchen — not in it, for the hired men, the neighbors, cattle buyers, peddlers, in fact all sorts and conditions — will be crowding into your kitchen to phone. . . . Why is it that just as something is boiling over on the kitchen stove the phone rings? I would put the phone just inside the laundry door; that is the nearest place to the kitchen where Ben and the men can most conveniently accommodate themselves. This is bad for your city visitors, but for the greatest good to the greatest number, I believe it is the best place.

. . . Unlike the city woman, the farm woman cannot phone for any thing any time she wants it from the grocery, bakery, or delicatessen and have the delivery boy come with it on the run, nor can she in a pinch send the family for their meals to the restaurant just around the corner, so she must keep plenty of provisions on hand all the time. . . .

Your affectionate,
Aunt Nellie


Dear Janet:

. . . A little kitchen is the right thing on a farm, but you must have a large dining room, for often you will have to feed a crew of men. . . .

. . . When you have a crew to feed, you must bring in what I call the "annex" table, simply a table top made of pine boards resting on a pair of horses. . . .

The dining-room chairs are a real problem, but do not buy till you find the right thing. Remember that nine out of ten hired men will tilt back on the hind legs of a chair and in no time a graceful spindle-legged chair is out of commission.

The fact is, the woman who has the conveniences and begins the right kind of cooking early enough can handle a big crowd of farmers at table with but one woman helper. With the food once cooked and on the table, the men prefer to wait on themselves. The speed with which they will stow away an enormous amount of food will be one of the big surprises awaiting you as a farmer's wife.

There are many solutions offered for lighting in the country, and electric lights or some system of gas lighting is not in the distant future for you; but now the inexpensive thing and probably the most practical is bracket oil lamps with reflectors. . . .

Then get a good broad-based lamp for your dining-room table. . . . This will be your reading lamp in the evening when you and Ben sit in the "cozy end."

The next thing in importance is the living room. Without any alteration whatever you can take the old parlor for your bedroom — you do not want a parlor anyway — and the old sitting room for your living room. I never could understand why people who could as well as not have a downstairs bedroom would persist in climbing stairs!

In losing your parlor you will lose nothing, for the old parlor idea was dead wrong. Our grandmothers took the "front room" for a parlor, and because the blinds were kept tightly closed the room was always dark and the carpet, therefore, did not fade so soon. It was to be opened, of course, for weddings and funerals, when the minister called, and on only a few other special occasions. . . . By some strange perversion of thrift the best room was least used. . . .

. . . During the coldest three months of the year the "cozy end" of the dining room will be your living room to save you much hard work and to save fuel, for that large front room would heat very slowly and take a great deal of wood which ought not to be wasted; but nine months in the year heating will not trouble. . . .

. . . I would strongly advise a . . . [bedroom] stove so that you may have a little fire whenever you feel the least bit chilly. Wood on that farm certainly is cheaper than human vitality.

. . . Many farmers' wives go to bed and shiver. You want a warm bed to get into, but you ought not to sleep in a warm room. An air-tight stove can be dampered down so effectually that with an opened window one can soon have a cool room.

Let me add, be sure to get the bureau so placed that its mirror will have the best possible light, for when you run in, after you have got a meal on the table, to smooth your hair, I want you to be sure to see that smutch on the side of your nose!

Do not try to furnish all of that great upstairs — one guest room is enough for now. This also will need a stove. . . . I would give each room a number and then mark all my bedroom linen with the proper number. This is a very great saving and convenience, for the hired girl you will have to have now and then probably would mix the linen of the guest room and that of the hired man's room. Bear in mind in the winter to empty the water pitchers as soon as a guest leaves a room, or they may freeze and break. Extra bedding should be kept in the closet, for some guests require an astonishing amount.

Ben will always have a hired man or two. Take that large room over the kitchen and put a stove in it. . . .

While you are planning to do your own work, there will be times when you will have to have help, so I would take that little south room over the dining room for a hired girl's room. An iron bed is essential, a stove if she is with you in the winter, and a well-furnished washstand. . . .

. . . Let her decorate it according to her own taste. If she wants advertising chromos and colored postals galore, all well and good. It is her room, not yours.

This whole problem of the hired help is a knotty one. Any combination you can make has its drawbacks, but for the present you must have your helpers under your roof and at your table. In time you will have a tenant house with a good farmer and family in it, but that is several years ahead. . . . Inasmuch as the hired man must board and lodge with you for the present, make up your mind to pay about top wages and get the best to be had. In the long run this will be a real economy. You not only get more work but far better work.

Your affectionate,
Aunt Nellie

Dear Janet:

Really the housewife's day begins yesterday though a man's day begins shortly before breakfast. That means you must do as much of the breakfast work as possible the night before. . . . Eternities have been wasted by women waiting on slow fires. . . . Ben or the hired man will make your fire, so that steam will be generating while the engineer of the day is dressing herself. . . .

Do not let two great big jobs land on you in the same day. Do not be caught so that you will have to bake on the same day that Ben has extra hired men on hand for you to cook for. He must let you know in time. . . .

A batch of unbaked bread buried in the far corner of the garden may be a good investment. By that I mean, be ready to sacrifice the less for the greater. Ben may be suddenly called to town and comes in and begs you to go with him just when your bread ought to go into the oven. . . .

Two or three hours together in the open air, measured in health, happiness and mutual planning for farm and home, might have results worth many batches of bread. Some women are so busy with little things they do not recognize a big thing when it stares them in the face. . . .

In dividing up the week, be sure to plan at least one play period. Have no set time for this. A surprise for Ben, bumping the old farm routine in a new place, is half the fun. Have some every week. Exuberance of spirit is not a farmer's failing. The fun may be a picnic lunch up in the back pasture where Ben is cutting brush, or phoning a neighbor to come over to supper, you and Ben taking her home afterward, or having the teacher spend Sunday with you — don't make company of her. . . .

In closing, dear Janet, let me say that Sunday must be the climax of your week. Devote that day to home and heaven. . . . If you are ever to devote yourselves to each other and the higher ends of living, it will be on Sunday. When you lose your Sunday these will go with it.

Your affectionate,
Aunt Nellie

Dear Janet:

In the old days, it took three women three days to get ready for threshers. . . .

In your part of the country, where threshers stay for but three or four meals at most, the farm wife will have to feed them for some time still [whereas, in the West, chuck wagons follow threshers]. And then there are silo fillers, hay balers, harvest hands, wood-sawing crews, and so on, so that you must make up your mind to cook for a crew of from five to fifteen men every now and then. . . .

The midday meal can be served in the field, picnic-fashion, to the real pleasure of the men, to the saving of their time and the lessening of your own work. I have served a mile and [a] half from the house and got the dinner there hot. Really this serving in the field is easier part of the time than in the house. The trick of it all is in getting rid of the nonessentials. Not frills but food fills the bill with the farm laborer. . . .

The question of suitable drinks for the men in the field in hot weather is an important one. In the old days grog aplenty was served with striking results, literally striking results, which were not at all on the program. That has most recently passed. . . .

To read of the rebellion of the hired man when you wanted him to help you wash was really very funny. His final unconditional surrender stamps Janet as a diplomat of high order.

However, do not be too puffed up about it, for the fact that Ben always has done it and would have washed had he been home that day, and the really deciding factor, the absence of another hired man to ridicule him for doing "woman's work," turned the scale in your favor. . . .

Having the help live right in the home with us is where we farmer-folks have it hard. In the city a man appears when the whistle blows and disappears when it blows again and that is the end of it. But not so on the farm. . . .

The hired man must be encouraged to buy more clothing so that he can make several changes between washings. . . . When we were washing only once in two weeks I discovered that a [hired] girl I had was washing her things twice a week. I told her she must quit it as she was wasting time, and then the secret was out. She had but one change, but had a commendable pride in keeping the fact to herself. . . .

. . . Give [a hired girl] a reason for what you do, and in turn expect her to reason about her work. Most women prefer to cook, dodging the dishwashing and wiping: but play fair with the hired girl, helping with the dishes. Some women, very efficient and executive, do all the important things and so keep their girls inefficient. Push the girl ahead just as fast as you can.

Big wages I would not pay. Give just the "going wage" of that neighborhood, such as the other farmers are paying; but in services as instructor, inspired and sympathetic associate I would try to make it well worth her while to stay with you. . . .

You will take a real interest in her family and make her feel that if she wants her younger brothers and sisters to visit her, they are very welcome. If she wants to have her sweetheart to visit her at your house, give her a place where she may receive him. . . . A real interest here will warm a girl's heart sooner than anything I know.

A nap in the afternoon is as much appreciated and as much needed by the maid as by the mistress. The day on the farm is long at both ends. . . . Never plan to "keep a girl busy," to "fill her time," meaning that as soon as one job is done another stands in line waiting for her. That sort of a program makes a drudge and a dawdler. . . .

A hired girl is entitled to her fun as much as a city "servant" is to hers. The town girl gets a chance to have some fun every night in the week. On the farm, there are no movies; the parks and beaches, if there are any, are too thinly populated to be any fun, so on "The Fourth," "County Fair week" or when the circus comes along, if she does not get an outside invitation to go, then you and Ben had better go and take her. . . .

Your affectionate,
Aunt Nellie

Dear Janet:

. . . Catch onto the country code as soon as you can. For one thing, it is good form in the country to borrow and lend, for there is no store just round the corner to be phoned to, with a delivery wagon waiting at the door. . . . This is not "nervy" in the country, just neighborly. . . .

In almost every rural neighborhood there is some one indiscreet enough to talk [imprudently] over the telephone, and there is often some one sneaky enough to listen in. . . . The only safe course is to talk over nothing over a party line that you would not be willing to proclaim from the housetop.

You might want to talk with your pastor or physician . . . and surely you have the right. In many neighborhoods it would be perfectly safe; in not a few neighborhoods it would be folly to do so. I am ashamed to say that the offender is more often a woman than a man. There is this excuse, however, for the woman — she is shut within four walls most of her time, while her husband can go to town or can exchange words with the neighbors; she is hungering for the news and in her loneliness she lets her curiosity get the better of her. . . .

Visiting on the party line is permissible. I believe in it as a great socializer. It banishes much of the loneliness and monotony of country life for the women. However, discretion must be used. I know of one party line with thirteen families on it. After supper and on Sundays it was almost impossible to get a chance on the telephone at all, there was such an interminable chatter. All these neighbors knew each other, and it was agreed that when the line was being used only for visiting, one who had business could ring in and say, "Please get off the line while I do this errand."

In the country the function of the telephone is even more social than commercial. Blessed be telephones! There is no excuse for farmers' being without them. The double wire, insulators and brackets do not cost $20 a mile, and the farmers can cut the poles in their own woods and set them in a slack time. . . .

The district schoolhouse ought not to be left off the line. In case of sickness or accident among the children the teacher can get help quickly. Sometimes fierce storms break suddenly [and] a wise teacher has kept the little children in rather than let them go out in a blizzard. . . . In such cases a telephone is a godsend indeed.

It is not a difficult matter nowadays to have a telephone line in any farm neighborhood. . . . The makers of telephone instruments and wire are anxious to broaden their markets and will gladly give directions for building spur branches from the main trunk lines. A private-party switchboard can be installed in a village store and a clerk employed to operate it at small cost. Such service is not the best, but it makes a beginning, and it will not be difficult to sell out to a larger company when a dozen parties have been signed up. . . .

Your affectionate,
Aunt Nellie

Dear Janet:

. . . You farm mothers are blessed with plenty of real work for yourselves and your little ones. Your duties call you out into the sunshine. You make many a trip during the day to the garden, the orchard, the henhouse, or the yard where the young chicks are. . . .

Have the little girls and boys play together. The work and play good for one are good for the other. . . . "Tomboys" make strong women. Never shame a girl for romping and scuffling with her brothers. Our New England mothers and grandmothers had prudish notions about what was proper for a girl. She did not have a fair chance; she was kept in the house and put at sewing, housework or dolls. Dolls are good on a rainy day for little girls, and boys, too, for that matter, but when the weather permits get the girls out for real athletics. Housework is not very good for the health of a growing girl.

I know this last statement will be disputed, but I want to repeat it in spite of the men who never did housework, but who constantly affirm that housework is the best thing in the world for a girl. They forget that it shuts her away from sun and air; that sweeping fills her lungs with dust; that the hot stove overheats her; that dishwashing makes her stoop-shouldered; that a few of her muscles are overstrained while most of them are underdeveloped; and above all there is the monotony of it which so many children hate. Give the girls a chance at some of the outdoor work, and make the boys do some of the inside work. If the girl feeds the hens and hunts the eggs let her brother help her do the dishes. . . .

Girls are coming into their own. Makers of women's garments report that young women nowadays require larger sizes than they did a generation ago. We are on the eve of a revival in physical training for women. There is a good chance to begin with the little girl on the farm. . . .

. . . Go slowly with sewing even for a girl. The place for her in her childhood is out of doors. . . .

Your affectionate,
Aunt Nellie . . .

❧ ❦

*Nellie Kedzie Jones and her family left Smoky Hill Farm in 1918. At sixty years old, she accepted a new position of state leader in home economics for the University of Wisconsin Extension in Madison. While her husband taught history for the university, she worked throughout the state, "initiating a variety of efforts to improve rural life in general and especially the lot of the farm woman," Delgado writes of Jones's "final official position" in a pioneering career of "organizing and defining traditional 'woman's work' into the rational scheme of modern home economics."*

*Among her many honors was an honorary doctorate awarded by her alma mater, Kansas State, in 1925. Upon her retirement in 1933, Jones was the first woman to be granted professor emerita status by the University of Wisconsin. However, "her less official work of lectures and radio talks continued" even into her nineties, writes Delgado, when Jones gave "lectures on growing old gracefully." In 1956, at the age of ninety-seven, Nellie Kedzie Jones died.*

*By then, more than half a century after Jones had inspired clubwomen to work for study in her field at the University of Wisconsin in Madison, its Department of Home Economics had gained academic stature in 1951 as the School of Home Economics within the College of Agriculture. Since then, the program has been reorganized twice, first as the School of Family Resources and Consumer Sciences and then as the separate School of Human Ecology before its centennial in 2003.*

## NOTES

1. McBride, *On Wisconsin Women*, 185.
2. Joyce E. Coleman, Rima D. Apple, and Greta Marie Zenner, "From Home Economics to Human Ecology: A One-Hundred Year History at the University of Wisconsin–Madison," School of Human Ecology Web site, University of Wisconsin–Madison, http://www.sohe.wisc.edu/depts/history/.
3. Nellie Kedzie Jones, "Pioneering in Home Economics," *K-Stater* (October 1954): 6; Charles M. Correll, "Three Great Teachers," *K-Stater* (October 1953): 18.

# The Wisconsin Idea of Dance

## A Decade of Progress, 1917–1926

MARY LOU REMLEY

*WMH* 58, No. 3 (Spring 1975): 179–195

❧

The impulse to dance is as old as civilization. . . . As an integral part of education, however, dance had little impact until the advent of Margaret N. H'Doubler and her "Wisconsin Idea of Dance," an idea which eventually culminated in the introduction of dance into physical education curricula throughout the United States.

Miss H'Doubler was born April 26, 1889, in Beloit, Kansas, the daughter of a Swiss artist-photographer-inventor (the H-apostrophe-Doubler is an Americanized version of the original Swiss family name Hougen-Doubler). Her early childhood years were spent in Warren, Illinois, where she attended elementary and high schools. Her family then moved to Madison, and in 1906 she enrolled at the University of Wisconsin, earning a B.A. degree in biology four years later. A program of physical education for women had become an established part of the University curriculum by this time, and women's sports activities had emerged at the turn of the century to augment the department offerings of gymnastics and calisthenics. . . . In this early period when the physical education profession was developing, teacher preparation programs were limited, and teachers were sometimes selected for their expertise in the performance of gymnastics, calisthenics, and sports activities. Thus, upon completion of her degree in 1910 and without special formal training, Miss H'Doubler was invited to remain at the University as an assistant in the department of physical education with primary responsibilities for basketball and baseball. Because of her keen interest and active involvement in the department program as a student, she readily accepted the challenge and opportunity to continue as a teacher. In spite of her lack of pedagogical training she was probably more ably prepared than many other teachers, owing to her background in the biological sciences and her varied sports and gymnastics experiences.

Miss H'Doubler had some limited experience with dance as a student through the department offerings of the aesthetic dance forms developed by Louis Chalif and Melvin B. Gilbert. But the imitative movements of these styles held no appeal for her nor for the director of the University's physical education department for women, Blanche M. Trilling. The stimulus that detoured Miss H'Doubler from her favorite pursuit of coaching girls on a basketball court into the world of dance came in 1916 when she left teaching to study philosophy for a year as a graduate student at Columbia University in New York. Miss Trilling sensed there was something more to dance than the "fancy steps," the "five stilted positions" of the classical ballet, and the artificialities of dance as it was then being taught.[1] Consequently, she asked Miss H'Doubler to make a study of dance during her stay in New York in an attempt to find some appropriate method for providing "something worth a college woman's time."[2]. . . . Miss H'Doubler remembered the pleasure and frustration with what she found:

> 1917 . . . was a very interesting time to be in New York . . . because there was a re-
> volt in all the arts. In music . . . new forms were appearing, . . . the same kind of
> thing in painting, and it was also happening in dance, but that was not very well
> known. There were a few who were dissenting, not teaching ballet, but the more I
> saw, the more I disliked it. It was merely miming; it was different movement, but
> imitating and being told what to do. The people who were dissenting and trying
> something different . . . were as limited in their thinking as the ballet in theirs.[3]

In response to Miss H'Doubler's comments that she would never teach dance, that she could find nothing that she would even want to teach, Miss Trilling continued to write from Wisconsin encouraging her to keep searching.

. . . Miss H'Doubler went to the studio of Alys E. Bentley, a teacher of music, not dance, and asked to work with her. . . . Miss H'Doubler recognized that her search "for something worthwhile in dance" had ended.[4]

In teaching music to young children, Miss Bentley had developed a unique, creative approach which utilized the child's natural impulses for expression and the use of movement in the learning process.[5] Lessons often began with students lying on the floor, each responding in his own way to a stimulus provided by Miss Bentley. Miss H'Doubler recalled that this aspect of teaching hit her like a flash. "Of course, get on the floor where you are relieved from the pull of gravity . . . and see what the natural, structural movements are."[6] The approach differed markedly from the usual imitative methods so prevalent for teaching movement forms of any kind. And while her observations of other dance forms that defied all the natural laws of the body offered her no solution in her search for a theory of dance, Miss H'Doubler found in Miss Bentley's logical techniques and ideas the spark for the beginnings of a full-blown philosophy of educational dance. In 1917, however, it was merely a spark. Miss H'Doubler . . . attempted to find support for her fledgling thoughts from physical education notables — Dudley Sargent, Carl Schrader, and Amy M. Homans — who she believed would "know what I am talking about and trying to do."[7] None of them confirmed or supported her far-fetched ideas, however, and Miss Homans was reported to have written Miss Trilling that "sad as it was, Miss H'Doubler was not quite sane."[8] Inflexible adherents to old dance forms and teaching methods could not abide teaching students to dance by having them first lie on the floor.

Despite the obstacles Miss H'Doubler returned to Wisconsin with her nebulous idea for a new approach to dance. . . . Her approach rested on the premises that dance must evolve from the experiences of each individual, be performed within the structural possibilities and limitations of each body, and serve as a means of self-realization for the student. . . .

In the summer of 1917 Miss H'Doubler first began teaching the "new dancing" to a group of summer session students, implementing "an idea not completely formed, only just a hopeful one."[9] The hopeful idea continued to develop, nurtured by experimentation during the summer, and Miss H'Doubler again offered "interpretative dancing" as one of the activities in the physical education program during the 1917–1918 school year. By second semester a special course, Dancing Methods, was established for teacher-training students, and physical education majors had their first exposure to the "new dancing."[10]

. . . Classes began with a series of exercises based on the body's natural movements. "Because of the muscular activity involved in the upright position, many of the fundamentals are executed lying on the floor, with the pull of gravity at a minimum. When the fundamental principles of movement have been mastered . . . in this position, the next step is . . . to carry these principles over into the upright position."[11]

Attention was then turned to the locomotor movements — walking, running, leaping, hopping, skipping, sliding, and combinations of these. As fundamentals were mastered, students attempted to combine them into more intricate movements. . . . Students also began to work at very early stages with application of Miss H'Doubler's theoretical concepts about what she called time-space-force: any movement takes place in terms of time intervals, involves force, and occurs in space.

After mastering the dance fundamentals, students were ready to move to the creative aspects of dance. Short verses were read sometimes, and students created personal interpretations of the words, using their movement experiences and imaginations. . . .

As students progressed to the more advanced levels of dance composition, Miss H'Doubler emphasized the importance of each dancer's expressing her own personality artistically. She insisted upon skilled performance in executing a dance, but that performance was not to be an imitation of a routine devised by someone else. . . .[12]

Miss H'Doubler went quickly about her work of developing this new approach to dance while continuing to teach basketball, baseball, and other sports. Visitors were not allowed in the dance classes, and emphasis was placed upon the value of the activity for the individual student rather than upon its entertainment potential. From the beginning, however, the students recognized its appeal to spectators. . . . By January, 1918, a small group of students had prepared a "series of interpretative dances . . . novel and interesting in the extreme . . . of a type never before seen at the University of Wisconsin."[13] These were presented at "Vodvil," the annual University talent show, and marked the first of many public performances which later became a tradition on the Madison campus. . . .

. . . [T]he new dancing, with its freedom of expression and naturalness of movement, received its strongest support from the general student in physical education classes. The closing of Lathrop Hall because of a fuel shortage in January, 1918, eliminated the usual classes in basketball, volleyball, indoor baseball, swimming, and gymnastics, and they were replaced by skating, coasting, tobogganing, skiing, ice hockey, and hiking. But students in dance classes expressed acute reluctance to curtail their new physical education activity, and they pleaded for other arrangements. Since space was the only requisite, Miss H'Doubler's dancing class, "limited to the first forty signing up, . . . met in the parlors of [the women's residence,] Chadbourne Hall."[14]

. . . The Women's Athletic Association (WAA) had provided strong leadership and a highly organized sports program for women for a number of years. In cooperation with the department faculty, WAA sponsored interclass tournaments throughout the year, had a point system for awarding a university athletic letter or pin or emblem through sports participation, and concluded the year with a Field Day for competition among classes in all sports. The festivities ended with the selection of varsity teams for each activity. As dance became popular, the logical niche for it, too, seemed to be within the department's sports format. Thus, in spring, 1918, just a year after its introduction within the physical education program, dance was accepted by WAA "as a sport" and given a point reward equal to other sports. Each class, freshman through senior, had its own dancing team, and a head of dancing was elected to serve with other sports heads on the governing board of WAA.[15] Dance Drama, the first full-length public exhibition, concluded the 1918 Field Day. Just prior to that performance, however, Miss Trilling began to have some misgivings about placing Miss H'Doubler's dance "in the public eye." At the time of dress rehearsal she suggested that the material for the performance was not what she had hoped for and should be canceled. Undaunted even in the face of opposition, Miss H'Doubler pleaded for permission to continue the program. Miss Trilling acquiesced. At the conclusion of the performance, she . . . report[ed] that she had never seen anything so beautiful and would never doubt her work again. . . .[16]

Local newsmen also heard of the new dancing at the University and interest in the novel took them to the physical education department in search of a story. No interviews were given, however, for Miss H'Doubler was not yet satisfied that her theories were either sound or perfected. . . . From her point of view the dance idea "had not been proven yet."[17] A news story was not forthcoming, and a local paper carried only a brief notice about the varied display of interpretative dancing by "dancers coached according to studies Miss H'Doubler made. . . ."[18]

. . . The course continued to be popular, and within a short time Miss H'Doubler was teaching as many as five hundred to six hundred students. . . .[19] Because class size was large, senior physical education majors were enlisted to assist, providing teaching aid to Miss H'Doubler and themselves an opportunity to learn how to teach the new dance. . . .[20]

Two years after the introduction of the new dancing it was fast becoming one of the most popular activities offered by the physical education department. Students were interested in and enthusiastic about Miss H'Doubler's approach, and large numbers registered for the department's newest "athletic work." Miss Trilling, too, was well pleased with the "splendid and constructive work" which Miss H'Doubler accomplished.[21] Knowledge of these attainments soon created widespread interest among other physical educators throughout the country, and requests began to arrive for demonstrations of the new educational dance form. At a time when the University carefully monitored the conduct and affairs of students and when it rarely allowed women students to leave campus, the administration granted Miss H'Doubler permission to travel to Detroit with a group of women from her classes to give a demonstration for directors of physical education in Michigan.[22] This was the first of many such requests, and, as Miss H'Doubler's reputation spread, groups of her dancers traveled throughout the Midwest demonstrating the theories and techniques developed in her classes. . . . Miss H'Doubler thereby maintained her intent to present dance as an educational endeavor for students rather than as polished entertainment for spectators.

As the number of requests for dance demonstrations increased — in one year the total was forty-six — Edward A. Birge, the University president, expressed concern about the amount students traveled and the length of time they spent away from campus. He finally informed Miss H'Doubler that the University could not become known as a "dancing school," and he put a stop to all travel. The ban did not, however, halt the demonstrations. So well known was Miss H'Doubler's approach to dance, that persons interested in learning more about it traveled to Madison themselves to observe her classes and discuss ideas with her.[23]

As other colleges and universities began to look for teachers of the new educational dance, inquiries came to the University of Wisconsin where it had originated. The inquiries mounted, and Miss Trilling commented to the University administration about them and pointed out the need for relieving Miss H'Doubler of some of her routine work so she could devote more time to teaching students majoring in physical education, which required some work in interpretive dance under Miss H'Doubler.[24] Many of these young women left the University with teaching certificates in physical education and became teachers of dance at major colleges and universities throughout the country. Long before the establishment of the dance major, alumnae from 1919, 1920, 1921, and 1922 were teaching "Miss H'Doubler's dancing" at Northwestern University, the University of Washington, Michigan State Normal School, the University of Texas, Illinois State Normal University, North Carolina College for Women, and Wellesley College.[25]

Miss H'Doubler's continual emphasis was not to prepare polished dancers for the stage and public performance, but to provide each student the opportunity to feel, move, and interpret within her own range of capabilities. . . .

. . . For some time before 1918, each school year had concluded with the May Fête, an elaborate outdoor program of singing and dancing, including a Maypole dance. . . . But as the country moved into the war years, the May Fête was discontinued. With the great interest in Miss H'Doubler's new dancing and perhaps the students' desire to display their talent, Dance Drama replaced the program. An admission fee was charged, and the proceeds donated to the War Orphan Fund. From that beginning Dance Drama developed into an annual event, almost always well-attended and a financial success. . . . With the establishment in 1921 of Orchesis, the dance club, Dance Drama came under the auspices of that organization and continued as an annual production for many years. . . .[26]

. . . Orchesis [was] "an honorary dancing organization . . . for banding together all the interests pertaining to the further development of dancing."[27] Several names for it had been submitted, but the students chose Miss H'Doubler's suggestion, Orchesis, from *orcheisthai,* a Greek word meaning "to dance." Members were selected by tryouts, and requirements were eventually refined to include knowledge of fundamental motor control, realization and appreciation of music through movement, and dance composition. . . .

Miss H'Doubler's concern for offering the benefits of dance to all individuals led her to keep attendance for Orchesis meetings and to give preference for Dance Drama parts to those girls who had attended regularly.[28]

Orchesis provided additional opportunities for highly skilled dancers, but less talented students also wanted to meet outside regular class time. Saturday morning sessions were begun, again on a volunteer basis, conducted by the president of Orchesis with the help of senior physical education majors. Formation of a junior Orchesis encouraged further interest among students. . . .[29]

As Wisconsin graduates accepted physical education faculty positions in colleges and universities across the country, Miss H'Doubler's philosophy of dance and the ideas of Orchesis and Dance Drama traveled with them. No written material concerning her approach to dance was available, and dancing teachers had to rely on classroom methods and experiences learned in Miss H'Doubler's classes in planning their own lessons. Thus, the first of several textbooks came "as a result of insistent demands from her pupils in various parts of the country."[30] With the publication of *A Manual of Dancing* in 1921 Miss H'Doubler's philosophy and teaching methods were readily available to anyone interested in educational dance.

Lesser known among Miss H'Doubler's theories at this time was the development of corrective dancing at the University. A physical examination was required of all women entering the physical education program, and students who failed to meet the qualifications for the usual activities were placed in corrective classes. Individuals were assigned corrective exercise, posture class, walking, or rest according to need. Another dimension was added in 1921 with an experimental class in corrective dancing. . . . Although Louisa Lippitt, head of the correctives department, was doubtful about the success of the method, she believed it should at least be tried. The experiment proved to be sufficiently valuable to continue, and the interest of students enrolled in the corrective work testified to its success.[31] Within a few years several classes in corrective dancing were offered by a department instructor in co-operation with Miss H'Doubler. Again her influence was far-reaching, for on both the East Coast at Wellesley College and the West Coast at the University of Oregon, University alumnae soon introduced similar corrective courses.[32]

Men, too, got involved with the new dance at an early date under Miss H'Doubler's guidance, but the program received little publicity. Early women's physical education department files and reports give no indication that men students attended classes, except for the professional preparation courses offered for both men and women. A local newspaper headline proclaimed in 1922, however, "Ye Gods, Male Students Take Up Aesthetic Dancing at U.W." This shocking affront to the masculine image came to light after a "peeping Tom" climbed onto a window ledge at Lathrop Hall and discovered not ladies dancing to the musical strains he had heard, but "about 15 men attired in Grecian costumes 'tripping the light fantastic' as daintily as you please." Queried about dancing classes for men, and why their existence had been concealed from the public, Miss H'Doubler explained that they were organized at the request of several men students. Classes were separate from those for women, and a decision had been made in conference with

University deans not to discuss the dance work of either men or women in the department.[33] Although men were performing in ballet and other professional dance forms at the time, it was surprising, perhaps, that male university students might be interested in a new kind of creative dance that appeared the exclusive realm of women.

Owing to the requests for teachers of the new dance from all parts of the country, the need for some in-depth preparation beyond the general dance classes became increasingly apparent. The development of a minor in interpretative dancing for women resulted. Most of the twelve credits of course work were selected from those offered physical education majors, with additional courses recommended in philosophy, psychology, music, and speech. . . .[34]

Miss H'Doubler's concerns, however, included making dance a full partner academically, and she hoped to see a dance major the fulfillment of that goal. She had gained full support from her avant garde ideas about dance from Miss Trilling and had an influential protagonist in George C. Sellery, dean of Letters and Science, the college which encompassed physical education. Nonetheless, she approached the challenge of a dance major with some trepidation, knowing that the proposal might well be rejected by the total university faculty. . . .[35]

A detailed document outlining requirements for a dance major was presented to the School of Education faculty for approval on June 8, 1926. Minor aspects apparently met with some resistance, for faculty approval was not forthcoming until the following October. . . . One final endorsement remained to complete establishment of an academic major in dancing, and on November 12, 1926, the Board of Regents approved [the action]. . . . Thus Miss H'Doubler's dream of academic respectability for dance became a reality.[36] The first dance major in any institution of higher learning had been launched. . . .

. . . Its complete implementation occurred the following year. . . . And for the first time, such courses as Rhythmic Form and Analysis, Dance Composition, and Theory of the Dance appeared as class offerings. Thirty students were registered in the "major course in dancing" in 1927–1928, and foundations for the further development and refinement of the Wisconsin Idea of Dance were well established. . . .[37]

. . . Miss H'Doubler's ideas matured and expanded and are still very much alive today. Her time-space-force concepts are utilized in dance classes across the country, and students continue to work with variations of her dance fundamentals in developing a vocabulary of movements for progressing toward the more complicated problems of composition and choreography. The Wisconsin Idea of Dance, or, perhaps more appropriately, Miss H'Doubler's Idea of Dance, is a viable theory even today. . . .

Miss H'Doubler taught at the University of Wisconsin until her retirement in 1954, advancing from an assistant in physical education in 1910 to professor in 1942. In the years following the establishment of the dance major she was widely sought as a guest lecturer throughout the United States and she taught in many major colleges and universities. Internationally, she . . . taught at colleges in Canada, England, Luxembourg, Austria, and Sweden. She [wrote] five books and several articles which explicate her theory and philosophy of educational dance. . . . She received the Wisconsin Governor's Council on the

Arts award in 1964; the Luther Halsey Gulick Award in 1971, the highest honor bestowed by the American Association for Health, Physical Education, and Recreation; and in 1972 received the honorary Doctor of Fine Arts degree from the University of Wisconsin.

Following her retirement in 1954 Miss H'Doubler continued to lecture and conduct special workshop sessions at the University of Wisconsin, and as recently as 1967 could be seen dressed in dance attire and seated on the floor of the dance studio in Lathrop hall. Young students surrounded her and listened attentively to the theories of "the grand old lady of modern dance in education" who could still move across the studio as gracefully and agilely as most of them, though nearing the age of eighty. . . .[38]

*By the mid-1970s, H'Doubler and her husband of forty years, an artist, had moved to Arizona, where she died in 1982. The pioneering dance program she established continues to thrive at the University of Wisconsin–Madison, where Lathrop Hall recently was remodeled for the opening in 1998 of the Margaret N. H'Doubler Performance Space.*

## NOTES

1. Miss Trilling came to the University of Wisconsin in 1912 as director of the Women's Gymnasium (later director of the Department of Physical Education for Women) and continued as the chief administrator of the department until her retirement in 1946. . . .
2. Taped interview with H'Doubler.
3. Ibid.
4. Miss Bentley directed a music studio for children. . . . [H]er unique approach to teaching was later referred to as "motor mental rhythmics."
5. Alys E. Bentley, *Child Life in Song and Speech* (New York, 1910), 13–14.
6. Taped interview with H'Doubler.
7. . . . Amy M. Homans directed the Boston Normal School of Gymnastics (later the Department of Hygiene and Physical Education of Wellesley College), one of only five early physical education teacher training institutions. Many of the leading physical educators in the United States, including Blanche M. Trilling, were graduates of BNSG. Taped interview with H'Doubler.
8. Margaret N. H'Doubler, Untitled Manuscript (undated, ca. 1937), Historical Files, Department of Physical Education for Women.
9. Taped interview with H'Doubler.
10. *Timetable*, Semester II, 1917–1918, University Archives, University of Wisconsin–Madison.
11. Margaret N. H'Doubler, *The Dance and Its Place in Education* (New York, 1925), 44.
12. . . . [See Margaret N. H'Doubler,] *The Dance and Its Place in Education; Movement and Its Rhythmic Structure* (Madison, 1946); and *Dance: A Creative Art Experience* (New York, 1940). . . . [See also] *A Manual of Dance* (Madison, 1921) and *Rhythmic Form and Analysis* (Madison, 1956).
13. *Madison Daily Cardinal,* January 23, 1918.
14. Ibid., January 19, 1918.
15. Ibid., April 10, May 21, 1918.
16. Taped interview with H'Doubler. . . .
17. Ibid.
18. *Wisconsin State Journal,* May 24, 1918.
19. . . . Since class rosters are not available for these early years, it is difficult to ascertain the exact number of *different* individuals registered for dance courses. . . .
20. *Madison Daily Cardinal,* October 28, 1918.

21. Blanche M. Trilling, "Biennial Report of the Director of the Women's Gymnasium," 1918–1920. . . . [All reports, handbooks, correspondence, and other primary sources herein, unless cited otherwise, are in the Historical Files, Department of Physical Education for Women, University of Wisconsin–Madison].

22. *Madison Daily Cardinal,* October 30, 1919.

23. Ibid., July 22, 1921; taped interview with H'Doubler.

24. Trilling, "Biennial Report," 1918–1920.

25. Lillian Stupp, ed., *Bulletin of the Alumnae Association,* 1925, 59–62. . . .

26. Margaret N. H'Doubler, "Dancing Report," in "Instructional Report," 1919–1920, 15; 1922–1923, 33; 1925–1926, 49. . . .

27. Taped interview with H'Doubler; Margaret N. H'Doubler, "Dancing Report," in "Instructional Report," 1920–1921, 20. . . .

28. Margaret N. H'Doubler, "Handbook of Department of Physical Education," 1924–1925, 21–22; . . . Stupp, *Bulletin of the Alumnae Association,* 1925, 24.

29. H'Doubler, "Dancing Report," in "Instructional Report," 1925–1926, 48; H'Doubler, "Dancing Report," in "Handbook of Department of Physical Education," 1924–1925, 20. . . .

30. Blanche M. Trilling to J. H. McCurdy, October 7, 1921. . . .

31. Louisa C. Lippitt, "Report of the Correctives Department," in "Instructional Report," 1920–1921, 9; Esther W. Klein and Carol S. Keay, "Corrective Report," Ibid., 1922–1923, 25. . . .

32. Stupp, *Bulletin of the Alumnae Association,* 1925, 18, 62.

33. *Wisconsin State Journal,* February 23, 1922.

34. *Catalogue of the University of Wisconsin,* 1922–1923, 307. University Archives.

35. Taped interview with H'Doubler.

36. "Physical Education Major in Dancing" (mimeographed), June 8, 1926; . . . Minutes of the Regular Letters and Science Faculty Meeting, October 18, 1926, University Archives; M. E. McCaffrey to Blanche M. Trilling, November 13, 1926. . . .

37. . . . H'Doubler, "Report on Dancing," in "Instructional Report," 1927–1928, 47. . . .

38. *Wisconsin State Journal,* April 30, 1967.

# Julia Grace Wales and the Wisconsin Plan for Peace

WALTER I. TRATTNER

WMH 44, No. 3 (Spring 1961): 203–213

"There she was at dinner, this girl with the great idea, painfully embarrassed, and trying to keep in the background."

The modest girl was Julia Grace Wales, Canadian-born instructor of English at the University of Wisconsin. The idea referred to had been revealed in her recently published pamphlet containing a plan to hasten the end of the Great War which now, in its first seven months, had already cost the belligerents almost a million casualties and a hundred million dollars. The speaker was Hamilton Holt, crusading, pacifist editor-owner of the influential journal, *The Independent*.

That afternoon, February 24, 1915, Holt had addressed an audience in Music Hall on the University campus, choosing as his topic "International Peace." After the lecture E. A. Ross, one of the nation's leading sociologists, took him to dinner at a friend's house where Miss Wales was also a guest. "She told us," Holt vividly recalled later, "the horrors of the war had sickened her physically. . . . She dreamed of them. She pondered over the crisis until finally she evolved a plan which — at the very least — offers the most feasible way to end the war." Thereafter, on a lecture tour which took him from Los Angeles to Boston, Holt devoted at least fifteen minutes of each lecture to a discussion of what was becoming known as the Wisconsin Peace Plan. . . .[1]

Julia Grace Wales was born on July 14, 1881, in the small town of Bury, Quebec, in eastern Canada between the St. Lawrence and New England. The eldest of three talented daughters of a dedicated rural physician, she could trace her ancestry to New Englanders who had emigrated to America before the Revolutionary War. One sister wrote music; one became a nurse in a Montreal hospital. Julia Grace, after having been educated in part at home, entered McGill University in Montreal and in 1903 was graduated, after having secured the coveted class honor — the Shakespeare gold medal — and having been awarded a scholarship to Radcliffe College [in Boston]. Following a year of graduate study, she received her master's degree and . . . came to the University of Wisconsin as an instructor in the English department. She was serving in that capacity in August of 1914 when the war broke out in Europe. . . .

. . . A month after hostilities began she wrote in a letter to Dr. Graham Taylor, prominent settlement worker and editor of *The Survey*, that she was convinced that in the "spiritual suffering of the multitudes of the warring countries, multitudes were . . . trying to take the Christian attitude" and that "there are currents of hidden energy that need *in some way* to be liberated, liberated and combined, and made active."[2]

In the words of Louise Phelps Kellogg, senior research associate of the State Historical Society of Wisconsin, secretary of the Wisconsin Peace Society, and intimate friend of Julia Grace Wales: "The pity and horror of it seized upon her . . . [and she] said to herself

and others, 'There must be some way out.' Gifted with great sympathy and a philosophi-
cal love for getting at the bottom of things, she thought night and day of some possible
exit from the entanglement in which she felt the world had been unwittingly plunged."[3]

Was it not possible, Miss Wales increasingly wondered, that the nations now at war had
been paralyzed by a conventional mode of thinking and were mistaken in supposing that
they were helpless in the face of a calamity which they had brought upon themselves? . . .

Sometime during the University's 1914 Christmas recess Julia Grace Wales conceived
and wrote in longhand the first draft of her plan — a proposal which if applied might be
the means of averting what she believed to be a prolonged, irrational, and un-Christian
war. The plan's basic idea was embodied in the title she assigned the manuscript, "Continuous Mediation Without Armistice," and in her opening paragraph she posed the question her plan was designed to answer:

"Can a means be found by which a conference of the neutral powers may bring the
moral forces of the world to bear upon the present war situation and offer to the belligerents some opportunity, involving neither committal to an arbitrary programme nor humiliation on the part of any one of them, to consider the possibility of peace?"[4]

In essence, Miss Wales's plan as it was finally evolved urged that the United States call
a conference to which each of the then thirty-five neutral nations of the world would send
delegates. The conference, or International Commission of experts, would mediate —
with armistice if possible, without it if necessary — but in such a way as to not endanger
the neutrality of any nation. It would constitute a court of continuous mediation, the
members of which were to have a scientific rather than a diplomatic function: they were
to be without the power to commit their respective governments to any proposals. This International Commission of inquiry, or "world thinking organ" as Miss Wales often referred
to it, was to sit as long as the war continued. It would invite suggestions from all the warring nations and simultaneously submit to all of them reasonable proposals to end the
war. . . . Each proposal would be based on two principles: first, that peace must not mean
humiliation to any nation; and second, that it must not involve compromise which might
later result in a renewal of the war. Such a conference would exert every possible effort
to prevent any of the neutral nations from being drawn into the conflict.[5]

Thus Miss Wales's plan, as she conceived it, was not in itself an actual plan for peace,
since it lacked any specific indication of the precise areas to be mediated, such as indem-
nification, boundary disputes, colonial settlements, and the like. Rather it was a proposal
for the creation of machinery whereby thoughtful proposals could be formulated and
then communicated to all the belligerents. In a sense, it was an attempt to extend the Wisconsin Idea — drawing upon technical experts to help the state formulate public policy
— to the realm of international relations.

Although the idea of "continuous mediation without armistice" as eventually formulated by Julia Wales was somewhat novel, the proposal that the United States call a conference of neutrals was not original with her. Hamilton Holt had long advocated such a
meeting in *The Independent,* and bills had been introduced in the Senate by [Wisconsin's
Robert M.] La Follette and [Nevada's Francis G.] Newlands asking the President to
convoke such a conference. . . .[6] Miss Wales acknowledged her indebtedness to others

for many of her basic points. . . . To the editor of the University's student newspaper, she wrote:

"Although so far as I know, my pamphlet was the first detached development of some aspects of the plan of continuous-mediation and some arguments in its favor to appear in print, I was not even the first to publish the idea. During the autumn of last year — I think almost immediately after the outbreak of war — a small folder was issued by Madame Rosika Schwimmer, containing in a few lines a proposal for a conference of neutrals. . . . [Schwimmer was an internationally known Hungarian pacifist and suffragist who had toured Wisconsin for both causes.] Not being in touch with the international movement I had not, however, heard of her proposal at the time my pamphlet was printed. Various presentations have been worked out independently by persons of various nationalities, showing that the idea is 'in the air' the world over."[7]

Having summoned the courage to commit her plan to paper, Miss Wales first showed it to Louise Phelps Kellogg, who was immediately won over by the scheme and arranged for Miss Wales to present it to the Wisconsin Peace Society. The Society at once incorporated the plan into its charter, and under its auspices had it printed in pamphlet form. From early in 1915, "Continuous Mediation Without Armistice," thereafter known as the Wisconsin Plan, spread rapidly, attracting numerous converts and advocates and achieving both partial success and widespread acclaim.

. . . Joseph Tumulty, President [Woodrow] Wilson's friend and private secretary, acknowledged receipt of a copy on January 13, 1915, and stated that ". . . at the first opportunity I shall bring it to the attention of the President." A few weeks later Tumulty once again wrote to the supporters of the Plan, saying that President Wilson was calling it to the attention of the Secretary of State. Joseph E. Davies, [a] former Wisconsin resident and Chairman of the Federal Trade Commission, acknowledged interest in [the Plan for] Continuous Mediation, and conveyed the news that he, too, would talk to the President about the Plan.[8] David Starr Jordan, internationally prominent scientist and Chancellor of Stanford University, as well as one of the nation's leading pacifists, after having read a copy of the pamphlet, wrote, "It seems to me the most forceful and practical thing I have yet seen." . . . Jordan was so enthusiastic that he suggested that the Wisconsin Plan be presented at the National Peace Conference to be held in Chicago, February 27 and 28, 1915. . . .[9]

. . . Julia Grace Wales, modestly preferring not to let it be known that she was the plan's creator, did not even attend the Chicago Conference. Her desire for anonymity stemmed partly from the fact that as a Canadian citizen and a belligerent in the struggle she thought it best to keep in the background, and partly because she felt that her ideas would receive more careful consideration if they were believed to have originated with a man.

Put on the program for the first session of the Conference, the Wisconsin Plan was presented to the delegates. . . . It received instant acclaim, and . . . was unanimously approved and embodied in the platform of the Conference. . . .[10]

Following its adoption by the National Peace Conference, the Wisconsin Plan met with further success. Hamilton Holt wrote to Miss Wales, saying: "Now that I have had time to mull over the 'Wisconsin Plan' I am coming to believe it has fewer objections than anything yet suggested. I hope and pray that somehow your ideas will prevail. You have done a great thing."[11] He also vowed to give the Plan much favorable publicity in the pages of *The Independent*. Although Woodrow Wilson refused to receive the National Peace Conference delegation,[12] [the Plan for] Continuous Mediation was adopted by the Wisconsin Legislature in the form of a resolution which was to be forwarded to the President. . . .[13]

. . . [A] campaign was started to spread the idea of Continuous Mediation throughout both America and Europe. Numerous press notices were secured, as well as favorable resolutions in state legislatures. Miss Wales received many letters of encouragement and congratulation, all taking an optimistic view of the Plan's future. . . . Secretary of State William Jennings Bryan replied that ". . . other copies of the so-called Wisconsin Plan have come to my attention. It has created a great deal of interest."[14]

A month after the Chicago conference [its chairman] Jane Addams wrote Miss Wales, inviting her to attend an international congress called by women of both the neutral and warring nations and to be held at The Hague. "It might," Miss Addams wrote, "be the one [great] opportunity to push forward your plan."[15] Accordingly, on April 13, 1915, Miss Wales sailed for Europe aboard the Dutch-American liner *Noordam*. . . .

However, the prospect of getting her Plan adopted at the Women's International Peace Congress was not very promising. . . . "You see," wrote Miss Wales on the eve of the Congress' termination, "the neutrals here are *scared to death*; they don't dare to *breathe* — much less try to do anything. . . ." But in her characteristic manner the optimistic Miss Wales vigorously continued, "In spite of the almost certain defeat of the resolution . . . I do not feel discouraged in the least. . . . We are going 'to keep on and keep on keeping on.'"[16]

Much to her surprise and delight, the highlight of her dangerous trip across the Atlantic was reached the very next day when, on the last day of the Congress, the Wisconsin Plan for Continuous Mediation was unanimously accepted by all the women delegates. The pamphlet, which had by then undergone several editions, was reprinted at The Hague in three foreign languages and distributed throughout Europe. The *Wisconsin State Journal* reported that someone suggested that the University of Wisconsin establish a permanent Chair of Peace, with Miss Wales as the first incumbent,[17] and a leading Chicago newspaper announced that "There is much interest at the State Department and in diplomatic circles over the proposal . . . presented by Miss Julia Grace Wales of the University of Wisconsin. This . . . will be given consideration at the State Department as soon as official copies can be received from The Hague."[18]

After organizing the International Committee for Permanent Peace, with Jane Addams as its chairman, The Hague Conference disbanded. The delegates, however, were divided into several groups, each of which travelled to different parts of Europe talking on behalf of [the Plan for] Continuous Mediation. Julia Wales travelled as secretary of the delegation to Scandinavia and Russia. . . .

. . . After wide travel, many interviews, and much discussion throughout a large part of the Continent, the envoys . . . issued the following Manifesto: "Our visit to the war capitals convinced us that the belligerent governments would not be opposed to a conference of neutral nations; that while the belligerents have rejected offers of mediation by single neutral nations, and while no belligerents could ask for mediation, the creation of a continuous conference of neutral nations might provide the machinery which could lead to peace."[19]

Miss Wales wrote that "those who were able to get into Germany . . . report much latent international sentiment, which, however, is denied a voice. . . ." In addition, there was a good deal of agitation and favorable sentiment for the Wisconsin Plan in Australia, Canada, England, Norway, Belgium, Holland, Sweden, Switzerland, and Denmark.[20]

By no means was all of the European reaction to the Plan favorable, however. Ever since the sinking of the *Lusitania* and the resultant loss of nearly 1,200 lives, Miss Wales had been forced to devote some of her limitless energy to rebutting her critics at home and abroad. Increasingly, as the opposition made itself heard, she clarified and restated her ideas. She constantly emphasized that the conference of neutrals would have no power to *will* or *decide* anything; its official function was merely to *think*, for it was meant to be a world brain. The interested governments in their official capacity could accept or refuse any proposal. In reply to the argument that mediation had already been offered and refused, Miss Wales stoutly declared that, on the contrary, her Plan was new and had never been tried. . . .

. . . The Plan neither stated nor implied any moral judgments. "It was the earnest desire of the writer of the pamphlet," she asserted, "to find some common ground, however slight, on which estranged friends could meet. . . ."[21]

In addition, she once again took the opportunity of making it clear to her critics that she did not consider herself a mere dispassionate onlooker in the struggle — nor, for that matter, was anyone else — and that she truly believed that the whole world had a stake in the outcome of the war. It was true that [the Plan for] Continuous Mediation was "neutral" in that it did not dogmatize about which side was "right," and in that sense it appeared too visionary to many of those people who were caught up in what they believed was a just war. Julia Wales agreed and admitted that she felt England was fighting for "eternal principles of freedom and justice," and she confided to a close friend that she had sympathized with England from the beginning. But uppermost in her mind were the innocent human lives which were being destroyed each day. The fighting must be brought to an end. . . . Julia Grace Wales was certain that "In the end, some such plan, if carried out, would tend to give speedy victory to the right — would tend to thwart wrong motives and to assist and reward right motives in every country."[22]

In spite of the criticism, the peace advocates did not slacken their efforts to persuade the Administration to endorse the Wisconsin Plan and call a neutral conference. President Wilson received thousands of telegrams from individuals and groups all over the United States, urging him to offer mediation. In October, 1915, the San Francisco International Peace Conference endorsed the Wisconsin Plan and commissioned David Starr Jordan to see the President about the possibility of its implementation.[23]

Louis Lochner was to accompany Jordan to the White House for his Presidential interview. On the way from the West Coast to Washington, the two men stopped in Madison for two days to speak with Miss Wales about her Plan and to visit with [University of Wisconsin] President [Charles] Van Hise, another of the Plan's supporters. Dr. Jordan endorsed the Plan in Madison and again commended its author at an all-University convocation before an immense audience on November 9. . . .[24]

David Starr Jordan's forty-minute interview with President Wilson was encouraging to the friends of peace. The President refused to commit himself to [the Plan for] Continuous Mediation, but, according to Jordan, he was "mellow" and "more inclined to listen than ever before." He seemed to grasp what Jordan said and even to "like" the idea. Wilson ended the interview by remarking, "I assure you gentlemen that you have done me real good." . . .[25]

When in Washington, Jordan and Lochner were also cordially received by Chairman Davies and former Secretary of State Bryan, both of whom still expressed considerable interest in the Plan. Their interview with Secretary of State Robert Lansing, however, was unsatisfactory. . . .[26]

Meanwhile, the peace advocates made a powerful convert. . . . [Automobile manufacturer] Henry Ford was persuaded to endorse [the Plan for] Continuous Mediation. He also announced that he would see the President on the matter of a neutral conference.[27] Ford entered the ranks just in time, for by then money was desperately needed by the friends of peace. . . .

Once again, President Wilson appeared to be swayed by the idea of a conference of neutrals, and within two weeks granted three separate interviews to advocates of [the Plan for] Continuous Mediation. At the least, his interest in the subject must have been aroused.

The story of Henry Ford's Peace Ship is a familiar one. When it became apparent that Wilson would not take the initiative in an attempt to bring the war to an end, Ford decided to do it himself. His plan included a spectacular end-the-war drive to "get the boys out of the trenches by Christmas," mainly by organizing a crusade of publicists and leading American advocates of peace who would arouse public opinion in such a fashion that the neutral nations would be forced to call a mediating conference. The venture was also to include the choosing of an unofficial international committee which would meet in Stockholm [in neutral Sweden]. Acting in a private capacity it would draw up peace proposals and work out all the necessary arrangements for the official conference of neutrals which would then, hopefully, be called.

At first Miss Wales, chosen as a delegate, was skeptical, although she admitted that "the sincerity, earnestness, and generosity of the enterprise, [was] . . . of course, beyond question." . . .[28] Evidently she was reassured, because when the *Oscar III* sailed from Hoboken, Julia Grace Wales, having received a leave of absence from the University, was aboard.

Regardless of what can be said of the Peace Ship's objectives or the reasons for its failure, the Stockholm Conference was somewhat of a success. . . .

But from then on the peace movement in the United States rapidly disintegrated. While the idea of a league of nations was not new to Americans, the idea of a League to

Enforce Peace was, and in attracting many people to its program of using force to insure peace, the League helped deplete the ranks of the staunch pacifists. President Wilson vaguely endorsed the League's principles, and . . . more followers were attracted. Later, Wilson's Fourteen Points and his proposal for a League of Nations turned the war into a struggle to "make the world safe for democracy" and a "war to end all wars." Wilson's idealistic preachments were much too persuasive for the dwindling band of peace advocates, and many Americans abandoned pacifism to support the President's calls for preparedness, reconciling their opposition to war and their support of preparedness by their interest in the proposed League of Nations. . . . By March 1917, most Americans were ready to go to war, end it, and return to a permanent peace. Only a few uncompromising and courageous pacifists, often exposing themselves to danger, stood their ground.

Julia Grace Wales was one of the victims of the President's idealism, and even she was caught up in the course of events. . . . [S]he said: "It seems to me that the idea of the standing challenge . . . which was the kernel of the theory of mediation without armistice, has now prevailed and become the definite policy of the governments. . . ."[29] Moreover, the President's call for a League of Nations appeared to her to be a close enough application of the principle for which she had fought. She did hope, however, that the specific idea of [the Plan for] Continuous Mediation would be made a permanent device of the League.[30]

It is quite clear that there was no single cause for the defeat of the peace movement in the period of the First World War. Most pacifists did not perceive or question the economic relationship between war and profit-making in America. They rarely attacked the yellow press or American loans and shipments of supplies to the belligerents. The pacifists also dissipated some of their energies in internal rivalries and conflicts. Furthermore, many pacifist leaders tended to oversimplify certain forces which draw men to war. As Merle Curti has pointed out, the pacifists failed to understand the glamour and lure that war exerts on the great masses of people.[31]

The failure of the Wisconsin Plan for Peace was, however, the result of several very distinct factors. In the first place, [the Plan for] Continuous Mediation never really succeeded in winning the support or approval of the public. Those favoring the Plan were mostly members of the educated classes, and there is no evidence of support from the middle and working classes. The majority of Americans, in fact, were not aroused by the issue of peace. . . . Miss Wales herself made an implied recognition of this deficiency when she confessed that "the strength of our cause has been in its very weakness, in the fact that it has been led by a few idealistic citizens of the world. . . ."[32] In addition, and probably most important, the Wisconsin Plan never won the Administration's support. On the whole, only a few public officials ever really believed in the Plan or exerted any official pressure in its behalf. Although at times Wilson seemed receptive to [the Plan for] Continuous Mediation, in the end he remained aloof to the idea. Without official support the Plan had little chance of success.

Also, the Plan was too passive: it offered the American public little that was positive or material. Julia Grace Wales was aware of this defect in 1915 when she perceptively observed: "That is the funny part of peace work; it is harmless. . . . I hope, however, that we shall soon be taken seriously as well as kindly."[33]

From 1914 to 1917 the war did not seem to threaten most Americans, the majority of whom, feeling that they had nothing to lose in the "European War," were not ready to act unless their interests were directly challenged. Many others, while opposed to war, were even more opposed to a German victory and feared that mediation by the neutrals, especially after the initial German military successes, would insure the Kaiser's victory.

America's entry into the war completed the disintegration of the peace forces and sounded the death knell of [the Plan for] Continuous Mediation. By 1917 the war was popular with most Americans. National war hysteria had closed the door to any rational decisions on the war issue, and the great majority of the peace advocates, including Julia Grace Wales, became interventionists and supported the war effort. . . . By 1918 the author of the Wisconsin Plan for Peace was able to write that "The community of nations as a whole has a duty to resist any aggressor who vitally threatens the freedom of future generations."[34]

After 1919 Julia Grace Wales' efforts on behalf of international friendship, understanding, and peace were submerged in her dedication to the teaching of literature. From 1919 to 1921 she was in England, teaching. . . . Returning to Madison in 1921, she resumed her responsibilities at the University, giving courses in Shakespeare, the Bible, and advanced composition. . . . [H]er publications were mainly in the field of Shakespearean criticism in scholarly journals. . . .[35]

. . . In 1942, as the world found itself engulfed in a second and more terrible war, Miss Wales again took up her pen in the defense of her ideals. Her small book, *Democracy Needs Education*,[36] published in Canada, awakens echoes of her Wisconsin Plan for Peace and suggests that she never entirely abandoned her earlier convictions. Five years later she retired . . . and returned to Canada where she died on July 15, 1957. . . .

## NOTES

1. *Wisconsin State Journal*, February 25, May 12, 1915; *Kansas City Star*, March 6, 1915. . . .

2. Julia Grace Wales to Dr. Graham Taylor, September 14, 1914, in the Wales Papers, WHS Archives [as are all sources cited herein, unless otherwise cited].

3. Louise Phelps Kellogg, "A Brief Sketch of the Life and Work of Julia Grace Wales."

4. Julia Grace Wales, "Supplementary Notes on a Plan for Continuous Mediation."

5. Mimeographed pamphlet written by Julia Grace Wales, "Continuous Mediation Without Armistice" (Madison, 1915).

6. *The Independent* 81 (March 29, 1915):434–444.

7. Julia Grace Wales to the editor of the *Madison Daily Cardinal*, October, 1915.

8. Joseph Tumulty to Joseph Jastrow, January 16, 1915; idem to Ralph Owen, February 5, 1915; Joseph E. Davies to Ralph Owen, February 5 and 15, 1915. . . .

9. David Starr Jordan to John K. Bonnell, February 16 and 17, 1915; . . . Jordan to Bonnell, February 18, 1915.

10. *Platform* of the National Peace Conference, in the Wales Papers; *Wisconsin State Journal*, February 27, 1915. . . .

11. Hamilton Holt to Julia Grace Wales, March 6, 1915.

12. . . . Louis Lochner to Julia Grace Wales, March 11, 1915.

13. Jt. Res. No. 39 S, passed March 16, 1915.

14. William Jennings Bryan to John A. Aylward, April 6, 1915.

15. Jane Addams to Julia Grace Wales, March 25, 1915.

16. Julia Grace Wales to Louise Phelps Kellogg, April 30, 1915; *idem* to Committee, May 11, 1915. . . .

17. *Wisconsin State Journal,* May 12, 1915.

18. *Chicago Herald,* May 3, 1915.

19. See Louis P. Lochner, *Always the Unexpected* (New York, 1956), 51, and Jane Addams, "The Revolt Against War," in *The Survey,* 34: 355–359 (July 17, 1915); *Text of the Manifesto Issued by the Envoys to the International Congress of Women at the Hague,* October 15, 1915, 15.

20. Julia Grace Wales to William Drysdale, October 25, 1915. . . .

21. Julia Grace Wales, "Continuous Mediation Without Armistice," in *The Nation* 101:434 (October 7, 1915).

22. Julia Grace Wales to Louise Phelps Kellogg, August 28, 1915; Wales, "Continuous Mediation," 435.

23. David Starr Jordan to Julia Grace Wales, October 20, 1915.

24. *Wisconsin State Journal,* November 10, 1915.

25. Louis Lochner, "White House Interview, President Wilson and D. S. Jordan," November 12, 1915.

26. Louis Lochner, "Additional Data Regarding Our Interview." . . .

27. Louis Lochner to Julia Grace Wales, November 20, 1915; Roger Burlingame, *Henry Ford* (New York, 1955), 82–83; "The New Kind of Militant Peace Plans," in *The Survey* 35 (December 4, 1915): 227–228.

28. Julia Grace Wales to David Starr Jordan, November 26, 1915.

29. Julia Grace Wales, "A Statement of My Present Position, September, 1917."

30. Julia Grace Wales to Jane Addams, November 27, 1917.

31. Merle Curti, *Peace or War* (New York, 1936), 306.

32. Julia Grace Wales to Louis Lochner, November, 1915.

33. Julia Grace Wales to the Committee, May 13, 1915.

34. Julia Grace Wales, "The Conscientious Objector and the Principle of International Defense," reprint from *The Advocate of Peace* (American Peace Society, Washington, D.C., 1918), 10.

35. *Writings of Grace Wales,* a bound volume in the University of Wisconsin Archives, contains a comprehensive collection of Miss Wales's published works. . . . [See also] "Memorial Resolutions of the Faculty of the University of Wisconsin on the Death of Emeritus Associate Professor Julia Grace Wales." Document 1190, November 4, 1957, WHS Archives.

36. *Democracy Needs Education* (Macmillan, 1942).

# Wisconsin and the Great Spanish Flu Epidemic of 1918

STEVEN BURG

*WMH* 84, No. 1 (Autumn 2000): 36–56

In December 1918, the State Board of Health declared that the "Spanish flu" epidemic that had just swept the state would "forever be remembered as the most disastrous calamity that has ever been visited upon the people of Wisconsin or any of the other states."[1] Eighty years later, the terror and devastation wrought by the tiny influenza virus still ranks it as one of the most terrible tragedies in the state's history. Even by modern standards, the scope of the epidemic remains staggering. Between September and the end of December 1918, influenza and related pneumonia debilitated almost 103,000 Wisconsin residents and killed 8,459 — approximately 7,500 more fatalities than would be expected from those causes in a normal year.[2] To gauge the magnitude of the crisis, consider that more Wisconsin residents died during the six months of the influenza epidemic than were killed in World War I, the Korean War, and the Vietnam conflict combined.[3] Only the Civil War (1861–1865) and World War II (1941–1945) claimed more Wisconsin lives.

The influenza epidemic was, of course, not simply a Wisconsin tragedy but a global pandemic that killed more than 20 million people worldwide during the summer and fall of 1918, more than the total number of soldiers who died in four years of unremitting slaughter during World War I. . . .

Surprisingly, however, the influenza epidemic lacks a place in the collective memory of Wisconsin similar to other notable local disasters, such as the Peshtigo Fire of 1871 or the sinking of the *Edmund Fitzgerald* in 1975, or even such national tragedies as the Great Depression or the Civil War. In part, this can be attributed to the elusive nature of the disease and the way it slowly and quietly spread across the Wisconsin landscape. No great ship sank, no armies clashed, no conflagration consumed a community. Instead, the flu spread insidiously by means of ordinary coughs and sneezes, borne through communities along the channels of human contact, sending both young and old retreating to their beds. At the time, no one even knew exactly what caused the disease — the influenza virus would not be viewed under an electron microscope for another fifteen years — nor how it spread, nor if it could be stopped. . . .

Moreover, the disease struck Wisconsin about six weeks before World War I ended on November 11, 1918, when newspapers were dominated by the rapid, victorious advance of Allied armies into Germany . . . , events that displaced other less dramatic news. There was little drama to the flu epidemic, particularly in its opening stages. The flu was silent, stealthy, invisible. It lacked the color of wartime exploits or the intrigue of diplomatic machinations. Other than reporting the number of sick or dead, new regulations, obituaries, or the speculations of overwhelmed health officers, there was little the newspapers could say about the crisis. Compared to the war, the epidemic lacked neat objectives, glamorous heroes, or odious villains. Its competition with the war for public attention probably contributed to its faint presence in the popular memory.

Yet the great epidemic is worth remembering, not only for the terrible swath it cut through Wisconsin but also because the crisis it engendered permits unique insights into the nature of government, citizenship, civic life, and public health at the beginning of the twentieth century. A state-level study is particularly apt. Wisconsin was the only state in the nation to meet the crisis with uniform, statewide measures that were unusual both for their aggressiveness and the public's willingness to comply with them. Undoubtedly, those measures helped reduce the loss of life from the disease. The states of the Upper Midwest proved most successful at preventing flu deaths, and though Wisconsin experienced a higher mortality rate than some other states in the region such as Michigan, Minnesota, and Indiana, it still emerged from the epidemic with one of the lowest death rates in the nation: 2.91 per thousand, compared with a national average of 4.39 per thousand. . . .[4]

. . . The swift and effective campaign against influenza in Wisconsin reflected merely the latest fruits of a forty-year effort to improve the overall quality of life by protecting citizens from the scourge of infectious disease. . . .

. . . What made the 1918 strain of influenza different, and deadly, were its rapid onset and dire complications. Common flu was ordinarily foreshadowed by symptoms and set in gradually. In 1918, the flu spread rapidly and often incapacitated its victims without warning. People in apparent good health would suddenly collapse with the flu; some died within hours. Furthermore, 20 percent of infected individuals — mostly those who resumed normal activities before the disease had fully passed — developed pneumonia. Up to half of those who caught pneumonia developed heliotrope cyanosis — a condition that filled victims' lungs with a thick blackish liquid, turned their skin bluish-black, and usually proved fatal within forty-eight hours. While the common flu often caused fatalities among the very old or the very young, the influenza epidemic of 1918 paradoxically took its most severe toll on those between the ages of twenty-five and forty — men and women in their physical prime.[5] There was no cure for the Spanish flu, and the only effective treatment was two weeks of undisturbed bed rest. . . .

. . . The disease probably traveled from Europe to the United States with returning servicemen. On September 14, 1918, Boston reported the first case of the Spanish flu in the United States. . . . By the third week in September, the Great Lakes Naval Training Station near Chicago reported 4,500 cases and 100 deaths. . . .[6]

During the week of September 28, 1918, one of the first cases of influenza in Wisconsin appeared when two sailors from the Great Lakes Naval Training Station fell ill while visiting Milwaukee. . . .[7] The health department requested physicians to report any new influenza cases immediately. Six cases were reported on September 26, twenty-four on September 27, sixty-two on September 28, and ninety-seven on September 30. On October 2, 1918, a two-day decline in the number of cases was followed by the first four influenza deaths. Five days later, 256 new cases were reported, together with nine additional deaths. The flu then ripped through Milwaukee, infecting hundreds of people each day, peaking on October 22 with 588 new cases. After a brief lull in early November, the disease returned and infected thousands more Milwaukee residents before it finally trailed off in late December.[8]

About the same time, other communities in southern Wisconsin reported outbreaks. Madison had its first cases in early October. The flu began on the University of Wisconsin campus among participants in the military-run Student Army Training Corps (SATC). . . .[9]

Influenza appeared in the Wisconsin communities and in the Lake Michigan port cities, then radiated along railway routes and highways. Madison's first death (October 9, 1918) occurred a full week after Milwaukee's first death; communities in the central and northern portions of the state often did not discover their first cases of influenza until the second or third week of October. . . .

During the second week of October, just as the fall potato harvest hit full swing in that region of Wisconsin, influenza tore through Waupaca. . . . The editor of the *Waupaca County Post* encouraged his readers to use positive thinking to beat the flu. He reminded the city's residents of their good fortune, noting that "few cases have appeared here, none yet fatal" and predicting that it was "very probable" the city would escape the epidemic.[10] About the time he was writing that editorial, fourteen-year-old Grace Larson caught a cold while picking potatoes with her sister. Following a quick recovery, she suddenly fell ill with pneumonia and died at her home on the evening of Tuesday, October 15, 1918. She was the city's first flu casualty. . . .[11]

Yet Wisconsin did not flinch in the face of the epidemic. Indeed, the state responded with one of the most comprehensive anti-influenza programs in the nation, one made possible by the existence of a strong state public health board and a well-coordinated statewide public health network, some forty years in the making. . . .

. . . Teachers were instructed to send sick pupils home and to report any illness immediately to the local public health officer. The board also recommended against public viewing of corpses at flu-victims' funerals or the holding of wakes in the homes where they had fallen ill. Sanctions were issued against public coughing, public spitting laws were to be strictly enforced, and kissing was discouraged as a potentially dangerous activity.[12]

On October 10, 1918, the deteriorating situation statewide led Dr. Cornelius Harper [the state health officer] to take the more drastic step of ordering all public institutions closed. This followed a recommendation by U.S. Surgeon General Dr. Rupert Blue suggesting that public health officers might consider closing public institutions should local conditions warrant such action; but nowhere except in Wisconsin was such an order issued statewide or in such a comprehensive fashion. After conferring with Governor Emanuel Philipp, Dr. Harper issued a statewide advisory, ordering all boards of health "to immediately close all schools, theaters, moving picture houses, other places of amusement and public gatherings for an indefinite period of time."[13] Within a day, virtually every local government in Wisconsin had cooperated and put the order into effect. . . .[14]

This is not to say there was absolute compliance. . . . In the exact center of the state, for example, Wausau delayed closing its schools for several days because local officials did not realize that the order was mandatory. The confusion stemmed from the poor wording of the telegram Harper had sent. . . .

The confusion had its most dire consequences in Wausau. . . . [T]he Wausau board of health decided to keep the city's schools open for a week. . . . [A]s a result of the mingling of the sick and well the city experienced a large number of cases all at once. Dr. Harper . . . conceded that the flu onslaught in Wausau "became one of the most difficult problems of any community in the state."[15]

A more deliberate form of opposition to the closing order came from a handful of religious leaders who questioned the wisdom of closing churches in a time of crisis. Virtually all churches of every denomination closed, though at least one priest, Father J. M. Naughtin of St. Rose Church in Racine, refused to close the church even amid demands from concerned local residents and the State Board of Health. Dr. Harper eventually raised the issue with Archbishop Sebastian Messmer of Milwaukee, who assured him, "Doctor, that church will be closed." . . .[16] He then decreed: "Hence, until the order is recalled, there will be no public services in our churches, Sundays or weekdays. The main doors of our churches will be locked. Bells may not be rung except for the Angelus, but funerals may be held and marriages performed in the churches, with a low Mass, provided only near relatives of the parties be present." . . .[17]

Archbishop Messmer's actions did not completely silence opposition to the closing of churches. For example, an editorial in Milwaukee's *Catholic Citizen* questioned placing churches "on a par with theaters, moving pictures, and dance halls, saloons and the like" and declared that the "closing of houses of worship is practical apostasy."[18] The Reverend H. C. Hengell, rector of St. Paul's University Chapel in Madison, emerged as an equally vocal critic. He declared that the closing order exceeded "Prussian bureaucracy at its worst" — strong words indeed when wartime anti-German sentiments were at their height. Hengell also believed that the order would do "irreparable harm to religion" and that its enforcement represented "the crying sin of the age."[19]

Yet overall, opposition to the closing order was rare, and deliberate refusals to enact its provisions were even rarer. Overwhelmingly, the people and institutions of Wisconsin observed the regulations, and many went even further by mobilizing their own local efforts to educate the public about the disease and to assist the afflicted. Perhaps the most impressive effort took place in Milwaukee, the city that posed the greatest health risk with . . . one-fifth of the state's population. . . .[20] The course of the epidemic in Milwaukee would be a significant factor in determining how the state would fare.

In fact, Milwaukee proved to be one of the best-prepared cities in America for meeting a major public health crisis. . . .

. . . Early in the campaign, health department officials met with the city's newspaper editors, all of whom agreed to help by not publishing stories that might create a panic and by printing educational stories and editorials urging compliance with the influenza campaign. The city's health department complemented the newspaper coverage by producing informational posters, placards, and pamphlets. . . . The streetcar companies printed and posted cards in all their cars admonishing the public: "Don't cough, don't sneeze, don't spit; use your handkerchief." . . . [W]ith the schools closed, the city's teachers selflessly conducted a house-to-house canvass to visit the sick and count the number of influenza cases. The canvass risked exposing teachers to the virus, but more importantly, it helped spread information and enabled the health department to monitor closely the state of the epidemic.[21]

Like the rest of the state, Milwaukee faced a shortage of hospital beds and medical personnel, a crisis compounded by the large numbers of doctors and nurses who were serving in the armed forces. Those who remained worked long hours and treated enormous numbers of patients, aided predominantly by women volunteers and civic groups who helped establish emergency medical facilities and who provided volunteer labor. The city secured two large private residences and the city auditorium as emergency hospitals; these were outfitted as hospitals by the members of the Citizens' Bureau of Municipal Efficiency. To free up the county health nurses to help flu victims at the emergency hospitals, the student nurses and instructors of the Wisconsin Anti-Tuberculosis Association took over their day-to-day duties. A large number of volunteer Red Cross nurses' aides joined the public health nurses at the hospitals, as did many school nurses, volunteers from the Wisconsin State Guard, and ten sailors from the Great Lakes Naval Training Station. Young women from wealthy families who owned automobiles volunteered as ambulance drivers with the Red Cross motor corps. Their responsibilities proved particularly arduous, including "driving the ambulances from early morning until way after midnight on some occasions" and "carrying patients rolled up in blankets down narrow stairs where the stretchers cannot be used." These citizen volunteers provided resources that allowed Milwaukee health officials to manage the crisis far better than would have been possible with only health professionals and their limited staff. Undoubtedly they saved thousands of lives.

Cities elsewhere in Wisconsin mobilized for the crisis on a smaller scale but with equal vigor. . . . Seventy women volunteers began touring the homes of [Wausau], whisked about in the automobiles of the Woman's Motor Squad, distributing health literature, recording the number and condition of sick persons, and noting whether they needed assistance. They soon discovered that the epidemic was taking a heavy toll on domestic life. In many homes, overworked, exhausted mothers were struggling to care for multiple sick children; in others, not one adult was fit to cook, clean, or tend the sick and dying. In response, the women's committee of the Wausau Defense Council and the Federated Charities began recruiting volunteers to aid sick families and assist overtaxed mothers with household chores. Several of the young women who volunteered in the homes of the sick took time off from their jobs, including about a dozen volunteers from the Girls' Training Corps who explained to their employers that their anti-influenza labor contributed to the war effort. . . .[22]

Other groups also aided the Wausau effort. The Ladies' Literary Society sewed gauze masks for public health workers; the Red Cross Home Service recruited young women to work as volunteer nurses; the Woman's Benefit Association of the Lady Maccabees printed and distributed informational cards. The domestic science teachers of the public schools and the Marathon County Training School for Teachers prepared meals for those too sick to cook for themselves. . . .[23]

Even with such a community effort, the severity of conditions in Wausau led the Red Cross to request additional assistance from the State Board of Health. . . .[24]

The state's smaller cities, towns, villages, and rural hamlets were of course far less likely to mount formal anti-influenza campaigns. Instead, most local governments enforced the closing order, then relied on local doctors, nurses, hospitals, and clinics to care for the sick, a response that often proved inadequate because of the shortage of health professionals and the great distances that often existed between patients' homes and the homes of caregivers. In Waupaca, just fifty miles south and east of Wausau, fully one-quarter of the city's 2,789 residents came down with the flu, and though the city's doctors and nurses worked almost nonstop, they still could not visit all the sick people. As one reporter commented, following three months of intense work battling influenza, the city's "doctors and nurses have been driven to their limit."[25] And as busy as the doctors were, the undertaker was even busier. He found himself conducting funerals almost every day — sometimes several a day — leading the *Waupaca County Post* to note "the strain on the undertaker has been enormous."[26] In some communities, of course, the undertaker himself fell ill or died, creating a nightmarish backlog of postponed funerals and stockpiled coffins awaiting burial. A resident of Waupun, on the Fond du Lac–Dodge County border, long afterward recalled his baby sister's funeral:

> Never within my memory were so many people of the town stricken at the same time. . . . So heavy were the fatalities that the sole undertaker in town could no longer cope. . . . Father Paul, our priest, had buckled under the weight of the flu and thus could not give words of comfort to the survivors. Margaret's tiny coffin — it was no more than a simple box — had rested on a little table by a window. Mother, crying softly, whispered that we should say goodbye to our sister. We chorused her name and then my Father, almost casually, tucked the coffin under his arm and left the room. That was our sister's funeral, stripped to the one absolute essential: burial. . . .[27]

Although the efforts of the state's large and small communities relieved enormous amounts of human misery, they could not stop the spread of the disease or reverse its symptoms. . . .

The only real cure for the epidemic was time. After the second wave of influenza swept through the state in November and December, the numbers of influenza and pneumonia deaths and illnesses gradually returned to normal. But the epidemic had taken a fearsome toll on Wisconsin. The larger cities suffered the greatest number of the deaths, with 41 percent of all deaths occurring in the state's nine largest cities (containing just under one-third of the state's population). Twenty-three percent of all deaths occurred exclusively in the city of Milwaukee. Virtually all the counties with the highest death totals — Milwaukee, Dane, Rock, Brown, Marathon, Kenosha, Sheboygan, and Racine — had significant urban centers. . . . Almost one-half of the deaths (49 percent) occurred in rural towns, villages, and unincorporated areas even though those areas held only 45 percent of the state's population. In some rural areas — such as the northern rural counties of Ashland, Forest, Lincoln, Chippewa, and Iron — the death toll ran from one-and-a-half times to double the state average per capita. . . .[28]

The untimely deaths of almost 8,500 Wisconsinites, many in the prime of their lives, affected families, communities, and the state in a multitude of ways that extended far beyond the statistical toll. Emotionally, families mourned the loss of beloved children, parents, and relatives. Because the epidemic took such a heavy toll among the state's young people, it stole the untapped potential of prematurely ended lives. The loss of breadwinners also brought financial hardship, and even if the breadwinner survived, waiting to fully recover from the flu could result in two weeks of lost pay — an enormous burden for working-class families who lived from paycheck to paycheck. As a result, thousands of families were thrown into poverty and forced to seek charity in the wake of the disease. . . .

The epidemic also took a severe toll on the civic life of the state. All the major centers of community interaction — schools, churches, civic organizations, sports teams, saloons, public meetings — shut down for the duration. Sporting events, parades, and holiday parties were canceled. Combined with a general curtailment of friendly visits, this decline in socializing noticeably weakened the social fabric. For almost three months, isolation rather than socialization became the norm, leading one newspaper editor to note that the epidemic and resulting bans "isolated families to a degree seldom known in city life," creating a sense of "forced retirement into oneself." . . .[29]

. . . [But] there can be no doubt that compliance spelled the difference between life and death for hundreds, perhaps thousands, of Wisconsin citizens. . . .

Combined with the advantages of a strong [statewide] health network and public support were the additional benefits of wartime mobilization. . . . [T]he wartime demand for personal sacrifice and cooperation carried over into compliance with public health edicts and aiding the sick. Fighting influenza became as important a patriotic duty as cursing the Kaiser. . . .

. . . It is well to remember that in 1918, millions sacrificed their individual wishes for the general welfare, and tens of thousands risked infection and possible death trying to alleviate the suffering of others. It was just such a popular impulse that helped reduce the destruction of the epidemic, and which would be equally important for combating a modern-day pandemic. In an age of apathy, cynicism, and individualism, it is worth reflecting long and hard that voluntarism, public cooperation, and an activist government prevented the worst public health calamity in modern Wisconsin history from being much, much worse.

## NOTES

1. Wisconsin State Board of Health, "Influenza," *State Board of Health Bulletin* 3, no. 4 (October–December 1918): 6.

2. . . . Bureau of the Census, *Mortality Statistics, 1919* (Washington, D.C., 1921), 30. . . .

3. *Wisconsin Blue Book, 1995–1996,* 759.

4. These figures are based on estimated excess deaths for the last four months of 1918, and the national average covers only the registration area in 1919, which included thirty-three states . . . and eighteen cities in non-registration states, comprising 81.1 percent of the nation's population. . . .

5. William Ian Beardmore Beveridge, *Influenza: The Last Great Plague: An Unfinished Story of Discovery* (New York: Prodist, 1977), 11–15. [See also Alfred Crosby, *America's Forgotten Pandemic: The Influenza of 1918* (Cambridge: Cambridge University Press, 1990).]

6. "Influenza Is Under Control at Great Lakes," *Capital Times,* 23 September 1918, 2.

7. For date of arrival, see "Influenza Epidemic," *Science* 48 (December 1918): 594; for the outbreak of influenza in Milwaukee, see Judith Walzer Leavitt, *The Healthiest City: Milwaukee and the Politics of Health Reform* (Madison: University of Wisconsin Press, 1996), 227.

8. "How Milwaukee Organized Its Fight Against the Flu," *Wisconsin Medical Journal* 17 (November 1918): 250–251.

9. "University Club to be Infirmary," *Madison Daily Cardinal,* 2 October 1918, 1. [See also "Varsity S.A.T.C. Man Dies from Pneumonia," *Capital Times,* 9 October 1918, 3.]

10. "Health Commissioner Says Worry Is Factor in Influenza Danger" and "Take Care," *Waupaca County Post,* 3 October 1918, p. 5, and 10 October 1918, 3.

11. "Young Girl Dies from Pneumonia at Home in Waupaca," *Waupaca County Post,* 17 October 1918, 1. . . .

12. Wisconsin Health Department, *Epidemic Influenza: Instructions for Its Prevention and Control* (Madison, 1918).

13. Cornelius A. Harper, "History of the State Board of Health" (unpublished manuscript, 1948), 343, in box 2, Cornelius A. Harper Papers, WHS Archives. . . .

14. "Influenza," *State Board of Health Bulletin,* 6–7.

15. Harper, "History of the State Board of Health," 346.

16. Ibid. Harper does not specifically mention Father Naughtin or St. Rose Church. . . . By consulting the list of priests with churches in Racine . . . [and comparing this with other information] the identity of the priest mentioned by Harper became apparent.

17. "Catholic Churches Closed Last Sunday," *Milwaukee Catholic Citizen,* 19 October 1918, 3.

18. "Closing the Churches," *Milwaukee Catholic Citizen,* 26 October 1918, 4.

19. "Protests Against Closing of Churches," ibid., 2 November 1918, 3.

20. *Wisconsin Blue Book, 1917,* 37, 65, 71.

21. Information in this paragraph and the next . . . was drawn from "How Milwaukee Organized Its Fight Against the Flu," 251–252, and Leavitt, *Healthiest City.* [On the Wisconsin Anti-Tuberculosis Association, see "Consumptive Citadel" in chapter 5.]

22. "Homes Canvassed for 'Flu' Census" and "Four Hundred Influenza Cases," *Wausaw Record-Herald,* 16 October 1918, 1, and 8 October, 1918, 2.

23. "Officers Urge Use of Masks" and "Warning Issued to all Emloyees," *Wausaw Record-Herald,* 14 October 1918, 1, and 8 October 1918, 2.

24. "State Men in Charge," *Wausau Pilot,* 5 November 1918, 1.

25. "Influenza Rages with Much Severity in City and County," *Waupaca County Post,* 12 December 1918, 1.

26. "Epidemic Decreasing in Vicinity," *Waupaca County Post,* 19 December 1918, 1.

27. Victor P. Hass, "Looking Homeward: A Memoir of Small-Town Life in Wisconsin," *WMH* 65 (Spring 1982): 184.

28. Statistics derived from State Board of Health, *Annual Report, 1919–1920* . . . [Madison, 1920], 57, 286–287, 304–305.

29. Untitled editorial, *Waupaca County Post,* 12 December 1918, 4. [Women were especially isolated, being less likely than men to leave home for work and more likely to care for ill children or others home from closed schools.]

# Theodora Winton Youmans and the Wisconsin Woman Movement

GENEVIEVE G. McBRIDE

*WMH* 71, No. 4 (Summer 1988): 243–275

In May 1919, in Washington, D.C., a Wisconsin visitor to the House of Representatives told the gallery doorkeeper that she was with "Mrs. Catt's ladies." Theodora Winton Youmans was directed to seats reserved for Carrie Chapman Catt's National American Woman Suffrage Association (NAWSA), between the press section and the National Woman's Party. It was apt placement. A pioneer woman journalist, Youmans had enlisted enthusiastically, if belatedly, in the suffrage cause. She was never to go so far as the militant Woman's Party. Women in that "party of picketing and bonfires and jails," as she wrote in her coverage of the historic House vote on woman suffrage,[1] were nobody's ladies. . . .

From the middle of the gallery, Youmans had a good view of the proceedings as the House passed and sent to the Senate the "Anthony amendment." Youmans wrote, "there was no excitement, no jubilee on our side." The year before, House approval of the same bill had caused a spontaneous hymn-sing by women in the galleries, but the bill had died in the Senate. This time, when the House passed the bill, suffragists held their hallelujahs. A week later, in June 1919, they were exultant when the Senate at last passed the Nineteenth Amendment to the Constitution and sent it to the states.[2] By then, Youmans was back home, rallying for ratification in her dual roles as president of the Wisconsin Woman Suffrage Association (WWSA) and as assistant editor and "suffrage writer" of the *Waukesha Freeman*.

From the middle of the woman movement, Youmans had a good view of its century of struggle. . . .

Youmans's moderate perspective and modest portrayal of her own role have influenced accounts of the Wisconsin woman movement because she was its first historian. . . . She [wrote] an article, "How Wisconsin Women Won the Ballot," in the *Wisconsin Magazine of History*. She wrote a shorter version for the state's chapter in the last volume in the massive six-volume *History of Woman Suffrage* begun by Susan B. Anthony.[3]

. . . Unconcerned about guaranteeing her place in state suffrage history, Youmans ensured Wisconsin's place in national suffrage history as the first state to ratify the Nineteenth Amendment.

Historians relying on Youmans's accounts published after 1920 have only a sketchy portrait of her contribution to the Wisconsin woman movement. . . . Ironically, because Youmans downplayed her own part in the woman suffrage campaign, the Reverend Olympia Brown, Youmans's militant predecessor as president of the WWSA, is better known. Youmans credited Brown with the state's progress toward woman suffrage. Yet as late as 1912, Wisconsin voters sent woman suffrage down to resounding defeat in a statewide referendum.[4] Brown deserves her due, but the remarkable turnaround in public opinion came during Youmans's triumphant but troubled WWSA presidency.

Youmans's histories minimized dissension in the suffrage movement nationally and in Wisconsin, where suffragists were especially polarized by World War I. The suffrage platform historically had been pacifist, but war was an opportunity for pragmatic women to win the vote. . . . Long a prominent pacifist in print but loyal to NAWSA and its leaders, the moderate Youmans led the WWSA to war. . . . By 1919, when Youmans sat with "Mrs. Catt's ladies" in the House gallery, she stood for a calculated patriotism which won suffrage, at a cost.

The suffragists' open disunity during World War I was the final battle in a long, internal war between the movement's generations. The second generation adopted methods of political compromise which won woman suffrage at the cost of moral compromise of the movement's original ideology, and its dignity. "First-generation" suffragists demanded the vote as their right. The second generation, Youmans's generation, reiterated earlier rhetoric justifying woman suffrage, but promised that women would earn it. . . .[5] In abandoning the movement's original ends, the means by which Youmans and her generation won suffrage carried within it a tragic flaw. World War I heightened the drama of the suffragists' generation gap, when the unyielding Brown was a perfect foil for the pragmatic Youmans.

Brown exemplified the first-generation suffragists; she was ahead of her time and out of place, the "domestic sphere" which was women's place in the nineteenth century [see "Olympia Brown and the Woman's Suffrage Movement" in chapter 4]. . . .

Youmans was always in the right place at the right time to realize her ambitions. Born in 1863 in Ashippun, she was . . . the only daughter of Theodore Sumner Winton and Emily Tillson Winton. Youmans's mother, formerly a schoolteacher, and father encouraged education for "Dora." He also gave her an early interest in politics. . . . The family moved in 1866 to Prospect Hill, now part of New Berlin, where Winton reigned as the crossroads settlement's postmaster, a prestigious federal post. . . . The Wintons sent their daughter to Waukesha's Carroll Academy, which was equivalent to a high school and the best education available in the county. She graduated as class valedictorian.[6] In the 1880s, she was a freelance writer for the weekly *Waukesha Freeman* and soon joined its staff. In 1889, she married *Freeman* editor and publisher Henry Mott Youmans. . . . She was named associate editor.[7]

At this point, Theodora Winton Youmans — known to her readers by the byline "TWY" — was unusual but not unique in the late nineteenth century. She was the first woman on the *Freeman* staff, but journalism was one of the first fields open to women. . . . In Wisconsin, by her own count, Youmans was one of about thirty women in newspapering, if one of only a handful in management. Most of her counterparts apparently came into the field upon marriage and rose to management upon widowhood.[8] Youmans was one of the few in her era who began a journalism career before she married her boss. . . . [L]ike other women journalists of the time, she covered meetings and social events rather

than crime or backroom politics. However, she increasingly contributed her own specialties. . . . A leader in Waukesha's women's clubs, she covered their contributions. . . .

She was elected a district president and to the board of the Wisconsin Federation of
Women's Clubs at its first convention [in 1896]. In 1898, Youmans was the federation's
president. . . .[9]

In 1898, before she could run or even vote for office, Youmans began her political career. She was an attractive appointee: In her own right, she was one of the most prominent clubwomen and woman journalists in Wisconsin, and she was the wife of an
influential man. . . . In 1898, Governor Edward Scofield appointed her to the committee
for the semicentennial celebration of Wisconsin statehood. In 1903, she was one of two
women appointed by Governor Robert M. La Follette to the Wisconsin board of managers for the St. Louis World's Fair. In 1905, she was the first woman named to the state
board of regents of normal schools. . . . In 1908, Youmans was a founder of the Wisconsin
Anti-Tuberculosis Association and the only woman on the state committee promoting
a national campaign for tuberculosis prevention [see "Consumptive Citadel" in chapter
5]. . . .[10]

By 1910, Youmans had outgrown her town. . . . From 1911 to 1920, Youmans turned
her energies to "suffrage work" — for her, as much a new career as it was a cause. During
her "suffrage decade," Youmans wrote a revealing appeal for recruits which suggests why
she, who seemed to least need the vote, worked so hard for women's enfranchisement.
The injustice of being denied the ballot affronted Youmans, but it had not held her back.
The injustices suffered by other women appalled Youmans, but she wrote that the vote
alone would not save them. . . . Youmans had a personal reason for enlisting actively in the
suffrage cause after 1910. She was apparently, if surprisingly, bored.

> The first experience of the woman who becomes interested in woman suffrage is
> the sense of loosening the petty restrictions about her. . . . She looks outside her
> little social clique, and finds to her surprise that there are numbers of 'nice' peo-
> ple beyond the sacred pale. . . . This enlarging of her acquaintanceship is even
> more enlarging to her mental horizon. She begins to see how extremely narrow
> and restricting her outlook has been. . . . She has seen the light; she has started in
> the right direction.[11]

Youmans's first experience in woman suffrage came in 1911, when the moribund Wisconsin woman suffrage movement was itself starting in a new direction. . . .

The second generation of Wisconsin suffragists was preparing a campaign to bypass
the legislature, and Brown. . . . Ada James left the WWSA, which had dwindled to seventy
members statewide. She founded the Political Equality League (PEL). . . . Youmans enlisted as "press correspondent" of the Political Equality League and also served on its
board. From 1911 on, Youmans worked three days a week at the *Freeman* and, officially, two
days a week — she admitted it was "most of my time" — for suffrage.[12]

. . . The referendum would fail in 1912. However, historians identify the campaign as
a turning point in the Wisconsin woman suffrage movement for two reasons: It attracted

new leaders, and it created publicity for the cause. . . .[13] Youmans was responsible for the publicity which, despite defeat of the referendum, was a remarkable success.

. . . She started a "suffrage column" in 1911 in the weekly *Freeman*. The column was syndicated, in a sense, because Youmans duplicated it in a suffrage *Press Bulletin* . . . sent every week to at least six hundred papers. . . . Daily releases went to the few daily papers in Wisconsin, and releases in several languages went to the many foreign-language papers. . . . [In her column,] she countered religious and ethnic resistance to woman suffrage with endorsements from Catholic cardinals and German Turners. . . .

Youmans surveyed editors in the state with a "post-card questionnaire" about their opinions of woman suffrage. She reported that journalists sympathetic to woman suffrage ran papers from Bloomer and Brillion to Viola and Wauzeka. . . . Youmans castigated editors less supportive of suffrage. She called the *Milwaukee Free Press* "an intelligent newspaper with the most astonishing if unintelligible streaks that it is possible to imagine." . . .[14]

Youmans publicized the suffragists' ceaseless fund-raising drives in the state. . . . Women raised [funds] from coins collected by streetcorner speakers, ticket sales to suffrage events, and other enterprises. A "society" theater party in Milwaukee raised $175, but scheduled speakers sent by the National American Woman Suffrage Association sometimes barely broke even. Suffragists also sold washing machines for $3.50 "to make money without begging for it," Youmans wrote. . . .[15]

Wisconsin suffragists staged a prolonged sideshow for publicity. Youmans later wrote, "That campaign was as lively as we — some trained, some untrained, in suffrage campaigns — could make it. . . ." [W]omen were "rather shy at first" about public speaking, Youmans wrote. However, state suffragists soon were holding mass "street meetings" and speaking to passersby who "under any circumstances" would not enter a "suffrage hall. . . ." Women in matching tunics of "suffrage yellow" motored around [the state] in automobiles festooned in the same color. Youmans went on tour in Wisconsin and later recalled that "the native Badger experienced the destructive shock of seeing a woman stand up in an automobile on a street corner and plead for political freedom."[16]

Suffragists reached Wisconsin voters by every mode of transportation and technological wonder available in 1912. At the state fair, the famous pacing horse Dan Patch paraded a yellow suffrage banner around the grounds, an "airship" scattered suffrage flyers overhead, and both the WWSA and the Political Equality League sponsored booths. . . . At Green Bay, Buffalo Bill Cody carried a suffragist banner as he led his Wild West circus into town. On the Wolf River, women cruised fifty miles upstream and stopped at landings to speak. Larger towns saw a twentieth-century marvel, moving pictures, when a two-reel "photo-play" entitled *Votes for Women* toured vaudeville theaters. A traveling stereopticon lantern slide show on women's working conditions went to storefronts around the state.[17]

Youmans publicized a news event of her own making when she singlehandedly engineered the endorsement of suffrage by Wisconsin clubwomen. . . . In 1912, the national federation avoided the issue, and the illogic exasperated Youmans. Clubwomen, she wrote, were "headed for the ballot box . . . from the beginning" and had been "in training long enough." She surveyed other state federations and found seven which had already

endorsed woman suffrage. . . . She spoke fervently for the endorsement against the sentiment of other state leaders and won members' support, two-to-one.[18]

The Wisconsin clubwomen's endorsement, almost on the eve of the referendum, was
a coup for the campaign. . . . Youmans's coverage of the convention in the *Freeman* suggested her elation: . . . "Club women, who are generally home-keeping wives and mothers,
are among the most conservative people in the world. A few years ago they would have
held up their hands in horror at the idea of endorsing equal suffrage. And yet by a vote
so decisive that there can be no question of their sentiments, they now go on record in
favor of it. . . ." [19]

Youmans exulted in the "indication of the growth of suffrage sentiment," but clubwomen could not be counted at the polls. She predicted that the referendum would fail
in 1912, and she was right. . . . Reasons for the referendum's failure were complex. A
hint of political corruption [at the polls] was not satisfactorily explained by a federal investigation. . . .[20]

Suffragists also faced organized opposition from two important state groups, Germans
and brewers. Both feared that if women could vote, they would impose temperance. . . .
Breweries funded anti-suffrage leagues organized by prominent women and by wives of
politicians or professional men to counter the state clubwomen's endorsement. . . .[21]

Suffrage leaders knew that a significant reason for the failure of the 1912 referendum
lay within the divided Wisconsin movement itself. . . .

After the referendum, James successfully negotiated a merger of the older WWSA and
the larger Political Equality League. The merger agreement excluded from the presidency of the new WWSA a specific roster of women, including James and Brown. . . .[22]

. . . Youmans agreed to take the presidency [in 1913]. . . . Olympia Brown, WWSA president since 1885, was named honorary president. Youmans later ruled that Brown's post
was for life. . . .[23]

The apparent unity of the new WWSA in 1913 was superficial, and even its show of
unity was short-lived. National schism in the suffrage movement would surface by 1914
and seep down to the state level by 1915. . . .

The year 1915 was perhaps Youmans's most difficult as president of the WWSA, with
no orders from "the National" above and disorder in the ranks below. She failed to forestall the membership's decision to lobby the legislature again [as in 1913] for another futile referendum attempt. . . .[24]

Youmans escaped Wisconsin . . . to assist in "press work" for the New York state referendum. . . . [For six weeks] Youmans wrote home to her readers that she was exhilarated
by suffragists' "great parade" in New York City streets and by working with Carrie Chapman Catt [who had been born in Ripon and also worked as a journalist]. Catt had been
president of NAWSA from 1900 to 1904, then left to lead international and New York state
suffrage organizations. . . . New York's referendum was defeated, freeing Catt to return to
the presidency of NAWSA. . . . From 1916 on, Catt would rescue the national organization
from schism and apathy.[25]

At a secret meeting late in 1916, Youmans along with other state presidents pledged allegiance to Catt's "Winning Plan." It would live up to its name. Catt's two-pronged plan reconciled suffragists' long-standing internal debate by encompassing [both] strategies. . . . First, there would be state-by-state campaigns to accrue sufficient electoral pressure to win a federal amendment. Then, the amendment would be sent back to the state level to be ratified. There would be no more "hopeless campaigns" in hostile states, Catt ordered. But in every state, suffragists were to remain organized for ratification. Wisconsin was clearly in the "hopeless" category. . . .[26]

Youmans's pledge that the WWSA would abide by national directives promised more than she could deliver, at first. Other suffragists, less willing to regard Wisconsin as hopelessly hostile, wanted another referendum campaign. . . . Catt censured the WWSA. Chagrined members backed down, not even lobbying for their own referendum bill which, predictably, failed in February, 1917. By then, Wisconsin suffragists were caught up in a national crisis. . . . It was "the certainty that war, real war, war that is bloody and brutal beyond words, is coming to this country," Youmans wrote.[27]

War would have a bloody and brutal impact on the fragile peace between the moderate WWSA and the state branch of the militant Woman's Party. In Wisconsin, divisive wartime tensions escalated sooner than in other states, and lasted longer. . . . Many members were of German ancestry; some like WWSA officer Meta Berger were Socialists [see "A Milwaukee Woman's Life on the Left" in chapter 5]. When war began in Europe, Youmans made immediate and impassioned pleas for peace. . . .[28]

Until war came to her country, Youmans found it possible to be both a pacifist and a suffragist. However, Youmans's pacifism was less an intellectual decision than an extension of her personality. Her WWSA presidency was characterized by a repeated preference for conciliation over confrontation. . . . [H]er writings suggest — well before Youmans admitted it to herself — that she was a suffragist first. The suffrage banner was, she made clear, no longer symbolic of a wide moral crusade for a better world. The crusade had become a single-interest coalition, prey to political shifts.

. . . By 1917, she was desperately seeking a way for suffrage organizations to "go on effectively with their regular work." . . . Catt proposed that women win [President Woodrow] Wilson's support for suffrage by supporting him in peace or war.[29] It was the logical result of the shift in suffrage arguments, made in the movement decades before, from justice to expediency. Instead of demanding the vote as their right, women had promised to earn the privilege of their suffrage. War put their promises to the test.

Youmans had to explain the apparent illogic of a very public pacifist turning to war, of a moderate in suffragism turning to militarism in politics. . . . [S]he was embracing the "preparedness" of the progressive president, Wilson, who was anti-suffrage. Wilson would explain his decision to go to war as a desire to make the world safe, and Youmans adopted his pragmatic rationale. Youmans did not admit that, even more, she wanted to save the suffrage movement. . . . The ingenious and convoluted reasoning was the opposite of her usual clarity, and she discussed herself in the third person, a departure from Youmans's very personal style of journalism: "The editor of this column is a pacifist. . . . She believes that this is not the time to push the peace propaganda and that those who insist upon doing so are in fact using their influence against peace . . . in favor of the antithesis of peace. . . . I insist that my pacifism is just as genuine as theirs — and far more practical."[30]

Youmans's action precipitated, at last, open repudiation by the last survivor of the suffrage movement's first generation. Olympia Brown had supported the militant tactics of the National Woman's Party since its inception . . . and she served on its advisory council. Still, Brown had retained her WWSA membership and generally refrained from outspoken opposition to her successor as president. . . . Like Youmans, Brown placed suffragism ahead of pacifism. But she would not abandon one belief for the other. . . . . Brown attacked members of NAWSA for their "unthinking subservience." Nearly eighty years old in 1917, Brown picketed the White House with the Woman's Party, a month after Youmans endorsed Wilson and war.[31]

Second-generation suffrage leaders also left the WWSA in 1917. . . . Zona Gale quit the WWSA, in June, 1917, in protest of its wartime stance. [So did] her successor as WWSA first vice-president, Meta Berger. . . . From Richland Center, James wrote that she wished she was with militant suffragists in the jails of Washington, D.C.[32] James followed Gale and Berger out of the WWSA.

. . . Years earlier, a hopeful Youmans had written that enlisting in the suffrage movement expanded a woman's "mental horizon" beyond "her little social clique." . . . [But] she had not been able to see beyond the horizon . . . to the battlefields of Europe where the nineteenth-century world was dying, or even to Washington where women battled to keep alive the suffrage movement's nineteenth-century goals. Youmans had "seen the light," she had "started in the right direction" in 1911 — and then she had directed the WWSA away from the pacifism and radicalism of the woman movement's founders. . . .

The loss of WWSA leaders to the Woman's Party in 1917 left Youmans with a WWSA membership less divided and more determined to win the war, and the vote, on the homefront. The departure of the women with whom she had worked most closely since 1911 was a personal blow to Youmans, but it was not devastating to the WWSA. . . . Youmans delegated lobbying to her second-in-command, Jessie Jack Hooper of Oshkosh. Hooper was the WWSA's first vice-president from 1917 on, and an effective lobbyist at cultivating legislators and tracking bills.[33]

Youmans's task was marshaling WWSA members to do "double duty" for suffrage and for war. . . . The WWSA was the first woman's group in Wisconsin to offer its services to the government, and Youmans was the WWSA representative on the Wisconsin Council for Defense. . . .[34]

Across the country, state after state yielded to similar displays of women's patriotic worth and gave them the vote. Women became a significant new constituency in suffrage states in numbers sufficient to put pressure on Congress. In January 1918, with Wilson's private support, the House passed the "Anthony amendment" first brought before it in 1878. . . . Youmans exulted in print with a wartime metaphor. "We have won. We are over the top," she wrote. "We have captured one of the three most important trenches on the way to complete enfranchisement."[35] There remained Senate passage of the amendment and ratification by the states.

The suffrage momentum finally reached Wisconsin in February, 1919. Legislators at last granted women the right to vote in presidential elections and power in the electoral college. . . . Wisconsin was one of the last "suffrage states," and the victory was anticlimactic, even distracting. Youmans was watching Washington. Despite Wilson's appearance before the Senate to plead passage of woman suffrage as a war measure, senators had voted down the bill in October 1918 and defeated it again, by one vote, in February 1919. . . . By May 1919, suffragists had amassed 314 of a total of 531 electoral votes in state-by-state campaigns, such as Wisconsin's. When Wilson called Congress to Washington for a special session, Catt called Youmans and other states' leaders to Washington to lobby their congressmen. Sitting sedately with "Mrs. Catt's ladies," Youmans watched as the House sent the amendment to the Senate again. "We knew the outcome beforehand," Youmans wrote. "The fight had been so long and the victory had some so gradually that it was difficult to grasp. We filed out smiling quietly at each other and that was all."[36]

A week later, when suffragists in Washington celebrated Senate passage of the Anthony amendment, Youmans was back in Wisconsin to be ready for the ratification fight. She was determined that her state, deemed "hopeless" by Catt, would redeem itself. . . . On June 10, 1919 — only six days after the Senate vote — Wisconsin and Illinois acted in a rush for the honor of being the first to ratify the Nineteenth Amendment to the Constitution. . . . Ada James came to the capitol in Madison with a suitcase packed for her father, who was retired from the legislature where he had proposed the 1912 referendum bill. David G. James raced Wisconsin's ratification to Washington first. . . .[37]

In many other states, organizations had disbanded after winning their own suffrage. . . . Youmans is singled out by a leading historian of the movement for following Catt's directives: "Before the end was in sight elsewhere, the woman who had served as president of the Wisconsin Woman Suffrage Association for six grueling years could write to a friend that they were . . . used to bearing the burden of the campaign. . . ." The last state was not secured until more than a year later, on August 26, 1920, when woman suffrage became law.[38]

The woman suffrage movement was not over. . . . [T]he campaign to "educate" public opinion continued without pause. Catt founded the League of Women Voters in February, 1920, and was its first president. In Wisconsin, Youmans stepped down from the presidency of the WWSA and presided over its transition to the League's state chapter. Hooper was the first president of the state League, and Youmans was the first vice-president. . . .[39]

Theodora Winton Youmans and Jessie Jack Hooper both ran for office, and lost, and deduced that women would spend decades earning their way into the inner circles of politics. Hooper ran as a Democrat for La Follette's Senate seat in 1922 and lost when the promised party support did not materialize. . . Youmans ran for the state senate in 1922 as a Republican. After she lost, she wrote bitterly in the League of Women Voters' newsletter of her disappointment in the "disgracefully small" turnout of women at the polls. Youmans redoubled her work in the League of Women Voters and in the Republican party, serving as first vice-president of the Republican women's organization in Wisconsin.

But Youmans knew she would not make history again, so she turned to writing it. . . . [She] began the several revisions of her last WWSA address, which became the standard histories of the Wisconsin woman suffrage movement. . . .[40]

. . . She wrote, "the careless world will probably continue to think that woman suffrage just happened, that it was 'in the air'; but we know that the changes in the opinions of society which made it possible are the result of ceaseless, unremitting toil." Youmans aptly described her . . . "sober record of doing the day's work as well as one could, educating and organizing, raising money and expending it, writing and exhorting, and never for one moment failing in faith as to the justice of our cause. . . ."[41] To Brown, woman suffrage was truly a cause. Youmans could adopt the first-generation's phrasing, but what she called "suffrage work" was just that: another job to be done. . . .

. . . Youmans was a clubwoman first, last, and always. . . .

Youmans in her modesty, and historians since in her footsteps, did not address the impact of Youmans and her "second generation" on the state woman suffrage campaign. . . . [T]heir common denominator was club work which encouraged their abilities, independence, and connections to power. They were swayed by neither sentiment nor gratitude to the leaders of the past, such as Olympia Brown, who scorned the "age of organization." Younger suffrage workers in Wisconsin, in the movement's last years, wanted an organizer like Youmans.

. . . Youmans's major success as the state suffrage movement's leader was due to her ability at organization, gained from her experience in women's clubs. Paradoxically, Youmans's major failure arose from her clubwoman's belief in collective action. . . . Youmans could not forever defer the confrontations over practices and principles between the militant Woman's Party and the moderate state suffragists. The same controversies at the national level came to a similar result. . . .

Youmans lacked the reflection and introspection which kept many suffragists true to the woman movement's original commitment to peace. . . . Youmans apparently never understood the difference between the contributions of herself and her predecessor, each an extreme example of her generation and each necessary to her era. Brown was ever the inflexible evangelist for a moral cause which Youmans perceived as political, requiring compromise. Youmans's political achievement must be balanced by her compromise with the movement's integrity.

But just as Youmans was kind in her account of Brown, Youmans herself should not be judged too harshly. She was a chronicler but not a student of suffrage history, and she paused little over lessons from the past. Youmans was conscious of posterity but not burdened by it, rarely fretting over the unforeseeable future for women whose lives she helped to change forever. She approached suffrage as "doing a day's work" and believed it was but a job to be done "as well as one could." If Youmans did not win woman suffrage wisely, she won it well.

⁓⁓

*At her death in 1932, Youmans was president of the Waukesha Women's Club for the third time and chaired the state federation's civics committee. Her will endowed the federation with the Theodora Winton Youmans Award, still given annually in her name to women for work in clubs, careers, or both — but, by her wishes, they must have contributed to their communities. For her contributions, historians and others in a survey cited Youmans as among the most significant Wisconsinites of the twentieth century. Among few women listed, she ranked after only Golda Meir and Carrie Chapman Catt; unlike them, Youmans stayed in Wisconsin to make history.*[42]

⁓⁓

## NOTES

1. Theodora W. Youmans, "Good Citizenship for Women," *Waukesha Freeman,* June 5, 1919, 2. . . Theodora Winton Youmans is hereafter identified as TWY and the *Waukesha Freeman* as *Freeman.* . . . [From 1911 through 1920, her column was variously called "Votes for Women," "Woman Suffrage and Women's War Work," and "Good Citizenship for Women."]

2. Ibid.; Eleanor Flexner, *Century of Struggle: The Women's Rights Movement in the United States* (rev. ed., Cambridge, 1975), 302–303, 327–328. [Until the amendment was passed and numbered, suffragists referred to the bill by its author, Susan B. Anthony.]

3. . . . TWY, "How Wisconsin Women Won the Ballot," *WMH* 5 (September 1921): 13, 23, 28, 31; TWY, "Wisconsin," in Ida Husted Harper, ed, *History of Woman Suffrage* (New York, 1922), vol. 6, 704–706. . . .

4. TWY, "Wisconsin Women," 14, 16.

5. Aileen S. Kraditor, *The Ideas of the Woman Suffrage Movement, 1890–1920* (New York, 1982; reprint of Columbia University Press, 1965), 44–45.

6. Pioneer Notebooks, Waukesha County Historical Society Research Center, Waukesha; . . . TWY, "A Pioneer Church at Prospect," *WMH* 9 (March 1926): 322; . . . *1880 Carroll College Catalogue,* Carroll College Archives, Waukesha. . . . [The Winton home and store, now moved from the original site, are restored landmarks in the New Berlin Historic Park.]

7. . . . Henry M. Youmans, "Fifty Years," *Freeman,* October 28, 1920. . . .

8. TWY, "Women as Journalists: Some Who Conduct Successful Papers in Wisconsin," *Milwaukee Sentinel,* March 15, 1891, 14. . . .

9. . . . "Theodora Youmans Dies Suddenly at Noon," *Freeman,* August 18, 1932. . . .

10. Ibid.

11. TWY, *Freeman,* February 26, 1914.

12. Ibid. January 25, 1912; Lawrence L. Graves, "The Wisconsin Woman Suffrage Movement, 1846–1920" (doctoral dissertation, University of Wisconsin, 1954), 115–117 . . . TWY, *Freeman,* June 5, 1919.

13. Graves, "Wisconsin Woman Suffrage Movement," 213–214; Marilyn Grant, "The 1912 Suffrage Referendum: An Exercise in Political Action," *WMH* 64, no. 2 (Winter 1980–1981): 116.

14. TWY, "Wisconsin Women," 16–17; TWY, *Freeman,* March 14, 21, May 9, 23, July 11, 18, 25, August 8, 22, 1912. . . .

15. . . . TWY, *Freeman,* February 22, March 7, April 11, May 2, 9, July 18, August 22, 1912.

16. TWY, "Wisconsin Women," 21; . . . TWY, *Freeman,* June 27, 1912. . . .

17. TWY, "Wisconsin Women," 21; TWY, *Freeman,* March 21, August 15, September 5, 26, 1912; Kenneth W. Duckett, "Suffragettes on the Stump: Letter from the Political Equality League of Wisconsin, 1912," *WMH,* 38, no. 1 (Autumn 1954): 32.

18. . . . TWY, *Freeman,* July 11, October 3, 17, 1912.

19. TWY, *Freeman,* October 17, 1912.

20. TWY, *Freeman,* September 12, 1912; Carrie Chapman Catt and Nettie Rogers Shuler, *Woman Suffrage and Politics* (New York, 1923), 186–188.

21. Graves, "Wisconsin Woman Suffrage Movement," 137–138, 223. . . .

22. Ibid., 137–138.

23. Ibid., 185, 229–230, 288, 378.

24. TWY, *Freeman*, February 25, March 25, April 8, May 20, July 8, 1915, November 16, 20, 1916. . . .

25. TWY, *Freeman*, September 23, November 11, 1915. . . .

26. Flexner, *Century of Struggle*, 240, 283, 289–292. . . .

27. TWY, *Freeman*, February 17, 1916, May 3, 1917. . . .

28. . . . TWY, *Freeman*, September 17, December 10, 1914.

29. TWY, *Freeman*, February 1, 15, November 3, 1917; Flexner, *Century of Struggle*, 294.

30. TWY, *Freeman*, June 21, 1917.

31. See "Olympia Brown and the Woman's Suffrage Movement" in chapter 4.

32. Graves, "Wisconsin Woman Suffrage Movement," 285–290; Ada James to Theodora Youmans, November 20, 1917, in the James Papers.

33. . . . See "Two Noteworthy Wisconsin Women" in this chapter.

34. TWY, *Freeman*, November 3, 1917; "Youmans Dies," *Freeman*, August 18, 1932.

35. TWY, *Freeman*, January 17, 1918.

36. TWY, *Freeman*, February 13, June 5, 1919; Flexner, *Century of Struggle*, 327–328.

37. Flexner, *Century of Struggle*, 327–328; TWY, *Freeman*, June 12, 19, 26, 1919.

38. Flexner, *Century of Struggle*, 329, citing Theodora Youmans to Sara Van Dusen, June 13, 1919, in the WWSA Papers, WHS.

39. TWY, *Freeman*, January 8, 29, February 12, March 5, 1920.

40. . . . TWY, "What Ails Wisconsin," *Forward* 3:6–7 (October 1924).

41. TWY, "Wisconsin Women," 24, 31.

42. "Youmans Dies," *Freeman*, August 18, 1932; Jim Stingl, "La Follette Shaped Century in State, Experts Say," *Milwaukee Journal Sentinel*, December 30, 1999.

# Two Noteworthy Wisconsin Women

## *Mrs. Ben Hooper and Ada James*

LAWRENCE L. GRAVES

*WMH* 42, No. 3 (Spring 1958): 174–180

When the women of Wisconsin gained the right to vote it was only after more than half a century of strenuous effort, and despite the most determined opposition by the men of the state. One of the most often-heard arguments against enfranchising women was that they had no desire for the ballot and if given the opportunity to vote, would refuse to do so. Even after they participated in their first presidential election in 1920, women had still to demonstrate what they would make of their new status. . . .

. . . On gaining victory [the Wisconsin Woman Suffrage Association] . . . became the Wisconsin League of Women Voters. Many suffragists moved over into the Wisconsin branch of the new league and under the leadership of their president, Mrs. Ben Hooper, of Oshkosh, soon began the rather formidable task of realizing the league's motto of "every woman an intelligent voter."

Skepticism over the extent to which women would interest themselves in politics seemed justified by the league's initial difficulties. . . . By 1922, two years after its founding, only forty-four local leagues had been organized in the state, with a combined membership of only about three thousand. For this condition there were several reasons. One was the continuing timidity and inertia of women who had not yet learned to be concerned with community affairs and were now reluctant either to vote or to join the League of Women Voters. . . .[1]

. . . Although it was intended to include members of various political persuasions, women were reluctant to commit themselves until certain that the organization was not attached to either the Republican or Democratic party. One woman wrote Mrs. Hooper from Appleton that her woman's club wanted to know more about the league before joining in order to avoid becoming politically involved; and, as late as 1926, one member expressed the fear that Republican women were using it for political purposes, whereas the Democratic women had bent over backwards in their effort to be nonpartisan.[2] Still another difficulty was that the League of Women Voters was torn by internal dissensions, as had been the case with the woman suffrage societies that preceded it.

Perhaps another and equally important reason why some Wisconsin women were unenthusiastic about further agitation was [the 1921 Wisconsin Equal Rights Amendment]. . . . This measure extended to women the same rights as men in such matters as voting, freedom of contract, holding office, jury service, holding and conveying property, care and custody of children, and in all other respects. The courts soon held that under these provisions a woman who cosigned a note with her husband was liable in her personal property for the debt.[3] If these modifications in their legal status seemed distasteful to

some women, such decisions as that a woman might vote in her own district if her husband lived far away in another state, or that a son would be exempt from non-resident tuition fees at the University of Wisconsin if his mother was a resident of the state while his
father was not, were much more appealing to others. . . .[4]

. . . Some did indeed want the right to vote — primarily to protect themselves from unjust legislation — but a more compelling reason with the majority was the fact that increasing numbers of women were developing a social consciousness which brought with it an
awareness of community problems. . . . Some women fairly seethed with desire to participate in politics and movements of one kind or another aimed at social betterment, and
many different individuals might be cited as representative of the new thinking on the
part of twentieth-century Wisconsin women. But perhaps no two would better epitomize
this intellectual trend than Mrs. Ben Hooper and Ada James.

Jessie Jack Hooper illustrates the type of person who might be described as a "clubwoman" in the best sense of that term. Since her husband was a prosperous attorney and
wholesale grocer, she had the opportunity early in her married life to develop a zeal for
public affairs, an interest which never appreciably diminished. One of her first ventures
was in the 1890s when, in concert with other women, she helped to finance and equip a
kindergarten in Oshkosh. The experiment was viewed with some skepticism at first, but
when it proved successful the city fathers soon took it over, going on to establish other
kindergartens in the city's schools. Mrs. Hooper also devoted several years' effort to induc-
ing Winnebago County to build a tuberculosis sanitorium, and participated in a project of
the women of Oshkosh to secure a nurse for the city's schools.[5]

*Hooper heard her first woman suffrage speech, by Susan B. Anthony, at the first International Con-
ference of Women in Chicago in 1893. However, she was motivated to suffragism more by frustration
with city fathers, writing to clubwomen that "the men in charge of our city government, while always
polite to us, had little interest in what we wanted because we had not votes." It was when she "tired
of joining pilgrimages to officials where we rarely got what we asked" that she "decided to concentrate
. . . on securing the vote for women" as of 1909 — ahead of her cohort in Oshkosh women's clubs.
As she wrote, "my friends were so ashamed of me that they did not even mention it."[6]*

Wearied of trying to "dig a hole with a teaspoon when a steam shovel was needed,"
Mrs. Hooper finally turned her attention to woman suffrage as a necessary tool, and campaigned actively for the Political Equality League during the months preceding the
woman suffrage referendum held in 1912. Thereafter, until ratification of the Nineteenth
Amendment in 1920, she continued her activities in the cause, serving for a time in Washington, D.C., with the National American Woman Suffrage Association as a lobbyist and
[member of the board of directors,] eventually becoming first vice-president of the Wisconsin Woman Suffrage Association. When the latter organization became the Wisconsin
League of Women Voters, Mrs. Hooper was the logical choice for its president, and in
1920 became the first occupant of that new office.[7]

She might have held her position indefinitely, had not the Democratic party leaders in 1922 asked her to challenge [Robert M.] La Follette for his senate seat. Mrs. Hooper wrestled with her conscience — briefly, for the men gave her only three hours to decide — and then accepted. She later declared that on entering the race she realized the tremendous appeal of La Follette in the state, but was unable to bring herself to decline the contest in view of the fact that having always censured men who shirked their responsibilities, she refused to commit the same offense. La Follette easily defeated her, and the election left Hooper with some bitterness towards her party. She claimed the Democratic State Central Committee had given her practically no support at all and was unable to cite any male who had spoken in her behalf. Excluding the money she spent herself, she received only about $500 from all other sources, and less than $200 from the men of the state. Nevertheless, she contended that the struggle had been worthwhile: she had maintained her self-respect, received a great many votes from women, and proved that women could stand for a political office and receive just treatment from the public. Actually, she had gotten over 78,000 votes — some 26,000 more than the Democratic candidate for governor.[8]

*"I have not learned anything about men in politics that I did not know before," Hooper wrote in the Wisconsin League of Women Voters* Woman Citizen. *"I have simply verified my former knowledge." The men of her party may not have taken seriously the futile contest against a La Follette landslide, but she did. She stumped the state from mid-August into November, hired campaign managers who were veteran suffragists from Illinois and New York, and personally funded much of the campaign's cost. After a favorable editorial in the* Milwaukee Journal, *the paper reprinted fifty thousand copies at no cost, since the party had provided her with no campaign literature.[9] However, upon her defeat, Hooper wrote in the* Woman Citizen *that she was "thoroughly convinced that women will have to make as hard a struggle for positions in our governing bodies as we did for suffrage." Her prediction was all too prophetic for Wisconsin, where no woman would run for such high office on a major-party ticket for almost half a century, and no woman would win a seat in Congress until the end of the twentieth century.[10]*

Her defeat by no means meant Mrs. Hooper's retirement. In addition to her feeling that making the senatorial campaign was a duty, she had also believed that if elected she could advance the cause of world peace more effectively than La Follette. As early as 1921 she had led the League of Women Voters into disarmament work and attempted to get 100,000 Wisconsin women to join her. Several years later she was responsible for the creation of a major women's peace society. In 1924 she wrote to prominent women in every state, inviting them to a luncheon to be given while the national convention of the League of Women Voters was assembled in Buffalo. A hundred and fifteen women responded to her overture and agreed to hold a Conference on the Cause and Cure of War, which was eventually sponsored by ten leading U.S. women's organizations. For a number of years in the late twenties the conference met annually in Washington in the cause of world peace.

During the last decade of her life Mrs. Hooper devoted herself mainly to attempts to achieve international peace. Her contributions were recognized in 1928 when she was given the chairmanship of the Department of International Relations of the General Federation of Women's Clubs, a post she held for several years. As she had with her other pursuits, she took her peace activities very seriously, devoting the major part of her time to generating support for U.S. entry into the World Court and to increasing sentiment in favor of disarmament. She carried on a heavy correspondence with the state chairmen of her department, dispatched thousands of pieces of literature, made several radio broadcasts, and embarked on extensive speaking tours across the country.[11]

The Kellogg-Briand Pact [an international peace treaty] occupied most of Mrs. Hooper's energies in 1928, but by 1931 she had plunged deeply into the formidable task of securing signatures from one million members of the General Federation of Women's Clubs, to be sent to the World Conference on Disarmament scheduled to be held in Geneva [Switzerland] early in 1932. The goal was not reached, but Mrs. Hooper's devotion to her duty had been so conspicuous that Carrie Chapman Catt, chairman of the Conference on the Cause and Cure of War [and the Wisconsin-born founder and president of the national League of Women Voters], appointed her to head the committee taking petitions from all U.S. women's groups to Geneva. This trip marked the high point in her career, and she rightly considered it to be one of the most important episodes in her life.[12]

By the time of her death in May 1935, Mrs. Hooper had thoroughly demonstrated that a woman could take an informed and important part in public affairs and need not sit back and leave the solution of civic problems exclusively to men. . . .[13]

Miss Ada James was another Wisconsin woman who ably proved that members of her sex need not necessarily limit their abilities to the management of their own personal affairs. In contrast with Mrs. Hooper, whose interests to a considerable extent turned outward from her own state, Miss James confined her attention chiefly to state and local matters during the many years she was active on the Wisconsin scene. But although they differed somewhat in the fields they chose to emphasize, both women exemplified the potentialities women might display if given the opportunity.

*James had been raised in reform. Her mother, Laura Briggs James, was a founding member of the Wisconsin Woman Suffrage Association in 1869 and a state officer in the 1870s. An uncle in the legislature sponsored the bill for the first state referendum on woman suffrage in 1886. James's father, legislator David G. James, sponsored the bill in 1911 for the second referendum on a state woman suffrage amendment.[14]*

Ada James first attracted statewide attention for her vigorous direction of the unsuccessful campaign waged by the Political Equality League during 1911–12 for passage of [a state] woman suffrage amendment. Following this, she remained active in woman suffrage work, and during World War I . . . found[ed] a Wisconsin branch of the National Woman's Party. Throughout the conflict she remained steadfastly in opposition to U.S. participation, thus agreeing fully with the stand taken by Senator La Follette. But by the end of the war she had become disillusioned with the two major parties in the state, and for a time entertained the vain hope that a third party might rise to [permanently] displace them. When this failed to occur she continued in the Republican party, serving from 1920 to 1926 as vice-chairman of its State Central Committee while that party was still firmly in control of the La Follette forces. In addition, she served as president of the Wisconsin League of Progressive Women for several years until she resigned in 1924 in order to enjoy the freedom to express her political opinions without the restraints of office.[15]

Mainly she wanted the liberty to criticize Governor John J. Blaine and his administration for the deficiencies she found in both. The decision was characteristic of her and was adhered to in spite of the fact that from 1921 to 1923 she had been a firm supporter of the governor and had often been consulted by him on policies and appointments. Her correspondence reveals that she had some influence, not only with him, but also with his wife [Anna Carrier McSpaden Blaine] and the lieutenant governor as well. But by 1923 she had cooled perceptibly in her enthusiasm toward Blaine, chiefly because he had failed to abolish the National Guard, and she no longer considered him a real Progressive. . . .[16]

In later years Miss James occupied herself chiefly with affairs in her native Richland County. In 1922 her father, D. G. James, set up a memorial trust fund for the relief of the needy, and much of his daughter's time was subsequently spent in its administration. Her primary interest lay in helping neglected and underprivileged children, wayward girls, and unmarried mothers. . . .

When the legislature passed an act authorizing the formation of county children's boards, Richland County was one of the first in the state to take advantage of the new statute. From the inception of such a board in her county in 1930, Ada James was its chairman, retaining her position until its merger into the county welfare board in 1948. The board had as its function the protection of needy children — mentally defective, neglected, illegitimate, or delinquent — making certain that aid was given them and that their legal rights were protected. Miss James discharged her duties with vigor and compassion. . . . Gradually, she became convinced that sterilization of the mentally unfit, together with the dissemination of birth control information, was necessary to prevent tragedy in the homes of parents unable to rear their children properly. Naturally, there was much opposition to both schemes; but Miss James remained their staunch advocate during the last years of her life [until her death in 1952].[17]

Ada James had become imbued with Progressive doctrines early in her life, which explains why she became such a devout supporter of La Follette after he had appeared to articulate those same ideas. She defined a Progressive as one not afraid to try something new. . . .[18]

. . . [D]uring the early twentieth century, progressive concepts swept over women as well as men. . . . [W]omen were concerned with the welfare of their communities — mothers whose children needed better schools and playgrounds; working women anxious for their own welfare; still others with the leisure and money to devote themselves to civic betterment. Not all women accepted the challenge and concerned themselves with such matters, it is true, but Jessie Jack Hooper and Ada L. James were typical of the growing number who did.

## NOTES

1. Mrs. Margaret D. Schorger to Mrs. Ben Hooper, December 28, 1920; undated memorandum, both in the Jessie Jack Hooper Papers, WHS Archives. . . .

2. Mrs. B. W. Wells to Mrs. Ben Hooper, March 7, 1921; Mrs. Margaret Fragstein to Hooper, November 26, 1926, both in the Hooper Papers. [One immediate issue was the campaign for the Wisconsin Equal Rights Amendment in 1921.]

3. *Forward* 2 (March 1923):10.

4. Jessie Jack Hooper, "Equality in Wisconsin," in the *Woman Citizen* 7 (February 24, 1923):11; Mrs. Frank [Mabel Raef] Putnam, "Equality in Wisconsin," in ibid., 7 (March 10, 1923):11; Putnam, "In Reply to Mrs. Hooper," in ibid., 7 (May 5, 1923):23–24.

5. *Oshkosh Daily Northwestern,* May 8, 1935; Jessie Jack Hooper, "The Autobiography of Jessie Jack Hooper," typescript copy, 9–10, Hooper Papers. [Born in Iowa in 1865, she was in college when she visited a sister who had married and moved to Oshkosh. Hooper did the same, moving to Oshkosh and marrying in 1888; see James Howell Smith, "Mrs. Ben Hooper of Oshkosh: Peace Worker and Politician," *WMH* 46, no. 2 (Winter 1962–1963): 124–135.]

6. Smith, "Mrs. Ben Hooper," 126; Hooper to *General Federation News,* March 16, 1929, in Hooper, "Autobiography," 102.

7. Hooper, "Autobiography," 11, 31.

8. Hooper to Ada James, July 4, 1922, James Family Papers, WHS Archives; Hooper to Mrs. M. F. Cunningham, November 13, 1922, Hooper Papers. . . . [Regarding the time frame, Hooper had not put her name in nomination but was selected by the state Democratic convention without her knowledge and notified by telephone; see Smith, "Mrs. Ben Hooper," 127.]

9. Smith, "Mrs. Ben Hooper," 127.

10. Hooper to the *Woman Citizen,* 7:12 (December 2, 1922).

11. Hooper to Mrs. Lucy Morris, June 23, 1928; Hooper to Mrs. Howard Kissam Pell, December 14, 1931, both in the Hooper Papers.

12. Hooper to Mrs. Edgar N. Bowker, October 1, 1928; Hooper to Mrs. John J. Louis, November 2, 1931; Hooper to Mrs. Henry Fradkin, December 20, 1931, all in the Hooper Papers. [On the petition campaign and opposition from anti-Communists, see Smith, "Mrs. Ben Hooper," 131.]

13. *Oshkosh Daily Northwestern,* May 8, 1935.

14. McBride, *On Wisconsin Women,* 101.

15. Diary of Ada James, James Papers, entries for March 20 and 28, 1920; *Milwaukee Journal,* April 21, 1924.

16. Governor John J. Blaine to James, February 24, 1922; Lt. Governor George F. Comings to James, February 15, 1921, both in the James Papers; *Milwaukee Journal,* April 18, 1924. [On Anna Carrier McSpaden Blaine, also a political protégé of the La Follettes and an unsuccessful candidate for her late husband's seat in the state senate in 1936, see Nancy Greenwood Williams, *First Ladies of Wisconsin: The Governors' Wives* (Kalamazoo, MI: Ana Publishing, 1991), 141–145.]

17. [*Richland Center Democrat,* October 2, 1952.]

18. *Milwaukee Journal,* January 16, 1927.

*Gwendolyn (Dodge) Washinawatok, second from right, was the first woman from the Menominee tribe to enter the Navy, pictured here in January 1944.*

# ~7~

# WOMEN AT WAR, 1930–1950

## INTRODUCTION

After decades of population growth and economic prosperity — or at least the promise of it — the period from 1930 to 1950 provided challenges for many Wisconsin families beyond the ken of previous generations. From the Great Depression years through the most devastating war yet seen, women in Wisconsin and elsewhere struggled for survival against despair as they faced decisions and new choices, which forever changed them but also freed them in ways no one could foresee. Women everywhere emerged as far different after the war, as did Wisconsin.

During the Great Depression, fewer women in Wisconsin worked for wages than in most states. Many working women, who rarely were unionized, lost their jobs — although they seldom lost jobs to men, countering a popular belief at the time that women and men competed for the same work. By contrast, in World War II, women found themselves sought after in the workplace, but then forced out again afterward, although a majority of women wartime workers wanted to keep their jobs, and some eventually found other employment. As historian William F. Thompson writes, "domestic turmoil brought on by the war frequently led men and women — but perhaps particularly women — to question that which they had previously taken for granted," at a time when women themselves were taken for granted.[1]

Amid the turmoil of the times, one of the few certainties of life in Wisconsin was a La Follette on the ballot — and it was taken for granted that the La Follette women would serve the state as well, if unofficially. That pattern had been set by matriarch Belle Case La Follette (see "The Two Worlds of Belle Case La Follette" in chapter 5) before her husband's death and continued beyond him. Their oldest son had succeeded him in the U.S. Senate in 1925; in 1930, their younger son Phil won the race for governor. Like his father, whose "loyal inner circle" began with Belle, according to historian John D. Buenker, Phil included among his advisors his wife, Isabel Bacon La Follette. Like Belle, "Isen" acted as an unpaid political confidante and as a columnist for *La Follette's Magazine*. Her work as a writer hardly was surprising, since she came from a famed literary family and had a career of her own before marrying into Wisconsin's most famous family. However, on the stump and in her column, Isen La Follette acted at Belle's behest despite her own generation's different "changes and choices," the title of Bernard A. Weisberger's article, excerpted in this chapter. As First Lady of Wisconsin, Isen La Follette served the state during the worst of the Great Depression — and as a columnist, she served her husband by promoting his programs to restore the economy by turning them to "women's issues" of domestic economies. With her help, he later returned to office for two more terms, and the political dynasty extended into the next decade as, all told, the

La Follette men ran in twenty-one statewide campaigns in twenty-six years — and the La Follette women helped them win.[2]

Less well-known women also exerted influence in "informal politics" in Wisconsin, where few won at the polls but many won on their issues. Conservationist Wilhelmine Diefenthaler La Budde of Milwaukee left an extraordinary legacy of her leadership of clubwomen in the campaign that saved Horicon Marsh as a wildlife preserve. She led lobbying for reforestation in northern Wisconsin, for protection of the porcupine, beaver, and great blue heron, and for a fishing license bill and a steel trap ban, and almost single-handedly won conservation education in schools statewide. The first woman appointed to the Wisconsin Conservation Congress and an officer in other organizations, she continued to connect them to the formidable force of the state federation of women's clubs for decades to come. That clubwomen sought public funding for conservation during the Great Depression — or that Isen La Follette's column neglected issues of working women, according to Weisberger — suggests that they were impervious to the problems of the poor. However, La Budde led the Izaak Walton League's efforts for Native Americans, and she also wrote of a tree-planting for schoolchildren where a dairy donated hundreds of milk bottles that disappeared. "The only explanation," she wrote, "is that the children ran home with the milk, possibly to feed a hungry baby." Clubwomen reimbursed the company because "under the circumstances, we are happy to make up the deficiency."[3]

That women's employment opportunities were deficient during the decade of the Great Depression owed in part to the federal government's New Deal make-work programs that primarily provided for men, based on the belief that only they supported their families, while unskilled women who headed households became increasingly destitute and desperately looked for work. Thousands in Milwaukee not only found work but made artwork for pay in an unusual program, initiated by women for women, in the federal Work Projects Administration in the 1930s. Extant examples of their work that were donated to the Wisconsin Historical Society led curator Leslie A. Bellais to write the history excerpted here of the Milwaukee Handicraft Project, "a story of hope and beauty during a time primarily known for barrenness," as she writes. From the first "motley, careworn and harassed group of women" weak from malnutrition, as described by project organizer and art professor Elsa Ulbricht, more than five thousand workers gained training in the production of textiles that were sold across the country to support the costs of the program, so that they could support their families. Some women became so skilled that they were hired away, which made room for more. Begun in 1935, the low point of employment in the decade, the handicraft project ended only when other work for women became available with the onset of war.

In Wisconsin, where women comprised one-fifth of the state labor force by 1940, "the war brought more women into the labor force than ever before," as Thompson writes. A decade later, women comprised one-fourth of the state workforce and became "a larger factor in the labor market." A significant factor for women was opportunity for new occupations opened to them in the war, as more found work in the well-paying manufacturing sector. Fewer served as maids in domestic service, and a few women of color found positions in professions, including Mabel Raimey of Milwaukee. The great-granddaughter of Sully and Susanna Costello Watson, who migrated to Milwaukee in 1851, Raimey became Wisconsin's first African American woman lawyer in the late 1920s, apparently by "passing" as white at the Marquette law school and bypassing the national bar's racial ban then. But no firm would hire her as a lawyer, and Raimey remained a legal secretary into the 1930s as she built a private practice. Her first choice had been teaching, and she was hired by Milwaukee public schools in the 1920s — for three days, until her race was discovered, and Raimey was fired. A decade later, with the growth of the black community and growing numbers of African American graduates from Milwaukee State Teachers College, the city's schools knowingly hired the first teachers of color, Susie Bazzell and Millie White. However, fewer women nationwide in the 1940s were in the professions than in the previous decade as discrimination increased in the few areas in which women competed with men.[4]

One of Wisconsin's most well-known physicians from the mid-1930s forward had withstood discrimination in her medical studies, when doctors at Yale University attempted to dissuade her from a career in public health administration. "In 1935, however, a single woman who worked in a male-dominated field could consider herself lucky to practice medicine in any form," as her biographer Sean Patrick Adams writes in his article excerpted here. Dr. Amy Louise Hunter held to her plan for a public health career "to reach a great many people" and helped to win "no less than a public health revolution" for hundreds of thousands of mothers and children. She served as director of the state Bureau for Maternal and Child Health for a quarter of a century — a pivotal period in the state and in her field — and her "innovative use of statistics," so persuasive to bureaucrats and medical men, especially improved rural practice.

Another who served Wisconsin's poorest people, her people, was only the second Native American woman physician in the nation. Dr. Lillie Rosa Minoka-Hill of Brown County was born in 1876 in New York on a Mohawk reservation, where her mother died soon after childbirth. Her adoptive father — a physician — discouraged her hope to become a nurse, because he feared that the long hours and heavy lifting would harm her health, and recommended his apparently less strenuous field. She graduated from medical school in 1899, came west to Wisconsin, married Charles Hill in 1905, and made his Oneida reservation her home. Widowed in 1916 with six children, Minoka-Hill often took patients' payments in food or firewood from the reservation at Duck Creek. In her later years, Minoka-Hill often had to rest en route for her heart or rest her eyes owing to poor vision since childhood. Another reminder of her childhood and Quaker schooling, her use of "thee" and "thy," also remained with Minoka-Hill until her death in 1952. Before her death, she was honored with membership in the Oneida nation, which, after her death, established the Dr. Rosa Minoka-Hill Fund to honor her memory with scholarships to Native American students.[5]

In the 1930s, more than 90 percent of Native Americans in Wisconsin remained rural — "resolutely rural (and poor) during the urbanizing era," Buenker writes — but they began to rebound and rebuild with the beginning of the "Indian New Deal" ending the worst governmental intervention in their lives. Their population had hit the lowest level in state history in 1920, with fewer than ten thousand Indians overall and barely two hundred living in cities. But their numbers increased by 1930, even before reform of assimilationist policies that had alienated many Native Americans from their tribal cultures. The 1934 act restored tribal control, if not tribal traditions that had accorded women an equal role; women did gain increased access to job training, if in traditional "female" roles such as secretarial work. The act ended the governmental removal of Native girls and boys to boarding schools at Gresham, Hayward, Tomah, and elsewhere in and out of the state. For those from "landless 'lost bands,'" the act also ended allotment, the private sale of tribal lands. Only the Menominee had held onto their land against allotment, but other federal practices devastated their forests during the Great Depression. They became among the poorest tribes by the end of the period and part of a migration to urban areas that would increase after another change in federal policy.[6]

The 1930 census found that the rest of Wisconsin finally had become more urban than rural, a decade after the country did, and the Great Depression accelerated the demise of the state's "golden age of agriculture" — and delayed overdue improvements for rural women. Only a fourth of farmhouses in the state had central heating, a fifth had indoor tap water, and a tenth had indoor toilets in 1940. "Long hours of hard labor which were the daily lot of farm women — whether income-producing or not — were due in large part to the common lack of these very basic conveniences," Thompson writes. By comparison, three-fourths of urban homes had central heating, and almost all had indoor taps and toilets. "The farmwife had to make do," according to Thompson, "with drawing water from a pump, cleaning and filling kerosene lamps, and preserving food and other perishables in iceboxes and fruit cellars" while awaiting rural electrification even to hear radio advertising for the new "electric servants," kitchen appliances.[7]

However, World War II further deferred the "good life" of modern consumption for many women in Wisconsin, where some farmwives would have settled for old-fashioned forms of help. A state study in 1943 found that as sons and hired men went into the service or to wartime work, the "typical farm" no longer was worked by the stereotypical man with a wife and children to do chores but often was left to single women or widows as well as widowers, single, or partly disabled men. In an era well before widespread mechanization in farm work, at least automobiles and trucks became more affordable by 1940, even for farm families. Most lived "within easy driving and hauling range" of "hamlets" of "a dozen or so to upwards of 150 inhabitants," Thompson observes. The new mobility by auto presaged the postwar mobility of the population when many immigrants' sons and daughters did not return to family farms and homes, "which had a dramatic impact on old ethnic communities."[8]

Many areas deemed "urban" by the census bureau's definition of twenty-five hundred residents had the ambience of "hamlets" or "small towns writ large," as Thompson writes. A fourth of Wisconsin's "rural" population lived in the most urban part of the state, the southeast, where farm women were among almost eight hundred thousand residents of metropolitan Milwaukee, which by 1940 included six cities topping ten thousand in population, even before the postwar boom for Milwaukee suburbs not only made rural areas urban but also meant an end to some of the city's ethnic enclaves. Immigrants' children "came out of the war with new confidence" and were "less self-conscious about their 'foreign' origins" and "more likely to marry someone from a different ethnic background" than before the war, according to Thompson.[9]

But the postwar boom would pass by most African Americans in Wisconsin, where most lived in Milwaukee's "Bronzeville." They remained in poor housing owing to the restrictive covenants of many subdivisions and suburbs of Milwaukee but also remained poor because most New Deal programs — unlike the Milwaukee Handicraft Project — practiced racial as well as gender discrimination. War work drew more migrants, but the total of little more than ten thousand African Americans by 1945 remained less than two percent of Milwaukee's population — although almost 90 percent of African Americans in the state lived in its largest city. Six of every ten African Americans in the state lived in a single state assembly district of the city, a legislative seat won by African American in 1944 and ever since. Residents of color also would come out of the war "proud of the contributions which they and their people had made" and "more willing than before to assert themselves in politics and other areas," as Thompson notes.[10]

No matter their heritage, American women made extraordinary contributions to the homefront in World War II. As Sara M. Evans writes, "women's most mundane activities were suffused with nationalistic fervor," from recycling tin cans to rationing food to buying war bonds to volunteering for the Red Cross and Civil Defense. Many women went to work for wages for the first time, including in federal day care centers — although there were few in Wisconsin — established so that more women could work in factories and wartime munitions plants, of which there were many in the state. Propaganda campaigns targeted women to assure them that less traditional tasks "once viewed as inappropriate," writes Evans, "suddenly became patriotic duties for which women were perfectly suited." Almost eight thousand Wisconsin women soon suited up in uniform, most enlisting as military nurses.[11]

Military nurses numbered more than half of the more than four hundred American women killed in action in World War II, including a Wisconsin woman among the first Army women awarded the Silver Star, the nation's third-highest honor. Army Lieutenant Ellen Ainsworth of Glenwood City was twenty-four years old in 1944 and on duty in a hospital during the battle of Anzio, Italy. She moved her patients to safety although wounded herself; six days later, she was one of the six nurses who died at Anzio. A nursing care facility at the Wisconsin Veterans Home in King is named in her honor, as is a conference room in the Pentagon.[12]

A Milwaukeean who served and died heroically, if unofficially as a spy, is honored annually in Wisconsin on Mildred Fish Harnack Day. She met and married a German when both were college students in the 1920s in Madison and moved to his homeland, where both taught in Berlin throughout the 1930s, as the Nazis rose to power. Both she and her husband became leaders in the resistance, saving Jews and spying for the Allies, until both were betrayed. In 1943, two months after the Nazis executed her husband, they beheaded

"Mili" Fish Harnack, who became the only United States civilian to die by direct order of Adolf Hitler against the woman he called the "meddling American."[13]

Thousands served in the Red Cross, including Elizabeth Richardson of Milwaukee. As an award-winning art student at Milwaukee-Downer College, she became beloved for satirizing campus life with her cartoon character, "Beulah," clad in cardigan and saddle shoes typical of "co-eds" of the era. In 1944, Richardson gave up an advertising career at Gimbels and then Schuster's department stores to serve in the Red Cross. She served in England until D-Day, the massive landing of Allied forces in France, where she served next though V-E Day, victory in Europe in May 1945. Only weeks later, on a trip to Red Cross headquarters in Paris, her plane crashed. Richardson was buried in a military cemetery in France, far from Milwaukee.[14]

Some Wisconsin women, serving or working in the Pacific, survived capture by the Japanese, including military nurse Ruth Marie Straub of Milwaukee. Her wartime diary also survived. "We are burying the dead in sheets," she wrote after days of bombing of an American base and only days before a bomb killed her fiancé. She had a nervous breakdown and was not recovered when captured and forced to walk hundreds of miles in the Bataan "death march." Decades before, teacher Ethel Thomas Herold and her husband had made their home in the Philippines, where she was imprisoned in a Japanese camp. Although she never returned to Wisconsin after her release, she also "never disavowed her rural roots" in Potosi, according to a biographer.[15]

Many Wisconsin women who returned from the war, or remained on the home front as war wives or war workers, recalled their experiences from the extraordinary to the mundane for a Wisconsin Historical Society oral history project, excerpted here. The story of Alice DeNomie of Milwaukee, an Ojibwe teenager who left school for wartime factory work, opens her niece Patty Loew's work on "the back of the homefront," where Native and African American women, like other Americans, "suffered wartime deprivation and loss." However, women of color also suffered discrimination, from fewer work opportunities to lower pay to poor housing. The demand for housing was especially high in cities, such as Kenosha, where a federal study found that although twice as many women worked there in 1944 than had held income-producing jobs before the war, far more lived with their parents than did working women in other states studied.[16]

During a time of transition for women from ethnic enclaves or communities, many also found that the war freed them from traditional constraints of their cultures, as is evident in their oral histories, edited by Michael E. Stevens and Ellen D. Goldlust and excerpted here. Some went overseas as nurses, and some went out of the state for the first time to follow spouses to military camps in the South, where they also encountered people of color — and discrimination — for the first time. Some stayed in Wisconsin for wartime work and their first encounters with other cultures closer to home. One young woman with a child stayed home yet served on the homefront within her culture by translating letters in English for immigrants with sons overseas. Despite the diversity of their experiences during and after the war, a commonality in women's stories is the collective strength they found on the home front with so many men gone to war — and when so many women worried, as the wife of a Wisconsin prisoner of war recalls here, whether their men would come home.

Some women came to Wisconsin after the war, as they never could go home again after surviving the Holocaust. In another Wisconsin Historical Society project, Stevens and Ellen Goldlust-Gingrich edited women survivors' stories as told in their own words, excerpted in this chapter. As the editors write, "the interviews show the ways in which the war disrupted and forever changed the lives" of Holocaust survivors, for whom the freedom they found in the postwar period held a different meaning than for other Wisconsin women who lived through World War II. "Despite their differences," note Stevens and Goldlust-Gingrich, the women "tell stories of triumph" as Jews who "defeated the Nazi dream of annihilation," held onto their own dreams, and defied a tendency to turn them into victims of the horror they had seen rather than victors over the hatred they had survived.

Hatreds closer to home also caused incidents of anti-Semitism and anti-Japanese sentiment in Wisconsin. Asian immigration was new to the state, where fewer than two dozen Japanese Americans lived in 1940. The war temporarily brought more, although all men, to Camp McCoy where infantrymen from Hawaii trained for six months in 1942, and residents made them so welcome that some returned to settle after the war. However, thousands of Japanese prisoners of war faced hostility when Camp McCoy called on nearby residents of Sparta to help defend "homeland security." Worst were mass meetings in Mequon to protest the relocation to Wisconsin of fifteen Japanese Americans among more than a hundred thousand — many of them Nisei, or native-born citizens — from the West Coast who already had been made homeless when "relocated" by the government to internment camps. However, several hundred more Japanese Americans were made welcome, almost half of them in Milwaukee but many in communities across Wisconsin. Few similar acts of anti-Semitism arose, although the state sued a "Gentile League" in Watertown in 1944 for organizing to deny the rights of Jewish residents. After the war, in 1945, a state Commission on Human Rights convened, although it lacked legal authority.[17]

Fittingly, the first Holocaust survivors immigrated as Wisconsin celebrated its centennial as the new homeland of hundreds of thousands of immigrants since statehood in 1848. The stories of immigrant and migrant women in state history were not forgotten, nor those of Native American women before them, owing to Ruth De Young Kohler, who chaired the Committee on Wisconsin Women for the 1948 Centennial Commission and organized displays at the state fair on a hundred years of women's history. She then preserved their research for posterity in the first major historical work on Wisconsin women. Kohler's *The Story of Wisconsin Women* remains a remarkable work for many reasons. Her years as women's editor of the *Chicago Tribune* made her work readable for a wider public. However, she also made a scholarly contribution to knowledge of the state's past — a part of the past that previous state histories by men somehow had missed.[18]

An inclusive, perceptive history of women from Wisconsin's diverse cultures, without prejudice, her prescient history holds stories of hundreds of women other than the wealthy, the powerful, and the prominent, like herself. Kohler wrote with empathy for women's everyday lives and thoughts in an earlier day — and with a streak of her own feminist thought and wit. No historian, before her or since, has succeeded half as well in telling women's half of Wisconsin history.

Yet Kohler was a woman of her time, and she wrote her history of women in Wisconsin while they still were recovering from more than four years of wartime "domestic turmoil" with fatherless families, food rationing, housing shortages, and other hardships on the homefront. She also wrote amid worsening news of the world with still-unfolding stories of the Holocaust's horrors and the aftermath of America's atom-bomb attacks at Hiroshima and Nagasaki, inaugurating the coming nuclear age. As well as she knew the past, her readers knew the unpredictability of the future. She concluded *The Story of Wisconsin Women* as only a woman of her generation could: "Once in this country, in this state, a full day of life could not be taken for granted, much less food and lodging and safety from attack."[19]

Her generation had been tested more than once, through the Great Depression and the "good war," by many challenges, choices, and changes almost unimaginable in their childhoods. They had not made a perfect world, or even a Wisconsin without prejudice. However, women and men in World War II became aware of a world beyond Wisconsin that had changed greatly since generations before them had left the "Old World" behind. In the new postwar world, Kohler wondered whether her generation and those that followed would have "the same vision and faith and courage of the mothers and daughters of Wisconsin's first century" and would succeed as well in "succeeding chapters" yet to be written.[20] Ruth De Young Kohler would not live to write the next chapter in state history; she died soon afterward, after having lived less than half a century. In their next half-century, Wisconsin women at times would take for granted the lessons of their past. However, by the time of their state sesquicentennial, and on the eve of a new millennium for Wisconsin, they would rewrite their history once again.

## NOTES

1. Sara M. Evans, *Born for Liberty: A History of Women in America* (New York: Free Press, 1989), 202; William F. Thompson, *HOW,* vol. 6, *Continuity and Change, 1940–1965* (Madison: SHSW, 1988), 99–101.

2. John D. Buenker, *HOW,* vol. 4, *The Progressive Era, 1893–1914* (Madison: SHSW, 1998), 439; Paul W. Glad, *HOW,* vol. 5 *War, A New Era, and Depression, 1914–1940* (Madison: SHSW, 1990), 298.

3. Wilhelmine La Budde to Golden Guernsey, November 3, 1931, Wilhelmine D. La Budde Papers, 1924–1956, WHS Archives, Milwaukee Area Research Center, Golda Meir Library, University of Wisconsin–Milwaukee; see also Amanda J. Bruesewitz, "Wilhelmine La Budde: Conservation Advocate" (honors thesis, University of Wisconsin–Milwaukee, 1999).

4. Thompson, *HOW,* 101; Phoebe Weaver Williams, "A Black Woman's Voice: The Story of Mabel Raimey, 'Shero,'" *Marquette Law Review* 74 (Winter 1991–1992), 345(–376); Albert Muchka, "Thirty Dollars Down and a Lifetime to Buy: The Watson-Raimey Collection," *Lore* 43, no. 4 (December 1993), 5–9; Jack Dougherty, *More Than One Struggle: The Evolution of Black School Reform in Milwaukee* (Chapel Hill: University of North Carolina Press, 2004), 20–21; Evans, *Born for Liberty,* 202.

5. Rima D. Apple, "Lillie Rosa Minoka-Hill," *Women and Health* 4, no. 4 (Winter 1979), 329–331. Granddaughter Carol O'Loughlin Smart of Waukesha authored a play on Minoka-Hill that she performed throughout Wisconsin; see Laurel Walker, "Waukesha Woman Honors Beloved Grandmother in 'Song!'" *Milwaukee Journal Sentinel,* April 13, 2003. Granddaughter Roberta Hill, a poet and professor of English

and Native American studies at the University of Wisconsin–Madison, authored a forthcoming biography on their foremother; twenty-one other grandchildren included the late Oneida artist Jim Hill.

6. Buenker, *HOW,* 86, 192; Glad, *HOW,* 486–488; Evans, *Born for Liberty,* 209–210; Patty Loew, *Indian Nations of Wisconsin: Histories of Endurance and Renewal* (Madison: WHS, 2001), 31–34, 94–95, 120.

7. Robert C. Nesbit, *Wisconsin: A History,* 2nd ed.(Madison: University of Wisconsin Press, 1989), 478; Thompson, *HOW,* 87; Evans, *Born for Liberty,* 219.

8. Thompson, *HOW,* 55, 87.

9. Ibid., 18, 55.

10. Joe William Trotter Jr., *Black Milwaukee: The Making of an Industrial Proletariat, 1915–1945* (Urbana: University of Illinois Press, 1985), 149; Thompson, *HOW,* 58, 322.

11. Evans, *Born for Liberty,* 219.

12. Tom Brokaw, *The Greatest Generation* (New York: Random House, 1998), 177; see also Avis Dagit Schorer, *A Half Acre of Hell: A Combat Nurse in World War II* (Lakeville, MN: Galde Press, 2000).

13. Shareen Blair Brysac, *Resisting Hitler: Mildred Harnack and the Red Orchestra* (New York: Oxford University Press, 2000). Brysac is a great-niece of Harnack by marriage.

14. Gordon Brown, "A Life Cut Short, A Life Remembered: Elizabeth Richardson, Milwaukee-Downer '40, 1918–1945," *Lawrence Today* 81, no. 4 (Summer 2001), 20–23.

15. Elizabeth M. Norman, *We Band of Angels: The Untold Story of American Nurses Trapped on Bataan* (New York: Simon and Schuster, 1999),14–15, 21–23; Theresa Kaminski, "From Potosi to the Philippines: The Rural Borders of Ethel Thomas Herold," paper presented to the Rural Women's Studies Conference, Las Cruces, New Mexico, February 21, 2003, 1–14.

16. Thompson, *HOW,* 99–100.

17. Ibid., 65, 325–327.

18. Clark G. Kuebler, "Mrs. Herbert V. Kohler (1906–1953)," *WMH* 37, no. 3 (Spring 1954): 186–187.

19. Ruth De Young Kohler, *The Story of Wisconsin Women* (Madison: Committee on Wisconsin Women, 1948), 135. She also authored *Wisconsin Historic Sites* for the centennial, served on the Board of Curators of the Wisconsin Historical Society, and founded the Society's Women's Auxiliary, now the Friends of the Wisconsin Historical Society.

20. Ibid.

# Changes and Choices

*Two and a Half Generations of La Follette Women*

BERNARD A. WEISBERGER

*WMH* 76, No. 4 (Summer 1993): 248–270

❧☙

*Two generations of La Follette men dominated progressive politics in Wisconsin from the 1890s through the 1940s. Robert M. La Follette Sr. ("Old Bob") served as Wisconsin governor from 1901 to 1905 and as a U.S. senator from 1905 until his death in 1925, after running as an independent presidential candidate in 1924. His oldest son Robert Jr. filled his father's seat in the U.S. Senate for the next two decades, while younger son Philip served as Wisconsin governor from 1931 to 1933 and again from 1935 to 1939.*

*"There were La Follette women, too," writes Bernard A. Weisberger — generations of women with their own traditions of public service, including two gubernatorial wives who led "independent public lives" and also campaigned for progressive women's causes. Belle Case La Follette (see "The Two Worlds of Belle Case La Follette" in chapter 5) and her daughter-in-law Isabel both "took a deliberate role as counselor, advocate, and organizer in their husbands' battles" and "could be described as 'new' or 'emancipated' women" in the context of their different times, he writes. However, that Isabel came to maturity in the post-suffrage period, he suggests, made the women's similarities less significant than their generational differences and meant "a huge difference in her sense of the world's priorities." She also served as the governor's wife during the Great Depression and, in the mid-1930s between her husband's tenures in office, traveled extensively in Europe and witnessed signs of the rise of Nazism that would lead to another world war.[1]*

*Weisberger does not suggest that generational differences explain how suffragists' daughters differed in facing the challenges of their decades between the wars, whether they were La Follettes or from less famous families. In his original article, he also focuses on Belle's daughters, Fola and Mary, as well as another daughter-in-law. Only Fola La Follette, an actress whose life largely was spent outside Wisconsin, also led a "public life." In contrast, Mary's "private and artistic temperament kept her in the wings," while daughter-in-law Rachel Young "disliked the engulfing rigors and rituals of campaigning" and "avoided them as much as possible."*

*But Isabel rose to the challenges of life as a political wife and of living up to the La Follette legacy — not only in support of her husband who followed his father's footsteps but also in her own right, as Weisberger writes in this excerpt, in following another La Follette woman who was among Wisconsin's most memorable and lively "first ladies."*

❧☙

. . . Isabel Bacon La Follette [was] known within the family by the nickname Isen. She, too, earned her bachelor's degree from the University of Wisconsin in 1921. It was there that she first saw Senator La Follette's handsome younger son, of whom she confided to a friend: "I'd surely like to vamp him."[2] She and Phil were married in 1923, a pair well-matched in bookish earnestness. Though from Salt Lake City, her background was uplift-ingly Bostonian, and she was the granddaughter of one of the founders of the educational publishing house of Allyn and Bacon. Between her graduation and wedding days she held a social-work job at a settlement house in Bayonne, New Jersey — much as Belle had be-come a schoolteacher thirty years earlier, while waiting for La Follette, Senior, to estab-lish himself in his new job as district attorney of Dane County. In 1924 Phil exactly followed the paternal pattern by running for and winning the same job. Isabel then and there became and remained his political consort.

Essentially her visible job was to organize the progressive women of the state for Phil's benefit. She kept in touch with and made speeches to their various organizations, arranged the candidates' social events during campaigns, and did the traditional enter-taining-with-a-political-purpose expected of the governor's wife. Meanwhile she was rais-ing three young children, the last of them born during Phil's second term.

She did have one position in her own right. Belle spotted her talent for writing and put her to work on the editorial staff of the family house organ, *La Follette's Magazine*, founded in 1909 (ultimately to evolve into *The Progressive*, still alive under other owner-ship). In time Isen began to write regular, signed columns of commentary on topics of the day. But though she spoke in a clearly identifiable woman's voice, the subjects she ad-dressed were rarely gender-specific. By the 1930s there was a general assumption that "woman's" political equality had been established by the Nineteenth Amendment. Nor were tips on "scientific homemaking" any longer news from a women's frontier. The do-mestic advice most appreciated by readers after 1930 dealt with how to make do on scanty salaries, for poverty dogged both sexes. Isabel's concerns were inexorably squeezed into the pigeonholes of Phil's agenda for economic regeneration; sooner or later she always got back to what women needed to know and do about pocketbook issues. Belle . . . had the luxury of seeing the "woman question" as part of an overall drive to free society from corruption, injustice, or mere stuffiness. Isabel's contemporaries, by contrast, agonized about war and fascism abroad and a stalled production system at home. Circumstances seemed to dictate that their most useful role would be to support the men who were, by custom and prerogative, leading the progressive fight.

It is hard to find a label for such women that does not sound dismissive, but "facilita-tors," or perhaps "cooperators" might do. For them, as for the welfare-state liberals who, under the New Deal, replaced the progressives as exemplars of reform in America, clean politics and personal emancipation had to take second place to activist government and social planning.

. . . The First World War [had] murderously unraveled the assumptions of improvers like Belle. . . . And the anticipations of those later cooperators in building a good society, like Isabel, also ended in war, followed by a long flight into domesticity. . . .

Isabel comes into the picture in 1920, the year of brightness shed by the final passage of the amendment that gave women the vote. To many women on the threshold of life it seemed that the battle was already won, and what remained was a mopping-up campaign. Young Miss Bacon, who gave the commencement address at her 1917 high school graduation, appeared to think so. Herself one of five daughters, she rattled off a list of improvements in "women's conditions" in the "advanced" nations of the world, and asked: "If such changes have taken place in the past half century, have we not a great deal to hope from the Future?" With all the confidence of her eighteen years she declared that the day of the spinning wheel was over, and therefore that an abstract being whom she referred to as "the woman" now had "more time for outside interests," more "surplus energy" to expend for the public welfare, and new power to "clear away the parasitic forms that . . . drag her down."[3]

Her letters home from college bubbled deliciously with the same kind of assurance. "I am taking political ethics," she told her family. "I'm crazy about it. It deals with the causes of the war, its results and problems, and how to deal with them."[4] Surely, dealing with them would be possible for a generation of men and women trained in such courses as Economics, and Leadership in a Democracy. She was also enthused about an undergraduate course in law, in which she was "learning stuff that absolutely everybody should know. . . . It's a men's class, supposedly, with about a dozen girls and two hundred men, and the men expect the girls to flunk out in three weeks. For that if for no other reason I'll show 'em." She expected to go "to New York or some big city to work" after graduation. "Sometimes," she said, "I get so anxious to get out and to work that I don't know what to do." But she likewise admitted to an occasional thought of "how nice it would be to get married as soon as I leave school."[5]

In the end that idea prevailed, after she met Phil in November of 1920. "[H]e is about as fas-kinating as you could wish for," she wrote home.[6] By the following spring they were engaged, and dreams of work took second place. Isabel's post-graduation job was clearly seen by both as a temporary pattern rather than a career choice. She was waiting in the time-approved way for Phil to be able to support a family. He seemed hesitant to declare himself ready for that, and Belle may have put Isabel on the staff of *La Follette's Magazine* early in 1923 in order to remind him more forcefully than love letters could of his young fiancée's presence. The two were married in April of that year.

Isen La Follette presumably shared the family's excitement and preoccupation with her father-in-law's valiant but doomed 1924 presidential race — she later recalled that they all felt like soldiers in a cause — but there is no record of her taking any active part. Her first child, Robert La Follette III, was born in 1926; daughter Judith arrived two years later. These commanded her full attention, given without inner conflict according to Isen herself. In her unpublished autobiography she wrote: "Real home-making is an expression of the creative urge and gives genuine satisfaction, even with the inevitable drudgery involved, as in all work."[7] Her initiation into campaigning does not seem to have begun until 1930, and then at Belle's behest. Belle wanted Isen's opinion of a draft platform that Phil had drawn up at the start of his run for the governorship. Isen protested that she knew nothing of politics — in fact, had a "natural distaste for it." Belle ignored the claim of ignorance. "You are an intelligent woman," she said. "If what Phil writes doesn't appeal to you, rest assured it will not appeal to others."[8] Then and thereafter Isen was present at the creation of speeches and documents, and in subsequent election years was sent out to speak to and cultivate gatherings of women on her husband's behalf.

On the platform, in the pages of *The Progressive*, and in whatever subtle ways were available as the official hostess at the governor's mansion, Isen rallied support for Phil's programs. These included measures to restore and modernize Wisconsin's economy and administrative machinery, to win it a share of federal assistance, to open its gates to main currents of New Deal thought. Phil talked of public power, bank regulation, protection for dairy farmers, unemployment relief, conservation, financial aid to strapped local governments, rural road improvement, an end to the use of injunctions in labor disputes, curbs on corrupt election practices, better conditions in the state's asylums and jails. Some of his proposals were based on his father's blueprints for a vital democracy. More of them, however, were designed to fight economic stagnation and to provide jobs as the needed precursors of freedom. And none of them dealt with "women's issues."

Isen La Follette spoke about them, of course, from a woman's viewpoint — that is, she tried to show how they would improve women's capacities to function in their customary family settings and jobs. This is not said in condemnation. She could hardly be expected to anticipate by thirty years or more the concerns of present-day feminism with professional, political, and social empowerment of women. Nor had she really abandoned Belle's insistence that educated women shared with men the duty to change the world. As a political consort to Phil she shared in the reading, the travels, the conferences and interviews by which he kept himself informed on every possible domestic and international issue. Her horizons were not bounded by the kitchen, the nursery, or even the borders of Wisconsin.

Nonetheless, it was always as a clearly labeled junior partner that she operated, like most of her women contemporaries in politics. And as a partner with very sharply defined and limited standing. A story in her private memoir tells it all. Some time around 1940 a number of Madison women organized an "entertainment" for the Progressive party members of the state legislature — all men — at which they might "talk informally on the problems facing them, so that the group could better understand and back them up in their fight." Proudly, Isen noted that the women planned and ran the entire affair. "They prepared and served a delicious meal furnished by themselves, and rushed through the dishes to participate in the evening's program."[9]

During World War II she sank deeper into domesticity. Despite having been an isolationist, Phil volunteered for the Army and spent two-and-a-half years in the Pacific Theater as a member of General Douglas MacArthur's staff. Isen, doubly wounded by the war both as an isolationist *and* a pacifist, spent the time like millions of other lonely women, raising her children. She lived in semi-isolation on a farm outside Madison that Phil had bought over her misgivings. After his return, they remained private citizens for the rest of their lives. Towards the end of hers, she organized a Women's Service Exchange in Madison, matching up retired women with employers who needed their particular skills.

In a general way, the threefold story of [the La Follette women] fits without too much tugging or stretching into the current generalizations about "women's history" in the twentieth-century United States. There was indeed a pre-1914 reformist feminism, typified by Belle, that did not challenge the stereotypes of all women as being inexorably maternal and domestic, and therefore especially fit to "clean up" society. And that movement did indeed fade from prominence in the flaming 1920s, the agonized 1930s and 1940s, and the complacent 1950s, carrying . . . Isabel's youthful idealisms with it.

But the delights as well as the deeper lessons of history are often to be found in the individual departures, the local variations on the main script . . . . Be that as it may, the La Follette women, however they may match scholarly "profiles," were intriguing separate personalities — literate, warm, and humorous in their private letters as often as they were opinionated and insular. Like their men, they espoused political rebellion; but when it came to family portraits they struck quite conventional attitudes as devoted spouses. Yet within each was a kind of innate contrariness — a generic La Follette trait that made them so irritating to their enemies, and keeps them so fascinating to a biographer.

## NOTES

1. Nancy Greenwood Williams, *First Ladies of Wisconsin: The Governor's Wives* (Kalamazoo, MI: Ana Publishing, 1991), 160–161.
2. Philip La Follette, *Adventure in Politics: The Memoirs of Philip La Follette,* edited by Donald Young (New York, 1970), 78.
3. Isabel La Follette, May 11, 1916, series 3, box 160, Philip Fox La Follette Papers, WHS Archives.
4. Ibid., Isabel La Follette to "Dearest Family," undated, "Sunday night," 1918.
5. Ibid., Isabel to "Dearest Family," April 11, 1919.
6. Young, ed., *Adventure in Politics,* 78.
7. Quoted in Ibid.,174. The comment on feeling like a soldier . . . is in the draft of "If You Can Take It" [draft of an unpublished autobiography by Isabel Bacon La Follette, with penciled note, "written 1947–48," of three drafts in the Philip Fox La Follette Papers, boxes 164 and 165].
8. Lucy Freeman, Sherry La Follette, and George A. Zabriskie, *Belle: The Biography of Belle Case La Follette* (New York, 1986), 235. [Born in 1936 and the fifth girl in the family named Isabel before becoming known by her nickname, Sherry La Follette was the third child of Isabel Bacon and Philip Fox La Follette.]
9. Isabel Bacon La Follette, "If You Can Take It," 371.

# "Who Guards Our Mothers, Who Champions Our Kids?"

## Amy Louise Hunter and Maternal and Child Health in Wisconsin, 1935–1960

SEAN PATRICK ADAMS

WMH 83, No. 3 (Spring 2000): 181–201

*Dr. Amy Louise Hunter "improved life in Wisconsin for countless families," writes Sean Patrick Adams of the director of the Wisconsin Bureau for Maternal and Child Health (originally, the Bureau for Child Health Welfare) from 1935 to 1960. Born in New York City in 1898, Hunter earned her first degree from Vassar on scholarship, defying her family. Her mother delayed Hunter's higher education by a year, keeping her at home "to acquire proficiency in housekeeping," according to Adams, and attempting to rid her daughter of "any ideas of going to college" as "inappropriate for young ladies"; Hunter's well-off family funded higher education only for her brothers.*

*Hunter had to work for tuition for a master's degree at Cornell and a medical degree from Yale University as well as a doctorate in public health from Yale that she pursued despite the advice of doctors at the school. "Every time I got out of school, everybody told me I couldn't get a job because of the Great Depression," Hunter later recalled. Her higher education ended in the mid-1930s, when she was in her mid-thirties, and a woman in the "male-dominated field could consider herself lucky to practice medicine in any form," as Adams writes. Hunter happily came to Wisconsin to head the bureau that "allowed her to reach a great many people." Created in 1919, the bureau had "focused solely on educating potential mothers in Wisconsin" through such means as "its high school course in infant hygiene, with the slogan 'Every Wisconsin Girl Educated for Intelligent Motherhood,'" that soon annually reached thousands of students in the state.*

*By the mid-1930s, the bureau became a national leader under Dr. Charlotte Calvert as the director from 1929 to 1935. From 1930 to 1932 alone, local and state health centers demonstrated basic child care to more than thirty thousand Wisconsin parents. The bureau also sent mailings of prenatal advice to expectant mothers and published manuals and handbooks on hygiene to teachers and others. But such programs still reflected "the conventional wisdom," according to Adams, of a bureaucracy of benevolence. "It was Calvert who first began to move the agency away from its progressive reformist roots and toward a more quantitative approach," he writes, although the concept of comparing infant and maternal mortality rates initially caused "indignation and outrage" from the medical profession. However, for the next quarter of a century, it was Dr. Amy Louise Hunter who "would bring to full fruition" the "budding use of statistical studies in public health" for the betterment of Wisconsin women and families.*

. . . In Wisconsin, Dr. Calvert had completed an intensive study of maternal mortality, and she wanted to conduct a survey similar to that of the New York Academy of Medicine [in

1933 in New York City].[1] The intense suffering of so many children during the early years of the Great Depression made such a survey urgent. In 1934, Dr. Calvert helped develop a statewide program to assess the status of Wisconsin's children in terms of malnourishment, food, clothing, and health care, and she began collecting data so that the resources of her division might be employed with greater efficiency.[2] Calvert's career as director lasted only six years, but by the time she retired in March of 1935, the state's infant mortality rate had dropped from 68.7 to 48.4 infants per 1,000 live births, and the maternal mortality rate had dropped from 4.9 to 4.68 per 1,000 live births.[3]

Amy Louise Hunter picked up the statistical program where her predecessor left off and expanded the use of statistical studies to isolate problem areas and, in her words, obtain "a little more understanding of the problem and attention to the details of prenatal care and delivery."[4] When she arrived in 1935, her program focused upon two major phases: the continual collection of data and the publication of statistical profiles into an accessible form. Although the amount of data in the form of birth and death certificates, local health questionnaires, and census material was immense, Dr. Hunter nonetheless insisted upon a hands-on approach to its analysis. She personally examined every Wisconsin maternal death certificate in order to assess major trends and problem areas. She constantly analyzed and redesigned the format of birth and death certificates in order to gather more relevant information.[5] One of her first major projects as director of what soon became the Bureau for Maternal and Child Health (BMCH) was to construct a series of maps breaking down both the infant and maternal mortality rates in Wisconsin by county. The maps were published by the State Board of Health in its annual report and reprinted in the *Wisconsin Medical Journal* in September of 1935.[6] By presenting state numbers in a disaggregate form, these maps allowed health professionals and the general public to see which counties were in the greatest need of attention.

Although Wisconsin enjoyed a relatively low infant and maternal mortality rate at the time Dr. Hunter took over the BMCH, she took a closer look at the numbers and discerned that they revealed previously hidden deficiencies in child care. In 1937, she used the new statistical data to demonstrate that although Wisconsin had a low infant mortality rate overall, it ranked a dismal twenty-second among the forty-eight states in neonatal deaths, those occurring within the first month of infancy. In fact, from 1934 to 1936, some 65 percent of infant deaths in the state occurred within the first month of birth, with the highest neonatal death rate taking place in rural counties that had no large cities.[7] Dr. Hunter's solution to this problem was for the BMCH to stress the essentials of routine prenatal care in those rural counties and to work toward increasing the percentage of births taking place in hospitals. She always viewed the state's achievements in maternal and child health with guarded optimism and eternal vigilance. "Wisconsin has a record in this field that is equaled by no large country in the world," noted the editors of the *Wisconsin Medical Journal* in 1940 in response to the impact of the BMCH's findings. . . .[8] Without Dr. Hunter's breakdown of infant mortality numbers, Wisconsin's problem in neonatal mortality might not have been spotted. . . .

. . . The challenge to public health of the "baby boom" years following World War II was of particular interest to Dr. Hunter. Live births in Wisconsin from 1941 to 1945 exceeded those of the preceding five years by 13.7 percent. Accordingly she warned in 1946, "Obviously the presence of numerous new citizens calls for increased vigilance in *immediate* health problems as well as *long-range* planning for a substantially increased pre-school and school age population."[9] Collecting statistical data on this group not only could help the future of maternal and child health in Wisconsin, it could also prepare the BMCH for the increased demand on state resources. In 1949, Dr. Hunter continued to direct attention to particular areas of the state when a lengthy article she contributed to the *Wisconsin Medical Journal* used the state average rate of maternal death as a baseline, then recommended that counties that were still above this rate receive specific programs, including special postgraduate programs in obstetrics, the upgrading of hospital facilities, and obstetric training for nurses. . . .[10]

. . . "Over the years," Dr. Hunter reflected in 1954, "statistics from births and deaths have been helpful in locating special problems and providing information on which to base postgraduate programs and research."[11]

The solid reputation of the bureau's statistical information and the cooperative style of its staff allowed Hunter to guide the direction of the medical community's choices. This same reputation also supplied Hunter with the opportunity to promote the achievements of the BMCH. Her gentle but firm way of keeping pressure on Wisconsin's medical community became a hallmark of her managerial style. . . .

Although the involvement of the United States in World War II brought an end to the Great Depression, it also brought new challenges for American maternal and child health. The swelling number of military dependents and working women strained the resources of many state health agencies, and, as during the Great Depression, states looked to the federal government for assistance. In February of 1943 the Children's Bureau requested funds to distribute to states needing help with enlisted men's family health care. By the time the 1943–1944 fiscal year ended on June 30, 1944, Congress had appropriated $29,700,000 to the Children's Bureau for this purpose and authorized another $42,800,000 for the 1944–1945 fiscal year.[12] Thus was born the Emergency Maternal and Infant Care Program (EMIC), in which Congress authorized over $130 million from March 18, 1943, to July 26, 1946, for the direct health care of wives and infants of men falling into the four lowest pay grades in the American armed forces.[13] This program, so different from earlier programs that provided only for health education, was a temporary measure designed to last only six months after the war ended. However, prior to its termination in 1947, the EMIC delivered an unprecedented level of federal intervention, serving 1.4 million American pregnant women and newborns.

As early as the fall of 1942, Wisconsin's State Board of Health anticipated the increased demand for health services around the military camps in the state and actually reserved funds for them. . . .[14] By keeping paperwork to a minimum and working with familiar hospitals and physicians, Dr. Hunter and her staff were able to process the vast majority of EMIC cases.[15] At the EMIC's end in 1947, Wisconsin accounted for 23,360 maternal cases and 3,720 infant cases, and had received $2,353,965 in federal funds.[16]

Despite the EMIC's success in administering to the nation's wartime needs in maternal and child care, the program drew criticism from doctors and their professional organizations. Much of this criticism paralleled the medical community's earlier rejection of the Sheppard-Towner Act [in the 1920s for maternal and infant care]. . . .[17] The fact that the Children's Bureau and the EMIC set billing procedures and rates for medical procedures intensified the fear that this temporary program would become permanent and undermine the autonomy of the individual physician. . . .

As the sole representatives of the EMIC in Wisconsin, Amy Louise Hunter and the BMCH were caught between the administrative demands of the federal program and the suspicions of its critics. Rather than choose one side over the other, Dr. Hunter balanced the temporary benefits of the EMIC against the suspicions of the obstetric and pediatric physicians. For example, when the State Medical Society of Wisconsin wanted to publish an anti-EMIC editorial in newspapers across the state, Dr. Hunter objected to criticism of a necessary wartime health program. "Would it not be better to emphasize the need for Wisconsin doctors to study carefully the issues involved in such programs as the Emergency Maternity and Infant Care," she asked of the State Medical Society, "in order to offer constructive suggestions to the Society and the State Board of Health as to how the State may best be served and sound policies of medical procedure retained?"[18] Although Dr. Hunter and the staff at the BMCH found the EMIC's complex regulations and their constant revision to be arduous and nettlesome throughout the duration of the program, they realized that the program did produce real benefits. For example, during the years in which the EMIC operated, a dramatic increase occurred in the number of births in hospitals, from 64.1 percent of Wisconsin births in 1940 to 93.7 percent in 1946.[19] Achieving this shift was one of the BMCH's major long-term objectives, because it resulted in lower infant mortality rates. . . .

But Dr. Hunter did not want to pin the future of Wisconsin's maternal and child health upon federal programs that she knew did not run smoothly or easily. . . .

. . . She also participated in a 1951 evaluation of the EMIC that stated, "the program was, as is characteristic of any national program, inflexible, burdened with red tape, and planned with disregard of the individual's needs as expressed in benefits offered."[20] Years later, a fellow physician remembered the EMIC as the "late lamented EMIC rat race," and said he admired Dr. Hunter for administering it with such patience and grace.[21] Although the EMIC represented a major initiative on the part of the federal government in maternal and child health, the major actor in this field remained the state agencies.[22]

In later years, Dr. Hunter continued her close contact with federal programs by keeping in touch with the Children's Bureau and participating in White House conferences on children and youth in 1950 and 1960. However, her experience with the EMIC had left her skeptical about the merit of placing responsibility for American maternal and child health in the federal realm.[23] She had much more faith in state-level agencies, and in the years following World War II, she embarked upon an ambitious outreach program that widened the scope and presence of the Bureau for Maternal and Child Health in the lives of Wisconsin women and children.

The expansion of the maternal and child health services in Wisconsin was perhaps the most innovative aspect of Dr. Hunter's career. When she arrived in Madison in 1935, the work of the bureau was largely confined to reducing maternal and infant mortality during childbirth through the use of educational programs. By the time she retired in 1961, the bureau had expanded to include a division of nutrition, a division of child development, and a division of school health. This administrative expansion reflected Dr. Hunter's vision of children's health needs as holistic, that is, as a combination of interdependent parts rather than individual symptoms or illness to be addressed separately. The immediate dangers of childbirth to mother and infant that spurred the creation of the bureau in 1919 had been significantly reduced by the 1940s and 1950s. Even then, Dr. Hunter did not rest on her laurels. For the remainder of her career, she worked to transform the BMCH into an agency that actively addressed the myriad medical, nutritional, and emotional needs of Wisconsin's children.

From its early years, the bureau had a few outreach programs in place. It ran maternal and child health centers, sponsored courses in infant hygiene, and distributed medical literature across the state. One of the most innovative programs in the years before 1935 was the prenatal letter campaign. In 1922, the bureau began sending expectant mothers a series of monthly letters with information and advice concerning pregnancy, childbirth, and early infant care. Whereas the group programs such as health center demonstrations or infant hygiene classes technically reached more people, the prenatal letters were the most effective means of getting vital information to those who needed it most. In the year that Dr. Hunter began her tenure as director, the BMCH sent out 4,754 letters.[24] She continued this program and experimented with new ways to reach a wider audience, such as exhibiting inexpensive wooden incubators in rural areas "to stimulate interest in saving the lives of premature babies" and to demonstrate the importance of maternal and child care.[25] Dr. Hunter assigned each incubator to a nurse in counties that had a large number of home deliveries. When a premature birth occurred, the county's public health nurse would aid both the mother and her physician in the use of the incubator — thus promoting both the use of hospital equipment and modern techniques in premature infant care. By 1940, thirty-eight incubators were assigned to thirty-four Wisconsin counties, and some of them remained in use for twenty years.[26]

During the 1940s, the BMCH's outreach program intensified as Dr. Hunter added to traditional services. In 1946 the agency hired a full-time illustrator to help with the over 1.3 million educational posters and publications distributed by the agency.[27] It also sponsored a trailer known as the "Little Blue Classroom on Wheels," in which public health nurses would travel to rural communities where modern health care was difficult to secure. Dr. Hunter explicitly designed this motorized clinic as a way to help "pick up the loose ends of health education" in Wisconsin and ensure that areas bereft of large hospitals were covered by the BMCH.[28] In its first two years of existence, the Little Blue Classroom visited fifty-three counties, provided over 400 sessions on maternal and child health, and reached over 18,000 Wisconsin residents.[29] Dr. Hunter also added new tactics in promoting maternal and child health. In 1940, she inaugurated a school health program,

developed teaching strategies for school health classes, and worked with local school officials to establish standards for sanitary conditions in Wisconsin schools. A nutrition program, in which BMCH staff members would train nurses, visit schools, and consult with
other state agencies on matters such as school lunch programs, blossomed during the
postwar years.

The BMCH also used films to reach both professional and lay audiences. Many films
designated for physicians were made in-house by the agency itself and demonstrated new
techniques in obstetric and pediatric care. For example, a sound film, *Appraisal of the Newborn,* was made with the cooperation of an actual practicing Wisconsin physician and the
Bureau of Visual Instruction of the Extension Division of the University of Wisconsin.[30] In
addition to these local productions, the BMCH distributed films made elsewhere, such as
*A Concept of Maternal and Neonatal Care* (1951), which demonstrated the ways in which a
hospital's professional staff, obstetricians, pediatricians, and nurses helped parents feel
safe and secure during childbirth.[31] Films represented an efficient way that the BMCH
could reach Wisconsin physicians, and cost less than sending actual BMCH employees
across the state to give lectures or workshops.

The BMCH also produced and distributed films for the general population. *Judy's
Diary,* an early example of this genre, first appeared in about 1936. Three short films
demonstrated the basics of child care to young mothers by illustrating three critical periods in Judy's life, including six months (*From Morning Until Night*), the toddler years (*By
Experience I Learn*), and two years of age (*Now I Am Two*).[32] These silent films illustrated
cleanliness and simplicity in infant and child care and included didactic statements such
as: "Father has a definite place in my life," "At seventeen months washing is no fun unless
I can help," and "Regular health examinations, proper food, and good health habits keep
me well and happy."[33] Judy's progress on film demonstrated the various stages of child development without the heavy-handed tone of a lecture or a pamphlet.

Just as films reduced the expense of reaching physicians, movies like the *Judy's Diary*
series could be played at schools, local health centers, and other venues at a low cost to
the BMCH. First-time mothers were especially appreciative of the opportunity to learn by
example rather than having to sit in a lecture hall and try to imagine what motherhood
would be like. As radio, film, and television grew more prominent in the daily lives of Wisconsin's population, they were the natural media to use to improve health care in the
state. The films also made a real impact upon the health of Wisconsin children. As Dr.
Hunter noted in 1950, films such as *Good Hearing Is Essential* and *Ears That Hear* played a
large role, especially in rural Wisconsin, in highlighting the general interest in preventing
hearing loss in children.[34]

Perhaps the greatest achievement in outreach during the postwar era was an expansion of the BMCH's mission to include the total health of the child. . . .

Dr. Hunter's sponsorship of mental health programs offers an excellent example of
this approach, based — like earlier BMCH programs — in education and consultation. In
1940, the BMCH established a division of mental health (renamed the division of child
guidance in 1952) and a year later it launched a program designed to improve mental

health facilities in Wisconsin. The BMCH's mental health specialist, Dr. Eugenia S. Cameron, organized mental health demonstrations across the state in order to "stimulate local interest in a preventive program and to show community organizations how they can establish their own clinical and educational services in mental hygiene."[35] The mental health program included direct-mail literature, mental health clinics in remote rural counties, and use of popular media such as radio and films to cover as much ground as possible. For example, the *Hi Neighbor!* series of radio programs aired in a number of cities. Titles included *The Bobby-soxer's Rebellion*, about adolescent rebellion, *Relax and Enjoy It*, regarding asocial behavior of young children, and *That's My Old Man!* about father-son relationships.[36]

By making these resources available, and by coordinating local groups rather than constructing its own statewide system, the BMCH took a flexible approach to its mental health outreach program. The result was a heightened awareness of the emotional needs of children and the realization in many Wisconsin communities that mental health was indeed an important goal for its young folk. Dr. Hunter did an excellent job of selling her concepts to the public. "Financially and economically this is sound thinking, inasmuch as the maladjusted adult produces a tremendous economic burden on the taxpayer," the editors of *Racine Labor* observed in 1951. "Preventing this by helping children adjust themselves properly to society and their fellow citizens is the primary function of the Child Guidance Clinic."[37] This acceptance of children's emotional needs represented a breakthrough in the 1950s. . . .

The idea that child care goes beyond simple survival formed the crux of BMCH outreach during Dr. Hunter's tenure. Her concept of total health, including both the emotional and the mental aspects of childhood, marked her as a pioneer in maternal and child health.[38]

When Amy Louise Hunter announced in 1960 that she would be retiring, her goal as a young doctor to help the "littlest ones who cried" had been fulfilled many times over. At the end of her career, a number of friends, colleagues, and admirers gathered for a large retirement luncheon in January of 1961. Among the various toasts and farewells was a poem offered by her friend Roy Ragatz, light-heartedly summarizing her work:

Who guards our mothers, who champions our kids?
Who, Amy, of course!
Who calms us down as we flip our lids?
Why, Amy, of course!
She reels off statistics, of state-wide gestation,
She counsels those pregnant (the pride of our nation); . . .[39]

. . . Dr. Hunter remained active throughout her eighties, helping create such institutions as Madison's Perinatal Foundation. One of the most satisfying activities for her in those years must have been the establishment of a fellowship in her name at her alma mater, the Yale Medical School, which had recommended that she not pursue a degree in public health. A half-century and many saved lives later, Wisconsin mothers and children were grateful that Dr. Hunter did not take Yale's advice.

On July 7, 1990, Amy Louise Hunter died at the age of ninety-two. Her career as director of the BMCH is characteristic of Wisconsin's longstanding tradition of an activist state government. By utilizing a flexible style of bureaucratic management with a keen eye toward outreach, Dr. Hunter was able to blend the best of both worlds in public and private health care. Her application of statistical research, her utilization of federal dollars for state programs, and her expansion of the BMCH's mission secured her a permanent niche in the history of maternal and child health. . . .

## NOTES

1. *State Board of Health Bulletin* 5 (April–June 1935): 19.
2. State Board of Health, *Annual Report,* 1936, 7.
3. *Capital Times,* March 1, 1935.
4. *State Board of Health Bulletin* 5 (July–September 1935): 4.
5. Amy Louise Hunter (hereinafter ALH) to Henrietta Herbolsheimer, July 31, 1945, State Board of Health Records, box 32, series 871, WHS Archives.
6. State Board of Health, *Annual Report,* 1936, 1601–1661; *Wisconsin Medical Journal* 34 (September 1935): 638–639.
7. *State Board of Health Bulletin* 6 (October–December 1937): 9–12.
8. *Wisconsin Medical Journal,* 39 (November 1940): 949.
9. *State Board of Health Bulletin* 8 (January–March 1946): 4–5.
10. *Wisconsin Medical Journal* 48 (September 1949): 819.
11. *Wisconsin Medical Journal* 53 (November 1954): 605.
12. Martha Elliot, "The EMIC Program for Wives and Infants of Enlisted Men," *State Government* 17 (September 1944): 404.
13. . . . [S]ee Joan Elizabeth Mulligan, "Three Federal Interventions on Behalf of Childbearing Women: The Sheppard-Towner Act, Emergency Maternity and Infant Care, and the Maternal and Child Health and Mental Retardation Planning Amendments of 1963" (doctoral dissertation, University of Michigan, 1976).
14. ALH to G. F. Burgardt, September 11, 1942, State Board of Health General Correspondence, box 5, series 871, WHS Archives.
15. ALH, "Emergency Maternity and Infant Care in Wisconsin [1944]," memo, State Board of Health General Correspondence, box 21, series 871, WHS Archives. . . .
16. Press release, July 23, 1947, Bureau of Maternal and Child Health Programs and Demonstrations File, box 2, series 2253, WHS Archives.
17. Kriste Lindenmeyer, *"A Right to Childhood": The U.S. Children's Bureau and Child Welfare, 1912–46* (Urbana, 1997), 239–247.
18. ALH to C. H. Crownhart, February 25, 1944, State Board of Health General Correspondence, box 21, series 871, WHS Archives.
19. State Board of Health, *Annual Report,* 1949, 61.
20. "An Evaluation of the EMIC Program," 1951, Bureau of Maternal and Child Health Programs and Demonstrations, box 2, series 2253, WHS Archives. . . .
21. H. Kent Tenney to ALH, January 9, 1961, Amy Louise Hunter Papers, WHS Archives.
22. Although the EMIC helped increase the national percentage of physician-attended hospital deliveries of white women from 55 percent to 92.8 percent of births and from 23 percent to 57.9 percent among women of color, it was hardly a comprehensive or even consistent program. For example, women who actually served in the military were ineligible for EMIC support! See Molly Ladd Taylor, "Women's Health and Public Policy," in Rima Apple, ed., *Women, Health, and Medicine in America* (New York, 1990), 405–406.

23. For more on the EMIC's performance, see Nathan Sinai and Odin Anderson, *EMIC: A Study of Administrative Experience* (Ann Arbor, 1948).

24. State Board of Health, *Annual Report,* 1936, 168.

25. State Board of Health, *Annual Report,* 1941, 58.

26. ALH, "Prematurity as a Factor in Wisconsin Infant Death Rates," *Wisconsin Medical Journal* 39 (1940): 562–566. . . .

27. Memo to Department Heads from ALH, September 28, 1946, State Board of Health Records, box 49, series 871, WHS Archives.

28. *State Board of Health Bulletin* 6 (October–December, 1941): 13–14.

29. State Board of Health, *Annual Report,* 1942, 56.

30. State Board of Health, *Annual Report,* 1941, 60.

31. "Film — A Concept of Maternal and Neonatal Care," memo, 1952, State Board of Health Collection, District Health Offices, General Correspondence, box 12, WHS Archives.

32. *State Board of Health Bulletin* 7 (April–June 1942): 14.

33. The *Judy's Diary* film series was produced by the University of Wisconsin Extension Division and sponsored and distributed by the BMCH. They may be viewed at the Visual Materials Archives, WHS.

34. ALH to Frank V. Powell, August 8, 1950, State Board of Health General Correspondence, box 112, series 871, WHS Archives.

35. Eugenia Cameron to C. N. Neupert, August 9, 1943, BMCH Child Guidance Reference and Program File, WHS Archives.

36. Eugenia Cameron to Harold Schroeder, March 3, 1950, BMCH Child Guidance Reference and Program File, WHS Archives.

37. *Racine Labor,* August 10, 1951.

38. *Health* 14 (January–March, 1960): 2.

39. The poem is in the Hunter Papers.

# No Idle Hands

## A Milwaukee WPA Handicraft Project

### LESLIE A. BELLAIS

WMH 84, No. 2 (Winter 2001–2002): 48–56

*In 1990, the Wisconsin Historical Museum acquired six mysterious artifacts: portfolios of block-printed fabrics. Leslie Bellais, curator of costumes and textiles, recalls that at first she "did not find the portfolios exciting to look at, bound as they were in faded coarse green cotton. Yet behind the drab covers, collages of color and dynamic patterns emanated from the . . . textile samples contained within each portfolio." She also found labels indicating that the portfolios were products of the Milwaukee Handicraft Project (MHP), a program sponsored by the Work Projects Administration (WPA). The federal government created the WPA in 1935, one of the worst years of the Great Depression in Wisconsin. As many as half of the wage-earners in the city of Milwaukee alone had lost their jobs and went on breadlines by 1930, and the county's public relief rolls had soared from a few thousand families to one in five households, and as many as forty thousand families went on welfare.[1]*

*However, the WPA and other programs helped few women compared to the many unemployed men who were the federal government's first priority, as Bellais also found when she finally could research the collection. In Wisconsin alone, the Civilian Conservation Corps (CCC) employed almost one hundred thousand men at forty-five camps where the "CCC boys" built bridges, roads, and trails, stocked streams and conducted a census of state deer during the Depression. While the "forest army" worked in the fresh air, received free health care and training for skilled work, and were fed, clothed, and housed by the federal government, New Deal programs provided few programs for minorities. The New Deal did even less for women during the Depression, when the government determined that families with two federal paychecks could survive on one and fired the wives — and then suggested that private employers follow suit. In Wisconsin, the percentage of women with paid work was well below the national average by the end of the decade.[2]*

*The far different story of several thousand women and minorities in Milwaukee who found work in the unique WPA program which was hidden within the portfolios puzzled Bellais, but she had other work projects. At last, "almost ten years later," as she recalls, Bellais had "the opportunity to look into their history, discover their purpose, and . . . learn the intriguing story of the Milwaukee Handicraft Project and its founder," Elsa Ulbricht. Born into one of Milwaukee's first German families, including a builder of memorable local landmarks to whom Ulbricht attributed her artistic abilities, she was born in 1885, the same year that doors opened at the Milwaukee State Normal School where she graduated in 1906 and gave most of her life. She taught kindergarten while taking night classes at the Wisconsin School of Art and then earned a two-year degree in art education from the Pratt Institute in New York City in 1911. She returned home to create an art education department at her alma mater, by then called Milwaukee State Teachers College, where she also earned a bachelor's degree in 1930 — as the Great Depression began. By 1935, Ulbricht had served on the faculty for a quarter of a century.[3]*

*Bellais also learned about Ulbricht's most unusual "students" during the Great Depression, mainly thousands of women in Milwaukee who were looking only for work but found an opportunity to make works of art — and to make history.*

... In the fall of 1935, the Wisconsin WPA Women's and Professional Division realized that unskilled women who headed their households desperately needed jobs. Harriet Clinton, director of the women's division, devised a plan to employ these women in making handicrafts. Clinton (1896–1975), an Iowa native with journalism degrees from the University of Wisconsin–Madison and Columbia University, had worked as a reporter for several Milwaukee papers before starting her job at the WPA. By 1935 she knew the Milwaukee community well and had demonstrated a flair for public relations work.

To make her handicraft project a reality, Clinton first approached the Milwaukee State Teachers College (MSTC) to act as sponsor. She chose MSTC because the school specialized in art education. Once the MSTC agreed to sponsorship, Clinton turned to Elsa Ulbricht, an art teacher at the college, to organize and run the program. The fifty-year-old Ulbricht was the perfect candidate for the job. Besides teaching arts and crafts at MSTC, she taught at the Art Institute of Chicago's summer school, was a founding member of the Wisconsin Designer-Craftsmen organization, and had served on Milwaukee's Public Works of Art projects committee, another WPA program. She also brought to the job enthusiasm, organization, a philosophy of craft as art, a strong belief in the project's benefits, and a forceful personality.

Clinton had envisioned women workers cutting up magazines and creating scrapbooks for educational institutions. Ulbricht responded that she was not interested in running a make-work project. Instead, she wanted the workers to produce objects of superior design and craftsmanship that contributed to "the cultural development of the individual and the community." To that end, she would expose the unskilled women workers to the idea "that a thing worth doing is a thing worth doing beautifully." Their products, which by WPA regulations could be sold only at cost to educational and tax-supported institutions, would raise standards of artistic taste throughout Milwaukee, the state of Wisconsin, and the nation wherever they were sold. Ulbricht summed up her policy in the craft project's official proposal, where she stated that the project had two purposes: to produce handicrafts made from wood, paper, yarn, or cloth that incorporated artistic design; and to influence taste and disseminate culture by distributing the handicrafts through public institutions.

To create artistic products, the project required artists. By late 1935 almost every established artist in Wisconsin had been put to work in various other WPA projects. Ulbricht looked through relief lists but did not find anyone who met her qualifications. She wanted people who had experience with crafts and craft materials, a history of original and creative work, a liberal arts education, and an ability to work with people. Eventually she received permission to hire her own four-year art students or graduates from the MSTC. Most of these young men and women had not found jobs in their chosen field, so Ulbricht felt they would bring an understanding and sympathy of the workers' plight with them. The students, hired as "designer-foremen," were to design the handicrafts, create a production line, and oversee the workers. (In later years the designer and foremen functions were split among different people.) Ulbricht had nothing but praise for these women and men, whom she described as "enthusiastic and energetic" with a willingness to experiment and a desire to produce the best products.

On November 6, 1935, the Milwaukee Handicraft Project opened its doors at the Veterans' Administration Hospital. Originally Ulbricht had expected workers with at least a rudimentary knowledge of sewing. Instead, she found completely unskilled women at the door, "the dregs of the unemployed" as Ulbricht later described them, whom WPA staff had randomly chosen from the relief lists. She remembered her heart sinking when she saw the "motley, careworn and harassed group of women"; most were poorly clothed, unkempt, and weak from malnutrition. Yet she thought they had an air of excitement about them, perhaps from knowing that the WPA might fulfill their need for work. Since many had not even handled scissors, she temporarily resorted to Harriet Clinton's idea of making scrapbooks to teach them how. Once they acquired the basic skills, the women quickly moved to more productive tasks.

The WPA women's division had told the MHP staff to plan materials and accommodations for 250 workers. However, during the first week Harriet Clinton approached Elsa Ulbricht and asked if she would mind having "Negroes" on the project. According to Ulbricht, she replied, "no, I like them." Once word was out that the MHP would accept male and female African Americans, workers arrived in increasing numbers with the total reaching 800 after two weeks. To make room for this flood of workers, the staff created two shifts of 400 employees each. By 1943, when it was disbanded, the project had employed more than 5,000 workers. Usually 600 to 900 people worked at a time, though the numbers peaked at 1,350 in 1939. Almost all of these workers were women, and more than half were African Americans.

Both women and African Americans had been barred from many WPA projects. . . . WPA administrators saw both groups as generally unskilled and inexperienced. They feared that women had become too eager "to be the family breadwinner, wage recipient, and controller of the family pocketbook," and wanted to discourage this attitude. The administrators also worried that the public would criticize them for "employing 'too many women.'" As for African Americans, WPA officials at federal and local levels argued that this group was "accustomed to relatively low standards of living" and therefore did not need work relief as much as those used to higher standards. WPA officials who disagreed with this approach found it difficult to secure sponsors for all–African American projects. Sponsors simply did not want to train black workers for jobs that would normally go to white men. Ulbricht's agreement to hire African American men and women made this project one of the few nationally integrated WPA programs.

However, integration did not always go smoothly. In an interview, years later, Clarice (George) Logan, a "designer-foreman," remembered her unit consisting primarily of Polish and African American women. She recalled that the two groups voluntarily segregated themselves, and she sometimes had to arbitrate fights between them. At one point Ul-bricht assigned a black man as foreman of the evening workshop. One of her two assis-tants, a woman who had handled administrative procedures since the beginning, eventually resigned over this decision. Ultimately, however, integration did not cause se-rious problems for the project. Instead, Ulbricht later declared that the most discourag-ing aspect of the workers' situation was the constant turnover. Once the MHP had taught women a skill and how to work in a factory-like setting, private industries and other WPA projects quickly hired them away.

The skill a worker would learn depended on her aptitude and interests. The MHP ul-timately had eleven work units, and after learning basic skills, a worker could choose which unit appealed to her. Each unit, headed by a designer-foreman, made a different product. Products included books, rugs, quilts, costumes, wooden toys, cloth toys, dolls, furniture, weavings, screen-printed textiles, and block-printed textiles. The textiles could be used for wall hangings, drapes, and covers for bound books. The portfolios that I cat-alogued in 1990 included samples of the block-printed textiles and were bound by the bookbinding unit.

The MHP staff designed the block-printing unit to be labor intensive, since many steps were involved, from initial design to finished fabrics. As Clarice Logan explained, "the primitive methods were most useful to the objectives of the WPA as a whole because it ne-cessitated a great quantity of workers with few variations of skills." In the early weeks work-ers practiced the craft using blocks borrowed from the MSTC art education department. Once the first blockprinting designer-foreman, Barbara Warren Weisman, had painted original designs on paper, production began in earnest. "Junior Artists" traced the designs onto linoleum or wood blocks and cut the master blocks. Other workers cut any other re-quired color blocks. A separate group of women mixed the oil-based inks, though in later years Artko Inc. of Milwaukee supplied premixed inks. Finally, another group of six women printed the blocks onto three-yard lengths of cotton, either osnaberg or percale, by pounding the inked blocks with rubber and wooden mallets. They used a press for larger blocks. Clarice Logan described this unit as being "filled with people, activity, and lots and lots of noise."

Logan's primary job as a designer-foreman in the block-printing unit was to create the graphic designs. Raised in Milwaukee since the age of eight, she had been a student of Elsa Ulbricht's and came to the project because of a strong affection for and sense of ob-ligation to her teacher. . . .

Ulbricht's design theories, which emphasized "form following function," strongly in-fluenced Logan. In speeches and unpublished papers, Ulbricht argued that the best-designed forms eliminated nonessentials and reflected the object's purpose. She also made it clear to the designer-foremen that a product "would be well designed or it would not be made." Early designers created original graphic motifs based on their own creativ-ity and interests. Once orders started arriving, Ulbricht asked her designers to produce designs appropriate to the purchasing institution's environment. To do this, the design-ers studied the sites, taking under consideration the institution's purpose, as well as the age, socioeconomic status, and artistic awareness of the people who would be using the objects.

Approximately 80 percent of the MHP's products were made for Milwaukee Public Schools. As a result, the designers of block prints created a line of children's prints for classroom use. All of these designs, which primarily consisted of child-related themes in bright colors, went through a testing phase before being put into mass production. Teachers and designers evaluated prototypes, especially their suitability for different age groups and grade levels. Once a design had been approved and printed, the MHP staff sent the completed textiles to the WPA sewing center to be made into curtains, wall hangings, and slipcovers.

The Milwaukee Handicraft Project quickly gained a reputation for its well-made and custom-designed products. Orders from institutions throughout the country as well as the state poured in, and the MHP staff had trouble keeping up. Customers from other states included Western Michigan University in Kalamazoo; the Franklin D. Roosevelt Library in Hyde Park, New York; the St. Louis County Rural Schools in Virginia, Minnesota; and the Crow Island School in Winnetka, Illinois. The University of Wisconsin–Madison had the MHP staff decorate the Memorial Union, the president's home, the College of Agriculture's short course dormitories, and the law school dean's office. MHP products appeared in the Milwaukee Public Library, Milwaukee's Whitnall Park Pavilion, and schools in Shorewood. The MHP also created exhibits of its products that traveled to most major cities in the United States, including New York and Chicago. Famous visitors, such as Frank Lloyd Wright, Eliel Saarinen, Russel Wright, and Eleanor Roosevelt, stopped by the workshop, intrigued by the combination of work relief for unskilled women and artistically designed objects. By 1944 the *Milwaukee Journal* declared that the MHP was "the project that made Milwaukee famous." . . .

Whether or not the MHP met Elsa Ulbricht's goal of improving taste, contemporaries generally regarded the project as successful. In 1937, when the Milwaukee State Teachers College withdrew itself as the MHP's sponsor, Ulbricht easily was able to convince Milwaukee County to take over sponsorship. The county leaders already were aware of the benefits the project had brought to the community. Their belief in the MHP was tested in 1941 when Congress disbanded the WPA, but the county leaders decided to continue the project without federal help. World War II and the flood of jobs it brought finally closed the door of the Milwaukee Handicraft Project in 1943. . . .

Today we can recognize the MHP portfolios as important historical and artistic documents that not only illustrate graphic design of the 1930s, but also relate a story of hope and beauty during a time known primarily for despair and barrenness.[4]

❧

*In its eight years, at a dozen sites — as many as seven at one time — the Milwaukee Handicraft Project employed more than five thousand workers, most of them women, at $50 per month, and approximately fifty artists were paid $75 a month. As for Ulbricht, in 1942, she was the first woman ever elected as president of the prestigious organization of the Wisconsin Painters and Sculptors and soon* *also served as president of the board of directors of the Art Institute of Chicago's prestigious Summer School of Painting. Ulbricht rose to director of the art division of Milwaukee State Teachers College from 1943 until her retirement in 1955 — at the age of seventy and after more than forty years on the faculty — a year before her alma mater became the University of Wisconsin–Milwaukee. She received the Wisconsin Arts Foundation Award for service, in 1966, and UW–Milwaukee's Alumna of the Year Award in 1973, when almost a hundred of her works were exhibited in a retrospective at the nearby Charles Allis Art Library. In the last decade before her death in 1980, at the age of ninety-five, Ulbricht also helped to organize two exhibits on the Milwaukee Handicraft Project at her alma mater, which still awards Elsa Ulbricht Scholarships to art students.[5]*

*Ulbricht's legacy also lives on in the Wisconsin Historical Society's collections, and her project still inspires students. Bellais solved the puzzle of the six portfolios of textiles acquired by the Society when she matched "many of the motifs, patterns, and borders" to other artifacts in its collections — not only wall hangings but also an undated scrapbook about the Milwaukee Handicraft Project. "The last pages of the book feature a photograph and description of the portfolios, and their purpose is clearly stated," she writes. "Ulbricht intended these books as educational aids for teachers, especially those teaching art or design." Bellais also found a later interview with Ulbricht describing the portfolios' purpose: "When I taught," said Ulbricht, "I could never find enough illustrative material to inspire my students."*

*Bellais traced the provenance of the portfolios through a 1939 Milwaukee Handicraft Project catalog that listed the "Educational Series" for sale at prices varying from $1.75 to $2.75. The portfolios came from Madison Area Technical College (then called the Madison Vocational School), which "probably used them in art design or home economics courses," Bellais suggests. "In the late 1930s the patterns would have seemed modern . . . and probably did inspire some students." But "by the time they came to the Wisconsin Historical Museum, the portfolios looked old-fashioned, outdated, and tired," writes Bellais. "They were no longer serving their original function of inspiration and education," at least for art students. However, the portfolios of patterns still inspire those interested in the history of textiles, such as Bellais — or in the history of how some Wisconsin women survived and supported themselves and their families during the Great Depression.*

# NOTES

1. Nesbit, *Wisconsin*, 477; John Gurda, *The Making of Milwaukee*, (Milwaukee: Milwaukee County Historical Society, 1999), 282; Glad, *HOW*, 426.

2. Glad, *HOW*, 494; Thompson, *HOW*, 97–98.

3. Peter C. Merrill, "Elsa Ulbricht: A Career in Art," *Milwaukee History* 16, no.1 (Spring 1993): 22–28; see also Peter C. Merrill, *German-American Artists in Early Milwaukee: A Biographical Dictionary* (Madison: Max Kade Institute, 1997), 131; Gertrude M. Copp, "Elsa Ulbricht," *Design* 45, no. 6 (February 1944): 4; Jackie Eaton, "Elsa Ulbricht and the WPA Project That She Made Famous," unpublished paper in the possession of the editor. Ulbricht's grandfather, Henry Buestrin, built Milwaukee's pillared Northwestern Mutual Life Insurance Company building and North Avenue Water Tower.

4. Sources for the original article include Elsa Ulbricht, "The Story of the Milwaukee Handicraft Project," *Design* 45, no. 6 (February, 1944): 6–7; Lois M. Quinn, *Jobs for Workers on Relief in Milwaukee County, 1930–1994* (Milwaukee: Employment and Training Institute, UW–Milwaukee, 1995); Kathryn E. Maier, "A New Deal for Local Crafts: Textiles from the Milwaukee Handicraft Project" (master's thesis, UW–Milwaukee, 1994); Nancy Reston, "The Federal Arts Project in Wisconsin, 1936–1939" (master's thesis,

UW–Madison, 1977); Barbara Jean Stein, "An Examination of the Design Style of the WPA Milwaukee Handicraft Block Printed Textiles, 1935–1944" (master's thesis, UW–Madison, 1979). [See also an account since published by one of Ulbricht's student "designer-foremen," Mary Kellogg Rice, *Useful Work for Unskilled Women: A Unique Milwaukee WPA Project* (Milwaukee: Milwaukee County Historical Society, 2003), and the Elsa Emile Ulbricht Papers, University Manuscript Collection 59, Golda Meir Library, UW–Milwaukee, which also holds taped interviews by and about Ulbricht; a report by Harriet Pettibone Clinton, *The First Year of Women's and Professional Projects*, privately printed in 1936; and related sources in the Charlotte Russell Partridge Papers and Miriam Frink Papers.]
5. Merrill, "Elsa Ulbricht," 22–28; Copp, "Elsa Ulbricht," 4.

# The Back of the Homefront

*Black and American Indian Women in Wisconsin during World War II*

PATTY LOEW

WMH 82, No. 2 (Winter 1998–1999): 82–103

It was an uncertain time and, like thousands of American Indian women on the eve of World War II, Alice DeNomie was uncertain about her future. In 1944 the Ojibwe teenager had been studying dress design at Milwaukee's Layton School of Art and working full time for the telephone company. A year later, however, she traded her patterns for blueprints and went to work at the Perfex Corporation, which produced the Norden bomb sight.

For her generation, war memories are visceral. DeNomie grieved with her oldest sister, whose young husband was killed in Italy, and worried about her own sweetheart on a ship somewhere in the north Atlantic. . . .

. . . White Americans struggled to adjust to wartime shortages. They rushed across the continent to fill an expanding, militarily driven labor market. They entered a postwar frenzy of technological advancement, material consumption, and suburban childbearing. But what about America's minority cultures? Was Alice DeNomie's life, for example, immeasurably changed? What about women in other minority cultures?

By war's end, more than a million black Americans had served in largely segregated units, but only a handful of books document what they experienced. Twenty-five thousand American Indians saw service, but few accounts chronicle their experience.[1] If the written record of black and American Indian service during World War II is thin, the historical literature on their families and loved ones on the homefront is emaciated.

An oral history project commemorating the fiftieth anniversary of World War II has helped to flesh out the experience of minority women. . . . The oral history project contributed, in a small way, to the history that has not yet been written: the stories of black and Native women who, like all Americans, suffered wartime deprivation and loss; and who, as an added ordeal, struggled with the inconsistencies of America's racial policies during the war.

There was a great irony, or perhaps a brutal consistency, in the racial policies of the armed forces during World War II. Blacks, most of whom wanted to serve in integrated units, were segregated. Indians, who wanted to serve in segregated units, were integrated. . . .

If black men were fighting at the back of the war, their wives and girlfriends were languishing at the back of the homefront. More than half of all black women ages twenty-four to forty-four were employed during the war, yet only 14 percent of them had white-collar jobs; one-third of American Indian women had jobs, but only one in three was a white-collar worker. . . .[2]

The image of Rosie the Riveter, created by the government and promoted through the media, was that of a white, middle-class woman holding an important job directly related to the war effort. . . .[3]

It is clear that Rosie did not typify the black women who were confined to the lowest-paying jobs, like domestic service and unskilled factory work. . . . In reality, Rosie did not typify most *white* female workers, either. Most women workers who entered the labor force during the war were poorly educated. They sought employment not because they *wanted* to work, but because they *had* to work. And the jobs that most women held did not involve actual production. Typically they were jobs that lacked glamour, like clerical work and telephone operating. Still, the war opened doors for all women. The annual income for black families more than doubled during the war. It may have been far below that of white families, but it was a beginning.[4]

Nellie [Sweet] Wilson of Milwaukee was twenty-five years old when Pearl Harbor was bombed. A single parent with two daughters, she tried for two years to find a job in the defense industry. "Being black and female, you weren't expecting too much," she observed with some irony. Wilson recalled that she was told by Milwaukee factory officials on more than one occasion that they weren't hiring, only to see white women behind her invited in for interviews. Wilson applied three times to the A.O. Smith Corporation, which made propellers for the B-29 bomber. Eventually the company hired her as a precision inspector for its blueprint division: "the best job of my life," as she described it. "Made the magnificent sum of $33 a week all through World War II. But at that time that $33 a week paid my rent and my groceries and my phone bills, everything. Independent living and loving every moment of it."[5] Wilson's annual wage was three-quarters of the median salary earned by a white female worker and little more than half that earned by a white male in Milwaukee. Still, she was considerably better off than most black women in her city.[6]

Alice DeNomie had a similar job at Milwaukee's Perfex Corporation, which made torpedo valves and the Norden bomb sight. DeNomie was the daughter of an Ojibwe father and Irish mother and had grown up in an Irish neighborhood. She left art school to take a job in the blueprint division of Perfex at thirty dollars a week — twice the salary she had earned in her pre-war job at the telephone company. Much of it went to her mother and father, who were trying to keep a family of eight afloat during the stormy days of World War II. "School seemed pointless when all this was going on," DeNomie remembered. "I was learning how to make formal evening dresses. I put away the *Vogue* magazines and never went back to them."[7]

She worked in relative comfort in a clean, well-lit, drafting room overlooking the production area, a place she described as dark, greasy, and foundry-like. "Most of the people sitting down, screwing things together, soldering, doing spot welding — were women. All the foremen were men. There wasn't one woman who was in charge of anyone."[8]

Alice DeNomie's oldest sister, Mary Jane Aynes, like most working women during the war years, had an office job. [While her husband was serving overseas,] Aynes was living in Alexandria, Virginia, with her sister-in-law, an army nurse. . . .[9]

Jobs like the ones DeNomie, Aynes, and Wilson had were the exception, not the rule, for minority women. Nationally, an additional 6 million women entered the workforce between 1940 and 1944, bringing the total female workforce to over 18.2 million. In Madison, however, black women who sought working-class jobs were six times more likely to work as domestic servants than to find a job in the capital city's small industrial base. . . .[10] Mary Caire, a black woman, had a day job for a white family in Madison. "I would cook and wash clothes and clean the house," she recalled, "and I only made $4 a week."[11]

In 1940, there were more black domestic servants in Wisconsin than there were black teachers and nurses combined. By 1950, half of all private household workers had left their jobs, but census figures suggest that most of them were doing the same work — cooking, cleaning, and waiting tables — for companies instead of families. The number of "charwomen," for example, nearly tripled over the decade. [12]

It is difficult to know for sure how many Wisconsin women overall were in the labor force during the war. . . . It is likely that some women operated cottage industries out of their homes. Frances Reneau, for example, an African American woman, was an accomplished seamstress — a skill that allowed her to remain at home in Beloit with her two children. Business was by word of mouth and brisk, sometimes too brisk. "Many times [I'd work] into the night because I'd have to stagger between meals, and the home housework and whatever," Reneau remembered. "I put many, many hours in and sometimes I wonder how I did it.". . .[13]

. . . [T]wo Ojibwe women, Cecilia DeFoe and Reva Chapman, . . . spent the war years on the Lac du Flambeau reservation in Vilas and Iron counties. DeFoe recalled that she had powerful feelings when her brother told her he and his cousins had signed up. "I felt sad because they were going. They're not going to fight close here, they were going to fight what I considered none of our business," DeFoe said. "Not too long ago they were killing us and we're going over there to take their part."[14] Reva Chapman's cousin was the first casualty from the reservation. To Chapman and DeFoe, this was a white man's war, and Indians had already lost enough to the white man.

But not all reservation women felt that way. Marge Pascale not only supported the military, she joined it. She enlisted in the Women's Auxiliary Air Corps (WAAC) in 1943 and spent the war as a photo lab technician, a parachute inspector, and a nurse's aide. She was one of several hundred American Indian women who saw the armed forces as a way to escape the extreme poverty of their reservations.[15] To Pascale, who had grown up poor in a large family on the Red Cliff Ojibwe reservation in Bayfield County, the WAACs represented opportunity and security. "One thing about the service," she observed, [was that] "you get two pair of shoes and you get a bed and you get to eat." . . .[16]

During the bleakest hours of the war, many black women sought spiritual strength in their churches. The black diaspora to the North, precipitated by wartime jobs and opportunity, had left more than a few transplants feeling isolated. Mary Caire found few other blacks in Madison. In fact, she said "people would fall off the street looking at us" because they had not seen that many blacks." Blacks comprised less than four-tenths of 1 percent of Madison's labor force by the war's end.[17] Caire found the fellowship she was seeking in the African Methodist Episcopal Church on Blount Street, where she taught Sunday school, sang in the choir, and eventually became a deaconess. Most of the members had migrated from Mississippi, Texas, and Arkansas. A.M.E. represented not simply a place to "get our minds together," but a place to mix socially.

Frances Reneau, the seamstress who moved to Beloit in 1938 from Indiana, was on her way to church when she heard the news about Pearl Harbor. Looking back, she said it was where she needed to be "to realize what had really happened that day." For her, church-going was uplifting, a necessity rooted in her ancestry: "Because, when you think back on slavery, if we didn't have the church or the religion where would we be today?"[18] Good ser-mons, songs, and prayer helped keep her community together and sustain it during the war years. Like Caire, Reneau's black church offered fellowship. She had fond memories of "family nights" which featured potlucks, amateur programs, and games for the younger people.

The churches Caire and Reneau belonged to were all-black. Rubie Bond [of Beloit], who attended both segregated and integrated churches, said she had mixed feelings about the black Baptist church where she sent her children to Sunday school. Bond, whose four great-grandfathers were white, was born on a plantation in Mississippi. . . . Ac-cording to Bond, [her children's] light complexions made them the targets of discrimi-nation by other black children, who spat at them in church. So, at the invitation of the minister of the United Brethren Church, she agreed to send her children to his Sunday school, an all-white congregation. "And one white family didn't like it, so they were going to draw out if my children went," Bond remembered. The reaction bothered her enough to keep her children home from Sunday school for a few weeks. When asked about it by her minister, Bond shared her concerns about the white family. "'Well, let them quit,' he said. 'And let your children come on.'"[19]

In addition to their churches, black women took refuge in all-black social clubs. Mary Caire belonged to several, including the Utopia, Lesjoyo, and Mary McLeod Bethune clubs . . . under the umbrella of the Wisconsin State Association of Colored Women's Clubs. Membership was a calling card. Black women who visited or relocated to another city found a black community ready to receive them. The clubs offered political lectures, philanthropic projects, and state conventions once a year. They also offered women an op-portunity to help the war effort.

The [clubs] organized USO dances for black servicemen stationed at Truax Field north of Madison. Once a week, club ladies would invite the soldiers to their churches for dinner. Most of the servicemen were from the South. "We cooked greens and we would cook cakes and pies and different things," Claire said, "and just have a big dinner, a big spread. Then they'd go into their dance and then they would go back out to Truax Field."[20] Caire's oldest daughter married one of those soldiers.

Alice DeNomie was active in USO activities as well, largely because of her parents, who were charter members of the Corporal Henry J. Schafer VFW Post on 28th and Clark streets in Milwaukee. Sally DeNomie, Alice's mother, was the post's musical director — an "enthusiastic pianist" with a penchant for Sousa and Gershwin who "more than made up in patriotism what she lacked in talent," according to her daughter. Sally DeNomie always dressed in white stockings and a white dress for her performances and might have been mistaken for a nurse if not for the "bemedaled blue cap with gold piping that distinguished her as a veteran's wife." Alice DeNomie, who was seventeen years old when the war broke out, went to the post with her. "I was really young and it was pretty innocent. You'd dance with them, play cards, that sort of thing." . . .[21]

Marge Pascale's social life in the Women's Auxiliary Air Corps revolved around a group of five close "crazy" girlfriends. "One time we kissed 250 guys that were going overseas from the second photo squadron," she confessed. "Our lips were chapped."[22] She dated judiciously. There were strict rules against enlisted men and women fraternizing with officers. She remembered some WAACs dating officers, but it was always "on the QT" [covert]. Pascale liked enlisted men better, because they were "real." In 1945, while working at a hospital in Atlantic City, she met and married her husband, Joe, who had just left the service. At the end of the war, she re-enlisted and served until 1947.

It might be argued that American Indians were well prepared for the deprivation that accompanied the war years. DeNomie's father, for example, when asked what the Great Depression was like on his Keweenaw Bay Reservation in Michigan, laughed and replied, "it's *always* depression on an Indian reservation." To ask black and American Indian women: "What was it like to do with less during the war?" seems a similar question. Less of nothing is still nothing. Like white women, blacks and urban Indians saved bacon fat for the war effort (it was used to make explosives), used eyebrow pencil to draw a "seam" on their bare legs in lieu of silk stockings, and rode the streetcar in order to save gasoline in the cars they did not own. Some things made sense. Some things did not. Relying on each other made the most sense of all. Rubie Bond had a neighbor whose little boy was on a special diet and had to have bananas. Because Bond had nine children, she received more ration stamps, which she used to buy bananas for her neighbor's son.

Alice DeNomie remembered that rationing produced a real sense of community in her neighborhood. "You'd get together and pool the sugar you had and make treats. Everything was in short supply — coffee, sugar — because all of that was going to the servicemen. And gasoline, forget gasoline."[23] Eggs, Jello, and especially meat were difficult to get. Like most other Americans, her family of eight maintained a "Victory Garden" which kept them fed during the war.

Rubie Bond's family had a big garden on Highway 51 some distance from her Madison home. Whenever she and her husband had free time they would drive down there and work their plot: "I remember one year, I canned 200 quarts of tomatoes, and string beans and corn and what have you."[24] Those who did not raise their own food often knew someone who did. Frances Reneau remembered getting food from her father-in-law's garden. World War II was a time of casseroles and "improvising," as Nellie Wilson put it. . . .[25]

In some respects, reservation Indians were better prepared for wartime deprivation than their urban cousins. During the war years, many Indian families survived as they had always survived — by hunting, fishing, and gathering on a subsistence basis. On some reservations, Hitler was less an enemy than the state conservation warden. During World War II, the state illegally restricted Indian hunters, not only *off*-reservation in violation of Ojibwe treaties with the U.S., but *on*-reservation as well. . . .

Fines for violating conservation laws in the 1940s could cost hundreds of dollars or one to six months in jail. Tribal members rarely had the money for fines and almost always spent time in jail, which placed a tremendous burden on their wives and children. Women hunted too and were arrested along with the men. Most had their firearms confiscated, but escaped prosecution because northern counties had no place to confine them.[26]

Cranberry and blueberry picking represented the only wage work for most reservation women. Wild rice, a staple of the Ojibwe diet, was sometimes sold to commercial processors. Cecilia DeFoe remembered that nearly everyone had gardens — not necessarily Victory Gardens, just gardens. DeFoe said there were people on the reservation who were particularly generous during the war. "Like if the man died, and there was a widow and had kids, they'd go and give her all them vegetables, everything that she needed. That's the way they did and that's the way during the war; lot of men gone, lot of women were still here and having a hard time."[27] DeFoe and Chapman recalled that some things, like butter, were too expensive to buy. Instead, they'd use salt pork and add deer tallow to make a sort of shortening. It would harden in a large pan. "Just chip it off, how much we wanted for some flavoring for potato soup or something like that," DeFoe said. "And that was good. And that could keep. Of course, we didn't have no refrigerators and stuff like that."[28] Government commodities — including rancid mutton, spoiled oranges, and rotten eggs — arrived monthly, much to the disgust of tribal members.[29] Neither Cecilia DeFoe nor Reva Chapman remembered buying any clothes during World War II. Their mothers bought bolts of material and made their own dresses and shirts. Blankets shipped in by the army were turned into woolen jackets. No one missed gasoline on the reservations since few had cars. DeFoe and Chapman said everyone got around Lac du Flambeau by walking.

Wartime deprivation was bearable, if only because there was so much that was not. Each woman defined herself in some way by the personal loss she suffered during the war — husbands, sons, fiancés, and friends. DeNomie said she was reminded of it every time she walked through her neighborhood. "A blue star hanging in the window meant the family had a son in the service. A gold star meant he wasn't coming home," she said sadly. "You'd walk along and you'd look at these windows and it was hanging in every window. Every window had a star — either a blue or a gold. My parents were grieving through most of the war for their friends and for our friends."[30]

There were gold stars hanging from the window sashes in Nellie Wilson's neighborhood too. "A gold star mother in the black community was as valuable as a gold star mother anywhere," Wilson said.[31] Everyone in her neighborhood had someone or knew of someone overseas. . . .

Mary Jane Aynes was living in Alexandria, Virginia, with her eighteen-month-old daughter when she received the news that every wife dreaded. Her husband, Bob Aynes, had been killed while flying a training mission over Caserta, Italy. "He was killed only three weeks after he got over there. The fighting in Italy was intense," she explained. "He and these flyers had just gotten their wings. They knew how to fly, but they didn't know how to fight with these planes," she said.[32] Her sister, Alice, actually received the news before she did. One of the men in Aynes' squadron sent DeNomie a letter with ten dollars enclosed "for the widow Aynes." DeNomie described the letter as "too terrible to share," and said nothing about it to her parents or brothers and sisters. When Aynes phoned her with the news, she took a "deplorable" train from Milwaukee to Washington, D.C. DeNomie's recollections of that long train ride are of dust and death — coal dust and ashes to ashes: "It was so sad. I remember I couldn't even say anything. She [her sister] was wearing white gloves and when I got off the train, she hugged me and her hand went on my hair. And my hair, sitting on this window where this coal dust was — when her glove came down it was all black."[33]

An estimated 550 Indians from around the country died in combat during World War II, or about 5 percent of the total number of Indians who saw service. Another 700 were wounded.[34] The Lac du Flambeau community lost three of its boys, including its most accomplished musician — Reva Chapman's cousin. . . .

Some of the men who returned had physical wounds, of course, but others bore psychological scars. Several of the black women spoke of friends and relatives who were never "quite right" again after the war. Nellie Wilson blamed Southern boot camps. . . . "The black men who had been exposed to that [discrimination] all their lives, they accepted it as a matter of course, but for these fellows who left here and went down there, it was rough for them. It was really rough for them."[35]

When word came on August 14, 1945, that the war was over, Nellie Wilson dropped her tools, her blueprints, and rushed out on the street with her co-workers at the A. O. Smith Company to celebrate. "The loneliness, the heartaches, and [families] separating" was over and life would return to . . . to what?" Wilson worried that she would have to go on public assistance again. "You have this sobering thought, now what am I going to do for a living? When they told us to go home, nobody said anything about tomorrow, next week, next month, anything."[36] Just as Wilson feared would happen, she was laid off. For the next year, she worked as a cocktail waitress at the club she used to go to when she was making good money during the war. As a patron, she remembered having felt sorry for those girls who had a job that was "degrading" and wondering why they did not just go out and get a better job. "Ignorance is truly bliss isn't it?" Wilson stated. Under pressure from the union to rehire its female employees, A. O. Smith called Wilson back to work as a "handyman," a job she kept until she worked up to the punch press. "It was just awful," Wilson remembered, "plus it's a wonder I still got my fingers because I'd be down there often all night long at the club till two o'clock in the morning. I'd get up and go out there and run those punch presses and I was half asleep. Afraid to quit each one of them [jobs]."[37] She eventually gave up waitressing for the "hard, dirty" job at A. O. Smith that gave her a sense of independence as well as the resources to put both her daughters through college.

For many women, the most pressing problem after the war was finding a place to live. There was a critical shortage of housing for all the returning veterans who were getting married and starting families. In 1948, Alice DeNomie Loew found herself staring out of a one-room trailer, thinking wistfully about a better home. . . .[38] The city [of Milwaukee] did build public housing projects. In the meantime, however, some veterans and their families were sheltered in a large city park in makeshift trailers, like the one in which Alice and her husband Marvin lived. After the oil stove blew, sending "parachutes of soot" floating through their postage-stamp-sized living space, not to mention all over their six-month-old baby, the Loews gave up and moved in with Marvin's parents.

Moving in with in-laws, of course, meant a loss of privacy. . . . Mary Jane Aynes faced many of the same problems her sister faced, but she confronted them alone, with a toddler. Aynes moved back in with her parents. She found a job with Milwaukee's media dynasty, the Journal Company, and rode the first wave into television. Aynes eventually remarried and had two more children. The daughter of the husband she had lost went to Marquette University on a federal war orphans scholarship. . . . "I cannot remember how young I was when I heard my mother's voice saying, 'You're going to college because the government is paying for it,'" Judy Calder recalled. . . . [Calder] wondered, "How many of us were there nationwide . . . and how many might have been minority women, women who might not have otherwise gone to school?" . . .[39]

World War II was a defining moment for the black and American Indian women who experienced it. They encountered the same hardship and heartbreak that their white counterparts did, but minority women, blacks in particular, endured the added indignity of discrimination in employment and housing, as well as lower incomes. There were no "Rosie the Riveters" among this group of women. Rosie was a middle-class myth created to generate enthusiasm and instill a sense of national pride in those who served on the homefront. From where Wisconsin's minority women were serving — at the back of the homefront — Rosie was a long way away. . . .

It takes nothing away from the men who fought and died during World War II to recognize the contributions of the capable women who ran the country in their absence. Among them were black and American Indian women about whom the history books tell us little — women like Nellie Wilson, Mary Caire, Ruby Bond, Frances Reneau, Cecilia DeFoe, Reva Chapman, Marge Pascale, my mother, and my aunt. There are more women of color out there with fascinating stories to tell, but oral historians must move quickly to gather their narratives. Many of these women are in their seventies and beyond. If their stories are not collected soon, they may never be told at all.

*Patty Loew writes, "I have been researching two of my 'subjects' all my life" — two sisters who "have shared an intense but loving rivalry that has lasted more than seventy years": her mother, Alice De-Nomie Loew, and her aunt, Mary Jane Aynes Kahl. Loew also is an enrolled member of the Bad River Band of Lake Superior Ojibwe and a descendant of the founder of one of the first Native American newspapers in Wisconsin, Antoine Denomie's* Odanah Star.[40] *She has followed her grandfather and aunt into the Wisconsin media as an award-winning public television producer.*

*Also a member of the University of Wisconsin–Madison faculty, Loew has received scholarly recognition for her research, most recently for her book published in 2001 by the Wisconsin Historical Society Press,* Indian Nations of Wisconsin: Histories of Endurance and Renewal *(see Introduction to chapter 1).*

# NOTES

1. Alison Bernstein, *American Indians and World War II* (Norman, 1991).

2. D'Ann Campbell, *Women at War with America* (Cambridge, 1984), 252.

3. Maureen Honey, *Creating Rosie the Riveter* (Amherst, 1984), 113.

4. Campbell, *Women at War with America*, 218–219.

5. Nellie Wilson, interviewed by Kathryn Borkowski, Wisconsin Women During World War II Oral History Project, hereafter known as OHP, transcript, 7.

6. U.S. Department of Commerce, Bureau of the Census, *A Report of the Seventeenth Decennial Census of the United States, Census of Population, 1950*, vol. 2, *Characteristics of the Population, Part 49, Wisconsin* (Washington, D.C., 1950), 49-221. In Milwaukee the median annual income for female black workers in 1950 was $1072 — about $300 less than what white women earned and less than a third of what white men earned.

7. Alice DeNomie Loew, author interview, October 23, 1995. Tapes reside with the author.

8. Ibid.

9. Mary Jane Kahl, author interview, October 17, 1995.

10. Thompson, *HOW*, 341–342.

11. Mary Caire, interviewed by Steve Kolman, September 3, 1993, OHP, transcript, 18.

12. U.S. Bureau of the Census, *A Report of the Seventeenth Decennial Census of the United States* Table 74, 49-176.

13. Reneau, interview, OHP, 6–7.

14. Cecilia DeFoe and Reva Chapman, interviewed by Kristina Ackley, July 10, 1992, OHP, transcript, 5–6.

15. Campbell, *Women at War with America*, 219.

16. Marge Pascale, interviewed by Kristina Ackley, August 24, 1992, OHP, transcript, 5–6.

17. U.S. Bureau of the Census, *A Report of the Seventeenth Decennial Census of the United States*, Table 77, 49-188.

18. Reneau interview, OHP, 17.

19. Rubie Bond, interviewed by Steve Kolman, March 19, 1992, OHP, transcript, 15–16.

20. Caire OHP interview, 34.

21. Loew interview.

22. Pascale OHP interview, 26.

23. Loew interview.

24. Bond OHP interview, 9.

25. Wilson OHP interview, 19.

26. Great Lakes Indian Fish and Wildlife Commission interview 900913C transcript, 89.

27. DeFoe and Chapman OHP interview, 11.

28. Ibid., 13. . . .

29. During the GLIFWC interviews, half a dozen tribal members mentioned the unpalatable wartime commodities.

30. Loew interview.

31. Wilson OHP interview, 24.

32. Kahl interview.

33. Loew interview.

34. Bernstein, *American Indians and WWII*, 61.

35. Wilson OHP interview, 25.

36. Ibid., 29–30.

37. Ibid., 36.

38. Loew interview. . . .

39. Judy Calder, letter to author, November 10, 1995.

40. Patty Loew, "Natives, Newspapers, and 'Fighting Bob': Wisconsin Chippewa in the 'Unprogressive' Era," *Journalism History* 23, no. 4 (1997): 149–158.

# Remembering the Holocaust

## MICHAEL E. STEVENS, EDITOR;
## ELLEN D. GOLDLUST-GINGRICH, ASSISTANT EDITOR

Remembering the Holocaust, *a volume in the Voices of the Wisconsin Past series, contains recollections of Holocaust survivors who immigrated to Wisconsin after World War II. These excerpts on their horrific experiences are taken from a remarkable oral history collection that preserves the memories of some of as many as two thousand Holocaust survivors in Wisconsin among one hundred forty thousand who resettled in the United States.*

*The interviews dispel assumptions on the homogeneity of European Jews and the similarity of survivors' experiences in the Holocaust. Likewise, the interviews reflect the rich individual lives of these women rather than simply portraying them as victims. As editor Michael Stevens notes, these "women tell stories of triumph, because each survivor defeated the Nazi dream of annihilation."*

## Germany and Austria

[In] 1933, the German Jewish population numbered about 550,000 (around 1 percent of the population). Although Jews had been integrated into all aspects of German life . . . anti-Semitic legislation was enacted throughout the 1930s. Jews were excluded from the professions, universities, and public service (1933); deprived of German citizenship (1935); and required to register property and to carry passports marked with a *J* for *Jude* (1938).

After Austria's incorporation into Greater Germany in March 1938, Austria's population of 185,000 Jews . . . became subject to Germany's anti-Semitic laws. Eight months later, the events of *Kristallnacht* (the Night of Broken Glass) marked the beginning of real peril for Europe's Jewry. On the night of November 9–10, widespread anti-Jewish rioting occurred in Berlin and in other cities throughout Germany and Austria. . . . [P]ogroms were organized and initiated by the Nazis. Mobs destroyed hundreds of Jewish homes, businesses, and synagogues.

. . . [N]ew legislation expelled all Jews from public schools, confiscated any businesses that remained in Jewish hands, and effectively eliminated Jews from the economy. . . .

After the events of *Kristallnacht*, German Jews knew that the situation had become perilous, and many of them frantically sought to emigrate. By 1941, some 240,000 Jews remained in Germany/Austria, and only about 30,000 of them survived the war. . . . [Some] escaped Nazi Germany; Eva Deutschkron was among those who did not.

### Eva Lauffer Deutschkron

Eva Lauffer was born in Posen, Germany (now Poznan, Poland), on November 12, 1918, to a widowed mother who remarried in the early 1920s, moved the family to Berlin, and established a retail clothing business. Terrified by *Kristallnacht*, Eva's family unsuccessfully attempted to leave Germany. . . .

On May 4, 1939, Eva Lauffer married Martin Deutschkron. While he worked as a tailor, she performed forced labor for the Siemens munitions factory. . . .

. . . We had an apartment, . . . and our janitor was against Hitler. And [the Nazis] had come to our janitor and asked where the Deutschkrons lived. . . . [The janitor] watched for my husband to come home. He came home [as] she was coming down the stairs from talking to them, and with her hands she motioned that he should go back, shouldn't go upstairs. . . .

My husband took off his Jewish star and went to the factory, into Gartenfeld, where I worked, to Siemens, and stood outside waiting for me where we were taken to work like prisoners. . . . He didn't look Jewish. So then I came from work, and I of course had the star on, and I saw him standing there without a star. I knew something was wrong. . . . So when he was there without the star, we never talked. I couldn't go up to him because I would have given him away.

So I got on the train and he got on the same train and we rode back, and at the railroad station there was my mother standing, a little farther over at the corner there was my father standing. They were so afraid. . . . We all went then to my parents' apartment to decide what to do now. My sister had been taken away already for almost six months — by this time you realize what was going on. . . .

. . . So we had taken our star off and we're going around to see who would give us shelter, who would help us in any way. . . . [A family physician] got me shelter . . . to be the maid [for his mistress, the wife of an SS officer], to take care of the child so the woman would be free and could spend time with him, which I found out later as I lived there.

And Martin wandered through the streets to see where he could find shelter . . . and a fellow saw him that he had worked with. . . . This Franz Gomber needed tailors so he says, "I give you a job. You can work here, and you can sleep here on the ironing table. . . ."

I eventually moved completely [into the tailor shop with Martin] and produced from morning to night these jackets and helped with other chores around. At night we would have a little heating plate where we would make a water soup. . . .

. . . [T]his Franz Gomber would see that he got [on the] black market some food for us. He would use his money for our survival. . . .

. . . [W]e were lucky enough, we had gotten out. My mother had given me a very small suitcase, [and] everything we had fit into that little suitcase. . . .

. . . My parents were picked up [in February 1943]; they showed up a few Sundays and then they didn't come anymore. . . . And I never heard of them again. . . .

The Deutschkrons [were betrayed,] left Gomber and stayed briefly with [a cousin] in Spandau before their hiding place was again betrayed. They returned to Berlin, where several families helped to hide them, including the Peltzers . . . who lived in Borkheide, a suburb just outside the city. . . .

. . . [As the war's end neared,] Mr. Peltzer came up to us and said, "I want from you a statement that I brought you through the war. . . . [A]nd if you don't give me this paper I will turn you over to the Germans." So we said, "Mr. Peltzer, we have to be honest. Let's go back, and you turn us over." We had somehow thought either he doesn't have the courage, because if he turns us over to the Germans, he's in trouble, too, because why does he have us here on his hands? Or we would run away. I don't know what we had planned for that moment. And as we walked back into the city, the Russian tanks rolled along the streets. It was May 5, 1945. And Mr. Peltzer became frantic and said to us, "Forget what I said. The war is over." And we said, "Mr. Peltzer, we will forget what you said, but get out of our lives. Right now we are parting paths, and just don't ever enter our lives again. You have helped us. This is fine; for this we leave you off the hook now. But don't enter our lives ever again."

After the Nazi surrender in the spring of 1945, Eva and Martin Deutschkron remained in Berlin, hoping to find surviving relatives. With the help of American soldiers, the Deutschkrons reestablished contact with family in the United States, and they immigrated in early 1947. Eva's brother had attended the University of Wisconsin in Madison prior to the war, and the Deutschkron family, which grew to include two children, moved there in November, 1948, and established a tailoring and retail clothing business. Martin Deutschkron died in 1985. . . .

## The Netherlands

. . . At the time of the German occupation in 1940, about 140,000 Jews (including refugees who had fled the Nazis in Germany, Austria, and Czechoslovakia) lived in the Netherlands, constituting 1.6 percent of the country's total population. More than half of all Dutch Jews lived in Amsterdam.

. . . In February, 1941, the Dutch Nazis intensified the anti-Semitic campaign, rounding up a . . . small number of Jews from Amsterdam's Jewish quarter and deporting them to Buchenwald and Mauthausen. As a result of these arrests, a general strike took place in Amsterdam, and the city was shut down for two days until the Nazis quashed the rebellion. In the summer of 1941, the government imposed a curfew on Jews. . . . In subsequent months, Jews were removed from public schools, barred from public places, and had their property confiscated. On April 29, 1942, Jews were required to wear a yellow star. . . .

. . . Beginning in the summer of 1942, men, women, and children were sent . . . to Westerbork and Vught, concentration camps within the Netherlands; from there, they were transferred to Auschwitz, Sobibór, and other camps in Eastern Europe. Of approximately 107,000 Dutch Jews who were deported, only 5,200 survived the war.

About 25,000 Jews in the Netherlands — the most famous of them being Anne Frank and her family — went into hiding with the aid of the Dutch underground, which was quite active. Roughly two-thirds of the Jews in hiding escaped detection and survived the war, among them . . . Flora Bader.

### Flora Melkman van Brink Hony Bader

Born in Amsterdam on June 20, 1919, Flora Melkman was the oldest of three children in an affluent Dutch Jewish family.

... [W]e Dutch Jews were very, very fortunate because our population was very beautiful. Jews were very assimilated. We were allowed to have any profession we wanted, our schools were wide open, our universities did not even at times ask what your religion was. Nobody bothered to know if you were Jewish or not Jewish, but you didn't hide it either. . . . [T]his was how I saw Holland. We were as free as you feel yourself to be [in the United States]. We had freedom there, totally. . . .

. . . I read the paper fervently, I was aware [of the Nazis] because of the people who came in great streams to Holland [as refugees]. . . . I was strongly inclined to believe that this doom would not just pass us by. I had a feeling it would come to Holland. . . .

. . . I would tell my family that it would be wise if we could try to leave Europe, and my mother said, "Stop reading those books." I was without my fiancé. He was in British India, and I wanted to get away and I wanted to marry him, but I had promised [to wait]. . . .

. . . We did hear the concentration camp stories of the people that came from Europe. . . . I personally believed everything of it, but there were many people who refused to believe the stories. . . . To think that human beings could inflict [such horror] upon others was unbelievable. . . .

Germany invaded Holland in May 1940, and despite the danger, Israel van Brink, Flora's fiancé, returned to Holland. The couple married on November 27, 1940.

[The wedding] was all in black, because I was well aware that Europe was in mourning. It was no time to celebrate a wedding. . . . I said, "mother, this is only for our household. I will marry without a great ado." And she told me, "Flory, you are my oldest, and you will be the only child that I will see into marriage. I will not see my other children marry. Will you allow me to have a family dinner in my house with my sisters?" I thought, "my very, very dumb mother is not aware of how serious our condition is." However, I didn't find it in my heart to say no because I knew this would be also a goodbye to the whole family. . . .

Over the next two years, restrictions on Jews mounted. . . . [T]he Melkmans and the van Brinks . . . were aware that it was only a matter of time before they, too, would fall victim to the Nazis. . . .

[My parents] had to close down the business. That meant no income. . . . [N]o gentile person was allowed to work for Jews. Then [the law] came [that] no Jews should have people working for them, even other Jews. . . .

. . . [W]e ate every evening with my parents and then [would] leave at a quarter to eight to go to my house, because after eight you were not allowed in the streets. . . . I thought, if this is the only thing that they bother us with, we can overcome.

Until in 1942 we all of a sudden heard that there were camps being made in Poland and Germany and that the intention was not to keep us in Holland. A lot of Jews did not believe it, and I also thought this is just malicious undermining of our capacity to survive the war.

I thought we could survive there, but the *razzias* [terror raids] started. My brother was taken from a library on the corner where we lived. . . . [He] went to the corner and didn't come home. Days, days, days, weeks. . . . And then my brother came back. . . . They just let him go free. . . .

We heard . . . what was happening in the Jewish *Viertel* [quarter]. . . . The first *razzia* was there. They halted the boys, made them do exercises in the open, and as they were doing that they were kicked in the face. . . . [S]ome were sent to Mauthausen, I believe, was the concentration camp. . . .

. . . We were stunned, we were horrified. . . . [When the city went on strike, this] was gentile people who were totally free to do whatever they want; they were so one with the Jewish population. . . . [But the Nazis] took out, at eight in the morning, six in the morning, all the male population of that square, placed them in front of the beautiful flower parks that we have in Holland, and killed them in front of their wives and children. After that, the strike broke. Nobody dared to lift a finger for the Jewish population, except a very, very strong underground movement. . . .

. . . There was no knowledge of the concentration camps. That came in 1942, when we were told to make a sack ready to take the most necessary belongings and to leave. That was when in our block, people would jump out of windows, mainly people that . . . came from Germany and that had more knowledge than we had. A lot of people in our block committed suicide. . . . And that set my mood for escaping them. . . .

In January, 1943, assisted by non-Jewish friends, Flora and Israel van Brink went into hiding. Flora's parents, Salomon and Duifje Melkman, and her sister, Anneke (Anne), were captured in a March, 1943 *razzia*. . . . [Salomon and Duifje] died in Nazi captivity; Anneke . . . took the opportunity to escape and joined Israel van Brink's mother in hiding. . . .

And now tragedy comes. . . . I was so eager to see my sister to tell me about my mother, I appealed to my husband to please go a few days to be with his mother and I would meet my sister. This was in April. . . . [W]e decided in the evening we would take off our David Stars and we would walk to this house where his mother was. We did that. He rebelled. I said no rebellion; we do it. . . .

. . . I saw my sister, who told me about my mother and father, how they had left. . . . At around eight o'clock, [we were] gathered in the living room, there was a knock at the door, and three people stepped in. Men from a dream. Creatures that you see in horror movies. [A] Dutch [man] with a mustache telling us, "you are all Jews. You are all arrested." None of us had a star. And I said, "no, we are not," and he said, "show me your identification." Now, I had the right identification because I was in the underground. My sister, who was very nervous, stood up and said to the man, "it's I that you are looking for. Take me. My family has nothing to do with it." Then she gave me away that I was Jewish, of course, but I never blamed her. . . .

. . . She was crying, "I did this to you, I did this to you. . . ." My husband went in the kitchen and he told him . . . "I can work, but I will be very handicapped if I had my wife there. Why don't you take me? It's more than you bargained for" — they were paid money for Jews — "Let my wife free. . . ." He gave the man all the money we had, all the gold, all the jewels we had, and he had also our identification papers. I had nothing. All of a sudden when I was dressing to go out with my sister, I was called to the kitchen. . . . [M]y husband said, "Flory, I just made a deal. I want you to leave." . . . I went to the front room, joined the others, looked for the last time at my sister, and he did so. I don't know how I had strength. I walked through the room . . . I heard my husband, my sister, and my cousin — the cousin of my mother-in-law — go down the steps to jail. . . .

I was not afraid anymore because I was alone. . . . Now [on Dutch underground] radio, one night I heard, "We want the world to know that the concentration camps where the European Jews are being referred to, also our Dutch Jews, are in essence death camps. Roofs are being opened and gas is poured in and people are dying like cattle." And on it went. I was paralyzed. I thought [it must be] propaganda. The blood went down to my feet. I became so sick that I hardly could get out of the closet that evening. . . . That was only in 1944 that first word came.

. . . And the fact for me was at that time when I heard those messages, [I realized] maybe I don't see Israel back with me soon, and certainly not Anne with her sickness, and my father, who had written me in deep despair that life had no meaning without my mother. He was partially paralyzed, had no chance. I was sure that my brother would return and my mother, who was in her forties and very beautiful and very strong-minded and healthy. So I wanted to live for them and be there when they would come to Amsterdam. . . .

. . . Flora van Brink spent the remainder of the war in the homes of other members of the Dutch underground. After the Allies liberated Holland in May, 1945, she learned that her husband and her entire immediate family had perished. She then joined with her mother-in-law to establish a new life in Amsterdam. In the following year, she married Josef Hony, who had spent three years at Auschwitz and had lost his wife and child. Josef and Flora had a daughter, Anneke (Anne), in 1947. The family immigrated to the United States in 1954 and settled in Milwaukee, where both Honys obtained work. After Josef died in 1967, Flora married Aron Bader, who died in 1979. . . .

# Poland and Ukraine

. . . Although Jews had lived in Poland, Russia, Ukraine, Belorussia, and the Baltic States as early as the tenth century, anti-Semitism was common, as were official discrimination and pogroms.

Poland's 3.3 million Jews constituted 10 percent of the country's population and 30 percent of its urban residents. . . . [In] 1938, the government announced its sponsorship of legislation to reduce the number of Jews in Poland and to eliminate Jewish social, political, and economic influence. . . . World War II began on September 1, [1939,] when Germany invaded Poland; the Soviet Union sent its troops into Poland two weeks later. The fighting ended quickly. . . . Jews in the German-controlled areas were immediately ghettoized and required to wear badges identifying them as Jews. Mass deportations began in December, 1941, and continued throughout the next three-and-a-half years. When the war ended in May, 1945, only 380,000 Polish Jews had survived. . . .

## Lucy Rothstein Baras

Lucy Rothstein was born on August 15, 1913, in Skalat, a half-Polish, half-Ukrainian town that was part of Poland until 1939 but is now in Ukraine. . . . After graduating from high school in nearby Ternopol, she attended law school in Lvov. In 1933 a law banning Jews from the legal profession forced her to abandon her schooling, and she learned the tailoring trade, returning to Skalat to open her own shop. . . .

In September, 1939, the Russians occupied Skalat, and the condition of Jews in the city improved. Rothstein acquired a position as a credit officer in a bank. But circumstances changed rapidly after June 22, 1941, when Germany declared war on Russia and moved troops eastward. In July, 1941, Nazi forces overran Skalat and murdered about 400 men, including Rothstein's father.

> And then the German soldiers started to come in with young Ukrainian boys, because the Germans didn't know where the Jews lived. Don't forget that they don't speak the same language, the Germans and the Ukrainians. The Ukrainians knew only the word *Jude* [Jew], so they showed [the Germans] with a finger where a *Jude* lived, and of course they broke into our house and there were no men. They didn't ask questions, they just opened the basement and hauled out [her father and brother in hiding]. . . .
>
> . . . [S]o women started to run around the marketplace and look for the men. And of course there were already all kinds of rumors that many Jews were killed and some are working hard. Oh, about four o'clock in the afternoon my brother came back in his pants and barefoot. So what happened? Where is father? "I don't know," he said. "Right away they separated us." My brother worked washing cars and trucks, so the Germans took off all his clothes, left him only his pants. They said a Jew didn't need such good clothes, and then one German told him he may go home, sent him home. But he said not everybody was sent home. That was Saturday. My father didn't come back.

Sunday morning, we heard that there were bodies in the basements of one of the towers [of an old castle on the outskirts of the city]. And one young boy came out and told the story. They put in a few hundred men — statistics later showed it was 400 — they pushed all these men inside and threw a few hand grenades. . . . [M]y father didn't come back, but . . . every day, the Germans would catch a group of Jewish men to dig graves and bury those, and at the end of the day, they shot these. . . .

German persecution of Jews increased, and a ghetto was established in Skalat. Nazi troops would periodically sweep through the ghetto and forcibly remove people. Fearing for their lives, many people, including the Rothsteins, constructed hiding places in their houses. The Rothsteins constructed a bunker under a false outhouse attached to their residence. Upon hearing that the Nazis were rounding up Jews in Skalat, the Rothsteins and a neighbor boy named David entered the bunker.

> . . . [W]e sat there for two days and two nights. Mother had prepared water and bread and a candle and matches there. They were always in there. And we heard upstairs, they had broken into the house and they broke dishes and there was jingling and clattering and everything else and then we heard screaming. Where our basement was, on the other side of the wall was the basement of David's family, and they were taken out and we heard them scream. Imagine what was going on. And of course [we] covered the boy's mouth so he doesn't scream because he heard all that.
>
> . . . And then we found out that 2,000 Jews were taken out on that day.

A labor camp was established in Skalat in early 1943. Lucy Rothstein was appointed personal seamstress to the local Nazi overseer; her husband-to-be, Edward Baras, was the overseer's farm administrator. Several months later, Lucy, her mother, and her brother, Milo, fled the camp and hid in a nearby forest because of rumors that the camp was to be liquidated. . . .

After about two weeks in the forest, Lucy's mother returned to town to dispose of some of the Rothsteins' goods so that they could buy food. She never returned. Later the forester told Lucy and Milo that their mother had been captured by the Nazis. . . .

[He took them to join a group of Jews in the forest, where they] hid in the woods until the winter of 1943, when they were liberated by the Russians. Milo joined the Russian army and was killed in March, 1945. Lucy returned to Skalat and married Eddie Baras on April 7, 1944. The couple had a son, Victor, the following January. The Baras family left Skalat in late 1945 and made their way to a displaced persons camp in Bamberg, Germany, where they remained until May, 1949. . . .

After leaving Germany, the Baras family spent nine months in New York before moving to Sheboygan, Wisconsin, to join Eddie's brother and sister, who had been sent there directly from Germany. The couple's daughter, Ellen, was born in 1954. Eddie Baras worked as a machinist at the Kohler Company in Kohler, Wisconsin, from 1953 until 1974; Lucy Baras worked part-time as a seamstress until her retirement in 1987. . . .

## Rosa Goldberg Katz

Rachel (Rosa) Goldberg was born in Lodz, Poland, on May 6, 1924, to a financially comfortable, liberal Jewish family. . . .

In November, 1939, two months after the Germans occupied Lodz, Rosa Goldberg, her parents, and her brother were moved into the Jewish ghetto, where they shared a two-room apartment with eight other people.

> . . . [T]hey just came in and they just chased the people out during the night, so I remember several nights I slept [with] several dresses on, just in case they come during the night so we have some change of clothing with us. We slept in our coats, in our shoes, with a bag right next to the bed in case if they come in the middle of the night. . . .
>
> We didn't know anything about concentration camps, just that they would come into our block in the middle of the night and shouting, shooting with machine guns, with horrible voices, "*Raus, Juden! Raus, raus, Schweinehund!*" ["Get out, Jews! Get out, get out, swine!"], swearing, and people just walked out of their houses — from their beds, really — in their nightgowns and piled on the buses. They took babies away from the mothers' arms and just put them on the buses and nobody ever saw them again. And they made lists of children. Parents disappeared and then there were children without parents. . . .
>
> . . . I think it was in July, 1942, my brother and I and my parents went out, and they picked my mom and my father. And whoever screamed or made a noise they took them, too. They stood there with those big, huge rubber things hitting the people to climb on those trucks, and I saw my mom being pushed and my father being hit. He was trying to help my mother to get up, and I started to scream, and my brother and another neighbor pushed me down so they wouldn't notice me and my brother just put his hand on my mouth. If they would have heard me, they would have taken me too. I don't know how my parents got on the truck, and all of a sudden I see my mother and father just waving to us from the truck.
>
> . . . With all the turmoil and all that confusion and screaming and crying they were separated, and father came back, but not my mother. And this was the last time I saw her.
>
> This was 1942, and from then on, every day they took people away. We didn't know where they were shipping them. Didn't know anything about them. We just knew that people just disappeared. My cousins we lived with — they took their children at the same time when they took my mom and father. . . .
>
> Finally, at one time they liquidated the part where we were living. We were supposed to go someplace else because there was nobody left where we were. The people were gone, disappeared. . . . They had dogs, wild dogs. They took babies away from the mothers and just threw them in the air, and they were shooting at them. When the babies dropped down onto the ground, the dogs tore them apart. . . .

... So we just took whatever was left and we walked to those wagons and we were shipped to Auschwitz. ...

It was absolutely bewildering. All of a sudden the train stops and the doors open. ... [T]here were soldiers with dogs and machine guns, pushing here, pushing there, screaming. People crying, people being kicked, people being beaten. It was such a bewildering feeling, and I kept saying, "Where are we? What's going on? What's happened?" It was just like you dream, and you're trying to wake up. I kept saying, "No, this must be a nightmare. I'm going to wake up any minute. ..."

... [F]inally they told us to get out, to line up, men here, women here, and all of a sudden I realized that my brother and my father went in one direction and Hela, my sister-in-law, and her mother and I went in a different direction, and I realized we won't be seeing each other anymore. We are being separated. ...

... I cannot describe it. A horrible nightmare is not as horrible as what was going on then. This was Auschwitz. ...

... Then they marched us into a huge building and they told us to get undressed, strip all our clothes, and then came soldiers in and out, in and out, pushing us around like we were cattle, not human beings. ...

Then they shaved our heads. ...

... [T]hen out again, shouts and screaming and shooting with the machine guns, always machine guns. ... They marched us off to a field right next to where we arrived, where the crematoriums were, and they told us to wait on that field right next to the crematorium. ... We looked at our arms — we didn't get any [tattooed] number. Usually for the people who didn't get the numbers, [if] they didn't bother to give a number, we were destined for the ovens. We didn't care — faster the better, sooner the better.

They must have forgotten about us because wagons kept rolling in night and day continuously, and the ovens, the smoke was going from those ovens. The smell, it was just terrible. During the day we were lying with no food, no water. It must have been about forty-eight hours we were lying in that field like they'd forgotten. They had completely forgotten about us. Apparently that's what happened because they were so busy with so many transports coming in with people and crying and screaming — you could hear night and day. It never stopped. It never stopped. They were so busy burning those poor, poor, wretched people. ...

After two days in the field, Rosa Goldberg escaped death when she was among five hundred Jewish women who were shipped to Berlin, by mistake — instead of five hundred French women, who apparently replaced them in the camp crematorium — to work as *Häuptlinge* (slaves) in the Krupps armament factory, making bombs.

Apparently they were afraid to let anybody know who we were, so they just left it alone. This probably saved our lives. Left us alone and gave us a big speech that we're going to be working at Krupps, and we have to work hard if we want to stay here, if we want to be surviving, otherwise we [were] going to be sent back to concentration camps. . . .

Goldberg assembled timing mechanisms for German bombs during the next eight months. In March, 1945, she and her sister-in-law were shipped to the concentration camp at Ravensbrück, Germany. The Swedish Red Cross liberated the camp a month later, and Goldberg was sent [to Denmark and then] Sweden.

> . . . The Danish people, then they saw us in our condition, and they were crying just looking at us. And they couldn't be kinder. . . .
> . . . [T]hen we went to Copenhagen. And oh, the people were greeting us on the railroad station with flags and trying to give us cigarettes, trying to give us food. We weren't even able to reach out and take any cigarettes, but we could see their kindness, their fear, the way we looked in the uniforms we had on, and the way we looked. It was just horror and we could see their horror. . . .

Goldberg worked as a tailor in Sweden until March, 1948, when she married Bernard Katz, also a survivor. The couple immigrated to the United States the following month and . . . mov[ed] to Oshkosh, Wisconsin, in 1953. The couple had two sons and two daughters before Rosa returned to school and received a degree in nursing. Bernard died in 1983; Rosa [Goldberg Katz] continued to work as a nursing assistant in Oshkosh until her retirement in 1994.

*The initial 160 hours of interviews by participants in the Wisconsin Survivors Oral History Project are available as transcripts or on tape in the WHS Archives. The survivors' "powerful testimonies," writes editor Michael E. Stevens in* Remembering the Holocaust, *"are testaments to hope."*

# Women Remember the War, 1941–1945

MICHAEL E. STEVENS, EDITOR;
ELLEN D. GOLDLUST, ASSISTANT EDITOR

☙ ❧

Women Remember the War, 1941–1945, *a volume in the Voices of the Wisconsin Past series, includes the experiences of Wisconsin women in World War II in their own words. The following excerpts from oral history interviews provide the perspectives of women in factories, offices, and farms across Wisconsin, and of mothers who stayed home as well as military women who went overseas among almost 8,000 who enlisted from Wisconsin. With more than 300,000 men from the state in uniform — almost one in five of the its male population of 1.6 million — women had new responsibilities on the Wisconsin homefront in World War II.*

*Women wage-earners were not new to Wisconsin, but wartime labor shortages accelerated the trend. Of 1.2 million Wisconsin women aged fourteen and above in 1940, more than 260,000 already worked for wages, approximately one in five women of working age in the state. Their numbers increased to as many as one in three Wisconsin women by 1944, when approximately 400,000 were in the workforce. Most had work more traditionally held by women, such as clerical and service-sector jobs, according to editor Michael E. Stevens; comparatively few women "found themselves in industrial settings for the first time." However, he writes, "their importance lies in the way that they challenged established stereotypes and served as models for later generations."*

☙ ❧

## Rose Kaminski

Born to Polish immigrants in Kenosha in 1918, Rose (Gudynowski) Kaminski moved to Milwaukee at age ten. She married John Kaminski in 1937 and had two daughters, one born in 1941 and the second in 1948. Her husband was drafted in early 1944. . . . Beginning in early 1943, she worked [at three factories including Rex Chain Belt Company] and Harnischfeger Corporation, remaining there until March, 1946, when she was released from her job to accommodate a returning veteran. She returned to Harnischfeger in 1950, working there until she retired in February, 1981. . . .

. . . I went in to apply for work [at Rex Chain Belt] as an inspector. . . . [T]his gentleman came up and said, "Well, we're going to be hiring inspectors, and we're also going to be needing several crane operators." And my ears perked up right away because my stepfather was a crane operator for years, and I always heard about it but never knew what it was. I was not familiar with the shop positions. . . . [We] walked into the factory, and here was this great big ordnance plant. . . . They were making great big howitzer barrels for the guns. Overhead were the cranes, and he showed us what we'd have to do.

. . . I said, "I'd like to try and see if I could do it." . . . He said, "We'll train you. It will take you three weeks and you'll be able to run a crane yourself." Well, I was running one in three days. It just came to me; I loved it. There was no problem. It was not difficult, and here I thought, "You can see the gun barrels. You know that it's part of the war.". . .

. . . [When the plant closed,] there was three [women] crane operators and . . . we went together to [Harnischfeger to] apply for work. Because in numbers there's a little strength, and you need a little moral support. You're not used to looking for a job, and you didn't know what you were getting into; you were afraid at that time. We were not as bold as we are now. . . .

## Emily Koplin

Born in Milwaukee in 1926, Emily Koplin grew up in an ethnically diverse neighborhood on Milwaukee's south side. . . . Koplin ha[d] worked in the office at the Allen-Bradley Company since graduating from high school in 1943, and at age sixty-seven she continues to postpone retirement.

. . . I spent a lot of time with the girls that I worked with . . . who had boyfriends or husbands overseas. . . . We waited for our men to come home. We didn't do any dating — those were the years where we would go to dances and girls would dance with girls. We had good times; we had a lot of fun. We were very, very close because we were all waiting. . . .

. . . I don't think [my parents] completely understood . . . this USO business. When I told my mother that I was going downtown to dance with sailors she almost had a nervous breakdown because nice girls just didn't do that kind of thing. You have to appreciate that was the thinking back then. . . .

. . . We spent a lot of time walking, just showing them the different sights of Milwaukee. . . . We just had a very enjoyable time just being friends. . . .

## Signe Cooper

Born in Clinton County, Iowa, in 1921, Signe (Skott) Cooper moved with her family to McFarland, just outside Madison, in 1937. Cooper was graduated from the University of Wisconsin's nursing school in 1943. She joined the Army Nurse Corps in May, 1943. . . . [In August, 1944] she was sent to the China-Burma-India theater. . . . After her discharge at the end of 1945, she returned to Madison, where she worked at Wisconsin General Hospital (now the University of Wisconsin Hospital) and later became a professor of nursing at the university. She retired in 1983. . . .

When I went into the service, there wasn't such a thing as basic training for nurses [by the military]. . . .

I think the role of the nurse changed after World War II because I think that many of the nurses who served in the army were not willing to subject themselves to some of the kinds of subservice, I guess, that had been evident before that. . . . [T]hey were given a lot more responsibilities. They were very often essentially on their own. I think there were many, many changes, some subtle and some not so subtle. But I think the experience of war really made a difference to nursing. . . .

. . . [S]ome of those experiences that we had, we probably wouldn't have survived without sort of helping each other through it. I think we were very much a support group for each other, even though we didn't call it that. It's like we didn't talk about culture shock, but we had culture shock.

# Jean Lechnir

Jean (Hahn) Lechnir was born in 1917 in Prairie du Chien and lived there her entire life. She received a B.S. degree from La Crosse State Teachers College before marrying Ray Lechnir in 1940. The Lechnirs had two small children and Jean was pregnant with a third when her husband was drafted for military duty in 1944 and sent to Europe, where he served until 1945. The Lechnirs later had three more children, and when their youngest child entered school in the early 1960s, Jean returned to work, holding a variety of jobs until her retirement in 1978. Her husband died in 1981. . . .

. . . By the time my husband went into the war . . . he was getting maybe forty, fifty dollars a week then, and we were feeding two youngsters. . . .

. . . [T]he government paid me eighty dollars a month. And then for each child I think I got ten dollars extra, and it was tough, real tough, but I had wonderful people over in the grocery store that helped us out a lot. . . .

. . . I also had a victory garden, and my husband left me with a whole passel of pigeons that he was raising. So I decided I'd better kill those, that's something we could eat, because I couldn't go uptown and buy beef roast or anything like that. . . .

. . . So I got out there and I grabbed the pigeons and I had a block of wood and a hatchet and I was standing out in the back yard and I'd come up with the hatchet and I'd just get to the pigeon's neck and I couldn't do it. . . . [My uncle killed them and] I cleaned them up and I cooked them and do you know, I had the worst time talking my little girls into eating them. They were pets, so — but we ate them anyway because I couldn't afford to do anything else. You ate anything that swam, crawled, or flew in order to eat cheaply. . . .

. . . [E]verything was rationed, and you had to wait in line to get butter or coffee . . . because we would hoard that. That's a horrible word to say — hoard. But we'd save our ration stamps and, of course, with our little babies and kids we didn't use a lot of coffee at times, not like we drink it now, and the butter was something else used very sparingly. . . .

. . . At first, you feel abandoned [when a husband was drafted] and you feel angry because they took him when you needed him more at home. Then you turn around and you feel proud because he was not afraid to go. He was afraid — they were all afraid — but he went and he was doing his duty, and we figured that was

part of our job . . . to give our husband to the war effort and to do the best we
could without him. . . . [Y]ou have lonely times — and especially when I had my
son and my husband wasn't with me, and the lady in the bed next to me or across
the hall, her husband was allowed to come home to be with her with his sailor suit
on, and I was alone and that was a very traumatic time. . . .

## Rose Truckey

Born to Armenian immigrants in 1924 in Racine, Rose (Arakelian) Truckey was originally
named Nazeli, but her father changed her name to Rose because a grade school teacher
could not spell or pronounce the more traditional Armenian name. During World War
II, Truckey got a job at the J. I. Case Company in Racine, working as a riveter on a production line that manufactured bomb bay doors for aircraft. While working at Case, she
met Sy Truckey, who was on medical leave from the army. They married in June, 1944,
and moved briefly to Rockford, Illinois. When her husband was again shipped overseas,
Truckey, who had become pregnant, returned to Racine and found a job at Zahn's Department Store. Following the war, Truckey worked in a Racine bank and advanced as far
as vice-president prior to her retirement in 1992.

Most of my friends were also married and/or having a child, so we kind of were
our own little group. We protected one another. When one of the girls was to go
have her child, she was just eighteen, and, gee, I was nineteen. Her mother had
died and so a group of us took her to the hospital and she had the baby, a little boy,
and I think a week later her husband was killed in action. Imagine: eighteen, a new
baby — those were not very nice times. I remember when Nancy [Truckey's
daughter] was born on April 11, [1945,] and then on April 12, President Roosevelt
died and the gal in the bed opposite me, her husband was in the navy and we were
frightened. We said, "my God, now that he's dead, will our husbands come home?"
. . . We were frightened. But it all worked out, they came home. . . . You could always make sure that somebody would be there if you needed them because you
couldn't depend on a man, there weren't any around. So it was really what we
could do for ourselves.

## Anne Dinsmore

Born in Madison in 1916 to Sicilian immigrants, Anne (Aparatore) Dinsmore was graduated from the University of Wisconsin in 1938 with a degree in social work. She worked for
several years with the Girl Scouts. . . . She married in 1943 and gave birth to a son in 1944,
after her husband left to serve in the war. They later divorced, and in 1966 she joined the
Peace Corps, spending two years in South America. After she returned to the United
States, Anne remarried and lived for the next several years in the Middle East. . . .

So I was at home with a child, and my job primarily was to read the letters [to
immigrant neighbors] that all the sons wrote home, to write letters, and to inter-

pret the news, what was happening. When [the older people in the community] couldn't read it in English and it wasn't coming to [them] in Italian, I'm sure it was frightening. And so I would explain [the news]. . . . [Y]ou had to do geography lessons. "I know where Italy is, but where is England?" "It's over here; see this map."

We put up a map. It was almost like a command post, just to try to explain where their children were, where our brothers were. That was a very poignant time. The women had some fears that after the Japanese [immigrants and descendants in the U.S.] were rounded up and sent to internment camps, they began to fear — when Italy was still on the side of the Axis, the German Axis — they began to fear that if things got really tough in Italy, [if people there] persisted in supporting Hitler, their lives would be pretty miserable here, and maybe we'd all be interned for one reason or another. And I kept saying, "No, that can't be. You see, your sons, our brothers, are fighting in this war." Well, of course, so were the Japanese [Americans]. . . .

. . . The community was held together by women. Women are pretty strong and our mothers were like the Rock of Gibraltar. They had always coped. Italian women had always coped. They had the nitty-gritty of family problems. Men always tended to shy away. The men — in the context of World War II, we're talking about the young men of fighting age — but their fathers fell apart when they saw them going off to war. . . . And it was the women who stood very strong and kept families together. . . .

## Gene Gutkowski

Eugenia ("Gene") (Amrhein) Gutkowski was born in Milwaukee in 1927 to Catholics of German descent. She left high school in 1943 to help her family financially when her brother left for military service, working at Steinmeyer's Grocery Store until the late 1940s. She then worked at Sealtest Dairy until her marriage to Alfred Gutkowski in 1953. Since that time she has been a homemaker . . . in Milwaukee with her husband.

We were strictly German. Even our church had words in German written in it. Our neighboring area was very Polish. . . . [A]nd in those days [most people] did not intermix. The Germans stuck together and the Polish, etc. So my sister had gotten married to this very fine young Polish man the month before, at Thanksgiving [1941], right before the war started. So my dad was really upset that she married a Polish person, because my father was pro-German. All his relatives were in Germany. His father came over, and some of his brothers were even born over there. So when the war started after a while with Germany, then my father — he just didn't think it was right for us to be fighting the Germans. And the teenagers, being what teenagers are, we weren't afraid to stand up to my father and we were trying to explain to him that there are Germans, and there are Germans. They were not all Nazis, and some did not like it any more than the rest of us. But it took

him a long time. He was praying that our brother, his son, would not have to go
and fight his own relatives. So I'm thankful my brother was sent to Japan and New
Guinea. . . .

. . . There was a Jew that was across the street from us that we weren't even allowed to play with, which I think is wrong — I think it's very wrong. But that's the
way it was in those days. . . .

## Annastasia Batikis

Born in 1927 in Kaukauna, Annastasia Batikis was [the] youngest of three children of
Greek immigrants from Constantinople. Her parents, who moved the family to Racine in
1929, spoke little English and emphasized Greek customs in the home. Batikis's mother
died during World War II. . . . [I]n the spring of 1945 [Batikis] tried out for the All-
American Girls' Professional Baseball League and won a position on the Racine Belles,
playing for one season. . . . [She earned] a B.S. in 1952 and a master's degree in 1960.
She taught in the Manitowoc schools from 1952 to 1954 and in the Racine public schools
from 1954 until her retirement in 1985. . . .

. . . I went to a couple of the USO dances, but more than that I was always either
making cookies or writing letters. . . .

Because my mother died when I was still so very young, I leaned pretty heavily
on my church background and the faith that I had and the friends that I had in
the church. . . .

. . . [E]verybody that had somebody in the service from the church [worked in
the war effort] one way or another. There was a lot of knitting going on, too. I did-
n't know how to knit so I didn't do that, but there was knitting, and then of course
a lot of the women that would be my mom's age, they rolled bandages — did
things with old sheets and stuff that they had. Some of them drove the Red Cross
wagons around. And then again, when the servicemen came into town, there was
always coffee and doughnuts for them. More than anything else I think it was just
the idea of sharing your home with some kid that was away from home, so whenever the kids would come to church that were around the area that were in service or if one of the sons brought somebody home with them, why, they were always
welcomed. Somehow they were taken in by the church family.

## Loa Fergot

Born in Neenah in 1924, Loa (Hutchins) Fergot met Paul Fergot in December, 1941,
while she was a high school senior. The couple married during the following September,
shortly before he left to join the Army Air Corps. Like many other cadet wives, Loa followed her husband . . . to various training sites [including in the South for] two years. Because of her secretarial skills, she easily found work. . . . When Paul completed his training
and went to Europe in August, 1944, Loa returned to Wisconsin, where she worked and
attended Oshkosh State Teachers College. Paul, a navigator on a B-24, was shot down over

Italy in October, 1944. The army listed him as missing in action until March, 1945, when Loa learned that he was a prisoner-of-war in Germany. The Fergots were reunited in June, 1945, in Milwaukee, and they subsequently settled in Oshkosh. . . .

I had never been down South in winter. . . .

The only thing I really didn't [expect] — I was so naive — was discrimination. We didn't know what it was, because my parents treated everybody in the very same way. . . . It was about that time that [African American singer] Marian Anderson tried to stay overnight in Appleton, and they wouldn't let her. And my grandmother, who was quite liberal, the one who taught music, was so upset. . . . [T]he vast amount of discrimination there was in the South, it really [upset me]. . . .

But one of the most difficult cities I had to find a place in was Lancaster, California [the future Edwards Air Force Base] . . . and the town had about five hundred people, I think. And I knocked on doors and knocked on doors and couldn't find a place. And Paul had been told that it would be like that — we knew that, we were aware of it. I spent the first night in a chicken coop, and I think the landlord really took pity on me and said, well, in a day or two, he'd have a place, but if I wanted to sleep in the coop out back, I could. And that's what it was — it was a chicken coop. It didn't have chickens in it, but I was sure it had rats and everything else. And there was an old bunk bed there, and it was in terrible condition. That's where I spent that night, and I didn't sleep much that night, either. There were some nights like that. I think it was the next day that he found me a room. When I look back at some of that, I wonder how I ever had the courage to do all that. . . .

. . . [We cadet wives] really bonded and really had some wonderful friendships. We played cards, we went downtown, we went to movies. We went out to the base whenever we were allowed to, which was not very often and usually amounted to about once a week. Our husbands, after a certain length of time, might be able to get off the base on the weekends. But we lived to see them, really. And we had good times together, because we were in such like situations. And I think that we didn't really believe that our husbands would ever go overseas. Not really. We thought the war'd be over before they finished their training, because that's quite a lengthy training. And if we did think about it, we probably just shoved it into the back of our minds, so we had a pretty good time. And in Lakeland, for instance, . . . of the four cadet wives and their husbands, one husband was shot down — after he got his commission — over Europe and was killed. And one was shot down over Germany, became a prisoner-of-war, and died in prison camp. And one was shot down in the Pacific and died. And Paul was the only one who lived, and he became a prisoner. So you can see what the chances were for airmen in those days. . . .

After Paul was sent overseas, Loa returned to Oshkosh, where she attended college.

I got a telegram. It came to Neenah, to my folks' house, and — I don't even know if I can talk about this. I was in school and it was between classes and I was standing by my locker, putting my books in, and I saw my folks walking down the hall. I knew right away what had happened, so — it was really tough, because I just slid down to the floor and sat there for a long time. And, of course, then my dad got down next to me, and he said, "He's only missing, you know, so there's lots of hope yet."...

...I went home with my folks to Neenah, and I can remember not wanting to do anything or think or move, even. I kind of just sat. ...

...I'm not sure when I started working, but I started working for the Menasha Woodenware, in the office....

...[I]t wasn't until March that I found out that [Paul] was [a] prisoner, and from then on, I can remember, every day was beautiful. I'd walk to work and it would be just gorgeous out, and oh, it felt so good. ... Even though I didn't hear from him for a long time, at least I knew that he was a prisoner. ...

...[When he was released and returned, it] seemed like my life was beginning again.

News of Germany's surrender received a quiet welcome in Wisconsin on May 8, 1945. ... As a Madison woman put it, "I won't do any cheering until it's over in the Pacific because that's where my husband is."

Victory over Japan provoked a wildly different reaction. News of the war's end hit Wisconsin at six o'clock in the evening on Tuesday, August 14, 1945, and celebrations took place throughout the state. In Madison, Milwaukee, Oshkosh, Racine, and in almost every other community, people gravitated to downtown business districts and celebrated for most of the night. The spirit of rejoicing seemed the same, whether in Milwaukee, where a quarter of a million people crowded onto Wisconsin Avenue, or in tiny Mishicot, where crowds went from tavern to tavern drinking toasts and a band of World War I veterans played. ...

Despite the communal nature of the celebration, the war's end had a deeply personal meaning for most citizens of the state. A young woman in Valders hugged a reporter from a nearby Manitowoc paper and told him, "My boyfriend is on Iwo Jima — now he will come home and we can get married — ain't it wonderful." A four-year-old boy in Appleton informed everyone who would listen, "my Daddy's coming home." A young mother, with two children holding her hands, walked down a Milwaukee street, her cheeks wet with tears, repeating, "just think, no more war. No more war."

The end of the war left an indelible impression [on Wisconsin women]....

## Rose Kaminski

... [E]verybody was out in the streets [of Milwaukee], and shouting, and yelling, and hugging, and kissing each other. We were going to go out and we were going to celebrate because my husband was home on leave — it was cause for celebration. Six of us piled into one car, and we headed for one of the taverns. We started out in Bay View, where my sister lived, and we stopped at one of the neighborhood taverns, and it was just jam-packed. Everybody hugging and kissing and buying drinks for one another. . . . We headed downtown. The nearer you got to Wisconsin Avenue, the more jammed it was — cars bumper to bumper. You could not even drive three or four feet, and you'd stop and people would get out of the cars, hug one another, kiss one another, yelling and hollering. It was pandemonium. It was just unbelievable.

## Dorothy Zumda

Everybody in the office said, "Everybody's going to be downtown in Milwaukee. . . ." So after work we all got on the streetcars. The streetcars were just jammed with people. I can remember one streetcar after another jammed, and people, I think, had flags and they were yelling and screaming. Everybody was so happy the war was over. And the streetcar was going down National Avenue, and it come in front of Wood Hospital [founded as the Old Soldiers Home]. . . . But here on the grounds are sitting all these veterans, some without legs, in wheelchairs with their legs covered with a blanket, and they're just sitting there watching us, watching these streetcars of mad people going past, yelling and screaming. Well, when the people spotted them everybody just quieted down and it [was] just flat [silence], and then a couple blocks later they started up again. That I remember; I could never forget that.

The end of more than three years of global conflict meant a resumption of normal life. Men came back from military service, many women left their jobs, and couples reunited and began families. . . . The American work force would never be the same, as women assumed a larger part in it than ever before. . . .

In addition to these societal differences, the war altered Americans on a personal level as well — no one could live through such a time and come out unchanged.

## Rose Kaminski

I think I became a most self-sufficient person. I know that I had to do a lot of things that I would not maybe have done had there been a man around the house. I was an independent person. . . .

I think we women were getting braver right along [before the war]. We were in a man's world, and I think we resented being told what to do. I think women were told what to do long enough. . . . So every month when I get my pension check, I know what I was working for. I feel pretty independent right now. My daughters were brought up to feel independent, too. They are both working. Like grandmother, like mother, like daughter, sent down the line.

*More than a hundred participants in the Wisconsin Women during World War II Oral History Pro-ject provided hundreds of hours of taped interviews that are available as transcripts or on tape in the WHS Archives.*

*Even so, many women could not voice all of their memories. They lost husbands, sons, or broth-ers among the more than eight thousand Wisconsin men who died in World War II. In* Women Re-member the War, *editor Michael E. Stevens observes that queries on "losing a loved one . . . elicited strong emotions from many women" and their requests to turn off the tape recorders. "Their relative silence," writes Stevens, "speaks eloquently of how deeply the pain of war still cuts," more than half a century later, when Wisconsin women remember the war.*

# 8

# NEVER DONE

## WOMEN'S WORK FROM THE WISCONSIN CENTENNIAL INTO THE NEW MILLENNIUM

*Women's work in making history is never done, nor is the work of historians in retelling women's stories in Wisconsin. However, the more recent past has yet to be researched and written, much less published in the principal resource for this anthology, the* Wisconsin Magazine of History. *With so few secondary sources available, this essay relies mainly on primary sources of the period, from newspaper accounts to televised interviews to Web sites, to summarize the story of women in Wisconsin since the centennial of statehood and take it to the end of the twentieth century and into the new millennium. This essay is offered in the hope that readers will find inspiration for further research as the next historians of women's work and will submit their works to the* Wisconsin Magazine of History — *toward the next anthology on women's work in Wisconsin.*[1]

I n the last half of the twentieth century, Wisconsin women at last made substantive progress on many fronts, from workplaces to campuses to politics, as did women nationwide. But by the end of the century, women elsewhere would move farther ahead, while Wisconsin would fall well behind most other states in women's working conditions, educational and employment prospects, and political progress. Yet by mid-century, early in the era, extraordinary women leaders — the likes of whom had not been seen since woman suffragists had made history — emerged from many sectors of life in Wisconsin. In the modern women's movement and in the new millennium, Wisconsin women would make history again.

In the centennial year of statehood, 1948, Wisconsin women already had made history on the state teams that dominated "a league of their own," the title of a later film on the All-American Girls Professional Baseball League that was created in wartime when male players went overseas. The film focused on only the first season, when the first four teams included two in Wisconsin, and the championship went to the Racine Belles; the fifth team in the league, the Milwaukee Chicks, took the title in the second season. But the league's best years came in the postwar period, peaking in the 1948 season with attendance of almost a million fans — almost a quarter of a century before Title IX started to set minimal standards for schools to level the playing field for women. The state's teams still "set the standard for women in baseball and in sports in general," said Jacqueline Mattson Baumgart of Brookfield, the Kenosha Comets' catcher in 1951. "We opened the eyes of the world to the fact that women have athletic skills," she declared with pride, decades later.

Although the league finally folded in 1954, many of the women stayed active in athletics, including Joyce Hill-Westerman, who had debuted with the league and the Racine Belles in 1943. Almost half a century later, she would make her film debut among almost fifty former AAGPBL players featured in closing scenes on the field at the Baseball Hall of Fame, where an exhibit had opened on the onetime league of women's own.[2]

The possibilities for women in the postwar period, after their service on battlefronts and on the homefront, seemed sky-high to one of the country's first female military pilots. Jeanette Kapus of Germantown was one of eight Wisconsin women in the Women's Air Service Pilots, or WASPs, an auxiliary of the Army Air Force but officially in the civil service. To free men in the military for combat, most of the women flew servicemen around the country or flew planes from factories to bases. However, Kapus was part of the elite group of test pilots who put planes through maneuvers to ensure the safety of the men who took them into battle. "It was dangerous, sure," she recalled decades later. "We just did it. . . . We all did it for our country, and we were and are very proud of that." But the military ended the WASPs even before the war's end. Kapus wanted to be a pilot, but neither the military nor airlines wanted women pilots. She took another civil service job but stayed in the military reserves to stay in the air. She also flew in exhibitions, including one at a veterans' convention in 1949, when she broke the women's flying record for the most spins — sixty-four spins, far more than the previous record of forty-eight. Kapus "wasn't even dizzy," she recalled, during her spectacular descent over Manitowoc. By the 1950s, with the Korean War, the new Air Force wanted the former WASPs back. Kapus re-enlisted, with a military commission, although women still were not allowed to be military pilots. For the next two decades, Kapus did personnel duties around the world and received many military awards. However, she rarely flew again, although her record still stood into the next millennium. "I suppose I was ahead of my time, too, because I really wanted to fly, that's all," she said. "It just wasn't the right time."[3]

Wartime-era options for women were few in postwar Wisconsin — and feminists even fewer. Women like Margaret Walsh of Appleton, a secretary who wanted to be her own boss, created their own options. "The only part of that job I liked was being on the phone," she would recall. Forgoing marriage and family, Walsh founded the first telephone-answering service in the Fox Valley, only the third such firm in the field in the state in 1949. She added branches in several cities, adapted to newer technologies, such as mobile phones and voice mail, and served as president of her national trade association before selling her pioneering enterprise after almost half a century. She hoped to be "an example for entrepreneurs" of either gender, Walsh later said, to "to prove that everybody can do it — men or women." Virginia Altenhofen Klecka of Milwaukee had to disprove more than myths about women's ability, especially in math; she also had to dispel doubts about disabilities after a diagnosis of diabetes in 1950, before she was thirty years old. A Marquette University instructor, not on the tenure track, Klecka faced health care costs and left teaching for the financial security of year-round paychecks. At Rex Chainbelt, later Rexnord, where most women worked in the secretarial pool, Klecka started as a statistician. But she became the company's corporate economist and nationally known as one of the first women in management in the heavy machinery industry. In the classroom or the boardroom, Klecka also taught by example and "encouraged women to go into fields that were not usually open to them," as she later recalled.[4]

In another unusual career for the era, Ernestine O'Bee was co-owner with her husband of Milwaukee's oldest African American-owned funeral home even before she enrolled in mortuary school. In 1952, she became the first licensed, female mortician in Wisconsin as well as the first woman appointed to the state board of examiners for funeral directors. She enlisted in many causes in her community and endowed a scholarship fund for students of color because a dean of women at her college had denied O'Bee her dream of being a journalist. "She said for black women, there were only two fields open, social work and teaching," O'Bee recalled. "That was evil. The trouble is, I believed her." O'Bee studied social work. However, in an interview on her personal history, "Milwaukee's matriarch of the funeral industry" showed that she also had learned women's history. "Women were the caregivers of the dead" in ancient times, she said, so "it should never have been unusual for women to be in the funeral business" in the modern era. Another future leader, Catherine Conroy, schooled herself for her field after hard lessons in life. Adopted into a family of eleven children, she had a comfortable suburban childhood until the Great Depression. The family moved often into ever-declining housing in the city, where Conroy attended eight different schools and did not consider college. She worked first in domestic service and then for the local telephone company, a typical employer of the time with women at clerical levels and men in management. By 1950, Conroy was a union organizer and a captain on picket lines in the first nationwide strike against "Ma Bell." After the strike, Conroy served as president of her Milwaukee local, a position in the labor movement that would make hers an important voice for workers in the later women's movement.[5]

Nor would rural women remain distant from the women's movement in the decades ahead, even one who chose a life of isolation on an island in the Rock River near Lake Koshkonong. One of the period's most important avant-garde poets lived in poverty, without electricity or plumbing, while penning paeans to her "life by water," as Lorine Niedecker titled one of her volumes. Comparing her life to those of earlier women writers, she wrote that "the Brontes had their moors" but "I have my marshes." After she had to leave college to care for her mother and a brief marriage that ended badly, Niedecker became a self-taught "folk poet" and an early feminist poet who wished for less housework and more time for writing. Her poems on gender and sexual politics brought friendships by correspondence with poets far from Fort Atkinson, where she had to walk five miles to work as a hospital cleaning woman in the 1950s. Almost thirty years after the publication of her first poems and fifteen years after the publication of her first volume of collected works, the success of her second volume and a successful second marriage came late in a life lived in constant struggle for survival. However, it was a life lived simply and well in a Wisconsin that also would survive for decades despite modern "improvements," from telephone services to freeways, where marshes were drained to make way for progress.[6]

If few, the new generation of feminists, born as the Nineteenth Amendment became law and the earlier "wave" of the women's movement ended, nevertheless bridged generations to found the next — and a tidal wave it would be. Even fewer made waves by running for elective office in the postwar era, which was "not especially noteworthy for women in state politics," as historian William F. Thompson states. No woman ever had served in the state senate, and only six had won seats in the assembly — including three at the same time in the mid-1920s, the first time that women held legislative office (see Introduction to chapter 6). Most had won only one term, and only one had served more than two terms: Mary O. Kryszak of Milwaukee, with a total of seven terms since 1929. She had left office twice, for a two-year term each time, until she left for the last time in 1947. The legislature again went without any women for a term. In 1949, two women won assembly seats, including Ruth Bachhuber Doyle of Madison, only the second Democratic woman to serve but from the fourth generation of her Wausau family in the Wisconsin legislature. However, she left after two terms because her husband became a gubernatorial candidate. He lost, and she did not run again. Decades would pass "before women would again achieve positions of comparable importance" in the Democratic party, according to Thompson — and before a Doyle, their son, would become governor of Wisconsin.[7]

In postwar Wisconsin, few Republican women fared better. Also sworn into office in the assembly in 1949 was the stalwart Sylvia Havre Raihle from Chippewa County, who would win four terms and serve the last two as the sole female "assemblyman," a term that long would remain unaltered. The state legislature returned in 1957 to men-only status for the next six years into the 1960s, the longest hiatus without women legislators since the first had served almost four decades before. By then, two other Republican women had held high office — but both only briefly, to fill vacancies, and only by appointment: Secretary of State Glenn M. Wise in 1955 and Dena A. Smith as state treasurer in 1957. The latter filled out her late husband's term, although she later would win back her office with her own name on the party ballot for four terms in the 1960s.[8]

The next woman in high office in Wisconsin, a Democrat, would not win her state post for another decade, when the phenomenal career of Vel Phillips would bridge both the women's movement and the civil rights movement, making history nationwide for her race as well as her gender. She began her rise even before Rosa Parks refused to go to the back of a bus in the South, the beginning of the modern civil rights movement. Phillips' story is less well-known but better exemplifies her people's struggle in the North. She also faced personal struggles as a woman who had to overcome her middle-class milieu and mores to serve as a bridge between women across social classes in her city. Born into Milwaukee's black elite — but on the South Side, where she would lead civil rights marches — Velvalea Rodgers grew up in the ghetto called "Bronzeville" in her increasingly segregated city. She earned her higher education by winning a national scholarship to Howard University and returned to Wisconsin for law school in the late 1940s, when even her engagement made history in her hometown as the first of an African American in the *Milwaukee Journal* women's pages. Phillips became the University of Wisconsin law school's first African American woman graduate as well as half of the first husband-and-wife team

admitted before federal courts in Milwaukee. She ran for a school board seat in 1953 and
again made history as the first candidate of color to make the ballot past the primary, although she lost in the later election. Both Phillipses became active locally in the National
Association for the Advancement of Colored People to support the NAACP's landmark
Supreme Court lawsuit to desegregate schools nationwide.[9]

By the mid-1950s, women became the majority of voters in the country, and Phillips
later credited her historic first victory to the local League of Women Voters (LWV) and
its work for minorities in Milwaukee. The local LWV served as a multicultural force for
racial progress in a Milwaukee much changed since her childhood and the city's "late
Great Migration" of African Americans, after they had moved to other cities in the North.
As they remained under-represented politically, the LWV worked for a referendum on redistricting and led voter registration drives. Phillips participated in the "doorbell-ringing
swings" and saw, "for the first time, the full story of crowded living conditions, blight, disease and ignorance" in her district. Decades later, she still recalled seeing "such poverty
— poverty like I did not know existed. I just was not aware of it." She also saw that "there
was no alderman, no county board member, no nothing" fighting for her neighborhood.
When redistricting was won and resulted in an open seat in her ward, the LWV redoubled
its work to register voters door to door, as did Phillips in running for office. She was not
deterred by a few "rebuffs" from residents, although one man "told her that as a woman,
she didn't need the salary" when men wanted the work. She also was not deterred by her
first pregnancy, although Phillips maintained her privacy and delayed a press announce-
ment until the day after the election. The expected resistance to her gender and race was
a sufficient political obstacle, and persuading voters to back an expectant mother probably was a hurdle beyond hope in the era. But every doorbell made a difference. In 1956,
Phillips became the first woman and first African American "alderman" in Milwaukee.[10]

Perceptions of women in politics in the 1950s are clearly evident in the post-election
coverage of Phillips's success, because the local press focused less on her race than on her
gender. Milwaukeeans read reassurances that she did not espouse egalitarian feminism to
effect complete equality. Instead, she embraced the "social feminist" perspective of the
League of Women Voters, which emphasized gender difference. "Women do bring something to public office that men do not," she declared, because women were "not thinking
of selfish motives and must have a real feeling for the work." Speaking in Sheboygan, she
won over clubwomen with a traditional appeal. "Women must be a conscience in politics,
as motherhood must go beyond the kitchen," she said, "in a rapidly changing world where
a woman's voice must be heard." However, Milwaukee's mainstream media did not hear
her message. Their stories focused instead on frivolous issues, tut-tutting about the title
that officials bestowed upon Phillips: "Madam Alderman." Milwaukee's more sympathetic
black press commented that she "had to constantly overcome double prejudices of racism
and sexism," proving herself not only to the media but also to "council members, constituents and others who felt a woman should be at home or engaged in brewing coffee or
taking shorthand for a male employer."[11]

Most women did not so openly defy "the feminine mystique," the title of a later book by Betty Friedan that would look back unfavorably on the 1950s and identify the media as largely responsible for a generation's dissatisfaction with domesticity and their gendered roles. An increasingly influential factor in the 1950s, the media promulgated the "dominant domestic ideology" of the decade that "defined women's place in the postwar, family-centered, prosperous, middle-class lifestyle," as historian Sara M. Evans writes. That ideology conflicted with the reality for many women in Wisconsin. Their numbers in the state workforce more than doubled, comprising more than a third of working-age women in the decade, despite "high marriage rates after the war and through the 1950s, when the cult of domesticity was at its height" across the country, according to historian Robert C. Nesbit. More than half of women in the previous generation had remained unmarried at the age of twenty-five, while less than a third of their daughters risked the stigma of remaining single at the same age. So most women in Wisconsin and nationwide in the 1950s married earlier than had their mothers.[12]

The resultant rise in the birth rate meant that many became working mothers, working outside the homes where the media told women that they belonged. Magazines and newspapers dominated the marketplace and targeted women with advice on fashion and food and with advice columns, including one read statewide in the *Milwaukee Journal* and written by the beloved "IQG," Ione Quinby Griggs, who was named Wisconsin's outstanding woman journalist in 1949. As a colleague wrote of the paper's most popular columnist, "thousands of letters crossed her desk from people seeking help, everyone from battered wives to unwed mothers." Their correspondence reflected the daily worries of Wisconsin women, from a Milwaukee woman who found a long-lost granddaughter with the help of other readers to a "runaway wife" whose lovelorn husband threatened suicide until the *Journal* columnist personally reconciled the couple. Never without her hat in the newsroom, "Dear Mrs. Griggs" was a fixture of daily life in Wisconsin, well into her nineties, as a source of unchanging solace and comfort for readers of all ages in the fast-changing decades to come.[13]

Girls growing up in the 1950s were more susceptible to the new media technology of television that targeted impressionable minds with advice through advertising, an insidious and incessant means to instill the ideology of "the feminine mystique." Only decades later did women's words emerge to counter the unrealistic vision of families and women that they had seen on their flickering screens. Sara Hellerud De Luca attests to the impact of television and its reach even into rural Wisconsin in her autobiographical *Dancing the Cows Home*. She regales her readers with tales of twin sisters' adolescent fantasies on a Polk County dairy farm where, inspired by a commercial, both girls aspired to be ballerinas and practiced by leaping barbed-wire bales or pirouetting around milk cans. Her recollection serves as a reminder that, despite postwar population shifts and the prevalence of urban and suburban lifestyles portrayed on television, rural Wisconsin was not "doomed to extinction," as Nesbit also suggests.[14]

A Wisconsin already more urban than rural soon also became more suburban as commuters lived far from workplaces while their families found new places such as shopping malls to form community life. Postwar population growth accelerated for the fastest rate in the state in fifty years, especially in the southeastern region. The cities of Milwaukee and Madison benefited from massive population shifts, while almost half of the counties in the rest of the state lost residents. Milwaukee County alone attracted numbers of new-comers equivalent to the entire population of Madison, and metropolitan Milwaukee sur-passed more than a million residents by 1960. However, the significant turning point for the new suburban mothers in Wisconsin may have come sooner, in 1957, when their turnout for a statewide referendum finally won the day for daylight saving time. Long de-layed by farmers whose workday began by dawn, daylight saving time meant more outdoor leisure time at the end of the workday for businessmen commuting from cities to suburbs. They also wanted their clocks set to be more compatible with their counterparts who al-ready had won daylight saving time in many bordering states and in the eastern time zone. For urban and suburban mothers, the issue was safety in school zones. Many children in rural districts rode school buses, while more urban and suburban children walked to school — and did so in the dark during Wisconsin winters until daylight saving time was won. "But for more and more mothers," as Thompson writes, "suburban life had its dis-contents" that led many women into more campaigns to move Wisconsin ahead of the times, like its clocks every spring ever since.[15]

The cities would be only one center of the modern women's movement soon to come, if not soon enough for the feminists of the 1950s from suburbs to dairy farms — and their daughters. The state's postwar birth rate peaked at almost one hundred thousand births per year by the end of the 1950s, and public school enrollments had almost doubled in the decade. More "baby boomers" graduated from high school in Wisconsin than in most states, and more girls earned diplomas than did boys. But the gender ratio reversed when their generation went on to college. More in Wisconsin went to college than elsewhere or in earlier eras: a third of the high school graduates in the state by the end of the 1950s, which was four times as many as in their parents' generation and twice the national aver-age in their own. But more men than women went to college, in part because men bene-fited from federal financial aid through the G.I. Bill, when women were not as welcome in the military. Most women veterans had served in auxiliary forces, not covered by the bill, although they were not exempt from the costs of war; nurse Doris Brown of Milwau-kee had served and died in the Korean conflict in the early 1950s. By the mid-1950s, more women went to college, and their numbers on state campuses would almost double in the next decade. The number of campuses also increased as the ten state teachers colleges — the former normal schools — became state universities in the mid-1950s. But women were less likely than men to complete college degrees — and less likely than their mothers' generation to complete advanced degrees. Many who became mothers were prevented from earning even high school degrees; state law did not forbid school districts from forc-ing pregnant girls to drop out until decades later. By the 1960s, women still comprised lit-tle more than a third of the students at the University of Wisconsin–Madison and would remain a minority on state campuses for decades more.[16]

For women to earn the education and employment they wanted would take a revolu-tion — or several revolutions, from the women's movement to women's studies, which would come from a collaboration in Madison of unlikely revolutionaries who hardly looked the part: Ruth Bachhuber Doyle, the former legislator, and Kathryn Frederick Clarenbach. Both dressed conservatively but fashionably, both were married and mothers, and both would raise sons who would rise in state politics. Both women were well-educated, and both found work in the educational bureaucracy that boomed in the state capital with the state birth rate. But both also had trained in the traditional role of women in Madison, where they learned the lessons of grassroots politics that were deemed unimportant by many men of the town. According to Nesbit, professors — almost all of whom were men at that time — "tended to be long on political conscience but shunned canvassing a block. Their wives were better at this."[17]

Clarenbach, a Sparta native and an alumna of the University of Wisconsin with three degrees including a Ph.D., had been a professor of political science before returning to Madison in the 1950s, but not as a faculty member. With Doyle, she worked in what many thought of as the University of Wisconsin's longtime limbo for women, the Extension. However, the Extension's "homemakers clubs" had evolved into an effective and statewide network of women, especially after their experience in collaborating on exhibits for the state centennial in 1948. Clubs "from farm areas and cities were active in creating displays regarding women's role in state history," according to an account of the start of women's studies in the state. The Extension "drew more and more women into public roles" as well as its noncredit courses in the 1950s and encouraged the homemakers who "yearned for a way to better themselves, for an outlet outside their homes, or for a return to school or job."[18]

A canvass of women students statewide in the UW Extension in 1958 found that most worked outside their homes and wanted more courses for career advancement and educational enrichment, as only a third had completed high school. Doyle and Clarenbach expanded the study with a second survey in Madison of faculty wives and other married women, finding that many had interrupted their own educations for husbands and families and wanted to complete their degrees. However, the women felt unwelcome on the Madison campus, where men comprised more than two-thirds of students. The potential market persuaded the university to take its "Wisconsin Idea" to women at last, with a professorship and a new administrative post for Clarenbach to create programs from career counseling to flexible scheduling. She coordinated her work with women already running a similar program in place at Milwaukee's UW Extension, where women students still outnumbered men, although the transformation in the mid-1950s of the former Milwaukee State Teachers College to a state university was reversing the gender ratio there as well. While the UW Extension would continue to serve women statewide beyond academe, Clarenbach would become "Wisconsin's leading spokeswoman for women's causes," according to Thompson, for almost forty years.[19]

Clarenbach was positioned in Madison for prominence in the coming movement as events raised women's consciousness of their issues nationwide. In 1963, journalist Betty Friedan's book, *The Feminine Mystique,* became a bestseller for her analysis of media and other societal forces that had "forced women out of public life and into a passive and infantilizing domesticity," as Evans writes. Passage of the Equal Pay Act in 1963 followed a presidential order against gender discrimination in federal hiring, following in turn from the final report of the first Presidential Commission on the Status of Women. Primarily middle-aged, middle-class professional women, the members of the commission could not bring themselves to support an Equal Rights Amendment, writes Evans. But their report "spelled out the realities of inequality" in existing laws from health care to child care, and from employment to holding political office, and called for similar studies at the state level.[20]

The national commission placed a priority on continuing education for women, which was the role of the UW Extension and led to a gubernatorial appointment for Clarenbach as chair of a state Commission on the Status of Women in 1963. Although Wisconsin was "light years ahead of other states" in having a commission, as she later recalled, the state had much work ahead as well. A sign of hope came in 1963 with the return of women to the floor of the state legislature for the first time in three terms. One of two women in the assembly at the time was Esther Doughty Luckhardt of Dodge County. Her opponent had campaigned on the slogan "It's a man's job," Luckhardt said, at a time when the only state-issued occupational licenses for women were in nursing and teaching. She also recalled the absence of a women's restroom near the assembly chamber until her second term, forty years after the first women had served in the Wisconsin legislature. Luckhardt would serve eleven terms, a record for women legislators not surpassed for forty years after she first won her seat in the assembly.[21]

Although Wisconsin also was almost forty years away from sending a woman to the U.S. Congress, several events encouraged the few congresswomen from elsewhere to improve opportunities for women everywhere in the country. The League of Women Voters became more activist in support of the cause of reapportionment, won when the U.S. Supreme Court issued what became known — without intentional irony, which is revealing of the time before women joined the justices — as the "One Man, One Vote" doctrine. Two congresswomen won inclusion of gender discrimination in Title VII of the Civil Rights Act of 1964, "the strongest legal tool yet available to women," according to Evans, although a new Equal Employment Opportunity Commission refused to enforce the amendment. However, one sponsor of the amendment, Senator Margaret Chase Smith, saw her name placed in nomination for the presidency at the 1964 Republican convention. "Despite condescending comments from males in the party," according to a reporter, the first presidential nomination of a woman by a major party "turned the convention into a college pep rally" as women students took to the floor, waving signs and Smith's trademark red roses. Breaking tradition by coming to the convention to see her nominating speech, Smith said she would not miss the moment and hoped she had won a "breakthrough" for "younger women of this country, as suffragettes helped pave the way for me."[22]

However, the significance of the series of historic events and the serious-minded states' commissions was not yet evident in 1964, when an even younger female cohort arose across the country in a seemingly frivolous phenomenon called "Beatlemania" by the media. At the time, meetings of middle-aged matrons mapping the future of women apparently had nothing in common with gangs of screaming teenaged girls in the streets of Milwaukee who mobbed the mop-topped group from Britain on "America's first modern rock 'n' roll tour," according to historian Jonathan Kasparek. The Beatles had an important role in more than music history, writes media studies scholar Susan J. Douglas, who suggests their significance in women's history. For the first generation raised on television and with transistor radios, the tour of the "Fab Four" came at "a critical point in the evolution of girl culture" and created a "sense of cultural and social collectivity" through the media, writes Douglas. In the frenzy of adolescent girls, she sees the "seeds of female yearning and female revolt" that the media-savvy generation soon would transform into a movement for women. Douglas also suggests that the boyish Beatles served to lessen a sense of loss among girls who saw a president assassinated and fathers and brothers sent overseas to serve in Vietnam. [23]

Women again went to war, with many from Wisconsin among the almost eight thousand who served in the military in Vietnam, although not yet in combat roles. Some served as air traffic controllers, as intelligence officers, and in other support positions. A few were physicians or physical therapists, although most served as nurses or in other nurturing roles, as did more than eight hundred civilian women in the Red Cross and Special Services. One Wisconsin woman worked as a war correspondent, and photojournalist Georgette "Dickey" Chapelle became the first female correspondent killed in action in her country's history. A nonconformist from her girlhood in the "staid," "stifling," and "conservative" midwestern community of Shorewood, she had "dreamed of flying airplanes," instead of playing with dolls, according to a biographer. The "feisty combat reporter" first gained fame in World War II for her coverage of Iwo Jima and Okinawa, then covered more major wars for *Life, Look, National Geographic,* and other magazines, and spent five weeks in a Budapest prison. She won major awards from media for decades, "despite difficulties with military men unused to a woman at the front — especially a tiny, "middle-aged woman with the voice of a Marine drill instructor" who "hit her stride at the age of forty." She was known for her "signature uniform" of fatigues paired with a bush hat and more feminine accessories, although a male colleague recalled Chapelle as a reporter "who refused to trade on her femininity to get stories — and didn't need" to do so. She was wearing her trademark pearl earrings on patrol with troops in Vietnam in 1965, when a landmine was tripped. The last words of the woman who had "stayed the longest and gone further forward than any reporter, man or woman," were: "I guess it was bound to happen." Marines named a hospital in Vietnam for Chapelle, while state university students in Madison supported a drive in her memory for CARE packages for troops in Vietnam.[24]

Many women who stayed in Wisconsin would support the more than fifty-seven thousand men from the state to serve in Vietnam by the war's end; thousands of Wisconsin women would be widowed, while others mourned fallen sons, brothers, and fathers. However, other women would march in the antiwar movement called the "war at home" that came to the Madison campus only in 1965, when the first ground troops — still a volunteer force — went to Vietnam. The movement spread slowly to other state campuses as women saw male classmates drafted if they lost college deferments or lost out in the dreaded draft lottery instituted at the end of the decade — or if they left the country as "draft dodgers" fleeing to Canada. Women of color in Wisconsin saw minority men drafted and dying in disproportionate numbers, as few had college deferments. By the mid-1960s, more than thirty-five thousand University of Wisconsin students statewide included barely more than three hundred African Americans, most of them at the Milwaukee campus, according to a survey by the UW System's Ruth Bachhuber Doyle. She reported that the results "came as a shock to officials" in Madison, who never had made a count of minorities. Her report and others on the status of minorities in the state helped the civil rights movement in cities such as Madison and Milwaukee to gain momentum.[25]

Amid media attention to other movements, the state commission on women's status competed for the public agenda in Wisconsin. In 1965, women won legislative approval to amend an example of "archaic views of equality" in state statutes, as Clarenbach labeled a law that did not allow mothers to sign minors' applications for drivers' licenses. But the governor vetoed the bill based on a legal opinion — not from a lawyer but from the motor vehicle department — that only fathers were "heads of households." Clarenbach publicly vowed to research other state laws that also "reflected poorly on the intelligence and responsibility of women." She also promoted the commission's agenda from issues in the workplace to the placement of advertising for employment in the first place. To a state industrial commission member who worried that women would get "jobs where they just get dirty," Clarenbach responded in the press that "women get into some pretty dirty jobs right in their own homes." To a federal recommendation that newspapers no longer list "help wanted" advertising under "male" or "female" categories, she responded in an interview in Milwaukee that "one big newspaper in this city has said that over its dead body would it change the format on classified advertising" — to which the Journal Company replied that it was not up to the newspaper but "up to the advertiser if he wants to discriminate." Only after many newspapers in the state decided it was up to them and dropped gendered advertising by the mid-1970s would Milwaukee's major newspapers do so.[26]

Although all states' commissions on women's status convened annually in the nation's capital, the meetings merited little media coverage because participants repeatedly refused any resolutions that actually required action — until 1966, when some of the members met on their own to found an advocacy group: the National Organization for Women. NOW's founders included Clarenbach and Conroy, who were unknown to most women from the East. They initially distrusted "the tall, dignified Wisconsin women's leader" — Clarenbach — and "her Wisconsin cronies," who were suspected of being spies from "hostile government agencies," according to historian Marcia Cohen. As for Betty Friedan, who named NOW and served as president, she saw Clarenbach as "a slow-witted Midwesterner." However, others came to appreciate "the cool-headed Clarenbach" and nominated her as the first chair of NOW. Conroy made the first donation — five dollars — to the treasury. At the day's end, NOW began its existence with $135. At the year's end, Wisconsin women comprised more than a third of the fewer than thirty founding members at the first convention, and three from Milwaukee served on the first board of NOW with Clarenbach. As Cohen notes, Clarenbach's "prestige far outweighed [Friedan's] media-oriented flamboyance" for midwestern women, although Friedan's attention-getting tactics and media access in the East eventually meshed well with the "sweat-labor organizational work" that "poured out of Kay's Wisconsin office" — her UW Extension ofice that served NOW in sending news releases, "letters, notices, minutes," and more.[27]

The need for advocacy for working women made news in Wisconsin and nationwide in newsrooms in 1966. The country's oldest press club, in existence in Milwaukee since 1885, denied equal access to women journalists, although many had won its awards for excellence in the field. Restricted from press conferences and crucial contacts at the press club, several newswomen asked for access with no success and then picketed the site, carrying signs guaranteed to capture news coverage. But their brethren in the media withstood progress for five more years, and the Milwaukee Press Club would become not only the oldest but also the only such men-only media organization in the country. Not until the next decade would the first woman, a fashion editor, enter the club during daytime. However, news photographers awaited the arrival of Ione Quinby Griggs, by then in her eighties but still writing her daily advice column. They snapped her on a barstool next to a female "copyboy," the term still used at the time for women college students who ran newsroom errands.[28]

Another media campaign across Wisconsin actually succeeded in changing state law to set back women in the law-and-order workplace. Progress for women in policing had been a cause for clubwomen since the previous century, when they won appointment in Milwaukee of a police matron for women prisoners (see Introduction to chapter 5), and a few Wisconsin counties had elected the first women sheriffs soon after full suffrage in 1920. However, research by Dorothy Moses Schulz and Steve Houghton reveals that most of the pioneering women in policing actually were "married to the job" as "unpaid jail assistants." They sought office only for the benefit of their husbands, who were incumbent sheriffs barred by state law from seeking successive terms. That lawmen bypassed the law by putting their wives on the ballot, as well as their male undersheriffs, long received little notice until "newspaper coverage of five wives replacing their husbands in 1966" resulted in a statewide referendum on the issue. The "growing demands by women for equal rights may have caused voters to view a past practice in a new light," as Schulz and Houghton write. An unenlightened sheriffs' association unleashed a media blitz to abolish term limits, and a typical commentary by a male columnist held that the office of sheriff was "peculiarly masculine" and no place for a wife and mother. Voters agreed. No women won office as sheriff in Wisconsin for the next fifteen years.[29]

The movement for women's rights made few more headlines for a time, as African Americans' advocacy for civil rights eclipsed other causes when urban riots erupted nationwide and in Wisconsin in 1967, the worst year of violence in many cities' streets. Years of nonviolent protests in Vel Phillips's city and hundreds of nights of marches against discrimination in housing, education, and employment ended in the "long, hot summer" of 1967 and one long night of disorder that led to three deaths, more than a hundred injuries, and mass arrests of more than seventeen hundred Milwaukeeans. The mayor called in five thousand armed National Guardsmen and sent them into Phillips's neighborhood, while the city was placed under curfew for a week and a half. The marches then resumed — as did racist reactions. At a rally following the firebombing of the NAACP youth center, Phillips was arrested, along with more than a hundred other activists. One was Father James Groppi, a local civil rights leader also born on the South Side, like Phillips, but assigned to an inner-city parish a few years before. The arrests of an African American city official and a white priest brought national media to the city that they called the "Selma of the North." As a broadcaster said, Milwaukee had become "held up to the nation as a symbol of hatred and bigotry." Phillips would recall that "our marches were a different kind than Selma, but in many ways just as terrifying."[30]

Days after the arrest of the city's only alderwoman, Milwaukee aldermen — and all of the rest were men, and white, more than a decade after her historic election — continued to unanimously oppose even consideration of a housing ordinance, the Fair Housing Law that Phillips had proposed for more than five years. "Physically and emotionally fatigued by the past week's events," according to a reporter, Phillips "fought to hold back tears of anger and sorrow." She would not cry in public, although she admitted years later to "many, many teary nights. It was as simple as that. I'd cry myself to sleep. . . . Wherever I was the first black, I was also usually the first woman. And there were certain things you just couldn't do. You couldn't show a tear because that, of course, would be too female." Instead, she escaped Wisconsin to lead a women's antiwar march in Washington with the Jeannette Rankin Brigade. Not until 1968, following the national tragedy of the assassination of Martin Luther King Jr., would Congress finally pass a federal open housing law. A week later, Milwaukee aldermen finally approved her Fair Housing Law. By then, the election of the city's first African American alderman also had brought an end to her twelve years of standing alone as the representative for her race, although Phillips long remained the lone alderwoman in the largest city in Wisconsin.[31]

However, in her neighborhood, Phillips hardly worked alone. Other women not born into Milwaukee's "black elite" but who also had higher education, most also at historically black colleges, had moved to the city and become community leaders. Ardie Clark Halyard, the first woman president of the local NAACP chapter in the early 1950s, also worked as half of the husband-and-wife ownership of a savings and loan company that built the community when no banks would back black businesses. She became bank president after her husband's death. Her successor in the NAACP, Thalia Winfield, would finance a program to build housing for moderate-income families in Milwaukee's inner city that was pioneered by the Reverend Gertrude Norris Pitts. The pastor since the 1950s of a Pentecostal congregation, in a church that she had built on Halyard Street in Milwaukee, Pitts would become the first female bishop in the Pentecostal faith. Mary Ellen Shadd Jones, a direct descendant of the first African American woman publisher, was the first woman publisher in Milwaukee's black press in the late 1950s and early 1960s, followed by Patricia O'Flynn Thomas Patillo, the publisher of a newspaper that endured for decades. Mildred Harpole, a lawyer and public schoolteacher who had helped to organize a boycott of the city's schools in 1964 and alternative "Freedom Schools" for a day, also helped to found an enduring alternative, Harambee School, as its first head administrator in 1970. Clara New of the University of Wisconsin–Milwaukee and Marian McEvilly of the local black press both won election to the Milwaukee School Board in 1975.[32]

The matriarch of Milwaukee's black press, Mattiebelle Woods, came to the city early in the twentieth century and continued to cover her community into the next millennium, when she was called the country's oldest working journalist. She wrote her first society column in 1950 and her last one fifty-four years later, only weeks before Woods died at the age of 102. More than a society columnist, she also served as "the community conscience," according to a member of Congress among the many women she mentored, no matter their race. Woods met with civil rights leaders from W.E.B. DuBois to Desmond Tutu to Martin Luther King Jr. and went to the White House at the invitation of the president when she was in her nineties. More typical of Milwaukee's women of color after the late Great Migration to the city was Claretta Simpson, called "Mother Freedom" in her community. She moved from Mississippi in the 1950s and was in her sixties in the 1960s, when she marched with Martin Luther King Jr. In 1970, she founded the Career Development Center to train youth of color for employment. Her agency helped hundreds of young women and men and would continue into the next millennium, as did she, when hundreds celebrated her hundredth birthday. "It was just what I wanted," said "Mother Freedom" of having an audience again. "There is still plenty I can tell people that they don't already know."[33]

African Americans were not alone in marching for their civil rights, as the city's South Side Hispanic community also protested employment discrimination. A march in 1968 marked "the opening salvo for the Latino protest movement" in the city, according to historian Joseph Rodriguez. The movement was brought north from Texas by Mexican Americans raised in the migrant rights movement, whom Rodriguez calls the "new generation of Latino leaders" — and Latinas including Rose Balderos, Josephine Chacon, Juanita Renteria, Gloria Salas, and Lalo Valdez. The generation ahead of them already had founded agencies such as the Council for the Spanish Speaking and the United Community Center, called the UCC, and faced a critical time for the community in 1969. The Milwaukee archdiocese closed the beloved Our Lady of Guadalupe school, which innovative women religious helped to save by running it with residents as a nonsectarian institution. The community also took control of the UCC in 1969, when it also became resident-run, although the "transition committee" was almost all male, and reopened it as a recreational center promoting primarily male sports. But one member of the committee was Rose Guajardo, a native of Mexico who had moved to Milwaukee at the age of fourteen, entered a convent three years later, earned a degree from Alverno College, and then left the order and began her career as a substitute teacher in city schools. In 1969, she became the first bilingual education supervisor in the Milwaukee Public Schools. She soon also became more influential in both the city's schools and her community's center, as the UCC evolved into an agency providing multiple services to all members of her community, eventually including counseling and housing programs for Hispanic women.[34]

The end of a decade dominated by the civil rights and antiwar movements was also a turning point in media attention to the women's movement. NOW and other new organizations led the way, but their numbers were low compared to legions of women in the more conservative League of Women Voters — more conservative nationwide than in Wisconsin. Yet even the national LWV called for action by its more than one hundred fifty thousand members in all fifty states and several territories in 1969. The call came amid celebrations of the centennial of its founding by Susan B. Anthony and Elizabeth Cady Stanton as the first woman suffrage organization. The year 1969 also marked the fiftieth anniversary of its reorganization as the League of Women Voters by Wisconsin native Carrie Chapman Catt upon passage of the Nineteenth Amendment (see "Theodora Winton Youmans and the Wisconsin Woman Movement" in chapter 6). The national LWV historically had lagged behind that of the Wisconsin chapter as early as the 1920s over the state's historic Equal Rights Amendment and the federal ERA proposed by the National Woman's Party. However, in the 1960s, state leaders played significant roles in "swinging" the national LWV to "come full circle in fifty years" from "study clubs," a member wrote. "Women armed with knowledge learned through the League often ache[d] to work for candidates," which was not allowed for officers under the official policy of nonpartisanship, she said. So state leaders already had answered a "groundswell" of demands to stop studying issues and start acting on reforms, from state finance statutes to fair housing laws. The national LWV — soon led by Ruth Chickering Clusen of Allouez — followed Wisconsin women's lead after a survey found, according to the local member's account, that "young women were mostly diffident about the League" compared to campus organizations.[35]

In the late 1960s, the first courses in women's studies surfaced on campuses in Wisconsin, as did resistance. Some women faculty were turned down for tenure even for volunteering their teaching time or sponsoring noncredit courses self-taught by students, but other women stepped in and would not be stopped. Credit courses soon arose almost simultaneously on several UW campuses as women fought for funding for full curricular programs. The first program came at the Milwaukee campus in 1971, the year of the first national conference in women's studies and a regional conference at Alverno College. That year, the first women's studies course came to the Madison campus, followed in 1972 by the first women's history course. Approval of the federal Title IX act, also in 1972, fueled colorful protests over the century-old issue of athletic facilities for women on the Madison campus (see "The University in 1874–1887" in chapter 4). They gained access to most facilities and approval of a full women's studies program in 1975. The first women's resource center — for support services, not studies — arose at the Green Bay campus in the mid-1970s, followed by others whose impact on campuses proved formative even for women students who were not in women's studies. Shirley Krug, a daughter of immigrants with eighth-grade educations who could not speak English when they came to Milwaukee, came to UW–Milwaukee and became active in campus politics, starting a women's resource center and winning the presidency of the student association. Krug stayed to earn a master's degree in economics — and would graduate from student government to state government when she won a seat in the assembly.[36]

However, the state with "Forward" as its motto, Wisconsin, went backward on women's status in the 1970s in a harbinger of the conservative backlash to come across the country.

Despite state legislators' early ratification in 1972 of the federal ERA, Wisconsin voters went against the same wording in their own state constitution. The state's schizophrenic split on the ERA was recalled in a later account by former Madison legislator Marjorie "Midge" Leeper Miller, who had won election to the state assembly in 1971 and served on the board of the new, nationwide Women's Political Caucus. "With the new surge of feminism, there was talk of the ERA across the country" as well as on the floor of Congress, so she introduced a new "state ERA" in Wisconsin — the state with the country's first ERA, half a century earlier. Her version, like the law proposed at the federal level, would have eliminated essentially only the "protective clause" in the 1921 Wisconsin ERA (see Introduction to chapter 6) to more closely match the wording of the federal amendment.[37]

In 1972, after Congress passed the federal ERA and sent it to the states, Wisconsin's legislature and many others ratified swiftly. Miller's bill already had won the first of two legislative approvals in successive sessions required for state constitutional amendments; she recalled that ratification of the federal ERA "was easy because we already had our discussions when we approved the first state passage" and also "went rather smoothly because it was assumed that ERA would soon be the law." Then an anti-ERA campaign arose nationwide from nearby Illinois, where "Phyllis Schlafly and other ultraconservatives began creating a backlash by claiming all sorts of dire consequences" to come from amending the Constitution to include equality for women. Faced with putting the state amendment to voters at the polls, Wisconsin's optimistic ERA backers opted to go on the ballot as soon as possible rather than "give the growing anti-ERA forces more time to fight it," Miller later wrote. However, her side had miscalculated. "We made a great mistake to let that constitutional declaration of equality slip through our fingers," she wrote, when the referendum went against a new state ERA in 1973. Worse, the result of Wisconsin's referendum was seen as "the first defeat of a state ERA in the country," rather than as a refusal to amend only a clause in a state ERA that stayed on the books. The anti-ERA campaign in Wisconsin had an incalculable cost countrywide, as it energized Schlafly and her forces to defeat the federal ERA in Illinois and elsewhere. Even after extension of the time limit for ratification — the first time limit ever required for a federal amendment — the ERA fell short, although by only a few states. "It was lost," as Miller recalled, "despite being overwhelmingly supported by the American people," if not those in Wisconsin.[38]

Legislators would act over time to essentially implement the lost ERA, improving the existing Wisconsin ERA with new statutes on sexual assault, divorce reform, and marital property rights. As Miller wrote, "the women's movement went on to achieve passage of many important pieces of legislation that brought equality to both sexes" and "corrected many of the most grievous discriminations" in state law, adding that "some of the problems that had worried opponents, such as women in the military, have also come about, anyway." She was not embittered by the ERA defeats because, in her view, "we did a lot to move women towards equality and to make their lives better," as had many women before her.[39]

Miller wrote that she had learned from the legacy left by her foremothers — including her own mother — who also had learned hard lessons when they led an earlier "wave" of the women's movement for their daughters to follow.

We feminists have been weakened more by our successes than by our failures. Many women . . . now take for granted their improved position. I was like that at the time. I never really talked to my mother about women getting the vote, even though she had the interesting experience of being elected county superintend-ent of schools in 1911 — nine years before the suffrage guarantee. . . . I grew up thinking we were born with voting rights and not even realizing my own mother was a pioneer.[40]

Watching as "women have continued to be elected in increasing numbers and have moved into many positions previously held only by men," Miller passed on the family's political legacy to her son Mark, who followed her into the legislature and said her example showed him "how one who sticks to values can really cause change."[41]

His mother had helped to set a record of four women legislators for the first time in 1971; two years later, in the same year that Wisconsin voters vetoed the ERA, they elected more women into high office than ever before. In 1973, Barbara S. Thompson became the first woman state superintendent of public instruction, while Miller served among seven women in the assembly. In the next term, their number in the assembly went into double digits, and the number never dropped into single digits again. Even more significant in 1975 was the election of the first woman to the upper house of the state legislature, Kathryn Morrison of Platteville; she won reelection two years later and welcomed a sec-ond woman, also a Democrat, to the state senate. By the end of the 1970s and the begin-ning of a conservative comeback, Republicans returned to their customary dominance of Wisconsin politics, winning in part with the next several women in the state senate while also gaining on Democrats' edge in the number of women in the assembly in the next decade.

Many women probably cared less about political agendas than "pocketbook issues" of stretching paychecks to put food on the table, including the "oleo wars" in the Dairy State that finally ended in the 1970s. For the sake of farmers, their rural legislators had fought to retain Wisconsin's ban on butter substitutes since the previous century. Well after wartime shortages had made less costly oleomargarine acceptable for many consumers and repeals after 1950 of taxes and bans elsewhere, "pro-butter" men in the state legisla-ture would not budge. Wisconsin housewives had only "white oleo," which came with packets of yellow food coloring and required laborious stirring. The law turned the state lawless as even church groups organized "oleo smuggling" by owners of station wagons, who crossed state borders to bring back colored oleo by the case for the sizeable families of the "baby boom." By the mid-1960s, as redistricting had begun to reduce the dispropor-tionate power of the rural bloc in the legislature, women had become involved in a "pro-oleo" campaign, and the women's pages of one major Milwaukee newspaper had published a series on "The Oleo Revolt." Repeal of the ban had been won in 1967 in a bill signed by the governor, with yellow pens given to women and others present. But the "pro-oleo" contingent continued to campaign against a state tax that made margarine more costly than butter, and they finally won repeal in the 1970s with the support of several newly elected women legislators. More women in Wisconsin had developed a taste for politics, if not for dairy products.[42]

Wisconsin women also made inroads in the legal system in the 1970s. After fifteen years as an alderwoman, Vel Phillips resigned in 1971, upon her appointment as the first woman in the Milwaukee County judiciary — and the first African American judge in Wisconsin — but later she lost her bid for reelection to the bench in her own right. In 1976, at the highest level of the state judiciary, Shirley S. Abrahamson became the first woman on the bench of the Wisconsin Supreme Court, although also by appointment and more than half a century after the first woman justice was elected to a state supreme court elsewhere. As Abrahamson later noted in a lecture on legal history, women lawyers and judges were "still 'tokens' in the courtroom and profession," despite progress made since her years in law school in the 1950s. One of her teachers had refused to hire her even for part-time work in his law firm, fearing that "people would gossip if he worked with a woman," she said. "The fact that his secretary was a woman seemed irrelevant." When she graduated at the top of her class, the law school dean warned that a woman would not "land a job with a law firm . . . except perhaps as the firm's law librarian." But women on the bench could be "beacons for change and progress," because their presence "conveys the message that women can play important roles" in the law, she said, and conferred "a sense of empowerment, a sense of what is within reach for women in any field." She faced her first election only a few years after Phillips's run but won with bipartisan support from women statewide. However, Abrahamson would remain the only woman on the state's high court for fifteen years.[43]

After fifteen years of chairing the state commission on women's status and changing their status in the UW System, Kay Clarenbach took a leave as a consultant in planning two watershed events for women worldwide and in her country in the 1970s. The International Women's Year celebration in 1975 concluded with a call for conferences in every country, and Clarenbach worked for conferences in every state. Her own state served as a model in 1977, when more than twelve hundred Wisconsin women convened in Madison to elect delegates to the historic National Women's Conference to be held in Houston that year. Not all in attendance in Madison were in agreement on proposals for the agenda at the national event; according to an account by Clarenbach, "the Equal Rights Amendment and abortion rights were the most controversial issues," and "although the opponents were few in number, they were very vocal with their views." Four regional events in the state followed for rural women whose concerns Clarenbach summarized in a report to a national council on women's education that described "the diversity of needs of rural women from farmwife entrepreneurs to Spanish-speaking migrants to tribal women on reservations." All were represented among twenty thousand attendees in Houston that year. By bringing together women statewide, nationwide, and worldwide, the conferences in the 1970s awakened a new generation to mutual concerns as well as "contacts and conflicts," according to Evans, and "generated moving stories of change and reconciliation" across cultures.[44]

A Wisconsin more measurably multicultural with every census also saw a continued rise of women from many cultures, including one woman who had been raised on one of the tribal reservations described in the report on the diversity of rural areas' needs. Ada E. Deer later testified to a congressional committee that growing up on the Keshena reservation in a cabin without the "conveniences" of electricity and plumbing, she "never felt poor in spirit," owing to her mother. A non-Native, Deer's mother had served the reservation as a nurse and instilled her "commitment to service" and educational aims in her daughter. Deer earned a tribal scholarship to the University of Wisconsin–Madison in the mid-1950s and became its first Menominee graduate, then the first Native American to earn a master's degree at Columbia University. In her years away from the reservation, her nation was first to face another federal turnabout in the treatment of Native Americans, this time terminating tribal rights in 1961. To preserve their identity, the Menominee asked the state to turn the reservation into a county for a ten-year trial period, pending review. As the decade ended and the deadline neared, Deer returned to Wisconsin. But she soon went to Washington as the lobbyist in Congress for the Menominee, who won their fight for self-determination, repeal of termination, and restoration of tribal status. The Memoninee elected Deer as their tribal council chair in 1974, the first woman to lead her nation. In the next year, the Forest County Potawatomi followed by electing Lois Crow as their tribal council chair.[45]

In Milwaukee, the home of the majority of minorities including Native Americans in the state, significant strides forward for women seemed to follow annually in the 1970s. An expansion in educational opportunities for teachers as well as students of color came with the promotion of the first African American principal in the Milwaukee Public Schools, Sarah A. Scott, for whom a middle school in the city was named as well as an annual award for outstanding school administrators. In 1977, the matriarch of an African American family dynasty in Milwaukee, Marcia P. Coggs, followed her late husband into the state legislature; she repeatedly was elected in her own right to the assembly, where she served for sixteen years, first with one grandnephew and then with two at the same time, while her daughter Elizabeth Coggs-Jones became a Milwaukee County supervisor.[46]

In 1978, Vel Phillips made history nationwide as the first woman and first African American elected secretary of state in Wisconsin — and as the first African American woman ever to win a statewide election to executive office in the country. In Wisconsin, the only woman who previously had held the office, by appointment, never had stepped up as the next in gubernatorial succession. During the absence of both the governor and the lieutenant governor, Phillips actually served as acting governor, if only briefly. As she delighted in recalling decades later, "the men hurried back" when they realized that she was the first woman governor of Wisconsin, for a few days — and that almost no one had noticed any difference. Phillips lost her bid for reelection, but remained the highest-ranking woman in state history for the rest of the century, although not for lack of women trying for high office in ensuing decades.[47]

One future candidate for Wisconsin secretary of state and for Congress, Ada Deer, had completed three years as chair of the Menominee Nation and returned to UW–Madison to teach in social work and the American Indian studies program that she would lead by the end of the century. Similar programs soon began at other campuses, not only in the north but also at UW–Milwaukee for a generation of Native American women and men raised far from reservations as a result of urban relocation, a federal attempt at forcing assimilation. The migration of African Americans and Mexican Americans, with a new influx from Puerto Rico, also continued to Milwaukee and other southeastern cities, where Hispanic communities campaigned for self-determination in schools. In Racine, Sara Morales managed a bilingual program, and in Milwaukee, pioneering bilingual program supervisor Rose Guajardo became an assistant principal. Guajardo recalled for a reporter her first sight of the United States, after crossing the border only to witness African Americans being denied a drink of water at a "whites only" fountain. "I had heard how the U.S. was the land of opportunity and freedom and respect," she said, but the incident made her "feel betrayed, hurt, and frustrated." In her school, Guajardo worked to welcome Wisconsin's newest immigrants: the Hmong.[48]

A once-minuscule Asian American community increased in size and complexity statewide after the Vietnam War, when Hmong Americans came to a new home in Wisconsin. Many settled in Milwaukee and Madison, while others dispersed to Appleton, Green Bay, La Crosse, Sheboygan, and Wausau, soon comprising a third of all residents of Asian heritage in the state and a fifth of all Hmong Americans nationwide. When their loyalty to the United States during the war had forced families to flee from Laos to refugee camps and then their new country, women's significance as historians of the Hmong was crucial in retaining their culture. In an oral culture without a written language and in which girls did not go to school until recent decades, Hmong women recorded the story of their people through their artistry in stitchery, or *paj ntaub*, long hidden in the Laotian highlands. Amid acculturation in Wisconsin, women's "story cloths" preserved their heritage by depicting their homeland, where many Hmong had been massacred, and then their diaspora. Like earlier newcomers, women of Asian heritage who arrived in the 1970s would emerge as leaders only later and become eloquent in their new language. Kyoko Mori earned master's and doctoral degrees at UW–Milwaukee in creative writing, then returned home to Green Bay to teach before she was hired by Harvard University. In her autobiographical account called *Polite Lies,* she wrote that Asian women were "caught between cultures." Her native language allowed women only words that signified subservience to men, she said. "In Japanese, I don't have a voice for speaking my mind."[49]

From Native Americans to newcomers, most Wisconsin women measured progress by far more than the footholds won by a few. However, fewer prospered in the 1970s, even as more women entered the workforce. While the proportion of women in well-paid professional work had not altered since 1940, more than half of the women who headed households alone and raised young children also worked, while the proportion of working wives in Wisconsin more than doubled from 1950 to 1970. The introduction of the birth-control pill in 1960 had liberated women, including Marge Engelman of Green Bay, a Methodist minister's wife who was moved to craft a commemoration of the freedom she felt from using the Pill and getting her first job. She made an American flag by using contraceptive dispensers as stars and dozens of bras for the stripes. However, a change in state law that allowed physicians to prescribe the Pill for unmarried women in Wisconsin was not won until the mid-1970s.[50]

Other churchwomen marked progress more seriously. The ordination by Presbyterians in the East of the Reverend Margaret E. Towner had made *Life* magazine in the mid-1950s, although she was allowed in a pulpit in her first church only once, and only to offer a benediction. By the mid-1970s, Towner answered a call to a pastorate in Waukesha County, the home of Lois Harkrider Stair, who had been elected as the first woman moderator — the national lay leader — by Presbyterians in 1971. However, a high school senior from Wisconsin who witnessed the election, hopeful for a new chapter in church history and aspiring to the ministry, later recalled her reception upon starting divinity studies in the mid-1970s. "At orientation we were told that all students must wear a necktie and jacket" to internship interviews, she said, calling the incident "just a preview of coming attractions at the seminary." The church's "door had been open to women" since the mid-1950s, she said, "but hearts and minds and pulpits were closed." She found a mentor in Towner, who ordained the Reverend Deborah A. Block to serve the state's oldest Presbyterian congregation, where she would become pastor by the end of the millennium. By then, her friend Dena Feingold from Janesville had served as rabbi of a Reform congregation in Kenosha since 1985 — the first woman rabbi in the state that sent her brother, Russ Feingold, to the U.S. Senate seven years later.[51]

By the 1980s, more than half of the working-age women in Wisconsin worked for pay, although most earned low pay. Families' economic need accounted in part for their numbers, according to Nesbit, who also cites the movement's success in the "beginning of a change of attitudes about working women" as a factor. However, a Milwaukee survey found that men valued housework as higher in prestige than did the women who did it — and any change in attitudes had not altered women's incomes. Statewide, men averaged significantly higher incomes than those of women in similar work, owing to fewer women in categories covered by collective bargaining. In a highly feminized field, some state teachers won collective bargaining by law only after a historic strike in Hortonville in the 1970s — and after almost a hundred had lost their jobs. Teaching would remain a predominantly female field, although men had increasingly usurped women in the prized school principal posts since 1950. By the 1970s, as the "baby boom" bust and the birth rate declined, men outnumbered women as school principals by four to one in Wisconsin.[52]

Even workers in union-protected plants lost economic security in widespread layoffs in Wisconsin, a part of the region known as the "Rustbelt" for reversals in the heavy machinery industries that long had been the state's strength. "No city collapsed during the 1980s more than Milwaukee," according to urban studies scholar Myron Orfield in a national analysis of the "most distressed cities in America." Other cities near Milwaukee, although not studied, also suffered. The closing of the country's oldest auto assembly plant put six thousand out of work in Kenosha, where women comprised more than 40 percent of the workforce. However, blue-collar men were as likely as their white-collar counterparts to expect wives to stay at home, even though those homes were made possible by working women in two-income families, suggests scholar Kathryn Marie Dudley in her study of Kenosha. One worker, a wife and mother of four, had "enabled her husband to take the risk of buying a tavern and going into business for himself," a business imperiled by the plant closing. "The contribution a working wife makes," writes Dudley, made "the difference between a precarious place just above the nation's poverty line and middle-class status," because many women earned "as much as the men they marry, or more." Moreover, many women autoworkers were "divorced or widowed, struggling to support children on their own."[53]

Many women had entered well-paid employment so late that they were the first to be let go. Sue Doro, the only woman machinist at Allis-Chalmers in West Allis in the 1970s, credited the women's movement and the Equal Employment Opportunity Commission, because the EEOC had threatened a lawsuit to win her hiring. Doro had taken the training for her nontraditional job after a divorce because, she said, "I knew I'd never be able to support a family of five kids as a receptionist." Her father had been a welder, so she "knew what blue-collar work was, and it paid real good" — but that was before the massive layoffs of her era. A tractor-shop steward until the company closed, Doro moved on to become a machine-lathe operator and safety captain at the Milwaukee Road. The only other woman there had stayed since World War II, "a 'Rosie the Riveter' who would not go away," as Doro described her coworker whose war never ended because she "fought a battle every day they didn't want you there." In her autobiographical *Blue Collar Goodbyes,* Doro wrote that older men treated her as "a daughter or a curiosity," but younger men saw her as a threat because "if a woman could do what they could do, perhaps it wasn't as hard as they thought." When the railroad was sold in the mid-1980s, Doro adapted again. She published her poetry on the human cost of plant closings, left town to lead a national organization for women in blue-collar work, and later worked for the EEOC to help others at the end of "the line."[54]

But by the 1980s, while many women had faced the loss of their livelihoods, few had faced the issues of basic survival that forever changed the women of Barneveld, where Wisconsin weather at its worst proved that it could erase the progress of centuries in seconds. In 1984, high winds hit Barneveld without warning in the night and ended nine lives, a level of loss in the little village of six hundred that would have been proportionate by population to nine thousand deaths in the city of Milwaukee at the time. Oral histories with survivors in one leveled Barneveld subdivision recorded women's words that could have been spoken by their foremothers whose accounts have not come down the decades to speak for themselves: the women in Peshtigo in 1871, when tornado-level winds turned a prairie fire into an inferno that left more than two thousand dead, or the women in New Richmond in 1899, when more than a hundred died in the worst tornado in state history. Four tornadoes had struck Dunn, Chippewa, and Clark counties on one day in 1958, taking a total of twenty-eight lives, but Barneveld's infamous twister caused more fatalities than any other tornado in Wisconsin for the rest of the century.[55]

One survivor, Mary Ann Myers, later recalled when the hail and winds hit her subdivision in Barneveld: "I knew that I must get out of bed and get my girls. . . . When I opened the door into that hallway, that side of the house had already blown away, and all I could see was a tree bending in the wind. . . . I screamed, and I gasped, and I prayed to God. There was nothing there. I was at the edge of nowhere. . . . I prayed: 'What am I going to do — my girls — where are they?' . . . I didn't know what I was going to do. I couldn't imagine what life would be like without my family."[56]

Of the four generations of her family in the village, all survived, although a grandson and his great-grandmother were among two hundred injured. Myers, other residents, and neighboring Mennonites helped for months to rebuild Barneveld, where she would become village president. Women's work — finding children separated from parents, caring for neighbors injured, mourning family members lost — is not always recorded by historians who chronicle the cost of buildings lost and rebuilt after disasters. But by their words, the women of Barneveld bring a reminder of the contribution that women have brought to Wisconsin from the beginning: rebuilding community.[57]

Across Wisconsin, as the winds of change of the 1960s and 1970s calmed, women rose to leadership in their communities and then in the legislature, where they won landmark laws. In La Crosse, where Jean Gitz Bassett was co-owner of a radio station with Evelyn Rohrer and her husband for two decades and also found time for a second career as a community volunteer, Bassett became the first woman president of the local chamber of commerce in 1977. In the political arena, Appleton apparently became the first of the state's largest cities with a woman mayor, Dorothy Johnson, as the next decade opened, and women in smaller municipalities won top political posts, from town boards to county boards, in the 1980s. In legislative leadership, the first woman co-chair of the powerful joint finance committee in 1983, assemblywoman Mary Lou Munts of Madison, had attempted to ameliorate the financial impact of divorce on women and children. Her no-fault divorce law had passed in 1977, and she had introduced the state's landmark Marital Property Act or "community property" rights bill in 1979. But the bill almost died on the floor in 1984 until its rescue by a bipartisan coalition led by two male state senators: Democrat Lynn Adelman of New Berlin, later a federal judge, and Republican Donald Hanaway of De Pere, later the state attorney general. Hanaway made an impassioned speech to save the law because, according to legal historian June Weisberger, "he decided this was the way he wanted his daughters to be treated."[58]

In the mid-1980s, Republican women began to reach legislative leadership, although representing the party out of power. Susan Shannon Engeleiter of Brookfield was the youngest woman in legislative history when she went into the assembly in 1975 at twenty-two years old and became the state senate's first woman minority leader a decade later. In 1987, Republican Betty Jo Nelsen of Shorewood became the assembly's first woman minority leader. But the legislature lost Engeleiter in 1988 to her second run for Congress, which she lost to a millionaire businessman with no political experience, although both went to Washington because she became the head of the Small Business Administration. Her loss in the legislature was balanced by the results of a special election, when a Republican assemblywoman won the state senate seat: Margaret Farrow, who had followed the traditional route to the legislature by beginning at the local level, if by breaking tradition in Elm Grove to become the first woman on the village board and then the first woman village president. However, compared to the number of women in high office elsewhere, Wisconsin fell well behind by 1990, when a national study ranked the state in the lowest fifth of all fifty states. No woman would be named majority leader of a party in power in the Wisconsin legislature until the next millennium.[59]

In the 1980s, progress also came in academe for women across the state as well as for women's studies programs. Few of the last four-year UW campuses that still had lacked women's studies programs in the mid-1970s faced the level of backlash that existed at the campus in Platteville, predominantly populated by men since its origins as a trade school in mining and proud to be a "bastion of the traditional male specialties." The gender wars at the onetime mining school may have inspired an account of the campaign in the 1980s at the last UW campus to approve a women's studies program. At River Falls, wrote a professor quoting another feminist scholar, winning a program was a process of "dancing through the minefield" of obstacles to women's studies. But by the mid-1980s, even the Jesuit institution of Marquette University in Milwaukee had sufficient faculty women to offer an interdisciplinary minor, as did other private colleges in Wisconsin. Marquette followed with a full major, also offered at Beloit College and Lawrence University. By the end of the decade, with women's studies established throughout the UW System, the aim became recruitment of more women faculty, especially after the hiring in 1988 of Donna Shalala as the chancellor at the Madison campus, the first woman to head a Big Ten school. The widespread recruitment of minorities as well as women was credited to the first woman of color on the UW Board of Regents, Edith Norman Finlayson, who already had made history as the first African American nurse at the veterans' hospital near Milwaukee and as a founder of her city's NOW chapter.[60]

Tumultuous times returned nationwide in the next decade as political prognosticators predicted "the year of the woman" in 1992, when many factors confounded women's expectations in an increasingly conservative Wisconsin. As the decade opened, the issue of abortion became politicized locally amid attacks by national anti-abortion organizations on women's clinics in Milwaukee. Another polarizing political issue was women's place in the military when they went into combat areas as support troops for the first time in the Gulf War in 1991, when fatalities included Sergeant Cheryl La Beau O'Brien of Caledonia. Of immeasurable impact on women were congressional hearings in 1991 on Supreme Court nominee Clarence Thomas, when a former employee, law professor Anita Hill, had to testify on sexual harassment to an all-male committee — and on television nationwide. The Thomas-Hill debacle "galvanized the resolve of women" to run for office, according to political scientist Georgia Duerst-Lahti of Beloit College. But another local political observer wrote that "events that triggered the year of the women don't play well in the conservative farm fields and factories" of Wisconsin.[61]

In 1992, more women went to Congress from across the country, but not from Wisconsin. For the first time, two women went to Congress from one state, California, while the first African American woman in the Senate, Carol Mosely Braun, won in nearby Illinois. In Wisconsin, a record number of five women ran for Congress in 1992 — as women had since 1922 — but not one won. The cost of political campaigns also contributed to the fate of women candidates for Congress, including Ada Deer. Although she had won in the primary, defeating a Democratic contender with more funding and experience as a state legislator, Kay Clarenbach's son, Deer had lost in the regular election to a far better-funded Republican. Another candidate for Congress, Margaret "Peg" Lautenschlager of Fond du Lac, later attested that political success was "fundamentally dependent on one's ability to raise money" and especially "difficult for women"; she had raised less than half of her opponent's treasury of almost half a million dollars. However, she also noted, he had not heard concern about his child-care arrangements, while Lautenschlager, like Engeleiter before her, constantly had faced constituents who worried whether a wife and mother ought to go to Washington.[62]

In 1992, when the number of women in state legislatures increased elsewhere, Wisconsin voters did not even want more women to go as far as Madison. Although women had gained seats in the state senate with every session since the mid-1980s, they lost more seats in the assembly. The total number of women winning seats in the Wisconsin legislature declined in 1992 and throughout the decade, despite the "year of the woman." However, progress was seen for women in sectors other than politics. The "year of the woman" even came to the Evangelical Lutheran Church of America when the Reverend April Ulring Larson of the La Crosse synod became that denomination's first woman bishop in the country.[63]

The "year of the woman" seemed to come to the University of Wisconsin in 1992, when the regents selected Katherine C. Lyall as the first woman president of the system serving more than one hundred fifty thousand students statewide. However, her appointment was an anomaly, according to a report that found comparatively few women faculty advancing at the main Madison campus, which still was dominated by men. Her success especially contrasted with the case of Ceil Pillsbury, a business professor denied tenure at the University of Wisconsin–Milwaukee, which captured the widespread support of women who were surprised at a paradoxical lack of progress for women faculty in the last decade of the century. Pillsbury's appeal of the tenure decision made *New York Times* headlines and brought national networks to the Milwaukee campus. However, she no longer taught there, as denial of tenure necessitated her departure. She taught at the University of Wisconsin–Green Bay, far from her home and family, for years until federal investigators came to the Milwaukee campus, found a hostile climate for women, and threatened the UW System statewide with the loss of federal funding, almost four million dollars. Pillsbury soon won tenure and part of a settlement of almost half a million dollars to a handful of women faculty. However, the university system soon had to settle more on male faculty who filed reverse-discrimination claims.[64]

The excellence of women faculty throughout Wisconsin was evident when a Lawrence professor won both unprecedented acclaim and catcalls by men in the audience at an international competition in 1995. Bridget-Michaele Reischl, conductor of the Lawrence University Symphony, became the first woman and the first American to win Italy's prestigious Pedrotti award. She also was the sole American and one of only a few women among sixty conductors. But the audience favorite was a man, and her award was met by "a smattering of boos," according to reviews. Reischl returned to her campus, redoubling her duties in the next decade as a guest conductor with major orchestras in Europe and across the country, in addition to serving as the conductor of the Green Bay Symphony. Her mother, also a musician, was not surprised by this success. She recalled giving her daughter "dolls and tea sets," but "instead of cuddling them and liking to change outfits, when I peeked into her bedroom, she'd be giving them instructions."[65]

Two of the most prominent women faculty at UW–Madison left Wisconsin for Washington in the 1990s, while a former woman professor who stayed in the state attained the highest honor on its high court. Madison chancellor Donna Shalala and American Indian studies lecturer Ada Deer went into the Clinton administration in 1992, Shalala in the cabinet as secretary of health and human services and Deer as the first woman to serve as assistant secretary of the interior over the Bureau of Indian Affairs. After three years of facing critics who felt that even she could not improve the troubled agency amid lawsuits against the federal government for mismanagement of tribal trust funds, Deer returned to campus politics in Madison. In 1996, former law school professor Shirley S. Abrahamson, who had served for twenty years on the Wisconsin Supreme Court, became Wisconsin's first woman chief justice. "I have watched the ranks of women judges grow from one" — herself — "to thirty . . . almost 12 percent of the judges" in Wisconsin in two decades, she said. "We have made great strides." However, she also noted that neighboring Minnesota had made history five years before, in 1991, as the first state with a female majority of justices on its high court.[66]

Also serving in Washington, as commissioner of immigration, was Milwaukee-born Doris Borst Meissner, while progress continued slowly but with certainty for immigrant women in her hometown. Milwaukee remained one of the most segregated cities in the country not only racially but also ethnically. Milwaukee's diversity increased after an influx in the 1980s of South Americans into the Hispanic community, which previously had been composed primarily of people with Central American heritage. In 1990, the United Community Center served Latina women with a bilingual day-care center, and the state's first Spanish-speaking day-care center opened at Esperanza Unida, where concern that too few women took advantage of job training would translate into a program to prepare hundreds as licensed home day-care practitioners. The Hispanic Chamber of Commerce also departed from cultural norms in naming a woman as executive officer: Maria Monreal-Cameron, the ninth child of immigrants to Milwaukee in the 1940s. Her mother had worked at a cannery and her father in a foundry, saving to open the first Mexican restaurants beyond the *barrio*. Their bilingual daughter, who had been "instilled with a fierce pride" by her mother and grandmother, soon inaugurated an annual Salute to Hispanic Women.[67]

Milwaukee women of color also would have lasting impact on their community, city and state in coming decades. Edith Norman Finlayson chaired the city's most important foundation throughout the 1980s, with a separate Women's Fund to support programs to improve economic self-sufficiency, prevent domestic violence, and promote better health. The fund began in 1985, just as Milwaukee's Jane Bradley Pettit became heiress to the Allen-Bradley fortune, and many women and girls became beneficiaries of more than two hundred fifty million dollars in her seed money to a wide range of causes. In the next decade, the Women's Fund countered the impact in the city of the onset of welfare reform

in Wisconsin — as would two women of color in Milwaukee who had been "welfare mothers" and emerged as leaders in 1990: Gwendolynne Moore began her first term in the assembly, and Jeanette Mitchell became the first African American woman to lead the
Milwaukee School Board after thirty years at the telephone company. She had started on
the switchboard but rose to management at the much-changed "Ma Bell." Moore moved
up to become the first African American woman state senator by the mid-1990s, and
Mitchell became head of Milwaukee's Helen Bader Foundation — but neither woman forgot how she had gotten to the top. Both spoke out about welfare reforms in Wisconsin,
from "Learnfare" to increase school attendance by penalizing absentee students' parents,
especially single mothers, to "Bridefare" to force women to wed or face state cuts in federal Aid to Families with Dependent Children, to "Wisconsin Works," which became more
famed by the name "W-2."[68]

W-2 became infamous among critics because of its impact on women and families, first
in Wisconsin and then nationwide, as federal reforms followed the state's model. The
state program promised to provide welfare recipients with job training to become employ-
able or face an end to financial assistance. Welfare rolls were reduced as many women and
men did find work, at first. But as a result, some became the "working poor," underpaid
and with fewer benefits. Told by a state official to "live with less," many families lived with
far less than promised, owing to mismanagement by private providers contracted by the
state. Caseloads dropped, but taxpayers' costs per case doubled compared to previous
welfare programs — as did salaries of administrators, whose costs averaged two-thirds of
funding meant for needy families. State child-care funding also soared from fifty-three
million dollars to more than three hundred million dollars to put mothers to work. Some
agencies ran out of funds and filed for state relief themselves after fines and other penalties for improperly penalizing recipients for infractions of new welfare rules, while the de-
serving families were denied rent payments, faced eviction, and resorted to food pantries.
That racial discrimination factored in the alleged infractions became evident. A state investigation revealed that families of color faced funding cuts far more often than non-
minorities — the majority of recipients — for the same causes. State officials retracted
long-standing denials of discriminatory decisions and admitted that race apparently was
a "factor in W-2 sanctions." But whether gender bias against the much-maligned "welfare
mothers" also factored in the fate of women and families was not studied.[69]

At the end of the century, the effect on women's progress of a decade of W-2 and other
welfare programs was evident: Wisconsin women remained well below national norms in
education and income. Nationwide, some signs seen as improvements were attributed in
part to federal welfare reform programs — and fear of sexually transmitted diseases. The
number of married teenagers rose nearly 50 percent during the decade, to 4.5 percent,
reversing a decline in their marriage rate in every decade since the 1950s. But the state that
started "Bridefare" lagged behind at 3.8 percent. Wisconsin girls were far more likely to
be single mothers, which often ended their educations early. They had fewer children than
others their age in most states, and federal reforms also provided better enforcement of
child support orders across the country, including Wisconsin, where a fourth of children

were to receive support. However, 12 percent of the state's parents — forty thousand — still owed ten million dollars in child support at the end of the decade. A statewide survey of families on federal assistance found widespread fear of poverty; for example, a fourth of families in La Crosse County — the highest proportion in the state — recently had gone hungry. "People have gotten off welfare, and they're working low-wage jobs," said the head of the local hunger task force. But their wages often were insufficient to meet families' most minimal needs. "Nobody's going to pay their rent," she said.[70]

Another factor in the finding on women's education and income became evident by the end of the century in Wisconsin, where studies of a "brain drain" found that women college graduates left the state at twice the rate of male classmates. Women became a majority of UW students statewide only in the 1990s, decades behind the rest of the country, where women were the majority on campuses in the 1970s and the majority of college graduates in the 1980s. In the 1990s, women's numbers declined in law and other lucrative fields of study in Wisconsin; in Milwaukee law firms, the percentage of women partners fell slightly below national averages, although a major firm had a female managing partner and others followed. In Madison, the University of Wisconsin Hospital and Clinics hired a woman president and chief executive officer, and the numbers of women continued to increase in the UW Medical School and science departments. However, their impact on medical treatment in the state would come only incrementally over time — and only if they stayed in the state — as fewer than one in six Wisconsin physicians were women, well below national norms. Other opportunities in health care swelled enrollments at technical colleges to record levels, including women such as Julie Strelow of La Crosse, who had been laid off after almost two decades when a local brewery closed; five years later, after retraining, she was back at work as a respiratory therapist.[71]

Women also increased in business schools statewide by 1990, when a hundred Milwaukee business leaders met on progress in a campaign to promote women into management. But all were men. The only women in the room were the waitresses serving them. A notable exception in the city's male-dominated business circles came with the naming of Mary Jo Meisner in 1993 as the eighth editor of the *Milwaukee Journal* in more than a century, although she left after one of the shortest editorial tenures in its history. In 1994, the hiring by the Brady Corporation in Milwaukee of Katherine Hudson, the first woman chief executive officer of a major publicly owned company in Wisconsin, had more lasting impact. She became a "local hero" to women but "a villain" to men, according to a media account, for admonishing executives at another meeting on corporate culture. "I speak to women all the time, so this is for the guys," said Hudson. "You miss out on one-half of the potential of your worlds, your markets," by not promoting women within their companies to reach potential women customers. But businesswomen would gain little more than a series of hand-wringing studies on their status in the state.[72]

A decade later, in a new millennium, "doors to the corporate boardroom remain mostly closed for Wisconsin women," according to one study. Another found that women's enrollments in master's programs in business schools had increased in Wisconsin beyond national levels. But another study's findings did not bode well for their future, if they stayed in the state. In Milwaukee, although most new managerial jobs went to women in the 1990s, most came at small companies and carried "ambiguous job titles" such as the ubiquitous positions in personnel and public relations that had become highly feminized fields. Statewide, women had made only minimal gains at the top, comprising less than 10 percent of board members and 12 percent of corporate officers at Wisconsin's fifty largest companies, well below the percentage of board seats and management positions held by women in Fortune 500 firms nationwide. One of the first women in top management at a major Milwaukee firm decades before, retired Rexnord economist Virginia Altenhofen Klecka, offered her own analysis: "Companies say there aren't many women qualified to sit on boards. One wonders what they mean by qualified. I suspect they aren't looking very hard or very far."[73]

That few firms looked beyond traditional resources for board members became evident from a study's findings that few women found their way into the "pipeline" to for-profit firms' boards because few found a welcome on the powerful nonprofit community organizations' boards that proved a crucial path for advancement for men. Some organizations that provided a means for advancement for men would not welcome women as members, much less as board members. An example arose in La Crosse, where the Fraternal Order of the Eagles — called the Eagles Club — had more than eight hundred men among its members but only one woman in 1997, when the club rejected more women applicants from its "auxiliary" in a secret ballot. Although the club accepted several men as members at the same time, apparently without question, the women were subjected to "unusually lengthy screening" that apparently included a background search for criminal records as well as interviews, according to the press. A member told a reporter that a woman applicant was "branded as kind of a troublemaker." However, another member who sponsored several of the women said that he could not recall a similar refusal of any applicant to the club that helped men move up in La Crosse.[74]

In banking, despite the long career of the legendary Catherine B. Cleary of Milwaukee, a woman headed only one of the city's top two dozen banks by the start of the millennium, when women comprised barely 5 percent of banks' boards of directors statewide. According to a study, state-based banks had not "let many women into the boardroom" because "tradition, slow turnover [and] cronyism contribute to disparity" in the state, compared to better gender diversity across the country. However, race also had factored in holding back women in banking until the end of the century and the founding of the first bank in Wisconsin run by African American women. All banking veterans in Milwaukee, they won startup funding in part from the bank where Cleary had worked — and they opened their bank at the former branch where Cleary had begun her career half a century before (see Cleary's "Married Women's Property Rights in Wisconsin, 1846–1872" in chapter 3).[75]

Wisconsin scored well below other states in women's business ownership, despite a few standouts. Most unusual may have been the first woman general manager and part-owner of a professional basketball franchise, Diane Bosshard of the La Crosse Bobcats. Better known was Pleasant Rowland of Middleton, founder of the Pleasant Company and creator of "American Girls" dolls to counter the Barbie and Cabbage Patch dolls, which she called a choice between "a brainless teen beauty queen and an adopted child." Formerly an elementary schoolteacher and textbook author, Rowland also drew on memories of her grandmother and of a family trip to a historic site for her concept of dolls accompanied by historically based books that introduced women's history to the next generation. Rowland reached annual sales of more than three hundred million dollars and became one of the richest women in the country when she sold her enterprise for seven hundred million dollars — to the company that made Barbie dolls. The onetime teacher had taught the toy industry that many American girls and their mothers wanted a more realistic alternative.[76]

Even in education, once the only sector of the workforce where women had held top positions, women schoolteachers were regaining their place only slowly in Wisconsin by the end of the century. A survey of school principals statewide found men still outnumbering women two to one, although women held an edge in elementary education and were a fourth of principals at the middle school level. However, at the high school level, women were only one-seventh of the principals statewide — fewer than the number of female school district superintendents. Their numbers had almost quadrupled in little more than a decade to seventy in Wisconsin and included the state's first African American woman school superintendent, Rosa A. Smith, in Beloit. The post of state school superintendent again went to men in the 1980s and 1990s. But at the postsecondary level, Katherine Lyall set a longevity record as UW System president, and women served in leadership of some UW campuses and technical colleges.[77]

But Milwaukee remained almost a male bastion in academe, except for women religious, almost until the new millennium. Most notable was Sister Joel Read, known nationwide for innovative programs for women students at Alverno College, where she had served as president for thirty years by 1998. No woman ever had so served at the city's oldest major university, Marquette, and none won similar status at the city's largest university until 1998, when Nancy L. Zimpher became chancellor of UW–Milwaukee. However, she was not the first woman to head a campus on the site. Her office was in the historic Milwaukee-Downer buildings that had been home to a woman president more than a century before (see "Milwaukee-Downer College Rediscovers Its Past" in chapter 3). Early in the new millennium, Zimpher left the state to lead another university, Read retired, and Lyall returned to research. But the status of women in the state, and the state of education nationwide, would never be the same.

Progress for women, whether in academic politics or state politics, had impact for others because every one who opened a door benefited others behind her — at least in theory, if not in Wisconsin. In practice, the so-called progressive state was surpassed by every other state in many measures of political progress by the end of the century. Only in Wisconsin had women never won office as governor or lieutenant governor or in Congress. That Wisconsin women voters participated at the polls more than in most states only added to the frustration for women in line to move up from the legislature, where their numbers declined throughout the decade to a level well below national norms.[78]

Several legislators returned to local politics, where women made more progress. In

1996, Jeannette Bell left the assembly after seven terms to serve as the first woman mayor of one of the state's largest cities, West Allis. The same decade saw a small city, Fitchburg, make history by electing its first woman common council president, Frances Huntley-Cooper, as the first African American mayor in Wisconsin. In the city of Waukesha, voters even elected two women in succession as mayor. In the state's second-largest city, Madison, Sue Bauman became the first woman mayor in 1997, when Kathleen Falk won as the first woman executive of the second-largest county, Dane. Other counties already had women executives, particularly Brown County, where two women served in succession; the first was a former mayor, followed by a former legislator.[79]

One woman legislator attempted the apparently impossible in Wisconsin, the last state without a woman in Congress, until Tammy Baldwin of Madison won her historic seat in 1999 in the U.S. House of Representatives, where the first woman had served in 1916. Baldwin won more progress for many women by publicly praising her upbringing by a single mother and, because Baldwin was a lesbian, by openly raising issues of sexual orientation to a new level. A prescient political analyst predicted that "Wisconsin Democrats are in an unusual position: rich in talent, with a surprising number of women in their next generation of leaders." That gender — or gender orientation — factored in delaying progress for generations of women in many sectors in the state caused a gubernatorial task force and then a commission to again study the ongoing effects of the "glass ceiling," a term for subtle barriers faced by women who could see to the top in their workplaces but were stopped from getting there. But the commission was underfunded, understaffed, ineffective, and effectively disbanded by the end of the century.[80]

While the commission had charted the lack of change at the top, women in Wisconsin had to live with the result — and while women aspiring to management were bumping up against a glass ceiling, working-class women were stuck to the factory floor. Some made strides, including union steward Elisa Ortiz of Madison, who was elected a vice president — and the first Hispanic woman — on the executive board of her local at Oscar Mayer Company; Ortiz called Tammy Baldwin her role model in calling for women's voices to be heard on issues such as flexible hours to allow for care of children and aging parents. Milwaukee's Ellen Bravo had founded and headed 9to5, The National Association of Working Women, to battle for issues from fair pay to "family-friendly" policies such as child care and flexible hours. But as she testified to a congressional committee at the end of the century, most workers still had "no say in their hours or working conditions." As another Wisconsin woman said, "When women do well, families tend to do well. When families do well, communities do well." However, many women were not doing well in Wisconsin.[81]

A landmark analysis of the status of the state's more than 2.7 million women at the end of the millennium found more women working for less in Wisconsin than almost anywhere in the country. Women comprised more than two-thirds of the state workforce in 2000, and two-thirds of state women were in the workforce in Wisconsin. Women in Wisconsin were "more likely to work than women in all but two states," according to the national Institute for Women's Policy Research. Worse, the impact of lagging educational levels on many Wisconsin women's incomes became evident by comparison with data from every state. The gender gap in wages in Wisconsin was "among the worst third of the states," according to the report, with women averaging less than seventy cents for every dollar earned by men. Annually, the disparity added up to an average of more than four thousand dollars in wages for women. As state workforce development secretary Roberta Gassman said, "the women of our state should not have to work for sixteen months to earn what men earn in twelve months, with less going into [women's] pensions and future security."[82]

In a state more rural than many but less diverse than most, women's status also depended in part upon where they lived in Wisconsin. The report found that families headed by single mothers fared the worst, with a third living in poverty in Wisconsin; only three states had worse poverty rates for women. Not surprisingly, the result was that women in Wisconsin also reported worse mental health, with higher rates of alcoholism and domestic violence, than in most states. Women far from cities had less access to services for health care as well as domestic violence shelters and family planning providers. At the same time, attacks on women's health care clinics had closed many sites in the early 1990s. The number that provided abortions dropped in the decade from sixteen to four, including two in Milwaukee and none west of Madison or north of Appleton in the state that the report on women's status ranked forty-eighth among all states for lack of reproductive rights.[83]

According to the report, women of color experienced the worst of the "overwhelming disparities in the status of women" in Wisconsin. Most were African Americans, who comprised almost 6 percent of the state's population, only half the proportion found in the rest of the country, and most lived in Milwaukee. The number of Hispanic Americans, the largest minority nationwide with more than 12 percent of the population, had doubled in a decade in the state but remained less than 4 percent of residents. Also scattered across the state were Asian Americans and other newcomers of non-European descent, comprising almost 2 percent of the population. Native Americans accounted for less than 1 percent of the population in their ancient land. By contrast, almost 90 percent of state residents had solely European heritage, including most of the recent immigrants, compared to less than 70 percent of the population nationwide. In Wisconsin, women and men of color comprised most of the population only in the state's only "majority minority" city, Milwaukee.[84]

Amid the homogeneity of most of Wisconsin, obstacles to equality escalated in the 1990s for women of other cultures, from Hispanics to Hmong to three hundred refugee Somalians who comprised one-tenth of one Barron County community, although the most recent immigrants comprised less than 4 percent of the population statewide. Still, a third of state counties approved English-only campaigns until Brown County's first woman executive, Nancy Nusbaum, vetoed her board of supervisors' resolution as "resonating with 'angry white men.'" After supervisors voted to sue and censure Nusbaum, she did not run for reelection. Worse than words were hate crimes in Manitowoc, where seven men faced charges from a firebombing that left a Hmong American family homeless, and in Milwaukee, where five men targeted Hmong Americans in a series of robberies. As one woman who was victimized in Milwaukee said, "I thought leaving Laos and coming to a place without war, I would be in a peaceful place." However, women across the state helped Hmong Americans acculturate to women's place in their new country. In Madison, coordinators of a cookbook worked to welcome newcomers, especially women unfamiliar with written recipes, who were "shy about sharing their favorite dishes," said one coordinator of the project. It was reminiscent of the legendary *Settlement Cookbook* begun by Milwaukee women for Jewish immigrants a century before (see Introduction to chapter 5).[85]

*The Status of Women in Wisconsin* report recognized the diversity of women's lives and lifestyles from city streets to farm fields in the new millennium, as many worked toward a different future for Wisconsin. Some worked for political progress, which seemed to come swiftly in the state that for so long had lagged behind others with more women in high office. First came the appointment in 2001 of state senator Margaret Farrow to fill out a term as the first woman lieutenant governor of Wisconsin — and as the first woman to surpass the rank of Vel Phillips as secretary of state two decades before. Within a month, with two women in the running, the state elected Elizabeth Burmaster of Madison as superintendent of public instruction, only the second woman to win the post in decades. Within a year, with Farrow up for reelection, five women vied for the top five slots in the state, including the first on a major-party ballot for governor: Democrat Kathleen Falk of Madison. Both Farrow and Falk lost, but another first for Wisconsin came in 2002 when both major parties put women on the ballot for lieutenant governor. The first ever to win election to the state's second-highest post was Barbara Lawton of Green Bay, and the 2003 inaugural brought together a trio of women whose service spanned generations in Wisconsin political history: Lawton was sworn in by Chief Justice Shirley Abrahamson while Ruth Bachhuber Doyle watched. "Believe me, she wasn't going to miss this," said her son, James E. Doyle, who was inaugurated as governor in the state capitol where she had served in the legislature half a century before.[86]

In 2003, also sworn in was the first woman to serve as state attorney general, Peg Lautenschlager of Fond du Lac, the former candidate for Congress who had faced concerns from voters about child care but a decade before. Other women in the law-and-order field in Wisconsin marked a milestone of a hundred members in their police association. Charter member Lieutenant Penny Kiefer acknowledged progress after almost a quarter of a century on the Portage force, although "there is still some apprehension about our capabilities," she said. "But it's slowly being conquered." In 2003, Milwaukee policewoman Nan Hegerty conquered another pinnacle of law enforcement with her appointment as the first woman police chief in the state's largest city. Women comprised only one-seventh of officers in eighteen thousand police departments across the country, and only one hundred and fifty had female chiefs, primarily serving in small towns. Hegerty was one of only four women chiefs in the country's sixty largest cities. Her success required the respect of men on the force, she said, but not by being "one of the guys." Although "they understand that women officers are essential," especially in the new trend called community policing, "they really want you to be women," asserted Hegerty. "On the other hand, they don't want you to be afraid to mix it up when the situation calls for it."[87]

In the legislature, the situation was mixed for women. Their numbers continued to decline from the record set more than a decade before, but Republican Mary Panzer of West Bend, previously the minority leader in the state senate, moved up in 2003 as its first woman majority leader. She was the daughter of a longtime legislative leader who "believed his daughters should have the same advantages as his sons" Panzer said. However, her tenure in leadership was short-lived, and she lost her try for re-election in 2004. At the same time, Annette Polly Williams, an African American assemblywoman from Milwaukee, set a record for longevity with her twelfth term, surpassing the service of almost a hundred women in the history of the Wisconsin legislature — among more than five thousand male legislators. In 2005, eighty years after the first women served, their number in legislative history at last surpassed one hundred, as several women won seats vacated by others who left the legislature. One was state senator Gwendolynne Moore of Milwaukee, who became the first African American and second woman from Wisconsin in Congress after her election to the House of Representatives.[88]

Many women across Wisconsin moved up in the new millennium. Frances Huntley-Cooper, who had been the first African American mayor in Wisconsin a dozen years before, left Fitchburg for a statewide post in Madison in 2003 as administrator of the workers' compensation division. Women became mayors in small cities from Sun Prairie to Prairie du Chien, and West Allis mayor Jeannette Bell became the first woman president of the statewide League of Wisconsin Municipalities. In the state's largest city, the first woman to run for mayor lost in the primary. But Julia Taylor became the first woman executive of the politically powerful Greater Milwaukee Committee, and corporate leaders also chose Katherine Hudson, by then Brady Corporation's chair of the board, to head a strategic planning committee mapping Milwaukee's future. Their counterpart in agriculture, the Wisconsin Farmers Union that functioned as a counterforce to big agribusiness, selected Sue Beitlich of Stoddard as its first woman president. Her family's Vernon County dairy farm hosted a gubernatorial press conference to promote the preservation of small farms that harked back to the era of the area's early settlement because, Beitlich said, "when family farms are prospering, it helps everybody."[89]

Whether in agriculture or other cultures that had become part of Wisconsin's colorful heritage, women continued to help others in their communities. Women always had led one of the oldest community agencies in Wisconsin, the Milwaukee Christian Center, founded in 1882 by Baptist missionary Mamie Passolt McKinney. She had come to the city to help the new immigrants then, providing preschool programs for German, Polish, Serb, and Greek children. She stayed active at her center, by serving children and others in the Hispanic community, past her hundredth birthday. In the new millennium, McKinney's work remained the center's mission. The agency grew to an annual budget of four million dollars and a staff of almost a hundred in programs from preschool to senior activities, and an emergency food pantry alone annually served more than four thousand needy residents. According to McKinney's successor, the agency hoped to expand to provide new services, from home-ownership counseling to fiscal literacy, because the center was "bursting at the seams" amid an economic downturn as the decade opened.[90]

As the Hispanic community matured, the *machismo* once dominant in its culture declined as more women rose to leadership statewide. Andrea-Teresa Arenas, from a Mexican migrant family in Milwaukee, served as a special assistant to the president of the UW System in Madison. In Milwaukee, Latina leader Lutecia Gonzalez served as an administrative law judge for the Equal Employment Opportunity Commission, and headlines hailed the first "Latinos" to win local elective offices, including three Latinas: circuit court judge Elsa Lamelas, school board member Jennifer Morales, and county supervisor Peggy West. Named one of the nation's most influential Latinas was Christine Rodriguez of nearby Shorewood, a Rockwell International Corporation vice president. She had started as a clerk-typist at less than two dollars an hour, rose to administering millions of dollars in charitable donations for Rockwell, then left in 2005 to lead a nonprofit educational project on the Great Lakes. A Latina Resource Center for victims of domestic violence opened in 2001 under the first woman president of United Migrant Opportunity Services, Lupe Martinez. The city's oldest Hispanic community service agency, the Council for the Spanish Speaking, named its first woman director, Rosa Dominguez. She could recall living in a railroad boxcar in rural Wisconsin when her family migrated from Texas, and her agency provided new migrants with educational programs such as Head Start and social services from food and clothing banks to job counseling to senior housing.[91]

A new generation of Hmong American women also emerged as leaders across the state in the new millennium. A refugee raised in Eau Claire, Dr. Pa Foua Yang, opened a clinic in Milwaukee that was the first in the state staffed by a Hmong physician to help women of her culture overcome modesty that prevented medical care. "Hmong women don't speak as much as I do," she said. "I say what I want, and I do what I want." In 2002, restaurateur Judy Xiong joined a new Hmong Chamber of Commerce in Milwaukee, one of many self-help groups that met at a national Hmong American conference held in the city. Mai Kao Moua of Wausau spoke at the conference on her "circle program" to help teenaged girls resolve tensions between their traditional and American cultures as they pursued professional careers and leadership roles. Another Wausau woman, Bao Xiong, won a national award in 2003 as a "hometown hero" for leadership in her Hmong community. Before television cameras on stage in New York City's Times Square, she stood with her "story cloth" depicting her family's flight from Laos and their arrival in Wisconsin, where she worked nights to earn a high school diploma during the day, then opened a day-care center to help other Hmong American women do the same. More than a hundred Hmong American families also became "hometown heroes" in Milwaukee as they found another way to serve their new country when at war again and overwhelmed the Milwaukee Red Cross with a collection for Wisconsin troops sent overseas.[92]

The "war on terror" in the new millennium came home to many women and men when their mothers, daughters, sisters, and friends died tragic deaths far from Wisconsin, at Ground Zero in New York City and in Iraq. On September 11, 2001, among the thousands trapped in the World Trade Center towers was Andrea Haberman of West Bend, a recent graduate of St. Norbert College and on her first business trip almost a hundred floors above the site that became Ground Zero. Even higher in the towers was Michell Callum Robotham, a young mother, formerly of Land o' Lakes, Neenah, and Milwaukee. In Washington, D.C., civilians Janice Scott and Patricia J. Statz were at work on the first floor of the Pentagon when they heard the news of the World Trade Center attacks. Scott called her husband, an army officer; they were planning to celebrate their twenty-fifth wedding anniversary with their daughters and her mother in Milwaukee within months. However, within minutes, Scott died at her desk when terrorists flew an airplane into the Pentagon. Patty Statz, who was married, a mother of two sons, and an alumna of University of Wisconsin–Stevens Point, still had family in Chippewa Falls, and she also was among almost two hundred others in the Pentagon and on the plane to die that day.[93]

As the terrible costs of the "war on terror" turned the country toward war in Iraq, Wisconsin women went to prison for protesting for peace at another "ground zero." Joyce Ellwanger of Milwaukee, Sister Caryl Hartjes of Fond du Lac, and Katherine Bjorkman of Burlington joined hundreds of antiwar activists in 2002 at a military base, Fort Benning in Georgia, that a reporter described as a "ground zero for annual protests and non-violent civil disobedience" because of its training school for armies from other countries. The women defied court orders barring them from the base and were among hundreds of protesters, including dozens convicted of criminal behavior for trespassing and sentenced to federal prison in the East. Hartjes, at sixty-seven years old, and Bjorkman, at nineteen years old, served three months. Ellwanger, a veteran of civil rights and peace protests since the 1960s and "a woman willing to go to prison for her beliefs," a reporter wrote, had been arrested most often before. At sixty-six years old, Ellwanger served six months in prison, where she continued to "wage peace" by posting peace statements in the prison.[94]

Others from Wisconsin served in the military in 2003, when the country went to war in Iraq, and women comprised more than 15 percent of the armed forces. However, one woman from Wisconsin at the Air Force academy in Colorado would not see combat, because she became embroiled in the gender war within the training schools as dozens of women reported sexual assaults by male cadets. In the case of Andrea Prasse of Elm Grove, she was expelled and stripped of her commission and her pay only eight days from graduation, and only on the word of a male cadet who accused her of cheating. Prasse provided evidence that he was motivated by revenge after she rejected his advances. For two years, she also rejected compromises offered by the Air Force and went to UW–Madison for a master's degree in engineering physics and astronomic science, wearing a uniform with unranked shoulder boards that were "a symbol of shame that she was made to wear," as a reporter wrote. Finally, Prasse was fully exonerated. At her home in Wisconsin, rather than at academy ceremonies, she received her diploma and her commission, and her parents replaced the shameful shoulder boards with the honor boards that Second Lieutenant Andrea Prasse had earned.[95]

Other women from across Wisconsin went to war in Iraq and earned their nation's highest honors, because they would not come back. Women were not yet to serve in ground combat, but Private Rachel Bosveld wrote from Iraq to family in Waupun that she was "anxious to be in battle" — until an attack on her unit. "Believe me, we want to go home," Bosveld wrote only days before she died in another attack, a week before her twentieth birthday. Within months, her stepbrother and sister-in-law also left home to serve in Iraq, where more than a dozen state soldiers died in the first year of the war. Private Nichole Frye of Lena served in a support unit in the reserves, supposedly not in combat; she emailed her mother that she was only delivering supplies to civilians such as food, water, and "books to the kids." Days after her arrival in Iraq, Frye died in a roadside attack on her convoy. Two sisters serving in Iraq soon did come home, although only to accompany the military casket of a third sister, Specialist Michelle Witmer of New Berlin. A college freshman for only weeks when her reserves unit had been called up the year before, Witmer had endured her off-duty hours by befriending children at a Baghdad orphanage, the beneficiary of a memorial fund in her honor. The sisters' service made headlines nationwide, as Witmer was the first woman to die in action in the National Guard's history of almost four hundred years and was the third fatality of a woman soldier from Wisconsin, more than from any other state in the first year of the war.[96]

The world had mourned the tragic death on the Columbia space shuttle of another Wisconsin woman in the military — the first woman astronaut from Wisconsin, twenty years after Sally Ride became the first American woman in space. Raised in Racine, Dr. Laurel Blair Salton Clark had graduated from UW–Madison's medical school and enlisted as a military flight surgeon. Only days before the disaster in 2003, she had scripted her own epitaph from space. In a poignant comment made to Milwaukee media and quoted in a presidential memorial for the Columbia crew, Clark spoke of her scientific experiments that brought roses into bloom high above her planet: "Life continues in lots of places, and life is a magical thing."[97]

Wherever they lived and worked, Wisconsin women had done more in the first few years of the new millennium than even their mothers' generation had accomplished in the half-century before. Whether they were stay-at-home mothers or traveled farther than their foremothers could have imagined, Wisconsin women had made history throughout the centuries of Native settlement and through the many waves of immigrants and migrants to Wisconsin in the centuries since. However, whether a new millennium had brought a "new wave" of feminism to further expand "women's place" in future in the state remained to be seen, because women's work was never done in Wisconsin. As former legislator Midge Leeper Miller said with hope, looking back on her era's lost ERA and looking forward to a better future for Wisconsin women, "we will have to wait for some new awareness and for a new wave of feminism to finish the task."[98]

☙ ❧

## NOTES

1. References used throughout this essay, not individually footnoted, include women's own official biographies in *Wisconsin Blue Books* and published by their offices; Kathryn F. Clarenbach, "Chronology of Recent Highlights of Wisconsin Women's Movement" for the Wisconsin Women's Network, www.wiwomensnetwork.org/chronone1.html; "Wisconsin Women Legislators — A Historical List," begun by A. Peter Cannon and published biennially by the Wisconsin Legislative Reference Bureau in 2001, 2003, 2005; "State-by-State Facts," published by the Center for American Women and Politics at Rutgers University, at www.cawp.rutgers.edu; and "State Quick Facts," published by the U.S. Census Bureau, at www.census.gov.

2. Thomas J. Morgan and James R. Nitz, "Our Forgotten World Champions: The 1944 Milwaukee Chicks," *Milwaukee History* 18, no. 4 (Winter 1995), 30–45; Sue Macy, "All-American Girls Claim Their Place in His-

tory," National Baseball Hall of Fame, www.baseballhalloffame.org/membership/memories%5Fdreams /2003/fall/AAGPBL.htm; Sue Macy, *A Whole New Ball Game: The Story of the All-American Girls Professional Baseball League,* (New York: Puffin Books, 1995), 8, 18, 25–27, 41–47, 55–56, 63–64.

3. Kris Radish, "'I Did It for My Country': Pioneering Pilot Broke Barriers," *Milwaukee Journal Sentinel,* July 24, 1997.

4. Steve Prestegard, "The Phone Pioneer," *Waupaca Marketplace Magazine,* April 25, 1995, 12; Amy Rabideau Silvers, "Klecka 'Broke Barriers' in Business," *Milwaukee Journal Sentinel,* October 25, 2002.

5. "Ernestine O'Bee to Be Honored," *Milwaukee Community Journal,* August 6, 2003; Felicia Thomas-Lynn, "Her Dream Denied, She Broke a State Barrier," *Milwaukee Journal Sentinel,* August 21, 2003; Tony Carideo, "Catherine Conroy: Unionist and Feminist," *Milwaukee Journal,* July 9, 1978, in Darryl Holter, ed., *Workers and Unions in Wisconsin: A Labor History Anthology* (Madison: SHSW, 1999), 232–233.

6. Jennie Penberthy, ed., "Introduction: Life and Writing," in *Lorine Niedecker: Collected Works* (Berkeley: University of California Press, 2002), 1–11.

7. William F. Thompson, *HOW,* vol. 6, *Continuity and Change, 1940–1965* (Madison: SHSW, 1988), 477–478, 569.

8. Ibid., 478, 694.

9. Editor's interview with Vel Phillips, Milwaukee, March 1, 2003; Joe William Trotter Jr., *Black Milwaukee: The Making of an Industrial Proletariat, 1915–1945* (Urbana: University of Illinois Press, 1985), 39–79; Thompson, *HOW,* 368–369; "Three Enter School Race," December 24, 1952, "Negro Woman Enters Race," October 3, 1955, Ellen Gibson, "'Councilman' Phillips Now 'Twice Blessed,'" April 4, 1956, all in the *Milwaukee Journal;* Eugene Kane, "Elitism Is Elitism, No Matter What Color It Comes In," *Milwaukee Journal Sentinel,* February 21, 1999.

10. Marian McBride [mother of the editor], "Negro Emerges in Politics," November 26, 1964, and "The Big League," July 4, 1969, both in the *Milwaukee Sentinel;* "Mother, Lawyer, Politician," February 8, 1958, and "'Councilman' Phillips," April 4, 1956, both in the *Milwaukee Journal;* Patty Loew, interview with Vel Phillips for WHA-TV, Madison, April 2, 2000.

11. "Pants Suit 1st at City Hall," October 9, 1970, "Role as Political Pioneer," November 9, 1978, "Black Was Beautiful for JFK's Spin Doctors," December 30, 1993, all in the *Milwaukee Sentinel;* "Mother, Lawyer, Politician," February 9, 1958, Laurence C. Eklund, "Mrs. Phillips in Limelight," December (n.d.) 1958, "Mrs. Phillips for Kennedy," December (n.d.) 1959, "It's Definite Kennedy in the Race," January 21, 1960, Ira Kapenstein and William R. Bechtel, "Major Factors Sifted in Victory of Kennedy," April 6, 1960, all in the *Milwaukee Journal.*

12. Sara M. Evans, *Born for Liberty: A History of Women in America* (New York: Free Press, 1989), 246; Robert C. Nesbit, *Wisconsin: A History,* 2nd ed.(Madison: University of Wisconsin Press, 1989), 503–504; University of Wisconsin Women's Studies Consortium, *Transforming Women's Education: The History of Women's Studies in the University of Wisconsin System* (Madison: UW System, 1999), 37.

13. Jackie Loohauis, "Dear Mrs. Griggs: A Legend Dies," *Milwaukee Journal,* August 19, 1991.

14. Sara De Luca, *Dancing the Cows Home: A Wisconsin Girlhood* (St. Paul: Minnesota Historical Society Press, 1996); Nesbit, *Wisconsin,* 503.

15. Thompson, *HOW,* 226–231, 654–657, 716; Nesbit, *Wisconsin,* 500–501.

16. Thompson, *HOW,* 618, 624, 700; Nesbit, *Wisconsin,* 529–530; UW Women's Studies, *Transforming Women's Education,* 45.

17. Thompson, *HOW,* 568–569; Marian McBride, "Political Pioneer," *Milwaukee Sentinel,* February 24, 1965; Nesbit, *Wisconsin,* 547.

18. "Remembrances Celebrate a Pioneering Feminist," *Milwaukee Journal,* March 13, 1994; UW Women's Studies, *Transforming Women's Education,* 37, 41.

19. UW Women's Studies, *Transforming Women's Education,* 25, 41–45, citing interview in Gerda Lerner and Joyce Follet, "Documenting Midwestern Origins of the Twentieth-Century Women's Movement, Oral History Project," WHS Archives; Thompson, *HOW,* 767.

20. Evans, *Born for Liberty,* 274–276; Marian McBride, "Women to Work for Equal Break," *Milwaukee Sentinel,* October 13, 1963.

21. UW Women's Studies, *Transforming Women's Education,* 48–54; J. R. Ross, "From First Female Lawmakers to Farrow, Times Have Changed," *Milwaukee Journal Sentinel,* April 27, 2001.

22. Evans, *Born for Liberty,* 274–276; Marian McBride, "Margaret C. Smith Makes History," *Milwaukee Sentinel,* July 16, 1964.

23. Jonathan Kasparek, "A Day in the Life: The Beatles Descend on Milwaukee," *WMH* 84, no. 2 (Winter 2000–2001): 14–23; Susan J. Douglas, *Where the Girls Are: Growing Up Female with the Mass Media* (New York: Times Books, 1994), 98, 113–120.

24. Michael E. Stevens, ed., *Voices from Vietnam* (Madison: SHSW, 1996), 40; Roberta Ostroff, *Fire in the Wind: The Life of Dickey Chapelle* (New York: Ballantine, 1992), xi–xiii, 24–28, 388–390; Marilyn Stasio, "When Death Is a Constant Companion: Why Women Reporters Go to War," *On the Issues* 7, no. 2 (Spring 1998), 7; see also Dickey Chapelle, *What's a Woman Doing Here? A Reporter's Report on Herself* (New York: Morrow, 1961).

25. Stevens, *Voices from Vietnam,* v–vi; "Campus Census Yields Surprises," *Milwaukee Sentinel,* May 4, 1965.

26. Marian McBride, "Mothers Limited by Law," *Milwaukee Sentinel,* November 9, 1967.

27. Marcia Cohen, *The Sisterhood: The Inside Story of the Women's Movement and the Leaders Who Made It Happen* (New York: Fawcett Columbine, 1988), 133–142; Mary Bergin, "NOW, Again; Young Women Revitalize Feminist Movement Here," *Capital Times,* September 24, 2003; UW Women's Studies, *Transforming Women's Education,* 49–50. Cohen credits the first coverage of NOW to the *Milwaukee Sentinel,* reporting Clarenbach as chair but "noting Betty only at the end of a long roll of charter members." Others from Wisconsin at the first convention included Gene Boyer of Beaver Dam, Analoyce Clapp, Mary Eastwood, and Nancy Knaak of Madison, and Edith Norman Finlayson, Sister Austin Doherty, and Sister Joel Read of Milwaukee. Conroy, Read, and Doherty served on the first national board. Wisconsin continued to contribute national leaders in succeeding decades, including Judith Goldsmith of Manitowoc as NOW president and Mary Jean Collins of Milwaukee as vice president of action, while Clarenbach later headed the NOW Legal Defense and Education Fund, and Boyer was the fund's vice president.

28. Marian McBride, "Woman Reporter Out in Cold," *Milwaukee Sentinel,* November 5, 1966; see also Milwaukee Press Club, Records, 1885–present, UWM Manuscript Collection 146, Archives, Golda Meir Library, UW–Milwaukee. [The editor of this anthology made the picket signs and was the "copyboy," a term later changed to "editorial messenger."]

29. Dorothy Moses Schultz and Steven M Houghton, "Married to the Job: Wisconsin's Women Sheriffs," *WMH* 86, no. 3 (Spring 2003): 22–37.

30. John McCullough, manuscript of broadcast on WTMJ-TV and WTMJ Radio, September 26 and 27, 1967, Milwaukee Journal Stations Papers, Archives, Golda Meir Library, UW–Milwaukee. Anita Weier, "Civil Rights Activists Recall '60s," *Capital Times,* October 29, 2002; see also Frank A. Aukofer, *City with a Chance* (Milwaukee: Bruce, 1968), and a more recent study, Patrick D. Jones, "'The Selma of the North': Race Relations and Civil Rights Insurgency in Milwaukee, 1958–1970" (doctoral thesis, UW–Madison, 2002).

31. "Common Council Again Rejects Fair Housing," September 9, 1967, "Pitts Is Second Black Alderman," April 6, 1968, "Open Housing Ordinance Passed," May 4, 1968, all in the *Milwaukee Courier;* Leonard Sykes, "Price of the Ticket," *Milwaukee Journal Sentinel,* February 4, 2002.

32. Trotter, *Black Milwaukee,* 87–92, 109, 127, 203; Kawanza Griffin, "Bishop Poured Her Talents and Energy into Family, Church," *Milwaukee Journal Sentinel,* February 28, 2005; Jack Dougherty, *More Than One Struggle: The Evolution of Black School Reform in Milwaukee* (Chapel Hill: University of North Carolina Press, 2004), 115, 154; Genevieve G. McBride, "The Progress of 'Race Men' and 'Colored Women' in the Black Press in Wisconsin, 1892–1985," in Henry Lewis Suggs, ed., *The Black Press in the Middle West, 1895–1985* (Westport, CT: Greenwood Press, 1996), 325–348, 397–348.

33. Thomas E. Mitchell Jr., "Friends and Peers Remember Longtime Columnist Mattiebelle Woods," *Milwaukee Community Journal,* February 23, 2005; Eugene Kane, "Woods Was the Life of the City's Parties," February 20, 2005, Steve Schultze, "Woods' Zest for Life Was Key to Longevity," February 27, 2005, and Felicia Thomas-Lynn, "Claretta Simpson: Civil Rights Stalwart Savors Freedom," November 28, 2003, all in the *Milwaukee Journal Sentinel.* [The editor also relies on personal experience, having worked with Woods at the *Milwaukee Courier.*]

34. Joseph Rodriguez, *Nuestro Milwaukee: The Making of the United Community Center* (Milwaukee: United Community Center, 2000), 13–14, 22–23, 26, 42–43; Alan J. Borsuk, "Making a Difference," November 24, 1995, and Georgia Pabst, "Program Helps Hispanic Women," December 5, 2001, both in the *Milwaukee Journal Sentinel.*

35. McBride, "The Big League," *Milwaukee Sentinel,* July 4, 1969; Amy Rabideau Silvers, "Wisconsin Teacher Rose to National Leadership Roles," *Milwaukee Journal Sentinel,* March 17, 2005.

36. UW Women's Studies, *Transforming Women's Education,* 50, 69, 76–77, 80, 123, 128; Amy Rabideau Silvers, "Krug, a German Immigrant, Helped Children Win Office," *Milwaukee Journal Sentinel,* April 26, 2001.

37. Midge Leeper Miller, "Wisconsin's Struggle for the Equal Rights Amendment," for the Wisconsin Women's Network at www.wiwomensnetwork.org/wisconsinera.html.

38. Ibid.; Mary Frances Berry, *Why ERA Failed: Politics, Women's Rights, and the Amending Process of the Constitution* (Bloomington, IN: Indiana University Press, 1986), 63, 75.

39. Miller, "Wisconsin's Struggle for the Equal Rights Amendment."

40. Ibid.

41. Ibid.; Anita Weier, "For Some Legislators, Tradition of Politics Is All in the Family," *Capital Times*, December 30, 2003.

42. Gerry Strey, "The 'Oleo Wars,'" *WMH* 85, no. 1 (Autumn 2001): 3–15; Marian McBride, "The Oleo Revolt: Ban, Tax Costing State," *Milwaukee Sentinel*, December 24, 1964.

43. Ann Walsh Bradley and Joseph A. Ranney, "New Case and Changing Faces: The Wisconsin Supreme Court in 2003," *WMH* 86, no. 3 (Spring 2003): 4; Shirley S. Abrahamson, "A Courtroom of One's Own: The New Role of Women in the Legal System," paper presented to Midwest Women in Law Regional Conference, October 10, 1996.

44. UW Women's Studies, *Transforming Women's Education*, 50; Evans, *Born for Liberty*, 306–307.

45. Nancy Oestreich Lurie, "Ada Deer: Champion of Tribal Sovereignty," in Theda Perdue, ed., *Sifters: Native American Women's Lives* (New York: Oxford University Press, 2001), 223–240; Nesbit, *Wisconsin*, 539; Patty Loew, *Indian Nations of Wisconsin: Histories of Endurance and Renewal* (Madison: WHS, 2001), 33–37.

46. Tina Burnside, "Working in System Is Coggs Family Affair," *Milwaukee Sentinel*, February 8, 1993.

47. Editor's interview with Vel Phillips, Milwaukee, Wisconsin, March 1, 2003.

48. Kazimierz J. Zaniewski and Carol J. Rosen, *The Atlas of Ethnic Diversity in Wisconsin* (Madison: University of Wisconsin Press, 1998), 13–15, 42, 65; "Deer Named to Head UW–Madison Program," *Wisconsin State Journal*, October 22, 1999; Nesbit, *Wisconsin*, 536; Rodriguez, *Nuestro Milwaukee*, 6–7, 10–12; Georgia Pabst, "Discrimination: A Reminder of How Bias Affects Us All," September 26, 1993, and "Immigrant Moms Go to School, Too," March 20, 1994, both in the *Milwaukee Journal;* Georgia Pabst, "Family Members Honored for Dedication," *Milwaukee Journal Sentinel*, October 14, 2001.

49. Nahal Toosi, "English-only Issue Divides a Diverse Area," July 17, 2002, Mary Louise Schumacher, "Words Apart," May 19, 2003, Jo Sandin, "Caught between Cultures," January 25, 1998, Lois Blinkhorn, "Out of Tragedy, a Quiet Pursuit of Truth," March 22, 1998, all in the *Milwaukee Journal Sentinel;* Pat Schneider, "Hmong Story Cloths a Fading Art," *Capital Times*, January 29, 2002; Kyoko Mori, *Polite Lies: On Being a Woman Caught between Cultures* (New York: Henry Holt, 1998), 82–105.

50. Nesbit, *Wisconsin*, 504; Thompson, *HOW*, 260–268; Doug Erickson, "High School Class to Make Flag with Bras," *Wisconsin State Journal*, March 9, 2002.

51. Amy Starr Redwine, "The Church's Pioneering Women," *Presbyterians Today* 95, no. 3 (March 2005), 12–15; Deborah A. Block, "What Untied Presbyterians," address presented to the 215th General Assembly, Presbyterian Church, U.S.A., Denver, Colorado, May 23, 2003.

52. Nesbit, *Wisconsin*, 504; Thompson, *HOW*, 260–268; "Hortonville Teachers' Strike of 1974," in Holter, ed., *Workers and Unions*, 243.

53. Joe Williams, "MPS Mired in 'Distressed' City," *Milwaukee Journal Sentinel*, January 8, 1998; Kathleen Marie Dudley, *The End of the Line: Lost Jobs, New Lives in Postindustrial America* (Chicago: University of Chicago Press, 1994), 16, 38–39, 192, 214.

54. "Machinist Makes Poetry of Blue-collar Life," *Milwaukee Sentinel*, November 13, 1992; Sue Doro, *Blue Collar Goodbyes* (Watsonville, CA: Papier-Mache Press, 1992), 19–20; see also Sue Doro, *Of Birds and Factories* (Milwaukee: Peoples' Books and Crafts, 1983), and *Heart, Home & Hard Hats: The Non-traditional Work and Words of a Woman Machinist and Mother* (Minneapolis: Midwest Villages and Voices, 1986).

55. Peter A. Felknor, "Tornadoes in Wisconsin: Two Case Histories," *WMH* 73, no. 4 (Summer 1990): 258–273.

56. Ibid., 261.

57. Ibid., 268.

58. Margaret Larson, *For the Common Good: A History of Women's Roles in La Crosse County, 1920–1980* (League of Women Voters of La Crosse County, 1996), 156–158; Mary Bergin, "Marital Property Law Just Two Decades Old," *Capital Times*, March 4, 2004; see also Josephine Staab, *Marriage as an Economic Partnership: How One State Made It Happen* (Madison: Atwood, 1998). Staab was a member of the task force that lobbied for the law, which took effect in 1986.

59. Ross, "From First Female Lawmakers to Farrow," April 27, 2001; Mary Van de Kamp Nohl, "Women & Power," *Milwaukee Magazine*, April 2002, 48.

60. UW Women's Studies, *Transforming Women's Education*, 122–123, 137–138; interview with Diane Hoeveler, Milwaukee, Wisconsin, July 2003; Amy Rabideau Silvers, "Finlayson's Volunteerism Lifted Students, Schools," *Milwaukee Journal Sentinel*, September 21, 2001.

61. Trina Haag, "Lack of Women in State Politics Called Puzzling," June 8, 1995, and Richard A. Serrano, "Silencing Protests," December 9, 1996, both in the *Milwaukee Journal Sentinel;* Georgia Duerst-Lahti, "Gender, Redistricting, and Other Aspects of Election 2002," for the American Political Science Association, October 2002, at www.apsanet.org/~elections.

62. Katherine M. Skiba, "Women's Losses Tied to Finances," *Milwaukee Journal*, November 8, 1992.

63. Gayda Hollnagel, "In a Dual Calling, Bishop and Pastor Spouses Share Lives, Ministry," *La Crosse Tribune*, May 25, 2003.

64. UW Women's Studies, *Transforming Women's Education*, 16, 89, 117; Katherine M. Skiba, "Campus Lacks Women in Key Leadership Roles," June 24, 1994, and Tom Vanden Brook, "Agreement Ends Bias Probe at UWM," July 23, 1993, both in the *Milwaukee Journal;* Kevin Murphy, "UW Settles Reverse Bias Lawsuits," *Milwaukee Journal Sentinel*, November 3, 1999.

65. Tom Strini, "A First for Conductor," October 3, 1995, and Michelle Derus, "Concerted Action: Lawrence Conductor Wins Acclaim through Hard Work and High Expectations," December 10, 1995, both in the *Milwaukee Journal Sentinel.*.

66. Patrick Jasperse, "Clinton's Wisconsin Contingent at Center of Today's Issues," *Milwaukee Journal Sentinel*, April 30, 1995; Philip Brasher, "Ada Deer Acknowledges Pressures in Trying to Please All her Bosses," *Wisconsin State Journal*, January 25, 1997; Abrahamson, "A Courtroom of One's Own," October 10, 1996.

67. Jasperse, "Clinton's Wisconsin Contingent," April 30, 1995; Rodriguez, *Nuestro Milwaukee*, 7; Pabst, "Immigrant Moms," March 20, 1994, Jesse Garza, "Hispanic Community Leaders to Be Honored," October 14, 1994, Jesse Garza, "Esperanza Unida to Honor Hispanics Who Inspire Others to Succeed," October 26, 1996, all in the *Milwaukee Journal;* Tannette Johnson-Elie, "Hispanic Chamber CEO Breaks Barriers for Self, Others," *Milwaukee Journal Sentinel*, January 11, 2003.

68. Georgia Pabst, "Community Leader Stays Focused," *Milwaukee Journal*, May 8, 1994; Alan J. Borsuk, "Pettit Still Unmatched as Local Philanthropist," November 17, 2002, and Alan J. Borsuk, "From Phone Operator to Leadership Instructor," October 1, 2001, both in the *Milwaukee Journal Sentinel;* Stacey MacGlashan, "Nation Stands Back to Watch State's Welfare Experiments," *Milwaukee Journal*, July 18, 1994.

69. Holly Deshaw, "Live for Less," April 24, 2002, Tom Held, "Agency Late in Filing W-2 Extensions," September 28, 2002, Peter Maller, "Meeting a Growing Need," November 10, 2002, Steve Schultze, "Audit Says Unfair W-2 Sanctions Continue," December 11, 2002, Steve Schultze, "Study Questions Cost, Effectiveness of W-2," December 21, 2002, Steve Schultze, "Welfare Agencies Seeking State Relief," December 23, 2002, Meg Kissinger, "Top Pay at W-2 Agencies Jumps," March 16, 2003, Steve Schultze, "Agency Fined," March 25, 2003, Steve Schultze, "Minority W-2 Clients Faced More pPenalties, Study Says," March 29, 2003, Steve Schultze, "State Finds Evidence of Race Bias in W-2," February 21, 2005, all in the *Milwaukee Journal Sentinel.*

70. Andrew Blasko, "Wisconsin's Teens Have Fewer Babies Than Teens in Other States," January 21, 1999, Tom Kertscher, "State Taking Deadbeat Parents' Tax Rebates," August 1, 2001, Genaro C. Armas, "More Teens Getting Married," November 9, 2002, "More Moms Getting Full Child Support," October 26, 2002, all in the *Milwaukee Journal Sentinel;* Patricia Simms, "State Study: Many Births in '96 Were Unplanned," March 12, 1999, and "Hunger Worries High in La Crosse," April 9, 2001, both in the *Wisconsin State Journal.*

71. Michael A. Fletcher, "Women Outpacing Men among College Graduates," July 8, 2002, Sharif Durhams, "Report Finds UW Women Treated Better," February 11, 2000, Gina Barton, "Pioneering Women Lawyers Slowly Climb Power Ladder," July 27, 2003, all in the *Milwaukee Journal Sentinel;* Judy Newman, "Women Find Their Progress to the Executive Suite Slow," *Wisconsin State Journal*, September 14, 2003; Steve Cahalan, "The Job Shift," *La Crosse Tribune*, September 29, 2002.

72. Nohl, "Women & Power," 50; Tom Heinen, "Conductors: Journal Had 8 Editors in 112-year History," *Milwaukee Journal Sentinel*, March 31, 1995.

73. Kathleen Gallagher, "Women Knocking on Boardroom Doors," January 8, 2001, Kathleen Gallagher, "Wanted: More Women Executives," May 10, 2004, and Silvers, "Klecka 'Broke Barriers,'" October 25, 2002, all in the *Milwaukee Journal Sentinel;* Bill Dunn, "MBA Isn't a Degree of Separation Anymore," *Capi-*

*tal Times,* August 16, 2001; Jessica Steinhoff, "Milwaukee's Women Leaders Fight for Respect," *Milwaukee Shepherd Express,* October 10, 2002.

74. Jaci Gardell, "100 Years Old, But Still Living in Past? La Crosse Eagles Club Blasted for Blocking Women," *Wisconsin State Journal,* February 4, 1998.

75. Paul Gores, "State's Bank Boardrooms Welcome Few Women," June 6, 2003, Tannette Johnson-Elie, "Women: Head of Home, Head of Company," December 4, 2001, "Firstar Invests $1 Million in Legacy," October 20, 1998, all in the *Milwaukee Journal Sentinel.*

76. Jeff Brown, "Full Plate," *La Crosse Tribune,* December 28, 1998; Doris Hajewski, "Mattel Buying State Doll Maker," *Milwaukee Journal Sentinel,* June 16, 1998; Jeff Richgels, "American Girls, Meet Barbie," *Capital Times,* June 16, 1998.

77. Anne Davis, "Female Principals Remain Scarce," *Milwaukee Journal Sentinel,* July 28, 2003.

78. Meg Kissinger, "Status Slips for State Women," *Milwaukee Journal Sentinel,* November 19, 2002.

79. "West Allis Mayor Plans to Run for Re-election," September 30, 1999, and Ana Caban, "Waukesha Mayor to Seek Re-election Next April," June 20, 2001, both in the *Milwaukee Journal Sentinel;* Paul Norton, "The Struggle Must Continue," October 21, 1995, and Pat Schneider, "Dame County! Women Score Firsts for Mayor and County Exec," *Capital Times,* April 2, 1997.

80. Frank A. Aukofer, "Baldwin Strives for Balance," December 5, 1999, Steven Walters, "State Democrats See New Day Dawning," November 8, 1998, both in the *Milwaukee Journal Sentinel;* Nohl, "Women & Power," 49–51.

81. Debra Carr-Elsing, "Union VP Has Family History of Activism," *Capital Times,* October 19, 2000; Ellen Bravo, testimony to House Subcommittee on Workforce Protections, Washington, DC, March 12, 2003; Kissinger, "Status Slips," November 19, 2002.

82. Amy B. Caizza, *The Status of Women in Wisconsin* (Washington, DC: Institute for Women's Policy Research, 2002), 5–6, 33–62; Joel Dresang and Jason Gertzen, "Wage Gap Is Stubborn, Disparity Is Bigger in Wisconsin Than Nationally," *Milwaukee Journal Sentinel,* June 3, 2004.

83. Caizza, *Status of Women in Wisconsin,* 5–6, 63–80; Lucas Wall, "Wisconsin's Abortion Rate Sinks to Record Low," August 15, 2000, "Progress for Women in State Still Limited," and Barbara Lawton, "Give Women Room to Lead Economic Growth," May 9, 2004, all in the *Milwaukee Journal Sentinel.*

84. Caizza, *Status of Women in Wisconsin,* 80; Jack Norman and Georgia Pabst, "Majority Minority: Seeds of City's Future Lie in Its Diversity," *Milwaukee Journal Sentinel,* August 22, 1999.

85. Scott Williams, "Refugees Get Down to Business as Grant Program Doubles," September 30, 2002, Vikki Ortiz, "State's Foreign-born Population Jumps 60%," June 5, 2002, Georgia Pabst, "To Many, Figures Are No Surprise," January 22, 2003, Lisa Sink, "Board Targets County Executive," August 27, 2002, Gina Barton, "Witness in Hate Crime Accused of Lying to Grand Jury," September 13, 2002, Annysa Johnson, "Hmong Soldiers Join Table of Honor," May 28, 2002, James H. Burnett III, "War in Laos Echoes in Robbery Spree," April 9, 2002, all in *Milwaukee Journal Sentinel;* Pat Schneider, "Women's Group Offers No-budget Cookbook," *Capital Times,* January 4, 1999.

86. "The Job Is No. 2, but Farrow Is First," March 2, 2001, and Scott Milfred, "Another Banner Election Year for Women?" August 19, 2001, both in the *Wisconsin State Journal;* "Women Take the Helm," *Capital Times,* November 9, 2002.

87. "Women Take the Helm," November 9, 2002; Ann McBride, "Portage Rolls Out Carpet for Female Police Officers," *Portage Daily Register,* September 27, 2002; Melissa Trujillo, "Milwaukee Panel Picks Woman as Police Chief, City Becomes the Biggest in the Nation to Have a Female Chief," *Wisconsin State Journal,* October 17, 2003; "Women Rise to Top of Police Ranks," Time-Warner Cable News, Milwaukee, Wisconsin, May 27, 2004. By the time that Hegerty took office, a larger city — Detroit — also had selected a woman as police chief.

88. "Women Slowly Enter State's Political Arena," August 25, 2002, and Larry Sandler, "Moore Rewrites History, Mainstream Appeal Makes Her State's First Black Congresswoman," November 3, 2004, both in the *Milwaukee Journal Sentinel;* Anita Weier, "For Some Legislators, Tradition of Politics," *Capital Times,* December 30, 2003.

89. Judy Ettenhorfer, "Sun Prairie Can Thank Orfan," *Capital Times,* April 9, 2003; Richard W. Jaeger, "Unhappy Voter Emerges as Mayor," *Wisconsin State Journal,* April 6, 2000; Meg Jones, "Phillips Voters Return Elvis to Sender," April 6, 2000, Amy Rinard, "Municipalities Take Case to Capitol," November 2, 2001, Rick Barrett, "GMC Finds New President," October 22, 2002, John Schmid, "Leading a Charge to Shape the

City, Hudson Focuses on Civic Passion," June 8, 2003, Eugene Kane, "Plenty of Fish in the Mayoral Ocean," June 10, 2003, Tom Daykin, "Farmers Debate Fix for Milk Price Drop," June 30, 2003, Amy Rinard, "Doyle to Spare Family Farm Tax Credits," July 10, 2003, all in the *Milwaukee Journal Sentinel;* Steve Cahalan, "Wisconsin Farmers Union Elects First Female President," *La Crosse Tribune,* February 26, 2003.

90. Georgia Pabst, "A Simple Mission," October 3, 2001, and "Center's Director Takes Her Work Straight to the People," July 23, 2002, both in the *Milwaukee Journal Sentinel.*

91. Tannette Johnson-Elie, "Hispanic Chamber CEO Breaks Barriers for Self, Others," January 11, 2003, and "Latinas Cut Slice of American Pie," November 14, 2000, Georgia Pabst, "Executive Moves in Elite Circles," April 18, 2002, "Center to Help Abused Latinas," May 13, 2001, "Dominguez to Lead Spanish Center," June 25, 2003, and "Latinos Coming of Age in Politics," April 18, 2004, all in the *Milwaukee Journal Sentinel.*

92. Georgia Pabst, "Hmong Doctor's Vivid Memories Bring Her to a Career of Helping," March 6, 2000, Alan J. Borsuk, "A Foot in Two Cultures," April 15, 2002, Peter Maller, "Red Cross Awash in Aid," March 28, 2003, Jesse Garza, "Quilt Tells Story of the Journey of Bao Xiong," April 21, 2003, all in the *Milwaukee Journal Sentinel.*

93. Mike Nichols, "Couple's Sorrow — and Solace — Lingering at Sept. 11 Site," September 8, 2001, and Amy Silvers Rabideau, "Family Must Tell Girl Her Mother Is Lost," September 14, 2001, both in the *Milwaukee Journal Sentinel;* "Remembering the Fallen," *Stars and Stripes,* October 11, 2001.

94. Leonard Sykes Jr., "Tireless Protester Convicted, Faces Prison Without Fear," *Milwaukee Journal Sentinel,* January 28, 2003; Doug Hissom, "A Woman of Conscience Willing to Go to Prison for Her Beliefs," *Milwaukee Shepherd Express,* October 2, 2003.

95. Meg Kissinger, "From Outcast to Officer," *Milwaukee Journal Sentinel,* August 1, 2004.

96. Mark Johnson, "Her Heart Had Been Set on Army, But Now She Longed to Come Home," October 28, 2003, Dan Egan and Mark Johnson, "Roadside Bomb in Iraq Claims Another of Wisconsin's Own," February 17, 2004, and John Diedrich, "A Woman Warrior's Role," April 17, 2004, all in the *Milwaukee Journal Sentinel.*

97. Philip Chien, "Racine Astronaut Finds Space to Be Magical," January 31, 2003, and "'We Lost Them So Close to Home,'" February 9, 2003, both in the *Milwaukee Journal Sentinel.*

98. Miller, "Wisconsin's Struggle for the Equal Rights Amendment."

# INDEX